rmS

The Study Book for the NEBOSH Level 4 Diploma

in Occupational Health and Safety Practice

Workplace and Work Equipment

RMS Publishing
Victoria House
Lower High Street
Stourbridge
DY8 1TA

First Published May 2005

Cover design by Graham Scriven.

Cover images supplied by ACT Associates and Speedy Hire Plc.

Printed and bound in Great Britain by Antony Rowe Ltd, Chippenham, Wiltshire

ISBN 1 900420 61 9

Editor's Notes

Diagrams and photographs

A number of the diagrams included in the Study Book for the NEBOSH Level 4 Diploma in Occupational Health and Safety Practice have been produced in hand-drawn format. In particular these are diagrams that students studying for NEBOSH examinations may be required, or find it helpful, to produce by hand at the time of examination. They are provided to help the student to get an impression of how to do similar drawings of their own. I hope that these diagrams show that such drawings are achievable by hand and also assist in illustrating a standard that might be expected in examination.

We have taken particular care to support the text with a significant number of photographs. They are illustrative of both good and bad working practices and should always be considered in context with supporting text. I am sure that students will find this a useful aid when trying to relate their background and experience to the broad based NEBOSH Level 4 Diploma syllabus. They will give an insight into some of the technical areas of the syllabus that people have difficulty relating to when they do not have a strong technical background.

Where diagrams/text extracts are known to be drawn from other publications, a clear source reference is shown and ACT wish to emphasise that reproduction of such diagrams/text extracts within the Study Book is for educational purposes only and the original copyright has not been infringed.

Legal requirements

Legislation is referred to in context in the various elements that comprise the book. This reflects the interest of the NEBOSH Level 4 Diploma syllabus and requirements to study new/amended legislation under the rule from NEBOSH that it has to have been in force for six months before it becomes examinable.

The NEBOSH Level 4 Diploma examinations do not assess the students' knowledge of section numbers of the Health and Safety at Work Act or knowledge of regulation numbers in an unhelpful way. Instead questions ask the student to explain something about a section number, or significant regulation, by giving the number and the purpose of that section or regulation. In addition, it should be remembered that the student might choose to refer to a section number when answering a question that requires a broad knowledge of law. Knowledge of significant section and regulation numbers is important when answering the questions for the Level 4 examinations. Section and regulation numbers are referred to in the DK^{TM} Study Books in order to differentiate different components of the law and to aid the student in referencing legislation in the workplace, if required by their work or assignments.

Syllabus

Each element of the Study Book has a element overview that sets out the aims of the units, the content, learning outcomes and any connected sources of reference. The Study Book reflects the order and content of the NEBOSH Level 4 Diploma syllabus and in this way the student can be confident that the Study Book reflects the themes of the syllabus. In addition, the syllabus is structured in a very useful way, focusing on hazards, their control and core management of health and safety principles.

National Vocational Qualification

We are confident that those working to national vocational qualifications in occupational health and safety will find this Study Book a useful companion. For students working towards the revised NVQ Level 4 in Occupational Health and Safety Practice they will find a good correlation between the scope of the Study Book series for NEBOSH Level 4 Diploma and the domain knowledge needs at that level.

Acknowledgements

Managing Editor: Ian Coombes MIOSH – Managing Director, ACT; member of NEBOSH Advisory Committee; member IOSH professional Affairs Committee.

RMS Publishing and ACT Associates Ltd wish to acknowledge the following contributors and thank them for their assistance in the preparation of the Unit C Study Book for the NEBOSH Level 4 Diploma: Roger Chance, Paul Harvey, Dean Johnson, Geoff Littley, Janice McTiernan, Barrie Newell, Gordon Self, Clive Raybould, Julie Skett and Luane Steele.

NEBOSH Study Books also available from RMS:

NEBOSH General Certificate (2nd Edition)	ISBN 1 900420 38 4
NEBOSH Construction Certificate (1st Edition)	ISBN 1 900420 58 9
NEBOSH Level 4 Diploma (1st Edition):	
A. Managing Health and Safety	ISBN 1 900420 59 7
B. Hazardous Agents in the Workplace	ISBN 1 900420 60 0
NEBOSH Diploma Part 1 (6th Edition)	
Risk Management	ISBN 1 900420 39 2
Legal and Organisational	ISBN 1 900420 40 6
Workplace	ISBN 1 900420 41 4
Work Equipment	ISBN 1 900420 42 2
Agents	ISBN 1 900420 43 0
NEBOSH Diploma Part 2 (3rd Edition)	
Risk Management	ISBN 1 900420 44 9
Legal and Organisational	ISBN 1 900420 45 7
Workplace	ISBN 1 900420 46 5
Work Equipment	ISBN 1 900420 47 3
Agents	ISBN 1 900420 48 1

Contents

Figure List (including tables and quotes)

Element C6

Element C7

Element C8

Element C9

Element C10

Element C11

List of abbreviations

LEGISLATION

ASLIC	Asbestos (Licensing) Regulations 1983
BR	Building Regulations 2000
CAWR	Control of Asbestos at Work Regulations 2002
CDGUTPER	Carriage of Dangerous Goods and Use of Transportable Pressure Group Regulations 2004
CDM	Construction (Design and Management) Regulation 1994
CHIP	Chemicals (Hazard Information and Packaging for Supply) Regulations 2002
CHPR	Construction (Head Protection) Regulations 1989
CHSW	Construction (Health, Safety and Welfare) Regulations 1996
CLAW	Control of Lead at Work Regulations 2002
COER	Control of Explosives Regulations 1991
COMAH	Control of Major Accident Hazards Regulations 1999
CoPA	Control of Pollution Act 1974
COSHH	Control of Substances Hazardous to Health Regulations 2002
CPA	Consumer Protection Act 1987
CSR	Confined Spaces Regulations 1997
DSE	Health and Safety (Display Screen Equipment) Regulations 1992
DSEAR	Dangerous Substances and Explosive Atmospheres Regulations 2002
EESR	Electrical Equipment (Safety) Regulations 1994
ELCIA	Employers Liability (Compulsory) Insurance Act 1969
ELDEA	Employers Liability (Defective Equipment) Act 1969
ENVA	Environment Act 1995
EPA	Environmental Protection Act 1990
ERA	Employment Relations Act 1999
ESQCR	Electricity Safety, Quality and Continuity Regulations 2002
EWR	Electricity at Work Regulations 1989
FAA	Fatal Accidents Act 1976
FAR	Health and Safety (First-Aid) Regulations 1981
FPA	Fire Precautions Act 1971
FPSPR	Fire Certificates (Special Premises) Regulations 1976
FPWR	Fire Precautions (Workplace) Regulations 1997
HASAWA	Health and Safety at Work etc Act 1974
HSCER	Health and Safety (Consultation with Employees) Regulations 1996
IER	Health and Safety Information for Employees Regulations 1989
IRR	Ionising Radiations Regulations 1999
LA	Limitations Act 1980
LOLER	Lifting Operations and Lifting Equipment Regulations 1998
MHOR	Manual Handling Operations Regulations 1992
MHSWR	Management of Health and Safety at Work Regulations 1999
NIHHS	Notification of Installations Handling Hazardous Substances Regulations 1982
NNSR	Notification of New Substances Regulations 1993
NOMAS	Dangerous Substances (Notification and Marking of Sites) Regulations 1990
NRSWA	New Roads and Street Works Act 1991
NWR	Noise at Work Regulations 1989
PER	Pressure Equipment Regulations 1999
PPER	Personal Protective Equipment at Work Regulations 1992
PSSR	Pressure Systems Safety Regulations 2000
PUWER	Provision and Use of Work Equipment Regulations 1998
RIDDOR	Reporting of Injuries, Diseases and Dangerous Occurrences Regulations 1995
RRFSO	Regulatory Reform (Fire Safety) Order 2005
SD Act	Sex Discrimination Act 1974
SMSR	Supply of Machinery (Safety) Regulations 1992
SPVSR	Simple Pressure Vessels (Safety) Regulations 1991
SRSC	Safety Representatives and Safety Committees Regulations 1977
SSA	Social Security Act 1985
SSACPR	Social Security Act (Claims and Payments) Regulations 1979
SSIIPDR	Social Security (Industrial Injuries) (Prescribed Diseases) Regulations 1985
SSSA	Social Security Administration Act 1992
SSSR	Health and Safety (Safety Signs and Signals) Regulations 1996
SWR	Special Waste Regulations
WAH	Work at Height Regulations 2005
WAH	Working at Height Regulations 2005
WHSWR	Workplace (Health, Safety and Welfare) Regulations 1992

GENERAL

AC	Alternating Current
ACGIH	American Conference of Governmental Industrial Hygienists
ACOP	Approved Code of Practice
ADI	Acceptable Daily Intake
ADR	Alternate Dispute Resolution
AGIR	Advisory Group on Ionising Radiation
AGNIR	Advisory Group on Non-Ionising Radiation
AIDS	Acquired Immune Deficiency Syndrome
ALARP	As Low As is Reasonably Practicable
ANR	Active Noise Reduction
APF	Assigned Protection Factor
ASL	Approved Supply List
ATP	Automatic Train Protection
AWS	Automatic Warning System
AZDN	Azodiisobutyronitrate
BATNEEC	Best Available Techniques Not Entailing Excessive Cost
BBV	Bloodborne Virus
BCS	British Crime Survey
BEQ	Break-Even Quantity
BMGV	Biological Mandatory Avoidance Values
BPEO	Best Practicable Environmental Option
BS	British Standards
BSC	British Safety Council
BSI	British Standards Institution
CAT	Cable Avoidance Tool
CBA	Cost Benefit Analysis
CCF	Common Cause Failures
CCTV	Closed Circuit Television
CE	Conformité Européene
CFDR	Centre For Dispute Resolution
CFM	Cubic Feet per Minute
CITB	Construction Industry Training Board
CL	Control Limits
CNS	Central Nervous System
CPD	Continuing Professional Development
CPR	Cardio Pulmonary Resuscitation
CW	Continuous Wave
DA	Designing Authorities
dB	Decibel
DC	Direct Current
DIY	Do It Yourself
DLBA	Direct Line Breathing Apparatus
DNA	Deoxyribonucleic Acid
DoE	Department of the Environment
DSE	Display Screen Equipment
EA	Environmental Agency
EAT	Employment Appeal Tribunal
EC	European Community
ECJ	European Court of Justice
ED	Effective Dose
EEA	European Economic Area
EEF	Engineering Employers Federation
EFTA	European Free Trade Association
EH	Environmental Health
EHO	Environmental Health Office
EIA	Environmental Impact Assessment
EINECS	European Inventory of Existing Commercial Chemical Substances
EMAS	Employment Medical Advisory Service
EMS	Environmental Management Systems
ESD	Electrostatic Discharge
ET	Employment Tribunal
ETA	Event Tree Analysis
EU	European Union
FID	Flame Ionisation Detector
FLT	Fork Lift Truck
FMEA	Failure Mode and Effect Analysis
FMECA	Failure Modes Effects and Criticality Analysis
FRA	Fire Risk Assessment
FTA	Fault Tree Analysis
GIT	Gastro Intestinal Tract

GP	General Practitioner
GSR	General Safety Requirements
HAVS	Hand-arm Vibration Syndrome
HAZOP	Hazard and Operability Studies
HCL	Hydrogen Chloride
HEPA	High Efficiency Particulate Air
HIV	Human Immunodeficiency Virus
HMCE	Her Majesty's Customs and Excise
HMIP	Her Majesty's Inspectorate of Pollution
HML	High, Medium and Low
HMSO	Her Majesty's Stationary Office
HPLC	High Performance Liquid Chromatography
HRA	Human Reliability Analysis
HRT	Hormone Replacement Therapy
HSC	Health and Safety Commission
HSE	Health and Safety Executive
HSG	Health and Safety Guidance
HSMS	Health and Safety Management Systems
HST	High Speed Train
ICAEW	The Institute of Chartered Accountants in England and Wales
ICD	International Classification of Diseases Injuries and Cause of Deaths
ICRP	International Commission on Radiological Protection
IEE	Institute of Electrical Engineers
ILO	International Labour Office
IOSH	Institute of Occupational Safety and Health
IPC	Integrated Pollution Act
IQ	Intelligence Quotient
ISO	International Organisation for Standardization
IT	Information Technology
KPI	Key Performance Indicator
LAAPC	Local Authority Air Pollution Control
LCA	Life Cycle Assessment
LEFM	Linear Elastic Fracture Mechanics
LEV	Local Exhaust Ventilation
LPG	Liquefied Petroleum Gas
LTEL	Long Term Exposure Limit
MAPP	Major Accident Prevention Policy
MCE	Mixed Cellulose Ester
MDI	Methylene Bisphenyl Di-isocyanate
MEL	Maximum Exposure Limit
MEWP	Mobile Elevated Work Platform
MF	Medium Frequency
MSDS	Material Safety Data Sheet
MSW	Municipal Solid Wastes
NDT	Noise Destructive Testing
NEBOSH	National Examination Board in Occupational Safety and Health
NHL	Noise induced Hearing Loss
NHS	National Health Service
NOAEL	No Observed Adverse Effect Level
NRA	National Rivers Authority
NVQ	National Vocational Qualification
OEL	Occupational Exposure Limit
OES	Occupational Exposure Standard
OHS	Occupational Health Service
OHSA	Occupational Safety and Health Administration
OHSAS	Occupational Health and Safety Assessment Services
OLA	Occupiers Liability Act
OLSA	Occupiers Liability (Scotland) Act
OPCD	Overcurrent Protective Device
PAR	Population Attributable Risk
PAT	Portable Appliance Testing
PCLM	Phase Contrast Light Microscopy
PES	Programmable Electronic Systems
PLC	Public Limited Company
PLM	Polarised Light Microscopy
PNS	Peripheral Nervous System
PPE	Personal Protective Equipment
PTSD	Post Traumatic Stress Disorder
PTW	Permit To Work
PVC	Polyvinyl Chloride
RCD	Residual Current Device
RCS	Risk Control Systems

RES	Representatives of Employment Safety
RF	Radio Frequency
RIA	Regulatory Impact Assessments
RL	Recommended Limits
ROSPA	Royal Society for Prevention of Accidents
RPA	Radiation Protected Advisors
RPE	Respiratory Protective Equipment
RRO	Regulatory Reform Fire Safety Order
RRSAG	Radiation, Risk and Society Advisory Group
RSI	Repetitive Strain Injury
RTFLT	Rough Terrain Fork Lift Truck
SCBA	Self-Contained Breathing Apparatus
SELV	Separated Extra Low Voltage
SEPA	Scottish Environmental Protection Agency
SNR	Single Number Rating
SPL	Sound Pressure Level
SR	Safety Representatives
SSW	Safe System of Work
STEL	Short Term Exposure Limit
SVQ	Scottish Vocational Qualification
SWORD	Surveillance of Work related and Occupational Respiratory Disease
SWR	Steel Wire Rope
TDI	Toluene Di-isocyanate
TQM	Total Quality Management
TTS	Temporary Threshold Shift
TUC	Trade Union Congress
TWA	Time Weighted Average
UV	Ultra Violet
VCM	Vinyl Chloride Monomer
VDU	Visual Display Unit
VHF	Very High Frequency
VOSL	Value of Statistical Life
VWF	Vibration White Finger
WATCH	Working on Action to Control Chemicals
WBV	Whole Body Vibration
WCI	Wind Chill Index
WEL	Workplace Exposure Limits
WHO	World Health Organisation
WRULD	Work Related Upper Limb Disorder
XRD	X-Ray Diffraction

This page is intentionally blank

General workplace issues

Overall aims

On completion of this Element, the student will have knowledge and understanding of:

- the needs for, and factors involved in, the provision and maintenance of safe places of work.
- the needs for, and factors involved in, the provision of a safe and healthy work environment.
- safe working practices associated with work in confined spaces.
- structural safety of workplaces.

Content

Specific intended learning outcomes

The intended learning outcomes are that the student will be able to:

1. outline the requirements of, and advise on actions required to secure compliance with, the Workplace (Health, Safety and Welfare) Regulations 1992 and Health and Safety (First-Aid) Regulations 1981

2. advise on the risks associated with working in confined spaces and precautions to be taken

3. identify potential causes of structural failure of buildings used as workplaces and recommend actions to be taken to maintain structural integrity

4. advise on compliance with the Health and Safety (Safety Signs and Signals) Regulations 1996

Relevant statutory provisions

Health and Safety at Work etc. Act (HASAWA) 1974 - section 2(2) (d) + (e)

Workplace (Health, Safety and Welfare) Regulations (WHSWR) 1992 (and as amended 2002)

Work at Height Regulations (WAH) 2005

Health and Safety (First-Aid) Regulations (FAR) 1981 (and as amended 2002)

Health and Safety (Safety Signs and Signals) Regulations (SSSR) 1996

The Confined Spaces Regulations (CSR) 1997

The Management of Health and Safety at Work Regulations (MHSWR) 1999 (and as amended 2003)

1.1 - Safe place of work

SAFE PLACES OF WORK

Employer's common law duty to provide safe places of work

The position at common law is that employers must take reasonable care to protect employees from foreseeable injury. If an employer knows of or should have known of a hazard and fails to do anything about it in reasonable time, he may be in breach of his duty of care.

An employer's general duties were identified by the House of Lords in the case of Wilsons and Clyde Coal Co. v English (1938) as follows:

- A safe place of work, including safe access and egress.
- A safe system of work.
- Safe plant and appliances.
- Safe and competent fellow workers.

If the employees' workplace is unsafe because of a third party and the employer does nothing then the employer as well as the third party may be liable. This might happen where the employer is a contractor on a building site and his employees are working in unsafe conditions due to an act or omission by the main contractor. The duty of care is non-delegable and is not removed because the employee is working on someone else's premises.

SAFE MEANS OF ACCESS AND EGRESS

The duty to provide a reasonably safe place of work relates to such matters as clearly marked gangways which are free of obstruction, the maintenance of floors and staircases, a safe working environment and safe means of access and egress together with the organisation of traffic routes (including pedestrian traffic). A critical consideration when considering traffic systems is the safety interface between pedestrians and traffic. The routes that people use should be clearly defined and marked. This is a requirement of the Workplace Regulations which states that every workplace shall be organised in such a way that pedestrians and vehicles can circulate in a safe manner.

The workplace may be some distance from the ground as with construction workers or several miles underground as with miners. Therefore, such things as approach roads, portable access equipment (ladders, etc.), and shoring of underground workings must be considered. Particular thought should be given to emergency egress.

This duty may be fulfilled through regular inspection of the workplace. It does not extend to abnormal hazards that could not have been foreseen. If there is a sudden, unexpected snowfall, the employer is not liable until he has had reasonable time to deal with it. If the employee is working at a site not owned by the employer, circumstances will determine whether it is inspected. For example, the employer of a painter and decorator would not be expected to inspect every household prior to work being carried out.

GOOD HOUSEKEEPING

Maintenance of a safe workplace may be achieved through the development of a housekeeping procedure. Good housekeeping implies "a place for everything and everything in its place". Laid down procedures are necessary for preventing the spread of contamination, reducing the likelihood of accidents resulting in slips, trips, and falls and reducing the chances of unwanted fire caused by careless storage of flammable waste. Exposure to dust can cause health problems and is an explosion hazard. Dust can be reduced by keeping it damp so it is less likely to become airborne. It can be removed from floors and surfaces by wetting it before sweeping or by using a vacuum cleaner.

SAFE TRAFFIC ROUTES

Regulation 17(1) of the Workplace Regulations states "'Every workplace shall be organised in such a way that pedestrians and vehicles can circulate in a safe manner". Clearly defined and marked routes should be provided for people going about their business at work. These should be provided for access and egress: the workplace gate, car parks, bus or train services. Safe crossing places should be provided where people have to cross main traffic routes. In buildings where vehicles operate, separate doors and walkways should be provided for pedestrians to get from building to building. Meshed handrails can be used to channel people into the pedestrian route. Where it is not possible to have a pedestrian route with a safe clearance from vehicle movement, because of building and plant design, then a raised pedestrian walkway could be considered to help in segregation.

Accidents can be caused where vehicles are unsafely parked as they can be an obstruction and restrict visibility. There should be clear entrance and exit routes in parking areas and designated parking areas to allow outgoing transport to be checked before leaving. Checking the load, the sheeting, etc. on the works roads can be a hazard to the driver and to others.

There should be clear, well-marked and signposted vehicle traffic routes which avoid steep gradients where possible, especially where fork lift trucks operate. It is important to have speed limits that are practicable and effective. Speed limit signs should be posted and traffic slowing measures such as speed bumps and ramps may be necessary in certain situations. Monitoring speed limit compliance is necessary, along with some kind of action against persistent offenders.

Inside buildings, speed limits of 10 or 15 mph are usually considered appropriate, although 5 mph may be necessary in certain situations.

Internal transport requires clear routes to be designated, marked with painted lines and preferably barriered off from pedestrians. Accidents can occur when fork lift trucks (FLTs) and people collide: the pedestrian may be injured by contact and the driver injured if the FLT overturns. Separate doorways should be provided for FLT entry and blind spots should be dealt with by the careful positioning of mirrors on walls, plant or storage racking. Routes should be wide enough to allow manoeuvrability and passing.

Where it is unavoidable that pedestrians will come into proximity with internal transport, people should be reminded by briefings, signs, etc. of the hazards, so they are aware at all times.

INTERNAL TRANSPORT

Dangers

Over 100 people die each year as a result of works transport related accidents. There is also a high incidence of accidents causing serious injury, e.g. spinal damage, amputation and crush injuries. Very few accidents involving traffic result in minor injury. In addition, transport accidents cause damage to plant, infrastructure and vehicles. The causes of traffic accidents are well known and understood; the prevention measures are simple and, in the main, inexpensive.

Precautions

Precautionary measures to be taken must include:

- Provision of suitable equipment, e.g. capability of the vehicle, ergonomic design features, audible warning system.
- Careful selection and training of drivers.
- Monitoring of driver standards.
- Provision of parking areas.
- Provision of suitable battery charging areas if necessary.
- Careful design of traffic routes.
- Maintenance of traffic routes.
- Traffic control e.g. identification of "no go" areas.
- Vehicle maintenance.

1.2 - Work environment

TEMPERATURE

'Reasonable' temperature inside workplaces

The level of heating should be appropriate to provide physical comfort. The nature of the work and the working environment will need to be assessed to achieve the correct level. Whenever possible the individual should be able to adjust their workplace to achieve this objective.

Workplaces can vary greatly:

- Very cold and exposed, such as a frozen food, minus 25° Celsius (C), storage warehouse.
- General warehousing at ambient temperature, 5ºC to 30ºC.
- General office where the nature of the work is sedentary 16ºC to 24ºC.
- High temperature processing such as a laundry, bakery 30ºC to 38ºC.
- High temperature manufacturing such as with glass, steel or ceramics 30ºC to 45ºC production.

Several factors should be considered such as personal capability, degree of hot or cold, wind speed and humidity.

See also - Element B8: Physical agents 2, radiation and thermal environment - in Diploma Study Guide: Agents, where these factors are covered in more depth.

Figure C1-1: Cool areas.   Source: ACT.

Means to measure temperature

See also - Element B8: Physical agents 2, radiation and thermal environment - in Diploma Study Guide: Agents, where these factors are covered in more depth.

LIGHTING

The necessity for lighting in workplaces

Workplace (Health, Safety and Welfare) Regulations, Reg. 8

The safety problems associated with inadequate/unsuitable lighting or lighting arrangements fall into two main categories:

1. Deterioration of visual acuity.
2. Increased likelihood of accidents caused by incorrect perception.

Definition of 'suitable and sufficient lighting'

Lighting should be sufficient to allow people to work, use facilities and move from place to place safely.

Natural lighting

Where reasonably practicable, lighting should be provided from natural sources. Windows and skylights should be cleaned regularly and kept free from obstruction.

Artificial lighting

Low Temperature Operation

Standard of fluorescent fittings can be operated down to -20 degrees C if a 38mm lamp and special starter are used. Lumen output will be 20% of normal when lamp is at -10 degree C. The lower lumen output must be considered when calculating the number of fittings required. Plastic sleeves are available to provide some thermal insulation to a lamp operating in a low temperature environment. Lowest operational temperature of other types of discharge lamps is as follows:

- High pressure sodium (HPS)   satisfactory down to - 60 degree C.
- Metal Halide (MH)   satisfactory down to - 20 degree C.
- Mercury vapour (MV)   satisfactory down to - 5 degree C.

Source: www. ndlight.com.

Lumen Type	Typical Lumen Output
GLS 100 Watt	1300
12V50 Watt diachronic TH	950
1500 Watt QI	33000
Fluorescent: 18 Watt	1150
Fluorescent: 30 Watt	2400
36 Watt	3300
36 Watt Triphos	3300
58 Watt	4600
Mercury Vapour: 250 Watt	13700
Mercury Vapour: 400 Watt	24000
Metal Halide: 250 Watt	20500
Metal Halide: 400 Watt	38000
High Pressure Sodium: 250 Watt	27500
High Pressure Sodium: 400 Watt	47500

Figure C1-2: Lumen outputs of different lamp types.   *Source: www. ndlight.com.*

Impact of lighting levels on safety issues

Light levels will affect individuals in a number of ways, in particular if they have problems of sight impairment. Older people often develop sight problems of long sight (reduction in the ability to read small print) from the age of 40 to 50 years. Some common issues are discussed below.

Incorrect perception

Deterioration of visual acuity. For example, visual fatigue, glare, falls resulting from level changes which are not apparent.

Failure to perceive

Increased likelihood of accidents caused by incorrect perception. For example, slips, trips and falls, vehicle collision, etc.

Stroboscopic effects

Stroboscopic effect is not common with modern lighting, but where it does occur, it can be dangerous. Earlier types of fluorescent light gave the impression that machinery was stationary or moving in a different way. Wiring adjacent tubes to different supply phases overcomes this problem.

Colour assessment

Colour rendition refers to the fact that colours appear different under different light sources. Choice of lamp is important if a "warm" or "cool" effect is desired. Colours will appear different when viewed under 'sodium' light to natural daylight, a consideration when working outside at night using high visibility clothing in areas illuminated by 'Sodium' lights, when the high visibility will not be observed.

Effect on attitudes

The eye is sensitive to the blue band of natural light and many individuals are depressed when light levels are low or diffused by heavy cloud, reducing that portion of light. Natural daylight is preferred, but this will often need to be supplemented throughout the day for many tasks, for example, when work of a detailed nature is carried out, such as with watch repairs or copy typing small print. Poor or very bright lighting will cause fatigue and reduce willingness to work; light levels should be assessed and maintained at an appropriate level for the tasks to be done.

Effects of brightness contrast

Shadow will affect the amount of illumination. Its effect will depend on the task being performed. The answer is to use more powerful lights or provide more of them.

Disabling and discomfort glare

Glare causes discomfort or impairment of vision. Dazzling lights and glare should be avoided especially when people move from brightly to dimly lit areas and vice versa. Providing diffusers or screens will reduce the effect of glare from a lamp. Blinds or curtains will reduce glare from sunlight.

Tissue damage from light exposure

Exposure to very bright light sources such as exhibition lighting, stage and image projectors, may cause permanent damage to the light sensing region of the eye ('burn out'). Visible ultraviolet light will cause photo keretitis, infra red will cause cataracts. Natural light (sunlight) exposure will cause skin changes ranging from tanning or darkening, burns through to formation of melanomas (skin cancers).

Visual fatigue

The use of planned work breaks or changes in work task - before fatigue becomes evident - is an important factor to consider when managing visual fatigue; this is particularly important when work is of a detailed nature. If the work involves use of computer display screens, reflections need to be minimised, to reduce visual fatigue. Care should be taken to reduce reflections by elimination of bright light sources or strong reflected images onto operator screens. These sources will often include incandescent bulbs, fluorescent lights, vertical or venetian blinds and even reflection of the operators themselves, particularly if they are wearing light clothing. Fatigue occurs when the eye is involuntarily distracted from the task i.e. data entry to the sharp edge of the reflected image. This unconscious eye movement will add to visual fatigue.

Instrumentation

Units and measurement of light

The common measuring techniques and terms that are used by the lighting industry are as follows:

Candela

The unit of luminous intensity. One candela is defined as the luminous intensity of 1/600,000 square meter of projected area of a blackbody radiator operating at the temperature of solidification of platinum under pressure of 101,325 Newtons per square meter.

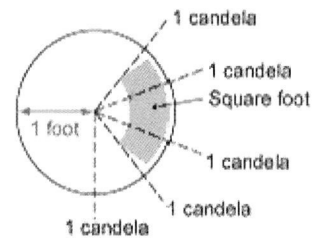

Figure C1-3: Candela.

Footcandle

A footcandle is a measure of light intensity. A footcandle is defined as the amount of light received by 1 square foot of a surface that is 1 foot from a point source of light equivalent to one candle of a certain type.

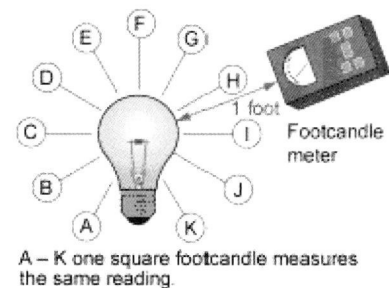

A – K one square footcandle measures the same reading.

Figure C1-4: Footcandle.

End footcandle

End footcandle measurements are based on the focused light beam only. The spherical energy or surrounding light output is not captured by or reflected back to the surface of the footcandle light meter. End footcandle is the focal light beam measurement from point A to point B at one-foot distance.

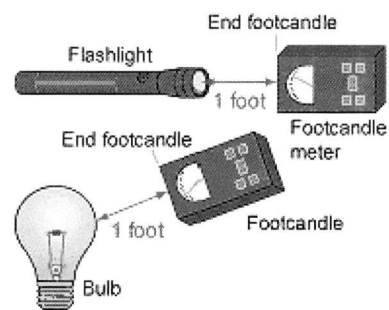

Figure C1-5: End footcandle.

Source: lightresource.com.

Lumen

A unit of light flow or luminous flux. The lumen rating of a lamp is a measure of the total light output of the lamp. The most common measurement of light output (or luminous flux) is the lumen. Light sources are labelled with an output rating in lumens. For example, a R30 65-Watt indoor flood lamp may have a rating of 750 lumens. Similarly, a light fixture's output can be expressed in lumens. As lamps and fixtures age and become dirty, their lumen output decreases (i.e., lumen depreciation occurs). Most lamp ratings are based on initial lumens (i.e., when lamp is new).

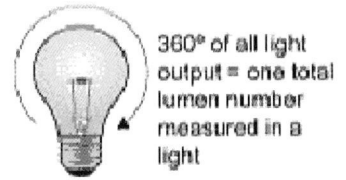

360° of all light output = one total lumen number measured in a light

Figure C1-6: Lumen.

End lumens

End Lumens measurements are based on a spot of light only. The spherical energy or surrounding light output is not captured by or reflected back to the surface of the lumen light meter. End lumens is the light measurement from point A to point B at one-foot distance.

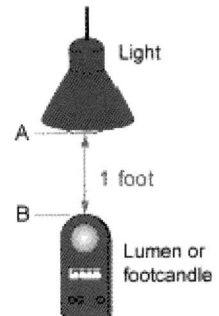

Figure C1-7: End lumens.

Source: lightresource.com.

Luminance

Luminous Flux (light output). This is the quantity of light that leaves the lamp, measured in lumens (lm). Lamps are rated in both initial and mean lumens.

Initial lumens indicate how much light is produced once the lamp has stabilized; for fluorescent and high-intensity discharge (HID) lamps, this is typically 100 hours.

Mean lumens indicate the average light output over the lamp's rated life, which reflects the gradual deterioration of performance due to the rigors of continued operation; for fluorescent lamps, this is usually determined at 40% of rated life.

Assessment of lighting levels

Luminous (light level)

This is the amount of light measured on the work plane in the lighted space. The work plane is an imaginary horizontal, tilted or vertical line where the most important tasks in the space are performed. Measured in footcandles (fc or lux in metric), light levels are either calculated, or in existing spaces, measured with a light meter. A footcandle is actually one lumen of light density per square foot; one lux is one lumen per square meter. Like lumens, footcandles can be produced as either initial or maintained quantities.

Work plane

The level at which work is done where illuminance is specified and measured. For office applications, this is typically a horizontal plane 30 inches above the floor (e.g. desk height).

Beam lumens

The total flux in that region of space where the intensity exceeds 50 percent of the maximum intensity.

Field lumens

The total flux in that region of space where the intensity exceeds ten percent of the maximum intensity.

Lux

The metric unit of measure for illuminance of a surface. One lux is equal to one lumen per square meter. One lux equals 0.0929 footcandles.

Light level

Light intensity measured on a plane at a specific location is called illuminance. Illuminance is measured in footcandles, which are workplane lumens per square foot. You can measure illuminance using a light meter located on the work surface where tasks are performed. Using simple arithmetic and manufacturers' photometric data, you can predict illuminance for a defined space. (Lux is the metric unit for illuminance, measured in lumens per square meter. To convert footcandles to lux, multiply footcandles by 10.76).

Efficacy

A measure of the luminous efficiency of a radiant flux, expressed in lumens per watt as the quotient of the total luminous flux by the total flux. For daylighting, this is the quotient of visible flux incident on a surface to radiant flux on that surface. For electric sources, this is the quotient of the total luminous flux emitted by the total lamp power input.

Efficacy of a light source

The total light output of a light source divided by the total power input. Efficacy is expressed in lumens per Watt.

Watt

The unit of measuring electrical power. Watt does not relate to the light output level. It defines the rate of energy consumption by an electrical device when it is in operation. The energy cost of operating an electrical device is calculated as its wattage time in hours of use. In single-phase circuits, it is related to volts and amps by the formula: Volts x Amps x Power Factor (PF) = Watts. (Note: For AC circuits, PF must be included).

Kilowatt hour (kWh) formula

The measure of electrical energy from which electricity billing is determined. For example, a 100-Watt bulb operated for 1000 hours would consume 100 kilowatt hours (100 Watts x 1000 hours = 100 kWh). At a billing rate of $0.10/kWh, this bulb would cost $10.00 (100 kWh x $0.10/kWh) to operate over 1000 hours.

Source: lightresource.com, Light Research Centre, Light Board, IES Lighting Handbook, 5th Edition.

Standards

Light types and measurement

Radiant flux is a measure of radiometric power. Flux, expressed in watts, is a measure of the rate of energy flow, in joules per second. Since photon energy is inversely proportional to wavelength, ultraviolet photons are more powerful than infrared.

Luminous flux is a measure of the power of visible light. Photopic flux, expressed in lumens, is weighted to match the responsivity of the human eye, which is most sensitive to yellow green. Scotopicflux is weighted to the sensitivity of the human eye in the dark adapted state.

Irradiance and illuminance

Irradiance is a measure of radiometric flux per unit area, or flux density. Irradiance is typically expressed in W/cm^2 (watts per square centimetre) or W/m2 (watts per square meter).

Illuminance is a measure of photometric flux per unit area, or visible flux density. Illuminance is typically expressed in lux (lumens per square metre) or foot candles (lumens per square foot).

Minimum lux levels

The following table represents only a small sample of workplaces. Many retail, exhibition and sports venues have lux levels over 1000.

Area	Lux (minimum)
■ Corridors ■ Passageways	40
■ Warehouses involving search and retrieval tasks ■ Stairs	80
■ Entrance halls ■ Foyers ■ Waiting rooms ■ Canteens ■ Machine shop general workbench	160
■ Counters ■ Kitchen (food preparation area)	240
■ Offices	320
■ Machine work high tolerance work bench	400
■ Electronic assembly work ■ Jewellery and watch repair	600

Figure C1-8: Lux levels.

Source: AS1680.2.4:1997 Table E1.

Emergency lighting

Standby lighting enables essential work to continue. It can be between 5 and 100 % of the illuminance produced by ambient lighting.

Escape lighting enables a building to be evacuated safely. Powered by either batteries or generator, the lighting should reach the required illuminance within 15 seconds. Battery powered lighting should last for between 1 and 3 hours.

1.3 - Welfare facilities and arrangements

Most workplaces are regulated by the Workplace (Health, Safety and Welfare) Regulations (WHSWR) 1992.

TOILET, WASHING AND CHANGING FACILITIES – WHSWR REGULATION 20

Readily accessible, suitable and sufficient sanitary conveniences must be provided. The conveniences must be adequately lit, kept clean and maintained in an orderly fashion. Separate conveniences for male and female workers must be provided except where the convenience is in a separate room and the door of which is capable of being locked from the inside.

The ACOP defines the following as minimum provision:

Number of people at work	Number of water closets	Number of wash stations
1 to 5	1	1
6 to 25	2	2
26 to 50	3	3
51 to 75	4	4
76 to 100	5	5
For every 25 above 100 (or fraction of)	+1	+1

Figure C1-9: Provision for toilet, washing and changing facilities. *Source: ACOP for the Workplace (Health, Safety and Welfare) Regulations 1992.*

STORAGE OF CLOTHING - WHSWR REGULATION 23

Suitable and sufficient accommodation must be provided for personal clothing not worn at work and clothing worn at work but not taken home. Such clothing accommodation must: be suitably secure when personal clothing not worn at work is being stored; separate work clothing and other clothing where necessary to avoid health risks or damage; be in a suitable location and so far as is reasonably practicable include drying facilities.

FACILITIES FOR CHANGING CLOTHING - WHSWR REGULATION 24

Where special clothing must be worn at work or for reasons of health or propriety a person cannot change in another room then suitable and sufficient changing facilities must be provided. Separate facilities or separate use of facilities for male and female workers must be taken into account.

The ACOP recommends that changing facilities should be readily accessible to workrooms (and eating facilities if provided) and should contain adequate seating arrangements. The facilities provided should be sufficiently large to enable the maximum number of workers to use them comfortably and quickly at any one time.

FACILITIES FOR EATING, REST ROOMS - WHSWR REGULATION 25

Readily accessible, suitable and sufficient rest facilities must be provided. Such rest facilities must be provided in one or more rest rooms (new and modified, etc. workplaces) or in rest rooms or rest areas (existing workplaces). Where food eaten in the workplace is liable to become contaminated, suitable facilities for eating meals must be included in the rest facilities.

Rest rooms and areas must include suitable arrangements for protecting non-smokers from the discomfort of tobacco smoke. Suitable rest facilities must also be provided for pregnant women and nursing mothers.

Where meals are regularly eaten in the workplace suitable and sufficient facilities must be provided for their consumption.

The ACOP recommends that rest facilities should include suitable and sufficient seats and tables for the number of workers likely to use them at any one time. Work seats in offices or other clean environments may be acceptable as rest facilities provided workers are not subjected to excessive disturbance during rest periods. Eating facilities should include a facility for preparing or obtaining a hot drink, and where hot food cannot be readily obtained, means should be provided to enable workers to heat their own food. Canteens, etc. may be used as rest facilities providing there is no obligation to buy food.

FACILITIES FOR PREGNANT WOMEN AND NURSING MOTHERS

Rest rooms and areas must include suitable arrangements for protecting non-smokers from the discomfort of tobacco smoke. Suitable rest facilities must also be provided for pregnant women and nursing mothers.

ARRANGEMENTS TO PROTECT NON-SMOKERS FROM TOBACCO SMOKE

Rest rooms and areas must include suitable arrangements for protecting non-smokers from the discomfort of tobacco smoke.

THE NEED TO TAKE ACCOUNT OF DISABLED PERSONS

Suitable toilet facilities will need to be provided for those who have physical disability and who rely on equipment to move about (crutches, walking sticks, frames and wheel chairs). The facility, typically a defined cubical, will need to have a wider than usual access door and sufficient room to turn around, in relation to the equipment fitted, i.e. wc, sink, refuse bins etc. located within. Means to summon assistance will also be required.

1.4 - First aid provision

BASIS OF PROVISION

The Health and Safety (First-Aid) Regulations 1981

Reg 2 First Aid provides treatment for the purpose of preserving life and minimising the consequences of injury or illness until medical (doctor or nurse) help can be obtained. Also, it provides treatment of minor injuries which would otherwise receive no treatment, or which do not need the help of a medical practitioner or nurse.

Reg 3 Requires that every employer must provide equipment and facilities that are adequate and appropriate in the circumstances for administering first aid to his employees.

Reg 4 An employer must inform his employees about the first-aid arrangements, including the location of equipment, facilities and identification of trained personnel.

Reg 5 Self-employed people must ensure that adequate and suitable provision is made for administering first-aid while at work.

To ensure compliance with Regulation 3, an employer must make an assessment to determine the needs. Under these regulations employers do not have to make first-aid provision for any person other than their employees (civil liability and any interpretation placed on the Health and Safety at Work etc Act may persuade an organisation to provide first aid to third parties that enter their premises). In situations where employees of more than one employer are working together, for example on a construction site, agreement can be made to share first aid facilities.

Numbers of employees

The number of employees that an employer has, and their distribution, is an important influence on the amount of first aid provision required. In small organisations the provision may be minimal, particularly if the workplace is located in easy access of emergency services. The smallest organisations will only need to establish an "appointed person", someone to take charge and ensure that the emergency services are alerted. They may have basic, emergency first aid knowledge to help sustain life. They are not classed as a "first aider". Where the number of employees at a given workplace increases then a fully qualified first aider is required e.g. when an office has 50 employees. In larger workplaces with more employees there would be a need for more than one first aider e.g. when an office has more than 100 employees the requirement for first aiders becomes one for every 100 employees. The workplace risk also determines the number of first aiders required.

Workplace risks

Any first aid provision made needs to reflect the workplace risks both in the level of risk and the type. Different work activities, for example offices, have relatively few hazards and low levels of risk. Others have a higher level of risk or more specific hazards, for example construction or chemical sites. In this case the construction site may anticipate a need for rapid local provision of first aid to deal with a wide range of injuries, particularly those impact and fracture injuries relating to falls of people or materials. The chemical site may anticipate exposure to specific chemicals which may need an antidote to be administered promptly or people being overcome needing oxygen. In addition, the site may be large and the first aid provision may have to travel large distances to respond to support a local first aider.

The number of first aiders needs to be determined and the workplace risks are a large influencing factor. For low risk workplaces the threshold which necessitates a first aider is 50 employees whereas for medium risk it is 20 employees and high risk 5 employees. The employer must ensure that adequate numbers of "suitable persons" are provided to administer first aid. "Suitable persons" are those who have received training and acquired qualifications approved by the HSE, and any additional training which might be appropriate under the circumstances, such as in relation to any special hazards. All relevant factors have to be taken into account when deciding how many "suitable persons" will be needed.

Proximity of emergency services

Where access to treatment is difficult first aiders will usually be required, such as where work activities are a long distance from accident and emergency facilities, for example when conducting forestry work. Where access to comprehensive treatment is difficult, for example where a chemical processing site is located away from towns and therefore away from emergency services, an equipped first-aid room may be required to offset the difficulty for ambulance access or to anticipate likely delay in treatment.

Having made an assessment the employer will then be able to work out the number and size of provision of first-aid equipment required. This may be a small personal first aid pouch, first aid boxes located at various points and on vehicles as necessary or a first aid room. The guidance to the Health and Safety (First Aid) Regulations suggests a minimum stock for the contents of first aid containers. The approved code of practice states that at least one first aid container will always be required for each work site.

LOCAL DEFAULT PROCEDURAL ARRANGEMENTS

- Sharing first-aiders - Arrangements can be made to share the expertise of personnel. Usually, as on a multi-contractor site, one contractor supplies the personnel.
- Employees regularly working away from the employer's premises.
- The numbers of the employees, including fluctuations caused by shift patterns. The more employees there are the higher the probability of injury.
- Absence of first-aiders through illness or annual leave.
- Shift patterns.

As described earlier in appropriate circumstances, an employer can provide an "appointed person" instead of a first-aider. The "appointed person" is someone appointed by the employer to take charge of the situation (for example, to call an ambulance) if a serious injury occurs in the absence of a first-aider. It is recommended that the "appointed person" be able to administer emergency first-aid and be responsible for the equipment provided.

Training of first aiders

Training courses for first aiders, including examinations, is controlled by the HSE. Approved courses should be of at least four full days duration. Certificates of qualification are valid for three years. A refresher course, followed by examination is required before re-certification.

PRINCIPLES OF FIRST AID

■ Sustain life.
■ Prevent deterioration.
■ Promote recovery.

1.5 - Safety signs

COMMON SIGNS AND THEIR CATEGORISATION

The Health and Safety (Safety Signs and Signals) Regulations 1996

The objective of the regulations is to provide a legal means to require that safety signs comply with BS 5378: Part 1 1980 where signs are directed at people at work.

The objectives are met by the following:

1. Signs are defined as those combining shape, colour and a pictorial symbol to provide specific health and safety information and instruction.

2. The regulations do not apply to road signs.

Supplementary safety strips can be yellow or fluorescent orange/red, but must not substitute signs as defined above.

Fire fighting, rescue equipment and emergency exit signs do not have to comply with BS 5378: Part 1 1980.

Requirements of regulations

The regulations require employers to provide specific safety signs whenever there is a risk which has not been avoided or controlled by other means, e.g. by engineering controls and safe systems of work. Where a safety sign would not help to reduce that risk, or where the sign is not significant, there is no need to provide a sign.

They require, where necessary, the use of road traffic signs within workplaces to regulate road traffic.

They also require employers to:

maintain the safety signs which are provided by them.

explain unfamiliar signs to their employees and tell them what they need to do when they see a safety sign.

The Regulations cover 4 main areas of signs:

1. **Prohibition** - circular signs, prime colours red and white, e.g. no pedestrian access.

2. **Warning** - triangular signs, prime colours black on yellow, e.g. overhead electrics.

3. **Mandatory** - circular signs, prime colours blue and white, e.g. safety helmets must be worn.

4. **Safe condition** - oblong/square signs, prime colours green and white, e.g. fire exit, first aid etc.

Supplementary signs provide additional information.

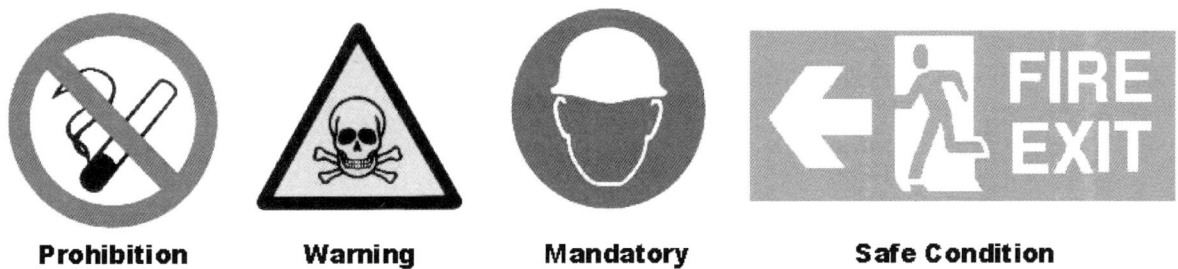

| Prohibition | Warning | Mandatory | Safe Condition |

Figure C1-10: Safety signs.   *Source: Safety Train.*

Figure C1-11: Mandatory.

Source: ACT.

Figure C1-12: Safe condition, warning & mandatory.   *Source: ACT.*

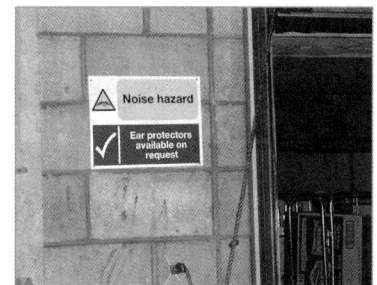

Figure C1-13: Warning & safe condition.

Source: ACT.

Hand signals

Hand signals must be precise, simple, expansive, easy to make and to understand, and clearly distinct from other such signals.

Meaning	Description	Illustration
General signals:		
START Attention Start of Command	both arms are extended horizontally with the palms facing forwards	
STOP Interruption End of movement	the right arm points upwards with the palm facing forwards	
END of the operation	both hands are clasped at chest height	
Vertical Movements:		
RAISE	the right arm points upwards with the palm facing forward and slowly makes a circle	
LOWER	the right arm points downwards with the palm facing inwards and slowly makes a circle	
VERTICAL DISTANCE	the hands indicate the relevant distance.	
Horizontal Movements:		
MOVE FORWARDS	both arms are bent with the palms facing upwards, and the forearms make slow movements towards the body	
MOVE BACKWARDS	both arms are bent with the palms facing downwards, and the forearms make slow movements away from the body	

Meaning	Description	Illustration
RIGHT to the signalman's	the right arm is extended more or less horizontally with the palm facing downwards and slowly makes small movements to the right	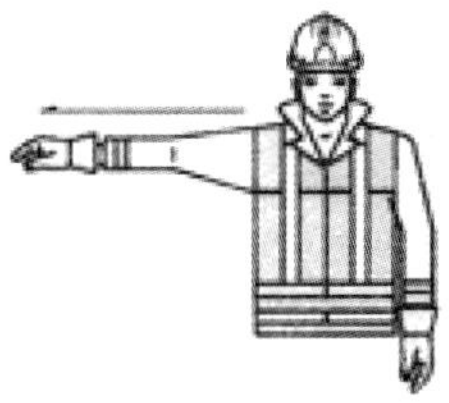
LEFT to the signalman's	the left arm is extended more or less horizontally with the palm facing downwards and slowly makes small movements to the left	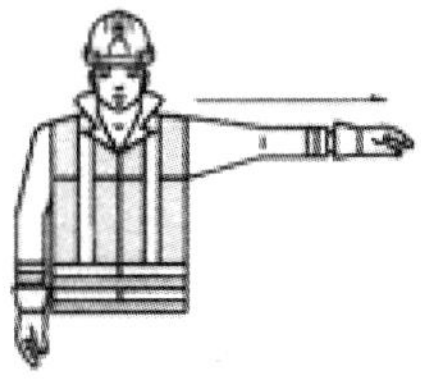
HORIZONTAL DISTANCE	the hands indicate the relevant distance.	
Danger: DANGER Emergency stop	both arms points upwards with the palms facing forwards	
QUICK	all movements faster	
SLOW	all movements slower	

Figure C1-14: Hand signals. *Source: Health and Safety (Safety Signs and Safety Signals) Regulations (SSSR) 1996.*

USE, LOCATION AND COMPLIANCE ISSUES

Safety signs and signals are not a substitute for other controls. Safety signs must be kept up to date, maintained in good condition and removed if they no longer apply.

1.6 - Confined spaces

DESCRIPTION OF CONDITIONS THAT CONSTITUTE A CONFINED SPACE

The Confined Spaces Regulations 1997, define a confined space as any place, including any chamber, tank, vat, silo, pit, pipe, sewer, flue, well, or other similar space, in which, by virtue of its enclosed nature, there is a foreseeable risk of a 'specified occurrence'.

A "specified occurrence" is defined as:

a. Fire or explosion.

b. Loss of consciousness or asphyxiation of any person at work arising from gas, fumes, vapour or lack of oxygen.

c. Drowning of any person at work.

d. Asphyxiation of any person at work arising from a free flowing solid.

e. Loss of consciousness of any person arising from a high ambient temperature.

Specific duties are placed on the employer (and self employed)

The employer must ensure compliance with the regulations in respect of work carried out by his employees. The employer must also ensure compliance so far as is reasonably practicable with the regulations in respect of work carried out by persons other than employees in so far as they relate to matters which are within the employer's control.

EXPLANATION OF CONFINED SPACE ENTRY RISK ASSESSMENT

Risk assessment will need to consider if entry is the only alternative to carry out the task, and if the task cannot be reasonably done by other means, the risks must be determined by analysis of each hazard and preventative control.

External factors such as weather conditions, temperature, proximity of other tasks, must also be included together with clear specification of the individuals responsible for isolation and making ready, those who need to enter and those who will monitor or might be required for rescue. The whole process should be documented and subject to a written permit to work.

FACTORS TO BE CONSIDERED WHEN ASSESSING RISK

A failure to appreciate the dangers associated with confined spaces has led not only to the deaths of many workers, but also to the demise of some of those who have attempted to rescue them. A confined space is not only a space which is small and difficult to enter, exit or work in; it can also be a large space, but with limited/restricted access. It can also be a space which is badly ventilated e.g. a tank or a large tunnel.

Need for access

Safe access to and egress from confined spaces

Openings affording safe access to confined spaces and through divisions, partitions or obstructions within such spaces need to be sufficiently large and free from obstruction to allow the passage of persons wearing the necessary protective clothing and equipment and to allow access for rescue purposes. Practice drills will help to check that the size of openings and entry procedures are satisfactory. Where entry to a confined space is necessary, employers will need to ensure that the necessary safety features are followed. For example, alongside openings which allow for safe access these might include a safety sign warning against unauthorised entry and platforms to enable safe working within the confined space.

Provision and maintenance of safe atmosphere

Testing the atmosphere

Testing of the atmosphere may be needed where knowledge of the confined space indicates that the atmosphere might be contaminated or to any extent abnormal. The appropriate choice of testing equipment will depend on particular circumstances. For example, when testing for toxic atmospheres, chemical detector tubes or portable atmospheric monitoring equipment is appropriate. However there may be cases requiring monitoring equipment specifically designed to measure for flammable atmospheres.

Testing should be carried out by persons experienced and competent in the practice and records of the findings should be kept. Personal gas detectors should be worn whenever appropriate to mitigate the hazard of local pockets of contaminates. Consideration needs to be given to:

- Deposits or sediments which may release toxic or flammable material when disturbed.
- Temperature changes may also cause materials to be released.
- Ingress of dangerous fumes from adjacent work.
- Failure of forced ventilation; in the event of failure of the ventilation either a back-up system should automatically take over or a system of work should be in place (e.g. alarm and air reservoir) to evacuate the confined space before anyone is put at risk.

Respiratory protective equipment (RPE)

Where RPE is provided or used in connection with confined space entry (including emergency rescue) it must be suitable for the purpose for which it is intended, i.e. correctly selected and matched both to the job and the wearer. RPE will not normally be suitable unless it is breathing apparatus with an independent air supply. Suitable breathing apparatus includes a properly fitting helmet or face-piece with necessary connections such that a person using it in poisonous, asphyxiating or irritant atmosphere breathes ordinary clean and dry air.

The task

Confined space entry should be subject to a procedure and permit to work system as discussed later. Whenever possible entry should be avoided by the use of, for example long reach tools for recovery of objects, pressure hoses for cleaning used from outside the confined space. The task must be clearly identified and described and subject to a formal assessment of needs.

Materials and equipment

Ropes, harnesses, lifelines, resuscitating apparatus, first aid equipment, protective clothing and other special equipment will usually need to be provided or used for or in connection with confined space entry or in case of emergency rescue. When a safety harness and line are used it is essential that the free end of the line is secured so that it can be used as part of the rescue procedure. The harness and line will need to be adjusted and worn so that the wearer can be drawn up head first through any manhole or opening. Power operated lifting equipment may be necessary for this purpose.

Persons at risk

Physical fitness, strength, agility are important attributes for those involved in confined space work together with low concern (claustrophobia) for work involving difficult or restricted access.

Reliability of safeguards

Typical safeguards include electrical isolation procedures. These will include lock off and / or fuse removal; removal of sections of pipe work to and from the vessel with the possible need to use blank off spades; removal and isolation of sources of heat (electrical, gas, steam) and the isolation of moving equipment such as mixers or turbines. All such safeguards will be subject to a company procedure and should be evaluated to ensure their effectiveness before entry is allowed. Where the use of breathing apparatus is required a standby person should monitor duration of exposure, within a 50% margin for air carried in a cylinder. For air supplied from a compressor a reservoir should be used, such that on failure of the compressor (and standby compressor) there is sufficient capacity for escape.

Operating procedures

Written procedures should be available for all confined space work; procedures may need to take account of work above ground (surface or gantry tanks) and work below ground (tanks, sewers etc). A procedure will normally require a formal document control system (permit to work certificate) to be used to describe (and restrict) the work to be done, a process to determine the hazards and define the controls to reduce the risk to an acceptable standard. The procedure will need to consider who is authorised to issue and establish controls and require those that enter to work to the controls. The form is signed by all parties to reinforce the gravity of the method of working. A possible permit to work certificate lay-out is shown below.

Example - entry into confined spaces

Possible Lay-Out For A Permit-To-Work Certificate

PLANT DETAILS (Location, identifying number, etc.		**ACCEPTANCE OF CERTIFICATE** Accepts all conditions of certificate		
WORK TO BE DONE			Signed Date Time	
WITHDRAWAL FROM SERVICE	Signed Date Time	**COMPLETION OF WORK** All work completed - equipment returned for use	Signed Date Time	
ISOLATION Dangerous fumes Electrical supply Sources of heat	Signed Date Time			
CLEANING AND PURGING Of all dangerous materials	Signed Date Time	**EXTENSION**	Signed Date Time	
TESTING For contamination	Contaminants tested Results Signed Date Time			
I CERTIFY THAT I HAVE PERSONALLY EXAMINED THE PLANT DETAILED ABOVE AND SATISFIED MYSELF THAT THE ABOVE PARTICULARS ARE CORRECT (1) THE PLANT IS SAFE FOR ENTRY WITHOUT BREATHING APPARATUS (2) BREATHING APPARATUS MUST BE WORN Other precautions necessary : Time of expiry of certificate : Signed Delete (1) or (2) Date Time		THIS PERMIT TO WORK IS NOW CANCELLED. A NEW PERMIT WILL BE REQUIRED IF WORK IS TO CONTINUE Signed Date Time		
		RETURN TO SERVICE	I accept the above plant back into service Signed Date Time	

Figure C1-15: Example PTW certificate (confined spaces).

Source: HSE Guidance note on permits to work.

Emergency arrangements

The Regulations prohibit any person to enter or carry out work in a confined space unless there are suitable and sufficient rescue arrangements in place. Emergency arrangements shall be suitable and sufficient provided they:

- Require the provision and maintenance of resuscitation equipment.
- Require the provision and maintenance of such equipment as is necessary to enable the emergency rescue to be carried out effectively.
- Restrict, so far as is reasonably practicable, the risks to health and safety of any rescuer.
- Shall immediately be put into operation when circumstances arise requiring a rescue.

The arrangements for emergency rescue will depend on the nature of the confined space, the risks identified and consequently the likely nature of an emergency rescue. The arrangements might need to cover:

1. Rescue and resuscitation equipment.
2. Special arrangements with local hospitals (e.g. for foreseeable poisoning).
3. Raising the alarm and rescue.
4. Safeguarding the rescuers.
5. Safeguarding the third parties.
6. Fire fighting.
7. Control of plant.
8. First aid.
9. Public emergency services.

STATUTORY REQUIREMENTS FOR TRAINING

Statutory requirements relate back to HASAWA, section (2) (C). Employers have a duty to provide such information, instruction, training and supervision to ensure the health and safety at work of employees. Specific training for work in confined spaces will include:

- Awareness of the Confined Space Regulations.
- The need to avoid entry unless it is not reasonably practicable to do so.
- Understand the work to be done (hazards and precautions).
- Understand the safe system of work, particularly permit to work.
- How emergencies arise, need to follow emergency procedures.

Specific training may include:

- Atmospheric testing equipment and interpretation of readings.
- Use, maintenance, cleaning of breathing apparatus or escape sets.
- Use of other PPE and limitations.
- Use of communication methods.
- Training in evacuation procedures.

Practical refresher training should be carried out at a suitable frequency. Standby team(s) for rescue would need to be trained additionally in:

- Use of rescue equipment, including lifelines, harness, lifting equipment.
- Dealing with failure of equipment whilst in use.
- Emergency arrangements and response.
- Resuscitation procedures and the use of any other related medical equipment.
- Emergency first aid.
- Use of fire fighting equipment.
- Liaison with local emergency services in the event of an incident.
- Training practice recovery with a full-weight dummy.

1.7 - Structural safety of workplaces

CAUSES OF DAMAGE TO THE STRUCTURE OF BUILDINGS

The biggest problems of deterioration met with in buildings are those caused by movement or the effects of water ingress. Softening of the ground from roof drainage may lead to settlement and consequential cracking of the wall. Erosion of soil due to rainwater runoff can undermine shallow foundations, leading to settlement and tilting of walls. Damaged drains and inspection chambers may also lead to ground softening. Tunnelling by vermin can also affect the stability of structures.

Lime mortar used with stone walls hardens over a period of time from the external face inwards. This surface hardening throws off rainwater, but, if the skin is ever damaged, water may penetrate through the joint and cause further deterioration.

Timber beams and roof trusses naturally deflect under load; joints and members may vary according to the moisture in the air. An increase in stress may occur due to overloading.

The ingress of water from whatever cause can lead to the deterioration of timber and mortar from the effects of wet rot. Dampness may come from driving rain, roof runoff or missing/damaged rainwater gutters. This concentrates water to a particular part of the wall. The results are clearly visible externally as stains and eroded mortar, etc. and any timber built into the wall is liable to be affected. Rusting of steelwork and reinforcement may cause cracking of surrounding masonry leading to further deterioration.

Adverse weather conditions

Severe weather conditions will often result in loss of roofing materials, collapse of signs and overturning of portable accommodation (portacabins).

Overloading of structures

Structures, racking and flooring may become overloaded and subject to collapse if materials stored are not managed correctly. Where storage racking is provided, each cell should be marked with the safe working load. Each vertical section of storage cells should be similarly plated with the safe working load for that group of cells. Prefabricated offices in work areas or warehouses should not be used to store materials on the roofs; such roofs should be signed to prevent this practice.

Consideration should be given to restricting total weight and identifying distribution of weight on all floors above ground level (where a cellar is below ground level, consider all floors above the cellar). Floors are particularly at risk during refurbishment when building materials might be concentrated within a small area, similarly during demolition, if materials are allowed to accumulate in large quantities.

Damage from moving plant

Damage may occur to walls, door edges, storage racking overhead pipe work and lights from a variety of vehicles both within and external to the building through contact with a variety of vehicles such as fork lift trucks, heavy goods vehicles and mobile plant. Protective devices include use of height, width clearance plates, physical barriers to protect overhead services, physical barriers and line marking to protect walls and doorways.

Hot and corrosive atmospheres

Work processes which evolve hot or corrosive atmospheres will progressively weaken structures with time. Temperature change will cause expansion and contraction of the building fabric, which may exceed the design specification over time. Corrosive atmospheres will erode the surface of the structure and may affect electrical insulation and cause hydrogen enbrittlement of steel supports if the levels exceed the design specification.

Vibration

Vibration from mobile and fixed equipment, if not suitably deadened with vibration buffers, may result in structural damage, or undermining of foundations.

Alteration to structural members

Before any building is modified or changed, a structural engineer should be involved in the design change phase; reference to the safety file for new builds will also be essential. Local building regulation / planning permission may be necessary; also liaison with the local fire authority and fire risk assessment is likely to be required.

Subsidence

Subsidence may occur over time due to natural ground movement. The design should have considered this possibility and footings suitable for the location should have been agreed with the local building regulation department and carried through into the build. Subsidence can occur as a result of extreme weather (or fracture of water supply main) resulting in flooding and subsoil erosion of the ground. New builds next to existing structures or other excavation works may weaken the subsoil and lead to subsidence.

Deterioration of building materials

Regular monitoring and maintenance of the building fabric will be required to ensure maximum life. Buildings will deteriorate from general wear and tear, from the effects of the environment, external issues will include sunlight, temperature change and ingress of rain, which will particularly affect cladding of wood and some synthetic materials. Internally, issues to consider will include changes in temperature, humidity and the corrosive effects of waste by products of processes.

Excavations

Excavations will need to be secured from collapse by the use of appropriate shoring, cross over points may be necessary and spoil and materials, vehicles should not be allowed to collect near the edge. Barriers must be used to prevent falls of people into the trench from the edge or cross over points. Adequate access and egress points should be established, together with suitable lighting.

Principles of fire and explosion

Overall aims

On completion of this Element, the student will have knowledge and understanding of:

■ the physics and chemistry of fire and explosion.

■ principles and prevention of fire spread.

■ the production of smoke and toxic fumes, their effects and control measures.

■ behaviour and performance of common building materials and structures in a fire and their relationship to the principles of prevention of fire spread in buildings.

Content

Specific intended learning outcomes

The intended learning outcomes are that the student will be able to:

1.   advise on the risks of fire and explosion in work premises

2.   advise on the implementation of appropriate control measures

Relevant statutory provisions

Dangerous Substances and Explosive Atmospheres Regulation (DSEAR) 2002

Electricity at Work Regulations (EWR) 1989

2.1 - Physics and chemistry of fire and explosion

Properties of solids, liquids and gases

FLASH POINT

The lowest temperature at which a substance will flash momentarily when a flame is applied.

FIRE POINT

The lowest temperature at which the heat produced will enable combustion to continue after a substance is ignited.

AUTO-IGNITION TEMPERATURE

The lowest temperature at which the substance will ignite spontaneously. It will burn without a flame or other ignition source.

VAPOUR DENSITY

This term is sometimes used in the 'fire world' and can cause confusion, as it is often mistaken for the 'density of a vapour' (relative density). Vapour density is the density of a gas or vapour compared to the density of hydrogen. This is worked out by using the molecular weights of the atoms concerned. Therefore the vapour density of, for example, oxygen is:

$$\frac{32}{2} = 16.$$

(Molecular weight oxygen = 32, hydrogen = 2).

This figure of vapour density is in a way therefore of little value, as it is a theoretical comparison to hydrogen.

For fire safety and fire protection reasons we are concerned with the comparison of a material and its vapours in relation to air (in the majority of cases). The vapour density of air at standard temperature and pressure is taken as 22.4. We can see therefore that the actual or relative density for oxygen when compared to air is:

$\frac{32}{22.4} = 1.43$ g/l a stp (i.e. approximately $1\frac{1}{2}$ times heavier than air).

As can be seen the difference is considerable and it must be ensured that the relative density of a vapour is used when considering its hazards and the necessary safety measures.

RELATIVE DENSITY

Density effects - liquids

Densities are determined by comparing the weight (mass) of a given volume of material with the weight (mass) of the same volume of water at the same temperature. Water is given a density of 1.0.

Some oils and fats have densities greater than one and would sink if mixed with water; materials such as petrol and benzene have densities less than one and would float on water. Low density liquids can spread and remain on top of denser liquids, Petrol and many organic solvents are less dense than water and when spilt or discharged into drainage systems may create a flammable or toxic hazard because they lie on the surface of the water. Selection of fire fighting equipment is important when dealing with fires involving solvents which are insoluble in water.

As indicated above density also varies with temperature. This is why the layering or stratification of immiscible liquids may occur in process and storage vessels upon heating. Increased temperatures may cause a reduction of density which increases the volume of the material. If the material is in a closed container the increased pressure exerted may cause the container to burst. Storage containers should therefore never be totally filled with liquids - an expansion gap is necessary to allow for changes in ambient temperature. The gap necessary should be calculated for the type of material to be stored and the maximum temperature likely to occur. The gap is referred to as the ullage space.

On a larger scale this phenomenon was overlooked and a major disaster occurred at the San Carlos campsite in Spain when a road tanker released product due to the effects of thermal expansion. The resultant ignition and explosion caused a fireball to travel through a busy camp site and beach area, causing serious burns and fatalities to hundreds of holiday makers, their injuries being worsened because they were in swim wear and did not have the protection of everyday clothing. The road tanker failure occurred due to overfilling at the depot. The tanker had been filled with 23 tonnes of propylene, but should have been filled to a maximum of 19 tonnes. For that density of material this would have left a substantial ullage for thermal expansion.

Density effects - gases and vapours

Few materials have a molecular weight less than air (approximately 29) so under normal conditions most gases and vapours are heavier than air. Hydrogen (1), methane (14) and ammonia (17) are exceptions.

The higher the molecular weight of a gas/vapour the greater its density at constant temperature. Vapours heavier than air can spread and accumulate at low level, e.g. in pits, sumps or drains and can give rise to:

- Fire/explosion hazards e.g. Propane, vapour density 1.5, air 1.0.
- A toxic hazard e.g. Chlorine.
- Oxygen deficiency in confined spaces e.g. Carbon Dioxide.

Densities of toxic gases and vapours relative to air at 20oC (ambient)			
	Density gas / density of air	**Boiling point oC**	**Molecular weight**
Ammonia	0.59	- 33.4	17
Propane	1.5	- 45	41
Carbon dioxide	1.98	- 79	44
Acetone vapour	2.00	56.5	58
Sulphur dioxide	2.22		64
Chlorine	2.46		71
Phosgene	3.43		99
Bromine vapour	5.54		160

Figure C2-1: Densities of toxic gases.   *Source: FST Consultancy.*

Vapours less dense than air at ambient temperature will spread at low level when cold, for example, vapours from liquid ammonia or propane spillage.

Accumulation of gases less dense than air e.g. hydrogen and methane can arise at high points in poorly ventilated buildings.

Consideration needs to be given to work activities where gas accumulation might occur e.g. maintenance work at a height.

Examples of saturated air are given below.

Relative densities of saturated air at 25°C	
Di-isobutyl ketone	1.01
Benzene	1.21
Carbon tetrachloride	1.65
Petrol	3.0

Figure C2-2: Relative densities of saturated air.   *Source: FST Consultancy.*

The relative density of a vapour or gas with air is important when considering local exhaust ventilation (LEV) requirements. We would normally position LEV at high level at filling points, but additional LEV at low level may be required for high relative density materials.

LIMITS OF FLAMMABILITY

A flammable gas or vapour will only burn in air if the mixture lies between certain limits. They are normally given as a percentage and are called:

- Upper Explosive Limit - the highest mixture of fuel and air that will just support a flame.
- Lower Explosive Limit - the lowest mixture of fuel and air that will just support a flame.

Remember, it is only vapour that burns; a solid or liquid must be heated to a temperature where the vapour given off can ignite before combustion takes place.

CRITICAL TEMPERATURE

Any liquid when heated will eventually boil. If this happens at atmospheric pressure it is known as the 'normal boiling point'. If the pressure is increased, a higher temperature must be reached before the liquid will boil. However, there comes a point where no matter what pressure is applied, the liquid will boil and vaporise. This is known as the 'critical temperature'. Some common examples are:

	Critical Temperature' oC
Butane	153
Chlorine	144
Ethylene	10
Hydrogen	-240
Methane	-83
Propane	96

Figure C2-3: Critical temperature examples.   *Source: FST Consultancy.*

Critical pressure

The pressure that must be applied to a gas fractionally below its critical temperature in order to liquefy it, is called its critical pressure.

	Critical Pressure (Atmosphere)
Butane	36
Chlorine	76
Ethylene	51
Hydrogen	13
Methane	46
Propane	43

Figure C2-4: Critical pressure examples.   *Source: FST Consultancy.*

When a gas with a fairly high critical temperature is kept as a liquid under pressure, such as Propane (LPG), it is important that ullage space is left inside the container. This is due to the expansion of the liquid as it is heated. The thermal expansion of the liquid alone may be sufficient to rupture the container. Assuming that correct ullage spaces are left, then the only increase in pressure will be due to the vapour pressure inside the ullage space for which the storage containers should be designed to withstand.

Obviously if stored incorrectly, e.g. aerosol in sunshine, a dangerous pressure rise occurs, and rupture/explosion can happen.

MAXIMUM EXPLOSION PRESSURE

The maximum explosion pressure is relevant in any area where flammable materials may be found and the potential for an explosion occurs.

Each mixture of flammable vapour with air will produce a different explosion pressure dependant upon the fuel / air mixture. The maximum explosion pressure is reached if the mixture is at its ideal or stoichiometric mixture.

The maximum explosion pressures will also be dictated by the material itself.

Fuel	Lower explosive limit kg/cu m	Maximum Explosive Pressure (Bars)
Coal	0.035	7.8
Aluminium	0.035	6.5
Starch	0.045	11.0

Figure C2-5: Maximum explosion pressures.   *Source: FST Consultancy.*

RATE OF PRESSURE RISE

Another consideration would be the rate of pressure rise. The slower the initial pressure rise occurs within an explosion, then the greater the chance of detecting the pressure rise and releasing an inerting agent to suppress the explosion.

When considering the effects of an explosion and the possible protection or prevention measures we need to consider the use of an inerting agent to suppress, provide sufficient blow out relief panels to vent the explosive force, or design the plant / machinery to withstand the maximum explosion pressure.

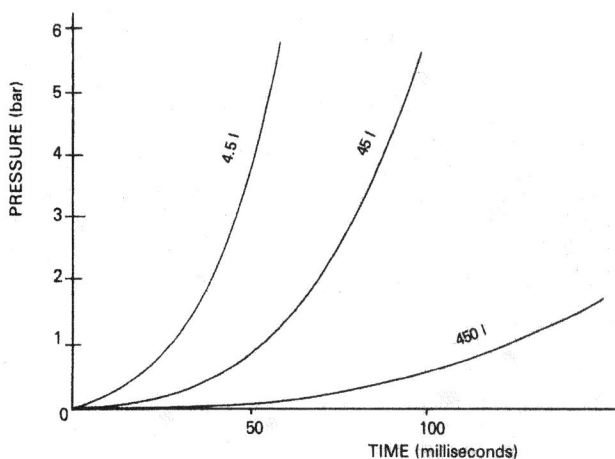

Figure C2-6: Explosion pressure curves for hexane/air mixtures in vessels of different sizes.   *Source: Ambiguous.*

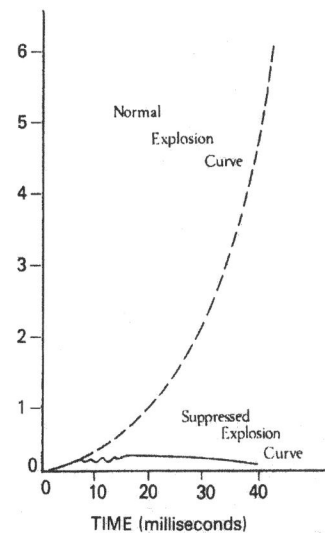

Figure C2-7: Suppressed explosion curve for a hexane/air mixture in a one gallon vessel.   *Source: Ambiguous.*

Mechanism of fire and explosion

THE FIRE TRIANGLE

Definition of combustion

Combustion is defined as being a chemical reaction during which heat energy and light energy are emitted.

The fire triangle

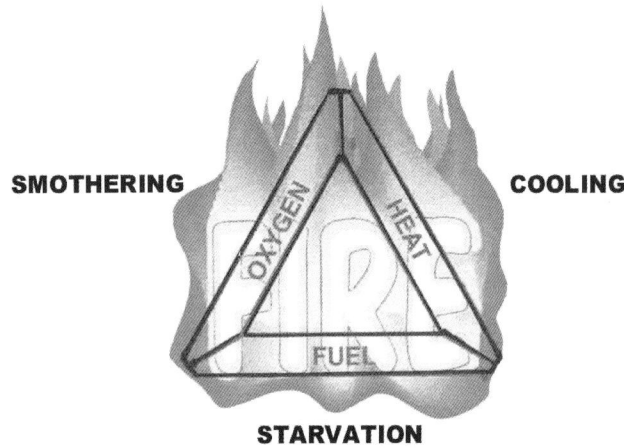

SMOTHERING

COOLING

STARVATION

Figure C2-8: The fire triangle.   Source: CorelDraw! 5.0 clipart.

A simple approach depicts fire as having three essential parts: fuel, oxygen and heat - this is called the fire triangle. When these three components form together in the right proportions, then the chemical reaction of combustion takes place. This traditional system is useful when you are considering the 'ingredients' needed to make a fire.

If one or more of these parts of the fire is removed, the fire will be extinguished.

This can be done by:

- **Cooling** the fire to remove the heat.
- **Starving** the fire of fuel.
- **Smothering** the fire by limiting its oxygen supply.
- **Chemical Interference** of the flame reactions.

The combustion process

As discussed above the combustion process is defined as a chemical reaction (or series of reactions) where heat and light energy are evolved. However, this is a very simplistic approach, and we would be better describing the chemical reactions in the combustion process as happening very quickly, at very high temperatures, and in very small volumes. The tiny reactions that take place will be exothermic and give out sufficient excess heat so as to 'fuel' the next chemical reaction. Combustion is therefore a chain reaction, or indeed a series of branching chain reactions. Many experts have studied the chemistry of fire, but it would probably still be true to say that all the chemical reactions that are occurring when a candle is burning cannot be written down. As an example of the complex nature of combustion we will consider the burning of hydrogen.

This reaction is simply denoted chemically as: **2 H2 + O2 = 2H2O**

This equation suggests that two molecules of hydrogen combine with one molecule of oxygen to form two molecules of water when they collide. Collisions like this must happen but they are very rare and do not explain the extremely rapid reactions in a hydrogen/oxygen explosion. In fact all flame reactions depend on the activities of 'broken off bits' of molecules. These tiny fragments are very reactive, very unstable, and can only exist for a fraction of a second. However, they are very mobile and capable of rapid reproduction. These fragments are known as 'free radicals'. If we consider the equation again we can see that the component parts can be broken up into hydrogen atoms (H), oxygen atoms (O), and hydroxyl radicals (OH). Inside a flame, all three components are very hot, in high concentrations and completely free to react. If we therefore consider these three separately:

If an oxygen atom collides with a hydrogen molecule, this can happen: ***O* + H2 →*OH + H***

(* denotes very energetic fragment or free radical)

A hydrogen atom will collide with oxygen to give: ***H + O2 → *OH + *O***

Finally, the *OH radical reacts with hydrogen to form water vapour plus one free radical: ***OH + H2 → H2O + H***

As you can see the combustion process is indeed a series of chain reactions and branching chain reactions. If we put the above reactions together we get an idea of the complex nature of combustion:

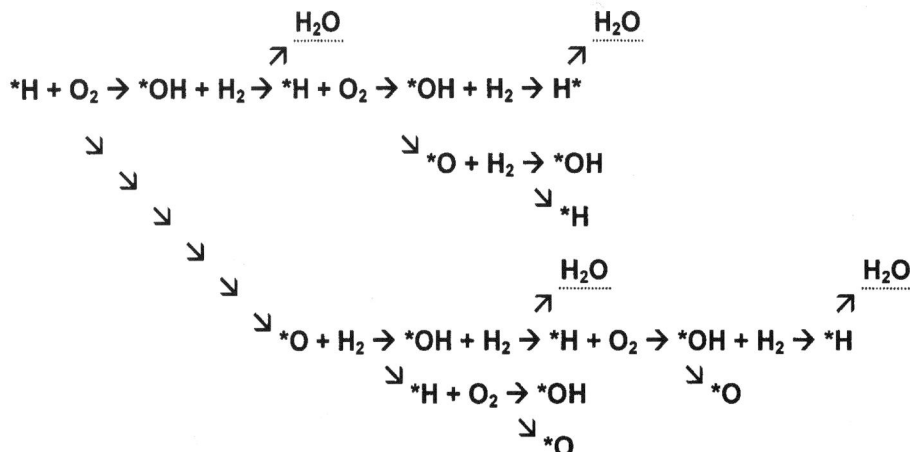

Points where water vapour is given off is denoted as **H_2O**.

In the above we have considered the exothermic reactions found in many fuels, which are stable compounds. They will only react (combust) if there is sufficient heat being produced to decompose the adjacent fuel molecule etc. We should also never forget the endothermic reactions found in certain materials where they absorb heat when they react. Thankfully these materials/compounds are infrequent, as they are unstable, as no heat has to be supplied to decompose them. Good examples of endothermic compounds would be carbon disulphide or more commonly, acetylene, as both explode readily.

THE EFFECTS OF ATOMISATION AND OXYGEN CONTENT

Atomisation

The size of the fuel droplets is an important parameter in combustion; the smaller the size of the droplet, the better the combustion. A 0.1 mm droplet burns in 0.01 seconds while a 0.2 mm droplet burns in 0.04 seconds. The combustion time is thus more or less square the value of the size of the droplet. As a consequence, a larger droplet may not burn internally when it starts to reach the cooler end of the flame. This causes the formation of soot and coke.

Oxygen content

Oxygen reacts with most elements. The initiation, speed, vigour and extent of these reactions depend in particular upon:

- The concentration, temperature and pressure of the reactants.
- Ignition energy and mode of ignition.

Oxygen enrichment of the atmosphere, even by a few percent, considerably increases the risk of fire. Sparks which would normally be regarded as harmless can cause fires, and materials which do not burn in air, including fireproofing materials, may burn vigorously or even spontaneously in enriched air. Oil and grease are particularly hazardous in the presence of oxygen as they can ignite spontaneously and burn with explosive violence. They should never be used to lubricate oxygen or enriched air equipment (special lubricants which are compatible with oxygen can be used under certain conditions). Many burning accidents which occur are triggered off by the lighting of a cigarette, therefore it is impossible to over-emphasise the danger of smoking in oxygen enriched atmospheres or where oxygen enrichment can occur. In such areas smoking must be forbidden.

IGNITION SOURCES

The majority of fires need an ignition source to enable them to start. It is imperative therefore that an assessment is made at your place of work to recognise all ignition sources that are, or are likely to be present. Once these ignition sources have been located, then the surrounding areas can be checked for combustible materials or gases that are normally or are likely to be present.

Having now identified all problem areas, a study can be made to assess the viability of removing the ignition source and the combustible material from each other. If this is not possible then some form of control measure should be taken so as to minimise the risk of fire. Ignition sources can be found in many varied ways. Some of the more common ways are listed below:

- Smokers, smokers' materials.
- Sparks from welding guns.
- Sparks from machinery.
- Static electricity.
- Electrical faults.
- Overheating machinery.
- Non-intrinsically safe equipment used in a flammable atmosphere.
- Radiated heat from a legitimate source.

It is also important that good housekeeping is maintained. If any of the above ignition sources are present and the housekeeping is poor, then the likelihood of a fire breaking out is dramatically increased. There are various types of ignition sources. The measures to control them are diverse.

Heat   This is present in many forms and anything that produces heat can be a source of ignition. The way to control this is to identify the source - then control it. Some examples of heat and control measures are:

- Friction - this can be controlled by good levels of maintenance and inspection.
- Conduction - metal is lagged to prevent heat transfer.
- Welding and Burning - safe systems of work are used with good levels of training and suspension and protection of combustible materials in areas of work.

Electrical
- Earth bonding - to prevent arcing of electricity, especially on supply pipes such as gas.
- Fuses and circuit breakers - to detect over current and prevent heating of machinery.

Smoking
- Disposal of cigarette ends in suitable containers.
- Disciplined staff and inspections to adhere to smoking policy.

Source of Ignition	Control Measure
Smoking materials	Good housekeeping, management control.
Sparks from welding gun	Hot work permits, management control.
Sparks from machinery	Good maintenance programmes, good housekeeping, correct choice of machinery.
Static electricity	Safe system of work, earthing straps/bonding, use of anti-static materials.
Electrical faults	Competent staff, good maintenance checks.
Overheating machinery	Good maintenance programmes, correct siting for airflows etc.
Radiated heat from legitimate source	Space separation, shielding / fire resistance.

Figure C2-9: Source of ignition & control measures.   *Source: FST Consultancy.*

Causes of ignition

Flammable materials may ignite in many ways, some familiar, some less so. Knowledge of the most important ignition scenarios is essential for designers seeking to reduce the likelihood of fire in buildings. The common element is heat transfer. Heat may be transferred by radiation through space, by conduction, upon direct contact with a heat source, or by convection (where air or other heated fluid moves to carry heat from source to sample). All ignitions are caused by a version of heat transfer, although other factors may influence them.

Sources of fuel

Anything that burns is a fuel for a fire:

- Flammable liquids.
- Flammable gases.
- Flammable chemicals.
- Wood.

- Paper and card.
- Plastics, rubber and foam.
- Loose packing materials.
- Waste materials.

Naked flame

The most common ignition source is flame. A match flame transfers heat primarily by convection and may be simply represented in laboratory testing. Larger flames, 0.5 m high or more, transfer heat primarily by radiative transfer and may ignite objects without coming into direct contact with them. The larger the flame the more probable radiative ignition becomes.

Hot surfaces

Hot surfaces can also cause fire. A heated metal block can transfer sufficient heat (by conduction) to raise the temperature of some materials above their ignition temperature. The most common case of ignition by this means is probably the kitchen fire in which a towel is ignited by contact with a cooking element.

Arcing

An electrically caused fire can occur if electrical energy is converted to thermal energy and the heat generated is transferred to a combustible material at a rate that will cause the material to reach its ignition temperature. One mechanism involved in converting electrical energy to thermal energy in an electrical distribution system is arc heating. "Arcing" is defined as a luminous discharge of electricity across an insulating medium. The electrical discharge of an arc can involve temperatures of several thousand degrees Celsius. In determining the heating effects of an arc, the classical Joule heating equation involving current squared multiplied by resistance (I^2R), however, does not fully explain the heating effects. Although the total power dissipated in the arc is equal to the total voltage drop in the arc multiplied by the arc current, power dissipation is not uniform throughout the arc. In general, arcing can be divided into two categories:

1. Non-contact arcing.

2. Contact arcing.

Non-contact arcing

This is arcing that does not require direct physical contact between the conductors or "electrodes" where the arcing is taking place. Two types of non-contact arcing involving lower voltages are:

1. Arcing between conductors separated by insulation that occurs across the surface of the insulation.

2. Arcing between conductors separated by pyrolyzed (carbonised) insulation.

With arcing between conductors separated by insulation, the mechanism of initiating an arc between stationary conductors separated by insulation will depend on the type and geometry of the conductors and insulation between them. In the case of typical air clearances found in an electrical residential distribution system, many kilovolts may be required to initiate arcing.

With arcing between conductors separated by carbonised insulation, arcing can occur at normal operational voltages. The resulting fault-current causes the carbon path to open and an arc is established similar to parting the conductors, as with contact arcing. Carbonised insulation between opposite polarity conductors or between a line-voltage conductor and ground can lead to an across-the-line arcing fault or a line-to-ground arcing fault.

Contact arcing

This is arcing that involves direct or indirect physical contact between the conductors, known as electrodes, where the arcing is taking place, such as arcing between closing or parting conductors making or breaking a circuit. With this type of arcing, the arc initiation mechanism involves a hot point (essentially from I2R heating) at the last point of contact when a circuit is being interrupted (i.e., conductors initially in contact are parting), or at the first point of contact where a circuit is being established (i.e., conductors that are initially separated and subsequently come into contact). Contact arcing is associated with normal operational arcing that occurs with any kind of air-gap type electrical switching device. Properly designed switching devices are capable of withstanding such arcing without excessive contact damage or generation of excessive heat. Contact arcing may also be associated with arcing faults due to the unintentional creation or interruption of current.

Technology for the 20th century - overcurrent protective devices

An overcurrent protective device (OCPD), such as a fuse or circuit breaker, is specifically designed to protect electrical circuits against the unwanted effects of overcurrents. For example, when too many products are plugged into the same electrical outlet, and the total load current exceeds the rating of the branch circuit, the OCPD will open the circuit before damage or a fire occurs. An OCPD, however, is not designed to protect a circuit against arcing faults. Because of the time-current characteristics of the OCPD necessary to provide effective protection against overcurrents, some arcing faults, including damaging arcing faults, may have time and/or current characteristics below the threshold levels necessary to open the OCPD.

The AFCI - technology for the 21st century

To offer additional protection to electrical circuits against the unwanted effects of electrical arcing, manufacturers have begun incorporating arc-fault detection technology into a product known as an arc-fault circuit interrupter, or AFCI. An AFCI is a device intended to reduce the number of arcing-fault fires by opening the electrical circuit when an arc fault is detected. What differentiates an AFCI from an OCPD is the complex electronic circuitry in the AFCI that can identify specific characteristics or signatures of the current or voltage waveform that are unique to electrical arcing.

Source: www.ul.com.

Sparking

Sparks generate very high temperatures in a very small space, but except when flammable gas mixtures are involved it is rare that a spark will cause ignition in the absence of other factors.

Smoking

Prohibition of smoking may be unreasonable and will lead to illicit smoking, but prohibition is essential where hazardous materials are dealt with, or processes are carried on which involve the release of ignitable or explosive dusts or vapours or the production of readily combustible waste. Smoking should be prohibited in stock rooms and other rooms not under continuous supervision. Any area where 'no smoking' is imposed should have the rule strictly enforced. Where smoking is allowed, provide easily accessible, non-combustible receptacles for cigarette ends and other smoking material and empty daily. Smoking should cease half an hour before closing down.

Electrostatic discharge

This is a transfer of electrostatic charges between bodies at different electrostatic potentials caused by direct contact or induced by an electrostatic field. Examples of electrostatic charges are:

- Walking across a nylon carpet on a dry day generates a static electrical charge of 35,000 volts.
- Opening a plastic bag generates a charge of 20,000 volts.

Fire control and navigation systems on military equipment such as the M-1 tank and F-18 aircraft are controlled by electronic microchips so sensitive that a static charge of 30-50 volts of static electricity may cause the equipment to malfunction during deployment or combat missions. Many of these defects are traced to careless handling and packaging of items sensitive to electrostatic discharge.

While microchips have grown smaller with greater functional capabilities, the components have become increasingly more complex requiring minute amounts of electrical current in terms of microvolts (one-millionth of a volt). These items are sensitive / susceptible to damage caused by static electricity and or electromagnetic forces, thus, requiring electrostatic/electromagnetic protective packaging materials, special marking, special workstations, clothing, equipment, and handling procedures.

Electrostatic discharge damage can take the form of:

- *Upset failures* result in gate leakage.
- *Catastrophic failures* occur in two forms: Direct and Latent failures.

Upset failures occur when an electrostatic discharge (ESD) has caused a current flow that is not significant to cause total failure. However, in use it may intermittently result in gate leakage causing loss of software or incorrect storage of information. Upset or latent failures may pass your company's quality control testing program.

Direct catastrophic failures occur when a component is damaged to the point where it is dead and will never again function. This is the easiest type of ESD damage to find, since it usually can be detected during testing.

Latent failures occur when ESD weakens or wounds the component to the point where it will still function properly during testing. However, over time the wounded component will cause poor system performance and eventually complete system failure. Because latent failures occur after final inspection or in the hands of our customers, the cost for repair is very high. Not only is this type of damage hard to find, it severely affects the performance of weapons systems and adversely affects the reputation of the supplying contractor's product. Therefore, it is imperative that ESD packaging and handling procedures be followed completely.

Source: www.dscc.dla.mil.

Exposure time

This can be critical. An intense heat source may cause a fire in a very short time, but so also may a much less intense heat source over a longer period. Thus fire in a waste paper basket may ignite a sofa very quickly, but a carelessly dropped cigarette may also cause ignition given more time.

Secondary ignition

The propagation of fire beyond the site of primary ignition will almost inevitably involve secondary ignition of surrounding materials. Now the ignition source is most often larger than before and may present an exposure different from the original. A lit match may not set a room on fire, but if it ignites the contents of a waste paper basket the room may become vulnerable.

When a fire has generated sufficient heat to make the upper reaches of a room very hot, there can eventually be sufficient radiation from this hot layer to ignite essentially all of the remaining unburnt materials in the area. This is termed flashover. Survival in the room would not now be possible.

Vapour phase explosions

Explosions can occur in flammable gases/vapours and also in certain types of dusts. An explosion is probably best defined as "rapid flame propagation throughout an area containing flammable vapours and dusts". For the explosion to occur the vapour/dust must be mixed with air in such proportions that the mixture is within the flammability range for that substance. Explosion can occur with such gases as hydrogen, propane, acetylene and examples of dusts that may cause explosion hazards are aluminium, coal, flour and polythene. In a dust explosion, there is an initial smaller Primary Explosion, which is then followed by a devastating Secondary Explosion. *See also - Dust explosions - later in this Element.*

CONFINED VAPOUR CLOUD EXPLOSIONS

Abbeystead, 1984

A confined explosion of methane gas in an underground pumping station resulted in the deaths of 16 people and injuries to 26 others. The water had not been pumped for 17 days and methane which had been released due to changes in temperature/vapour pressure over the period had accumulated in large quantities and was ignited with catastrophic effects. The methane had percolated from the surrounding ground through the concrete walls of the tunnel and become dissolved in the water supply. It had not been recognised that significant quantities of methane might be present through gas-liquid solubility effects.

Gas-liquid solubility effects

For dilute solutions the partial pressure exerted by a gas solute 1 in a liquid solvent 2 is given by:

P1 = H x m

where H is Henry's Law constant for the specific system and m is the mole fraction of the solute in the solvent.

Different values of H apply for each gas-liquid system. For a gas only slightly soluble in a liquid, e.g. oxygen in water, a much higher partial pressure of the gas is in equilibrium with a solution of given concentration, than with moderately soluble methane or highly soluble ammonia in water.

The solubility of a gas generally decreases with increasing temperature.

A simple example of how these circumstances may occur in any workplace is the storage of a gallon of petrol in a garage. If the container were to leak and spill its entire contents upon the floor then the following scenario could result:

One gallon of petrol on complete vaporisation under ambient conditions would fill a tank of volume 66m^3 with a vapour-air mixture at the lower flammable limit of 1.4% in air.

Relatively small quantities may result in:

- Significant explosions.
- Fireball.
- Spread of liquid (if liquid at normal temperature and pressure).
- Thermal radiation (heat).
- Projectiles.

UNCONFINED VAPOUR CLOUD EXPLOSIONS

The classic example of an unconfined vapour cloud explosion was that which occurred in 1974 at the Nypro UK chemical plant at Flixborough. The explosion occurred following the uncontrolled release of cyclohexane from a temporary pipe line which had been used to bypass a reactor taken out of service for repair *(see also - Actual incidents of vapour phase explosions - later in this Element).* The cyclohexane collected over the plant due to inversion conditions. Normally the air temperature decreases with altitude. In inversion conditions the reverse is true (i.e. temperature increases with altitude). The unusual condition did not allow the vapour cloud to disperse and it collected within explosive limits. The cloud was ignited from an unknown source and the resulting explosion killed 28 people and injured 36 others. Off site, several hundred were injured mainly by flying debris. There was:

- Damage to over 1,800 premises (ranging from structural failure through loss of roof tiles to broken windows).
- Damage to power transmission lines (several brought down).
- The fracture of a cooling water supply line to a steel works (2 miles away).

It should be noted that the presence, layout and design of structures within the area of the explosion can help to magnify its effects.

BOILING LIQUID EXPANDING VAPOUR EXPLOSIONS (BLEVES)

Gases, such as butane and propane, are stored in cylinders under pressure in their liquid phase. When the valve to the cylinder is opened the resulting drop in pressure restores the butane etc. to the gaseous state. If, however, the closed cylinder is in a fire, its contents will revert to the gaseous phase with a resulting increase in pressure inside the cylinder. As the heat turns the liquid into a vapour, the vapour is vented off and the liquid level drops. As there is less and less liquid to absorb the heat, the metal container just above the liquid level absorbs the heat and the structure of the metal starts to change and weaken. The metal melts and thins, can no longer contain the pressure of the contents and ruptures. The contents burst out catching fire as they go and sending chunks of the metal container into the surrounding area. This is known as a boiling liquid, expanding vapour explosion (BLEVE).

This will consist of :

- A blast wave (usually low).
- Radiation (thermal) high.

- Missiles (projectiles) long distance.

Severe burn range:

- Aerosol can   10 metres.
- LPG cylinder   35 metres.

- LPG rail transport   250 metres.

Pressure can build up in drums due to the difference between filling temperature and ambient temperature. If the ambient temperature is higher, ejection or splashing of the liquid contents, or vapour release, may occur on opening exposing the operator to the risk of splashing.

In June 1993 at Ste. Elizabeth de Warwick, Quebec, Canada, the fire brigade responded to a large cattle barn fire. A 4,900 litre propane tank was close to the fire with its relief vent operating, shooting flames over 5 metres into the air. The fire fighters applied water to the LPG tank in an effort to cool it, but the tank bleved and split into two large pieces. One piece was blasted into an open field while the other one travelled over 47 metres, struck a fire engine, then travelled a further 232 metres where it struck a passing vehicle trapping the occupant. Four fire fighters were killed when the metal struck the fire engine, one being thrown 47 metres. The blast also injured three fire fighters and four members of the public.

In April 1998 in Albert City, Iowa, two pipelines carrying liquid propane were struck by a vehicle; the LPG rapidly converted to gas and was ignited by a nearby ignition source. The fire impinged on the main LPG tank containing 83,000 litres, which was situated between three buildings. The tank vented allowing the gas to escape and was left to vent while water was applied in an attempt to keep the tank cool. However, the gas was not vented fast enough and the weakened metal tank split sending large sections in four directions. The blast extinguished the fire. Two fire fighters were killed and a number of people were badly burned including the fire chief. The pieces destroyed buildings and travelled up to 77 metres away.

Actual incidents of vapour phase explosions

FLIXBOROUGH 1974

On Saturday 1st June 1974 the Flixborough Works of Nypro (UK) Limited (Nypro) exploded killing 28 people and injuring 36 others on site. The explosion was estimated to be the equivalent of 15-45 tons of TNT. If the disaster had occurred during the normal working week the death toll would have certainly been greater. Outside the site, 53 casualties were recorded together with extensive property damage over a wide area (1,821 houses and 167 shops/factories).

Circumstances

- No 5 reactor (R2525) was discovered to be leaking on the cyclohexane train and was shut down in order to be depressurised and cooled prior to a full inspection. The next morning (28th March 1974) a 6 ft crack was found by the Plant Manager.
- The gap between the flanking reactors (No. 4 and No. 6) was bridged by a 20 inch dog leg pipe between 2 expansion bellows. The inlet and the outlet of the pipe were at different levels and unsupported.
- The assembly was subjected to temperature and pressure more severe than had been encountered since the dog leg was fitted but still within what should have been normal margins.
- The bridging pipe ruptured which released large quantities of cyclo-hexane which mixed with air to form an unconfined vapour cloud which then exploded.

Key factors

- No proper design study had been carried out, nor had the need for support of the bypass pipe been appreciated.
- British Standards were not consulted.
- No safety testing had been carried out.
- The key post of Works Engineer was vacant and none of the senior personnel, who were chemical engineers, were capable of recognising what should have been a simple engineering problem. A junior engineer was present but his concerns were discounted as was his latter sketch for supports.
- There was an inadequate nitrogen supply upon which the hazardous process system depended.
- There was nitrate stress corrosion on the reactor (R2525) thought to have initiated the sequence of events which led to disaster.
- Many of the stainless steel pipes had suffered from embrittlement due to contact with zinc. The stainless steel pipes had also suffered from creep cavitation fractures which can be produced in a relatively short time under temperature and pressure.
- Note that the events in the control room cannot be determined with certainty as all control room personnel were killed and the instruments destroyed.

SAN CARLOS 1978

San Carlos de la Rapita, Spain, July 11 1978. An overloaded truck carrying combustible propylene gas skidded around a bend in the road and slammed into a wall. The cargo was released, caught fire and bleved, sending 100-ft-high flames into a campsite where 780 tourists were eating, sunbathing and swimming. The fireball killed many lightly clad campers immediately and many others died later from burns. The death toll was 216 and it also injured 200 people.

See also - 'Relative Density' under '2.1 Physics and chemistry of fire and explosion' - earlier in this Element.

MEXICO CITY 1984

At approximately 05:35 hours on 19 November 1984 a major fire and a series of catastrophic explosions occurred at the government owned and operated PEMEX LPG Terminal at San Juan Ixhuatepec, Mexico City, Mexico. As a consequence of these events some 500 individuals were killed and the terminal destroyed. Three refineries supplied the facility with LPG on a daily basis. The plant was being filled from a refinery 400 km away, as on the previous day it had become almost empty. Two large spheres and 48 cylindrical vessels were filled to 90% and 4 smaller spheres to 50% full.

A drop in pressure was noticed in the control room and also at a pipeline pumping station. An 8-inch pipe between a sphere and a series of cylinders had ruptured. Unfortunately the operators could not identify the cause of the pressure drop. The release of LPG continued for about 5-10 minutes when the gas cloud, estimated at 200 m x 150 m x 2 m high, drifted to a flare stack. It ignited, causing violent ground shock. A number of ground fires occurred. Workers on the plant now tried to deal with the escape taking various actions. At a late stage somebody pressed the emergency shut down button.

About fifteen minutes after the initial release the first BLEVE occurred. For the next hour and a half there followed a series of BLEVEs as the LPG vessels violently exploded. LPG was said to rain down and surfaces covered in the liquid were set alight. The explosions were recorded on a seismograph at the University of Mexico.

Failings in technical measures

The total destruction of the terminal occurred because there was a failure of the overall basis of safety which included the layout of the plant and emergency isolation features.

- Plant Layout: positioning of the vessels.
- Isolation: emergency isolation means.

The terminal's fire water system was disabled in the initial blast. Also the water spray systems were inadequate.

- Active / Passive Fire Protection: survivability of critical systems, insulation thickness, and water deluge.

The installation of a more effective gas detection and emergency isolation system could have averted the incident. The plant had no gas detection system and therefore when the emergency isolation was initiated it was probably too late.

- Leak / Gas Detection: gas detection.

Hindering the arrival of the emergency services was the traffic chaos, which built up as local residents sought to escape the area.

- Emergency Response / Spill Control: site emergency plan, access of emergency vehicles.

Source: HSE, Hazardous Installations Directorate, Case Studies.

HICKSON AND WELCH 1992

At approximately 1.20pm on 21 September 1992 a jet of flame erupted from a manway (access opening) on the side of a batch still at the factory of Hickson & Welch Ltd, Wheldon Road, Castleford, West Yorkshire. The flame cut through an office/control building nearby killing two employees instantly. Three other employees in these offices sustained severe burns but escaped. Two later died in hospital.

The flame also struck a much larger four-storey office block, shattering windows and setting rooms on fire. There were 63 employees in this building including a number who were returning from lunch. All managed to escape with the exception of a young employee, who was overcome by smoke in a second floor toilet. Although she was rescued by fire service personnel approximately 40 minutes later, she died on 23 September 1992 from the effects of smoke inhalation.

At the time of the incident a process vessel known as '60 still base', used to distil an organic liquid in batches, was being raked out to remove an accumulation of semi-solid residue or sludge which was rich in dinitrotoluenes and nitrocresols. Before raking, heat was applied for about three hours to the residues through an internal steam coil. This started a self-heating (exothermic) runaway reaction in the residue leading, with disastrous consequences, to deflagration and a jet flame.

The incident could have been prevented if the hazards and the risks associated with this non-routine clean-out operation had been accurately assessed beforehand and suitable precautions taken. However, fundamental errors and incorrect assumptions were made, which led to an incident in which five people lost their lives. The incident also revealed defects in fire precautions affecting the means of escape from parts of the main office block.

In view of the nature of the incident, and public concern, the Health and Safety Commission (HSC) instructed the Health and Safety Executive (HSE) to carry out a formal investigation under Section 14(2) (a) of the Health and Safety at Work etc. Act 1974 and make a special report. For the sake of brevity this report concentrates on the cause of the incident and the precautions that should have been taken to prevent it but omits reference to many satisfactory arrangements identified during the investigation.

Following the investigation by the HSE, Hickson & Welch Ltd was prosecuted. The company was convicted for an offence under Section 2 of the Health and Safety at Work etc. Act 1974 at Leeds Crown Court on 30 July 1993 and was fined £250,000 with £150,000 costs awarded against it.

The investigation revealed several important lessons some of which are of general relevance to the chemical industry; these are summarised below.

Lessons

1. Where the batch distillation of highly energetic materials (such as mononitrotoluenes or other organic nitro compounds) is carried out still residues should be analysed, monitored and removed at regular intervals to prevent possible build up of unstable impurities.

2. The use of chemical plant for a different process or purpose should be treated as a plant change procedure requiring rigorous assessment. Consequently before plant is used to carry out non-routine operations authorisation should be obtained from an appropriate level of management who should ensure that plant hazards have been identified, risks assessed and the precautions determined.

3. Safe systems of work covering all aspects of operation and maintenance of all process plant should be established and defined in comprehensive instructions including those operations undertaken at infrequent intervals. These systems should be monitored by management and reviewed at appropriate intervals.

4. The nature, operation and limitations of control systems on process plant should be determined, and their implications for health and safety taken into account, before non-routine operations requiring their use are authorised.

5. Companies should assess and monitor the workload and other implications of restructuring levels of management and supervision to ensure that key personnel have adequate resources, including time and cover, to discharge their responsibilities.

6. Persons authorised to issue permits-to-work should be sufficiently knowledgeable about the hazards associated with relevant plant. If 'authorised' personnel are relocated to former workstations refresher training should be given and recorded before re-authorisation.

7. The design and location of control and other buildings near chemical plant which processes significant quantities of flammable and/or toxic substances should be based on the assessment of the potential for fire and explosion and/or toxic releases at these plants. Companies should assess the suitability of existing control buildings and if they are found to be vulnerable, reasonably practicable mitigating action should be taken.

8. Companies should regularly monitor and audit their own compliance with performance standards defined in their fire certificates. Particular attention should be paid to the effects of material alterations, e.g. installation of pipework and cable ducts and other work in areas concealed by false ceilings, to ensure that the fire-resisting integrity of protected routes is maintained and fire training records should be regularly updated.

9. When exercising their on-site emergency plans companies should ensure that roll call information on missing persons is passed immediately, accurately and directly to the Senior Fire Officer in charge. Roll call procedures should be practised routinely to ensure that they are effective when carried out at all periods of the working day.

Dust explosions

Dust explosions can occur in any building used for the manufacture or handling of fine particulate combustible material. This type of explosion can occur if a combustible dust is suspended in air as a dust cloud in such proportions that it will support combustion. In these conditions the surface area exposed to the air is very large in comparison to the mass of the powder. If ignition does occur the entire material may burn very rapidly. Energy can be released suddenly as heat and this can cause gaseous reaction products to be formed. If the dust cloud is contained, the rapid release of heat and gaseous products that are formed causes an increase in pressure that most industrial plant cannot withstand.

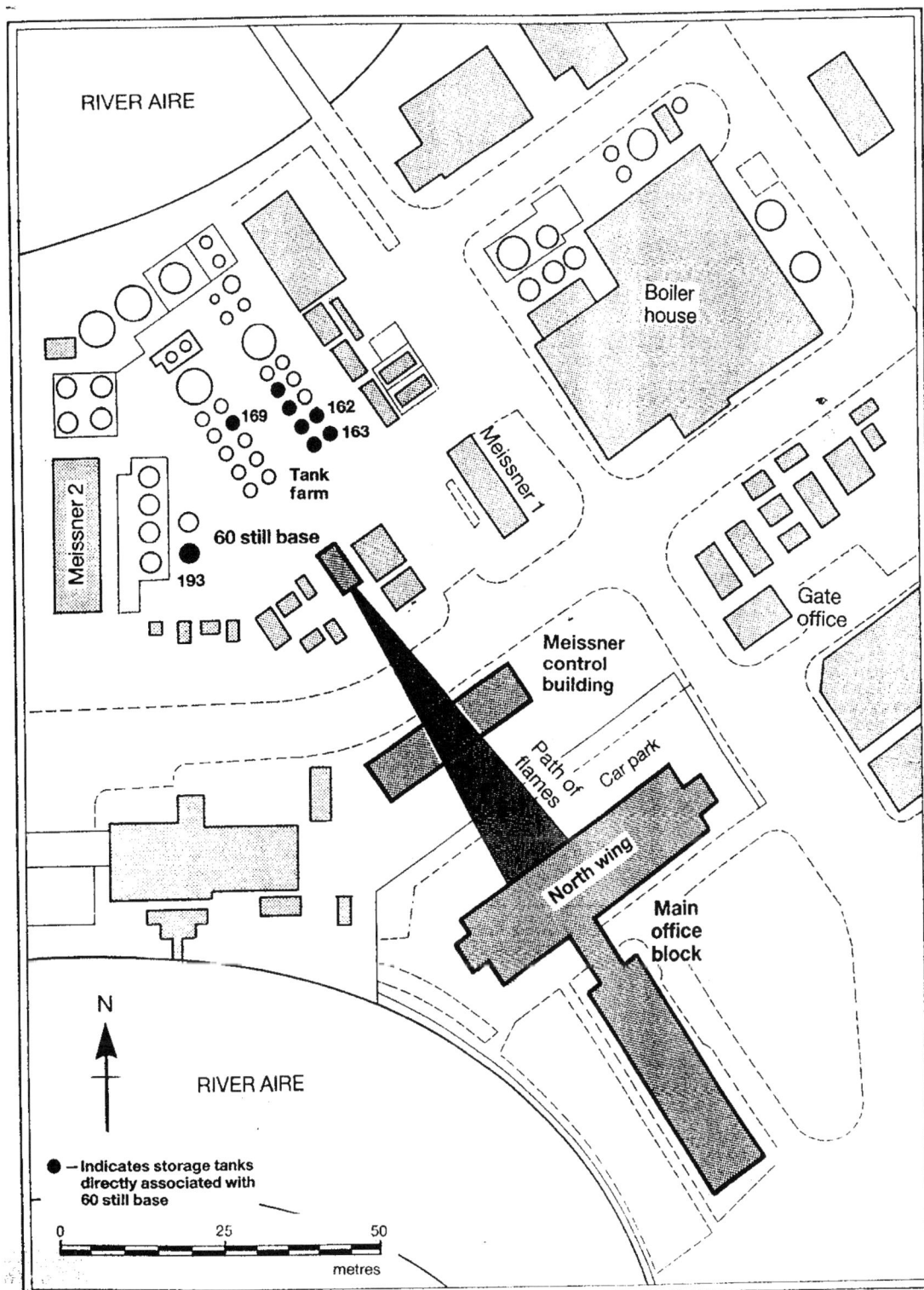

Figure C2-10: Hickson & Welch factory - plan of area around 60 still base showing path of the jet flame.

Source: HSE report of the investigation into the fatal fire at Hickson and Welch Ltd, Castleford, on 21 September 1992.

THE IMPORTANCE OF PARTICULATE SIZE, EXPLOSIVE CONCENTRATIONS AND IGNITION ENERGY

The severity of the explosion can depend on many things, to include:

Particle Size   As a general rule a dust will not explode if its particle size is greater than 500 microns and will give only weak explosions if over 200 microns.

Concentration   Although the explosive limits for dusts will vary for differing materials and circumstances, it has been found that for the majority of organic materials the lower explosive limit is 10-50 g/m^3. This would resemble a dense fog.

Ignition   The ignition temperature of most dust suspensions is between 200°C and 900°C, the majority falling between 300°C and 600°C.

The ignition source energy is usually above 5mJ.

Other factors which will effect the severity of explosion are:

Turbulence   Ignition of a highly turbulent dust suspension will result in a more severe explosion hazard.

Moisture Content   As the moisture content of the dust increases and reaches 16% by mass, the explosion severity decreases.

PRIMARY AND SECONDARY EXPLOSION

These explosions are normally started in specific items of a powder handling plant (primary explosion), but the effects on the building can be devastating if a vastly more powerful (secondary explosion) propagates throughout the building.

The types of industries that are typically at risk are those dealing with agricultural products, foodstuffs, pharmaceuticals, chemicals, pigments, polymeric materials, rubbers, coal and wood products.

Industrial dust explosions can be divided into two types. Firstly a primary explosion which usually occurs in an enclosure or handling plant located within a building. Structural damage of lightweight plant may occur at this stage, as pressures of 8-10 bars are produced, but more concerning is the consequent air turbulence created within the workplace. The pressure wave created combined with the air turbulence may dislodge dust off all horizontal surfaces within the workplace, and cause an airborne suspension of combustible dust throughout the entire workplace. This dust can then be ignited by either the initial ignition source, the combustion bi-products of the primary explosion or any other ignition source with sufficient heat energy. Secondly, a secondary explosion will then occur throughout the entire workplace with devastating effects. Entire buildings have been destroyed by such effects.

As an example of the problems of secondary explosion and the need for good housekeeping as prevention, a layer of flour 0.3 mm thick on the floor in a building would be capable of producing an explosive cloud 3 m high.

Dust explosions can only occur if certain conditions are present:

- The dust must be combustible.
- The dust must be capable of becoming airborne.
- The dust particle size and distribution must be capable of propagating flame.
- The concentration of dust must fall within the explosive range.
- An ignition source of sufficient heat energy must be in contact with the dust.
- The atmosphere must contain sufficient oxygen to sustain combustion.

Actual incidents of dust explosions

GENERAL FOODS, BANBURY 1981

Failure of plant in the General Foods Ltd. factory at Banbury, Oxfordshire, on Wednesday 18 November 1981, led to an emission and build-up of corn starch powder, which ignited and exploded, injuring nine workers and causing substantial damage. The emission was caused by a malfunction of a conveying system, which resulted in a feed bin being overfilled. The control system was not capable of detecting that the conveying system was attempting to fill an already full bin.

The results of an investigation into the process plant failure detailed the causes of the equipment failure and concluded with recommendations for preventing a repetition of this explosion at similar plants as follows:

"That those who design such plants or use existing plants should carry out analysis to identify possible modes of failure and to ensure that the necessary precautions to reduce the risk of failures and mitigate their effects; that users should have an adequate safety policy with effective organisation and arrangements to carry it out to ensure that the dangers are fully appreciated and that safe systems of work are established and implemented; that staff employed should be properly informed of the process hazards and adequately trained to ensure safe operation of the plant and properly instructed as to the action to be taken in the event of plant failure developing; that proper arrangements should be made for plant maintenance to ensure that plant failure cannot initiate conditions in which an explosion might occur; and that there should be provision of suitable buildings with adequate explosion relief to house plant of this type in the event of it not being practicable to install the plant external to buildings".

2.2 - Behaviour of materials

BEHAVIOUR OF BUILDING STRUCTURES AND MATERIALS IN FIRE

General considerations

The properties of building material vary considerably and may affect their choice in relation to fire hazards. However, the choice of materials used may be affected by other parameters such as economics, availability and aesthetics. The principal consideration should be to ensure that the material and its application complies with the law. All building works with very few exceptions are controlled by some form of building legislation. The principal aim of this legislation is that materials are used correctly so that the safety of life is ensured.

When considering the type of material to be used, and its application, the following criteria should be assessed:

- Ignitability.
- Flammability.
- Surface spread of flame.
- Heat release.

- Smoke (or gas) release.
- Fire resistance.
- Flame penetration.
- Smoke (or gas) penetration.

All the above relate to the safety of the occupants of a building, as they may affect the means of escape, whilst others are more important from the point of view of damage to the structure and contents.

Other considerations that may affect the choice of building materials include:

- The use or uses of the building.
- The dimensions (compartmentation) of the building.
- The design and layout, including escape routes.
- Whether or not the material will burn.

- The ability of the material to support and spread flame across its surface.
- The behaviour of the material when it is burning.
- The effects of high temperature on non-combustible materials.

The effects of fire on building materials will vary according to its application to the structure. Consideration must be given to the effects of materials being combined in use. The reaction of fire on an isolated material is likely to be entirely different if that material is used in a different format, applied differently, or used in conjunction with other materials.

FIRE PROPERTIES OF COMMON BUILDING MATERIALS AND STRUCTURAL ELEMENTS (AND THEIR LEVEL OF FIRE RESISTANCE)

Metals

Metals may require surface protection to minimise the danger of fire spreading by conduction. Unprotected metal used structurally may also present a danger of collapse in fire. All metals soften and melt at high temperature. Structural steel loses 2/3rd of its strength at 600°C and begins to sag and distort.

In addition metals expand when they get hot. A steel joist 10m long will expand by 8 cm when heated to 600°C. This expansion factor, especially as the length of the beam increases, can cause walls to be pushed out with a resultant structural collapse.

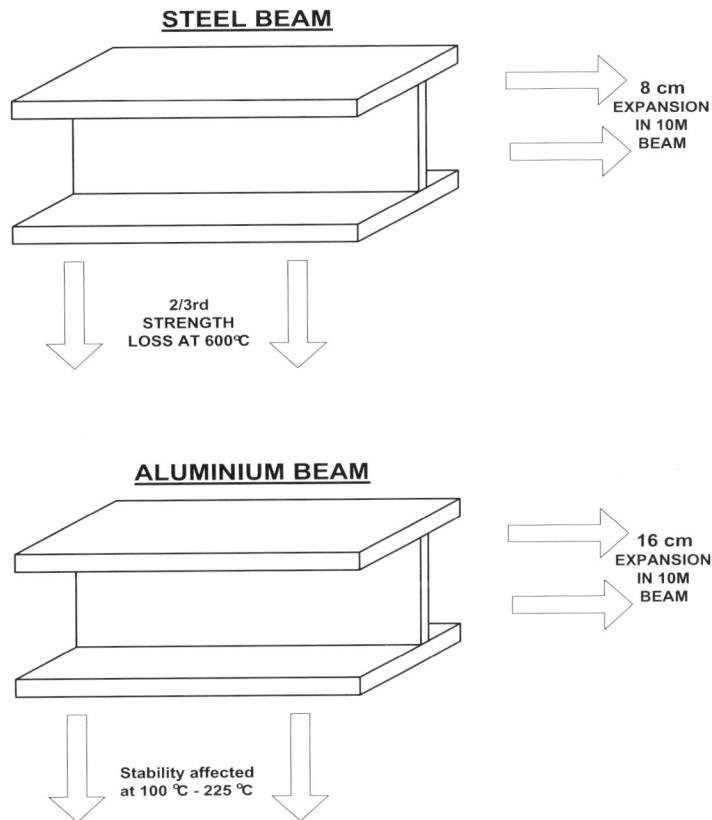

STEEL BEAM

8 cm EXPANSION IN 10M BEAM

2/3rd STRENGTH LOSS AT 600°C

ALUMINIUM BEAM

16 cm EXPANSION IN 10M BEAM

Stability affected at 100 °C - 225 °C

Figure C2-11: Properties of steel and aluminium beams.   *Source: FST Consultancy.*

Aluminium alloys are now being used in building construction owing to:

- The reduction in weight (aluminium is 1/3rd the weight of steel).
- Its resistance to corrosion.
- The ease of handling and working.
- Its high strength to weight ratio.

However these types of alloys have the following disadvantages:

1. Very rapid loss of strength in fire (stability affected at 100°C - 225°C).
2. High expansion rate (twice that of steel).
3. High thermal conductivity (3 times that of steel) giving a greater risk of fire spread.
4. Low melting points (pure aluminium 658°C).

Steel or metal alloy structural members must therefore be protected from the effects of fire. This can be done in one of the following ways:

1. Solid protection.
2. Hollow protection.
3. Sprayed or applied mineral coatings.
4. Intumescent coatings.
5. Hollow section filled with water.
6. By filling hollow webs of beams etc. with lightweight blocks of concrete.
7. By design features such as suspended ceilings.

Concrete

Concrete is strong in compression but weak in tension and is therefore reinforced with steel in areas which will be subject to tensile stress, e.g. lower half of a concrete beam. The fire resistance of concrete elements is influenced by the following:

- Size and shape of element.
- Disposition and properties of reinforcement.
- The load supported.
- The type of concrete and aggregate.
- Protective concrete cover provided to reinforcements.
- Conditions of end supports.

As already stated the concrete relies heavily on reinforcement steels for its fire resistance. If the steel reinforcement is allowed to heat up then it begins to lose strength. A point is reached at which reinforcing metals lose 50% of their strength - this point is called the 'critical temperature'. The critical temperature for mild steel reinforcements is 550°C and high yield steel reinforcements 400°C.

Bricks

Brickwork can provide a vital role as a non combustible and fire resistant element as part of the structure of a building, and can also be used to protect other elements of structure from the effects of fire, e.g. loadbearing columns, staircases, shafts and ducts. Load bearing brickwork has inherent fire resistance and requires no further protection. The duration of fire resistance is dependent upon the thickness of the wall: i.e.

- A 100 mm brick wall gives approx. 2 hours fire resistance.
- A 200 mm brick wall gives approx. 4 hours fire resistance.

The fire resistance is also affected by the type of construction of the brick itself. If the brick is hollow cast or has holes throughout its width, then it is more susceptible to spalling with the bottom face falling off. This would obviously reduce the fire resistance.

Wood

The fire resistance of timber as an element of structure depends upon the following:

- The density of the timber.
- Its thickness and cross sectional area.
- The quality of workmanship and/or detailing.

Timber has a very low thermal conductivity and this factor, combined with its production of a protective skin of charcoal in a fire, retards its rate of combustion. Carefully constructed joints which eliminate cracks and air spaces contribute substantially to fire resistance. Due to this slow rate of burning and the fact that timber will distort and sag for a considerable way before collapse occurs, it is a fairly good material to use when considering fire in buildings.

Timber can be treated with fire retardant materials to increase its safety within fires. Fire retardant coatings can be applied to timber with a class 3 or class 4 rating for surface spread of flame to raise the classification to class 1.

Building boards and slabs

Fire resistance and surface spread of flame characteristics are inherent qualities of board materials. If the performance qualities of boards is low then it may be desired to increase this by the addition or impregnation of a fire resistance substance either onto or into the board material.

Escape routes and circulation spaces within buildings should have both ceilings and walls comprising materials of class 'O' standard. Different materials are given differing classification, some examples of which are given below:

Plasterboard	Class 'O'
Woodwool slabs	Class 'O'
Mineral fibre board	Class 'O'
Chipboard	Class '3'
Softboard	Class '4'
Plywood	Class '3'

Figure C2-12: Material classifications.

Source: FST Consultancy.

As discussed, the room linings should be such that they are not easily ignitable. We should also consider the effects of the wall linings on the speed of development of a fully developed fire, e.g. flashover.

This is illustrated in the table below, which is extracted from test results achieved by the Building Research Establishment.

Wall Lining	**Flashover Time**
Dense non-combustible material, e.g. brick	23 minutes 30 seconds
Fibre insulating board with skim of plaster	12 minutes
Hardboard with 2 coats of flat oil paint	8 minutes 15 seconds
Non-combustible insulating material	8 minutes

Figure C2-13: Wall lining test results.

Source: Building Research Establishment.

As can be seen, even materials that are classed as being non-combustible can affect the development of a fire due to their insulating properties.

Sandwich panels

In modern buildings one type of construction which is commonly used, but is causing great concern, is 'sandwich panels'. These consist of two outer skins of sheet metal (normally a light alloy) with an infill of heat insulating foam. In some cases the foam used is polyurethane or styrene foam. This type of construction is causing problems in buildings which are on fire, due to sudden and unannounced building collapse, as the panels fall out of their framework. They can also cause very rapid fire spread once the internal foam is on fire. As a result of these problems, fire brigades may have to consider attacking a fire from outside the building, so as not to endanger the lives of fire-fighters.

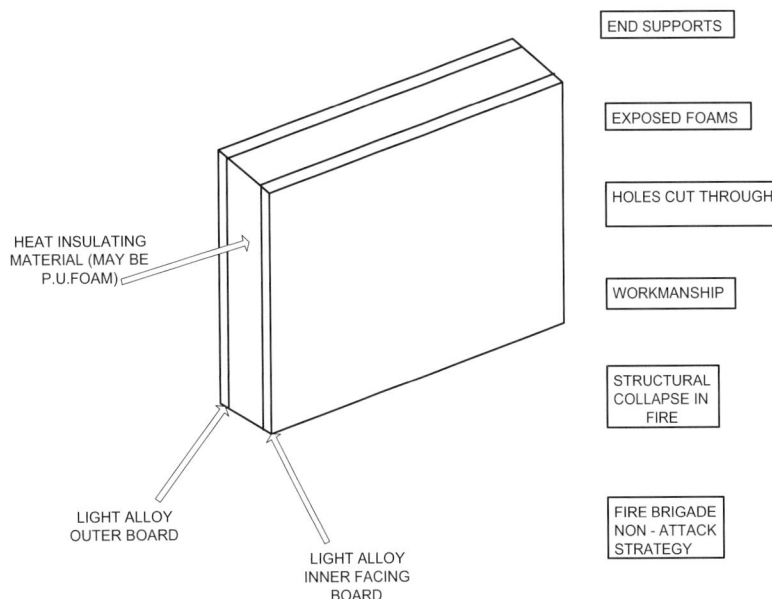

Figure C2-14: Sandwich panel.

Source: FST Consultancy.

Glazing materials

Glass is a non-combustible material and therefore will not contribute to the fire load of a building. However, glass panels in doors or walls do provide a weak point in fires due to their early collapse or their ability to pass radiated heat and thus allowing fire spread. Fire resisting glazing can be used to give up to 1½ hours' fire resistance. The actual figure is dependant upon the nature and dimensions of glass, the type of frame and the glazing detail.

Wired

This can be used to give up to 1½ hours fire resistance dependant upon the materials and design of the frame. The glass is usually 6mm thick and up to 1.6 square metres in area.

Laminated glass (pyran)

This type of glass is now becoming more common in use. It comprises 3 to 5 layers of glass with interlayers of intumescent material which reacts at 120° forming an opaque shield. This glass then prevents radiated heat passing through and can therefore be used in many more situations than the traditional wired glass.

BEHAVIOUR OF COMMON BUILDING CONTENTS IN FIRE

Fire spread due to materials

We also need to consider the possibilities and effects of fire spread within a building due to the types of materials that are stored and used within it. HSG64 assessment of fire hazards from solid materials gives guidance on this matter. This document subdivides materials into two categories, HIGH or NORMAL risk. However, it does this based on two different tests. The first test specifies materials high or normal risk dependent upon the maximum rate of temperature rise, the second test specifies on the volume of smoke produced. As can be expected some materials will be classified as high in one test but normal in another. These tests are used, as the rate of temperature rise and the amount of smoke being produced from a material will have a major influence on people's immediate ability to use the means of escape provided. They are therefore a useful test in helping to make a risk assessment of the risk to life.

The test results show a few materials which fall into the high category in both tests, and therefore present a great danger:

- Acrylic fibre.
- Acrylic mixture.
- Acrylic over locks.
- Expanded polystyrene.

- Flexible polyether (PU foam).
- Polypropylene silver.
- Rigid PU foam (low density).

One area of concern with flammable substances is the storage of such materials. ***See also - section 2.3, 'segregation and storage' later in this element.***

Paper-based materials and fabrics

Smooth hard surfaces normally will not spread flame as fast as soft or fuzzy surfaces. Thick surfacing materials will usually spread flame more slowly than thin materials, but studies indicate that flame spread is relatively independent of thickness for most materials thicker than 6mm (¼ inch). The absorption of heat by base materials to which a finish material may be applied will tend to reduce the rate of surface burning, provided there is intimate contact between the two surfaces. This is most significant where thin surfacing materials are concerned. The method of fastening the surfacing material to the base material is most important. The moisture content of a material can also affect the rate of surface spread of flame, particularly with cellulosic materials, as can the proportion of combustible matter it contains.

Plastics

Basically there are two types of plastic:

1. Thermoplastics - which when heated will soften and melt.
2. Thermosetting - sets to a hard infusible form.

The point to remember with most plastics when involved in fire is the amount of smoke and toxic fumes that will be emitted. Many types of expanded cellular plastics linings, if unprotected, can be a very serious hazard, and cause for concern may arise even when they are protected, if the protection provided is insufficient or ineffective. Unprotected expanded cellular plastics linings or those with only thin surface protection should be regarded as suspect unless their performance has been checked in large scale ad hoc experiments.

When considering the above factors, it is worth considering that a large proportion of materials can now be treated or enhanced is some way to make them less susceptible to fire. For example you can now obtain fire resistant paper which is intumescent based. With any fire treatment we need to know if the fire resistant properties are inherent and if they will therefore stay with the product throughout its life, or if the fire resistance is added so that it has a shelf life or can be affected by actions such as cleaning / washing.

2.3 - Fire and explosion prevention

Structural protection

The spread of fire from the room of origin to other parts of the same building results from the same processes as growth in the room of origin, i.e. by conduction, convection and radiation. The routes being firstly by passing through any existing gaps or openings in the surrounding construction (including doorways); secondly by burning through or opening up gaps within the construction and thirdly by heat conducted through the construction - so igniting combustible materials in direct contact or in close proximity to the other side. The fire and hot gases will then spread along any available routs such as corridors, stair and lift wells, service ducts and cavities.

OPENINGS

It is therefore important to ensure that the separating elements of construction (walls, floors, supporting elements and doors) have the necessary fire resistance and that gaps and other openings in or between elements are properly fire-stopped. Attention must also be paid to the design of details involving ducts, pipes and services passing through fire-resisting walls and floors - particularly those elements forming the enclosures to fire compartments and to escape routes.

VOIDS

A particular hazard exists in extensive cavities in horizontal or vertical constructions which, if fire penetrates them, act as 'chimneys' or 'flues', conveying flames and hot gases over considerable distances, a situation aggravated when they are lined with combustible materials.

COMPARTMENTATION

When designing to prevent the spread of fire from the room of origin, various parts of a building may be required to be enclosed or separated by fire-resisting construction, the most notable technique being called **compartmentation**. A fire compartment is defined as 'a building or part of a building, comprising one or more rooms, spaces or storeys, constructed to prevent the spread of fire to or from another part of the same building, or an adjoining building'. Requirements for compartmentation are generally based on the occupancy and size of the buildings. When considering the size of compartments, consideration can be given to the installation of a sprinkler system. In general the size of a compartment can be doubled if there is a sprinkler system installed.

Key features of plant design and process control

DESIGN OF PLANT

Risk assessments must be made to ascertain if an explosion risk exists. If this is the case, then prevention measures must be taken:

- Elimination of one of the conditions needed for an explosion to occur are removed or negated.
- Use of inert gases in enclosed plant/machinery.
- Removal of dust suspensions from the workplace, i.e. good ventilation.
- Regular cleaning of horizontal surfaces so as to remove accumulated dust and the secondary explosion risk.
- Design plant/workplace to negate horizontal surfaces, e.g. incline light fittings to at least $60°$.
- Use of false ceilings to prevent dust settling on roof beams.
- Internal walls should be smooth and washable.
- Floor/wall joints to be curved to prevent build up in corners.
- Regular and efficient housekeeping system.
- Use of a ventilation/extraction system incorporating dust collection, preferably outside the building.
- Removal of ignition sources - the main ones being:
  - Flames.
  - Hot surfaces.
  - Incandescent materials.
  - Spontaneous heating.
  - Welding or cutting operations.
  - Friction or impact sparks, e.g. foreign body in process.
  - Electric sparks.
  - Electrostatic discharge sparks.

Plant Separation: In order to minimise the total amount of dust available to the explosion, physical separation of one plant item to another is best. If, however, they need to be linked for production purposes then 'chokes' such as screw conveyors and rotary valves are recommended.

PROCESS CONTROLS

Various plant controls may be important in controlling the possibility of a dust explosion. Listed below are some typical issues that may need to be controlled.

- If powdered products are being dried, you need to know the maximum safe temperature that equipment can be operated at, so as to prevent auto-ignition of the powder.

- Overloading or blockage of feed systems may cause machinery to overheat. This may need to be detected by a system control, rather than reliance upon operators to spot the problem.
- Air pressures may need to be monitored to detect system failures such as faulty relief panels, or collection bag failure, both of which would cause large volumes of dust to escape into the air.
- Local exhaust ventilation should be interlocked so that the process can only run if the ventilation system is operating correctly.
- Detection may need to be installed after a grinding plant, so that any sparks or potential ignition sources can be detected and extinguished before they create an explosion.
- Storage bins and hoppers may need to be fitted with overfill alarms to prevent material being spilt.
- Process controls should be in place so that any deviation from a safe working condition will cause the operation to close down.

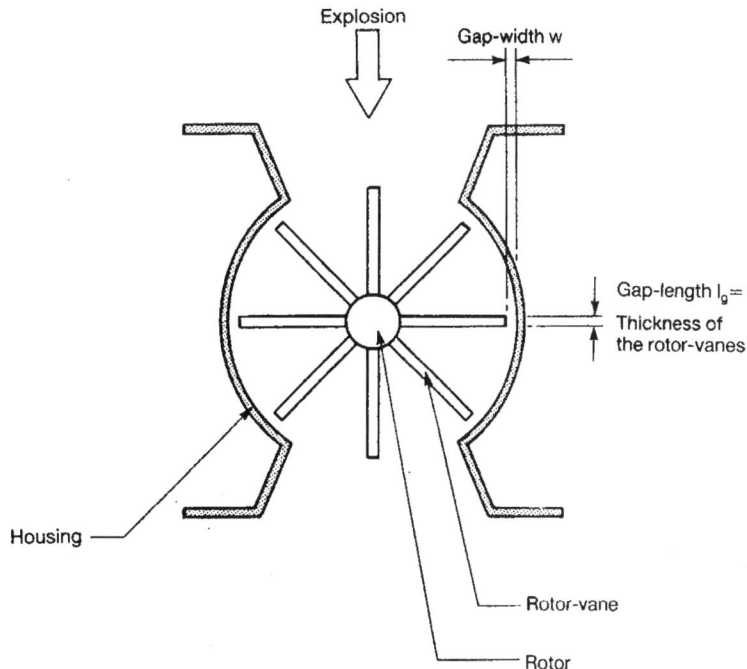

Figure C2-15: Important dimensions of rotary valves used as explosion chokes.   *Source: HSG103.*

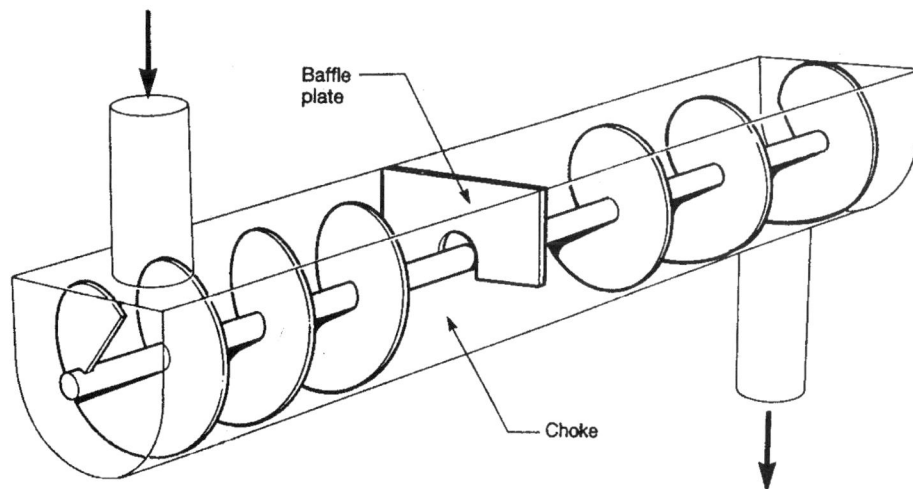

Figure C2-16: The use of a screw conveyor as a choke.   *Source: HSG103.*

Segregation and storage

STORAGE

In some cases precautions in the storage of a HIGH fire hazard material may be specified as a condition of the fire certificate under the Fire Precautions Act 1971. Where this is not the case, the general duties of the Health and Safety at Work Act 1974 should be followed and the material should be stored in a way that ensures safety, so far as is reasonably practicable.

Ideally, a material assessed as being a HIGH fire hazard should be stored in a separate area, either in a separate building or in a single storey extension to the main building or in a safe place in the open air - with suitable weather protection. Except as discussed below, where it is not reasonably practicable to avoid locating the storage area in an occupied building the store should be separated from the rest of the premises by partitions of not less than 30 minutes fire resisting construction. HIGH fire hazard materials should not normally be stored below an occupied floor or in a basement. Where such materials are kept in the same building as domestic or other occupied premises separation of not less than 1 hour fire resisting construction should be provided between storage and occupied areas.

In some premises it may not be reasonably practicable to provide a separate store but safe storage can be achieved by other means. In assessing whether the arrangements provided for storage are adequate in such cases it will be necessary to consider the characteristics and quantity of materials stored, the conditions of storage and use, the nature of the building and the adequacy of emergency procedures and fire precautions. Examples of situations where separate storage facilities may not be required include:

- Where the quantity stored is insignificant compared with that required for work in progress.
- Where finished or partly finished goods present a reduced fire risk because of their form, outer covering or packaging.
- Where a single storey building has a large volume of free space at ceiling level, so that there is no risk of smoke logging during the early stages of a fire; and where the disposition of stored materials has been taken into account in the general fire precautions.
- Where safe storage can be achieved by other means, e.g. by spatial separation, the provision of fire or smoke detectors, linked to an alarm system, water-spray protection, automatic smoke vents and smoke curtains (using one or more of these as circumstances dictate).

The layout and operation of the storage area require careful planning. The layout should provide for the stable and safe storage of all materials and should allow ready access to all parts of the store for both people and fork lift trucks. The methods of stacking and mechanical handling adopted will be determined by the needs of the business but when the store is designed, due regard should be given to the effect that a fire in the store could have on the premises and its occupants. Matters such as stack heights, clearance around and above the aisle widths and total quantities stored should be considered as part of the overall assessment of fire risk.

A store should be used exclusively for storage. Production and ancillary processes, especially any that might introduce sources of ignition, e.g. shrink wrapping of the product onto trays and fork lift truck battery charging, should be excluded. Where this standard cannot be achieved and it is necessary to carry out such operations, they should be separated from the materials stored by a safe distance or carried out in a separate bay set aside for the purpose.

Smoking should be prohibited in all storage areas and other ignition sources excluded. For example, direct fired heaters or heaters with high surface temperatures capable of igniting the material should not normally be used.

Where it is necessary to introduce a source of ignition, e.g. for maintenance work, there should be clear instructions on any additional fire precautions required and close supervision, preferably including a permit-to-work system for any 'hot work' - e.g. involving welding, cutting or grinding - required in the area. The work area should be inspected immediately on completion of the job and once or twice again during the next hour for signs of smouldering fires.

Access to storage areas should be restricted. The number of people working in the areas should be limited and where possible other staff in the premises should not have to pass through this area or use it as their only means of escape from the premises.

Process of assessment of fire hazards from solid materials

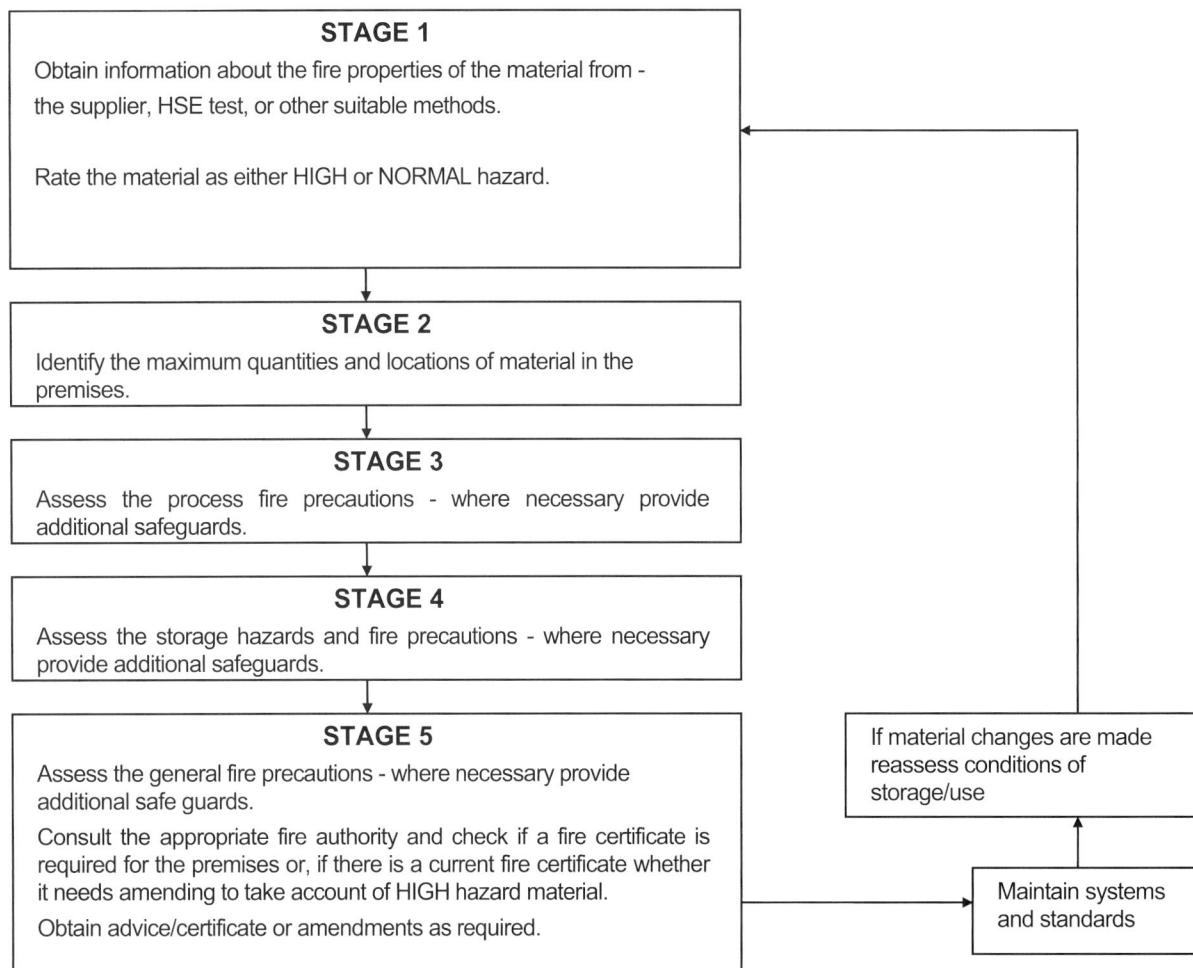

Figure C2-17: Process of assessment of fire hazards from solid materials.   *Source: FST Consultancy.*

FLAMMABLE

Capable of burning with a flame.

COMBUSTIBLE

Capable of burning.

INCOMPATIBLE MATERIALS

Materials which should not be mixed together due to the interaction/reaction between them.

HAZARDOUS AREA ZONING

Areas where explosions may occur are subdivided into zonal areas. Each zone is classified dependant upon the likelihood and persistence of an explosive atmosphere being created.

- **Zone 0** Explosive atmosphere in air with gas, vapour or mist present continuously, or for long periods of time.
- **Zone 1** Explosive atmosphere in air with gas, vapour or mist likely to occur in normal operation occasionally.
- **Zone 2** Explosive atmosphere in air with gas, vapour or mist not likely to occur in normal operation, but if it does it will be for a short period only.
- **Zone 20** Explosive atmosphere in air with a cloud of combustible dust present continuously or for long periods of time.
- **Zone 21** Explosive atmosphere in air with a cloud of combustible dust likely to occur in normal operation occasionally.
- **Zone 22** Explosive atmosphere in air with a cloud of combustible dust is not likely to occur in normal operation, but if it does it will be for a short period only.

EXCLUSION OF IGNITION SOURCES

To prevent a fire or explosion from starting it should be obvious that all ignition sources must be removed from the risk area. Knowledge of the product is needed, so that ignition sources relevant to the ignition energy required can be removed. This factor is linked into the hazardous area zoning above, as this dictates the type of control measures that are needed in each zone.

INERTING

'Inerting' means the displacement of the atmosphere in a confined space by a non-combustible gas (such as nitrogen) to such an extent that the resulting atmosphere is non-combustible. Note: that this procedure produces an IDLH oxygen-deficient atmosphere that can only be entered using self-contained breathing apparatus (SCBA).

Another definition would be: the process of purging a container or covering a product with a non-reactive atmosphere such as nitrogen, carbon dioxide, argon, or helium.

2.4 - Explosion mitigation

METHODS OF EXPLOSION RELIEF

Venting/ explosion panels

Explosion Relief Venting is the most common system used, and involves incorporating deliberate points of weakness. These normally take the form of explosion relief vents in the plant item and/or building. If the vents are of the correct size and in the correct place, an explosion will be vented to outside. The objective is to prevent the explosion pressure from exceeding the design strength of the plant or building. This is normally done by use of lightweight roofs, lightweight wall panels, louvres and vents. The size of vents required will depend upon the properties of the dust involved, the strength of the plant/building involved and the opening pressure of the vents.

Vent panels may become dangerous missiles in the event of an explosion, so they may need to be fixed to the plant or building with chains, or some similar device. Care needs to be taken with the siting of vents, so as to prevent the fireball or pressure wave that is produced from creating further dangers.

Bursting discs

Certain plant and machinery will have explosion relief built into it in the way of a bursting disc. This is a purpose designed weak spot that is designed to rupture at a predetermined pressure, which will therefore vent any pressure immediately and will prevent a more damaging explosion occurring.

Suppression (e.g. inerting)

It may not be possible or desirable to provide explosion relief venting, and a method of explosion containment or suppression may need to be installed.

An explosion may develop pressures up to 10 bars, which buildings cannot withstand, but small items of plant such as grinding equipment may be able to be designed to do so. However, this method is not often cost-effective on larger items of plant/machinery.

An explosion suppression system will detect an explosion in its early stages by detecting a pressure increase. The system will then inject an extinguishing agent (often dry powder) into the path of the explosion so that the flame front is extinguished, and the explosion is basically stopped in its tracks.

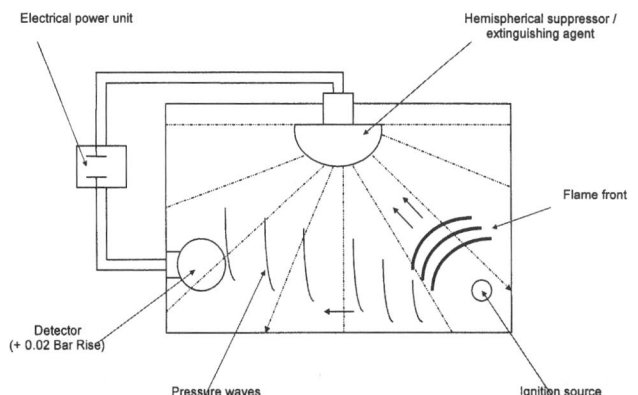

Figure C2-18: Explosion suppression. *Source: FST Consultancy.*

Overall assessment of dust explosibility - a simplified approach

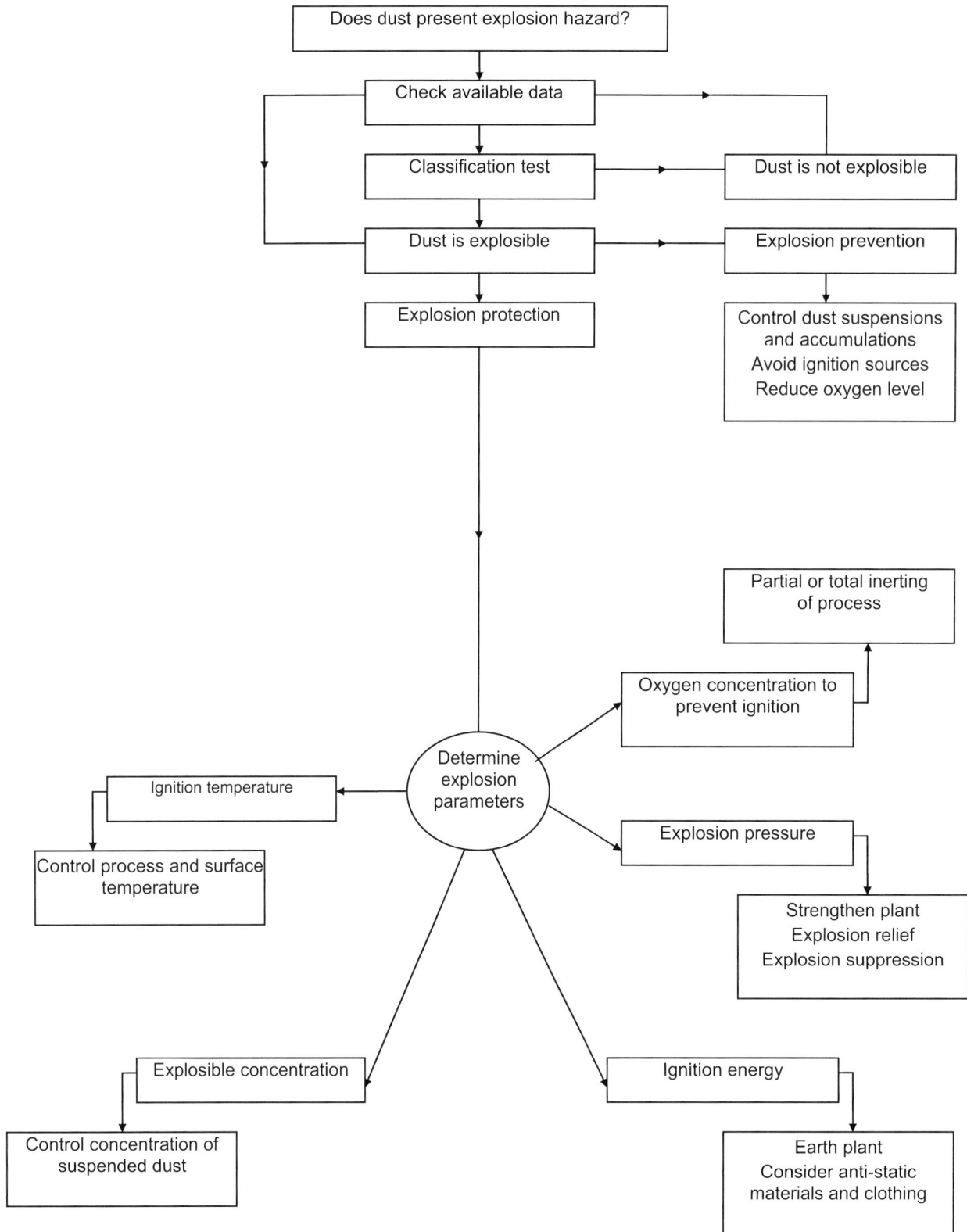

Figure C2-19: Overall assessment of dust explosibility.   *Source: FST Consultancy.*

Workplace fire risk assessment

Overall aims

On completion of this Element, the student will have knowledge and understanding of:

■ workplace fire risk assessment.

■ common fire detection and alarm systems and procedures.

■ fire fighting systems and equipment.

■ portable fire fighting equipment.

■ requirements for means of escape in case of fire.

■ emergency evacuation procedure.

Content

Specific intended learning outcomes

The intended learning outcomes are that the student will be able to:

1.   assess the risks of fire in work premises

2.   advise on the implementation of appropriate control measures

3.   advise on means of fire prevention and prevention of fire spread in buildings

4.   advise on the selection of fire fighting equipment and fire alarm systems

5.   advise on means of escape as part of fire precautions

6.   assist in the maintenance of a fire evacuation procedure

7.   advise on the statutory requirements relating to fire safety at the workplace

Relevant statutory provisions

Fire Precautions Act (FPA) 1971 (as amended by the Fire Safety and Safety of Places of Sport Act 1987)

Fire Precautions (Workplace) Regulations (FPWR) 1997 (and as amended 2003)

Fire Certificates (Special Premises) Regulations (FPSPR) 1976

Management of Health and Safety at Work Regulations (MHSWR) 1999 (and as amended 2003)

Building Regulations (BR) 2000, Approved Document B

3.1 - Fire risk assessment

COMMON FLAMMABLE SOLIDS

Flammable solids form the majority of fuels within workplaces and are certainly the most common type of fuel to be ignited first when a fire starts. There are very few solid materials that will not burn, the principal factors being the format that the fuel is in and the heat output of the available ignition sources. When assessing fuels within the workplace we need to consider the size of the particles of fuel and how they are presented in the workplace. For example, we could probably extinguish a small naked flame by dropping a cupful of sawdust on top of it from close range if we emptied the cups contents in one go. However, if the sawdust is fine enough and is suspended in the air in the right proportions a tiny static spark could be sufficient to cause a dust explosion. Common examples would be paper, plastics, foams and wood.

COMMON FLAMMABLE LIQUIDS

Flammable liquids are known fire problems due to their capability to ignite easily and spread fire quickly. The prime considerations would be the flashpoint for the liquid concerned, its rate of vaporisation and its flammable or explosive range. The lower the flashpoint, the higher the rate of vaporisation; and the wider the flammable range, the more dangerous the product. Common examples would be petrol, thinners and oils.

COMMON FLAMMABLE GASES

The most common flammable gases would be acetylene, propane, butane and natural gas. Any flammable gas has the potential of filling areas with gas/air mixture which can then ignite and cause an explosion throughout the entire space with devastating effects. As above one of the main considerations would be the explosive range of the gas as the wider the range, the greater he potential to ignite the gas cloud.

FIRE HAZARDS

A hazard can be described as something with the potential to cause injury to people, damage to property or impact on the environment. A severe fire has the potential to cause major loss, including injury or death to people. Millions of pounds of damage is caused by fire every week and the smoke from a fire or the run off of fire fighting water can cause environmental pollution. In the majority of cases it is sufficient to consider fire hazards as five distinct areas of concern:

- Sources of fuel - *as indicated above.*
- Sources of heat (or ignition sources) - must be identified and controlled, relevant to the nature and types of fuel within the workplace.
- Sources of oxygen - oxygen may be found in the workplace in the form of cylinders, piped oxygen or via chemicals such as oxidising agents. It may also be necessary to consider the effects of air movement within the workplace via air conditioning / air handling systems and the associated trunking. Such systems will provide additional air to any fire area and may spread fire or smoke to other areas within the workplace.
- Structural features that could lead to fire spread - unprotected openings in floors / walls and ceilings will easily allow fire to spread. Large voids below or above floors will allow fire / smoke to spread undetected and any unprotected vertical shaft will quickly allow fire / smoke to spread up through the building.
- Work practices - the management of the workplace, its contents, and the people within it are major factors in the number and type of fire hazards that are created. For example, a workplace where poor housekeeping standards are allowed and will easily lead to the obstruction of fire exits and fire equipment, and combustible materials will be allowed too near to sources of ignition with the resultant increased probability of fire occurring.

ASSESSMENT OF RISK

Having identified the fire hazards within the workplace and the people who may be harmed by any resultant fire, an assessment of the risk or probability of a fire occurring and its consequences on the people within the workplace must be made. When making this assessment the existing fire safety control measures should be considered. A decision needs to be made if the existing control measures are adequate, or if additional measures are required. Some people may prefer to allocate a risk rating to the workplace e.g. normal risk, but this is not necessary.

CONTROL OF IGNITION SOURCES

The ignition sources within the workplace need to be controlled in relation to the fuel sources. This can take many formats such as operating a safe smoking policy, instigating a 'hot work permit' system or installing electrical flameproof equipment into areas where flammable atmospheres exist.

CONTROL OF FUEL SOURCES

Fuel sources also need to be controlled in the workplace. Again this can be done in many ways; examples would be removal of combustible fuels, minimising stocks, replacement of existing materials with others that are less flammable and application of good housekeeping standards.

CONTROL OF OXYGEN SOURCES

The control of oxygen supplies is vital. This may be done by the safe use and storage of cylinders, not storing oxidising materials near any heat sources or combustible materials, shutting down unnecessary ventilation systems and simple measures such as ensuring that fire doors are closed.

RISK ASSESSMENT

The purpose of a fire risk assessment is to identify where fire may start in the workplace, the people who would be put at risk, and to reduce the risk where possible.

When undertaking a fire risk assessments there are five steps that need to be taken:-

Step 1 - Identify potential fire hazards.

Step 2 - Decide who may be in danger, and note their locations.

Step 3 - Evaluate the risks and carry out any necessary improvement measures.

Step 4 - Record findings and action taken.

Step 5 - Keep assessment under review.

Step 1 - Identify fire hazards

- *Identify sources of ignition -* Smokers' materials, naked flames, heaters, hot processes, cooking, machinery, boilers, faulty or misused electrical equipment, lighting equipment, hot surfaces, blocked vents, friction, static electricity, metal impact and arson.
- *Identify sources of fuel -* Flammable liquids, flammable chemicals, wood, paper and card, plastics, foam, flammable gases and LPG, furniture, textiles, packaging materials, waste materials including shavings, off cuts and dust.
- *Identify sources of oxygen -* Natural ventilation, doors, windows, forced ventilation systems, air conditioning, oxidising materials, oxygen cylinders or piped oxygen systems.
- *Identify structural features that may spread fire -* Combustible wall, floor or ceiling linings, open voids, open ducts, breeches in fire resistance.

Step 2 - Decide who could be harmed

- Consider people in workplace - staff, visitors, contractors, public, old, young, disabled, and level of discipline and training.
- How could fire, heat, smoke spread, how will people be warned of fire, could people be trapped by fire?
- Who may be at risk - where are people?

Step 3 - Evaluate the risks and carry out necessary improvements

- *Reduce sources of ignition -* Remove unnecessary sources of heat or replace with safer alternatives, ensure electrical fuses etc are of the correct rating, ensure safe and correct use of electrical equipment, enforcing a 'hot work' permit system, safe smoking policy, arson reduction measures.
- *Minimize potential fuel for a fire -* Remove or reduce amount of flammable materials, replace materials with safer alternatives, ensure safe handling, storage and use of materials, safe separation distances between flammable materials, use of fire resisting storage, repair or replace damaged or unsuitable furniture, control and removal of flammable waste, care of external storage due to arson, good housekeeping.
- *Reduce sources of oxygen -* Close all doors and windows not required for ventilation particularly out of working hours, shutting down non essential ventilation systems, not storing oxidizing materials near heat sources or flammable materials, controlling the use of oxygen cylinders and ensuring ventilation to areas where they are used.
- *Reducing unsatisfactory structural features -* Remove, cover or treat large areas of combustible wall and ceiling linings, improve fire resistance of workplace, install fire breaks into open voids.

Consider existing fire safety measures in the workplace and consider possible improvements.

Fire detection and warning
- Can fire be detected quickly enough to allow people to escape?
- Can means of warning be recognised and understood?
- Do staff know how to operate system?
- Will staff know what to do if alarm operates?
- Are fire notices around workplace?

Means of escape
- How long will it take for people to escape once they are aware of fire?
- Is this time reasonable?
- Are there enough exits?
- Are exits in right places?
- Do you have suitable means of escape for all people including disabled?
- Could a fire happen that would affect all escape routes?
- Are escape routes easily identifiable?
- Are exit routes free from obstructions and blockages?
- Are exit routes suitably lit at all times?
- Have staff been trained in the use of the escape routes?

Means of fighting fire
- Is the fire fighting equipment suitable for risk?
- Is it suitably located?
- Is it signed where necessary?
- Have people been trained to use equipment where necessary?

Maintenance and testing
- Do you regularly check all fire doors, escape routes, lighting and signs?
- Do you regularly check all fire fighting equipment?
- Do you regularly check all fire detectors and alarms?
- Do you regularly check any other equipment provided to help means of escape arrangements?
- Are there relevant instructions to staff re maintenance and testing?
- Are those who carry out maintenance and testing competent?

Fire procedures and training
- Do you have an emergency plan?
- Does the emergency plan take account of all reasonably foreseeable circumstances?
- Are all employees familiar with plan, trained in its use and involved in testing it?
- Is the emergency plan made available to staff?
- Are procedures to follow clearly indicated throughout workplace?
- Have you considered all people likely to be present?

Step 4 - Record findings and action taken

If you employ more than 5 staff you must keep a written record of the findings of your risk assessment, together with details of any people identified as being at particular risk. You also need to keep a record of action taken.

Significant Hazard	People at risk	Existing control measures	Further action needed	Projected completion date	Responsible person

Figure C3-1: Risk assessment record example. *Source: FST Consultancy.*

Step 5 - Review and monitor

You must review the fire risk assessment and your fire safety measures on a regular basis. This must be done in the event of:

- Changes to workplace.
- Changes to work process / activity.
- Changes to number or type of people present.
- If a near miss or a fire occurs, review system.

The purpose of the assessments under the FPWR 1997 is to identify where fire may start in the workplace, the people who would be put at risk, and to reduce the risks where possible. This type of assessment supplements those already carried out under existing legislation. The areas that need attention when carrying out assessments in the workplace are:

- Identify ignition sources and where possible reduce the risk of causing a fire.
- Identify combustible materials in the workplace and store them safely to reduce the risk of contact with ignition sources.
- Identify those substances, which are oxidising agents, and/or those that present a significant fire risk and store them safely away from sources of ignition.
- Identify those people who are at significant risk from fire and take steps to reduce that risk.
- Identify any structural features that could promote the spread of fire and, where possible take steps to reduce the potential for a fire to grow.
- Monitor during maintenance and refurbishment periods the introduction of ignition sources and combustible materials into the workplace.

Evaluate the workplace to ensure that the following are satisfactory:

- Fire detection / warning.
- Means of escape.
- Means of fighting fire.
- Fire safety training of employees.

Prepare an emergency plan and inform and instruct employees accordingly.

3.2 - Detection and alarm

FACTORS IN DESIGN AND APPLICATION OF FIRE DETECTION AND ALARM SYSTEMS

Fire detection equipment

The following are the types of fire detection equipment which have been used and which may be offered for use. These are described in order that the application and limitations of the various types may be appreciated. The amount of maintenance and the extent of electrical cabling and controls required for spot detectors of the ionisation chamber, photo-electric and thermal type only make the installation of these forms of detectors justifiable in certain locations, and application requires careful consideration of the risk area to be protected.

Type	Suitability	Speed / sensitivity	Other factors
Smoke detectors Ionisation Optical	Buildings with relatively clean, ambient atmospheres. Particularly effective for compartments containing electrical/electronic equipment.	Generally give the earliest warning. Ionisation detectors generally more sensitive to optically dense smoke, e.g. from burning PVC.	False alarms may be given by fumes, dusts, steam, smoke and other particulate matter. Fast air flows can cause Ionisation detectors to false alarm.
Heat detectors Rate of rise Fixed temperature	Most buildings. Not usually suitable for compartments containing electrical/electronic equipment.	Rate of rise detectors quicker than fixed temperature devices if a fire develops heat quickly. Fixed temperature includes Quatzoid glass bulbs.	Abnormal temperature increases may cause false alarms. Fixed temperature devices less prone to false alarms.

Type	Suitability	Speed / sensitivity	Other factors
Flame detectors Infra red Ultra violet	Generally for supplementing heat or smoke detectors in tall compartments where the view is unobstructed.	Quickest warning where flames are immediately present, e.g. fires involving flammable liquids.	Infra red detectors may be operated by gas flames and other heat sources under some conditions and the ultra violet may be operated by lightening, ultra violet lamps and flame cutting equipment.
Laser beam/infra red detector	Tall compartments. Cable tunnels.		One unit can cover a large volume.

Figure C3-2: Fire detection equipment.   *Source: FST Consultancy.*

Alarm systems

Fire alarms - purpose

The purpose of a fire alarm is to give an early warning of a fire in a building for two reasons:

1. To increase the safety of occupants by encouraging them to escape to a place of safety.

2. To increase the possibility of early extinction of the fire thus reducing the loss of or damage to the property.

BS 5839, Part 1: 2002 lays down set guidelines which should be followed when installing a fire alarm system. This note is designed to give guidance to the user when involved in design and maintenance of a fire alarm system.

Hand-operated alarm system

For example, a hand bell or whistle. Their limitation is with size of building and the need to be located conveniently. Some are portable and could, therefore, be prone to loss/theft.

Call points

Call points should be positioned 1.4m above floor level, on escape routes. The maximum distance a person has to reach a call point should not exceed 30m.

Wiring

A wide variety of different cables can be used in various parts of a fire alarm system. Because of their varying abilities to resist both fire and electrical or mechanical damage many of these cables may be restricted in their suitability for specific applications.

The following cables would be acceptable subject to their use:

- Mineral insulated copper clad.
- Pirelli F P 200.
- PVC in conduit.

However, in modern self monitoring systems, lower standards of wiring may be acceptable for certain components of the fire alarm system.

Sounders

The alarm system will utilise audible sounders, such as bells or sirens. The wiring of sounder circuits should be arranged such that, in the event of a short circuit, at least one alarm sounder will continue to sound.

Sound levels

The sound levels should be 65dB (A) or 5dB (A) above any other noise that is likely to persist for longer than 30 seconds. In sleeping risks the sound levels should be 75dB (A) at the bedhead. Noise levels of above 120dB (A) may cause hearing damage in these areas. Special provisions may be necessary (e.g. visual signals).

Single stage alarm

The alarm sounds throughout the whole of the building and calls for total evacuation.

Two-stage alarm

In certain large/high rise buildings, it may be better to evacuate first the areas of high risk, usually those closest to the fire or immediately above it. In this case, an evacuation signal is given in the restricted area, together with an alert signal in other areas. If this type of system is required, early consultation with the Fire Authority is essential.

Staff alarms

In some premises, an immediate total evacuation may not be desirable, e.g. Night clubs, shops, theatres, cinemas. A controlled evacuation by the staff may be preferred, to prevent distress and panic to the occupants. If such a system is used, the alarm must be restricted to the staff and only used where there are sufficient members of staff and they have been fully trained in the action of what to do in case of fire.

Control panel

This must show the state of the systems: Normal - fault - fire. The panel should be sited in an area of low fire risk. Preferably at ground level near to an entrance that is likely to be used by the Fire Brigade and ideally be visible to the Fire Brigade without having to enter the building.

Power supplies

Normal supply for the system is from public mains electrical system. Standby supplies are most commonly a battery with automatic charger (life of at least 4 years). Alternatively they may be batteries with a standby generator, the standby system should be able to maintain the system for a period of 24 hours.

Radio link systems - advantages

1. No wiring needed.

2. Easier, cheaper and quicker to install.

3. System can be extended beyond a single building.

4. No damage to existing surfaces of the building.

5. Each detector or call point can be identified.

6. Temporary cover for special risks can be arranged.

Radio link systems - disadvantages

1. Due to limits of allowed frequency spectrum this can lead to interference between simultaneous signals.

2. Each detector call point and sounder has to be supplied with its own power batteries or local mains.

3. Radio path may be interrupted by temporary or permanent screening.

4. The receiver may be blocked by interfering signals from other sources.

Zones

When a fire signal is given it is necessary that there should be no confusion as to its point of origin and to achieve this, it is necessary to sub-divide the building into zones.

The size and number of the zones should comply with the following:

■ The floor area of a single zone should not exceed 2000 m^2.

■ The search distance should not exceed 30 m.

Search Distance is defined as: the distance which has to be travelled by a searcher within a zone in order to visually determine the position of a fire.

(Remote indicator lamps outside of doors may be useful, especially if doors are likely to be locked). More sophisticated detector alarm systems have control panels which illustrate more clearly the location of fires.

If the total floor area of the building is 300 m2 or less, then it may be considered as a single zone.

If a total floor area exceeds 300 m2, then all zones should be restricted to a single storey.

Zone boundaries should (if possible) be boundaries of fire compartments. (However, it is permissible to have two complete fire compartments in one zone or two complete zones in one fire department.)

Where the building is in "multiple occupation", the zoning arrangement should take account of this and no zone should include areas in more than one occupancy.

When detectors and/or call points are fitted in stairways or lift shafts, they should be treated as separate zones.

Testing of the system by the user

Daily check - panel indicates normal operation; if not, record fault in the log book and actions taken.

Weekly check - one detector, call point or end of line switch should be operated to test control and indicating equipment and to test alarm sounders. If more than 13 zones, more than one zone may need to be tested to ensure the interval between tests on one circuit does not exceed 13 weeks.

Visual check on batteries - check oil, fuel and coolant on generators. Any defect recorded in log book with the action taken.

Quarterly, annual checks and after a fire - to be carried out by a competent person (e.g. installing engineer).

PRINCIPAL COMPONENTS OF SYSTEMS - DETECTION AND SIGNALLING

Smoke detection

Ionisation detectors

Ionisation type detectors consist of one or two ionisation chambers and the necessary amplification circuits. The ionisation detector has, as a sensing element, the ionisation chamber which utilises the principle of air being made electrically conductive (ionised) by bombardment of the nitrogen and oxygen molecules in the air with alpha particles emitted by a minute source of radioactive material. A voltage applied across the ionisation chamber causes a very small electrical current to flow as the ions move to the electrode of opposite polarity. When visible or invisible combustion particles enter the chamber they attach themselves to the ions and cause a reduction in mobility and thus a reduction in current flow. The reduced current flow increases the voltage on the electrodes which, at a pre-determined level, results in an alarm.

The device is very sensitive to smoke and to the products of combustion from various materials. This type of detector is unsuitable for use in cable ways in its present state of development since the products of heating PVC at relatively low temperatures contain only small quantities of particulate matter and thus are not easily detectable.

Photo-electric cell smoke detectors

Photo-electric detection of smoke in varying degrees of density has been employed for several years, particularly where the type of fire anticipated is expected to generate a substantial amount of smoke before temperature changes are sufficient to actuate a heat detection system. This type of detector operates on a principle where smoke entering a light beam either obscures the beam path or reflects light on to a photo cell.

Photo electric cell detectors may be used as individual sensing heads or grouped in a cubicle with air sampled from the protected zone.

Laser or beam type

The laser or beam type detector employs a beam carried between elements at extreme ends or sides of the protected area. Smoke between the light source and the receiving photo cell reduces the light reaching the cell, thus causing actuation. Given an unobstructed clear space, light beam detectors of the photo electric type have been installed for distances up to 90 m.

Sampling type

This system utilises large bore plastic pipework in the form of a bus line with spurs. Air inlet holes are drilled at suitable sampling points. A sample of the atmosphere within the risk area is drawn into the sampling pipework by the action of the sampling fan. Once a smoke contaminated sample enters the pipework there is rapid detection. Each bus line is separately monitored by a photo electric cell and an alarm is given by measurement of increases in obscuration values.

Flame detectors

A flame detector responds to the appearance of radiant energy visible to the human eye (a wavelength of approximately 4,000 to 7,000 angstroms) or to radiant energy outside the range of human vision. These detectors are sensitive to glowing embers, coals, or actual flames which radiate energy of sufficient intensity and spectral quality to initiate response of the detector. There are four basic types of flame detectors:

Infra Red - this device has a sensing element responsive to radiant energy outside the range of human vision (above 7,700 angstroms).

Ultra Violet - this device has a sensing element responsive to radiant energy outside the range of human vision (below approximately 4,000 angstroms).

Photo Electric - this device employs a photo cell which either changes its electrical conductivity or produces an electrical potential when exposed to radiant energy.

Flame Flicker - this device is a photo electric type which includes means to prevent response to visible light unless the observed light is modulated at a frequency characteristic of the flicker of a flame.

Thermal detectors

Fusible links

Fusible links are devices where a link is formed by solder which fuses under conditions of high temperature, thus allowing mechanical initiation of the fire protective equipment.

Fusible links have the disadvantages of being slow in action, the solder is permanently stressed mechanically and therefore subject to creep, and inaccuracies may develop due to corrosive effects. In more modern designs the solder is not permanently stressed mechanically, but is allowed to melt and flow to break an electrical circuit.

Bi-metallic strips

Bi-metallic strips are two metals joined together to form a composite strip. The individual metals have widely differing coefficients of expansion so that under the application of heat the composite strips will curve and thus can make or break a contact in a electrical circuit. The manufacturing process is complex in respect of the formation of the join between the two metals, and lack of sensitivity and inaccurate working can result from faulty production.

The firetec system

This system is based on the use of differential thermocouples. Each detector contains two thermocouples connected in opposition. One thermocouple is exposed directly to the heat whilst the other is shrouded in high alumina ceramic. The resultant output of the combined detectors is directly proportional to the temperature difference.

The firewire system

This system consists of a number of sensing elements connected in series to form a loop, the ends of which are connected by wiring to a monitoring and control unit which indicates a warning if overheating or a fire occurs. The sensing elements consist of flexible stainless steel capillaries of standard lengths. Each length of capillary contains a co-axial centre electrode separated from the capillary by a temperature sensitive material. The ends of the capillary are terminated by an end fitting assembly comprising stainless steel coupling mat, locating sleeve and a concentric pin which forces the connection to the central electrode.

Electrical resistance detector

This form of detector is based on the Wheatstone bridge principle and detects a change of voltage due to a change of resistance of a wire when heated. An alarm indication is initiated when the voltage reaches a certain level.

Heat energy detecting cables

Linear heat energy detection in the form of heat energy detecting cables can be used to detect abnormal temperatures in cable installations and other critical areas.

Rate of rise detectors

Fire detectors that operate on the rate-of-rise principle function when the rate of temperature increase at the detector exceeds a stated rate. Detectors of this type invariably combine two functioning elements, one of which initiates an alarm on a rapid rise of temperature. The various types of rate of rise detectors are as follows:

Contra-operating bi-metallic strips giving a rate-of-rise of temperature feature

This detector consists of one bi-metallic strip enclosed in a housing of high thermal capacity and another element open to the environmental conditions. The device remains immune to relatively slow changes of ambient temperature, but will operate to make or break an electrical circuit when a rapid rate-or-rise in temperature occurs.

Pneumatic detectors incorporating a rate-of-rise of temperature facility

In pneumatic detectors the heating effect on an enclosed quantity of air gives an increase in pressure which is exerted on a diaphragm which actuates the protection and alarm features. A compensating vent takes care of normal changes in ambient temperature.

Another type of pneumatic detector comprises a glass element with two spherical bulbs, one of these is exposed to external temperature, the other is contained within the case. These bulbs are joined by two connecting tubes. One of these tubes is blocked with a porous plug, and the other contains two electrical contacts bridged by a slug of mercury. Rapid rises in temperature cause the mercury to either make or break the circuit across the two contacts. The porous plug determines the sensitivity of the detector and acts as a compensator for small rates of rise of temperature above ambient.

Thermocouple detectors incorporating a rate-of-rise of temperature facility

Two dissimilar metals joined together at a point form a temperature sensitive junction which may be used to produce a thermo electric effect, corresponding to change in temperature. The device is extremely sensitive and has a high speed of response, but its efficiency depends on the condition of the junction which for this reason must be adequately protected against physical damage and atmospheric effects which may reduce the speed of response and sensitivity. The device also requires the use of compensating leads and it must be protected from any spurious effects such as induced voltage.

Exploding quartzoid glass bulb

The exploding glass bulb is essentially a temperature heat sensitive release valve. The bulb contains a liquid which has a freezing point below any natural climatic figure and a high co-efficient of expansion. A small amount of vapour is trapped when the bulb is hermetically sealed. When the liquid expands under the influence of heat energy from a fire, pressure in the bulb rises slowly until all the vapour is absorbed. Further rise of temperature causes a rapid rise in pressure sufficient to shatter the bulb. The detector bulbs are designed for various rupture temperatures, and are designated by the colour of the bulb.

In water spray installations of the "dry system" type the exploding glass bulb is used to control automatic water spray deluge valves. In this application the bulb acts as a detector in the compressed air detector line. Groups of detectors are mounted in separate systems of detector pipework which is charged with compressed air and connected to the water spray deluge valve control mechanism. Under normal conditions the air pressure in the detector pipework holds the deluge valve in the closed position. Rupture of a detector bulb automatically releases air pressure in the small bore detector pipework causing the water valve to open and water to flow to the projectors concerned.

In water spray installations of the "wet system" type the quartzoid bulb acts as a detector/activator and is mounted directly on the water spray control valve casing. Rupture of the detector bulb automatically opens the valve which distributes water to a limited group of spray projectors designed to cover the risk.

In automatic water sprinkler installations the quartzoid bulb is used to detect and extinguish or control an outbreak of fire be distributing water automatically over the area commanded by the individual sprinkler head.

MANUAL AND AUTOMATIC SYSTEMS

Automatic fire detection

The majority of serious fires occur at night when people are not present to deal with them. In the day time many large fires start in parts of buildings (e.g. store rooms) which are infrequently visited. It is dangerous to rely on people to detect fire because they may either not be there at the crucial moment or may well react incorrectly. The most effective precaution against delay in a fire being discovered and the alarm being raised is to install an automatic detection system, which is linked to an alarm company. In doing so 24 hour protection is given.

The purpose is to ensure that in the event of fire, occupants are warned so that they can be evacuated at an early stage, and to ensure that the Fire Brigade arrives at the premises before the fire has got out of control.

There are opportunities to detect fires at the four stages of a fire:

1. Invisible products of combustion.

2. Visible smoke.

3. Flame.

4. Heat.

The methods of detection tend to reflect these opportunities.

Systems should be installed by specialist firms and should conform to British Standard 5839, Part 1, 2002.

Manual call points

Regardless of the detection system that is installed, there should always be the opportunity for the building occupants to raise the alarm themselves. In anything other than very small buildings where manual fire alarms can be considered, there will normally be the traditional manual/electrical call points. The individual breaks the glass by pressing on it with their finger, an electrical contact is then made that causes the fire alarm warning devices to operate throughout the workplace. In very modern systems there may not even be any glass present, as the operation of the call point will cause the plastic front to rock backwards. It may be worth noting that call points may need two actions to operate them if fitted with anti-tamper devices. These can be found in the form of clear plastic covers which encase the call point. These may have to be lifted upwards (often breaking a seal or setting off a local alarm) to enable the call point to be accessed. This type of system is becoming more common in public areas where they have been installed as an attempt to reduce the number of malicious false alarms being made.

3.3 - Fire fighting

Design and application of fixed fire-fighting systems / equipment

HOSEREELS

Internal hose reel systems

Since only the amount of tubing required needs to be pulled off the reel before the water is turned on (in some cases the water can be turned on before any tubing is run out), only one person is needed to operate it. The comparative lightness and lack of back pressure from the nozzle makes the hose reel a suitable item of equipment for all staff to use. So many different types of hose reel are in use that it is impractical to describe them all. In principle, however, the equipment is very similar to the standard hose reel fitted to Fire Brigade fire appliances, and no difficulty should be experienced in using any type of hose reel found.

Hose reel connections

A connection is made to the nearest water supply which may be a branch from a wet riser, a connection via an adaptor to an internal hydrant or a specially installed hose reel main. A stop valve is fitted to control the supply of water to the hose reel. The reel itself is mounted on a hollow rotating shaft. Water is fed to the centre of the reel through a stuffing box gland, the tubing being connected to an outlet on this rotating shaft. Rubber tubing of 20 mm or 25 mm in diameter is employed and a light branch with a shut-off nozzle is fitted.

Hose reel operation

To operate this type of hose reel all that is necessary is to turn on the valve, and holding the branch, pull off as much tubing as necessary from the reel; the shut-off nozzle is opened when the fire is reached. On some types an automatic valve is fitted to obviate serious delay should the operator fail to turn on the valve before taking the branch to the fire. In one type the action of removing the branch from its holder opens the valve; in another the valve is automatically turned on by the rotation of the drum after a few turns of tubing have been pulled off. To ensure that the tubing pays out easily without kinking or fouling, some form of metal guide is provided, or alternatively, the whole reel swings in the direction in which the tubing is being unreeled. Hose reels are sometimes provided with a fixed metal cover to prevent the collection of dust and to protect the rubber tubing from exposure to light which will eventually cause deterioration of the rubber.

Hosereels - use on fire

Hosereels are designed for use on Class A - Carbonaceous fires. The hosereel acts as a replacement for water fire extinguishers and it is said that one hosereel equates to 4 x 9 litre water extinguishers. Modern hosereels have an adjustable nozzle and can be adjusted to give a jet of water, water spray or a combination of both. The water jet is normally used for its "striking power" in attacking the seat of a fire. The jet of water should be "played" across the fire surface and into the heart of the fire to extinguish embers, etc. The water spray can be used if the burning material is easily disturbed with the possibility of spreading the fire. The spray pattern produced allows larger areas to be covered in one go than if the water jet has been used and as it has less pressure behind it, it does not spread materials, i.e. dusts, as easily. The water spray can also be used for protection purposes by placing a curtain of water droplets between the fire and the person operating the hosereel and therefore cutting down on the radiated heat that is absorbed.

Hosereels - advantages/disadvantages

Advantages
- Continuous supply of water - no time constraint.
- Greater quantity of water is delivered than from an extinguisher which has a better effect at extinguishing the fire.
- The person who is attempting to extinguish the fire does not need to get as close as when using extinguishers.
- A spray pattern can be produced to protect the user from radiated heat.

Disadvantages
- Considerable physical effort may be required to pull the hosereel to the fire, especially if the route has lots of obstructions.
- Any doors through which the hosereel is pulled will become wedged open by the reel. This will present the possible problem of smoke travel within the building.
- Can only be used on Class 'A' Carbonaceous Material fires.
- People may stay in the fire area for too long, and put themselves at excessive risk.

Hosereels - limitations

Hosereels should be connected to a permanent water supply so they are not limited by discharge time factors as are extinguishers. The hosereel itself should comply to EN 671 which permits up to a maximum of 30 metres of hosereel in one piece. However at present BS 5306 is still in force which allows up to 45m on one drum of hosereel. This does limit the use of hosereels by virtue of the distance that it is located away from a fire. One limiting factor to the above is the friction drag created by pulling the hosereel along the floor. Considerable physical strength is required to pull 30 metres of hose, and for this reason consideration should be given to shorter lengths of hosereel being provided in more frequent locations. A second limiting factor is the likely route through which the hosereel will need to pass. If this route includes a lot or corners, turns or doors, then hosereels may not be the most suitable fire equipment to be provided. A point to remember is that every door between the fire room and the main escape route will be wedged open by the hosereel.

Hosereels - siting

- One hosereel should be provided for every 800m2 or part thereof.
- Hosereels should be sited in prominent and accessible positions at each floor level adjacent to exits in corridors on exit routes in such a way that the nozzle can be taken into every room and every part of the room.
- Preferably hosereels should be installed into recesses so as not to obstruct the means of escape.
- Any doors fitted to hosereel cupboards should open through 180 degrees.

Hosereels - maintenance

(A)   Monthly inspection

A check should be made to ensure that the hosereel system is intact and has no obvious signs of damage. The operating valves should be checked to ensure that they are in the correct position and that they are free moving. British standards recommend this check is completed monthly whereas the HSE guidance book 'Fire Safety an Employers Guide' recommends a weekly check.

(B)   Annual test

- The hosereel should be run out to its full length and checked for damage or defects.
- The hosereel valve and the nozzle should be checked to ensure free movement throughout its operating range.
- The water supply should be switched on and the nozzle operated to check that a suitable water jet is obtained.
- It would be good practice to check that 24 litres min. of water is supplied from the topmost reel - with the 2 topmost reels operating at the same time.
- Whilst the hosereel is pressurised, a check should be made for any leaks from the system.

AUTOMATIC SPRINKLER SYSTEMS

Function

An automatic sprinkler and fire alarm system is a device for extinguishing the fire in its early stages by the use of water and simultaneously sounding an alarm to summon such human aid as may be required to turn off the water after the sprinkler equipment has performed its task. It accomplishes the first purpose, the extinguishment of fire, by discharging water on to the seat of the fire and over the whole area involved immediately the fire causes a sufficient rise in temperature to operate the sensitive controls (known as "sprinkler heads") and before the fire has time to get out of hand.

The second function of the sprinkler system, that of sounding the alarm, is equally positive, as the ringing of the alarm gong is caused by the action of the water flowing through the pipes leading to the open sprinklers. The alarm that is sounded is only a local alarm on the external face of the building. Consideration should be given to linking the sprinkler to the fire alarm system and a call centre so that a guaranteed response is given.

Under normal conditions, the discharge of water is sufficient to effect complete extinguishment of the fire, but, if by reason of the presence of some obstruction which provides an "umbrella" for the fire and prevents the discharge falling directly on to the seat of the fire, the fire is not completely extinguished, the shower of water from the sprinklers will be sufficient to hold the blaze in check. Thus sprinklers prevent the spread of fire pending the arrival of the Fire Brigade.

Classification

Installations can be classified under four headings, each designed to protect buildings of certain occupancy risks, e.g. School (light), foam plastic store (extra high).

1. Light Hazard System.
2. Ordinary Hazard System.
3. High Hazard System.
4. Extra High Hazard System.

Each installation consists of a range of pipes, suitably graded in size and generally suspended from a roof or ceiling, connected through controlling valves to one or more water supplies. The pipework is fitted throughout the building; it is designed to protect with sprinkler heads, spaced between approximately 2 and 3 metres apart, according to the risk in the building. The sprinkler heads cover all parts of the building, including concealed spaces, stairways and passageways. The maximum area that one sprinkler head can cover varies between approximately 2.5m2 and 9m2 according to the classification of risk, type of system and location of the heads.

Types

Wet system

In this system the pipework is charged with water under pressure at all times. It is the system employed where there is no danger of frost, i.e. in climates where freezing is unknown or where the building is continuously heating during the winter months. With the wet system, the sprinklers are usually fitted pendant below the sprinkler pipework.

Dry system

In buildings where the water in the sprinkler pipes is likely to freeze, the "dry" pipe system is applied. All installation pipes which would normally carry water are charged with air at a moderate pressure and the water is held back out of the reach of frost by a differential air valve which lifts and allows water to enter the pipework system when a sprinkler opens and releases the air in the pipes.

Alternative wet and dry

This is the system which is adopted for the protection of buildings in which freezing is likely only over part of the year. In this system the pipework is charged with water in the summer and with compressed air in the winter.

In this system the pipework is arranged with a gradual fall towards the installation and the sprinkler heads are fitted above the pipes to facilitate draining.

Pre-action system

This is a combination of a standard dry, or alternative wet and dry, sprinkler system, and an independent approved system of heat or smoke detectors installed in the same area. The heat or smoke detectors will operate at a lower temperature than the sprinklers and the pre-action valve will allow water to flow into the pipework before the first sprinkler head operates.

In an extensive building there may be several installations, some of which may be wet and some alternate according to its susceptibility to frost, but the point to be borne in mind is that each installation is self-contained, having its own controlling valves and separate connections to the water supplies so that one system is unaffected by another, with a separate alarm gong for each system. In addition each system is numbered and painted a different colour. Apart from the obvious advantages of the foregoing it also serves as a reliable guide as to the section of the building involved and in many instances the room in which the fire originated.

Features of a sprinkler system

Controlling valves (wet system) - sprinkler stop valve

This valve is of the usual wedge type and is provided on the supply side as a means of cutting off the water supply to the installation following the extinguishment of the fire and is normally kept strapped and padlocked in the open position, a strap being used so that in the event of the key not being available to open the lock, the strap can be cut thus enabling the stop valve to be closed. Upon arrival at a fire or where a sprinkler system has actuated, the officer in charge of the first attendance will station a firefighter at the stop valve to ensure that it is **not** closed down until he/she gives orders to that effect.

Pressure gauges

Two pressure gauges are fitted to each set of valves; one is connected to the supply side of the stop valve and the other to the delivery or installation side of the valve. The former indicates the pressure in the mains or other sources of supply, the latter to record the pressure in the installation. Also in the case of the latter, to record the air pressure on the installation when the system is on air, in the case of the alternative system.

Sprinkler heads

Two main types of sprinkler heads are in use throughout the country, all conforming to a similar design and principle of operation. These are fusible soldered strut or quartzoid bulb. The main components of a sprinkler head are:

- Main body with screw thread for screwing into pipework.
- Yoke, i.e. 'V' shaped casting.
- Distributor at the base of the yoke.
- Diaphragm (a flexible metal plate with a hole in the centre secured between the yoke casting and the main body).
- Glass valve (a hemispherical glass valve which seats against the diaphragm).
- Glass valve cap (a small brass cap which butts against the underside of the glass valve and is recessed to house one end of a metal strut).

Fusible soldered strut

With a fusible soldered strut sprinkler head, the strut is composed of three pieces of metal joined together with a low melting point solder. When this solder is softened by the heat of the fire, the strut falls apart and the glass valve is thrown clear. The water escapes in a solid half inch jet, impinges upon the distributor plate and is scattered in all directions in the form of a drenching spray. In order to protect against deterioration in the operation, certain corrosive resistant coatings are applied to the sprinkler by the manufacturer. It is also recommended that petroleum jelly be applied to all heads periodically. The operating temperatures at which sprinkler heads are designed to operate are identified by various colours.

Soldered Strut	Colour of Yoke Arms
68/74°C	Uncoloured
93/100°C	White
141°C	Blue
182°C	Yellow
227°C	Red

Figure C3-3: Fusible soldered strut - operating temperatures for sprinkler heads.

Source: FST Consultancy.

Quartzoid bulb type

The main structure of the head is retained but in place of the struts a barrel shaped bulb made of Quartzoid (a transparent material) of unusual strength and toughness is used. This bulb is hermetically sealed after being filled with a highly expandable liquid (coloured). When the head is exposed to a rise in temperature pressure within the bulb rises quickly, and fracture of the bulb results. These sprinkler heads are made to operate at various temperatures. In temperate climates, the usual operating temperature for normal situations is 68°C, but for use in special conditions, such as are met in drying stoves, ovens, etc. higher operating temperatures are necessary.

The Quartzoid bulb is so strong that it can stand any hydraulic pressure which may be applied to the interior of the sprinkler head. The filling in the whole range of Quartzoid bulbs cannot freeze however severe the frost may be. These sprinklers are equally suitable for the coldest as well as the hottest climate. The bulb is completely resistant to acid or any corrosive action and in any situation will preserve its effectiveness unimpaired for an indefinitely long period. The operating temperatures at which sprinkler heads are designed to operate are identified by various colours.

Sprinkler rating	Colour of bulbs
57°C	Orange
68°C	Red
79°C	Yellow
93°C	Green
141°C	Blue
182°C	Mauve
204 to 260°C	Black

Figure C3-4: Quartzoid bulb type - operating temperatures for sprinkler heads.

Source: FST Consultancy.

Water supplies

The water supplies for a sprinkler system must be reliable under all conditions and adequate for the appropriate class of risk. They are divided into grades according to the number and type of water supplies available.

Testing of sprinkler systems

Daily checks

- The alarm connection to the Fire Brigade or the remote manned centre should be tested daily if it is not automatically monitored.
- Check water levels and air pressures in pressure tanks if not automatically monitored.

Weekly checks

Check and record:

- All water and air pressure gauge readings on installation, trunk mains and pressure tanks.
- All water levels in elevated private reservoirs, rivers, canals, lakes, water storage tanks and pressure tanks.
- Test each water motor alarm for 30 seconds.

Automatic pump starting tests:

- Check oil, fuel levels.
- Simulate a pressure fall to operate automatic start.
- Check pressure at which pump cuts in - is it correct?
- Check the electrolyte level and density of any lead acid batteries.
- If heating systems are fitted to prevent freezing, they should be checked.

Quarterly checks

A complete check is done normally by an engineer, plus a check should be made to ensure that there have been no structural changes or alteration of layout of contents that would impede the effectiveness of the sprinkler system.

In addition, there are checks at 6 month, 1 year, 3 year and 15 year intervals. These are normally completed by a service engineer.

Water systems

There are generally at least two separate water systems on site:

- Spray water system.
- Hydrant system (internal and / or external).

Spray water system

The spray water system is the main fire protection system comprising high velocity waterspray, medium velocity cooling sprays, sprinkler and selected internal / external hydrants. The system can also supply high velocity water to serve low expansion foam base injection equipment protecting gas turbines and fuel oil tanks.

The water systems form ring mains and are supplied from trunk mains pressurised from a tank charged partly with water from a jockey pump and partly with air from a compressor, with the fire pumps available to cut in on dropping mains pressure when water is being taken from the system. These systems generally use town or raw water supplies.

The pressure tank is a cylindrical steel vessel with convex ends filled with air under pressure and water. The general requirements for a pressure tank are:

- It must be housed in a readily accessible position in a sprinkler protected building or in a separate building of incombustible construction used for no purpose other than for the housing of fire protection water supplies. The tank must be adequately protected against mechanical damage. The temperature of the room should be maintained above 4°C.
- When used as a single water supply, the tank must be provided with an approved arrangement for maintaining automatically the required air pressure and water level in the tank under non-fire conditions. The arrangement should include an approved warning system to indicate failure of the devices to restore the correct pressure and water level. This arrangement is also advocated in cases where the tank provides the duplicate supply.
- The tank must be fitted with air pressure gauges and a gauge glass to show the level of the water. Stop valves and back pressure valves must be provided on both the water and air supply connections to the tank and they must be fixed as close to the tank as possible.

High velocity water sprays

Effective fire protection is afforded by projectors which project a fine spray. The main difference between a water spray projector system and a sprinkler system is that the projectors are not only located overhead but may be sited all around the area of risk. They can be installed to discharge in a horizontal, or even, in certain circumstances, an upward direction. The main application is for the protection and containment of plant using or storing insulating oil, lubricating oil, fuel oils and other flammable liquids. High velocity water sprays project water at high velocity to emulsify oils and liquids at risk. They may be used as an extinguishing system as well as for protection from fire.

The water sprays system is characterised by the type of water projectors selected and these characteristics vary in regard to their density of flow, discharge angle, maximum spacing between projectors and maximum range from the equipment to be protected. The type, characteristics and range of projectors differ with each manufacturer consequently projector coverage, design and configuration of systems offered will vary. Each water spray nozzle should include a thimble strainer integrated within the nozzle to prevent blockage of the nozzle exit by any debris in solution or inadvertently picked up in the pipework.

The point of projectors must not be moved once set, otherwise the area will no longer be fully protected.

Medium velocity water sprays

This system is used for protecting such risks as Bulk Hydrogen, Chlorine and Propane stores and has been used for cooling the external surface areas of bulk gas turbine fuel storage tanks. It is not an extinguishing system and unlike high pressure water spray systems operates at a lower pressure of 1.4 to 3.5 bar at the sprays. Volatile liquid fire situations cannot be extinguished by the application of medium velocity water sprays but close control of a fire can be obtained at the same time rendering adjacent plant and structures safe by the cooling effect of the water film. This form of protection also gives protection to personnel when fighting fires on this type of risk. Without it, close approach to the seat of the fire might not be possible.

Hydrant system

The main hydrant systems form ring mains and are for general use in protecting buildings and other such risks. The system is generally kept primed with clean water but not under pressure, with the pumps being on manual start. The water supply can be from a river or the sea. There are external manifolds into which the County Fire Brigade can connect their pumps to supplement the system.

Some hydrants are coupled to dry risers which are only pressurised when water is pumped into the low level inlet.

Carbon dioxide flooding

Fixed carbon dioxide installations in this country are usually of the high pressure type in which the gas is stored in liquid form in drawn steel cylinders each containing from 22 to 35 kg (50 to 80 lb) of CO_2 at a pressure of 48 - 58.5 bar depending on the atmospheric temperature. The cylinders may be used singly or may be connected to a manifold in batteries.

Characteristics of fixed installations

Carbon dioxide is stored in the cylinders as a liquid, and when released it travels in the same form through the pipework to the discharge nozzles. In the case of high-pressure systems, a discharge horn is fitted to the nozzle to prevent the entrainment of air with gas, minimise turbulence, and reduce the high velocity of the discharge. The release of pressure allows the liquid to turn partly to 'snow' (solid CO_2) and partly to gas; the 'snow' emerges at a temperature of -79°C.

Carbon dioxide extinguishes a fire principally by reducing the oxygen concentration in the vicinity of the burning material.

Operation of CO_2 systems

A single cylinder is often manually operated by a pull handle, provided either close to the cylinder or at a point outside the space protected. The handle is connected to a cable which, when pulled, withdraws a pin holding a weight in place above the operating level on the cylinder, so that the withdrawal of the pin allows the weight to drop on the lever and so open the cylinder. A battery of cylinders can be similarly operated. Above the lever of each cylinder is a weight and all the weights are held up by a common operating shaft. When the support, which keeps the shaft in place, is released (by pulling the releasing handle) the weights fall on the respective levels and so operate the cylinders.

A fixed CO_2 installation may be operated manually, as we have described above, or automatically by means of air-expansion thermostats or, more usually, by fusible links.

The systems are classified as manual or automatic according to the method of actuation, although the automatic system will also have some means of manual control. Before work or inspections are carried out in any enclosure protected by automatic CO_2, or other chemical extinguishing equipment, the automatic control is rendered inoperative and the equipment left on hand control; a notice to this effect is attached to the equipment, and a permit-to-work system is normally employed.

The automatic control is restored immediately after the persons engaged on the work or inspections have come out of the protected enclosure. Any precautions which are taken to render the automatic control inoperative are noted on any Permit for Work issued for work in the protected enclosure. If it is necessary to enter a space flooded with CO_2 breathing apparatus must be worn because CO_2, although not toxic, is an asphyxiant and excludes oxygen from the room.

Vaporising liquids (halon) flooding

Halon systems are now illegal due to the environmental damage.

Fixed foam installations

Fixed foam installations are used against flammable liquids, and generally consist of foam pourers or foam-making branches fed with a supply of foam.

The foam is normally the mechanical type foam produced by mixing foam-making compound and water and passing it through a foam-making generator. These generators are designed to mix the correct proportions of foam compound and air with the quantity of water which is flowing, to generate foam and then deliver it through pipework to the point of discharge. The foam so produced normally has an expansion ratio of approximately 8:1. High expansion foam with an expansion ratio of 1000:1 will be discussed at the end of this sub-section.

Method of operation

It is less easy to arrange for fixed foam installations to operate automatically than is the case with other extinguishing agents. Not only is it vital that the system should operate immediately a fire starts, but it is equally important that it should be shut down as soon as the supply of compound or solution is exhausted; otherwise water alone will reach the foam pourers, with potentially disastrous results.

It is because of this that completely self-contained fixed installations are generally limited to relatively small risks, such as isolated indoor transformers, etc. For large risks, like oil storage tanks, the fixed installation consists of fixed piping (arranged to suit the risk) terminating in foam pourers or fixed monitors; the piping is run back to an appropriate point and terminates in a coupling, usually protected by a glass panel marked with the words *foam inlet*, together with an indication of the particular risk involved.

This arrangement ensures that foam can be applied where it is required; as long as foam compound and water under pressure is available to a foam generator or foam inductor at this point, a continuous supply of foam can be channelled to the required spot.

Use of high expansion foam

It has been shown that high expansion foam is a practical method of fire protection, particularly for special risk areas which are otherwise difficult to protect effectively. High expansion foam can fill an entire building in a matter of minutes; the foam is a good heat insulator and it is effective on ordinary surface fires as well as on flammable liquids.

Dry powder installations

Dry powders, offer the advantage of a quick knock-down of fire and they have negligible toxic effects. Their major disadvantage is that they require a lot of clearing up once an installation has operated. Compacting of the powder is also a problem, due to heat or vibration or moist atmospheres during storage. This could present difficulties in the maintenance of the system especially after discharge when compacting could take place in valves, etc. Recently developed powders (e.g. 'Monnex') appear, however, to be free of this problem.

A dry powder installation consists of dry powder containers linked by pipework to discharge nozzles covering the areas of risk. When a fire occurs it is necessary to pressurise the powder so that it is forced through the pipework and discharge nozzles. This is usually done with CO^2. A line detector is linked to a lever which then actuated allows the head of a CO^2 cylinder to be pierced. The carbon dioxide thus released pressurises the dry powder and forces it over the protected area. Dry powder installations can usually be operated either automatically or manually.

Portable fire fighting equipment

CLASSIFICATION OF FIRES

A basic understanding of the classes of fire needs to be taught because many fire extinguishers state the classes of fire which may be attacked. There are 5 classes into which fires can fall:

CLASS A	Fire involving solids (wood, paper, plastics, usually of an organic nature).
CLASS B	Fires involving liquids or liquefiable solids (petrol, oil, paint, fat, wax).
CLASS C	Fires involving gases (liquefied petroleum gas, natural gas, and acetylene).
CLASS D	Fires involving metals (sodium, magnesium and many metal powders).
CLASS F	Fire involving cooking fats/oils.
ELECTRICAL FIRES	Although not a true class of fire, we should also consider fires in electrical equipment.

EXTINGUISHING MEDIA AND MODE OF ACTION

Fire extinguishers - Use

Water

Water extinguishers should only be used on Class A fires. Water works by cooling the burning material to below its ignition temperature therefore removing the heat part of the fire triangle and the fire goes out. In addition to the cooling effect, steam is produced in the fire area due to the effects of the heat on the water. This aids in the extinguishing process by tending to smother the fire. Water is the most common form of extinguishing media and can be used on the majority of fires involving solid materials

Must not be used on liquid fires or in the vicinity of live electrical equipment.

Foam

Foam is especially useful for extinguishing Class B fires - those involving burning liquids and solids which melt and turn to liquids as they burn. Foam works in several ways to extinguish the fire, the main way being to smother the burning liquid, i.e. to stop the oxygen reaching the fire zone. Foam can also be used to prevent flammable vapours escaping from spilled volatile liquids and also on Class A fires.

Must not be used in the vicinity of live electrical equipment unless electrically rated and then only with great care from a distance of more than one metre.

Steam drench

This extinguishing medium is rarely found but has been used on ships and in oil terminals due to its ready availability. It has an excellent knock down ability due to the vast amount of water droplets that are a feature of this medium. It is also electrically non-conductive. Steam is therefore preferred for use in live electrical environments. Unfortunately it has two distinct disadvantages:

- It has no cooling effect - so there is a chance of re-ignition.
- It is dangerous to human life whilst being used.

Therefore, it can only be used safely in total isolation, or in the form of steam lances in places such as oil refineries, for use by trained and protected staff.

Powder (dry powder)

Powder is excellent for the rapid knock down (flame suppression) of large flammable liquid spills. One of the ways in which powder works to extinguish a fire is the smothering effect. It forms a thin film of powder on the burning liquid thus excluding air. It also chemically interferes with the flame propagation process. The high performance powders now on the market can be used on Class A fires but the normal powders will only subdue this type of fire for a short while. Powders generally provide extinction faster than foam, but there is a greater risk of re-ignition and this should always be borne in mind. If used indoors, a powder extinguisher can cause problems for the operator due to the inhalation of the powder and obscuration of vision. It is therefore imperative that the exit route is clear and available before the extinguisher is operated.

Can be used on live electrical equipment, although damage to the equipment may occur.

Halon (halogenated hydrocarbons or vaporising liquid)

This type of extinguisher should no longer be found in the workplace as it has been withdrawn from use and is illegal to use.

Carbon Dioxide (CO^2)

Carbon Dioxide can be used on live electrical equipment. However the operator needs to get very close to the burning equipment as the carbon dioxide needs to be injected through any air vents that are present so that the electrical component is filled with CO^2. Can be used for small Class B fires in their early stages, indoors or outdoors, with little air movement.

Carbon dioxide replaces the oxygen in the atmosphere surrounding the fuel and the fire is extinguished. Because it replaces the oxygen, CO_2 is an asphyxiant and should not be used in very small, confined spaces unless the operator can withdraw quickly. When working correctly a CO_2 extinguisher is very noisy due to the rapid expansion of gas. This expansion causes severe cooling around the discharge horn and can freeze the skin. Operators should be aware of these occurrences.

Unless the fire is completely extinct, it will take hold again as soon as the CO_2 disperses, which usually occurs within a few seconds. As most carbon dioxide extinguishers last only a few seconds, it is obvious that only small fires should be tackled with this type of extinguisher.

Class C fires

It will be seen that only Class A and B fires have been dealt with above. Except in very small occurrences, a Class C fire should not normally be extinguished, and should only be extinguished if the gas supply can be isolated.

If a leak from a gas cylinder or pipework is burning, the danger area can be identified, i.e. the flames can be seen, and anything which is being affected by the flame can be seen. Where possible the area around the fire should be protected until the leak can be stopped at source by closing the valve, etc. This removes the third side of the fire triangle, the fuel. Any remaining small Class A or B fires can be dealt with using the correct extinguisher. If, however, the fire is extinguished before shutting off the supply, the area of danger cannot then be seen. The possibility of a highly flammable gas cloud spreading throughout the area must be appreciated.

Class D (metal) fires have not been dealt with, as they are, thankfully, rare. Industries which have a known metal fire risk, e.g. aluminium swarf, should have special powder extinguishers on site to deal with such a fire. The powder inside the extinguisher may vary depending upon the metal risks involved. It may also be possible to deal with metal fires by using a supply of dry sand to smother the fire. Powders such as graphite and talc can be used but specific extinguishing agents may be used dependant upon the metal fire risk. Dry sand can also be used to extinguish metal fires, as can bags or sacks of extinguishant.

Method of Operation

There are now only two basic methods by which fire extinguishers are operated - Stored Pressure type and Gas Cartridge type. The method of operation will be marked on the extinguisher.

Fire extinguishers - limitations

Fire classification

Fire extinguishers are limited firstly to the class of fire on which they can be successfully used. It would not be good practice and may indeed be dangerous to use extinguishers for types of fires for which they are not approved.

Duration of discharge

The effectiveness of a fire extinguisher is then limited by the duration of discharge. Some extinguishers only last for very small periods of time and for this reason can only be used on small fires. The minimum duration of discharge for extinguishers is as shown in the following table.

Class F (cooking fats/oils)

New style wet chemical extinguishers have been designed to specifically deal with this type of risk. The extinguishing agent saponifies the cooking oil and cuts off the oxygen supply to the fire.

Minimum duration of discharge

Nominal charge of extinguisher Kg or litres	Minimum duration of discharge of extinguisher (seconds)
Up to and including 3	6
More than 3 but less than or equal to 6	9
More than 6 but less than or equal to 10	12
More than 10	15

Figure C3-5: Minimum duration of discharge - extinguisher.   *Source: FST Consultancy.*

Range of discharge

The extinguisher is also limited by the range (or throw) of the discharge. This would affect the maximum distance that a person could be from a fire and still be effective in extinguishing the fire. Obviously persons would not wish to get too close to fires and therefore, if the range of discharge is too short, then it will be impossible to extinguish the fires.

Fire ratings

Some attempt is made at showing the limits of the fire extinguisher by stating its fire rating. However, this is only done for Class A, Class B and now Class F fires.

Class A fire ratings are achieved by an extinguisher successfully putting out a designated size of test fire. The test fire is made from Pinus Silvestris and the rating achieved relates directly to the length and number of pieces of timber used to construct the test fire, e.g. a 13A rated extinguisher, extinguished a fire constructed of 14 layers of sticks, each transverse layer consisting of 13 sticks (500 mm each), the test fire being 1.3 metres long.

Class B fire ratings are similarly achieved but the fires consist of specified containers of flammable liquid (aliphatic hydrocarbon). The test fire rating achieved relates directly to the volume in litres of fuel, e.g. A 55B rated extinguisher extinguished a fire consisting of 55 litres of fuel with a surface area of 1.73 square metres.

Obviously as can be seen from the illustrations given above, the procedure for test fire ratings is quite involved and further guidance on this matter should be sought from EN 3 1996. Fire extinguishers are installed into buildings in relation to their fire ratings:

Class A fires:	Minimum of 2 extinguishers per floor, unless maximum of 100 sqm on upper floor area and in single occupancy.
	Floor area m sq x 0.065 = Class A fire rating required in building / floor area
Class B fires:	Assess premises in four ways:
	each room / enclosure to be considered separately
	fire risks over 20 m apart consider separately
	fire risks under 20 m apart treat as an undivided or divided group
	Risk of a spillage fire.
Spillage:	Rating required = 10 x volume of spillage.
Undivided group:	Containers less than 2 m apart consider as a single container. Therefore total surface area of all containers is used.
Divided group:	Containers more than 2 m apart but less than 20 m apart consider as separate risks. Therefore surface area of largest containers is used.

Figure C3-6: Fire extinguishers in relation to their fire ratings. *Source: FST Consultancy.*

Extinguisher rating	Max area for 3 foam extinguishers m sq	Max area for 2 extinguishers m sq	Max area for 1 extinguisher m sq
21 B	0.42	0.26	0.14
55 B	1.1	0.69	0.37
144 B	2.88	1.8	0.96

Figures C3-7: Maximum area of a class B fire. (demonstration examples only, this is not a comprehensive list). *Source: FST Consultancy.*

SITING

Portable fire extinguishers should always be sited:

- On the line of escape routes.
- Near to room exits inside or outside according to occupancy and/or risk.
- Near, but not too near, to danger points.
- In multi-storey buildings, at same position on each floor, i.e. top of stair flights or at corners in corridors.
- Where possible in groups forming fire points.
- Where possible in shallow recesses.
- So that no person need travel more than 30 metres to reach an extinguisher.
- With the carrying handle about one metre from the floor to facilitate ease of handling, removal from wall bracket.
- Away from excesses of heat or cold.

MAINTENANCE

British Standard Code of Practice BS 5306, part 3, 2003, details the inspection, maintenance and testing of portable fire extinguishers as follows:

(A) Monthly inspection

A monthly check should be carried out to ensure that extinguishers are in their proper place and have not been discharged, lost pressure or suffered obvious damage.

(B) Annual inspection and maintenance

A more thorough inspection of extinguishers, spare gas cartridges and replacement charges should be carried out by a responsible person on an annual basis. This may include internal and external inspection dependent upon the type of extinguisher.

(C) Test by discharge

Extinguishers should be tested by discharge at intervals as detailed below. The time interval should be taken from the date of manufacture or the last actual discharge.

Extinguisher type	Interval of discharge
Water (stored pressure)	Every 5 years
Foam (all types)	Every 5 years
Water (gas cartridge)	Every 5 years
Powder (gas cartridge)	Every 5 years
Powder (stored pressure valve operated	Every 5 years
Carbon Dioxide (all types)	Every 10 years (20 years if annual inspections done),
Powder (stored pressure primary sealed)	then after 10 years, then every 5 years

Figure C3-8: Extinguisher type and interval of discharge. *Source: FST Consultancy.*

The above information is only a portion of the information on maintenance, inspections and testing. *For further details the British Standard should be consulted.*

TRAINING REQUIREMENTS

Careful consideration should be given to the wording in any company policies and or notices. Any information that is given out should reflect the company policy. It is from this that the training needs should be decided. Any staff that may be called upon to use fire fighting equipment should be trained in its application and use. It is strongly recommended that this training should include the practical use of the equipment on controlled fires.

3.4 - Means of escape

GENERAL REQUIREMENTS

In the main the guidance on acceptable means of escape will be found in published British Standards and Government Department Guides. No general code or 'rule book' has ever been produced which will give the answer to every problem, nor is such a code every likely to be written. However, a great deal of experience has been gained over the years and from this has evolved certain generally accepted principles. These principles are outlined below, however the points raised in this Element have been made for illustration purposes only, and have no legal standing. Individual codes of practice or risk assessment techniques should be used to assess the means of escape necessary in buildings.

Definition of means of escape

The following is a widely accepted definition of means of escape:

"Structural means forming an integral part of the building whereby persons can escape from fire by their own unaided efforts to a place of safety".

A careful study of each phrase in this definition will show that it can form a yardstick against which a solution to a means of escape problem can be judged.

Structural and integral

Good means of escape must be part of the structure of the building and made immovable. The effect of this is to generally rule out the use of most portable self rescue devices, which cannot be relied upon to be in position when required.

Escape

The word 'proceed' may better indicate what is required. It should be possible to turn one's back on the fire and walk away to a safe place. This should be aimed at from all parts of the building.

Fire

Whilst it is obvious that persons should be able to escape from fire, the question of safe escape from heated and toxic gases must also be considered. Protection against the products of fire is probably the most important part of means of escape.

Unaided

The use of this word indicates that, except in special cases such as non-ambulant patients, no mechanical or other devices should ever have to be operated or relied upon. This would certainly rule out the use of lifts or any form of escape which relies on other persons for its operation.

Place of safety

A place of safety is ideally in the open air from where dispersal can take place. This would be termed 'ultimate safety'. It is often necessary to devise a 'halfway' place of safety, for example, when evacuating high buildings. This may be defined as a place of 'comparative safety'.

STRATEGIC FACTORS AFFECTING MEANS OF ESCAPE

- Occupancy.
- Construction.
- Time of Evacuation.
- Exits.
- Travel Distance.
- Management.

Occupancy

This factor divides into:

1. The people in the building (population).   2. The use to which the building is put.

Population

- Number of occupants.
- Physical condition.
- Expected reactions.
- Asleep or awake.

Number of occupants

In existing occupied buildings the number of occupants can be determined by counting the people. However this is not always possible and the number may not remain constant. A figure also has to be established for proposed buildings.

To overcome this problem 'occupancy factors' have been calculated. These work on the basis that, depending on the type of situation, a person will require a certain amount of space (m^2). Space is calculated when the area is empty - before the installation of equipment and storage. Typical occupancy factors are:

- Coffee lounge, committee room   1.0.
- Conference room, dining room   1.0.
- Open plan offices   5.0.
- Library, other offices, kitchens   7.0.
- Shops and showrooms   2.0.
- Supermarkets   7.0.
- Bars   0.3.

Physical condition

It is important to ascertain the degree of agility that can be expected. A means of escape route that involves climbing through a window, for example, may be considered to be acceptable with the occupants in their present state, but will they remain agile?

Expected reactions

In a disciplined occupancy e.g. factory premises, office premises, etc. where regular fire drills may be carried out involving everyone, the reaction of the occupants will no doubt be different to a building occupied largely by members of the public.

Asleep or awake.

This is of vital importance as any sleeping occupancy must have time to react to the alarm and to then respond quickly.

Use of the building

- Nature of contents.
- Furnishings.
- Goods stored or used.
- Processes carried on.

It must be established what kind of occupancy is anticipated, what effect on the spread of fire the contents may have and whether or not smoke in large volumes is expected. Processes of hazardous nature, e.g. low flash point liquids, obviously require special consideration. The location of such processes adjacent to escape routes or the access thereto will also have to be carefully considered.

Construction

Primary Construction: This refers to the main fabric of the building, i.e. walls, floors, roof and internal dividing walls. The following classifications are awarded according to this primary construction.

Class A   Complete non combustible construction.

Class B   Traditional construction, i.e. non-combustible walls, combustible floors and/or roof.

Class C   Combustible construction.

Secondary Construction: This refers to internal partitioning, wall and ceiling linings, etc. The anticipated effect that the secondary construction would have upon a fire may well lower the original classification based on the primary construction.

Time of evacuation

Class A   3 minutes.

Class B   2½ minutes.

Class C   2 minutes.

Exits

Entrances, exits and circulation areas are provided in all buildings for normal everyday use and a means of escape should utilise, where possible, existing arrangements. The first approach to this factor should therefore be a question of disposition, number and width of existing exits. Only if they are insufficient in some respect should further steps be taken. Minimum width should be 750 mm, and more than one exit should be provided if there are more than 50 people in a room. (A unit of exit width = 525 mm.)

When the question of adequacy in number or width arises, a more detailed study of the movement of persons becomes necessary. This is usually so when dealing with places of public resort or those having a high density factor. In most other cases the width of exits is not a crucial factor as the number provided for normal use is generally adequate to cope with the number of persons involved (N.B. 40 people per unit). The Guide to Fire Precautions in existing places of work requiring a fire certificate gives further comment. Flow rate - assume largest exit not available and reduce allowable people accordingly.

Travel distances

This has been defined as:

"The distance to be traversed in order to reach a place of safety".

Place of safety in this context can be either ultimate or comparative. If evacuation times are to be maintained, then some limit has to be placed on the travel distance acceptable. It is not possible to set maximum distances which cover a variety of occupancies so it becomes essential to refer to the relative code of practice for guidance. This would include distances to:

- Final exits.
- Down stairs which are protected routes.
- Doors to a protected lobby.
- Doors in a compartment wall.

Management

One of the overriding factors affecting the means of escape from buildings is the management of fire safety measures. If the management are committed to safety then it should be relatively easy to implement and maintain fire safety measures. If the management are not committed to safety then fire safety standards will not be met or maintained. The maintenance of fire safety standards within buildings should be integral to the business with control of the workplace, work practices, staff training and maintenance of the building and fire systems to name but a few.

TECHNICAL FACTORS AFFECTING MEANS OF ESCAPE

Stairs

In the majority of cases stairs are enclosed in a fire resistant shaft. If the structure around the stairs is fire resistant, the doors onto the stairs are fire resistant doors and there is an exit (or two totally separated exit routes) from the base of the stairs, then the stairwell is described as a fire protected stairwell. This type of structure has special significance as it complies with the definition of a storey exit as described in building regulations and fire safety guidance. As such travel distances are measured to storey exits when deciding upon the compliance of a building design with recognised standards.

In certain buildings a special stairwell (usually called a fire-fighting shaft) is needed. Additional facilities including fire-fighting lifts, fire-fighting stairs and lobbies are included in a fire-fighting shaft. The addition of these measures will allow the Fire Service to quickly access the fire floor or to access the floor below a fire from which an operating base can be set up. In general buildings with floor levels over 18m above, or basements more than 10m below Fire Service vehicle access level, will need to provide fire-fighting shafts.

It may be possible to have an unprotected stairway in a building, but it is not usually counted for means of escape purposes. If an unprotected stairs does form part of the means of escape then the travel distances are measured up to and down the stairs. By taking this approach travel time is reduced before the effects of a fire can prevent people escaping down the stairs. It also usual in such circumstances to install compensating features into the building such as fire detection, sprinklers and/or smoke ventilation.

Gangways and passageways

In any area where people work or to which the public are admitted, the contents of that area should be arranged so as to allow free passageway for means of escape. It may be necessary for example in factories or large shops such as DIY shops to mark the gangways with paint. Where the areas used as gangways are subject to change then the marking may be of some other non-permanent but durable material.

Doors

In simple terminology there are two types of doors when considering fire safety - fire resisting doors and fire exit doors. Of course the fire exit door may also be a fire resisting door.

Fire resistant doors along with fire resistant structures serve two purposes:

1. Prevent the spread of fire.

2. Ensure that there is means of escape for persons using the building.

It is often difficult to tell visually what a fire door is. However, points to look for are:

■   The door will normally be fitted with three hinges.
■   The door will normally be fitted with a positive self closing device, e.g. swing arm device or percomatic closer.
■   New fire doors will be fitted with intumescent strips and cold smoke seals.
■   New doors should have a colour raw plug inserted into one of its side edges. The colours on the plug denote the standard of the door, e.g. white circle with red dot is an FD30/20 door which requires intumescent materials to be fitted. A white circle with a green dot is an FD30/20 door which does not require intumescent materials.

There are a few terms used in the statements above with which some people may not be familiar.

Swing arm device

Traditional type of door closer which fits at top of door and joins onto door frame. Once opened it should slowly close and latch the door.

Percomatic closer

A type of door closer which uses spring loaded pistons for its methods of operation. The door closer itself is mounted inside the leaf of the door after a hole has been routed out. The only visible portion is a single or double chain between the door and door frame (hinge side). Again this device is intended to close and latch the door.

Intumescent strips

Intumescent material is material that expands when it get hot. Strips of this material are fitted around both sides and the top of the door. If there is a fire the material intumesces (swells) and fills the gap between the door and door frame, thus preventing fire and smoke from passing through.

Cold smoke seals

Intumescent materials work well if a fire is close to a door or well developed. If the fire is small or distant from the door, by the time the smoke reaches the door it is cold and the intumescent material will not intumesce. Smoke would then pass around the edge of the door.

A cold smoke seal is a nylon brush or neoprene strip which again is introduced both sides and at the top of the door. This seal should constantly brush against the door/door frame and therefore prevent the cold smoke from passing through the gap.

FD20/20 and FD30/20 etc.

Fire doors are now denoted as shown above. FD stands for fire door. The first figure stands for stability test rating in minutes, the second figure stands for integrity in minutes.

- Stability - is the time at which collapse occurred.
- Integrity - is the time that cracks or other openings exist which flame or hot gases can pass and cause flaming of a cotton wool pad.

The major point to bring out in the use of fire doors is *that they should be not be wedged open.*

Fire exit doors are there to allow people to get out of the building in the event of fire. As discussed above re escape routes, they need to be wide enough for the number of people who may need to use them. The method of opening doors and any method of securing doors is critical.

Routes for escape

When talking of escape routes in case of fire, people often think of the stairwells and corridors within a building. Although these are both important aspects of the escape route, they are not the only factors to consider.

The escape route should be considered from every point of every room. It should therefore be considered from the individual desks, benches or workstations within a room. There should be a clear path or gangway from each individual's workplace to the exit from the room. Consideration should be given to the spacing between desks, workstations and items of plant or equipment within the building. If there is a main gangway or path through a room or floor, then it should be kept clear at all times.

A minimum clearance width of between 750mm and 1 metre should be maintained throughout the escape route. This minimum width may need to be increased, dependent upon the number of persons who may need to use the escape route. Consideration should be given to painting tramlines or hatched areas on the floor, or even the use of guardrails to denote the gangways within a workplace. If this is done, then it should make the escape route within the room itself more identifiable.

Once persons have escaped from the room itself, the escape route should utilise the normal means of egress from a building where possible. Only where these routes do not provide adequate means of escape are additional exits and escape routes required.

Having escaped from individual rooms, the normal escape route now consists of corridors, stairwells and possibly external staircases.

The route taken should be safe from fire and for this reason will normally be protected from the remainder of the building by fire resistant structures. The protection to the escape route should be such that persons will not be affected by the fire or smoke that is present. One exception to this would be ground floor open plan units where persons can walk away from fire and out of exit doors. Basically if a person can turn their back on a fire from any part and walk away to an exit door then fire resistance may not be required. If there is a possibility that persons could become trapped by fire, then fire resistance may be necessary.

Emergency lighting

After the design and provision of means of escape has been concluded, its safe and effective use in case of fire must be secured. Two factors that have to be considered with escape routes are the amount of natural light along the route, and the day / night hours worked by staff. Basically, if an escape route has no natural or borrowed light, or staff work out of normal hours, then escape lighting may be required. The escape lighting should adequately illuminate escape routes in the event of failure of the normal electrical supply to the lighting circuit due to fire.

Commonly, under the Fire Precautions Act premises require emergency lighting systems. Provision is made in the act for securing the means of escape, and emergency lighting is one part of this. Under other legislation the provision of emergency lighting may also be required, either directly as in B1 of the Building Regulations (BR) 2002, or as a result of conditions imposed by licences etc. Emergency lighting is usually provided on common access routes in commercial, industrial and multi storey premises.

Functions

Emergency lighting is required to fulfil the following functions:-

- To indicate clearly the escape routes.
- To provide illumination along such routes to allow safe movement towards and through the exits provided.
- To ensure that fire alarm call points and fire fighting equipment provided along escape routes can be readily located.

Types

Maintained	Operates at all times.
Non Maintained	Only lights up when power fails.
Sustained	Contains 2 lamps - 1 powered from mains 1 powered from emergency lighting supply (usually batteries).
Self Contained Luminaire	Luminaire containing everything:- lamp, battery, test facility and controls.
Low Level Lighting System	Lighting strips (continuous) at floor or skirting board height.

Siting

Emergency lighting luminaries should be sited near each exit door and emergency exit door and at points where it is necessary to emphasise the position of safety equipment and hazards e.g.

- Near each intersection of corridors.
- At each exit door.
- Near each change of direction.
- Near other changes in floor level.
- Outside each final exit door.
- Near each fire alarm call point.
- Near firefighting equipment.
- To illuminate exit and safety signs required by the enforcing authority.

Testing of emergency lighting system

Daily:

- Check no faults - normal power.
- If maintained system, check lamp is lit.
- Any faults to be rectified and action recorded.

Monthly:

- Simulate a power failure to the normal lighting circuit and check that self contained luminaries have energized.
- Simulate a power failure to the normal lighting circuit to check that central battery system energizes (if a central battery system if fitted).
- Simulate a power failure to lighting to check that generator starts up and energizes lights for a minimum of one hour (if generator system fitted).

6-monthly:

- Longer duration tests should be done, e.g. 3 hour self contained luminaries should be energized from battery for 1 hour.
- There are also additional tests after 3 years and thereafter annually.
- One other consideration when assessing the need for escape lighting may also be the use of photoluminescent signs and markings.

Exit and directional signs

Escape routes that form part of the everyday access/egress from a building are not normally identified as escape routes by use of signs etc. The reason for this is that it is recognised that persons working in a building would already know their way in and out of the building. However, consideration should be given to the access/egress used by different sections of the workforce and their knowledge of other personnel's access/egress. The statements made above do not apply if members of the public frequent the building. In this case exit signs etc. would need to be placed along all escape routes.

Escape routes which are not in normal use, e.g. external fire escape stairways must be indicated by use of exit signs and directional arrows. In addition, any door fastenings which may need to be opened should have signs to denote operation.

Any signs or notices which are used along the escape route should be readily visible and large enough to be read from the furthest point in the room, corridor etc. Exit signs are normally placed above doorways and openings to which they relate. If it is not possible to site an exit sign above a door, it should be sited immediately next to the doorway, not on the door itself. If the sign is put on the door and the door left open, then the sign will not be seen. Consideration should be given to suspended signs.

The following points should be considered before deciding on the type, size and position of any signs:

- The line of exit route changes direction - therefore a sign bearing a directional arrow is necessary.
- The sign must be capable of being read from both approaches to the exit and so may be required to be double sided.
- The sign must have letters/pictures large enough to be read from the extremities of the room or corridor.
- The sign must not be obscured by light fittings, items of plant, changes in ceiling level etc.
- On landings or at the base of staircases where there is doubt whether the escape route is up or down, a further directional sign is required.
- Signs must be conspicuous and if normal lighting is artificial or work is done in hours of darkness, the sign should be illuminated.

Notices

All notices should be checked as part of the fire audit procedure to ensure that they are present and that they are legible. Where safety signs are required then they must incorporate pictograms. Word only signs are now illegal.

General principles for means of escape planning

a. There should be alternative means of escape from most situations.

b. If it is not possible to have direct access to a place of total safety, e.g. final exit door, it should be possible to reach a place of comparative safety, e.g. fire protected stairway, within a reasonable distance. In these cases we have an unprotected portion of the escape route and a protected portion.

c. Any unprotected part of an escape route should be limited so that people do not have to travel excessive distances, possibly whilst exposed to the dangers of fire and smoke.

d. Horizontal protected escape routes should be limited in distance, as they do not provide protection indefinitely.

e. Corridors should be sub-divided by fire doors to prevent smoke travel.

f. If people cannot turn their backs on a fire and walk away, then fire protection of the escape route must be considered (dead end conditions).

g. Fire protected stairways are considered to be 'fire sterile' areas. Therefore flames, smoke and gases must be excluded from these areas. Fire risks should not be allowed into these areas, e.g. storage, photocopier, etc., and must not be allowed if they are the only stairs.

h. Once a person has entered a fire protected stairway, then they must be contained within a fire protective structure all the way to the final exit door.

i. Exits should not be close enough to each other, so that a fire starting between them will render them both unusable. This is accounted for by the application of the $45°$ rule, i.e. at the point from where a person is trying to escape, if both exits are within a $45°$ angle from that point, then they will only be considered as a single exit route.

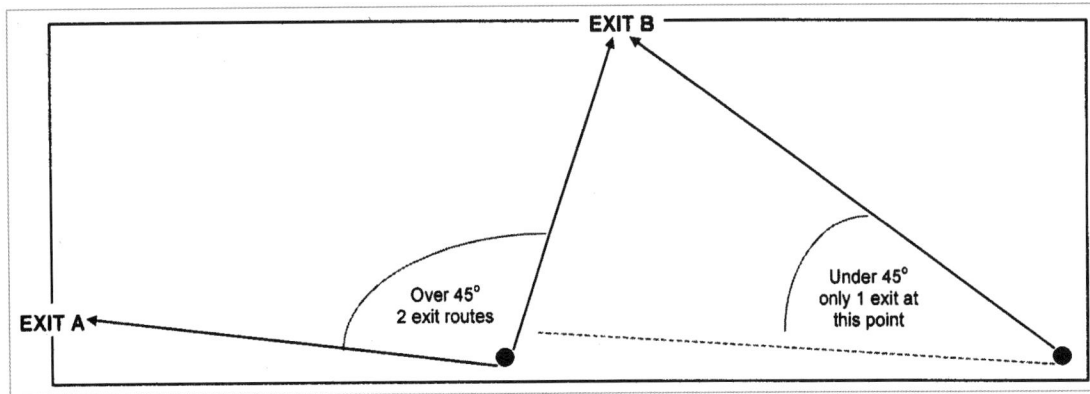

Figure C3-9: Exits - 45° rule. *Source: FST Consultancy.*

j.   Inner rooms (room within a room) are allowed with certain provisions. However, inner, inner rooms are not allowed.

k.   Any known fire risks should be located in the building, with consideration to the means of escape, and the effects that they would have on them, if on fire; e.g. if you have an access room and an inner room, the fire risk should ideally be in the inner room.

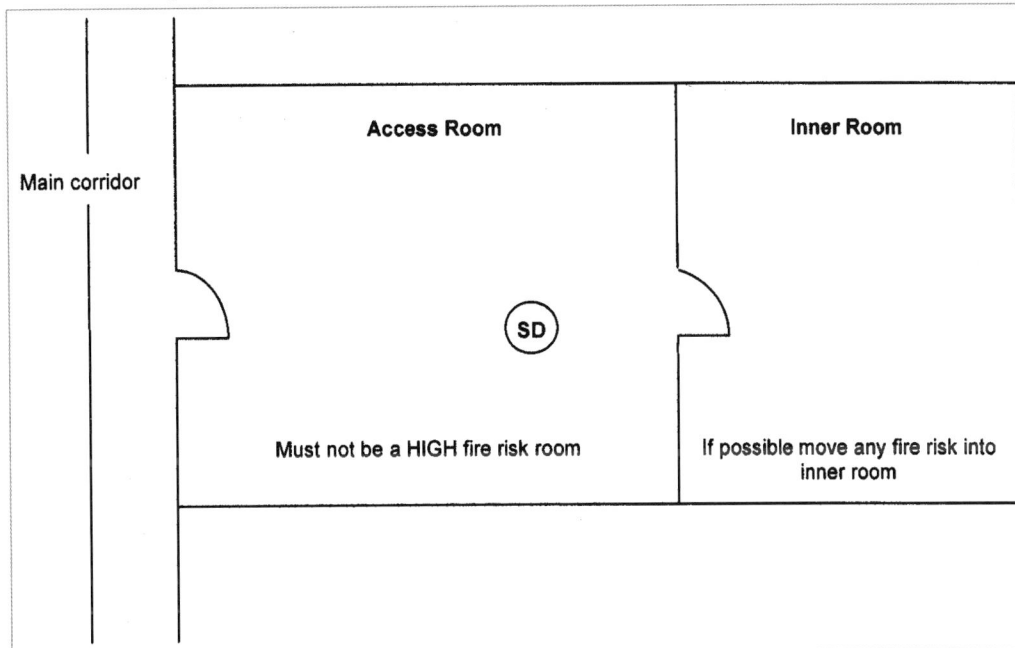

Figure C3-10: Known fire risks. *Source: FST Consultancy.*

l.   When planning for means of escape, if a room or storey has more than one exit, then you must assume and plan for the eventuality that one of the exits (the largest) will be blocked by fire or smoke.

m.   In a multi-stairway building, unless the stairway is approached via a protected lobby, i.e. two door protection to stairs, then it must be assumed that a stairway will be rendered unusable due to fire or smoke. Another exception to this would be if the stairway is fitted with a smoke control pressurisation system.

n.   Doors on escape routes should ideally open in the direction of travel, and must do so if more than 60 people may use the door.

REQUIREMENTS OF THE RELEVANT LEGISLATION

The two principal pieces of fire safety legislation that are applicable to buildings is the Fire Precautions Act (FPA) 1971 and the Fire Precautions (Workplace) Regulations (FPWR) 1997. The FPA is prescriptive legislation where the Fire Brigade dictates standards to the building owner and/or occupier. The FPWR 1997 are goal based with the employer conducting a fire risk assessment and implementing fire safety standards as they deem fit. At this point in time buildings that require fire certificates are under both pieces of legislation at the same time. *See also - "Relevant statutory provisions" - element C11.*

Fire certificates and their conditions

In buildings that require fire certificates the means of escape from fire and the maintenance of the means of escape are detailed in the certificate. This traditional prescriptive system of controlling fire safety standards in buildings has worked very well. The certificate sets out the minimum standards for means of escape in case of fire and makes it a legal requirement that the management within the workplace maintains them. Once a fire certificate is in force it is illegal for alterations to be made to the building without seeking approval of the local Fire Authority. Conditions will be imposed that prevent fire doors being wedged open, prevent fire exits being locked or obstructed and even controls the surface finishings that are put on walls and ceilings. Conditions will also be imposed on the fire alarm / fire detection, emergency lighting, fire fighting equipment and fire training standards within the building.

3.5 - Emergency evacuation procedures

EVACUATION PROCEDURES

The danger which may threaten persons if fire breaks out depends on many different factors. Consequently, it is not possible to construct a model procedure for action in the event of fire in all premises. Having thoroughly understood the fundamental principles, however, you should experience no difficulty in adapting them to the circumstances of each case.

To avoid delay in evacuating the premises when the fire alarm is sounded, there should be a pre-arranged procedure enabling persons to leave safely and quickly.

The essential factor is that all staff should be familiar with the escape route to be used in the event of fire and also with an alternative route, should the main escape route be impassable.

Every employee should therefore be given instruction about their action on hearing the fire alarm as a part of their induction training.

The instruction should state which route is to be followed, which alternative route is to be used if the first is impassable and where to assemble for a roll call on reaching open air.

The responsibility for ensuring that a department is evacuated quickly and safely should rest with the departmental manager or a nominated fire marshal. A search of the department including lavatories and cloakrooms should be made, and on reaching the assembly point, the roll should be called to ensure that everyone in the department is accounted for, taking particular care if flexible working hours are allowed.

There are a number of approaches to evacuation procedures this may include the following.

Single stage evacuation (total)

This involves the immediate evacuation of all the occupants of a building on the sounding of the alarm.

Horizontal evacuation

Certain types of premises may not be suitable for total evacuation due to the type of residents within the building e.g. Old Persons Homes, Hospitals. In this type of premise it is normal to only evacuate residents from the fire affected area in the initial stages. Residents should be evacuated to a place of safety, normally so that there is two fire door separation between the residents and the fire. The place of safety must then have another direction of escape that is away from the fire area. It is paramount that the building structure is maintained so that the fire or smoke cannot bypass the fire protection and jeopardise the safety of the people in the place of safety. If the situation gets worse, there must be a method of evacuating residents further away. This is normally done by moving them horizontally further away from the fire and behind additional fire resistance; however it may involve vertical evacuation and if necessary total evacuation.

Staff alarm controlled evacuation

In some premises, an immediate total evacuation may not be desirable, e.g. night clubs, shops, theatres, cinemas. A controlled evacuation by the staff may be preferred, to prevent distress and panic to the occupants. If such a system is used, the alarm must be restricted to the staff and only used where there are sufficient members of staff and they have been fully trained in the action of what to do in case of fire.

Two stage evacuation

This allows for a period of time, following the initial alarm and the evacuation of those in the proximity of the fire, for the incident to be investigated. The alarm is then either cancelled, if it is false, or the fire has been extinguished, or the remainder of the building is totally evacuated. In a two stage system a continuous bell or signal from the sounder indicates immediate evacuation, and an intermittent signal an alert, to enable shut-down operations and the evacuation of the disabled (where appropriate) to commence elsewhere.

Phased evacuation

Phased evacuation systems are becoming more common as buildings become taller and house increasing numbers of staff. The occupants of the floor on which a fire occurs together with the occupants of the floor directly above are evacuated immediately a fire is detected. The remainder of the occupants are alerted and remain in the building unless the fire is such that they need to evacuate. Further evacuations are carried out two floors at a time under the control of fire marshals or the fire brigade, and are determined by the way in which the fire develops.

- Good communications are essential if an orderly evacuation is to be undertaken. If a phased evacuation system is in operation, fire marshals will need to be able to communicate with the senior fire marshal in the control centre by fire telephones, which should be installed on each floor of the building.
- Buildings in which phased evacuation is proposed should incorporate the highest standards of fire protection, and staff should undergo comprehensive training. In particular, each floor should be constructed as a compartment floor, an automatic fire detection and alarm system should be installed, smoke control measures are recommended, and, if the building is over 28m high, an automatic sprinkler installation should be considered.

Allocation of responsibility

Allocation of specific responsibilities will vary according to circumstances. The most important requirements are that there should be no confusion as to who is responsible for each of the various measures that may need to be taken, and that decisions are not delayed unnecessarily because one or more of those responsible are not immediately available.

The ideal is that there should be a designated person in each department, or on each floor, responsible for taking immediate charge at the scene of the outbreak and for taking decisions which may be required pending the arrival of a more senior member of the managerial staff, the works fire officer, or the public fire brigade. It should be clearly understood that if the designated person is not available then the deputy, or next senior employee, takes charge.

The tasks of the designated people in the departments are to ensure the safety of the occupants, and, if the fire is in their department, to attempt to contain it, if trained. When in doubt, safety is the more important consideration.

Fire instruction notices

At conspicuous positions in all parts of the building, and adjacent to all fire alarm actuating (break glass) points, printed notices should be exhibited stating, in concise terms, the essentials of the action to be taken upon discovering a fire and on hearing the fire alarm.

Fire action

In the event of a fire, action upon discovery needs to be immediate and a simple fire action plan should be put into effect. A good plan of action would include the following points:

1. Sound the fire alarm (to warn others).
2. Call the fire brigade.
3. Tackle the fire (only if trained, and it is safe to do so).
4. Get out of the building and stay out.
5. Arrange a roll call or floorsweep.

However, be careful of the wording on fire routine notices, as they have legal implications, e.g. if Point 3 'Tackle Fire' is on the notice, you may need to train everyone to use fire equipment.

The roll call system

The roll call system is based on checking that everyone in a building has reached a place of safety. The names of all the building's occupants are recorded on a list. In the event of a fire or practice, following evacuation, a designated person checks that everyone on the list answers the roll call. This information is then passed to a central control point.

Advantages of this system include:

- Specific confirmation that staff are out and safe.
- The emphasis lies in getting people out then checking.

Disadvantages of this system include:

- It is dependent on complete and up-to-date lists of their building occupants, which are often difficult if not impossible to maintain at any one time.
- Reactive to evacuation - it doesn't help get people out.
- A lot of time is spent checking lists before the area can be declared clear.
- It assumes all personnel know where to go if the building is evacuated.

The fire marshal system

This system is based on splitting a building into small manageable areas. In the event of a fire, designated staff search their area to ensure that all staff leave the building. They then direct people who have not evacuated to the appropriate Fire Exit and onward to their assembly area. They then report that their area is clear (or otherwise) to an allocated person at the assembly point.

Advantages of this system include:

- It has been shown to be the quickest, most efficient way to evacuate a building.
- It allows the Fire Service in quickly to rescue people and reduce damage.
- Buildings are split into pre-defined areas for control - no 'grey' areas.
- Pro-active - Floor Marshals identify dangers and problems arising during - not after evacuation.
- It allows for a controlled search of an area, if necessary.

Disadvantages of this system include:

- It may only be in operation during the normal working day.
- It is normally voluntary - it relies on staff goodwill.

It is obviously important that all areas of the building are covered by Fire Marshals, and companies who choose to adopt this system must ensure that there are sufficient numbers of Marshals to cover the building at all times, bearing in mind that 'extra' Marshals will be required to cover absences, for example, leave, personnel who have to leave their normal place of work (e.g. delivering a report to another part of the building) and training courses! etc.

The actual system of work operated by the Fire Marshals will be dictated by the building layout, the work practices and number of staff available to conduct an evacuation. However, it has been found that one of the three options explained below, or an adaptation of these will normally suffice. In all cases the Fire Marshals will check areas within the workplace, and instruct staff to evacuate the building by the nearest safe exit. The Fire Marshals will basically be the last person to evacuate the area they are checking. It is always advisable to give Fire Marshals some visible form of identification such as high visibility jackets, and some form of communications would be advantageous.

Evacuation of disabled

Due to recent changes in the Discrimination Disabled Act alterations may need to have been made to enable people with disabilities to access buildings. This may mean that you may now find people with disabilities on floors where they were not originally. As the fire manager you need to ensure that all persons who enter your buildings can escape in the event of a fire. There is a misconception in some companies that it is satisfactory to evacuate the person with the disability to a safe refuge e.g. fire protected stairwell and to hold them there awaiting the arrival of the Fire Brigade, so that they can carry them down. This is not the case. If you have people with disabilities in your building, it is your responsibility to get them out should the need arise.

This issue is not however straightforward, as there are many forms of disability which may be encountered. The more common disabilities would be mobility impairment, vision impairment and hearing impairment.

Hearing Impairment - This may be solved by trembler alarms for staff, flashing lights and 'buddy' systems.

Vision Impairment - This may be solved by use of tactile signs and 'buddy' systems.

Mobility Impairment - This may vary from someone who is just slower than everyone else in escaping, to a person in a wheelchair. Solutions may vary from assisting the person out of the building immediately after the initial rush of occupants, to use of evacuation chairs and other escape systems. If you take the worse case scenario of a person in a wheelchair that you need to evacuate vertically, there are risk factors involved in moving them. The better system would include someone remaining with the person in the safe refuge, communication between this point and the fire panel, so that an informed judgement can be made on whether it is necessary to evacuate the individual or not.

FIRE DRILLS

The danger which may threaten persons if fire breaks out depends on many different factors. Consequently, it is not possible to construct a model procedure for action in the event of fire in all premises. Having thoroughly understood the fundamental principles, however, you should experience no difficulty in adapting them to the circumstances of each case. It is therefore important that before fire drills are planned, the following points must be considered.

The purpose of fire drills

The responsibility for carrying out fire drills rests on the occupier of the premises. A fire drill is intended to ensure, by means of training and rehearsal, that in the event of fire:

1. The people who may be in danger act in a calm and orderly manner.
2. Where necessary, those designated carry out their allotted duties to ensure the safety of all concerned.
3. The means of escape are used in accordance with a predetermined and practised plan.
4. If evacuation of a building becomes necessary, it is speedy and orderly.

Instruction

This should be given frequently at such intervals as will ensure that all employed persons are instructed at least once, in each period of twelve months. Instruction and training generally should provide for the following:

1. The action to be taken upon discovering a fire.
2. The action to be taken on hearing the fire alarm.
3. Raising the alarm, including the location of alarm call points, internal fire alarm telephones and alarm indicator panels.
4. The correct method of calling the fire brigade.
5. The location and use of fire fighting equipment.
6. Knowledge of escape routes.
7. Appreciation of the importance of fire doors and of the need to close all doors at the time of a fire and on hearing the fire alarm.
8. Stopping machines and processes and isolating power supplies where appropriate.
9. Evacuation of the building.

In addition to the above, certain categories of staff should be instructed and trained in any matters peculiar to their particular responsibilities at the time of a fire. Examples are:

- Department Heads.
- Engineering and Maintenance Staff.
- Floor Supervisors.
- Security Staff (including night security patrols).
- Telephonists.

At least once a year a practice fire drill should be carried out simulating conditions in which one or more of the escape routes from the building are obstructed. During these drills the fire alarm should be operated by a member of staff who is told of the supposed outbreak and, thereafter, the fire routine should be rehearsed as fully as circumstances allow.

Log books

Such details as are necessary to show the training and instruction given should be recorded. The following are examples of matters which may need to be included in such a record:

1. Date of the instruction or exercise.
2. Duration.
3. Name of the person giving the instruction.
4. Names of the persons receiving the instruction.
5. The nature of the instruction training or drill.

Organisation

In all premises one person should be responsible for organising fire instruction and training and in larger premises co-ordinate the actions of persons in the event of fire.

FIRE POLICY / FIRE PLAN

Policy

The management from each company should formulate a fire policy which would include its fire plans. All of the points mentioned in the previous notes on fire protection and fire prevention should be included, plus any other fire related subjects which are pertinent to the company but are not included in this note. As part of the fire policy, the management should evaluate the severity of fire risks, train and inform people what to do in the event of fire and how to prevent fire, organise a chain of management responsibility to reduce fire risks, and consider damage control should a fire occur.

Evaluation of fire risks

Management should be aware of the vulnerability of the premises to fire damage. Points that should be considered are:

a. The nature of the processes, contents and materials.

b. Structural and other measures to prevent the spread of fire.

c. The susceptibility of the firm to consequential losses following a fire due to:

- Interruption of business.
- Damage to key points, e.g. control panels.
- Loss of records, designs, plans and patterns.
- Delivery times for new equipment/goods.

- Difficulties in replacing stock/equipment.
- Reaction of customers when faced with a delay.
- Reaction of competitors during downtime.
- Staff attitudes.

Responsibilities

Crucial to the success of any fire prevention system is the organisation provided to maintain the fire safety system. There is an old saying "that safety must start at the top" and it's true. A brief outline of responsibilities is suggested below, but each company should formulate its own management structure for fire safety.

Managing director/directors

This tier of management is responsible by law for the safety of people, and the safety of premises. However, they normally delegate the direct responsibility for fire related matters to a lower management level. This is acceptable providing that they have given the nominated person sufficient training and information to carry out the tasks, and that the person concerned has sufficient managerial powers to implement their policies.

Fire safety manager

This is normally a full or part-time responsibility and is often twinned with safety and security. As pointed out above, this person should be given sufficient training and information and have sufficient managerial powers to carry out the job successfully.

Department heads and supervisors

They are normally responsible for day to day fire safety including the daily checking of their areas for fire dangers.

Safety representatives and safety committees

They should inform the management of any fire risks which come to their attention.

Fire/security staff

Normally responsible for routine security/fire safety, which they may achieve by frequent patrols, maintaining fire equipment and reporting fire dangers.

All employees

Should observe the company's rules for fire prevention, be familiar with the fire precautions relevant to their particular jobs and know the action to take in event of fire. Some employees many be trained to act as fire marshals or fire wardens.

Damage control

A good management team should also make contingency plans in advance of a fire to ensure a speedy return to normal working and to reduce the effects of fire in the premises.

Fire plan

When the fire risk has been assessed and the managerial responsibilities delegated, then the policy that has been formulated should be written down in the form of a fire plan or fire manual. The manual should detail the fire safety systems and equipment that have been provided and then actions needed to maintain standards day to day.

The manual should cover such areas as:

- Organisation of fire safety and managerial / employee responsibilities.
- Legal requirements.
- Insurance and other obligations.
- Structural precautions for fire prevention.
- Means of escape.
- Security.
- Storage.
- Precautions in production areas.
- Plant and equipment (design, installation, maintenance).
- Waste collection, removal, and disposal.
- General fire precautions.
- Smoking.
- Contractors.
- Fire protection equipment.
- Training.

In addition to the fire manual:

- A fire routine procedure should be formulated for all parts of the premises and staff trained to ensure the system works.
- Checklists for a routine checking system should be formulated.

Procedure to be adopted in the event of fire

In drawing up the procedure, care must be taken to ensure that:

- A senior member of staff is responsible for safety in avoiding fire and in the event of fire.
- All members of staff are issued with clear and comprehensive instructions.
- Responsibilities in the event of fire are clearly allocated.
- The design of the premises and the particular hazards of the materials and processes used in the premises are taken into account.
- The alarm system is clearly audible and distinguishable throughout the premises.
- The fire 'control centre' - probably the telephone switchboard - will come into operation in the event of fire with standing instructions as to the immediate actions to be taken - this includes summoning the fire brigade and notifying the management.
- The evacuation procedure is efficient and all employees are familiar with the main and alternative escape routes from their department.
- In the case of evacuation, provision is made for a search of every part of the premises.
- Practice fire drills are held at least once a year.

Work practices

When you consider that approximately 50% of all fires are caused by staff actions, then it is evident that when considering fire prevention, we should look at the working practices of the staff.

All staff should carry out their work with safety in mind. This awareness should not only cover health and safety, but fire safety. It should be obvious therefore that there is a direct link between work practices and training. It has been found in the past that, by training staff and making them more fire safety conscious, the number of fires caused by the careless actions of the staff or the tendency of staff to misuse equipment has reduced.

Work permits

One area of work practices that has caused fire problems, historically time and time again is the operation of work permits for hot work processes. Or, to be more precise, the lack of work permits has created problems. When staff (or contractors) need to use hot work processes, e.g. cutting and welding, a formal list of fire prevention rules should be implemented in the form of a permit to work system. The hot-work permit should cover such points as:

- Clearing up of combustible materials from around the work area.
- Ensuring there are no risks within the work area from liquids, vapours, gases or dusts.
- Sheeting up of any combustible materials that cannot be removed, by the use of fire blankets or other suitable materials.
- Fire extinguishing equipment on hand and a person trained in its use available.
- Workmen aware of nearest fire alarm call point and the fire routine procedure.
- Checking of area after work is completed to ensure that there are no smouldering fires.

3.6 - Enforcement

REGULATORY POWERS OF A FIRE AUTHORITY WITH RESPECT TO FIRE SAFETY

Enforcement can be taken at three levels:

1. *Prohibition Notice (FPA 1971) -* if persons at serious risk in case of fire.

2. *Serious Case Offence -* if staff at risk of serious injury.

3. *Enforcement Notice (Improvement Notice) -* if fire safety deficiency and improvements needed.

See also - "Relevant statutory provisions" - element C11.

The storage, handling and processing of dangerous substances

Overall aims

On completion of this Element, the student will have knowledge and understanding of:

■ the arrangements for ensuring the safe storage, handling, processing, disposal and transport of dangerous substances.

Content

Specific intended learning outcomes

The intended learning outcomes are that the student will be able to:

1. identify the design, planning and operational requirements for safe storage of dangerous, toxic, and corrosive substances

2. identify the design, planning and operational requirements for safe transport and handling of dangerous substances

Relevant statutory provisions

Fire Certificates (Special Premises) Regulations (FPSPR) 1976

Notification of Installations Handling Hazardous Substances Regulations (NIHHS) 1982 (and as amended 2002)

Dangerous Substances (Notification and Marking of Sites) Regulations (NOMAS) 1990

Chemicals (Hazard Information and Packaging for Supply) Regulations (CHIP) 2002

Health and Safety (Safety Signs and Signals) Regulations (SSSR) 1996

Dangerous Substances and Explosive Atmospheres Regulations (DSEAR) 2002

Control of Major Accident Hazards Regulations (COMAH) 1999

Carriage of Dangerous Goods and Use of Transportable Pressure Equipment Regulations (CDGUTPER) 2004

4.1 - Major accidents

EFFECT OF TEMPERATURE

Reaction rate is *exponential* to temperature and increases by a factor of 2 for every $10^{\circ}C$ rise, whereas available cooling rate (batch production) is *linear*.

The reaction rate increases with increasing concentration of reactant.

For chemical reactions which are exothermic (give out heat energy) it is essential to maintain the reactor temperature within a narrow band to prevent uncontrollable (run-away) conditions occurring.

For example consider a common manufacturing process, the production of urea formaldehyde adhesive resins for the manufacture of chip-board.

The process is relatively simple, urea is mixed with 36% formaldehyde, at a controlled ph and held for approximately 4 hours at $60^{0}C$. Polymerisation occurs and the viscosity of the material increases to a pre-determined value, which represents the molecular chain length required. If the temperature is allowed to rise much above $70^{0}C$, the reaction will become uncontrollable, resulting in solidification of the constituents and release of volatile toxic materials e.g. formaldehyde MEL 2 ppm.

Reaction temperature control is a very important issue when considering scale-up of production from laboratory through pilot plant to final production.

Exothermic reactions may follow inadvertent admixture of materials.

EFFECT OF PRESSURE

The most significant use of pressure is the production of compressed gases, the most common being compressed oxygen, liquid nitrogen, and solid carbon dioxide produced from the fractional distillation of compressed air. Other gases are produced either directly or indirectly from chemical processes and for convenience are stored under pressure: common gases are chlorine, liquefied petroleum gas (propane), sulphur dioxide, hydrogen, ammonia and acetylene. The main hazard with pressure processes is over pressurisation leading to catastrophic failure of the planet or storage container. Examples have been discussed earlier.

EFFECT OF CATALYSTS

Certain material will significantly promote or retard a chemical reaction. Common catalysts used to promote are platinum and nickel and they are used extensively to carry out chemical reactions at lower than would be necessary temperature or pressures. Some materials such as iron can have the reverse effect and 'poison' or stop certain chemical reactions.

Promotion catalysts are not consumed in the process, but provide a lower energy route for the reaction to proceed at the electron transfer level.

For the hydrogenation of castor oil [here hydrogen is added to castor oil under pressure to increase the molecular weight] to produce margarine, a platinum catalyst is used to promote the transition process at a temperature below which the product would decompose.

The purity of raw materials is important to ensure the desired reaction rate is achieved to prevent the possibility of run away reactions.

HEAT OF REACTION

Endothermic reactions - reactions which take in heat energy

Endothermic reactions accompanying large quantities of material may similarly consume large quantities of energy resulting in freezing of process pipe-work or equipment, e.g. dissolving urea in acetone at ambient will result in a temperature drop in excess of $20\,^{\circ}C$, well below freezing point.

Exothermic reactions - reactions which give out heat energy

The energy liberated can be considerable over a short space of time and if the quantities of material are large may result in ejection of the substances from equipment or if confined may result in explosions, e.g. mixing concentrated sulphuric acid with hydrochloric acid.

Effects of enthalpy changes on mixing of liquids

When of two or more substances of different molecular structure are combined an exothermic (release of heat energy) or endothermic (take up of heat energy) reaction may result. This internal energy change is called enthalpy.

Runaway reactions

During the manufacture of a chemical, starting materials will undergo chemical transformations resulting in the formation of the final product. These chemical changes normally involve the evolution or absorption of heat and are said to be exothermic or endothermic reactions, as outlined above. Of most concern in chemical processing is the exothermic process. If the heat released from such a process cannot be removed efficiently it presents a potential hazard to the operation by remaining in the reaction mass, with the consequence of raising the reaction mass temperature, and hence reaction rate, resulting in a runaway reaction.

If the chemical containment vessel is incorrectly designed or specified, a runaway will result in over pressurisation of the reactor and possible loss of containment and toxic release due to violent boiling and/or rapid gas generation.

In addition, where a runaway reaction occurs, the elevated temperature achieved may well initiate secondary, competing reactions, such as thermal decompositions, which will exacerbate the hazard resulting from a runaway.

Source: Chilworth Technology.

METHODS OF CONTROL OF TEMPERATURE AND PRESSURE

Representative measurement of temperature and pressure is an essential requirement to ensure safe processing of many substances and materials.

Where liquid materials are stored changes in ambient temperature will result in changes in temperature within the stored liquids, due to the movement of heat by convection currents. Many manufacturing processes are carried out at temperatures above ambient and reliance on convection currents alone could result in localised overheating and possibly loss of reaction control ('run away reactions) Where large volumes of liquids are to be heated, efficient agitation or circulation is essential to maintain even temperature rise Reaction rate will typically double or treble with each 10 degree centigrade rise. Control will rely on temperature detection (e.g. thermometer, thermocouple) and display or readout. For large vessels (or ones containing liquids of high viscosity) detection might need to be measured in more than one part of the liquid to determine efficiency of transfer of heat and to maintain temperature control.

Pressure, or overpressure measurement is particularly important where there is a risk of explosion. With many liquid processes over pressurisation will be measured by a detector and displayed in a similar way as with temperature. Such process vessels will rely on rapid (automatic release e.g. relief valves, bursting disc) venting to a safe area. Where processes involve flammable dusts are concerned control of explosion will be designed into the process and may consist of an over pressure detection device, which causes a suppressant to be released preventing structural failure of the process vessel. Other devices include weighted lids which lift to reduce the pressure, for example on grinding mills. These may be combined with workplace walls and other vents, which are designed to collapse in such away that they vent to a safe area.

THE CONTRIBUTION OF TYPICAL MECHANICAL AND SYSTEMS FAILURES TO MAJOR ACCIDENTS

Flixborough, Piper alpha and Hickson & Welch

Please refer to Element C2.

Grangemouth - 1987

BP Oil (Grangemouth) Refinery Ltd, set up in the early 1920s, is situated close to the River Forth. The refinery processes 8 million tons of crude oil per annum and employed 1200 full time employees and up to 1000 contractors may be employed on maintenance.

The HSE report *"The fires and explosion at BP Oil (Grangemouth) Refinery Ltd"* describes three separate maintenance related incidents which occurred in 1987. These are:

1. A fire involving flammable liquids released during maintenance of a flare system killing two men and seriously injuring two more on 13 March 1987. Potential ignition sources had not been rigorously excluded, means of escape were inadequate, and permit to work procedures had been devised and were being implemented without sufficient awareness of the hazards.

2. A major explosion and fire in the refinery hydrocracker plant on 22 March 1987 killed one man and caused extensive damage. The plant was being recommissioned after repairs. Rupture of the vessel occurred following breakthrough of high pressure hydrogen probably caused by inadequate operating practices and made possible by the disconnection of safety devices.

3. A fire within a crude oil storage tank in Dalmeny Oil Storage Terminal on 11 June 1987 killed one man who was removing the thick sludge which had accumulated at the bottom of the tank. Ignition was caused by smoking and there had been persistent deliberate evasion of safety rules by some of the contractor's team. Safety rules had not been effectively enforced by either the contractor or the refinery operator.

It should be noted that all four deaths caused were all contractors' men. The flare line incident arose when an operator tried to clear drainline blockages by disconnecting the pipework back to the shut-off valve from the distillation column. A hydrocarbon release occurred which he could not initially shut off. The emergency procedure was initiated which required the column to be depressurised by opening a pressure control valve to the flare system. However 30 tonnes of liquid had accumulated at a low point in the flare line over a long period because sludge and debris, including welding rods from the initial fabrication, were blocking the sump and drain. This liquid was then propelled at high speed down the flare line by the escaping vapour. The force dislodged the flare line and it fell and buckled. A factory inspector said that it was 'extremely fortunate' that the line was not totally ruptured.

The consequence could have been a disaster far worse than the 1974 Flixborough explosion.

Violations are highly susceptible to management influence as most underlying causes of violations are either created by management, accepted by management or condoned as normal working practice by management neglect.

Very often, a workforce believes that management would 'pressure' them to perform jobs more quickly - this belief being based, in part, on the evidence of management apparently turning a blind eye to any improvised methods. This could have been because management did not notice such improvisation, or management pressures may be real, rather than perceived. As a result, in many workplaces, violations have become the normal methods of working, rather than the laid down procedures. Not surprisingly these breaches in rules eventually lead to incidents.

An easy management response to an incident may be a hasty introduction or revision of rules and procedures, perhaps without consideration of the full practical implications. Such a response might have more to do with reinforcing the management's position, than with fully discharging their responsibilities for safety.

THE FIRE AT ALLIED COLLOIDS LTD - JULY 1992

At 2.20pm on Tuesday 21 July 1992 a series of explosions leading to an intense fire broke out in a storeroom in the raw materials warehouse of Allied Colloids Ltd, Cleckheaton Road, Low Moor, Bradford, West Yorkshire. The fire spread rapidly to the remainder of the warehouse and external chemical drum storage. Although none of the company employees were injured, 33 people, including 3 residents and 30 fire/police officers were taken to hospital where they were primarily treated for smoke inhalation. Six people were detained. Approximately 2000 local residents were confined to their houses and residents in eight properties immediately adjacent to the raw materials warehouses were evacuated. Firewater run-off caused significant river pollution. The incident gave rise to concern throughout Bradford, Kirklees and neighbouring areas and has been reported as a major accident to the EC as required by the SEVESO Directive. The total cost of company property damage was estimated at £4.25 million and substantial indirect costs were incurred.

The fire was preceded by the rupture of two or three containers of azodiisobutyronitrile (AZDN) about 50 minutes earlier. These were kept at high level in a storeroom within the raw materials warehouse and as far as can be determined were accidentally heated by an adjacent steam condensate pipe. AZDN is unstable when heated and has self-accelerating decomposition temperature (SADT) in 25 kg packages of 50°C. It is a flammable solid and incompatible with oxidising materials. HSE's investigation team concluded that powder released from rupturing drums came into contact with sodium persulphate and possibly other oxidising agents which were stored in the storeroom, causing delayed ignition followed by explosions and the subsequent major fire.

At Bradford Crown Court on 29 January 1993 Allied Colloids Ltd was convicted under the Heath and Safety at Work etc. Act 1974, Section 2 (two counts) and Section 3 and fined a total of £100,000 with costs of £62,324 awarded against them. The company was also prosecuted by the National Rivers Authority for causing pollution as a result of the escape to water courses of contaminated fire-fighting water run-off. They were convicted on 19 July 1993 at Bradford Magistrates Court under the Water Resources Ac 1991, Section 85.

What happened at Allied Colloids is an example of an incident where a number of apparently unrelated errors, omissions and failures (some of them relatively minor in nature) in various parts of the organisation resulted in a major fire that had serious safety, environmental and financial consequences. The fire caused considerable local anxiety. In view of this the HSE undertook to publish the findings of the investigation. For the sake of brevity this report concentrates on the defects which brought about the incident and the emergency actions taken, and omits reference to many perfectly satisfactory arrangements identified during the investigation. The investigation revealed several lessons to be learnt not just for this particular company, but for the chemical industry in general and others. These are listed below.

Lessons

1. Warehouses and other premises where chemicals are stored should be designed and operated in accordance with current legislation and guidance published by enforcing authorities and industry. In particular, attention should be paid to the need for segregation of incompatible substances, the warehouse management system, safe operating procedures, fire detection and fighting methods as well as recording systems for ensuring the safe operation within the storage facility.

2. Companies should not neglect non-production departments, or warehouses in particular, when providing heath and safety resources. Equal priority should be given to assessing risks in all areas and activities and resources allocated accordingly.

3. Safety policy statements should be re-appraised immediately following any company re-organisation and the revised policy statement should be issued to all employees promptly. The written job descriptions of managers should incorporate responsibility for safety and should correspond with the managerial duties described in the safety policy.

4. Companies should regularly monitor and audit their safety performance in storage facilities as well as compiling statistical data on accidents, ill-health and incidents.

5. Targets for good safety performance in storage facilities should be set by companies as part of a safety planning strategy.

6. Safety related maintenance/engineering requests should be specifically identified and give the necessary priority. Engineering management should monitor outstanding requests to ensure that they are dealt with on a timely basis.

7. Managers, supervisors and operators of chemical warehouses should receive adequate training in their duties and specifically in respect of the placement and segregation requirements for chemical storage. Records should be kept of the training given to each individual member of staff.

8. Companies should summon the emergency services immediately when incidents occur which have the potential to escalate. This procedure should be incorporated into the emergency plans.

9. At major hazard sites equipped with public warning sirens agreement should be reached between the company and the emergency services on the circumstances in which the alarm can be sounded and who can order its sounding. This procedure should be written into the off-site emergency plan. Companies should ensure that means of public warning are effective and reliable and that back-up power supplies are provided if necessary.

10. Statutory off-site emergency plans should state clearly the immediate actions needed to prevent or mitigate environmental contamination during or after a major accident, and which body has responsibility for undertaking them. There should also be provision for giving advice and necessary information to relevant bodies and the public.

11. Companies should ensure that they are able to advise emergency services and other relevant public authorities of the potential toxicity of products of combustion from mixed chemical fires on their premises.

12. The HSE and other interested parties should develop guidance on the control of fire water run-off at major hazard sites.

13. Sites where fire water run-off could create a major environmental accident should consider with relevant bodies how best to contain fire water run-off or to mitigate any effects run-off might have.

14. Major hazard sites should pay particular attention to site congestion, not merely because of risks created during normal operation but when planning extension of or modifications to existing plant.

4.2 - Storage of dangerous substances

DANGEROUS SUBSTANCES

Identification

The Chemicals Hazard Information and Packaging for Supply Regulations (CHIP 3) 2002 requires suppliers to classify substances in accordance with a specified scheme. This classification scheme applies to both the harmful effects on health of substances (e.g. toxic, corrosive, irritant etc.) and their physical properties (e.g. explosive, oxidising, flammable etc.). Suppliers must then provide health and safety information to users in the form of safety data sheets and labels.

In addition the Dangerous and Explosive Atmospheres Regulations (DSEAR) 2002 are also relevant to the storage of dangerous substances. DSEAR applies to any substance or preparation (mixture of substances) with the potential to create a risk to persons from energetic (energy-releasing) events such as fires, explosions, thermal runaway from exothermic reactions etc. Such substances, which are known in DSEAR as dangerous substances, include: petrol, liquefied petroleum gas (LPG), paints, varnishes and certain types of combustible and explosive dusts produced in, for example, machining and sanding operations.

It should be noted that many of these substances will also create a health risk as well. For example, many solvents are toxic as well as being flammable. DSEAR does not address these health risks; they are dealt with by the Control of Substances Hazardous to Health Regulations (COSHH) 2002. DSEAR is concerned with harmful physical effects from thermal radiation (burns); over-pressure effects (blast injuries) and oxygen depletion effects (asphyxiation) arising from fires and explosions. Annex 1 sets out the steps necessary to determine whether you have a dangerous substance present in your workplace.

DSEAR generally defines a 'highly flammable liquid' as one which has a flash point of less than 32°C. DSEAR also defines a 'liquefied flammable gas' as any substance which at a temperature of 20°C and a pressure of 760 millimetres of mercury would be a flammable gas, but which is in liquid form as a result of the application of pressure refrigeration or both.

Schedule 4 of DSEAR also identifies the following *warning sign for places where explosive atmospheres may occur:*

Figure C4-1: Warning sign - explosive atmospheres.

Source: DSEAR 2002.

The distinctive features of the above warning sign are:

- Triangular shape.
- Black letters on a yellow background with black edging (the yellow part to take up at least 50% of the area of the sign).

Hazards presented and assessment of risk

Risk assessments should consider the implications to health and the environment when assessing storage facilities for hazardous materials. Storage will be required at the point of receipt, at the point of use and at the point of disposal. This will apply to bulk supplies as well as those which are purchased in smaller containers.

Incidents such as the unconfined vapour cloud explosion at Flixborough and the fire at Allied Colloids have emphasised certain basic principles of storage which are:

- Minimum quantities held.
- Segregated storage of incompatible substances.
- Safe distances (i.e. remote from workforce).

Flammable materials should be stored in accordance with the requirements of relevant legislation. Typical features are:

- Substances stored in bulk containers which are piped to place of use.
- Adequate identification, bunding and protection by fire suppression equipment of storage arrangements.

STORAGE METHODS AND QUANTITIES

The issue of segregation is particularly relevant where both toxic and flammable materials are used together. Poor segregation substantially increases the risk (of both fire and from toxic fumes) to emergency response organisations and neighbours. Leakage or spillage of certain materials may act as a source of ignition when they come into contact with each other through an exothermic chemical reaction.

The plant should be designed to minimise the need for manual handling, process materials should be pumped whenever possible. Many chemical process facilities are conducted at a height in tall buildings and gravity is utilised to advantage in moving materials around.

Bulk

Transfer of solids, liquid and gases

Solids may be handled in a variety of ways: 25kg sacks, utilising manual handling,   1 tonne portable sacks, utilising mobile handling equipment such as pedestrian lift trucks, Archiemedian screw fed or air blown, from a powder silo. The latter mechanical methods are preferred because they reduce the operator interface and issues such as manual handling and exposure. Other factors to be considered are build-up of static charge and air entrainment either or both contributing to the risk of ignition. Earthing and the use of inert carrier gases may be used to minimise these risks.

Liquids are similarly available in a variety of packages, typically in drums up to 250 litres capacity, 1 tonne portable tanks, road tankers and fixed storage tanks. Whenever possible it is best to use bulk storage and piped systems to minimise the loss of the material particularly with the transfer of hazardous liquids. Particular care needs to be taken to ensure that the storage / transfer equipment is chemically suitable for the material to be stored. Precautions are necessary to prevent inadvertent mixing with other materials on filling and containment of any spillages which might foreseeably occur. Where flammable materials are stored provision to prevent sources of ignition are necessary; this will include earth bonding to common ground to reduce the risk of static build up on transfer. Other considerations include the provision of safe vents (flame traps etc.), the possible need to recycle vapours to reduce environmental pollution and the provision of adequate fire suppression equipment.

Gases are available in a variety of cylinder sizes through to bulk storage installations. Care needs to be taken to protect cylinders from damage. Gases not connected for use should not be stored in the work area unless suitable storage provision is available.

Piping

All process pipe work should be made from appropriate materials having regard for the process materials, e.g. flammable, corrosive and of sound construction with adequate support. All pipe work should be labelled with contents and direction of flow. Isolation valves should be provided appropriate to the risk. Earthing may be required to minimise ignition of flammable materials from static electricity (care should be taken to ensure earth bonding across flange connections).

Intermediate

Intermediate storage consists of work in progress. Often this will utilise fixed plant which may be used for different substances in accordance with the manufacturing process programme. Intermediate storage will need to be identified, usually in process logs, as distinct from labelling of primary storage raw materials. Consideration will need to be given to strict maintenance of emptying and refilling records; also the need for cleaning before refilling if residues may have an adverse chemical reaction with other materials which may be transferred.

Drum Storage

Where substances are supplied or used from containers the storage facility should meet above requirements as a minimum standard. They should be secure and adequately ventilated. Materials for immediate use in the workplace should not exceed 50 litres. Containers should be designed to reduce risk by the incorporation of self closing, spring loaded caps with a flame arrestor in the neck. The spring loaded cap will snap shut in the event of it being dropped and will act as a safety relief valve which prevents excess pressure rupturing the container. Safety storage cabinets should be used for storing flammable liquids in the workplace. Ideally, these should incorporate the following features:

- Double walls for improved thermal insulation.
- Fitted with low level vents housing flame arrestors in order for the vapours to be safely ducted away; and
- Liquid traps to collect any leaks and spills from stored containers within the cabinet.

Particular care should be taken to keep the floors of warehouse or bunded areas free of contamination. Drip trays or containers used for repackaging must be clean before use.

Specific locations

Specific locations include: external/internal bulk drum storage; external bulk storage of liquid raw materials; in process material, including reactors and intermediate storage; bulk storage of finished products for packaging or dispatch by road or rail.

SEGREGATION REQUIREMENTS AND ACCESS

Dangerous substances include: oxidising agents, flammable solids and liquids, toxic substances and corrosive materials. Consideration should be given to segregation to reduce the risk from mixed spillages or fire. Mixed spillages of oxidants and flammable materials could result in spontaneous ignition and possible explosion. Other substances if not segregated, such as toxic materials would endanger not only workers, but local emergency or fire fighting personnel called to the scene. Most substances are released as the result of damaged packaging. Safe storage (pallets in good condition, packages shrink wrapped to prevent falls of materials, drums, bagged material not stored too high resulting in damage from the weight of material above) and   access are important factors in managing chemical substances.

LEAKING AND SPILLAGE CONTAINMENT

Leaking and spillage can result from a number of sources: faulty valves or flanges to pipework; containers such as tins, drums or bags; loss from tanks (typically one tonne) of solids and liquids; road or rail freight containers; cargo vessels etc.

Typical techniques to contain spillage include: curbed areas for drum storage, tanker loading of liquids, bunded areas to contain sited tanks, drip trays at decanting points (piped systems and 40 gallon [255 litre] drums).

Portable tanks are available with two skins (a tank within a tank) to contain any spillage from the internal tank, often used where there is a need for portability such as with construction sites, to minimise the impact of spillage on the environment when storing materials such as fuel oils. Similarly cargo vessels may have duel skinned tanks or hulls.

Bunding

A bund often consists of an area contained by a rectangular wall built upon a concrete slab. The bund floor and walls should be treated to be impervious to any spillage. Storage tanks are located within this confined area. The capacity of the bund should be sufficient to contain a minimum of 110% of the contents of the largest tank.

Transfer

Factors to consider when transferring substances:

Liquids

- Zoning if flammable solvents or vapours involved.
- Correct positioning of valves.
- Destination container of suitable capacity.
- High level alarms.
- Starting and stopping of transfer pumps.

Powders

- Containment on conveyors.
- Use of inert gases when blown.
- Zoning if flammable dust is involved.
- Correct positioning of controls.
- Destination container of suitable capacity.

4.3 - Storage of toxic and corrosive substances

IDENTIFICATION OF TOXIC AND CORROSIVE SUBSTANCES

All toxic and corrosive substances should be labelled in accordance with the CHIP Regulations. Such materials should not be held in mixed storage, but segregated to prevent spillages becoming mixed and endangering workers or emergency service personnel when attending an incident.

IMPLICATIONS FOR STORAGE WITH EMPHASIS ON INCOMPATIBLE MATERIALS AND THEIR SEGREGATION

Some toxic materials will spontaneously react when in contact with water (isocyanates explosively decompose) or acids (cyanide compounds will release hydrogen cyanide, ferrous sulphide, hydrogen sulphide, both lethal in poisonous gases).

4.4 - Handling of dangerous substances

NOTIFICATION OF INSTALLATIONS HANDLING HAZARDOUS SUBSTANCES (NIHHS) REGULATIONS 1982 (AS AMENDED)

Under the *Notification of Installations Handling Hazardous Substances (NIHHS) Regulations 1982 (as amended 2002)*, an activity which involves a notifiable quantity of a hazardous substance at a site, in a pipeline, must be notified to the HSE at least 3 months before the activity commences; or at least 4 weeks before, in the case of *ammonium nitrate*. There is a list of notifiable hazardous substances and the notifiable quantities in Schedule 1 of these regulations.

FLOW THROUGH PIPELINES

All pipelines should be made of suitable material to withstand the corrosive effects of substances; typical materials include stainless steel, coated mild steel and glass (larger laboratory facilities, used to scale up processes). All pipework should be identified with the substance and direction of flow arrows. Pipe flanges should be chemically resistant and where the risk of static electricity is present from pumping non-conductive substances, earth bonding should be maintained across each flange or valve in the pipe run to ensure a common earth to reduce the risk of static sparks of sufficient energy to be a source of ignition.

SAFETY PRINCIPLES IN FILLING AND EMPTYING CONTAINERS

Factors to be considered when filling and emptying containers include:

- Overfill devices.
- Zoning if flammable solvents or vapours involved.
- Earthing receipt container to supply container.
- Need for ullage provision (compressible air void in sealed containers such as drums or tankers, to allow for contents volume changes with temperature).
- Spillage containment.
- Capture of any vapours.

SAFETY PRINCIPLES IN DISPENSING, SPRAYING AND DISPOSAL OF FLAMMABLE LIQUIDS

Dispensing principles are essentially as with filling and emptying, as above.

Spraying risks include inhalation and risk of explosion; factors to consider include:

- Suitable respiratory protection.
- Hand, forearm protection (to prevent skin inflammation or dermatitis, common with flammable liquid contacts).
- Suitable containment of material overspray (water washed exhaust systems to trap solids and solvents).

Disposal of flammable liquids should include consideration of the following:

- Segregation.
- Containment and labelling of waste.
- Use of a suitable solvent recovery company.
- Safe incineration or alternate disposal.

THE DANGERS OF ELECTRICITY IN HAZARDOUS AREAS

Where flammable dusts or vapours may be present, the work area will need to be assessed and areas identified as Zones to prevent or minimise electrical sources of heat or sparks.

Zone 0, where there is a risk of flammable dust or vapour all the time, e.g. within a reactor or storage tank.

Zone 1, where there is a foreseeable risk of flammable dust or vapour, e.g. within a processing plant occupied by operators.

Zone 2, where there is a remote risk of flammable dust or vapour, e.g. within a drum storage area.

See also - Dangerous and Explosive Atmospheres Regulations 2002 (DSEAR) - Element C11 Relevant statutory provisions.

4.5 - Transport of dangerous substances

SAFETY PRINCIPLES IN LOADING AND UNLOADING OF TANKERS AND TANK CONTAINERS

Drivers of tankers etc. must be in possession of sufficient written information which must allow them to know the nature of the dangers involved and the emergency action to be taken.

The 'Transport Emergency Card (Road)', known more commonly as a *Tremcard*. The *Tremcard* must be kept in the vehicle cab, so that this 'information in writing' can be easily located by the emergency services in the event of an accident. A *Tremcard* relating to the previous load should be put into a securable compartment or container which is clearly marked and capable of remaining closed even in the event of a vehicle roll-over.

Both drivers and recipients of materials are required to observe all the precautions necessary for preventing fire or explosion. Written procedures should be issued, laying down precautions which must be taken during various operations - particularly loading and unloading:

- Fire extinguishers should be carried when substances pose a risk of fire or explosion.
- Earth connections must be in use before and during loading and unloading, to prevent the possible build up and subsequent discharge of static electricity.
- No loading or unloading if there is an electrical storm overhead.
- No smoking in the vicinity during loading or unloading.
- For flammable substances (e.g. Petroleum spirit) no matches or lighters are to be carried by the driver.

It should not be forgotten that some manual handling will be involved even with bulk materials. This will occur for example, even where solids are transported from silos using conveyors or compressed gas as there may be a need to direct the flow from chutes. Where the loading/unloading of liquids are involved, manual handling will occur at the point of connection / disconnection. Where manual handling is carried out, other risks associated with close proximity to the substance need to be evaluated (e.g. exposure to toxic materials or dust, the risk of ignition).

There is a risk of cross contamination where bulk storage tanks used for different purposes are delivered to a multi storage area. The incident at Camelford which involved the inadvertent gross contamination of a service reservoir with aluminium sulphate is an extreme example of what can go wrong. In order to avoid this, couplings which are of a different design can be used in order to prevent errors.

Emergency site arrangements need to be established. Typically this will involve measures to:

- Raise the alarm.
- Initiate evacuation.
- Deal with contamination of individuals (safety drench showers) and the environment.

Wind socks may be necessary to indicate direction routes for air borne contaminants.

Prohibition against overfilling

Must ensure that sufficient room for expansion is allowed for when loading. This space for expansion is known as the ullage.

LABELLING OF VEHICLES AND PACKAGING OF SUBSTANCES

Tank containers used to carry dangerous substances must be fitted with the appropriate hazard warning panels. These are often referred to as '*hazchem*' panels. Each panel has five sections which provide information on:

- The emergency action code.
- The substance identification number.
- The symbol indicating the general nature of the substance.
- A source of specialist advice - usually a telephone number.
- The manufacturers or owner's name and logo - this is optional.

Where a number of substances are carried in compartments, a multi-load hazard warning panel should be displayed. These panels will contain a hazard warning symbol of a white diamond containing an exclamation mark, and the words '*multi-load*' instead of the substance identification number.

DRIVER TRAINING AND ROLE OF DANGEROUS GOODS SAFETY ADVISERS

Supervision of Vehicles

The driver must ensure that when the vehicle is not being driven, it is either:

- Parked in a safe place OR
- Supervised at all times by himself or some other competent person over the age of 18.

- 'Safe place', which can be approved local authority parks or other open air sites where the public have no access, e.g. factories or transport depots.

Training of Drivers

Drivers are given adequate instruction and training so that they are able to understand:

- The nature of the dangers posed by the substance.
- The action to take in an emergency.
- Their duties under the regulations.

Records of instruction and training, given to each driver during his employment, must be maintained. A copy must also be available to the driver.

Transport of Dangerous Goods (Safety Advisers) Regulations 1999

The Transport of Dangerous Goods (Safety Advisers) Regulations implement a European Directive (96/35/EC) on the appointment and vocational qualification of safety advisers for the transport of dangerous goods by road, rail and inland waterway.

The Regulations prohibit the transport of dangerous goods by road, railway and inland waterway unless one or more safety adviser(s) are appointed. The number of advisers must be sufficient to ensure that their functions and duties can be carried out effectively. Arrangements must be made to ensure adequate co-operation between the safety advisers appointed. Advisers must be provided with adequate time, means, information and facilities necessary to fulfil their functions and duties.

No one may be appointed as a safety adviser unless they hold a vocational training certificate appropriate to the modes of transport used and the dangerous goods specified and transported by the employer or one or more. The Regulations also impose requirements with regard to the issue, form, validity and renewal of certificates. Vocational training certificates are mutually recognised throughout the EU.

The function of the safety adviser is to:

- Monitor compliance with the rules governing the transport of dangerous goods.
- Advise the employer on the transport of dangerous goods.
- Ensure that an annual report to the employer is prepared on the activities of the employer concerning the transport of dangerous goods.
- Monitor the following practices and procedures relating to the activities of the employer which concern the transport of dangerous goods:
  - The procedures for compliance with the rules governing the identification of dangerous goods being transported.
  - The practice of the employer in taking into account, when purchasing means of transport, any special requirements in connection with the dangerous goods to be transported.
  - The procedures for checking the equipment used in connection with the transport of dangerous goods.
  - Proper training of the employer's employees and the maintenance of records of such training.
  - The implementation of proper emergency procedures in the event of any accident or incident that may affect safety during the transport of dangerous goods.
  - The investigation of and, where appropriate, preparation of reports on serious accidents, incidents or serious infringements recorded during the transport of dangerous goods.
  - The implementation of appropriate measures to avoid the recurrence of accidents, incidents or serious infringements.
  - The account taken of the legal prescriptions and special requirements associated with the transport of dangerous goods in the choice and use of sub-contractors or third parties.
  - Verification that employees involved in the transport of dangerous goods have detailed operational procedures and instructions.
  - The introduction of measures to increase awareness of the risks inherent in the transport of dangerous goods.
  - The implementation of verification procedures to ensure the presence, on board the means of transport, of the documents and safety equipment which must accompany transport and the compliance of such documents and equipment with health and safety regulations.

The implementation of verification procedures to ensure compliance with legislation governing loading and unloading of dangerous goods.

The safety adviser must also ensure the preparation of a report on any accident which affects the health or safety of any person or causes damage to the environment or to property and which occurs during the transport of dangerous goods by the employer who has appointed him. A copy of the report must also be provided to the employer.

The Secretary of State or any goods vehicle examiner must be provided on request with the name of any safety adviser, a copy of any accident and annual reports, and any vocational training certificate.

The Executive and the Secretary of State for Defence may grant exemptions from any requirement or prohibition of the Regulations in specified circumstances.

Work Equipment

Overall aims

On completion of this Element, the student will have knowledge and understanding of:

■ criteria for the selection of work equipment that is safe and without risk to health.

■ main legal duties on manufacturers and suppliers.

■ relevance of anthropometric, ergonomic and reliability data relating to safe work equipment.

■ properties of materials and failure prevention strategies including non-destructive testing techniques.

■ ways of ensuring continued safety in the use of work equipment.

■ work equipment which is subject to statutory inspection, and the purpose, nature and frequency of such examinations.

■ safety in the design and operation of pressure systems.

Content

Specific intended learning outcomes

The intended learning outcomes are that the student will be able to:

1. advise on the areas to be addressed to ensure the selection and use of work equipment that is safe and without risks to health

2. identify likely failure modes of components and recommend actions to minimise the probability of failure

3. assist with development of a programme of planned preventive maintenance

4. identify the principal requirements of statutory provisions relating to the provision and use of work equipment

5. identify items of equipment which are subject to a requirement for statutory examination and describe the nature of such examination

6. describe the components of pressure systems, common causes of failure and prevention strategies

Relevant statutory provisions

Simple Pressure Vessels (Safety) Regulations (SPVSR) 1991

Personal Protective Equipment at Work Regulations (PUWER) 1992

Lifting Operations and Lifting Equipment Regulations (LOLER) 1998

Pressure Equipment Regulations (PER) 1999

Pressure Systems Safety Regulations (PSSR) 2000

Carriage of Dangerous Goods and Use of Transportable Pressure Equipment Regulations (CDGUTPER) 2004

5.1 - Selection

SUITABILITY FOR TASK AND ENVIRONMENT

The Provision and Use of Work Equipment Regulations (PUWER) 1998 are concerned with most aspects relating to work equipment. PUWER 1998 broadly defines work equipment to include machines of all kinds, appliances, apparatus, tools or installation for use at work.

Work equipment includes:

- Air compressor.
- Automatic car wash.
- Automatic storage and retrieval equipment.
- Blast furnace.
- Butcher's knife.
- Car ramp.
- Check-out machine.
- Combine harvester.
- Computer.
- Crane.
- Drill bit.
- Dry cleaning unit.
- Fire engine turntable.
- Hammer.
- Hand saw.
- Laboratory apparatus.
- Ladder.
- Lawn-mower.
- Lift truck.
- Lifting sling.

- LPG filling plant.
- Mobile access platform.
- Overhead projector.
- Portable drill.
- Potato grading line.
- Power press.
- Pressure vessel.
- Quarry crushing plant.
- Resuscitator.
- Road tanker.
- Robot line.
- Scaffolding.
- Scalpel.
- Socket set.
- Soldering iron.
- Solvent degreasing bath.
- Tractor.
- Trench sheets.
- Vehicle hoist.
- X-ray baggage detector.

Not work equipment:

- Livestock.
- Substances.

- Structural items (buildings).
- Private car.

Provision and Use Of Work Equipment Regulation [PUWER] 1998 - Regulation 4

Suitability of work equipment

(1) Every employer shall ensure that work equipment is so constructed or adapted as to be suitable for the purpose for which it is used or provided.

(2) In selecting work equipment, every employer shall have regard to the working conditions and to the risks to the health and safety of persons which exist in the premises or undertaking in which that work equipment is to be used and any additional risk posed by the use of that work equipment.

(3) Every employer shall ensure that work equipment is used only for operations for which, and under conditions for which, it is suitable.

(4) In this regulation "suitable" means suitable in any respect which it is reasonably foreseeable will affect the health or safety of any person.

Suitability should consider:

- Its initial integrity.
- The place where it will be used.
- The purpose for which it will be used.

Integrity - equipment should be safe through its design, construction or adaptation e.g. sharp edges removed from the pen tray of a flip chart stand, 'Home made' tools may not comply as they are often a basic adaptation of scrap material. Equipment adapted to do a specific task should be considered carefully, e.g. the addition of a welded bracket may compromise integrity.

Place - equipment should be suitable for the different environments (risks) it is to be used in - wet or explosive. Account must be taken of the possibility that the equipment may cause a problem, e.g. a petrol generator used in a confined space, a hydraulic access platform used in a location with a low roof, or the environment may cause a problem to the equipment, e.g. lifting equipment used in an acidic atmosphere or a power tool used in a wet place.

Use - equipment should be suitable for the specific task it is used for - a hacksaw should not be used to cut metal straps that secure goods to a palette (instead, a purpose designed tool should be used to stop the straps suddenly moving when they are cut); the use of a ladder to do work at a height (instead of a scaffold or other access platform); exceeding the safe working load of a crane or fork lift truck, a swivel chair used as a means of access to a shelf.

CONFORMITY WITH RELEVANT STANDARDS

Work equipment should be designed and manufactured such that it conforms to all relevant standards. Historically this will have been British Standards. Though many British Standards remain in place today many new standards for work equipment are produced in conjunction with European and international standards organisations. Those that have been agreed at a European level will carry the letters 'EN' in addition to the familiar BS, for example, BS EN 60974 - Arc welding equipment. Those that have been agreed at an international level carry the letters 'ISO', for example, BS EN ISO 12100 Safety of machinery Part 1 - Basic terminology and methodology. Section 6 of The Health and Safety at Work Act (HASAWA) 1974 requires those involved in the supply of (including design and manufacture) equipment to ensure that it is safe and healthy, so far as is reasonably practicable. This will require them to take account of all relevant standards.

When providing work equipment for use in the workplace care must be taken to ensure that it has been manufactured to any product Directive which is relevant to the equipment. This means that in addition to specifying that work equipment should comply with specific health and safety legislation, such as the Electricity at Work (EWR) Regulation 1989, it is necessary to specify that it comply with legislation implementing any relevant EC product Directive, for example, the Supply of Machinery (Safety) Regulations SMSR) 1992. In addition PUWER 1998 requires that new equipment conform to European Community requirements, where they exist, prohibiting the use of equipment that does not comply.

PUWER - Regulation 10 conformity with Community requirements

Every employer shall ensure that an item of work equipment has been designed and constructed in compliance with any essential requirements, that is to say, requirements relating to its design or construction in any of the instruments listed in Schedule 1 of PUWER 1998 (being instruments which give effect to Community directives concerning the safety of products).

Where an essential requirement applied to the design or construction of an item of work equipment, the requirements of regulations 11 to 19 and 22 to 29 shall apply in respect of that item only to the extent that the essential requirement did not apply to it. Work equipment provided for use must conform with legislation made in the UK in response to EC directives relating to work equipment. Only those directives listed in schedule 1 of PUWER 1998 are to be considered and then only those that have been translated to UK law. Examples relate to:

■ The amount of noise emitted from a variety of equipment (e.g. Construction equipment or lawn mowers).
■ Electro-medical equipment.
■ Simple pressure vessels.
■ Machinery safety.
■ Personal protective equipment.

Directives tend to contain details of 'essential health and safety requirements' and a system whereby compliance may be demonstrated. Compliance is usually demonstrated by the attachment of a CE mark and the manufacturer/supplier holding an EC declaration of conformity. This declaration may, in the early days of the legislation, be a self declaration or a third party declaration. When a directive has been translated to UK legislation and it is fully in force only products which conform and bear the 'CE Mark' may be placed on the market or introduced into the UK. Employers carry this duty when providing equipment.

Not all work equipment is covered by a product directive. Directives and legislation derived from them are not retrospective. Second-hand equipment brought into use need not be modified to meet 'essential safety requirements', but will need to comply with regulations 11 to 24 of PUWER 1998. Second-hand equipment imported from outside the EU must comply with 'essential safety requirements' of the relevant product directive. When equipment is in compliance with specific directive (UK legislative) requirements regulations 11 to 24 of PUWER 1998 do not apply.

CE MARKING

Article 100A Directives seek to achieve free movement of goods in the European Community single market by removing different countries' national controls on the standards of goods and harmonising 'essential health and safety requirements'. Examples of Directives achieving this are shown above. Suppliers must ensure that their products comply with the legal requirements implementing the Directives, for example, the SMSR 1992. It is a common feature of these Directives that compliance is claimed by the manufacturer affixing a mark to the equipment - 'CE Marking'.

REQUIREMENTS FOR MAINTENANCE

When selecting work equipment it is important to establish what the requirements for maintenance are. It may be that the equipment has sealed components and must be returned to the manufacturer or periodic maintenance will mean taking the equipment to a specialist dealer/supplier rendering it out of use for this period. As such there can be added pressure put on the organisation who may not find it convenient to be without the equipment. It is essential that this sort of circumstance be considered and arrangements made to deal with it, for example, purchase or hire of extra equipment to be brought into use to allow for maintenance. Maintenance regimes should be carefully considered before selecting equipment. Maintenance staff may not have the specific expertise or skill to work on new equipment, leading to increased risk to themselves and others.

PUWER - Regulation 22 Maintenance operations

Every employer shall take appropriate measures to ensure that work equipment is so constructed or adapted that, so far as is reasonably practicable, maintenance operations which involve a risk to health or safety can be carried out while the work equipment is shut down or, in other cases -

(a) Maintenance operations can be carried out without exposing the person carrying them out to a risk to his health or safety; or

(b) Appropriate measures can be taken for the protection of any person carrying out maintenance operations which involve a risk to his health or safety.

Machinery should be designed to enable routine adjustments, lubrication, cleaning and maintenance to be carried out without the removal of guards. In this way effort should be taken to enable lubrication and adjustment to be applied from outside the guard.

AVAILABILITY OF EXPERTISE / SKILLS REQUIRED

The availability of expertise and skill must be considered for all new equipment planned for selection and use, whether this is for long term purchase or short term hire. It may be that the organisation has staff with similar expertise and that they only need a short period of orientation to familiarise themselves, but for many organisations new equipment can mean a radical step forward in technology. It is essential that operation and maintenance of equipment with specific risks be restricted to those that have appropriate skill and expertise.

PUWER - Regulation 7 Specific risks

(1) Where the use of work equipment is likely to involve a specific risk to health or safety, every employer shall ensure that

  (a) The use of that work equipment is restricted to those persons given the task of using it.

  (b) Repairs, modifications, maintenance or servicing of that work equipment is restricted to those persons who have been specifically designated to perform operations of that description (whether or not also authorised to perform other operations).

(2) The employer shall ensure that the persons designated for the purposes of sub-paragraph (b) of paragraph (1) have received adequate training related to any operations in respect of which they have been so designated.

Operators

It is dangerous to assume that because the method of use of new equipment is 'obvious' to those that looked into and sourced it that it will be so 'obvious' to the operators. It is also necessary to guard against the over enthusiastic operator that feels sure they have the expertise to operate something. It is essential to take a stepwise approach to the introduction of equipment, for example, driving a fork lift truck is very different to driving a van and the organisation has to anticipate the need to train someone in the use of a fork lift truck before it is put to use in the workplace. Not planning for this at the time of selection may cause the equipment to be used by operators without the appropriate skill or expertise. Even with what seems to be the same piece of work equipment, e.g. when a larger, different model of fork lift truck is hired, it is essential that the operator takes a period of time to formally familiarise with the truck and to practice in a safe place before putting it into use.

Maintenance personnel

As with operators it is essential to consider who is to maintain the equipment before it is selected. If the equipment represents a major leap in technology aspects of its maintenance may fall outside the skill and expertise of the current maintenance personnel. It may be necessary to train or recruit staff in good time before the maintenance is required. In addition, new facilities and equipment may be needed in order to conduct the maintenance safely. Accidents often occur because new equipment may appear to be similar to previous equipment. The small differences may be critical and must be emphasised as part of the training of maintenance personnel.

5.2 - Use

The definition of 'use' is wide and includes all activities involving the work equipment such as stopping or starting the equipment, programming or setting, transporting, repair, modification, maintenance, servicing and cleaning. In addition to operations normally considered as use, cleaning and transport of the equipment are also included. In this context 'transport' means, for example, using a lift truck to carry goods around a warehouse.

WORK EQUIPMENT RISK ASSESSMENT

The Management of Health and Safety at Work Regulations (MHSWR) 1999 places a specific requirement that general risk assessments be conducted. These must be suitable and sufficient. Implicit in this is the need, in some cases, to conduct an initial, detailed and technical risk assessment. In order to have sufficiently risk assessed the use of equipment it may be necessary to conduct very specific and technical risk assessments in order to confirm hazards and the suitability of controls.

The risk assessment process formalises and documents the way in which designers identify hazards, risks and select the appropriate safety measure. The level of risk influences the level and quantity of safety measures used. In deriving a suitable and sufficient risk assessment it may be necessary to address the need in three phases:

- **Initial** - to determine broad data on hazards, the consequences arising and the likelihood of the consequence occurring (the risks).
- **Detailed** - a specific assessment of the features which constitute a hazard, how they are encountered and the controlling effects of safety measures.
- **Technical** - a comprehensive assessment of the whole or part of the machine and safety measure systems considering the failure modes and their effects.

RISK CONTROL MEASURES

Intrinsic safety

This is the condition where safety is established by ensuring selection and/or design of components and equipment that ensures no potential to cause harm. In practice this may actually be reduction of potential to an acceptable level. For example, the reduction in speed of rotation of a shaft does not eliminate it as a hazard but may reduce the risk such that it may be considered to be insignificant. By reducing the energy available to the component or equipment e.g. the reduction of force or electrical power required may cause the power or force to be below normal human thresholds of tolerance, thus preventing harm.

Risk reduction by design

Equipment must be suitable, by design, construction or adaptation, for the actual work it is provided to do. This should mean in practice that when employers provide equipment they should ensure that it has been produced for the work to be undertaken and that it is used in accordance with the manufacturer's specifications and instructions. If employers choose to adapt equipment then they must ensure that it is still suitable for its intended purpose.

Designers should establish health and safety features that reduce risk at the design stage. Consideration should be given to all aspects of use. In addition, design should minimise risks at all phases of the life of the equipment including:

- Construction.
- Transport.
- Installation.
- Commissioning.

- De-commissioning.
- Dismantling.
- Disposal.
- Recycling.

Wherever practicable, dangerous parts should be eliminated or effectively enclosed at the initial design. If they cannot be eliminated, then suitable safeguards should be incorporated as part of the design. Provision should be made to facilitate the fitting of alternative types of safeguards on machinery where it is known that this will be necessary because the work to be done on it will vary.

At the design stage arrangements should be made where practicable to eliminate the need to expose any dangerous parts during operation, examination, lubrication, adjustment or maintenance.

There are then two principles to bear in mind:-

a.   As a first principle, as many hazards as possible should be avoided by suitable choice of design features.

b.   Secondly, where it is not possible to avoid these hazards, the factors which influence the magnitude of the risk should be examined, i.e. reducing speed or distance of movement, force, torque, inertia, and by use of surfaces that are as smooth as possible.

Guarding and safeguarding

Guards are physical barriers which prevent access to the danger zone. A safeguard is defined as 'a guard or device to protect persons from danger'. This term includes items classed as 'protective devices', which are devices which do not prevent access to the danger zone but stop the movement of dangerous parts before contact is made e.g. photoelectric trip device.

This includes 'protective appliances' which are used to hold or manipulate in a way which allows operators to control and feed a loose work piece at a machine while keeping their body clear of the danger zone e.g. jigs used with a band saw (normally used in conjunction with guards).

This term may be taken in a wider context to include any technical, procedural or behavioural measure provided for the purpose of health and safety. In the case of work equipment it may include the brakes on a mobile scaffold, the sheath on a knife, training of a user of a machine, an inspection procedure for excavations, space around equipment.

Other relevant safety features

Includes stop/start controls, emergency stop controls and isolation/lock off facilities.

PUWER 1998 - Regulation 12 Protection against specified hazards

(1)   Every employer shall take measures to ensure that the exposure of a person using work equipment to any risk to his health or safety from any hazard specified in paragraph (3) is either prevented, or, where that is not reasonably practicable, adequately controlled.

(2)   The measures required by paragraph (1) shall -

(a) Be measures other than the provision of personal protective equipment or of information, instruction, training and supervision, so far as is reasonably practicable.

(b) Include, where appropriate, measures to minimise the effects of the hazard as well as to reduce the likelihood of the hazard occurring.

(3)   The hazards referred to in paragraph (1) are -

(a) Any article or substance falling or being ejected from work equipment.

(b) Rupture or disintegration of parts of work equipment.

(c) Work equipment catching fire or overheating.

(d) The unintended or premature discharge of any article or of any gas, dust, liquid, vapour or other substance which, in each case, is produced, used or stored in the work equipment.

(e) The unintended or premature explosion of the work equipment or any article or substance produced, used or stored in it.

(4)   For the purposes of this regulation "adequately" means adequately having regard only to the nature of the hazard and the nature and degree of exposure to the risk.

(5)   This regulation shall not apply where any of the following Regulations apply in respect of any risk to a person's health or s safety for which such Regulations require measures to be taken to prevent or control such risk, namely -

(a) The Ionising Radiation Regulations (IRR) 1999.

(b) The Control of Asbestos at Work Regulations (CAWR) 2002.

(c) The Control of Substances Hazardous to Health Regulations (COSHH) 2002.

(d) The Noise at Work Regulations (NWR) 1989.

(e) The Construction (Head Protection) Regulations (CHPR) 1989.

(f) The Control of Lead at Work Regulations (CLAW) 2002.

This Regulation covers risks arising from certain listed hazards during the use of equipment. Examples of the hazards that the Regulation addresses are:

■   Material falling from equipment, e.g. molten metal spilling from a casting machine.
■   Material held in the equipment being unexpectedly thrown out, e.g. swarf ejected from a machine tool.
■   Parts of the equipment breaking off and being thrown out, e.g. an abrasive wheel bursting.
■   Part of the equipment coming apart, e.g. a machine tool working loose and flying off a lathe.
■   Overheating or fire due e.g. to friction (bearings running hot), electric motor burning out, cooling system failure.
■   Explosion of the equipment due to pressure build-up, e.g. due to the failure of a pressure-relief device.
■   Explosion of substance in the equipment, e.g. chemical reaction or unplanned ignition.

Where items of equipment have these risks present priority must be made to deal with these by means of guards to contain them. Where this is not practicable personal protective equipment should be provided.

Personal protective equipment (PPE)

The provision of PPE is governed by the Personal Protective Equipment at Work Regulations (PPER) 1992 *(see - Personal Protective Equipment at Work Regulations - later in this element)*, and various items of legislation including the:

- Control of Lead at Work Regulations (CLAW) 2002.
- Ionising Radiation Regulations (IRR) 1999.
- Control of Asbestos at Work Regulations (CAW) 2002
- Control of Substances Hazardous to Health Regulations (COSHH) 2002
- Noise at Work Regulations (NWR) 1989.
- Construction (Head Protection) Regulations (CHSW) 1989

The provision of PPE is as a last resort and should only be relied upon when other controls do not adequately control risks.

The hazards associated with machinery should be considered and minimised at the design, construction, transport and commissioning phases of the life of the machine. Risks associated with the use of the machine (i.e. setting, operation, cleaning, fault finding and maintenance) should be considered and the need for additional PPE assessed in order to identify need and to ensure that they are adequate and suitable for purpose. This may be done at the same time as a general risk assessment is carried out. In respect of machinery, the mechanical and non-mechanical hazards should be considered:

Mechanical	Non mechanical
Crushing.	Electricity.
Shearing.	Thermal.
Cutting or severing.	Noise.
Entanglement.	Vibration.
Drawing in or trapping.	Radiation.
Impact.	Materials and substances.
Stabbing or puncture.	Ergonomics.
Friction or abrasion.	
High pressure fluid injection.	

Figure C5-1: Mechanical and non-mechanical hazards of machinery.   *Source: ACT.*

Eye protection

Eye protection, as with other types of PPE, must be assessed for suitability. The appropriate standard is BS EN 166 (which replaced BS 2092). The standard covers many parameters including its optical class, mechanical strength, field of use. These must be marked on each piece of eye protection. Examples are as follows:

	PROPERTY	BS EN 166
Mechanical	General purpose.	S
Strength	■ Low energy (125 ft/s).	F
	■ Medium energy (360 ft/s).	B
	■ High energy (570 ft/s).	A
Field of Use	■ Chemical.	3
	■ Dust (large particles).	4
	■ Gas and fine dust.	5
	■ Electric arc.	8
	■ Molten metal.	9
Optional	Resistance to misting.	N
Requirements	Resistance to surface damage.	K

Figure C5-2: Examples of eye protection.   *Source: ACT.*

(Protectors conforming to more than one type should also be marked to reflect this).

Thus, if protection was required against chemical splash, dust and molten metal hazards, safety goggles conforming to BS EN 166 3.4.9.B.N might be provided.

More generally, there are three main types of eye protection:

- Safety spectacles / glasses.
- Goggles.
- Face shields.

Safety spectacles / glasses

These may have toughened glass or plastic lenses with plastic or metal frames. Lenses should not be removable as they could fall out. Spectacles can be supplied with side shields and should be fitted for the individual concerned, particularly if he or she has prescription lenses.

Advantages	Disadvantages
■ Lightweight, easy to wear.	■ Do not give all round protection.
■ Can incorporate prescription lenses.	■ Relies on the wearer for use.
■ Do not 'mist up'	

Safety goggles

Are generally cheaper and offer more protection against various hazards than do spectacles. Users can experience discomfort when they are worn for long periods. Some designs can be worn over prescription lenses but this, too, may cause discomfort.

Cup-type goggles protect against flying particles, welding glare or radiation, whereas wide-vision goggles (specific to purpose) give protection against flying particles, welding glare, radiation, dust, fumes and splashes.

Advantages	Disadvantages
■ Give all round protection.	■ Tendency to 'mist up'.
■ Can be worn over prescription lenses.	■ Uncomfortable when worn for long periods.
■ Capable of high impact protection.	
■ Can protect against other hazards e.g. dust, molten metal.	■ Can affect peripheral vision.

Face shields can be hand-held, fixed to the helmet or strapped to the head, protect the face and eyes.

Advantages	Disadvantages
■ Gives full face protection against splashes.	■ Require care in use otherwise can become dirty and scratched.
■ Can incorporate a fan which creates air movement for comfort and protection against low level contaminants.	■ Can affect peripheral vision.
■ Can be integrated into other PPE e.g. head protection.	

Other general protection

Head protection - safety helmets or scalp protectors (bump caps). Safety helmets have a useful life of three years and this can be shortened by prolonged exposure to ultra-violet light.

Protective outer clothing - may incorporate high visibility features near traffic routes (e.g. lift trucks operating in vicinity).

Protective inner clothing - overalls.

Gloves - must be suitable for both physical and chemical hazards.

Footwear - safety boots/shoes.

Ear protection - see also - 'Physical agents 1 - noise and vibration' - element B7 within Unit B: Hazardous agents in the workplace.

There are numerous types of body protection available mainly split into **full body** or **half body**. Boiler suits of old are still used but with technological breakthroughs in the textile industries there are extremely light weight fabrics available offering high levels of protection against a wide range of hazards. Fabrics such as Gortex lined coats offer good protection against wet processes and Nomex offers extremely good protection against fire. Hand and arm protection is available to protect against a variety of chemical and physical hazards. These include protection against cuts and abrasions by light weight chain mail gloves and sleeves as well as modern tough fabrics such as Kevlar. Chemical resistance should be assessed to ensure adequate protection. For example, fluorocarbon (Viton) material provides good protection when handling diesel fuel whereas natural rubber and butyl gloves are not recommended for this use.

As with all PPE footwear should be provided to meet the conditions and hazards which may be encountered. Obvious hazards such as falling materials can be protected against using footwear such as steel toecap shoes. Additional protection may be required for the ankles and for protection from acids, alkalis, oils etc. In addition soles may also be required to offer anti-slip protection and/or offer some protection against electric shock.

Here are some common examples of types of safety footwear:

■ Falling objects.		*steel toe-caps.*
■ Sharp objects.		*steel in-soles.*
■ Flammable atmospheres.		*anti-static footwear.*
■ Spread of contamination.		*washable boots.*
■ Molten metal.		*heat resistant boots and gaiters.*
■ Electricity.		*rubber soles.*
■ Wet environments.		*impermeable wellingtons.*
■ Slippery surfaces.		*non-slip soles.*
■ Cold environments.		*thermally insulated soles.*

TRAINING

In order to ensure the safe use and maintenance of work equipment it is essential that adequate training takes place. The need may be simple and short but it must take place. Operators of equipment will need different training to those that supervise safe operation or those that maintain the equipment, though there may be some overlap of need. For example, an operator of a fork lift truck will need to have knowledge and skill enough to do this safely, whereas a supervisor/manager does not need the skill to operate but must understand the hazards, precautions and rules of safe operation in order to have an expectation and to enforce safe standards. A maintenance person may not have to have all the skill of a fork lift truck operator but would usually need enough skill to test the equipment after maintenance.

Statutory requirements for training

The HASAWA 1974 places a duty on the employer to ensure, so far as is reasonably practicable, that employees receive adequate training, as necessary. In addition, it places a duty to not expose others to risk, so far as is reasonably practicable. Case law (R v Swan Hunter Shipbuilding Ltd and Another) clarifies that the duty may extend to the provision of information (and training), if it is reasonably practicable. This duty is further extended by PUWER 1998, in that the employer must ensure that all persons that use the equipment have received adequate training.

PUWER - Regulation 9 training

(1) Every employer shall ensure that all persons who use work equipment have received adequate training for purposes of health and safety, including training in the methods which may be adopted when using the work equipment, any risks which such use may entail and precautions to be taken.

(2) Every employer shall ensure that any of his employees who supervises or manages the use of work equipment has received adequate training for purposes of health and safety, including training in the methods which may be adopted when using the work equipment, any risks which such use may entail and precautions to be taken.

Statutory requirements for certification and authorisation

PUWER sets out general requirements for training and restriction of those that use equipment. The general statutory duty is not well defined and does not specify processes of certification and authorisation. Training and restriction requirements are developed in the approved code of practice (ACOPs) for wood working machines and power presses, which emphasises the need to restrict use of this equipment to those that have been adequately trained and are designated to the task of using it. The term designated remains unclear and relates in this context to a system of certification of competence and the giving of authorisation. In addition the ACOP for the Training of Drivers of Rider Operated Lift Trucks requires a well structured process of training, certification and authorisation of drivers. Instructors carrying out training to this ACOP are required to have been trained to a given standard. The HSE approves a small number of organisations who accredit and monitor training providers. These are the Construction Industry Training Board (CITB), Road Transport Industry Training Board (RTIB) the Association of Industrial Truck Trainers (AITT) and Lantra - Sector Skills Council for the Environmental and Land-based Sector. Drivers certified under this system are then trained and assessed to a standard expressed in the ACOP. When a driver is trained and certified it then falls to the employer of the driver to determine that they are competent and to authorise them. This authorisation is often represented by the provision of a licence depicting their competence and authorisation. A similar approach may be taken with other forms of work equipment.

STATUTORY RESTRICTIONS ON USE OF WORK EQUIPMENT

In many workplaces there is a variety of pieces of equipment. Until it is agreed that a person has received sufficient training and has appropriate skill to use the work equipment, they should be prevented from doing so. This may be by specific instruction or where the risks are particularly high by physical restraint preventing the equipment being put into use. For example, a wood working machine in a general workshop may be locked off and issue of the key controlled and restricted to those that are competent to use it. In the same way a mobile elevating work platform (MEWP) may be restricted, and a mobile scaffold or ladder restricted by a chain and padlock. In addition to requirements emphasising the need for training people PUWER 1998 sets out a requirement to restrict use to those 'given the task of using it' where specific risks exist. The term specific risks is not defined, but guidance to PUWER 1998 tends to support restriction where the risks of inappropriate use might lead to serious consequences, though this is not a limiting factor and the principle of restriction to those that adequately trained should be universally applied. Older legislation had identified, through experience of accidents, certain equipment that required restriction for 'young people' *(see below),* and though this is no longer mandatory some consideration to the inherent risks of this equipment should be made.

PUWER - Regulation 7 specific risks

(1) Where the use of work equipment is likely to involve a specific risk to health or safety, every employer shall ensure that

(a) The use of that work equipment is restricted to those persons given the task of using it.

(b) Repairs, modifications, maintenance or servicing of that work equipment is restricted to those persons who have been specifically designated to perform operations of that description (whether or not also authorised to perform other operations).

(2) The employer shall ensure that the persons designated for the purposes of sub-paragraph (b) of paragraph (1) have received adequate training related to any operations in respect of which they have been so designated.

Previous legislation has been quite prescriptive e.g. Factories Act restricted the use of what was called dangerous machinery such that people under the age of 18 could not clean specified moving machinery. Whilst this is no longer a specific requirement the list should be considered as a guide to what type of machinery would typically be considered to have specific risks under PUWER 1998, and would require restriction. The types of machine that were considered to be dangerous under this and similar legislation were:

- Brick and tile presses.
- Calenders.
- Carding machines used in wool textiles.
- Corner staying machines, as used in upholstery.
- Dough brakes and mixers.
- Food mixing machines when used with attachments for

machines being in any case machines used for cutting wood, wood products, fibreboard, plastic or similar material Milling machines used in the metal trades.

- Opening or teasing machines used for upholstery or bedding work.

mincing, slicing or chipping or any other cutting operation or for crumbling.

- Garment presses.
- Gill Boxes used in wool textiles.
- Hydro extractors.
- Loose knife punching machines.
- Machines of any type equipped with a circular saw blade or with a saw in a form of a continuous band or strip, planing machines, vertical spindle moulding machines and routing

The following machines whether power driven or not:

- Circular knife slicing machines used for cutting bacon and other foods (whether similar to bacon or not).
- Guillotine machines.

- Pie and tart making machines.
- Power presses including hydraulic and pneumatic presses.
- Rotary knife bowl chopping machines.
- Semi-automatic wood turning lathes.
- Vegetable slicing machines.
- Washing machines in use in laundries.
- Wire stitching machines.
- Worm pressure extruding machines.
- Wrapping and packing machines.

- Platen printing machines.
- Potato chipping machines.

Similarly, the Abrasive Wheels Regulations (now revoked) controlled who could fit abrasive wheels - people who did had to be trained and properly appointed. The use of this equipment was not restricted under this older legislation. However it might be considered that abrasive wheels represent a specific risk and would require restriction of use, as required by Regulation 7 of PUWER 1998.

5.3 - Duties in respect of machinery, pressure systems and electricity on manufacturers and suppliers

GENERAL DUTIES OF MANUFACTURERS, IMPORTERS AND SUPPLIERS

Health and Safety at Work etc. Act (HASAWA) 1974 - Section 6

1. It shall be the duty of any person who designs, manufactures, imports or supplies any article for use at work:

    a. To ensure, so far as is reasonably practicable, that the article is so designed and constructed as to be safe and without risk to health when properly used.

    b. To carry out or arrange for the carrying out of such testing and examination as may be necessary for the performance of the duty imposed on him by the preceding paragraph.

    c. To take such steps as are necessary to secure that there will be available in connection with the use of the article at work adequate information about the use for which it designed and has been tested and about any conditions necessary to ensure that, when put to that use it will be safe and without risks to health.

2. It shall be the duty of any person who undertakes the design or manufacture of any article for use at work to carry out or arrange for the carrying out of any necessary research with a view to the directory and, so far as is reasonably practicable, the elimination or minimisation of any risks to health or safety to which the design or article may give rise.

3. It shall be the duty of any person who erects or installs any article for use at work in any premises where that article is to be used by persons at work to ensure, so far as is reasonably practicable, that nothing about the way in which it is erected or installed makes it unsafe or a risk to health when it is properly used.

RISK ASSESSMENT

Risk assessments by designers are needed to allow them to improve the selection of safety measures for each type of hazard. The standard relating to the risk assessment of machinery is BS EN 1050:1996 'Safety of Machinery - Principles for Risk Assessment'. As with other forms of risk assessment the process first requires risk analysis:

- Determination of the limits of the machinery.
- Identifying hazards.
- Risk estimation.

The assessment process then requires risk evaluation to ensure that the machinery is safe. If machinery is not safe then further risk reduction measures will be required. This process taken from BS EN 1050 is outlined in the figure below. Risk is estimated by taking into account:

- The severity of harm.
- The probability of occurrence of that harm which involves:
    - The frequency and duration of exposure of persons to the hazard.
    - The probability occurrence of the hazardous event.
    - The technical and human factors which will allow the avoidance of the hazard or the limiting of harm.

The choice of an appropriate strategy will involve:

- Risk reduction by design.
- The need for safeguarding (including guarding and PPE).
- The provision of information for use (e.g. training, safe working procedures, supervision, permit to work systems).
- The need for additional precautions (e.g. emergency monitoring circuits).

ESSENTIAL HEALTH AND SAFETY REQUIREMENTS

Essential health and safety requirements for machinery

The specific requirements of Annex 1 of the Machinery Directive are listed in Schedule 3 of the SMSR 1992. **(See summary next page - EHSR were amended in 1993 to accommodate lifting equipment).**

Various product Directives are produced by the European Community to define and control the standards of products manufactured for use within the Community. They do this by setting out 'essential health and safety requirements' (EHSR). These are the features of the product that when it is manufactured will make it safe and healthy for supply into the Community. The requirements are set out in such a way that they express principles of health and safety and though they are quite specific they do not express how they may be technically fulfilled - this is left to the designer and manufacturer in the first instance. When applying the essential health and safety requirements it is possible to take account of technical and economic limitations at the time of construction. Conformity with specified published British/European standards (transposed harmonised standards) will be presumed to comply with essential health and safety requirements.

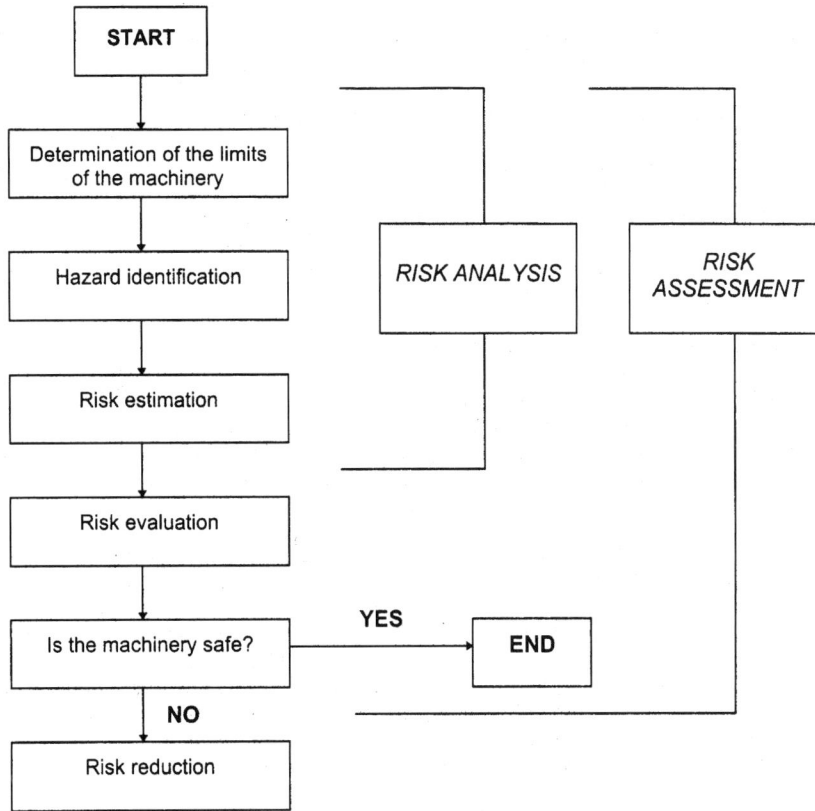

Figure C5-3: Risk assessment.   *Source: BS EN 1050.*

Section	Element (of essential health and safety requirement)	Relevant
1.1.	*General Remarks*	
1.1.1.	Definitions	
1.1.2.	Principles of Safety Integration	
1.1.3.	Materials and Products	
1.1.4.	Lighting Arrangements	
1.1.5.	Design of Component Handling	
1.2.	*Controls*	
1.2.1.	Safety and Reliability	
1.2.2.	Control Devices	
1.2.3.	Starting Arrangements	
1.2.4.	Stopping Devices	
	Normal Stopping	
	Emergency Stopping	
	Complex Installations	
1.2.5.	Mode control and selection	
1.2.6.	Failure of Power Supply	
1.2.7.	Failure of the Control Circuit	
1.2.8.	Software	

Section	Element	Relevant
1.3.	*Protection Against Mechanical Hazards*	
1.3.1.	Stability and Anchorage	
1.3.2.	Risks of Break-up during operation	
1.3.3.	Risks due to Falling or Ejected Objects	
1.3.4.	Risks due to Surfaces, Edges or Angles	
1.3.5.	Risk related to Combined Machinery	
1.3.6.	Risks due to Variable Speed	
1.3.7.	Risks due to Moving Parts	
1.3.8	Choice of Protection Arrangements	
1.4.	*Required Characteristics of Guards/Devices*	
1.4.1.	General Requirement	
1.4.2.1.	Fixed Guards	
1.4.2.2.	Movable Guards	
1.4.2.3.	Adjustable Guards	
1.4.3.	Special Requirements for Protective Devices	
1.5.	*Protection Against Other Hazards*	
1.5.1.	Electrical Supply	
1.5.2.	Static Electricity	
1.5.3.	Energy Supply other than Electricity	
1.5.4.	Errors of Fitting	
1.5.5.	Temperature	
1.5.6.	Fire	
1.5.7.	Explosion	
1.5.8.	Noise	
1.5.9.	Vibration	
1.5.10.	Radiation	
1.5.11.	External Radiation	
1.5.12.	Laser Equipment	
1.5.13.	Emissions of Dust, Gases etc.	
1.5.14.	Risk of Internal Trapping	
1.5.15	Risk of Slipping, Tripping or Falling	
1.6.	*Maintenance*	
1.6.1.	Machinery Maintenance	
1.6.2.	Access to Operating and Servicing Position	
1.6.3.	Isolation of Energy Sources	
1.6.4.	Operator Intervention	
1.6.5.	Cleaning of Internal Parts	
1.7.	*Indicators*	
1.7.0.	Information Devices	
1.7.1.	Warning Devices	
1.7.2.	Warning of Residual Risks	
1.7.3.	Marking	
1.7.4.	Instructions	

Figure C5-4: Sample document - list of residual risks for passing to the customer.   *Source: Supply of Machinery (Safety) Regulations - Guidance.*

ATTESTATION PROCEDURES

Supply of Machinery (Safety) Regulations 1992 (as amended)

The provision of machinery is specifically governed by the SMSR 1992 *(see HSE information sheet at Appendix 2 to this Unit)*. In order to understand the full scope of this legislation it is necessary to consider the various definitions contained within the regulations:

Safe

When the machinery is properly installed, maintained and used for the purpose for which it is intended, there is no risk (apart from one reduced to a minimum) of it being the cause or occasion of death or injury to persons or, where appropriate, to domestic animals or damage to property.

Supply

Read in conjunction with section 46 of the Consumer Protection Act (CPA) 1987 and includes offering to supply, agreeing to supply, exposing for supply and possessing for supply.

Responsible person under SMSR

This includes:

■ The manufacturer of the machinery.
■ The manufacturer's appointed representative in the community.
■ The person who first supplies the relevant machinery.

The term manufacturer includes any person who assembles machinery or parts thereof.

Machinery under SMSR

For the purposes of SMSR:

1. An assembly of linked parts or components, at least one of which moves including, without prejudice to the generality of the foregoing, the appropriate actuators, control and power circuits, joined together for a specific application, in particular for the processing, treatment, moving or packaging of a material.

2. An assembly of machines, that is to say, an assembly of items of machinery as referred to in paragraph 1 above, which, in order to achieve the same end, are arranged and controlled so that they function as an integral whole not withstanding that the terms of machinery may themselves be relevant machinery and are accordingly required to comply with these Regulations.

3. Interchangeable equipment modifying the function of a machine which is supplied for the purpose of being assembled with an item of machinery as referred to in paragraph 1 above or with a series of different items of machinery or with a tractor by the operator himself save for any equipment which is a spare part or tool.

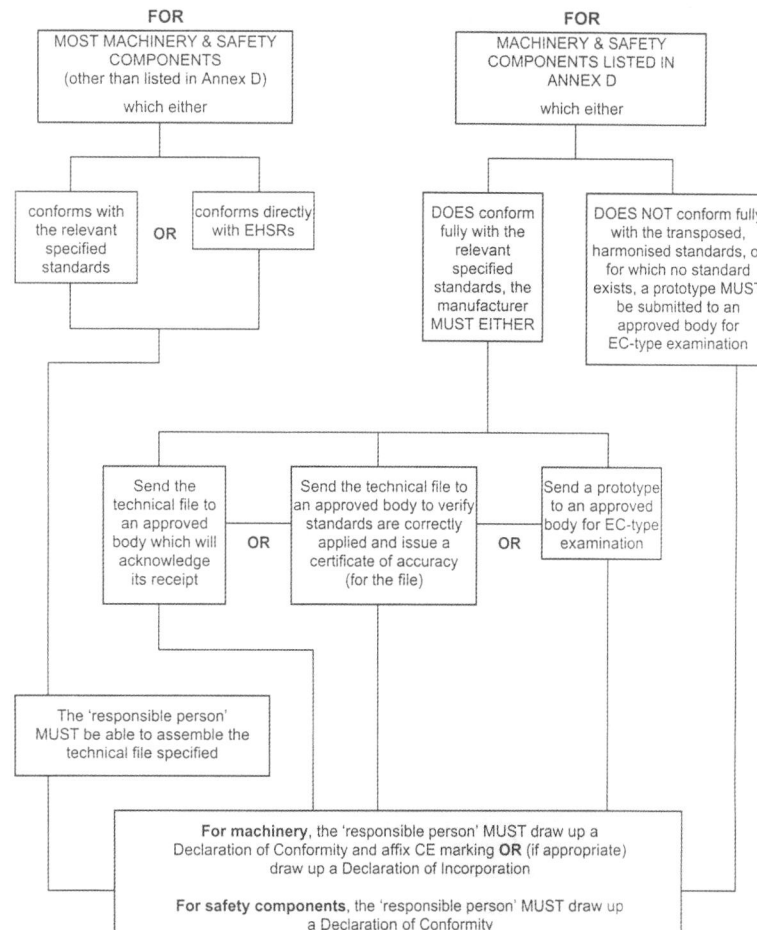

Figure C5-5: Machinery safety

Source: Ambiguous.

TECHNICAL FILE

A responsible person must compile or be able to assemble a technical file comprising the following information:

- Overall drawings of the machinery together with drawings of the control circuits.
- Full detailed drawings and calculations, test reports as may be required in order to check conformity with the essential health and safety requirements.
- A list of the essential health and safety requirements, the transposed harmonised standards applicable, standards adopted, any other technical specifications applied.
- A description of the methods adopted to eliminate hazards presented by the machinery.
- Any technical report or certificate from a competent body or laboratory.
- For declaration of conformity with a transposed harmonized standard any technical report on tests conducted by the responsible person or competent body or laboratory.
- A copy of the instructions drawn up in accordance with the provision of information.
- For series manufacture of machines the internal measures that will be implemented to ensure that all machines produced will be in conformity with the EHSR.

The information must be retained and kept available for at least 10 years from the date of manufacture, in the case of series manufacture from the last unit produced. If submitted to a UK approved body the documentation is to be in English, if to another Member State in a language acceptable to them.

DECLARATION OF CONFORMITY/INCORPORATION

Harmonised standards

A technical specification adopted by either the European Committee for Standardisation (CEN) or the European Committee for Electro-technical Standardisation (CENELEC) or both laying down a procedure for the provision of information in the field of technical standards and regulations.

Standard

A technical specification approved by a recognised standardising body for repeated or continuous application, with which compliance is not compulsory.

Series manufacturer

Means the manufacturer of more than one item of relevant machinery of the same type in accordance with a common design.

Declaration of conformity

The responsibility for demonstrating that machinery satisfies the EHSR rests with the manufacturer or importer into the European Community - the responsible person. The responsible person may be someone that manufactures specialist equipment for the sole use of their organisation - this is still supply. For most machinery the responsible person must be able to assemble the technical file.

For machinery listed in schedule 4 of the SMSR 1992, which is drawn from Annex 4 of the Machinery Directive and expresses a list of machinery posing special hazards, the process is slightly different. The list of machinery includes circular saws, portable chain saws, presses for the cold working of metal and injection moulding machines. For listed machinery that is *manufactured in conformity with transposed harmonised standards* the responsible person may choose between:

- Drawing up and forwarding a technical file to an approved body and have it assessed for conformity - the file will be kept and a receipt provided.
- Submitting the technical file to the approved body who will verify the standards have been appropriately applied - *a certificate of adequacy* will be issued.
- Submitting an example of the machinery to an approved body for EC type-examination.

For machinery that is *not manufactured in conformity with transposed harmonised standards* the responsible person must submit an example of the machinery for EC type-examination. Whichever attestation route is taken the responsible person must then draw up a declaration of conformity for each machine supplied. The declaration is issued with the machine and declares that the machine complies with the EHSR and entitles the responsible person to affix CE marking.

Declaration of incorporation

Where the machinery is intended for incorporation into other machinery or an assembly with other machines, for example, an electric motor or a conveyor belt section, a declaration of conformity is required. The responsible person draws up a declaration of incorporation for each machine, no "CE" marking is applied to the machinery. A declaration is applicable in the case of relevant machinery which is intended for:

- Incorporation into other machinery.
- Assembly with other machinery.
- Is not interchangeable equipment.
- Cannot function independently.

A declaration of conformity states that the machinery must not be put into service until the machinery that it is incorporated into has been declared in conformity with the EHSR.

Certificate of adequacy

A document drawn up by an approved body to which a manufacturer has submitted a Technical File which it has been verified and confirms the correct application of the appropriate transposed harmonised standards and that the technical file contains the necessary information.

Safety Components

Safety components should have a Declaration of Conformity but not a CE mark in respect of the Machinery directive.

EC DECLARATION OF INCORPORATION

We hereby declare that the following machinery is intended to be incorporated into other machinery and must not be put into service until the relevant machinery into which it is to be incorporated has been declared in conformity with the essential health and safety requirements of the Machinery Directive 89/392/EEC and 91/368/EEC.

Machine description _____

Make_____ Type _____

Serial Number _____

Manufactured by _____

Address _____

_____

This machinery has been designed and manufactured in accordance with the following transposed harmonised European standards

EN292 parts 1 and 2: 1991 Safety of Machinery - Basic concepts, general principles for design.
EN294: 1992, Safety of Machinery - Safety distances to prevent danger zones being reached by the upper limbs.
EN349: 1993, Safety of Machinery - Minimum gaps to avoid crushing of parts of the human body.
EN418: 1992, Safety of Machinery - Emergency stop equipment, functional aspects - Principles for design.
EN60204 part 1: 1993, Safety of machinery - electrical equipment of machines - Specification for general requirements

_____
_____
_____

In addition, this machinery has been designed and manufactured in accordance with British Standard BS5304: 1988, Safety of Machinery.

A technical construction file for this machinery is retained at the following address:

_____
_____

Signed _____ Date _____

Name _____ Position _____

Being the responsible person appointed by the manufacturer or nominated representative of the manufacturer established in the EC, and employed by

_____

EC DECLARATION OF CONFORMITY

We hereby declare that the following machinery complies with the essential health and safety requirements of the Machinery Directive 89/392/EEC and 91/368/EEC.

Machine description _____

Make_____ Type _____

Serial Number _____

Manufactured by _____

Address _____

_____

This machinery has been designed and manufactured in accordance with the following transposed harmonised European standards

EN292 parts 1 and 2: 1991 Safety of Machinery - Basic concepts, general principles for design.
EN294: 1992, Safety of Machinery - Safety distances to prevent danger zones being reached by the upper limbs.
EN349: 1993, Safety of Machinery - Minimum gaps to avoid crushing of parts of the human body.
EN418: 1992, Safety of Machinery - Emergency stop equipment, functional aspects - Principles for design.
EN60204 part 1: 1993, Safety of machinery - electrical equipment of machines - Specification for general requirements

_____
_____
_____

In addition, this machinery has been designed and manufactured in accordance with British Standard BS5304: 1988, Safety of Machinery.

A technical construction file for this machinery is retained at the following address:

_____
_____

Signed _____ Date _____

Name _____ Position _____

Being the responsible person appointed by the manufacturer or nominated representative of the manufacturer established in the EC, and employed by

_____

Figure C5-6: EC declaration of incorporation. *Source: ACT.* Figure C5-7: EC declaration of conformity. *Source: ACT.*

DECLARATION OF TYPE APPROVAL

European community (EC) type-examination

This is the procedure whereby an approved body ascertains and certifies that an example of relevant machinery satisfies the relevant provisions of the Machinery Directive. The procedure requires the following to be included in an application:

Details of the manufacturer, or representative in the Community, and place of manufacture.

- A technical file.
- A representative example of the machine or a statement of where it may be examined.

The approved body will

- Examine the technical file and verify its appropriateness and relation to the example machine.
- Examine the example machine to determine if it has been manufactured in accord with the technical file, check standards used (if applicable) have been properly applied, examine and test to determine compliance with EHSR.

If the example complies an EC type-examination certificate is issued. Conditions may be applied to the certificate and it will have sufficient information with it such that the approved example machine may be identified. If a certificate is refused the approved body informs other approved bodies. The responsible person must inform the approved body of modifications; they will consider the modifications and determine if the current certificate remains valid.

DECLARATION OF CE MARKING

CE marking can only be applied where conformity with EHSR has been determined. CE Marking consists of a symbol shown below and the last two figures of the year in which the mark is affixed. The letters "CE" are the abbreviation of the French phrase "Conformité Européene" which literally means "European Conformity". The term initially used was "EC Mark" and it was officially replaced by "CE Marking" in the Directive 93/68/EEC in 1993. "CE Marking" is now used in all EU official documents. "CE Mark" is also in use, but it is NOT the official term.

Figure C5-8: CE Mark.
Source: Ambiguous.

CE marking must be affixed in a distinct, visible, legible and indelible manner. It would not usually be smaller than 5mm and the component parts need to be in proportion.

It is an offence to affix the CE marking on a machine unless it satisfies the EHSR and is, in fact, safe. It is also an offence to affix any mark which can be confused with CE marking.

5.4 - Ergonomic, anthropometric and human reliability considerations

It is essential to have a balanced strategy in order to achieve safety with machinery. This means not having an over reliance on any one control but ensuring that they are integrated and complement each other, technical, procedural and behavioural controls working in harmony. A significant consideration in providing work equipment controls are ergonomic, anthropometric and human reliability considerations.

DESIGN OF CONTROLS AND EMERGENCY CONTROLS

Failure of any part of the control system or its power supply should lead to a 'fail-safe' condition (more correctly and realistically called 'minimised failure to danger'), and not impede the operation of the 'stop' or 'emergency stop' controls. The measures which should be taken in the design and application of a control system to mitigate against the effects of its failure will need to be balanced against the consequences of any failure. The greater the risk, the more resistant the control system should be to the effects of failure.

At the person-machine interface the operator will have to manipulate parts of the machine to pass a message to it, the machine will act according to the message received and pass a message back to the operator. The operator must be trained to communicate in a way the machine understands and the machine must be manufactured to be able to act according to instructions and communicate in an understandable way with the operator. It would be impossible to carry out a task if every time you pressed the red button you got a different response. We all know the frustration when using a computer and you cannot get it to do what you want simply because you do not know the right letter to press or the right icon to click on. There has been an attempt in recent years to make computer software 'user friendly', which means the operator and the computer can understand each other.

It should be possible to identify easily what each control does and on which equipment it takes effect. Both the controls and their markings should be clearly visible. As well as having legible wording or symbols, factors such as the colour, shape and position of controls are important. Any change in the operating conditions should only be possible by the use of a control, except if the change does not increase risk to health or safety. Examples of operating conditions include speed, pressure, temperature and power.

The controls provided should be designed and positioned so as to prevent, so far as possible, inadvertent or accidental operation. Buttons and levers should be of appropriate design, for example, including a shrouding or locking facility. It should not be possible for the control to 'operate itself', such as due to the effects of gravity, vibration, or failure of a spring mechanism.

The primary requirement is that the action of the stop control should bring the equipment to a safe condition in a safe manner. This acknowledges that it is not always desirable to bring all items of work equipment immediately to a complete or instantaneous stop; for example, to prevent the unsafe build-up of heat or pressure, or to allow a controlled run-down of large rotating parts. Similarly, stopping the mixing mechanism of a reactor during certain chemical reactions could lead to a dangerous exothermic reaction. Though there are a number of reasons to bring equipment to a controlled rather than immediate stop PUWER 1998 qualifies this general requirement by 'where necessary for reasons of health and safety' which provides an overriding drive to assure that it is brought to a complete stop in these circumstances. Therefore accessible dangerous parts must be rendered stationary; however parts of equipment which do not present a risk, such as suitably guarded cooling fans, do not need to be positively stopped and may be allowed to idle.

Emergency stops are intended to effect a rapid response to potentially dangerous situations and they should not be used as functional stops during normal operation. Emergency stop controls should be easily reached and actuated. Common types are mushroom-headed buttons, bars, levers, kick-plates, or pressure-sensitive cables.

Warnings given in accordance with PUWER 1998 Regulation 17(3) (c) should be given sufficiently in advance of the equipment actually starting to give those at risk time to get clear, and circumstances will affect the type of warning chosen. As well as time, suitable means of avoiding the risk should be provided. This may take the form of a device by means of which the person at risk can prevent start-up or warn the operator of his/her presence. Otherwise there must be adequate provision to enable people at risk to withdraw, e.g. sufficient space or exits.

REDUCING NEED FOR ACCESS (AUTOMATION, REMOTE SYSTEMS)

A key consideration in risk reduction by design of machinery can be achieved by reducing the need for operator intervention in danger zones. As the need for access increases, so does the need for more sophisticated safeguards. Automated and remote systems can be considered by the designer to meet the need to keep people away from danger areas. For example, effort should be made to automate such things as lubrication and machinery adjustment for production control. Materials can be fed automatically into machines, reducing the need for the operator's hands to access the danger area to place the materials, as, for example in the case of a power press. Where the operator of machinery may need to gain access to see part of the process, vision panels or remote cameras can be provided.

LIGHTING

Under the SMSR 1992, the manufacturer must supply integral lighting suitable for the operations concerned where its lack is likely to cause a risk despite ambient lighting of normal intensity.

The manufacturer must also ensure that there is no area of shadow likely to cause nuisance, that there is no irritating dazzle and that there are no dangerous stroboscopic effects due to the lighting provided by the manufacturer. Internal parts requiring frequent inspection, adjustment or maintenance must be provided with appropriate lighting. Local lighting may be needed to give sufficient view of a dangerous process or to reduce visual fatigue.

Additionally, PUWER 1998 (Regulation 21) requires that workplaces where people use work equipment should be suitably lit. PUWER 1998 also requires employers to ensure that work equipment, such as lighting, complies with relevant UK legislation implementing EC Directives, for example, the Electrical Equipment (Safety) Regulations (EESR) 1994 which implement the Low Voltage Directive.

If it is intended by the manufacturer to be used in dark places, self-propelled machinery must be fitted with a lighting device appropriate to the work to be carried out, without prejudice to any other regulations applicable (e.g. road traffic regulations, navigation rules, etc).

Users should ensure that workplaces housing machinery are suitably and sufficiently lit. If the ambient lighting is sufficient for the tasks involved in the use of the equipment, special lighting need not be provided. But if the task involves the perception of detail, for example, precision measurements, additional lighting should be provided to ensure it is adequate for the needs of the task.

Local lighting should be provided on the machine for the illumination of the work area when the construction of the machine and/or its guards render the normal lighting inadequate for the safe and efficient operation of the machine, for example, on sewing machines. Local lighting may be needed to give sufficient view of a dangerous process or to reduce visual fatigue. Travelling cranes may obscure overhead lighting for the driver and others, particularly when there is no natural light available (night working), and supplementary lighting may be necessary.

Additional lighting may be necessary in areas not covered by general lighting when work, such as maintenance or repairs, is carried out in them. The arrangements for the provision of lighting could be temporary, by means of hand or other portable lights, or by fixed lighting inside enclosures, such as lift shafts. The standard of lighting required will be related to the purpose for which the work equipment is used or to the work being carried out. Lighting levels should be checked periodically to ensure that the intensity is not diminished by dust and grime deposits on the fittings. Where necessary, the luminaries and reflectors should be cleaned at regular intervals to maintain lighting efficiency. Where access is foreseeable, on an intermittent but regular basis, permanent lighting should be provided.

LAYOUT OF PLANT AND MACHINERY

The layout of plant and machinery should be designed to promote:

- Efficient working.
- The orderly arrangement of goods and materials.
- Movement of people and, where applicable, handling and transport equipment.

Machines should be spaced to give ample room for the movements of operators, and to allow the work in progress to be stacked between operations. Gangways should be of adequate width to enable any work which departs from the normal sequence to be moved to the appropriate machine easily and quickly.

Conditions of layout which promote efficient working are also conducive to safety. Adequate working space and unrestricted freedom of movement allow a machinist to work more naturally, and therefore more safely than if his movements are cramped and unnatural. Energy spent in unnecessary handling and transport of material reduces that available for productive work and leads to fatigue, which is a likely cause of accidents, particularly on machines. Unimpeded gangways reduce the risk of injuries resulting from slipping or stumbling.

For safety and convenience of working there should be on three sides of every machine a clear space of 1 metre more than the maximum length of the material to be handled. Spacing of this standard will permit unrestricted freedom of movement for the machinist, both when working the machine and when handling the work, and will provide space for stacking work in progress without encroaching on gangways. This provision of adequate space around machines will also assist for periods when cleaning and maintenance are conducted.

In order to remind people to maintain space for its purpose, walkway or material staking, good practice encourages marking the floor with painted lines to identify the space.

TRAINING

Training needs are likely to be greatest on recruitment. However, training needs are also required:

- If the risks to which people are exposed change due to a change in their working tasks.
- Because new technology or equipment is introduced.
- If the system of work changes.

Refresher training should also be provided when necessary. Skills decline if they are not used regularly. Particular attention should be paid to people who deputise for others on occasions - as they may need more frequent refresher training than those who do the work regularly.

Training and proper supervision of young people is particularly important because of their relative immaturity and unfamiliarity with the working environment. Induction training is of particular importance for them. There are no general age restrictions in legislation relating to the use of work equipment although there is some cautionary comment concerning young people in the relevant ACOPs made under PUWER 1998 dealing with power presses and wood working. All employees should be competent to use work equipment with due regard to health and safety regardless of their age.

The MHSWR 1999 contain specific requirements relating to the employment of young people under the age of 18. These require employers to assess risks to young people before they start work, taking into account their inexperience, lack of awareness of potential risks and their immaturity. Employers must provide information to parents of school-age children (for example when they are on work experience) about the risks and the control measures introduced and take account of the risk assessment in determining whether the young person should undertake certain work activities. The operation of some machinery may present risks to young people that the MHSWR 1999 were anticipating. *See also - '5.2 Use, training' - earlier in this element.*

In determining the training requirements of a person account should be taken of the circumstances in which the employee works, for example, if the person works alone or under close supervision of a competent person, as well as the technical content of the training. It is important to note that PUWER 1988 requires *'adequate'* training and HASAWA 1974 section 2 requires training *'as necessary'*. It is therefore essential to fit the training provided to each individual's needs in order to take account of normal human reliability considerations. The training should also match the task the person conducts; they may operate or clean or maintain the equipment in each circumstance the training requirements will have some common elements and some differences.

Care also needs to be taken to ensure those that manage or supervise as well as those that use work equipment are included in the training strategy. The requirement should consist of the:

- Evaluation of the competence they need to manage or supervise the use of work equipment.
- Training of the employee to make up any shortfall between their competence and that required to carry out the work with due regard to health and safety.

IMPORTANCE OF SIZE OF OPENINGS

Where it is necessary to provide an opening in a guard, it should be at a sufficient distance to prevent any person from reaching the danger point. This may be achieved by positioning the guard at the required distance or by providing a tunnel which extends outwards from it. Access to a guard opening may also be prevented by the use of a false table. The effectiveness of a guard with an opening should be calculated using the distances laid down in BS EN 294/811. This should be reinforced by physical tests carried out with the machinery at rest and in a safe condition.

As with barriers, there are two dimensions of interest. These are the size of the opening and the distance to the dangerous part.

Anthropometrics is the study of human dimensions, and this form of study has enabled guided decisions on acceptable opening sizes.

The following table takes account of anthropometric data and gives the dimensions in millimetres for a regular shaped opening in respect of the fingertip of a person aged 14 years or over:

Part of body	Illustration	Opening (gap b) mm	Safety distance (sd)		mm
			Slot	Square	Round
Fingertip		$b \leq 4$	≥ 2	≥ 2	≥ 2
		$4 < b \leq 6$	≥ 10	≥ 5	≥ 5

Figure C5-9: Anthropometric data.

Source: Ambiguous.

The standards contain similar data in respect of people of 3 years of age and above and for most parts of the body including:

- The arm (with various limitations of movement - e.g. only at shoulder and armpit).
- The finger up to the knuckle joint.
- The hand.
- The toe and the toe tip.
- The toe.
- The foot.
- The leg (both up to the knee and up to the crotch).

Where openings are irregular then the smallest regular opening that the irregular opening can be completely inserted into are determined and the corresponding safety distances are calculated.

IMPORTANCE OF HEIGHT OF BARRIERS AND DISTANCE FROM DANGER

If the dangerous part of a machine cannot be reached then it may be considered safe by position.

Where it is not practicable to use enclosing guards, barriers may be used to prevent people reaching the danger point. These rely on a combination of height and distance to achieve their purpose. For example, for a danger zone where there is *low risk* from a friction or abrasion hazard extending up to 1.8m in height it may be protected from reach by the following combinations of barrier and distance:

Height of protective structure (barrier) mm	Distance from danger zone mm
1000	1100
1200	1200
1400	900
1600	900
1800	600
2000 and above	-

Figure C5-10: Low risk of a friction or abrasion hazard.

Source: BS EN 294.

These distances must be increased if there is a high risk, for example of entanglement:

Height of protective structure (barrier) mm	Distance from danger zone mm
1000	1500
1200	1400
1400	1100
1600	900
1800	800
2000	600

Figure C5-11: High risk of a friction or abrasion hazard.

Source: BS EN 294.

Barriers are not foolproof and they cannot prevent access to a person intent on gaining access. Therefore, as a person's intent on reaching a dangerous part increases, e.g. by climbing on chairs, ladders or the barrier itself, the protection provided by a barrier will decrease.

When reaching down over an edge, the safety distance is dependent on:

- Distance of danger point from floor.
- Height of edge of barrier.
- Horizontal distance from the edge of the barrier to the danger point.

Safety distances to prevent danger zones being reached by the upper and lower limbs are contained in two standards:

BS EN 294 : 1992   Safety of machinery - Safety distances to prevent danger zones being reached by the upper limbs

BS EN 811 : 1997   Safety of Machinery - Safety distances to prevent danger zones being reached by the lower limbs

These build on the data contained in the superseded standard 'British Standard Code of practice for Safety of Machinery BS 5305:1998'. They must be considered in conjunction with risk assessment. For example, if there is a low risk from a danger zone which is directly overhead, it may be considered out of reach if it is 2.5 m or more above ground. This *'acceptable'* distance is increased to 2.7 m or more if there is a high risk.

5. 5 - Failure modes and prevention

Main modes of failure and their causes

INFLUENCING FACTORS ON MODES OF FAILURE

Stress and strain

The properties of stress and strain relate to the strength and stiffness of a material.

Stress is the load (force) per unit area:

$$S = \frac{F}{A}$$

Where: S = stress

F = force

A = area

The unit of stress is the Newton per square metre (N/m^2) or the Pascal (Pa). This is more usually expressed in meganewtons per square metre (MN/m^2) or Newton's per square millimetre (N/mm^2). Stress is a measure of the *strength* of a material.

Thus a rod which is pulled in tension has a strength which is proportional to its cross sectional area. For example, a rod with a cross sectional area of 4 cm^2 breaks at a pull of 500 MN, then a rod of the same material of 8 cm^2 cross sectional area will break at a pull of 1000 MN force.

Strain is a measure of the *stiffness* of a material:

$$\text{Strain} = \frac{\text{change in length}}{\text{original length}}$$

As the units of length are the same they cancel each other out (e.g. mm/mm), thus strain has no units. The property of the stiffness of a material is the extent to which a material resists being deformed by a load or how springy it is. It is important to note that strength and stiffness are not the same thing. The amount of stress that a piece of material (member) is under relates to how *hard* the atoms in a solid are being pulled apart whereas the amount of strain relates to how *far* they are being pulled apart.

Tensile, compressive and shear stresses

Stress can result from a tensile force, a compressive force and from a shear force. Tensile forces are those internal forces which act on a member to pull it apart whereas compressive forces are those internal forces which push a member together:

Tension

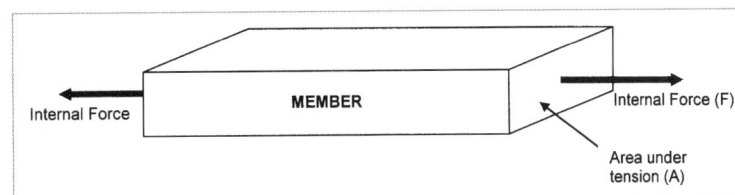

Figure C5-12: Tension.

Source: ACT.

Compression

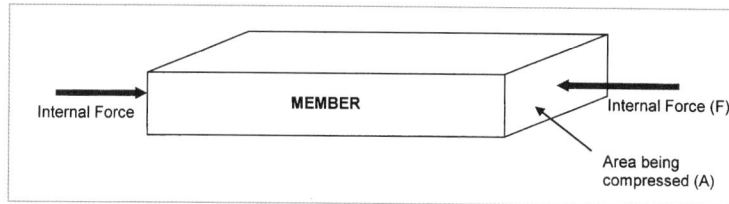

Figure C5-13: Compression.

Source: ACT.

The tensile strength of a material is measured in a tensile testing machine which pulls a test piece apart. Compressive strength is measured by placing a test piece under compressive forces until it fails explosively. In the building industry, designers are usually more concerned with tensile forces that compressive as most materials are able to withstand compressive forces better. For example, a brick is able to withstand compressive forces equivalent to a stack of bricks placed on top of it to a height of about 7 km! When compressive forces are applied to a slightly out of true member (e.g. a scaffold standard), a **bending moment** is created. A bending moment is a focus of stress at a particular point within the structure **(see section - buckling - later in this element).** The out of true standard will already have **residual** stresses due to its deformation (i.e. the bend). Residual stresses can be introduced by material defects such as impurities, pitting, corrosion crack and holes. This can also be shape dependant. A rounded corner tends to experience less residual stresses than a square corner. Thus defects and cracks in materials all represent stress concentrations which make failure more likely.

Shear stress

A shear stress is the measure of the tendency for one part of a solid to slide past the neighbouring part.

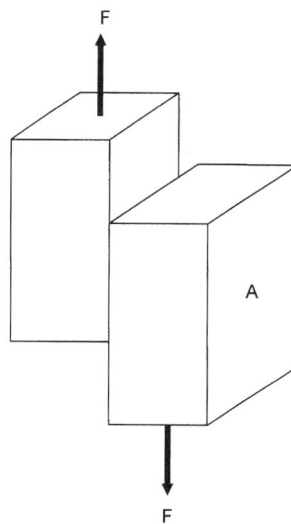

Figure C5-14: Shear stress.

Source: ACT.

$$\text{Shear stress} = \frac{\text{shearing load}}{\text{area being sheared}} = \frac{F}{A} = \text{MN m}^{-2}$$

Stress/strain relationships, yield point, breaking stress, ultimate tensile strength, elasticity and plasticity

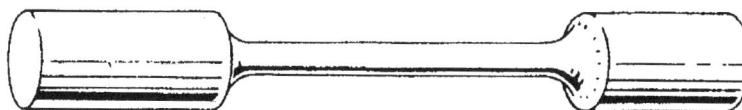

Figure C5-15: A tensile test-piece.

Source: Ambiguous.

When a test piece is placed in a tensile testing machine it will produce a load (force) - extension (i.e. change in length) graph. As the dimensions of the test piece are known this can be translated to a stress strain diagram. This will reveal a large amount of information about the properties of the material:

- The amount of elastic deformation. This is reversible deformation.
- The degree of permanent plastic deformation. This is not reversible.
- The yield point at which plastic deformation is initiated.
- The stress at which a material breaks is called the breaking stress.
- The maximum tensile stress that a material can support without breaking is called the ultimate tensile strength.

Brittle materials such as cast iron and glass display elastic behaviour until they break (i.e. they do not deform plastically). Thus they will revert back to their original shape once the stress on them is relaxed.

A stress strain curve for most materials will have an initial straight elastic region (see diagram). The slope of this elastic region is a measure of the stiffness of the material. i.e.:

$$E = \frac{stress}{strain}$$

where E is the elastic modulus or **Young's modulus** after Thomas Young (1773-1829). Young's modulus is the ability of a material to withstand elastic deformation (i.e. its stiffness or floppiness).

The stress-strain curve for many materials will also show plastic deformation in addition to elasticity. This is demonstrated by a curved region on a graph.

Another term used to describe a material is **ductility**. This is the property, possessed by a typical metal, of being able to be drawn out into a wire.

The Tensile Stress-Strain Curve of a Hypothetical Metal

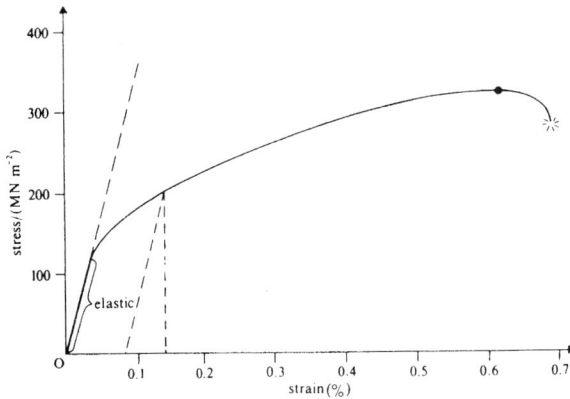

Sketches of the Stress-Strain Curves for Cast Iron and Glass

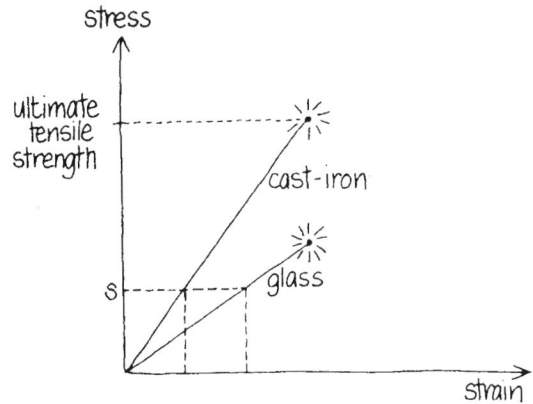

Figure C5-16: Tensile stress-strain curve.   *Source: Ambiguous.*   Figure C5-17: Stress-strain curve for iron and glass.   *Source: Ambiguous.*

Selected properties of some metallic solids at 20 °C (293 K)

Material	Density	Melting temp	Thermal Conductivity	Electrical Resistivity	Ultimate tensile strength	Yield Stress	Ductility (elongation)	Young's Modulus
	kg m^{-3}	K	W m^{-1} K m^{-1}	Ω m	MN m^{-2}	MN m^{-2}	%	GN m^{-2}
iron, pure	7870	1810	80	9.71	210	120	40	211
steel, mild	7860	1700	63	12	690	350	20	212
copper, pure	8960	1356	385	1.67	215	45	60	130
Zinc	7170	693	111	5.92	115	25	25	105

Figure C5-18: Properties of some metallic solids.   *Source: Ambiguous.*

Selected properties of some non metallic solids at 20 °C (293 K)

Material	Density	Melting temp	Thermal Conductivity	Electrical Resistivity	Ultimate tensile strength	Ductility (elongation)	Young's Modulus
	kg m^{-3}	K	W m^{-1} K m^{-1}	Ω m	MN m^{-2}	%	GN m^{-2}
carbon, diamond	3300	Λ	20	~10^{12}	-	0	1200
Concrete	2400	Λ	0.1	-	~5	0	14
glass, plate	2500	1400	1.0	~10^5	~100	0	71
Nylon	1150	470	0.25	~10^{16}	70	60-300	1.5
Polythene	920	410	0.2	~10^{16}	13	400-800	0.2

Figure C5-19: Properties of some non-metallic solids.   *Source: Ambiguous.*

Concrete and diamond breaks down by, for example, charring or burning rather than melting.

Dashes indicate data not available.

The main modes of failure of structural components are:

- Ductile failure.
- Brittle failure.
- Metal fatigue.
- Buckling.
- Corrosion.
- Wear.
- Creep.

DUCTILE

The property of ductility is the amount of plastic deformation which can take place before fracture. This property allows ductile materials to be shaped (e.g. mild steel body panel in a car). The adjacent atoms within the material slide over each other rather than come apart as in brittle failure *(see - brittle failure - below).* Ductile failure almost always occurs as the result of a single stress overload to a ductile material. These may be tensile or compressive forces and involve substantial plastic deformation prior to fracture and thus usually shows advance warning. Materials such as steel may become more ductile as temperature rises and then become subject to ductile failure.

BRITTLE FAILURE

Brittle failure is also known as fast fracture as this type of failure occurs without warning or prior evidence of distress. Brittle failure is caused by tensile stresses on brittle materials such as cast iron, glass and pottery. More ductile materials such as steel become brittle at low temperature and can also be subject to brittle failure.

The main feature of brittle materials is not the lack of tensile strength or lack of stiffness but rather a lack of toughness. That is the lack of resistance to the propagation of cracks. Once the force which causes fracture is applied, cracks propagate very quickly (usually at several thousand miles per hour) in a brittle material - thus to the naked eye the fracture appears instantaneous. The factors that promote brittle failure are:

- High tensile stresses.
- Residual (locked in) stresses.
- Impact loading which does not give the material time to deform plastically.
- Low and high temperatures.
- The embrittlement of materials through metallurgical changes.
- Work hardening.
- Inappropriate use of brittle materials.
- Welding joints (these may be brittle).
- Thick plated (>100mm) vessels are more prone to brittle failure than thin walled ones. Thick plates are more likely to incorporate defects and thick plate accentuates 'restraint' stress and stress concentrations.

Obviously brittle failure may be avoided by taking the above factors into consideration.

Figure C5-20: Tensile stress and ductile failure. *Source: Ambiguous.*

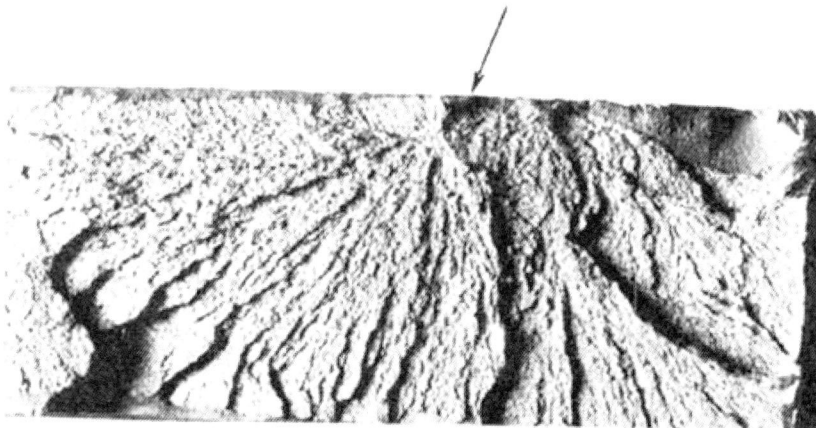

Figures C5-21 & 22: Tensile stress and brittle failure. *Source: Ambiguous.*

One example of the embrittlement of materials through metallurgical changes is hydrogen embitterment. This is an effect produced by the adsorption of hydrogen ions during plating or pickling operations. Pickling is the removal of mill scale, lime scale or salt water deposits with a dilute (usually sulphuric) acid containing inhibitors.

METAL FATIGUE

Notches, holes and irregularities within a material promotes the formation of notches or cracks. Providing the crack is below a 'critical length' it will not extend because making it spread requires too much energy. Metal fatigue occurs because the accumulating effects of fluctuating loads promote slow changes in the crystalline structure of the metal. Tiny cracks, which are difficult to detect, then start to extend very slowly through the metal until it reaches critical length. The crack then speeds up and runs across the material leading to failure. Prior to rupture fatigue failure may be practically impossible to spot with the naked eye.

The effect of metal fatigue was illustrated in 1953 and 1954 when two Comet aircraft crashed. A modern aircraft is basically a cylindrical pressure vessel which is pressurised and relaxed each time the aircraft takes off and lands. In these two accidents, cracks started from the same small hole in the fuselage and spread very slowly and undetected until they reached critical length.

The skin of the aircraft's fuselage then tore catastrophically apart and exploded. The aluminium alloy used in the design was particularly susceptible to metal fatigue.

As previously stated, fluctuating stresses are the main cause of metal fatigue. Metal fatigue is **promoted** by:

- Static tensile stresses.
- Stress concentration areas such as holes, notches, welds and cracks.
- Corrosive environments.
- Low tensile strength materials such as low tensile steels which have poor fatigue strength although high tensile steel is sensitive to stress concentrations.

Prevention of metal fatigue relies on:

- The reduction of stress concentrations.
- The reduction of fluctuating stresses.

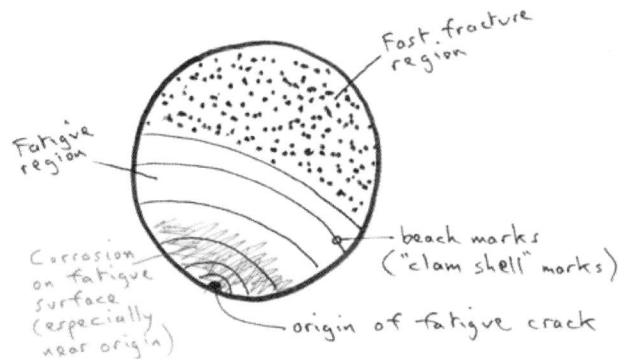

Figure C5-23: Stress-strain curve for Iron and Glass. *Source: ACT.*

BUCKLING

Buckling is caused by excessive compressive forces on a structural member (e.g. a crane jib). The ability of a material to resist buckling depends on its stiffness and therefore its ability to withstand stresses. A member will be stable only as long as the highest stresses do not exceed the yield stress (elastic stability). Where this does occur, plastic deformation takes place.

Buckling can be prevented by ensuring the appropriate material choice (i.e. stiffness) of the structural member and by ensuring that forces are not magnified by the member being 'out of true', (e.g. a scaffold standard which is not vertical will have the vertical forces placed upon it magnified by being 'out of true' thus a bending moment occurs) and buckle failure results.

Scaffold standard

Unloaded standard which is 'out of true' equal to α

When force 'F' is applied a bending moment is instantly created which increases the deflection still further

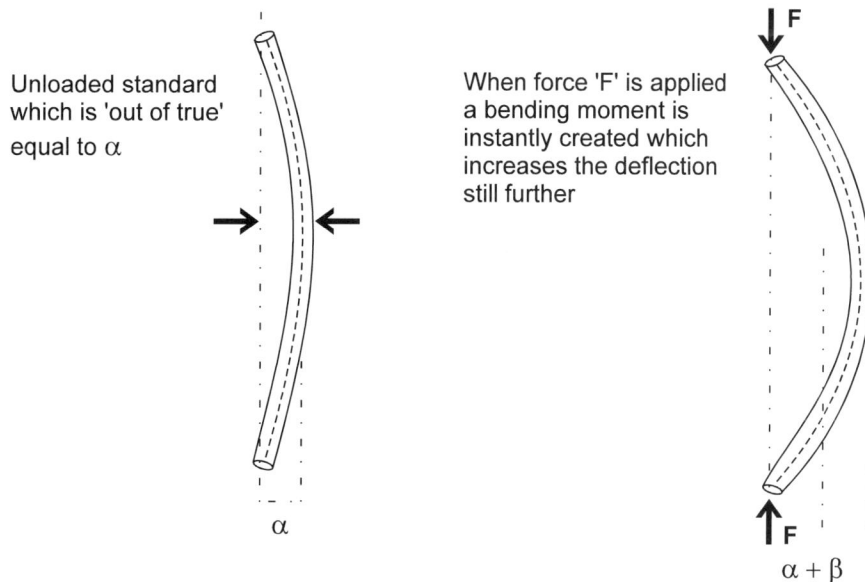

α

α + β

Figure C5-24: Scaffold standard. *Source: ACT.*

CORROSION

Corrosion is the deterioration of a metal through chemical or electro-chemical interaction with its environment. This follows when a material, such as mild steel, is attacked by agents such as polluted air and sea water which then leads to the formation of rust (oxides).

Corrosion is promoted via specific environmental factors including moisture (made worse by water-soluble pollutants or solid impurities) and high temperatures. Most corrosion involves an electro-chemical process. Here, a combination of moisture above a critical humidity level, oxygen and an electrolyte combine to promote the liberation, transfer and consumption of electrons. A small potential difference allows electrons to flows from one location (the anode) to another (the cathode).

Where two dissimilar metals are in electrical contact (this includes if it is through an electrolyte) galvanic corrosion can take place. Depending on the relationship of the two metals to each other in the galvanic table one establishes itself as the anode and the other the cathode. For example if steel and zinc were placed together then the steel would become the cathode and zinc the anode. In the process of galvanic corrosion the anode is corroded in preference to the cathode. Sometimes, in anticipation of this form of corrosion, it is arranged that zinc is placed in contact with steel structures. This would lead to the zinc material being corroded (sacrificed) in preference to the steel, for example in the case of a ship's hull or pipelines laid in the ground.

Damage to the material may take a combination of forms:

1. General thinning of the material e.g. rust.

2. Passive film formation (tarnishing) which forms a barrier to further corrosion.

3. High temperature oxidation which, for example, leads to blockages and overheating in pipe-work.

4. Pitting where the material is selectively attacked.

5. Cracking - selective attack forms deep cracks.

Precautions against corrosion include:

- Choice of materials.
- Protective coatings.
- Low pH and de-aeration of water.
- Cathodic protection where a sacrificial anode is incorporated into the design (e.g. a manganese strip is buried alongside a steel pipe and wired to protect the pipe from corrosion).
- Designing details to avoid crevices together with good drainage in places where water may collect.

Base	Magnesium		
	Zinc		
	Aluminium (commercial)		
	Cadmium		
	Duralumin (Al with $4\frac{1}{2}$% Cu)		
	Mild steel		
	Cast iron		
	Stainless steel		
	(Type 430; 18% Cr)		ACTIVE
	Stainless steel		
	(Type 304; 18% Cr 10% Ni)		ACTIVE
	Lead-tin solders		
	Lead		
	Tin		
	Nickel		
	Brasses		
	Copper		
	Bronze		
	Monel		
	Silver solders	(70% Ag 30% Cu)	
	Nickel		PASSIVE
	Stainless steel	(Type 430)	PASSIVE
	Stainless steel	(Type 304)	PASSIVE
	Silver		
	Titanium		
	Graphite	(Carbon) (non-metal)	
	Gold		
Noble	Platinum		

Figure C5-25: Galvanic series in sea water.

Source: 14 Bimetallic Corrosion, Dept .of Industry in association with the Institution of Corrosion, Science and Technology.

Courtesy of International Nickel Limited.

Figure C5-26: Corrosion of galvanised iron pipe.

Source: 14 Bimetallic Corrosion, Dept .of Industry in association with the Institution of Corrosion, Science and Technology.

The figure above shows the corrosion of a galvanised iron pipe near to a junction with a brass fitting and copper tube, showing the build-up of corrosion products resulting from exposure to hot, moderately soft water. At temperatures above 60°C iron is anodic to zinc. In addition, corrosion is enhanced by copper dissolved from the pipework depositing onto the zinc coating and exposed iron and setting up local bimetallic cells.

WEAR

Wear is the loss of material due to the sliding contact between two materials (e.g. metal to metal). Wear is promoted by a lack of lubrication and the presence of abrasive foreign matter (e.g. grit).

Lubrication prevents surface contact by separating them with a thick protective oil film under pressure (thick film lubrication) or by a thin layer of grease only a few molecules thick (boundary lubrication). Wear can be prevented either by maintaining lubrication and/or by choosing materials with compatible surface energies thereby reducing adhesion.

Abrasive wear can be reduced by the cleaning of surfaces, the keeping out or filtering of contaminant abrasives and the use of hard materials.

CREEP

Creep is most commonly found in plant and components which have been subjected to high temperatures such as gas turbines. The grains of the material slide over each other as time passes leading to excessive deformation or rupture. Essentially creep is plastic deformation which evolves with time.

Creep can be promoted with only minor variations in temperature. This can lead to drastically reduced component working life. A component with a 11 year life at 500ºC can be ruptured within an hour at 700ºC.

Measures to prevent creep include:

■ Temperature and stresses control in plant including the minimisation of thermal stresses (e.g. re-routing hot pipes).
■ Use of creep resistant materials (e.g. 1% chrome, ½ % molybdenum steel).
■ Regular inspection for cracks and signs of deformation such as bulges.
■ Maintenance - replacement of prone components.

Failure prevention strategies

The prevention of failures in materials depends on the:

■ Assessment of the foreseeable modes of failure under normal operating conditions.
■ The selection of appropriate materials and structural components.
■ The carrying out of appropriate design calculations and the incorporation of an appropriate factor of safety.
■ Manufacture using quality assurance techniques.
■ Installation that prevents damage and unplanned pre-stressing.
■ Determining an appropriate inspection, test and maintenance regime (including non-destructive testing and the use of fracture mechanics).
■ Avoiding alterations and ill conceived repairs.
■ Use within known and accepted limits.

METHODS OF IDENTIFYING POTENTIAL FAILURE MODES

Identifying potential failure modes

It is important that the designer understands and appreciates the conditions and use in the actual environment in which it is being used. For example, the fan blade fitted to the British Midland B737- 400 which crashed at Kegworth experienced flutter at altitude, a fact that had not been appreciated at the design and test stage. This led to catastrophic failure of the left engine when the blade snapped into the engine.

Use of fracture mechanics

Fracture mechanics is used to test the residual strength of materials which contain cracks or flaws. As stated previously there is a 'critical crack length' beyond which failure will result. For example, if a crack is observed during visual inspection of a pressure vessel, fracture mechanics can be used to predict the future development of the crack thus avoiding the need to scrap an expensive vessel. By knowing the crack's depth and length, the tensile strength of the material and the fluctuating pressures to which the vessel is subjected, the working life of the vessel can be predicted. Monitoring of the development of the crack serves to refine the model used and confirm its accuracy.

There are two techniques which can be used as a predictive tool:

■ Linear elastic fracture mechanics (LEFM).
■ General yielding fracture mechanics.

These techniques allow the working life of a component or system to be extended and minimise the risk of catastrophic failure. It is important to note that fracture mechanics do not deal with ductile failure, because this type of failure is not affected by cracks (unless they are huge!).

RELATED ENVIRONMENTAL FACTORS

The performance of a component or material is greatly influenced by the environment it is placed in. As can be seen by previous explanations of mode of failure, unsuitable materials placed in an offensive environment may be encouraged to fail. Examples given are simple forms of steel whose performance and ductility may be fine in a moderate temperature ambient at 200C but may fail in a brittle mode when put into service in the cold temperatures of the North Sea. Similarly, a steel sling used to lift hot forged items may be subject to long exposure to high temperature and the state of the material may become changed, leading to failure at a level below its rated safe working load. It is for this reason that materials suited to this environment need to be selected and in practice the sling may be assigned a *'working load limit'* below the usual safe working load when used in ambient temperatures of 200C.

Selection of materials

The selection of materials is therefore very important. For example, iron was commonly used for lifting chains. This has been replaced by high tensile steel because of the problem of work hardening and the expense of the annealing process that iron required in order to reduce the probability of brittle failure. As an added benefit, the factor of safety required to offset the fact that as the iron chains became work hardened they became brittle has been reduced through the use of high tensile steel chains.

Purpose of 'safety factors'

If a structure is designed to support three times its normally expected load then its *factor of safety* is 3. The purpose of safety factors is to allow for:

■ Sub-standard materials.
■ Poor quality workmanship.
■ Higher than expected loads.
■ Unusual/abnormal conditions.

This factor of safety is also called the *load factor* and is calculated by taking the normal maximum load to which the structure will be subjected and then multiplying by the factor of safety:

design load = normal maximum load x factor of safety

It should be noted that the safety factor does not represent a margin of spare capacity.

Role of testing

QUALITY ASSURANCE DURING MANUFACTURE AND INSTALLATION

ISO 9000 requires that:

■ Suppliers are to establish and maintain documented procedures to ensure that purchased product conforms to specified requirements.

■ Suppliers are to establish and maintain documented procedures for inspection and testing activities in order to verify that the specified requirements for the product are met.

■ That the required inspection and testing and the records to be established be detailed in the quality plan and documented procedures.

■ Suppliers ensure that incoming product is not used or processed (except in specific circumstances) until it has been inspected or tested or otherwise verified as conforming to specified requirements and requires that verification be in accordance with the quality plan or documented procedures.

■ When determining the amount and nature of receiving inspection, consideration should be given to the control exercised at the subcontractor's* premises and recorded evidence of conformance required.

■ Where incoming product is released for urgent production purposes, prior to verification, it shall be positively identified and recorded in order to permit immediate recall and replacement in the event of non-conformance to specified requirements.

■ The supplier to inspect, test and identify product as required by the quality plan or documented procedures.

■ The supplier is to hold product until the required inspection and tests have been received and verified except when product is released under positive recall procedures.

■ The supplier is to arrange for the protection of the quality of the product after final inspection and test and, where contractually specified, this protection shall extend to include delivery to destination.

* It should be noted that the term subcontractor is defined under ISO 9000-2 as an organisation that provides products (including services) to the supplier.

In addition where servicing is a specified requirement (e.g. vehicles, washing machines or a photocopier), then the supplier must establish and maintain documented procedures for performing these services.

TESTING DURING MANUFACTURE AND INSTALLATION

Final inspection and testing can have three main forms:

1. An inspection carried out on completion of the product.

2. A last inspection carried out prior to dispatch.

3. A last inspection the supplier carries out prior to transfer of ownership to the customer.

Final inspection should include ensuring that previous inspections and tests have been carried out and that the as-built configuration is the same as the issue status of all parts, sub assemblies etc. specified by the design standard. The inspection record must clearly show whether the product has passed or failed inspections and/or tests according to the defined acceptance criteria. Non-conforming products must be controlled to ensure that they are not used. Therefore they must be clearly identified and segregated to ensure this.

Inspection, measuring and test equipment used for inspection and test purposes must be controlled, calibrated and maintained. Similarly gauges, tools, jigs etc. must be verified to ensure accuracy. The aim of inspection and testing is to ensure that the product complies with specified requirements. The principle behind this is that inspection and test does not control quality but merely measures achieved quality in order to give the producer information for remedial action.

The trend in systems where materials failure is critical is towards a regime of written systems of inspection (examination) and test. Examples include pressure systems *(see also - '5.9 Pressure systems' - later in this element)* and lifting equipment. Here a system is broken down into its component parts and subjected to a routine of inspections and tests depending on its failure modes. Previous incidents, such as the hoist accident at Littlebrook 'D' Power Station and the crane accident at Brent Cross, and failures should be taken into account when determining the nature and frequency of such inspections and tests - as should the lessons learnt during the systems life. Perhaps the best example of this philosophy is in the aircraft industry where the identification of a failed component in one airframe can lead to the grounding of all of that type of aircraft world wide.

Forensic examination of failed components

Failed components can be forensically examined in order to determine the modes and causes of failure. The first consideration must be to ensure that evidence is not contaminated during any inspection or removal process and to ensure that the examination takes place quickly enough so that significant further corrosion etc. does not take place. Careful visual examination, possibly with the aid of a magnifying glass or low power microscope, can reveal much about the mode of failure. The following table considers the indicators that point towards failure modes.

Mode	Possible indicators
Tensile fracture	Local 'necking' or extension and decrease in sectional area in direction of load.
Shear fracture	Friction marks with a new-moon shaped gap on the unloaded side of a bolt etc.
Brittle failure	Clean break with no signs of necking. Surface has coarse, angular appearance with 'chevron' markings pointing back to the starting point.
Wear	Shiny new appearance, pitting and fretting of components
Corrosion	Pitting, colour changes (e.g. rust & tarnishing).
Fatigue crack	'Beach' marks

Figure C5-27: Failure modes.

Source: ACT.

Failure modes and prevention in relation to major incidents

See also – Vapour phase explosions Flixborough – Element 2

BRENT CROSS - 20 JUNE 1964

Facts

The jib on a 15 ton mobile crane failed and fell onto a passing coach killing seven passengers and injuring a further thirty two. At the time of the accident the crane was erecting a larger scotch derrick crane.

Background

The crane was manufactured by Sheds Engineering Products Ltd which was later to become the British Crane and Excavator Corporation Ltd (BCEC). The crane was a 15 ton mobile crane with a maximum safe working load (SWL) of 12.5 tons working with the minimum jib radius of 10 ft. This was reduced to 7.5 tons SWL with an 80 ft jib and 15 ft radius. The load factor/ margin of safety was 1.6. The jib was designed to withstand stresses induced by:

- Acceleration/deceleration of slewing motion.
- Wind pressure on the side of the jib.

The Road Traffic Act had been amended to allow a maximum allowable overhang of any crane of 6 ft. In order to comply the crane was fitted with a gate section (like a giant hinge) enabling the head and heel sections of the jib to fold back one against the other, and bringing the overhang to within the maximum 6 ft allowed.

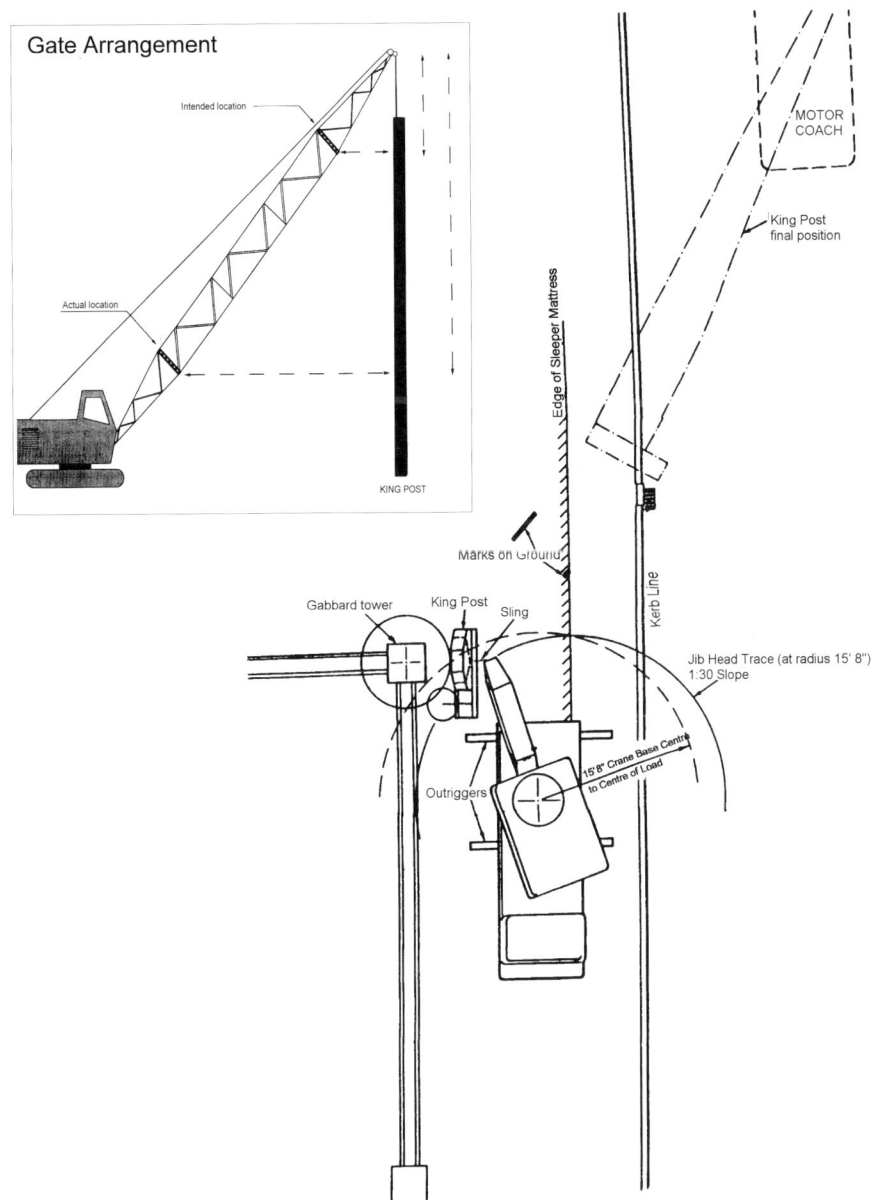

Figure C5-28: Crane failure at Brent Cross.   *Source: Ambiguous.*

The gate was designed by BCEC. The design calculations were destroyed; however the designer considered that two limitations should be incorporated into the use of the gate:

1. It should always be inserted next to the head section.

2. It should not be used with a jib longer than 40 ft plus the gate.

However no note of these considerations exists and the instructions were not communicated. The gate was made by Steels Process Plants Ltd, a subsidiary of BCEC.

The gate was designed to be fitted with 12 lugs:

- 4 rectangular 1 ¾" thick (no. 236667).
- 8 triangular - 1" thick (no. 236668).

During fabrication all 12 lugs were fabricated to the 1" triangular design (no. 236668). The thickness error was detected for the missing 4 x 1 ¾" lugs, however the shape was not. Thus 4 thicker 1 ¾" lugs were locally manufactured by Steels to a triangular shape - rather than the rectangular shape that the design called for.

The designer's specification of rectangular lugs was necessary to deal with the compressive forces within the jib. By using triangular lugs, the scissor-action created when the jib extended was over done on one side making the jib slightly out of skew.

BCEC did not fit the gate themselves. A service engineer fitted the gate next to the heel section, adjusted the radius indicator but did not otherwise recalibrate the crane nor was it subjected to a test.

The head and heel sections were 15 ft each which, together with the main section, brought the overall length of the jib to just over 80ft. The crane was lifting a king post which was estimated to weigh 6 ½ tons but actually weighed 7 tons 17 cwt. The safe working load of the jib length (82' 9") and at the assumed working radius (15' 8") was 7.5 tons. The actual radius was 19'.

The terrain did not permit the crane to face the lift - it was sited alongside and had to work over-side. The crane was sited on a 1:30 slope. The mis-manufacture of the gate resulted in lateral bending stresses in the jib. Had the gate been fitted next to the head section, then the bending forces would have been less than a quarter of those on the lower position. The jib failed and fell onto a passing coach killing seven passengers and injuring a further thirty-two.

Key factors

- Incorrect manufacture of the gate (wrong lugs, wrong shape of lugs).
- Incorrect positioning of the gate.
- Failure to inspect.
- Failure to test.
- Failure to notify designer's limitations on use to the user.
- Crane was operating on a 1:30 slope.
- Estimated weight of load was wrong.
- SWL exceeded.
- The safe load indicator was defective.

LITTLEBROOK D POWER STATION - 09 JANUARY 1978

Facts

Several contractors were involved in the construction of the Littlebrook 'D' power station in Dartford Kent on behalf of the Central Electricity Generating Board. One sub-contractor Edmund Nuttall Ltd (Nuttalls) was given the job of constructing the shafts and tunnel as part of the cooling system. Access to the two tunnels involved was via a hoist fitted in each of the two access shafts. On 9 January 1978 a single suspension rope of one of the hoist cages, in which nine men were travelling, broke. The safety gear failed to operate and the cage plunged more then 30m (100 ft) to the bottom of a 60m (200 ft) shaft. Four men were killed and five were seriously injured.

Key factors

- The hoist's suspension rope broke at a part weakened by corrosion and lacking lubrication. Later examination showed that a length of about 35m of the rope was completely devoid of lubricant and very corroded both internally and externally with many of its wires broken. Tests indicated that at the fracture all the wires had lost 50% of their tensile strength and the outer wires had lost 80%. It was also estimated that at the fracture position there was a loss in breaking strength of approximately 80% before the final fracture occurred.
- The deterioration took place over a relatively short period of time and was not detected.
- Analysis of the water in the shaft showed that it contained salt and the corrosion was consistent with the rope having been impregnated with salt water.
- Both clamping units of the cage safety mechanism were found to be corroded and coated with hard, cement like, material that prevented them from working.

Contributory factors

- The statutory six monthly examination of the hoist was overdue.
- The weekly site inspection had failed to record any defects.
- The maximum load for the hoist was eight passengers.
- The maintenance of the cage safety mechanism had been inadequate to maintain it in good working order in the environment to which it had been exposed.

The subsequent HSE investigation could not establish the exact pattern of routine maintenance on the hoist or if the hoist had been maintained in accordance with the manufacturer's (ACE Machinery Ltd) instructions since the operator (Nuttalls) kept no records. Many defects in Nuttalls' safety management system were noted (including policy, inspection, maintenance, training, resources and monitoring).

As a result of the investigation it was shown that similar hoists were defective. All known users were advised of the need to perform a free-fall (drop) test. One of the key recommendations of the investigation was that all rope suspended passenger hoists should be suspended by at least two ropes. In addition it was concluded that prototype testing of the maximum number of drop tests which types of safety gear may undergo before requiring replacement should be established.

(See diagram - next page)

General layout of shaft hoist and tunnel

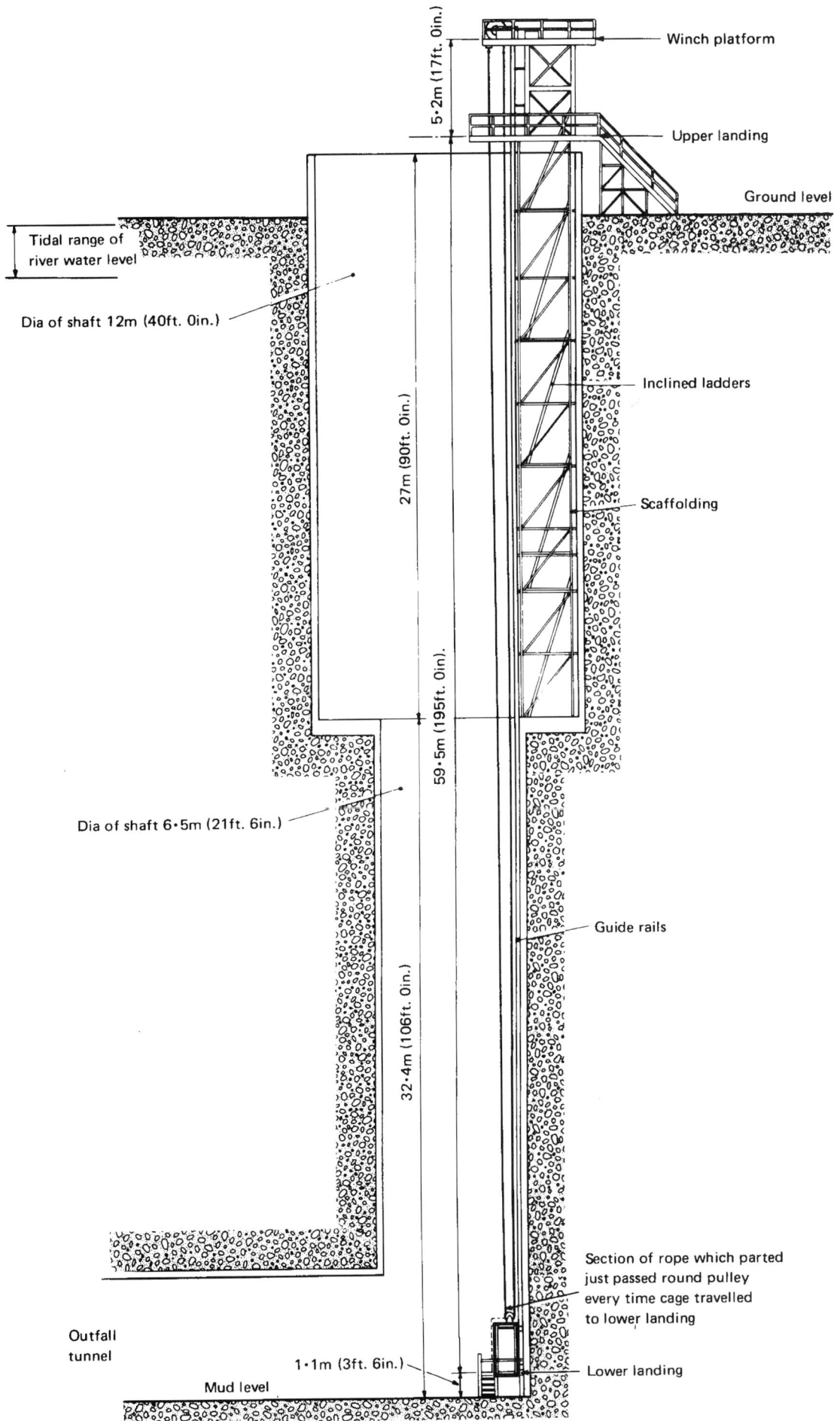

Figure C5-29: General layout of shaft hoist and tunnel.

Source: The hoist accident at Littlebrook 'D' Power Station, HSE Books.

MARKHAM COLLIERY - 30 JULY 1973

Facts

The day shift was being lowered at No. 3 upcast shaft at Markham Colliery, Derbyshire on 30 July 1973. A double deck cage containing 29 men crashed to the wooden baulks at the pit bottom killing 18 men and seriously injuring another 11.

The accident occurred due to an overwind. The ascending cage rose until it struck the roof girders of the airlock structure fracturing the surrounding concrete and brickwork. As there were no safety catches in the headframe, the cage then dropped back until it was hanging by its suspension chains from the detaching hook. The engineman applied the brake lever and 'saw some sparks under the brake cylinder' and heard a bang. The brake lever seemed to have little effect so he pressed the emergency stop button expecting to see the drum brought to a sudden stop but nothing happened.

The descending cage carrying the 29 men struck pit bottom with such force that it fractured 9 of the 17 of the wooden baulks (the speed of impact was estimated to be 27 miles per hour). Although power had been cut off before the crash, the momentum of the winding system unwound the spare coils of overlap rope and then the metal loop, with part of the drum side and brake path was torn away. The rope and loop were pulled over the headgear pulley and then fell down the shaft on top of and along side the cage containing the men. The drum continued to rotate and the flailing loop of the underlap rope seriously damaged the winding engine house and an adjoining workshop. The subsequent investigation found that:

1. There was a complete failure of the winding engine brake - the centre rod in the spring nest had broken.

2. The centre rod appeared to have failed due to fatigue.

The investigators fitted four strain gauges at 90° to each other to a replacement centre rod as near as possible to the position where the fracture occurred in the original rod. These tests showed that, in addition to tensile stresses at the gauge positions, there were substantial stresses due to bending when the brake was operated. The gauges at right angles to the winding drum indicated that the magnitude of stresses varied to such an extent that on the one furthest from the drum there was a change from tension to compression as the brake was released.

Later metallurgical examination of the spring nest showed that it had failed because of fatigue. There was evidence that three small cracks had existed for some time and had propagated to a depth of 1.1 inches before the rod broke. Numerous additional small cracks existed both above and below the fracture. These were found in the laboratory by magnetic particle inspection. Experiments showed that these small cracks would not have been revealed by an ultrasonic probe; however, this method would have detected the much larger cracks (of ~ 3/8 " depth).

The centre rod was made from good quality carbon steel. The ultimate tensile strength of the material was 38 tonf/in2 and the mean tensile stress induced by the spring nest at the minimum cross section was 6.2 tonf/ in2. Consequently the static factor of safety was 6.1. The investigation, however, revealed that the bending and alternating stresses with an amplitude of ± 6.6 tonf/ in2 were superimposed on the tensile stress. These stresses meant that the failure of the rod was inevitable. The centre rod which was 8 ft 11 7/8 in (2.74m) long and 2" (51 mm) in diameter had been in service for 21 years.

The investigation also showed that winding enginemen were trained 'on the job' and used different operating techniques which were inconsistent methods of controlling the gear.

Key factors

1. No provision had been made for non-destructive testing of the centre rod in the spring nest.

2. The centre rod was a 'single line' component and the safety of the cage was completely dependent upon it.

3. A similar rod had broken in Ollerton Colliery in January 1961. This was attributed to induced stresses. The subsequent instruction to examine centre rods did not give any guidance as to the nature and frequency of examinations or the use of NDT.

4. Ultrasonic tests, which can be carried out in situ, would have revealed large cracks (~3/8 inch depth) but would not have detected the small cracks in the rod. The probability of detecting the crack which led to failure using ultrasonic methods would therefore have depended on its rate of propagation and the interval between tests.

Recommendations

The investigation recommended that:

1. All winding engines be examined and modified.

2. Winding engines should not rely on 'single line' components or, if this is not possible, they be modified, operated and maintained so as to prevent danger.

3. Appropriate ndt testing be carried out on all safety critical components.

4. A design analysis, including an assessment of the working life of components, be carried out.

5. Control systems be reviewed to ensure that electrical braking be available after the initiation of an emergency or automatic trip device.

6. All solid landings in shafts be replaced by suitable arresting devices.

7. The training and examination of winding enginemen be reviewed and an operation manual be prepared.

8. Every winding engine which can attain a speed in excess of 7 ft/sec be provided with a rope speed indicator.

PORT RAMSGATE - SEPTEMBER 1994

Facts

At 0045 on 14 September 1994 a passenger walkway at Port Ramsgate collapsed killing six passengers and seriously injuring seven more.

In the collapse, one end of the walkway fell 10 metres, embedding itself in the deck of the pontoon that had provided the floating seaward support for the structure.

HSE's investigation established that the immediate cause of the collapse was the failure of a weld in a safety-critical support element of the structure. Further investigation revealed gross deficiencies in the design which would have ensured failure of safety-critical elements within a fairly short part of the structure's lifespan. HSE established that the collapsed walkway was of unique design and that similar risks of collapse did not exist at other British ferry ports.

The technical deficiencies arose from the failure of various parties involved in the procurement, design and installation of the walkway to manage the project effectively and in particular to carry out any reasonable risk assessment of the project.

The problem was that there was no allowance made for roll in the design, and the bearings were assumed to be able to accommodate torsion. This led to the bearings being under-designed. The independent, external checkers did not notice this problem. Other factors, such as the leaving out of some of the greasomatics, and problems during construction, accentuated the problem and speeded up the disaster. The constant swaying motion that the sea put on the bearings and welds of the walkway gradually caused a fatigue failure.

Background

The following is taken from "The Collapse of the Ramsgate Walkway" by J C Chapman.

The life of ship to shore structures is related more closely to the life of a ship, about 20 years, than to the notional 120 years of a highway bridge. Yet the operating conditions of ship-to-shore structures are exceptionally onerous. The support system must accommodate the tidal range, wave effects, and occasional ship impact. Large horizontal movements must also be accommodated.

A single-tier vehicle linkspan, supported at the seaward end on a pontoon had been operating at Ramsgate for several years. Transverse inclination (roll), caused by waves, wind, or eccentric loading was assumed (in accordance with common practice) to be accommodated by the torsional compliance of the linkspan.

When Belgian ferries were relocated to Ramsgate, a second linkspan was required above the existing one. The seaward end was supported on a portal frame erected on the pontoon, which had been designed for that possibility. A covered walkway was also required so that foot passengers could board without interrupting the flow of vehicles. The seaward end of the walkway span was supported on a cantilever platform on the outside of the portal frame. The shore end was supported within an aperture in the passenger access building.

The existing pontoon and vehicle linkspan were designed, fabricated and constructed by an experienced and respected firm of naval architects and engineers. The contract was for a design-and-build. They were certified by Lloyds Register. Similar arrangements were adopted for the new walkway and linkspan.

The walkway consisted of box section trusses with 6mm steel plate roof, lower sides and floor cladding welded to the trusses and cross members. This made the walkway very stiff, flexurally and torsionally. The shore bearings were steel plates with low friction pads attached. The bearings could slide on steel plates fixed to the web of channel sections, between the upstanding flanges. The slide clearance enabled the walkway to rotate about a vertical axis. The bearing was attached by vertical brackets to tubes within which stub axles, projecting transversely from the end of the walkway structure could rotate. The axles were welded within the central bore of vertical discs, which were site welded to the walkway structure. The seaward bearings were of similar design, but the right hand bearing had a vertical pin projecting downwards through the horizontal plate of the cantilever platform. Vertical movement was limited by a welded collar. This all meant that the articulation system allowed for the three translatory freedoms of the pontoon and two of the rotational freedoms, but there was no allowance for roll, which could be accommodated only by a bearing lifting from its seating, as was observed in service.

Key facts

At 0045, while passengers were boarding a ferry, the seaward end of the main walkway span dropped without warning, about 10m to the pontoon deck. The violent deceleration on impact caused the death of six passengers and serious injuries to seven others. The walkway had been in service for only 4 months. There were no unusual external circumstances

The right hand seaward bearing, including the axle remained on the platform being retained by the pin. The welds connecting the axle to the disc had fractured. The left hand seaward bearing struck the deck and was propelled into the dock. The walkway structure itself was intact.

As part of the certification procedure, the walkway had been tested under the design loading, without apparent damage. One month before the accident the walkway had been inspected by the insurers' inspector, who had been trained to inspect ship-to-shore structures; he had found nothing wrong.

HSE took the bearings and part of the support platform for examination. Calculations made by the designer/installation contractors and by Lloyds Register were also examined.

HSE found that the welded connection of the axle of the right hand seaward bearing to the disc had failed in fatigue, thereby detaching the walkway from the bearing. The connection of the left hand seaward axle had failed largely in fatigue, and final fracture had occurred when the bearing hit the pontoon deck. Both shore axles had extensive fatigue cracking but were still connected. This confirmed that an incident during construction involving the right hand seaward bearing was not the cause of failure, because when the incident occurred the shore bearings were not loaded. The lubrication of the axles was deficient, partly through poor design and partly because some automatic lubricating devices had not been fitted.

The prime cause became apparent from the calculations of the designers and checkers. Both had independently made the same conceptual mistake.

Instead of calculating the axle moment at the weld connecting the axle to the disc, they assumed the moment to be zero. They had designed on the basis of shear alone. A smaller but still major error was the assumption that all four reactions were equal, notwithstanding the rotational movement of the pontoon and the large torsional stiffness of the structure.

The bearings were not fabricated in the same factory as the structure and the drawings were separate. There were no assembly drawings, and this could have increased the risk of incorrect design assumptions.

Nothing new was learnt about the technical causes but there can be benefits from the lessons of this tragic incident. Those who could learn from this include client organisations and others who initiate structural projects, designers, manufacturers, contractors, operators and those who approve or verify such projects. HSE has published a report to draw attention to a set of circumstances in which large organisations with professional and technically well qualified staff allowed a series of errors to lead to disaster. These are summarised below:

HSE brought legal proceedings against Port Ramsgate, the operating company, Fartygsentreprenader AB (FEAB) Fartygskonstructioner AB (FKAB), the designers/installation contractors, and Lloyds Register of Shipping, the independent approval organisation. Lloyds Register pleaded guilty, the Port of Ramsgate pleaded not guilty and the Swedish contractors did not plead and did not attend. All parties were charged under the Health and Safety at Work etc Act and Port Ramsgate were also charged under the Docks Regulations. (CDM was not in force at the time). All parties were found guilty. The fines, a total of £1.25m, a record at the time, were in proportion of 5:2:1 to FEAB FKAB, Lloyds Register and Port Ramsgate. Costs to HSE of £713,000 were divided approximately equally. It has not been possible to recover the fines and costs from the Swedish contractors as they have gone bankrupt.

Consideration was given by the Crown Prosccution Service to manslaughter proceedings, but responsibility for the failings which caused the incident was divided between so many individuals and organisations that no clear case could be established against any of them.

Non-destructive testing

The principle of non-destructive testing (NDT) is to test the integrity of materials without causing damage in the process. Many of the techniques used rely on considerable skill and experience by the operator and rely on tests being carried out at appropriate intervals. Personnel carrying out inspection/s in relation to NDT must be properly trained and qualified.

Most NDT methods will only detect surface flaws (patent defects). Radiography used to carry out an internal inspection is very effective however in identifying sub-surface flaws (latent defects); it exposes operators to other dangers which must be considered.

NDT is used by manufacturers to:

- Ensure product integrity and reliability.
- Prevent failure and accidents, and save lives.
- Make profit for users.
- Ensure customer satisfaction.
- Aide better product design.

- Control manufacturing processes.
- Lower manufacturing costs.
- Maintain uniform quality level.
- Ensure operational readiness.

The selection of the most appropriate NDT method for a particular component depends on a number of factors such as:

- Material of construction.
- Thickness of section.
- Type of defect to be detected.

- Cost Inspection equipment available.
- Operator skill Level of inspection.

NDT TECHNIQUES SUITABLE FOR SURFACE DEFECTS

- Visual inspection.
- Liquid penetrant inspection.
- Magnetic particle inspection.
- Eddy current testing.

Visual inspection

Visual inspection involves direct or indirect inspecting for *surface* condition, defects, roughness and/or dimensional changes.

Despite many other more sophisticated NDT techniques, visual inspection plays an important role in the detection of surface flaws and damage. This can be done unaided or with the use of a microscope. Some signs of damage may be obvious (e.g. pitting and large surface cracks) but some are not (e.g. an increase of 1 mm in a 125 mm diameter tube may indicate imminent creep rupture).

Advantages

- A fast, cheap and relatively simple means of surface inspection.

Disadvantages

- Dependant upon the eyesight of the inspector; therefore regular eyesight tests for both visual acuity and colour differentiation are essential.
- Time for continuous viewing must be restricted with frequent rests to reduce fatigue.

Source: www.azom.com. NDT - Surface Examination Techniques.

Typical applications

Weld inspection -

- Verification of correct weld preparation.
- Inspection for surface defects, e.g. undercuts and cracks.
- Verification of completed weld profile (cap, root).

Condition monitoring in service -

- Detection of corrosion.
- Detection of defects and cracks.

Metrology -

- Measurement of component geometry.
- Measurement of surface roughness.

Etch inspection -

- Detection of grinding defects.
- Detection of incorrect heat treatment (case depth).
- Metallographic examination (weld profile, inclusions grain size, microstructure).

Visual inspection has many techniques to aid the operator and extend its capability.

- Lighting must be at an appropriate level and of the correct type.
- Magnifiers, from low power, x2 to x5, hand held lenses to high power microscopes.
- Borescopes are devices that permit inspection of internal surfaces in piping, engines, air frames etc. They contain systems of lenses, mirrors, prisms and lighting which illuminates the test area and transmits images to the inspector. They may be either rigid or flexible. The flexible type uses optical fibres, the smallest have outside diameters of just a few millimetres and can be steered into position around tight bends.
- Television cameras combined with borescopes, video recorders and image processing equipment permit the remote collection and storage of visual images. This permits inspection in difficult and hazardous sites, e.g. nuclear installations and underwater pipelines. Image enhancement by computer is also possible.
- Surface replication using strippable films also permits the remote inspection of surfaces.
- Etching for metallographic examination and to reveal cracks, inclusions and localised variations in composition and hardness.

Source: www.azom.com. NDT - Surface Examination Techniques.

Liquid penetrant inspection

Liquid penetrant inspection enhances visual inspection for ***surface*** flaws by the use of liquid dyes on any non-absorbent material's surface. A brightly coloured or fluorescent liquid is applied to a component surface and allowed to penetrate any surface-breaking cracks or cavities. After soaking (approximately 20 minutes), the excess liquid penetrant is wiped away from the surface and a developer applied. The developer draws penetrant out of any cracks by reverse capillary action to produce indications on the surface. These (coloured) indications are broader than the actual flaw and are therefore more easily visible. The types of defect that can be detected using this method include: cracks, porosity, seams and laps (defects highlighted in the surface) and leak detection (because the dye seeps out of cracks etc.). Dyes include:

- Low viscosity oil and chalk.
- Brilliant dye penetrants.
- Water washable fluorescent penetrants.

The surface of the test piece must be clean and undisturbed; can be used on both ferrous and non-ferrous metals.

Advantages

- The method has high sensitive to small surface discontinuities.
- The method has few material limitations, i.e. metallic and nonmetallic, magnetic and nonmagnetic, conductive and nonconductive materials may be inspected.
- Large areas and large volumes of parts/materials can be inspected rapidly and at low cost.
- Parts with complex geometric shapes are routinely inspected.
- Indications are produced directly on the surface of the part and constitute a visual representation of the flaw.
- Aerosol spray cans make penetrant materials very portable.
- Penetrant materials and associated equipment are relatively inexpensive.

Disadvantages

- Only surface breaking defects can be detected.
- Only materials with a relative nonporous surface can be inspected.
- Precleaning is critical as contaminants can mask defects.
- Metal smearing from machining, grinding and grit or vapor blasting must be removed prior to LPI.
- The inspector must have direct access to the surface being inspected.
- Surface finish and roughness can affect inspection sensitivity.
- The contact time between the penetrant and the test surface is important and must not be too short.
- Excess penetrant can be removed carelessly (I.e. from flaws as well as from the test surface).
- Multiple process operations must be performed and controlled.
- Post cleaning of acceptable parts or materials is required.
- Chemical handling and proper disposal is required

Source: www.corrosion-doctors.org (Liquid Penetrant).

Typical applications

Liquid penetrant inspection is used in a number of industries. The aerospace industry use automated fluorescent penetrant testing to look for fatigue cracking in turbine blades; the construction industry uses dye penetrant testing as a quick and simple method for checking that welds and other susceptible areas are free from surface-breaking flaws.

Magnetic particle inspection

An electromagnetic test method which provides for the detection of ***surface and near surface*** discontinuities in ferro-magnetic materials.

A magnetic field is induced in the test piece and a suitable medium (e.g. iron filings mixed with paraffin) is sprinkled on the surface. Defects are indicated by anomalies in the distribution of these particles. In order to aid detection the particles are often florescent when placed under ultraviolet light. The types of defect that can be detected using this method include: cracks, laps, seams, voids, pits and subsurface holes.

Advantages

- Test method is quick and simple.
- Highly sensitive to the detection of surface and slightly subsurface indications.
- Test method process may often work through contaminant layers and coating thickness.

Disadvantages

- Test material may be ferrous.
- Will not detect deep internal flaws.
- High currents applied to components may cause damage.
- Demagnetisation is often necessary after inspection.

Source: www.msb.intnet.mu/MSB/MSBHome.usf (Non-Destructive Testing).

Typical application: small steel forgings for use in safety-critical applications which need to be inspected for surface and near surface flaws which might propagate in service. Magnetic particle testing is widely used for this type of application since, in addition to offering adequate sensitivity to defects, the technique can be mechanised for volume production.

Eddy current testing

The most widely used and best-known of the electromagnetic methods is Eddy current testing. This method can be used on electrically conductive materials for detecting and characterising defects such as **surface and near surface** cracks, gouges and voids. It can also be used to verify a material's heat treat condition. In addition, wall thickness of thin wall tubing and thickness of conductive and non-conductive coatings on materials can also be determined using this method.

Defects are detected by observing the distribution of an electro-magnetic field flowing through the test piece. A search coil is moved over the material's surface. Any impedance changes in the coil could indicate the presence of a flaw.

Advantages

- High speed testing (can be automated).
- Accurate measuring of conductivity.
- Discontinuities at or near surface can be reliably detected.
- High-sensitivity to small discontinuities.
- Accurate coating thickness measurements.
- Direct go/no go answers can be quickly obtained.
- No physical contact required.
- Low cost.
- Portable.

Disadvantages

- Limited penetration into test article.
- Several variables simultaneously affect output indication.
- Discontinuities are qualitative not quantitative indications.
- Material must be conductive.
- Requires skill when many variables are involved.
- False indications can result from edge effects and parts geometry.

Source: NASA Preferred Reliability Practices, Practice No. PT-TE-1421.

Typical applications

The inspection of metal wires for surface and near surface defects at high speeds and high temperatures. During the manufacture of steel wire of speeds up to 100 m/s, it is necessary to feed back information on wire quality to the control station as quickly as possible so that actions can be taken before several thousand metres have been processed. An Eddy current inspection technique using a small coil probe is able to detect significant flaws, during the high speed inspection, even at wire surface temperatures of 1200°C.

NDT TECHNIQUES SUITABLE FOR SUB-SURFACE DEFECTS

- Radiography.
- Ultrasonic testing.

Radiography

Internal defects are highlighted by transmitting **X-rays or gamma rays** through a material to a film on the opposite side of the test-piece. These rays are highly penetrating and are used to expose the film which records the intensity of the radiation which it has received. As cracks and other flaws are hollow, these show as dark patches on the radiograph.

Used on both ferrous and non-ferrous materials; the types of defect that can be detected using this method are: porosity, slag inclusions in welds, tungsten inclusions, lack of fusion or penetration, forging laps and cracks (although this method is not particularly suitable for the latter).

Neutron radiography is another technique for photographing the interior structure of solid objects. Whereas X-rays cannot discriminate between materials of similar density; neutrons, on the other hand, can interact quite differently with materials of similar density and thus give a complementary view to that of X-rays.

Advantages

- Can be used with most materials.
- Discloses fabrication errors.
- Reveals structural discontinuities.
- Provides a permanent visual image.

Disadvantages

- High safety considerations.
- Specimen needs to be accessed on at least two sides.
- Difficult on complex geometry.

Source: www.msb.intnet.mu/MSB/MSBHome.usf (Non-Destructive Testing).

Typical applications

Radiography is important for ensuring that any welds are free of defects. *(X-ray radiography)* - used extensively in the testing of aircraft structures and components, welded assemblies, pressure vessels and piping, electronic circuitry, bridge girders, and similar materials. *(Gamma ray radiography)* - pipelines, bridge and building fabrications, pressure vessels, large forgings and castings, and armoured vehicle components. *(Neutron radiography)* - the testing of nuclear reactor fuel, detecting of hydrogenous materials, detecting of flaws in gas turbine blades and corrosion of aircraft components, quality control of ceramics, detecting of explosive charges, and detecting of the presence of lubrication films inside gear boxes or bearings.

Ultrasonic testing

Ultrasound is defined as (sound) waves at frequencies beyond the upper limit that the human ear can detect (i.e. above 20 kHz). An ultrasonic probe is used to detect cracks in a test-piece. This sends ultrasonic waves into the metal and picks up reflections from the internal boundaries within the metal. These reflected waves are normally observed on a screen with any flaws represented as 'blips'. Angled probes are used to more accurately locate cracks.

The types of defect that can be detected using this method include: cracks, misalignment, porosity, inclusions, surface conditions and pitting.

Advantages

- High sensitivity which permits detection of minute defects.
- High penetrating power (6-7 metres in steel).
- High accuracy of flaw positioning and sizing.
- Needs only one to one surface of the specimen.

Disadvantages

- Complex geometry of the test specimen causes problems during inspection.
- Defect orientation affects detection ability.

Source: www.msb.intnet.mu/MSB/MSBHome.usf (Non-Destructive Testing).

Typical application: in the aerospace and nuclear industries. Large airframe and rocket fuselage sections made up from fibre reinforced composites and honeycomb structures are examined using sequenced multi-probe equipment under computer control and operating to dimensional accuracies and repeatability in the order of one micron.

OTHER NDT TECHNIQUES

- *Acoustic methods* including: acoustic emission, tap testing, acoustic-ultrasonic testing and acoustic microsopy.
- *Electromagnetic methods* including: magnetic flux leakage, magnetograpgy, nuclear magnetic resonance, electric current testing, corona-discharge testing, potential drop testing, dielectric testing, and microwave-radiation testing.
- *Leak-test methods* including: tracer-gas leak detection, pressure-change testing, vacuum-system tests, bubble-leak detection and acoustic leak-testing.
- Hydrostatic and pneumatic testing.
- Cryogenic testing.
- Tensile tests.
- Hardness, impact and manipulating tests.
- Corrosion tests.
- Brittle (coating) laquer testing.
- Strain-gauge testing.
- Electrical resistivity.
- Thermography.
- Holography.

Note: other sources of information, besides ACT, for the above section on non-destructive testing include Kempe's Engineers Year-Book 2001, published by United Business Media.

5.6 - Maintenance

COMMON HAZARDS AND PRECAUTIONS ASSOCIATED WITH MAINTENANCE WORK

Many of the investigated process maintenance incidents were identified as due to lack of, or failure of, permit-to-work systems. These circumstances point to the need for greater attention being paid by management to checking the use of the permit systems.

Maintenance operations require careful consideration if they are to be undertaken without undue risk. More effort is needed by management and workers to control the substantial hazards that are inherent in maintenance operations.

In many of the investigated maintenance incidents the method of work used for the job was itself inherently unsafe and needed to be radically altered before work could be safely carried out. Procedures for handling likely plant failures or breakdown situations must be considered in advance so that the risks are controlled and minimised. Pre-planning of routine maintenance procedures could reduce the number of incidents and accidents.

A safe system of work is required for any maintenance activities which involve the removal of guards. Where the maintenance work involves access into the machine, this system should include a lock-off procedure. A safe system of work is a method of doing a job which eliminates identified hazards, controls others and plans to achieve the controlled completion of the work with minimum risk. A safe system of work may include a range of precautions from simple lock-off procedures and protective equipment through to a full written permit-to-work. It requires a systematic, imaginative analysis of the job and its hazards. The analysis should be practical and incorporate lessons learned from past experience

The following examples are features of safe working practices that reduce the risk of maintenance work:

- Isolation (e.g. disconnected or with fuses or keys removed).
- Isolation of equipment and pipelines containing pressurised gas, fluid, steam or hazardous substances. Isolating valves should be locked off and the system depressurised where possible, particularly if access to dangerous parts will be needed.
- Allowing moving equipment to stop.
- Supporting parts of equipment which could fall.
- Allowing components which operate at high temperatures time to cool.
- The switching off of mobile equipment, gear box in neutral, applying brakes and, where necessary, checking wheels.
- Cleaning of vessels that have contained flammable solids, liquids, gases or dusts and monitoring prior to hot work being carried out.

MAINTENANCE STRATEGIES

Two basic strategies are applied in maintenance. The first is the one that ensures that when a component comes to the end of its life this has the minimum impact on what surrounds it e.g. safety, productivity.

It is widely accepted that a maintenance strategy based solely on repair at the time of component breakdown is neither efficient nor effective. Its main advantage is the fact that it is fairly transparent that maintenance is required when components are broken. This then ensures no effort is wasted replacing parts that have some life left in them. This approach would also be unacceptable on health and safety grounds if a significant risk would arise from the failure of the component. This does not mean that this type of maintenance is unacceptable in all circumstances. Indeed some effort is being applied to maximise on this technique by the study of modes of failure and the classification of the failure on a risk basis. In conjunction with this is the design of equipment that fails to safety, thus allowing the use of breakdown maintenance techniques. The only other issue is the efficient replacement of the component. Once again considerable effort is going into the design of equipment that makes maintenance easy to conduct.

The other important strategy in maintenance is the one that maximises on the life of the component/equipment. This is done by a number of maintenance methods, planned, preventative, and monitored. The planned method seeks to inspect and replace components on a scheduled basis. Preventative maintenance seeks to take action which tries to keep the condition of the component at its best by carrying out frequent care of the component e.g. lubrication, adjustment, cleaning. Monitored maintenance seeks to monitor the conditions of components determining the point just before failure, at which point it would be replaced.

Maintenance often uses a blend of all methods and strategies in order to gain best results. Planned maintenance is frequently done by a specialist at intervals in the life of equipment; preventative maintenance is conducted frequently (each day or similar) by a non-specialist (operator); and monitored maintenance is particularly useful towards the end of its life and is conducted by specialists.

Although all maintenance is preventive in some respect, the primary aim of planned preventive maintenance is to prevent failures occurring while the equipment is in use.

When inadequate maintenance could cause the equipment, guards or other protection devices to fail in a dangerous way, a formal system of planned preventive maintenance may be necessary. A system of planned preventative maintenance could be introduced on a risk basis, highest risk equipment being done first. Over a period of time all equipment could be brought under the scheme. Thus if an item of equipment should fail on an unplanned basis this should be seen as an equipment based accident and may be investigated on the same basis as other accidents.

Breakdown maintenance involves carrying out maintenance only after faults or failures have occurred. It is appropriate only if the failure does not present an immediate risk and can be corrected before risk occurs, for example, through effective fault reporting and maintenance schemes.

Planned preventative maintenance involves replacing parts and consumables or making necessary adjustments to preset intervals so that risks do not occur as a result of the deterioration or failure of the equipment.

Condition-based maintenance involves monitoring the condition of safety-critical parts and carrying out maintenance whenever necessary to avoid hazards which could otherwise occur.

Figure C5- 30: Different maintenance management techniques.   *Source: HSC Approved code of practice for PUWER.*

Maintenance strategies - examples

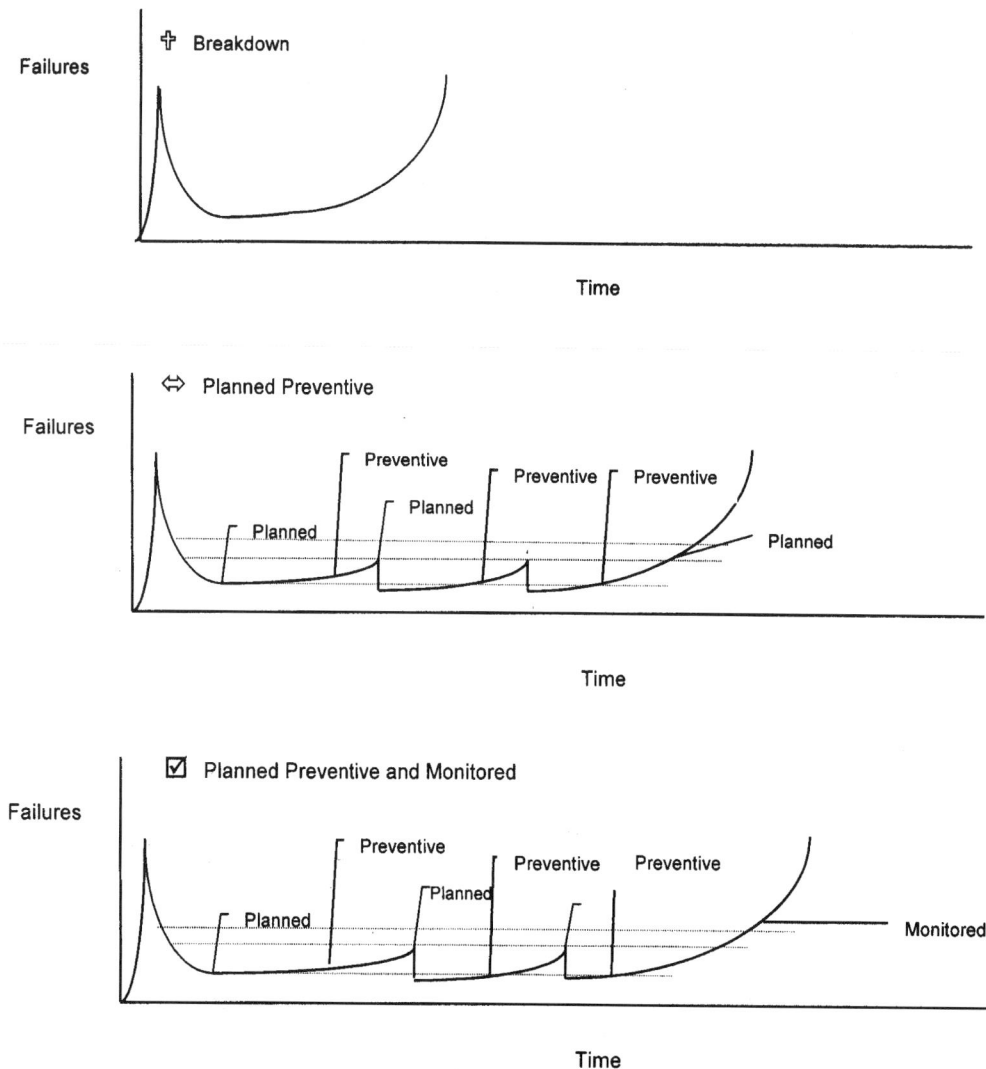

Figure C5-31: Examples of maintenance strategies.   *Source: Ambiguous.*

FACTORS TO BE CONSIDERED IN DEVELOPING A PLANNED MAINTENANCE PROGRAMME

Supplier information

Manufacturers and suppliers of work equipment are obliged by section 6 of HASAWA 1974 to provide information on the health and safety of their products. It is reasonable and practicable that they include information on expected maintenance necessary for the equipment when in foreseeable use. It is important when developing a planned maintenance programme to consult this data as a source. It should be remembered though that the specific use of the equipment may vary and could cause the programme to provide more frequent (or less) maintenance than that which is recommended.

Risk

In essence the risk from failure of equipment is one of the most important factors to consider in a programme of maintenance of work equipment. If the risk of failure is low then the programme may extend the period between maintenance to draw out the most use from the equipment with the least effort and cost. However, not all items of the same type of equipment are identical and some will fail within this averaged maintenance period, but as the risk is low it may be considered of little consequence. Where the risk from failure is high the periods between maintenance may be reduced to develop a higher degree of confidence that the equipment will not fail.

Frequency of use

Frequency of use can vary the wear out rate of equipment in that on average the more the equipment is in use the more maintenance is required. This is not always the case with some components of the equipment, for example, low use may mean more frequent starts and stops in using the equipment and might put additional burden on components like motors or fitting brackets whose main stress is caused at start of use. Equipment that remains in use after initial start up may not carry the same stresses as that which is taken in and out of use.

Competency availability

Depending on the equipment and maintenance required the maintenance programme may require specialist competencies. It is important to give this early consideration when developing a maintenance programme as it can take a considerable time to develop skill and expertise. If there is a competency gap it may be necessary to recruit or hire people to supplement the competency of current staff, particularly if a major maintenance programme with enhanced maintenance techniques is to be used.

Other factors

- Minimum legal requirements.
- Experiences of maintenance staff and users.
- Current best practice expectation for safeguards.
- Resource available.
- Time to introduce.
- Cost and benefit.
- Planning and work done records.
- Training of users/maintenance people.
- Control and confirmation of action through job sheets and procedures.

BENEFITS OF PLANNED PREVENTIVE MAINTENANCE

The main benefits are:

- Extended life of components.
- Assurance of reliability.
- Confirmation of condition of components.
- Reduced risk/loss producing failure events.
- Ability to carry out work at a suitable time.
- Better utilisation of maintenance staff.
- Less peaks and troughs.
- Less standby facility required.
- Less expensive (last minute) contracted facility required.
- Cost effective actions.

STATUTORY REQUIREMENTS FOR MAINTENANCE

HASAWA Section 2 places a duty on the employer to ensure the maintenance of plant *(equipment)*, so far as is reasonably practicable.

PUWER - Regulation 5 Maintenance

(1) every employer shall ensure that work equipment is maintained in an efficient state, in efficient working order and in good repair.

(2) every employer shall ensure that where any machinery has a maintenance log, the log is kept up to date.

The need to maintain is considered to be adequately dealt with by the HASAWA 1974. The obligation or outcome of the maintenance is dealt with in PUWER 1998.

'Efficient' refers to its ability to ensure health and safety (not production). As such parts that clearly protect people and provide health and safety e.g. guards, ventilation systems and pressure relief valves must be maintained such that they perform their function at all times. Efficiency though also relates to other parts whose condition might affect health and safety in a more subtle way e.g. a bearing that through poor lubrication may become a source for a fire or for a high level of noise.

Maintenance must ensure the condition of the equipment is kept above a threshold that would put people at risk. Deterioration to a low level before action should be prevented. Equipment may need to be checked frequently in order to allow maintenance above this threshold. The frequency of checking will depend on the equipment, task and the risks arising from the deterioration of the condition of the equipment.

The extent of the maintenance necessary to ensure efficiency will vary greatly dependent on similar factors to above.

In addition to PUWER 1998 other legislation sets out requirements for inspection/examination and maintenance e.g. for hoists and other lifting equipment, local exhaust ventilation equipment and pressure vessels. It is essential that these are seen as minimum requirements and that in addition to this the equipment must be maintained in an efficient state/working order and good repair.

In the same way PUWER 1998 does not require a log of maintenance. However the HASAWA 1974 requires 'ensure maintenance' with the burden of proof on doing so on the accused. Furthermore, some specific legislation will require a record of inspection and confirmation that deficiencies have been remedied e.g. scaffolds, excavations, power presses.

STATUTORY REQUIREMENTS FOR INSPECTION

PUWER 1998 Regulation 6 - Inspection

"Every employer shall ensure that work equipment exposed to conditions causing deterioration which is liable to result in dangerous situations is inspected:

a) At suitable intervals.

b) Each time that exceptional circumstances which are liable to jeopardise the safety of the work equipment have occurred, to ensure that health and safety conditions are maintained and that any deterioration can be detected and remedied in good time.

Every employer shall ensure that the result of an inspection made under this regulation is recorded and kept until the next inspection under this regulation is recorded."

This Regulation relates to the inspection of most work equipment. Only some power presses and their guards, lifting equipment and winding apparatus, and equipment which is subject to inspection under the Construction (Health, Safety and Welfare) Regulations (CHSWR) 1996 are not covered.

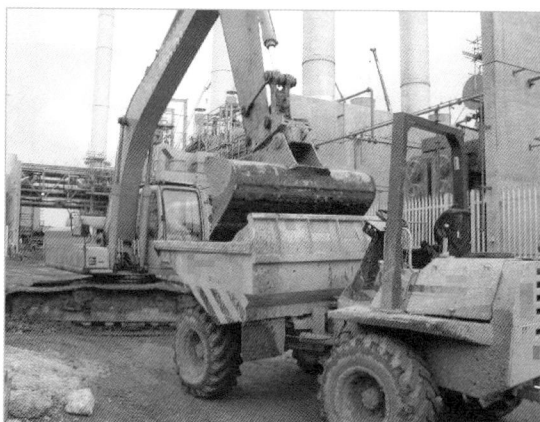

Figure C5-32: Equipment inspection. *Source: ACT.*

Work equipment must be inspected after installation and prior to first use or after assembly on a new site or location where its safety depends on installation conditions. Inspections must be recorded and carried out prior to removal from premises, sale, hire or loan to another employer.

Equipment must be inspected on a regular basis in order to confirm the condition that it is in. The inspection required is more than a simple daily pre-use check carried out by the operator. The person using equipment, who should be confirmed as competent, should carry out operator checks prior to the use of any equipment. Operator checks should include guards, cables, casing integrity, cutting or machine parts and safety devices such as cut-outs. The inspection required under this regulation should be significant and address a list of identifiable health and safety critical parts. The purpose of an inspection sheet is to determine deterioration of specific parts, abuse and misuse and also to ensure that all items are considered at the time of inspection, by serving as an aide memoire. The results of the inspection will confirm whether or not a piece of equipment is in a safe enough condition to use. Other regulations, such as the Lifting Operations and Lifting Equipment Regulations (LOLER) 1998 require and set certain statutory inspection requirements

5.7 - Statutory examinations

The purpose of statutory examinations is to provide a means to identify the condition of critical equipment that if not maintained to an acceptable standard would create serious risk. The examinations take the form of a physical examination of the equipment by a competent person to identify patent defects in the condition of equipment and its safety devices.

The implication of this measure is to oblige employers to ensure this equipment and its safety devices are maintained to an efficient and effective standard (with regard to safety).

In addition to the task of examination a competent person is often expected to conduct tests of the equipment.

The law requiring the tasks to be conducted by a competent person does not prescribe the attributes of the person or whether they should be independent of the employer. The tasks are expressed as an absolute duty on the employer and if the employer contracts with another party to carry it out this does not absolve the employer from responsibility to ensure that it is done.

NEED FOR COMPETENT PERSONS

The purpose of the competent person is to provide knowledge, skill and experience sufficient to achieve the specific examination that they are considered competent to conduct and to draw appropriate conclusions. This means that in some cases the person will be a specialist (often independent) engineer dealing with this matter e.g. pressure vessels or an engineer of the organisation e.g. automatic safe working load indicators.

NOTIFICATION AND RECORD KEEPING

The requirements to conduct examination and tests also carry obligations to maintain a record of the action, the outcome and conclusions about whether the equipment should remain in service.

With some specific equipment, e.g. power presses, there is a requirement to notify the HSE of equipment that falls below an acceptable standard sufficient to remain in service.

TYPES OF INSPECTION, FREQUENCIES AND STATUTORY BASES FOR EXAMINATION

Cranes and lifting equipment

Statutory requirements are set out in Regulation 9 of the LOLER 1998.

Used lifting equipment must be thoroughly examined before being put into service for the first time by a new user. This does not apply to new lifting equipment (unless its safety depends on installation conditions) or equipment that conforms to European Community requirements and has been certified as being examined within the previous 12 months. Suppliers of used lifting equipment are obliged to certify that a thorough examination has been carried out.

Where the safety of lifting equipment depends on the installation conditions it must be thoroughly examined prior to first use, after assembly and on change of location in order to ensure that it has been installed correctly and is safe to operate.

Lifting equipment exposed to conditions causing deterioration that is liable to result in dangerous situations is to be thoroughly examined by a competent person:

a) At least every 6 months - lifting equipment for lifting persons and lifting accessories.

b) At least every 12 months - other lifting equipment or

c) In either case, in accordance with an examination scheme and

d) On each occurrence of exceptional circumstances liable to jeopardise the safety of the lifting equipment.

Figure C5-33: Marking of equipment.   *Source: ACT.*

Where appropriate to ensure health and safety, inspections must be carried out at suitable intervals between thorough examinations. Examinations and inspections must ensure that the good condition of equipment is maintained and that any deterioration can be detected and remedied in good time.

Hoists and lifts

Scaffold hoists (persons/materials) should be inspected weekly, and thoroughly examined every six months by a competent person and the results of inspection recorded.

The legislation governing the construction, use and thorough examination of lifts and hoists, is the LOLER 1998 *(see above, plus further information on LOLER at the end of this Element).*

Simple pressure systems

Pressure Systems Safety Regulations (PSSR) 2000.

A written scheme of periodic examination by a competent person must be drawn up for pressure systems and implemented or certified as being suitable by a competent person before the system can be operated.

The user of installed systems must ensure that the examinations are carried out by a competent person as laid down in the scheme.

A pressure system is, as defined in the PSSR 2000, as follows:

■ "A system comprising one or more pressure vessels of rigid construction, and any associated pipework and protective devices.

■ The pipework with its protective devices to which a transportable gas container is or is intended to be connected.

■ A pipeline and its protective devices".

A pressure vessel is generally considered one which operates at a pressure greater than atmospheric pressure, e.g. steam boilers, receivers and air receivers.

Competent persons

The PSSR 2000 define the term competent person as a competent individual person (other than an employee) or a competent body of persons. There are three distinct functions of the competent person:

Figure C5-34: Air compressor.   *Source: Speedy Hire plc.*

1. Advising the user on the scope of the written scheme of examination.

2. Drawing up or certifying schemes of examination.

3. Carrying out examinations under the scheme.

It is the responsibility of all users to select a competent person who is capable of carrying out his duties in a proper manner. The competent person should have relevant knowledge and experience of the system. For complex systems, the competent person may be a number of different people for different parts of the system.

The examinations should be impartial and objective with the safety considerations and use of the system in mind.

Power presses

PUWER 1998, Part IV, Regulations 32-35

Presses must not be put into service for the first time, after installation or after assembly at a new site or in a new location, unless it has been thoroughly examined and any defects remedied. Parts of closed tools together with guards and other protection devices must be similarly examined. Power presses and guards etc. must be thoroughly examined at least every 12 months, where there are fixed guards only; or at least every 6 months in other cases or each time that exceptional circumstances have occurred which are liable to jeopardise the safety of the power press or its guards / protection devices. Defects must be remedied before the power press is used again.

Power presses must not be used after the setting, re-setting or adjustment of its tools, save in trying out its tools or save in die proving, unless the devices have been inspected and tested by a competent person appointed in writing (or a person undergoing training for that purpose and acting under the immediate supervision of a competent person). The inspector must sign an approved certificate.

Recorded in-situ inspection and test of guards / protection devices must be carried within the fourth hour of any working period (including days, nights or shift systems).

Inspectors making thorough examinations must report defects relating to guards or protection devices as soon as is practicable to the employer. Reports must be in a format contained in Schedule 3 of the PUWER 1998 and copied to the enforcing authority where defects in a power press or its guard or protection device which is or could become a danger to persons.

5.8- Pressure systems

COMPONENTS AND RELEVANT FLUIDS

See also - the Pressure Systems Safety Regulations (PSSR) 2000 in Element C11 - Relevant Statutory Provisions.

As defined in the PSSR 2000:

- A system comprising one or more pressure vessels of rigid construction, and any associated pipework and protective devices.
- The pipework with its protective devices to which a transportable gas container is or is intended to be connected.
- A pipeline and its protective devices.

A pressure vessel is generally considered to be one which operates at a pressure greater than atmospheric pressure, e.g. steam boilers, receivers and air receivers.

The four main types of pressure vessel are:

Steam Boiler - any closed vessel for any purpose steam is generated under pressure greater than atmospheric and includes any economiser used to heat water being fed to any such vessel, and any superheater used for heating steam.

The purpose of the steam boiler is to generate steam under pressure. This is achieved by using fuel, air and water. The fuel is burnt and its potential heat transmits this energy which heats the water into water vapour, which also stores heat in the form of sensible and latent heat. There are 2 common types of boiler - horizontal and vertical.

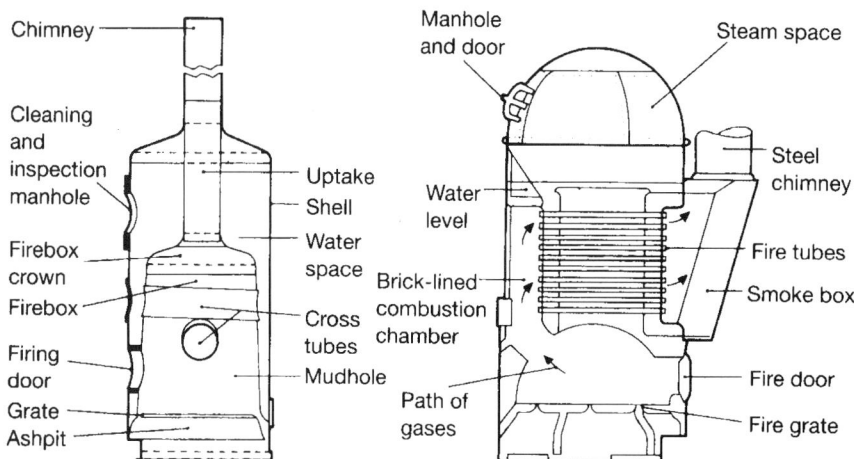

Figure C5-35: Pressure systems.　　　　*Source: J Stranks; Health & Safety in Practice (Safety Technology); Pitman Publishing; 1996.*

Steam Receiver - Any vessel or apparatus, other than a steam boiler, steam container, steam pipe or coil, or part of a prime mover, used for containing steam under pressure greater than atmospheric pressure.

Steam Container - Any vessel, other than a steam pipe or coil, constructed with a permanent outlet to atmosphere or into a space where pressure does not exceed atmospheric pressure, and through which steam is passed at atmospheric pressure, or at approximately that pressure, for the purpose of heating, boiling, drying, evaporating or other purpose similar.

Air Receiver - Any vessel or apparatus used for containing air under pressure greater than atmospheric pressure.

Other examples of pressure systems include: LPG bulk storage and compressed air systems.

TYPICAL CAUSES OF FAILURE

Pressure as in a boiler or other vessels, results in tensile stresses longitudinally and also circumferentially. Other stresses may also be present, such as residual stresses as a result of welding, thermal stresses from heating and cooling and restraint stresses such as form fixings holding the vessel in place.

Two of the most common causes of failure with boilers are

- Overheating caused by low boiler water levels.
- Long term effects of corrosion.

Both can lead to boiler failure or explosion due to a fracture under pressure.

Excessive stress

Ductility is the amount a material will stretch before fracture. The atoms in a material slide over one another, rather than splitting as in the brittle failure. Failure is usually the result of a single stress overload. A copper hot water cistern can balloon due to excessive pressure; this would be an example of ductile failure.

Abnormal external loading

Failure due to abnormal external loading may be due to factors like being struck by something such as a fork lift truck or fuel delivery vehicle all of which could create concentrated stresses from the impact. Where an accidental explosion, such as a dust explosion was to occur this too could provide abnormal stresses. If the vessel is restrained in such a way that it is not evenly held in place (perhaps mounting bolts have been fixed to the floor out of alignment with the fixing holes) the additional stress created when it is secured may be sufficient to cause failure.

Overpressure

Over pressurisation of systems can occur if pressure relief valves fail coupled with other devices failing. This will lead to the pressure level rising beyond safe working and design limits which normally leads to catastrophic results.

Overheating

Overheating can occur if alarms and controls fitted to prevent this have not been tested or maintained or inappropriate controls have been fitted originally. Pressure that rises beyond safe working and design limits can lead to catastrophic results. Although pressure vessels are usually manufactured to withstand 3 times its safe working pressure, fatigue can soon become a problem.

Mechanical fatigue and shock

Pressure within a system will cause tensile stresses in all directions. If the stresses are greater than the materials can cope with it will lead to ductile or brittle failure. Fatigue is the phenomenon leading to fracture under repeated or fluctuating stress. Fatigue stress is usually progressive, starting with minute cracks and grows under the action of fluctuating stress. Pressure system fatigue failure is often triggered by some surface interruption. In engineering components, these surface faults could be sharp changes in direction, threads, oxide inclusions, grinding marks, weld defects, gauge mounts and seal mounts, to name just a few. All these surface faults constitute what is known as 'notch' or 'stress raiser'. If a notch or fault is present in a component, stress concentration is produced at the root of the notch. A stress concentration effect is present near any fault or imperfection, and in the zone at the root of the fault.

Thermal fatigue and shock

Thermal shock is a situation where the water in a boiler is suddenly displaced by water with substantially different temperatures. It causes rapid expansion or contraction of tubes, boiler plate, pipes, valves and fittings causing stresses to the boiler or piping system. If this becomes a frequent event this can result in fatigue leading to such things as leaking tubes, cracked pressure vessels, and cracked cast iron sections.

Brittle fracture

This type of failure has a tendency to fracture without deformation. Brittle materials may be incredibly strong but lack resistance to the propagation of cracks. Failure is promoted by factors such as high tensile and residual stresses; impact loading; high/low temperatures; thick plated vessels (> 100mm) and welded joints. Precautions include the selection of notch tough material and the avoidance of notches in the structure. It must be understood that a normally ductile material can fail in a brittle manner when complex stress fields exist.

Creep

When a material is under constant load or stress, it may undergo progressive plastic (permanent) deformation over a period of time. This time dependent deformation is called 'creep'. The creep of materials used for pressure systems is very important, especially those at elevated temperatures. For such designs creep is the limiting factor with respect to the operating temperature. For some materials, such as lead, creep can occur at room temperature

Hydrogen attack

This occurs when hydrogen seeps into gaps in the molecular framework of the metal and causes stresses from within the framework causing embrittlement. Hydrogen attack can occur as a result of the cathode reaction during corrosion. Hydrogen can also be introduced during melting and entrapped during solidification. It can also occur during heat treatment, electroplating, acid pickling or welding. Systems are most susceptible at room temperature and as little as 0.0001% of hydrogen by weight can cause cracking in steel.

Corrosive failure

Corrosion is the deterioration of a material through chemical or electro-chemical attack by atmosphere, moisture or other agents. In pressure systems, corrosion can thin the material causing it to lose strength. Corrosion occurs where levels of oxygen or carbon dioxide are high, where pH values are low or high, where contact occurs between dissimilar metals and in damp environments or corrosive atmospheres. For this reason, any modification to the environment which makes it less aggressive will be beneficial.

Corrosion can take many forms, for example, aqueous, dissimilar metal, grain boundary, erosion, pitting and stress are all types of corrosion. Corrosion increases maintenance costs, results in premature replacement of equipment and causes unnecessary safety risks. Precautions against corrosion include correct choice of materials, good design, protective coatings, neutral pH environments, low reactive humidity and cathode protection by introducing a sacrificial anode (e.g. a manganese strip is buried alongside a steel pipe and wired to protect the pipe against corrosion).

Contributory factors

Design considerations

Design extends beyond the calculation of thickness and includes an assessment of materials to be used, together with manufacturing and welding processes to be employed. Service conditions should be carefully reviewed to ensure the design parameters are appropriate. Failures are usually associated with the influence of some element not envisaged or catered for at the design stage. Overload due to excessive pressures can be catered for by fitting adequate relief devices. The most common form of failure is fatigue and this is perhaps the least appreciated. It is important to assess the anticipated range and frequency of load cycling and to pay close attention to detailed design to minimise stress concentration effects.

Scale

Scale is an extremely hard substance created when mineral salts come out of solution as their solubility drops with a rise in water temperature. Scale forming salts adhere directly to heating surfaces, forming layers of insulation on the metal, substantially decreasing its heat transfer efficiency. One 1.5mm of scale in a boiler will increase fuel consumption by 12.5%. Scale results in metal fatigue/failure causing overheating, energy waste, high maintenance costs and unnecessary safety risks.

Fouling

This is very similar to scaling; fouling occurs when restriction develops in piping and equipment passages, creating inefficient water flow. The major consequences of fouling to boiler room equipment are energy waste and increased operating/maintenance costs.

Foaming

This is a condition in which concentrations of soluble salts (aggravated by grease, suspended solids or organic metal) create frothy bubbles (resembling the foam in a beer mug) in the steam space of a boiler. Foaming can cause priming, in which the bubbles break and create liquid that combines to form slugs of water that are carried over into the steam system. Pressure from the steam can create velocities as high as 80-100 miles per hour for slugs of water discharges into the steam lines. These slugs can wreak havoc with devices and piping downstream of the boiler (a similar version of this phenomena is 'water hammer' when air is the culprit).

Caustic embrittlement

This occurs when hairline cracks appear in highly stressed areas due to high concentrations of alkaline salts that liberate hydrogen which is then absorbed by the iron in steel, effectively changing its physical properties. This condition is caused largely by boiler water with pH values 11+ and manifests itself in high-temperature areas of the boiler. Unless embrittlement problems are constantly monitored and controlled, they will take their toll in higher fuel costs, increased safety risks, unnecessary downtime and equipment replaced.

Low water level

If this is not properly sensed and the burners do not shutdown the boiler will overheat due to exposed metal surfaces (i.e. not wetted). Overheated boilers will be permanently damaged. If the safety valve has not been serviced properly and does not relieve the pressure adequately, the boiler could explode violently and result in injury or death. Low water conditions are a significant cause of accidents involving pressure vessels.

Lamella tearing

This is a form of cracking that can occur in steel plates under large fillet welds. The cracking, which can destroy the integrity of the plate, can be difficult to detect as it may be entirely sub-surface. There is evidence that lamella tearing is caused by its association with inclusions in the plate.

Wear

This is the loss of material through friction. The pressure vessel itself does not usually suffer but components in the system do, for example pumps and motorised valves etc. Lubrication and the absence of foreign matter keeps wear under control.

Seal failures

Smaller scale failures commonly occur when seals such as 'o' rings or 'H' seals fail at joins or couplings in the system pipeline. This can be due to the heat effects produced in air systems or incorrect fitting during installation. Failures can also be found in high pressure systems where parts of the system are isolated and a section of pipeline is then drained of pressure. When the line is then re-pressurised it is carried out too quickly and the sudden pressurisation on the seal actually dislodges the seal from its seat in the coupling, producing a coupling seal failure and the system then leaks. Once this has occurred the seal is more susceptible to further damage.

Operator error and maintenance

Apart from low water conditions it would appear that good operator training and preventative maintenance procedures could drastically reduce the number of accidents involved with pressure systems. This would include the regular testing of all the protective devices on a regular basis.

Water hammer

Steam systems are very prone to water hammer which can have disastrous effects. Pipe work should therefore be designed and constructed so that any water only collects at suitable points in the system where drains are provided

Unsuitable material for pipes

Plastic pipes are often used on compressed air systems. Not all plastics are suitable for use where there is the possibility of their exposure to heat or becoming brittle. Care should therefore be taken that pipes are suitable for the intended use. Suitable moisture filters and/or drains should be provided where moisture would adversely affect the integrity of the system or the operation of any protective device.

PREVENTION STRATEGY

Design and construction

Designers should work to a clear specification and take account of current safe practice. The specification should set out the necessary operating and safety requirements. In some cases it will be provided by the user but in others the designer should draw up the specification. This information needs to be passed on by designers to clients and users.

Factors that the designer should consider and take account of are as follows:

- The expected life.
- The need for the system to be examined. Most vessels should be provided with adequately sized openings so as to permit adequate examination of the interior of the vessel. However with some systems, either because of size or the fluid which is contained, internal examination may be unnecessary or even harmful. In such cases the designer should consider what examinations are needed and provide other means for carrying them out.
- The conditions of operation and performance requirements of the system, allowing for the most onerous combination of temperature, pressure and other relevant parameters to which it may reasonably be subjected and taking into account the characteristics of the contents.

Account should also be taken of the conditions which will exist during start-up and shut-down of the system.

The designer should also ensure that the system can safely withstand the consequences of such conditions unless it is to be fitted with appropriate control and protective equipment which will either prevent the conditions arising or enable the stored energy to be safely dissipated.

Such devices should prevent unsafe pressure rises so that the device will commence to operate at its set pressure, which shall not exceed the system design pressure and will reach full discharge capacity within a set limit of overpressure (accumulation).

Consideration should also be given to the consequences of a pressure relief device operating and it should be ensured that the contents are released in as safe a manner as is practicable.

Additional features include warning devices to alert that the system failure may occur. Suitable control equipment should be provided to enable the system to be properly controlled within its safe operating limits. The equipment should allow for likely fluctuations in the operating conditions. Measuring devices should give adequate indications of relevant critical conditions within the system, e.g. temperatures, pressures.

The design should provide for corrosion allowances if some corrosion is unavoidable and foreseeable; for wear if stirrers or agitators are liable to cause wear which may give rise to danger; and generally provide for foreseeable changes in the equipment during normal use. This may include specifying process materials which may not be put into the system because they are incompatible with the materials of construction.

Pipework should be designed so as to allow for the forces due to thermal expansion and contraction, externally applied loads or any reasonably foreseeable vibration. Suitable expansion bends and/or joints should be incorporated in the pipework as necessary.

Additionally where it is used for some gases and vapours it has a tendency to accumulate liquids or condensates, the design should minimise the number of places such as low points where liquid can accumulate. All pipework drainage should be in a safe place.

The Pressure Systems Safety Regulations 2000 - Regulation 4

1. Any person who designs, manufactures, imports or supplies any pressure system or any article which is intended to be a component part of any pressure system shall ensure that paragraphs (2) to (5) are complied with.

2. The pressure system or article, as the case may be, shall be properly designed and properly constructed from suitable material, so as to prevent danger.

3. The pressure system or article, as the case may be, shall be so designed and constructed that all necessary examinations for preventing danger can be carried out.

4. Where the pressure system has any means of access to its interior, it shall be so designed and constructed as to ensure, so far as practicable, that access can be gained without danger.

5. The pressure system shall be provided with such protective devices as may be necessary for preventing danger; and any such device designed to release contents shall do so safely, so far as is practicable.

Protection devices

Steam systems

All systems have devices fitted for various purposes, some are functional, others are protective devices. Some of these devices are as follows:

Device	Protective Device	Description
Safety Valve	Yes	This is usually a spring loaded valve which is designed to lift at a predetermined pressure value to relieve excess pressure. These values should never be set at a higher value than the permissible working pressure or design pressure of the boiler.
Water Level Gauge	Yes	This indicates the amount of water in a system or boiler. The bottom of the gauge should be fitted at least 50mm above the uppermost heating surface in the boiler. Can have remote systems fitted with probes indicating levels by lighting red or green lights as appropriate. These should be tested once a shift or day as appropriate.
Water Level Controls	Yes	Two of these should be fitted to each boiler. They have a dual function: ■ To control the water at the correct operating level. ■ To shut down the burner in the event of a low water level warning. These should be tested once per shift or day as appropriate.
Blow Down Valve	No	This is situated at the bottom of the boiler and is used to discharge water/sludge from the boiler.
Feed Check Valves	No	Used to control feed water being pumped into the boiler. There are two valves, the first is a screw down valve the second a non-return valve which prevents water flowing back through the pump when it stops.
Pressure Gauge	Yes	This should have a range of 1.5-2 times the design pressure of the system
Main Stop Valve	No	Used to control the discharge of steam into the steam mains. The main stop valve is situated on top of the boiler.

Figure C5-36: Description of steam systems devices.   *Source: ACT.*

Air systems

Air is generated under pressure normally by the use of a compressor or similar device. Common devices fitted to air systems are as follows:

Device	Protective Device	Description
Pressure Gauge	Yes	Fitted to the compressor and at all stages of generation to show the working pressure in the line.
Oil and Temperature Gauge	Yes	Fitted to prevent the compressor overheating.
Safety Valves	Yes	Operation is the same as for steam systems and are fitted at various points of the system
Automatic Cut Out	Yes	Oil flooded compressors should have an automatic shutdown device to prevent the temperature of the compressor oil or air from exceeding safe limits.
Inter coolers and after coolers	Yes	Used to cool the air in the system at various stages as when generated the air becomes very hot. These devices are a form of heat exchangers

Figure C5-37: Description of air systems devices.   *Source: ACT.*

Air receivers

These have similar devices fitted, however they do have additional devices.

Device	Protective Device	Description
Drain Valve	No	Fitted to the bottom of the receiver, used to drain moisture from the receiver. Should be regularly and frequently used to prevent the build up of moisture and/or emulsified oil.
Stop Valve	Yes	Used to control the air outlet from the receiver.

Figure C5-38: Description of air receivers devices.   *Source: ACT.*

Repair and modification

When repairs or modifications to the pressurised parts of the system, whether temporary or otherwise, consideration should be given to the original design specification, the duty for which the system is to be used after the repair or modification, including any change in relevant fluid, and the effects any such work may have on the integrity of the pressure system, and whether the protective equipment is still adequate.

The Pressure Systems Safety Regulations 2000 - Regulation 13

The employer of a person who modifies or repairs a pressure system at work shall ensure that nothing about the way in which it is modified or repaired gives rise to danger or otherwise impairs the operation of any protective device or inspection facility.

Information and marking

The Pressure Systems Safety Regulations 2000 - Regulation 5

1. Any person who-

(a) Designs for another any pressure system or any article which is intended to be a component part thereof.

(b) Supplies (whether as manufacturer, importer or in any other capacity) any pressure system or any such article, shall provide sufficient written information concerning its design, construction, examination, operation and maintenance as may reasonably foreseeably be needed to enable the provisions of these Regulations to be complied with.

2. The employer of a person who modifies or repairs any pressure system shall provide sufficient written information concerning the modification or repair as may reasonably foreseeably be needed to enable the provisions of these Regulations to be complied with.

3. The information referred to in paragraph (1) shall-

(a) In the case of paragraph (1) (a), be provided with the design.

(b) In the case of paragraph (1) (b), be provided with the pressure system or article when it is supplied by that person.

(c) In the case of paragraph (2), be provided to the user of the system immediately after the modification or repair.

4. Any person who manufactures a pressure vessel shall ensure that before it is supplied by him the information specified in Schedule 3 is marked on the vessel, or on a plate attached to it, in a visible, legible and indelible form; and no person shall import a pressure vessel unless it is so marked.

5. No person shall remove from a pressure vessel any mark or plate containing any of the information specified in Schedule 3.

6. No person shall falsify any mark on a pressure system, or on a plate attached to it, relating to its design, construction, test or operation.

Adequate information about the pressure system must be passed on to the user. This should include:

- Safe operating limits.
- Scheme of examination.
- Design standards and constructional materials.
- Certificates of conformity.
- Design pressures and temperatures.
- Intended contents, flow rates, capacities, etc.

Pressure vessels should be marked with the following information, prescribed in schedule 3 of the Pressure Systems Safety Regulations:

1. Manufacturers name.

2. Serial number of vessel.

3. Date of manufacture.

4. Standard of built.

5. Maximum allowable pressure.

6. Minimum allowable pressure where it is other than atmospheric.

7. Design temperature.

Anyone operating a pressure system must be given adequate and suitable instructions for safe operation and emergency action. This instruction should form part of the operating instructions for the plant and should include information on start-up, shutdown, normal operation, functions of controls, emergency procedures, etc. Doors providing routine access should be dealt with by specific instructions covering interlocking checks, opening and closing precautions, failure signs, etc.

It should be noted that the supply of pressure equipment is also governed by the *Pressure Equipment Regulations (PER) 1999* which came into force on 29 November 1999. These set out the general requirements relating to the placing on the market or putting into service of pressure equipment and assemblies by a *responsible person* (a person who manufactures the pressure equipment or assemblies for his own use or imports pressure equipment or assemblies from a third country, where it is in the course of business). Pressure equipment or assemblies must satisfy the relevant essential health and safety requirements and be safe with the appropriate conformity assessment procedure carried out (unless the equipment is to be used for experimentation). A declaration of conformity must be drawn up and CE marking affixed.

Safe operating limits

Safe operating limits must be known to those that operate a pressure system and the system must only be operated within these limits. Clear marking on the system of the limits will help to communicate the safe operating limits and assist with compliance with the limits. Care will need to be taken to ensure that pressure relief valves are functional in order to respond to accidental over pressure.

They must be periodically inspected to ensure they have not been tampered with such that they operate at pressures greater than the safe operating limit or that they are not corroded/stuck closed.

The provision of a well placed, legible gauge which identifies the safe working pressure will assist with compliance to the safe operating limits.

The Pressure Systems Safety Regulations 2000 - Regulation 7

1. The user of an installed system and owner of a mobile system shall not operate the system or allow it to be operated unless he has established the safe operating limits of that system.
2. The owner of a mobile system shall, if he is not also the user of it:

(a) Supply the user with a written statement specifying the safe operating limits of that system established pursuant to paragraph (1).

(b) Ensure that the system is legibly and durably marked with such safe operating limits and that the mark is clearly visible.

Written scheme of examination

Examination means a careful and critical scrutiny of a pressure system or part of a pressure system, in or out of service as appropriate. It means using suitable techniques, including testing where appropriate, to assess its actual condition and whether, for the period up to the next examination, it will not cause danger when properly used if normal maintenance is carried out.

Normal maintenance means such maintenance as it is reasonable to expect the user (in the case of an installed system) or owner (in the case of a mobile system) to ensure is carried out independently of any advice from the competent person making the examination.

A written scheme of examination must be available before any system is used. This should be drawn up by a competent person and should include:

- Pressure vessels.
- Pipe work and valves.

- Protective devices.
- Pumps and compressors.

Examination intervals should be specified, though these may be different for different parts of the system, so that deterioration, etc. can be detected before danger arises. An initial examination should be done before use. Any repairs or modifications should be controlled. Factors to be taken into account when deciding upon the frequency of examination will include:

- Previous intervals and system records.
- Standards of supervision and routine checks.
- Type and quality of fluids in the system.

- The likelihood of creep, fatigue, etc. failures.
- Corrosion potential and effect.
- Presence of heat sources etc.

The type of examination should also be specified.

Examinations must be carried out in accordance with the written scheme and the system adequately assessed for fitness for continued use. Appropriate preparations for and precautions during examination should be arranged for by the user. A report with any conditions or limitations on use should be prepared on completion of the examination.

Where the competent person's examination identifies imminent danger then a report must be made to the user who should ensure the system is not used further and a report is sent to the relevant enforcing authority.

Anyone operating a pressure system must be given adequate and suitable instructions for safe operation and emergency action. This instruction should form part of the operating instructions for the plant and should include information on start-up, shutdown, normal operation, functions of controls, emergency procedures, etc. Doors providing routine access should be dealt with by specific instructions covering interlocking checks, opening and closing precautions, failure signs, etc. Precautions must be taken to prevent unintentional pressurisation of parts of any system not designed for pressure.

Routine and regular maintenance should be carried out including periodic checks and inspections of important parts or components.

Adequate records of examinations, repairs, modifications etc., should be kept at the premises where the system is used.

Maintenance and record keeping

Routine and regular maintenance should be carried out including periodic checks and inspections of important parts or components.

The Pressure Systems Safety Regulations 2000 - Regulation 12

The user of an installed system and the owner of a mobile system shall ensure that the system is properly maintained in good repair, so as to prevent danger.

Records of examinations in accordance with the written scheme must be kept for the last examination and any previous ones that contain material information relating to the systems safe operation, details of repairs or modifications. Records would usually be kept at the premises where the system is used, or the base for mobile systems.

Competent persons

The PSSR 2000 define the term competent person as a competent individual person (other than an employee) or a competent body of persons. There are 3 distinct functions of the competent person:

- Advising the user on the scope of the written scheme of examination.
- Drawing up or certifying schemes of examination.
- Carrying out examinations under the scheme.

It is the responsibility of all users to select a competent person who is capable of carrying out his duties in a proper manner. The competent person should have relevant knowledge and experience of the system. For complex systems the competent person may be a different number of people for different parts of the system.

The examinations should be impartial and objective with the safety considerations and use of the system in mind.

Machinery Safety

Overall aims

On completion of this Element, the student will have knowledge and understanding of:

■ risk assessment as applied to machinery.

■ the mechanical and non-mechanical hazards presented by machinery.

■ machinery safeguarding techniques and design.

■ the main hazards and safeguards in working with robots and computer controlled machinery and plant.

Content

Specific intended learning outcomes

The intended learning outcomes are that the student will be able to:

1. advise on the selection of proposed plant and machinery with reference to relevant legal requirements and standards

2. identify risks associated with machinery and advise on safeguards to minimise such risks

3. identify risks associated with programmable electronic systems and advise on safeguards to minimise such risks

Relevant statutory provisions

Supply of Machinery (Safety) Regulations (SMSR) 1992 - scope and application

Workplace (Health, Safety and Welfare) Regulations (WHSWR) 1992

Provision and Use of Work Equipment Regulations (PUWER) 1998

6.1 - Machinery risk assessment

The classification of machinery hazards

MECHANICAL HAZARDS

The main types of mechanical hazards as:

- Crushing.
- Shearing.
- Cutting/severing.
- Entanglement.
- Drawing in/trapping.
- Impact.
- Stabbing/puncture/ejection.
- Friction/abrasion.
- High pressure fluid injection.

Crushing

Caused when part of the body is caught between either two moving parts of machinery or a moving part and a stationary object e.g. the callipers of a spot welding machine.

Shearing

When two or more machine parts move towards/past one another a "trap" is created. This can result in a crush injury or even an amputation.

Examples of shearing/crushing action hazards include: power presses, guillotines, scissor lifts etc.

Figure C6-1: Bench cross-cut circular saw.　　*Source: ACT.*

Figure C6-2: Shear.　　*Source: ACT.*

Cutting/severing

Saw blades, knives and even rough edges, especially when moving at high speed, can result in serious cuts and even amputation injuries. The dangerous part can appear stationary!

Examples of cutting action hazards include: saws, slicing machines, abrasive cutting discs, chains (especially chainsaws) etc.

Entanglement

The mere fact that a machine part is revolving can in itself constitute a very real hazard. The risk of entanglement is increased by loose clothing, jewellery, long hair etc.

Examples of rotating action hazards include: couplings, drill chucks/ bits, flywheels, spindles and shafts (especially those with keys/bolts).

Figure C6-3: Entanglement in chuck of pedestal drill. *Source: ACT.*

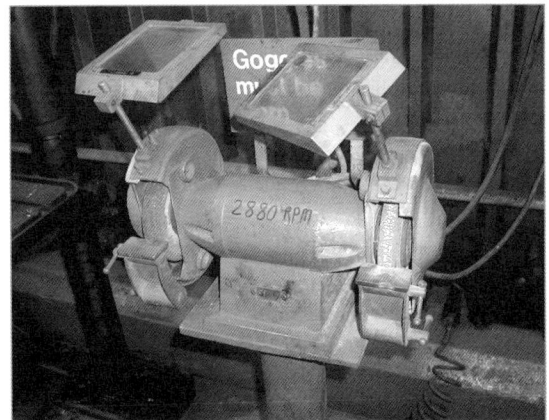

Figure C6-4: Abrasive wheel.　　*Source: ACT.*

Drawing in/trapping

When a belt runs round a roller an in-running nip is created between them (in the direction of travel). Examples of in-running nip hazards are V-belts, meshing gears and conveyors etc.

Impact

Caused by objects which strike the body but do not penetrate it (unlike stabbing and puncture wounds).

Stabbing/puncture/ejection

The body may be penetrated by a) flying objects such as broken pieces of machinery (e.g. a shattered grinding wheel) and ejection of material (e.g. swarf, sparks etc.) or b) sharp pieces of machinery e.g. drilling machines and sewing machines.

Friction/abrasion

Friction burns and abrasion injuries can be caused by coming into contact with smooth surfaces moving at high speed e.g. sanding machine, grinding wheel etc.

High pressure fluid injection

Injection of fluids through the skin may lead to soft tissue injuries similar to crushing. Air entering the blood stream through the skin may be fatal. Examples are diesel injectors, spray painting and compressed air jets.

NON-MECHANICAL HAZARDS

BS EN 292 identifies the main types of non-mechanical hazards as:

- Noise.
- Vibration.
- Electricity.

- High/low temperature.
- Radiation.
- Hazardous substances.

Others that may be considered are:

- Falling.
- Collision with equipment.

- Ergonomics - manual handling.
- Pressure.

Noise

Noise sources from equipment may be from such things as bearings that are loose or worn, materials falling into or out of equipment as part of the process or from air exhausted from equipment.

Vibration

Vibration may be designed as part of the process or a result of moving parts of the equipment such as conveyor systems and rotating parts.

Electricity

May arise as a hazard from the following sources:

- Power generated at a variety of voltages often 440v, 230v, 110v and alternating current or direct current, stored energy should also be considered.
- Static from movement of in particular non-conducting material.
- Chemically derived and used in, for example, batteries.

High/low temperature

Many processes rely on the input of high or low temperature as part of the process. It should be remembered that the process may evolve high or low temperature e.g. use of liquefied petroleum gas for fork lift trucks.

Radiation

Radiation may be emitted from processes in a number of forms and may be ionising or non-ionising.

Hazardous substances

Hazardous substances may be part of the process, evolved or introduced along with materials by mistake e.g. vapours released or substances carried on materials from a prior process.

HAZARDS FROM TYPICAL MACHINES

The way people work in relation to machinery can be a major contributory factor in machine related accidents. Care is required in the operation, maintenance and cleaning of machinery and, ideally, written safe procedures/permits should cover all three actions listed.

Drills (radial arms, pedestal) - main hazard of entanglement

The mere fact that a machine part is revolving can in itself constitute a very real hazard. Loose clothing, jewellery, long hair, etc. increase the risk of entanglement.

Hazards in setting: Hazards in setting are failure to remove chuck-key before use, failure to secure guard to drive pulleys.

Hazards in use: Hazards in use are entanglement, puncture, flying swarf.

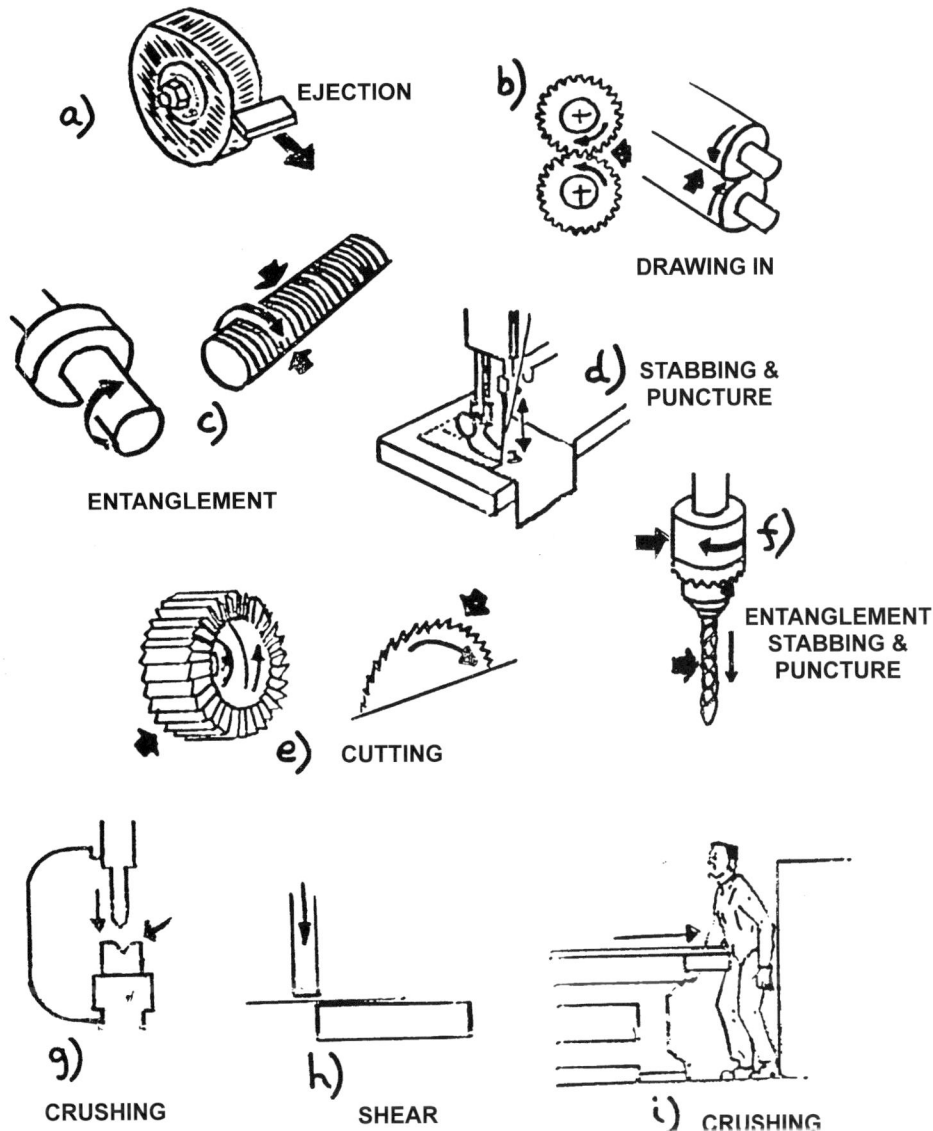

Figure C6-5: Examples of machinery hazards.

Source: ACT.

Circular saws - main hazard of cutting

Saw blades, knives and even rough edges, especially when moving at high speed, can result in serious cuts and even amputation injuries. The dangerous part can appear stationary!

Other examples of cutting action hazards include saws, slicing machines, abrasive cutting discs, chains (especially chainsaws) etc.

Guillotines - main hazard of shear

When two or more machine parts move towards/past, one another a "trap" is created. This can result in a crush injury or even an amputation.

Other examples of shearing/crushing action hazards include: power presses, guillotines, scissor lifts etc.

Paper shredders

Main hazards are drawing-in, cutting or crushing, also cuts from paper handling and potential electrical risks.

Abrasive wheels

Hazards include friction and abrasion, entanglement, drawing in, and possible ejection should parts of the wheel or work piece break. Other hazards are heat, sparks, noise and electricity.

Lathes

The main hazards are drawing in, entanglement, material being thrown off.

Simple robots

Main hazards are associated with setting up and maintenance. At set up the robotic equipment should be equipped with an operation one step (inching) facility to prevent rapid unpredictable movements. On maintenance similar arrangements are required to prevent a variety of injuries, such as crush, entanglement, shear, cutting electric shock or burns (welding heads). At breakdown the main issue is trapped potential energy which might cause the equipment to cycle, even when isolated from external energy sources, resulting in any of the above injuries.

Mechanical and hydraulic presses

Crush injuries, with similar problems to those highlighted for robotics.

Portable power tools

A huge variety of power tools is available. Typical injuries are cutting, stabbing, and eye injuries from waste material and deafness from noise. Portable tools include equipment powered by battery and compressed air (the latter for use in zones 1 and 2).

SUMMARY - MACHINERY HAZARDS

Examples of mechanical hazards	Examples of machines with this mechanical hazard	Examples of non mechanical
Entanglement	Drilling machine	Extremes of temperature
Friction and abrasion	Grinding wheel	Electricity
Cutting	Sharp edges	Noise
Shear	Guillotine	Radiation
Stabbing and Puncture	Sewing machine	Vibration
Impact	Shattered grinding wheel	Dust etc.
Crushing	The ram of a forge hammer	
Drawing in	Conveyor belt	
Injection	Compressed air	
Ejection	Grinding wheel - disintegration or sparks	

Figure C6-6: Machinery hazards.

Source: ACT.

Factors to be considered when assessing risk

- Persons at risk.
- Severity of possible injury.
- Probability of injury.
- Need for access.
- Duration of exposure.
- Reliability of safeguards.
- Operating procedures and personnel.

PERSONS AT RISK

The people that are at risk are those that encounter the machinery through its life and include:

- Manufacture and test.
- Installation and commissioning.
- Setting up and use.
- Adjustment, maintenance, clean and repair.

When in use people in the area of the machine must be considered along with those actually using it. People who would not usually be expected to encounter or use it must also be considered, for example those that supply products for work or remove them after work.

SEVERITY OF POSSIBLE INJURY

This will in the first instance depend on the level of energy relating to the hazard encountered. For example, the force exhibited by two moving parts closing together. The second factor influencing the severity of injury is any limitation on the extent to which parts or the whole of the body may encounter the hazard, e.g. finger in a gap, head between the parts of a press or the whole body entering an area used by a robot. The third factor is the duration of exposure to the hazard. A brief encounter with the surface of an abrasive wheel may be minor, but if a hand is retained in contact major injury will result.

The degree of potential injury has an important influence on the level of safety precautions. Where two machines present the same probability of injury, but in one case the injury is death and in the other a bruised or broken finger, clearly the former carries the higher risk and requires a higher level of safety precautions. Some types of injury, particularly those involving injury to health, are not immediately apparent and may be manifested some time after exposure to a hazard has ceased. Other injuries build up over a long period of exposure to a hazard.

PROBABILITY OF INJURY

Tends to be summarised as being dependent on three factors:

Technical factors

- Dangerous parts - type of hazard and the ease with which a hazard may trap, cut or entangle an individual (dependent on speed and surface of the moving part).
- Guards and other devices available.
- Controls and layout of equipment.

Procedural factors
- Planned cleaning and maintenance.
- Systems of working required for dangerous access.
- Lock off procedures.
- Permit to work.

Behavioural factors
- Information and understanding of hazards.
- Instruction.
- Training - skills and procedures.
- Supervision.
- Positive motivational work methods.
- Perception of hazards - accentuated.
- Human error through fatigue and repetition.

NEED FOR ACCESS

What is the frequency, proximity and duration of access?

What are the circumstances of access? - running, off, isolated, locked off.

What are the reasons for access? - operational / informal, setting, use or maintenance, unplanned encounter.

DURATION OF EXPOSURE

Duration of exposure to the hazard increases the probability of contact and then the extent of injury sustained. If duration is taken to be repetitive small exposures that are reliant only on the skill and attention of the individual it can be seen that this could quickly lead to error and injury.

RELIABILITY OF SAFEGUARDS

The greater the risk, the greater is the need to protect against it. The greater the probability or severity of injury resulting from failure of the safety measures, the greater should be the reliability of the measure.

The reliability of a safeguard can be improved by avoiding motives for its defeat and/or by making defeat more difficult.

The design of the safeguarding system should take full account of the human factor, during each phase of the machine's life. Where this aspect of the design is inadequate motives to defeat the interlock will commonly arise, displayed as the need to gain access inside the guards e.g. production problems. Where needs of this kind are identified the design should be modified to eliminate or reduce this need.

Designers should set out to establish likely operating difficulties and take account of them.

Ways by which defeat may be made more difficult include:

The use of interlocking devices or systems which are coded, e.g. mechanically, electrically, magnetically or optically;

Physical obstruction or shielding of the interlocking device while the guard is open.

Where systems rely on special actuators or keys (coded or not) care should be taken over the availability of spare actuators or keys and master keys.

OPERATING PROCEDURES AND PERSONNEL

It is not always possible to eliminate hazards or to design completely adequate safeguards to protect people against every hazard, particularly during such phases of machine life as commissioning, setting, process changeovers, programming, adjustment, cleaning and maintenance, where often direct access to the hazardous parts of the machine may be necessary. In situations like this safe working practices or probably better known as Safe Systems of Work must be devised and used.

Procedures
- Planned cleaning and maintenance.
- Systems of working required for dangerous access.
- Lock off procedures.
- Permit to work.

Personnel
- Selection of suitable personnel for the proposed tasks.
- Information and understanding of hazards.
- Instruction.
- Training - skills and procedures.
- Supervision.
- Restriction of use and maintenance tasks to those competent and authorised.
- Positive motivational work methods.
- Perception of hazards - accentuated.
- Human error through fatigue and repetition.

Main types of safeguarding devices

FACTORS AFFECTING CHOICE OF SAFEGUARDING METHOD

In selecting an appropriate safeguard for a particular type of machinery or danger area, it should be borne in mind that a fixed guard is simple, and should be used where access to the danger area is not required during operation of the machinery or for cleaning, setting or other activities.

As the need for access arises and increases in frequency, the importance of safety procedures for removal of a fixed guard increases until the frequency is such that interlocking should be used.

Where access to the danger area is not required during normal operation of the machinery, safeguards may be selected from the following.

■ Fixed enclosing guard.
■ Fixed distance guard.
■ Interlocking guard.
■ Trip device.

Where access to the danger area is required for normal operation, safeguards may be selected from the following:

■ Interlocking guard.
■ Automatic guard.
■ Trip device.
■ Adjustable guard.
■ Self-adjusting guard.
■ Two-hand control device.
■ Hold-to-run control.

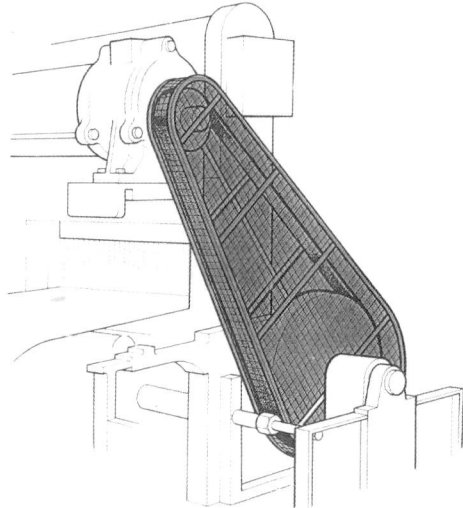

Figure C6-7: Fixed enclosing guard constructed of wire mesh and angle section preventing access to transmission machinery.   *Source: BS 5304: 1988.*

Hierarchy of safeguarding methods (PUWER - Regulation 11 dangerous parts of machinery)

(1)   Every employer shall ensure that measures are taken in accordance with paragraph (2) which are effective -

(a)   To prevent access to any dangerous part of machinery or to any rotating stock-bar; or

(b)   To stop the movement of any dangerous part of machinery or rotating stock-bar before any part of a person enters a danger zone.

(2)   The measures required by paragraph (1) shall consist of -

(a)   The provision of fixed guards enclosing every dangerous part or rotating stock-bar where and to the extent that it is practicable to do so, but where or to the extent that it is not, then;

(b)   The provision of other guards or protection devices where and to the extent that it is practicable to do so, but where or to the extent that it is not, then;

(c)   The provision of jigs, holders, push-sticks or similar protection appliances used in conjunction with the machinery where and to the extent that it is practicable to do so, but where or to the extent that it is not, then;

(d)   The provision of information, instruction, training and supervision.

(3)   All guards and protection devices provided under sub-paragraphs (a) or (b) of paragraph (2) shall:

(a)   Be suitable for the purpose for which they are provided;

(b)   Be of good construction, sound material and adequate strength;

(c)   Be maintained in an efficient state, in efficient working order and in good repair;

(d)   Not give rise to any increased risk to health or safety;

(e)   Not be easily bypassed or disabled;

(f)   Be situated at sufficient distance from the danger zone;

(g)   Not unduly restrict the view of the operating cycle of the machinery, where such a view is necessary;

(h)   Be so constructed or adapted that they allow operations necessary to fit or replace parts and for maintenance work, restricting access so that it is allowed only to the area where the work is to be carried out and, if possible, without having to dismantle the guard or protection device.

(4)   All protection appliances provided under sub-paragraph (c) of paragraph (2) shall comply with sub-paragraphs (a) to (d) and (g) of paragraph (3).

(5)   In this regulation -

"danger zone" means any zone in or around machinery in which a person is exposed to a risk to health or safety from contact with a dangerous part of machinery or a rotating stock-bar;

"stock-bar" means any part of a stock-bar which projects beyond the head-stock of a lathe.

Guard construction

Any guard selected should not itself present a hazard such as trapping or shear points, rough or sharp edges or other hazards likely to cause injury. Guard mounting should be compatible with the strength and duty of the guard. Power operated guards should be designed and constructed so that a hazard is not created. In selecting the material to be used for the construction of a guard, consideration should be given to the following:

- Its ability to withstand the force of ejection of part of the machinery or material being processed, where this is a foreseeable danger. Its ability to provide protection against hazards identified. In many cases, the guard may fulfil a combination of functions such as prevention of access and containment of hazards. This may apply where the hazards include ejected particles, liquids, dust, fumes, radiation, noise, etc. and one or more of these considerations may govern the selection of guard materials.
- Its weight and size in relation to the need to remove and replace it for routine maintenance.
- Its compatibility with the material being processed. This is particularly important in the food processing industry where the guard material should not constitute a source of contamination of the product.
- Its ability to maintain its physical and mechanical properties after coming into contact with potential contaminants such as cutting fluids used in machining operations or cleaning and sterilising agents used in food processing machinery.

Characteristics, key features, limitations and typical applications of

FIXED ENCLOSED GUARDS

A fixed guard is a guard that has no moving parts.

If the guard can be opened or removed, this should only be possible with the aid of a tool. Preferably the fastenings should be of the captive type.

Ideally the removal of a single fixing with the appropriate tool should give the access required.

Fixed enclosing guards. A fixed enclosing guard is a fixed guard which, when in position, prevents access to a danger point or area by enclosure.

When it is necessary for work to be fed through the guard, openings should be sufficient only to allow the passage of material but should not create a trap between the material and the guard. If access to the dangerous parts cannot be prevented by the use of a fixed enclosing guard with a plain opening, then a tunnel of sufficient length should be provided.

FIXED DISTANCE GUARDS

A fixed guard which does not completely cover the danger point but places it out of normal reach. The larger the opening (to feed in material) the greater must be the distance from the opening to the danger point.

A distance guard which completely surrounds machinery is commonly called a perimeter-fence type guard.

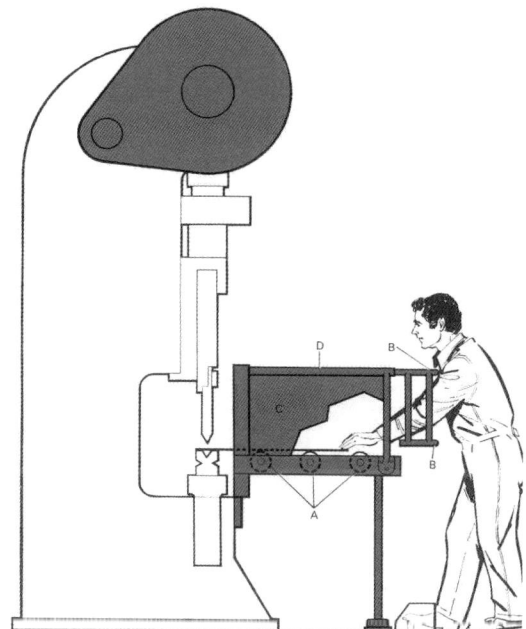

Figure C6-8: Fixed distance guard fitted to a press brake.
Source: BS 5304: 1988.

Anthropometric considerations

General

Guards should be designed and constructed with the object of preventing any part of the body from reaching a danger point or area. They should take account of the physical characteristics of the people involved, and in particular their abilities to reach through the openings, and over or around barriers or guards.

Openings in a guard

Where it is necessary to provide an opening in a guard, it should be at a sufficient distance to prevent any person from reaching the danger point. This may be achieved by positioning the guard at the required distance or by providing a tunnel which extends outwards from it.

The relationship between the size of the guard opening and the distance of the opening from the danger point may be described by the formula:

$$Y = \frac{X + 6}{12}$$ where Y = the opening in mm and X = distance from hazard in mm

Barriers

Where it is not practicable to use enclosing guards, barriers may be used to prevent people reaching the danger point. These rely on a combination of height and distance to achieve their purpose. A guide figure of 1.8m height is suggested for perimeter fencing. With the body upright and standing at full height, the safety distance when reaching upward is 2500 mm.

Barriers are not foolproof and they cannot prevent access to persons intent on gaining access. Therefore, as a person's intent on reaching a dangerous part increases, e.g. by climbing on chairs, ladders or the barrier itself, the protection provided by a barrier will decrease.

When reaching down over an edge, the safety distance is dependent on:

- Distance of danger point from floor.
- Height of edge of barrier.
- Horizontal distance from the edge of the barrier to the danger point.

INTERLOCKED GUARDS

A guard, similar to a fixed guard, but which has a movable (usually hinged) part so connected to the machine controls that if the movable part is in the open/lifted position, the dangerous moving part at the work point cannot operate. This can be arranged so that the act of closing the guard activates the working part (to speed up work). e.g. the front panel of a photocopier.

An interlocking guard should be so connected to the machine controls that:

- Until the guard is closed the interlock prevents the machinery from operating by interrupting the power medium;
- Either the guard remains locked closed until the risk of injury from the hazard has passed or opening the guard causes the hazard to be eliminated before access is possible.

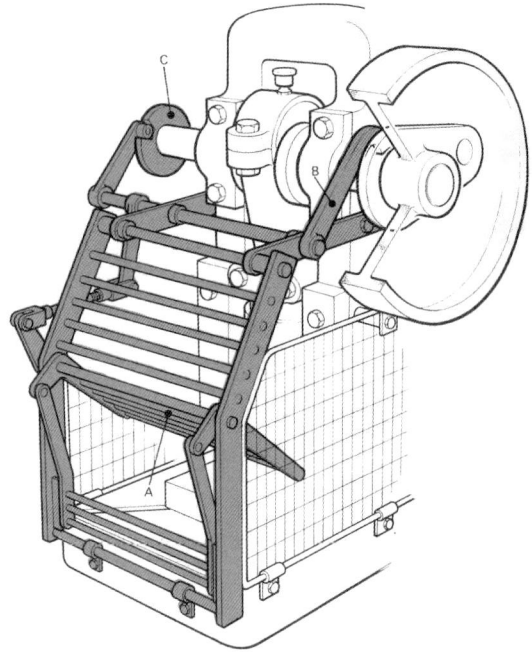

Functions of an interlock

An interlock provides the connection between a guard and the control or power system of the machinery to which the guard is fitted. The interlock and the guard with which it operates should be designed, installed and adjusted so that:

- Until the guard is closed the interlock prevents the machinery from operating by interrupting the power medium;
- Either the guard remains locked closed until the risk of injury from the hazard has passed, or opening the guard causes the hazard to be eliminated before access is possible.

Figure C6-9: Interlocking guard for positive clutch power press.
Source: BS 5304: 1988.

Interlocking media

The four media most commonly encountered in interlocking are electrical, mechanical, hydraulic and pneumatic. Electrical interlocking, particularly in control systems, is the most common and electrical components are often incorporated in hydraulic and pneumatic circuitry, e.g. solenoid operated valves. The principles of interlocking apply equally to all media. Each has advantages and disadvantages, and the choice of interlocking medium will depend on the type of machinery and the method of actuation of its dangerous parts.

Some interlocking systems have more than one control channel, e.g. dual control systems. It is often advantageous to design these systems so that the similar failures in both channels from the same cause (common cause failures) are minimised. One way of achieving this is by using a different control medium for each channel, e.g. one hydraulic and one electrical.

Interlocking methods

Methods of interlocking which ensure that the power medium is interrupted when a guard is open fall into two groups:

- Power interlocking.
- Control interlocking - illustrated by the following schematic diagrams (note: not actual circuit diagrams).

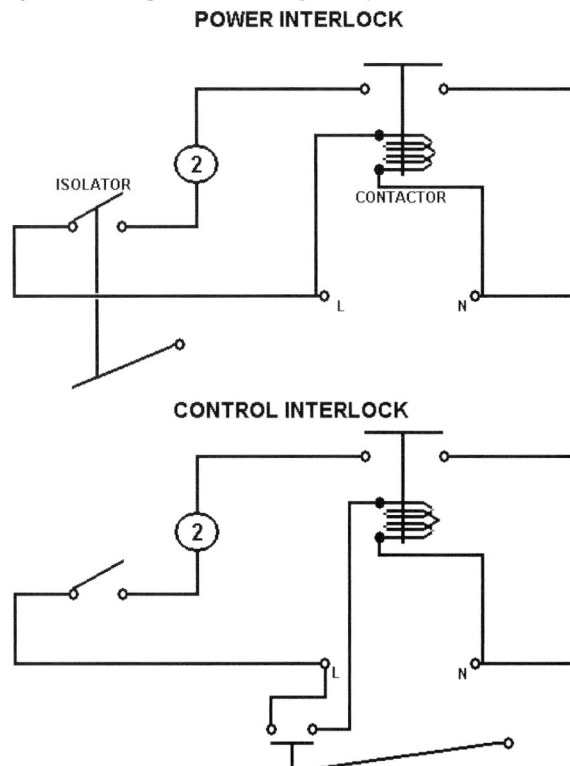

POWER INTERLOCK

CONTROL INTERLOCK

Figure C6-10: Schematic representation of power and control interlocking.

Source: Ambiguous.

Interlocking incorporating braking and/or guard locking

A hazard may exist after interruption of the power medium, for example, due to the continuing release of stored energy. Under these circumstances, systems should incorporate a device (or in dual systems, devices) to either:

1. Cause the hazard to be eliminated as the guard is opened (braking); or

2. Prevent the guard from being opened until the risk of injury from the hazard has passed (guard locking).

Guard locking systems.

Motion or position *sensing* devices:

a. Rotation sensing device which may be operated on various principles such a centrifugal force, friction, voltage generation;

b. Photoelectric beam;

c. Proximity device.

d. Position switch or valve.

Timing devices:

a. Mechanical, electric or electronic clocks.

b. Delay relay.

c. Sequence valve.

d. Threaded bolt.

e. Dashpot.

Guard *locking* devices:

a. Captive- key unit.

b. Trapped-key unit.

Types of failure of interlocking systems

The most common failures from which an interlocking system may suffer are as follows:

a. Failure, interruption or variation of externally supplied power medium, e.g. electrical supply, pneumatic or hydraulic ring main;

b. Malfunction due to power medium contamination;

c. Earth faults, i.e. accidental connection of a conductor to earth;

d. Open circuits in electrical systems;

e. Cross connection faults causing, for example, unintended starting or failure to stop.

f. Malfunction due to the electrical environment, i.e. mains borne or radiated interference. (This is normally less of a problem with electromagnetic and electromechanical devices than electronic devices.);

g. Disconnection or rupture of hoses or piping;

h. Mechanical failure, e.g. breakage or seizure;

i. Malfunction due to vibration;

j. Brake failure.

Measures can be taken to minimise the consequences of single failures in interlocking systems. These may include the use of additional control or monitoring channels:

1. Dual-control system interlocking with cross monitoring, which may or may not be self-checked;

2. Dual-control system interlocking without cross-monitoring;

3. Single-control system interlocking.

Probable effect of a failure to danger

Type of system	Probable effect of a failure to danger in a single channel	Action
Dual-control system interlocking with cross-monitoring. Monitoring function self-checked.	Guarding system remains effective.	None.
Dual-control system interlocking without cross-monitoring, but provided with indication of failure.	Machinery will continue to operate normally. Guarding system remains effective only on one channel.	Note indication failure. Take necessary remedial action.
Single-control system interlocking without indication of failure.	Machinery will continue to operate normally.	Guarding system is ineffective.

Figure C6-11: Probable effect of a failure to danger.   *Source: ACT.*

Choice of interlocking system

Selection of the preferred system of interlocking for a particular application should take account of:

a.   Frequency with which the approach to the danger area is required;

b.   Probability and severity of injury should the interlocking system fail;

c.   Resources required to reduce the risk of injury.

Power interlocking systems eliminate intermediate components used in control interlocking systems thereby reducing the probability of failure. Alternatively, the probability of failure of control interlocking systems can be reduced by incorporating additional interlocking and/or monitoring channels.

Interlocking switch types

a.   Cam-operated position switches.

b.   Tongue-operated switches.

c.   Captive-key switches.

d.   Trapped-key control of electrical switches.

e.   Inductive proximity switches.

f.   Magnetic switches.

g.   Diode links.

h.   Manually operated delay bolts.

i.   Solenoid operated shotbolts.

Mechanical interlocks

Can take a number of forms but usually involve discs, bars and levers arranged so that operation of the machine can only be carried out in a safe order. One such arrangement is used on positive clutch power presses. This utilises an arrangement where a cup type cam prevents the guard from opening until the press stops at the end of its cycle. This is used in conjunction with a lever connected to the guard which stops the clutch being operated while it is open.

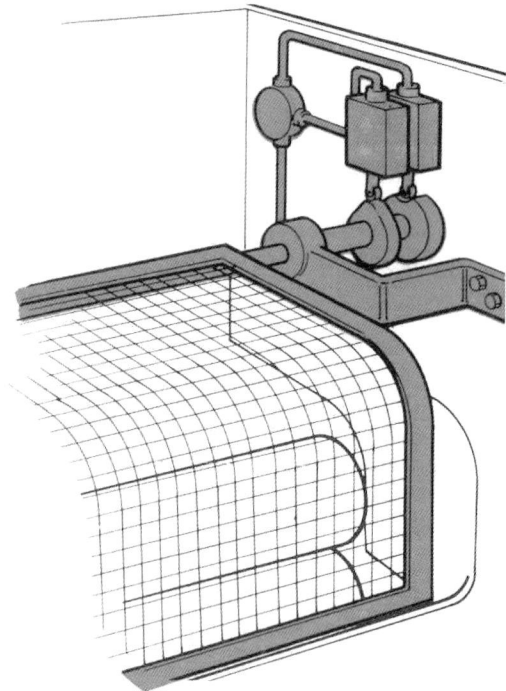

Figure C6-12: Two position switches operating in opposite modes, mounted side by side, each actuated by its own cam mounted on the guard hinge.   *Source: BS 5304: 1988.*

Cam-activated position switches and modes of operation

Cam-operated limit switch interlocks are versatile, effective and difficult to defeat. They can be rotary or linear and in each case the critical feature is that in the safe operating position the switch is relaxed, i.e. the switch plunger is not depressed. Any movement of the guard from the safe position causes the switch plunger to be depressed, tripping the controls and stopping the machine. Interlock switches should work in the 'positive mode'; negative mode is not acceptable. However for certain high risk areas, a combination of positive and negative mode is recommended and this arrangement can incorporate a switch failure monitoring circuit. The type of electrical switch used in interlocking is important.   They must be of the positive make-and-break type (known as 'limit' switches) that fail to safety and have contacts capable of carrying the maximum current in the circuit. Micro switches relying on leaf spring deflection for contact breaking are not acceptable.

A switch can be actuated in either of two modes, positive or negative. In the case of a cam operated electrical switch, positive means the contacts have been opened by a positive mechanical action of the cam (or similar). Negative means the contacts are opened by spring pressure when the cam is rotated. When used singularly positive mode is preferred.

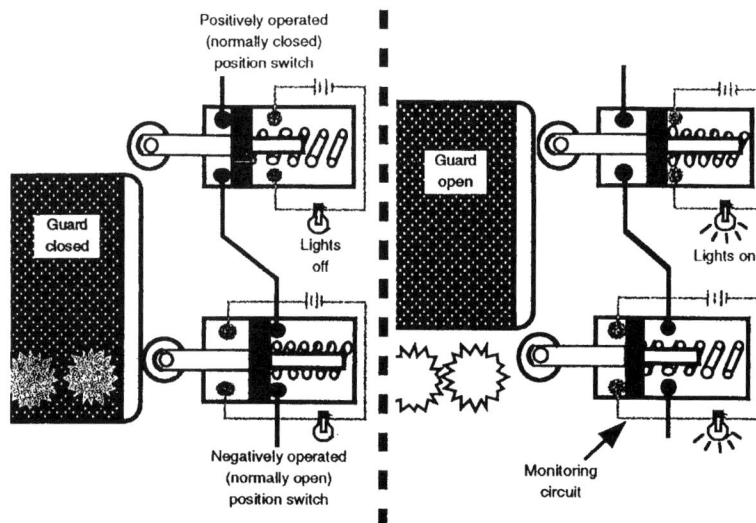

**Interlocking system incorporating two position switches operating in opposite modes
together with a simple self-monitoring arrangement**

Figure C6-13: Interlocking system.   *Source: Paper D (S Tech); Q5; June 1996 Previous NEBOSH Diploma.*

Magnetic switches

Magnetic switches with the actuating magnet attached to the guard have the disadvantage that they can be defeated easily. However, types using a shaped magnet have been accepted and in use for many years. Normal reed switches are not acceptable unless they incorporate special fail safe and current limiting features. Reed switches are often encapsulated and have application in flammable atmospheres. A similar type of switch relies on inductive circuits.

Captive and trapped key systems

Captive key systems

Captive key interlocking involves a combination of an electrical switch and a mechanical lock in a single assembly. Usually the key is attached to the movable guard. When the guard is closed, the key locates on the switch spindle. First movement of the key mechanically locks the guard shut and further movement actuates the electrical switch to complete the safety circuit.

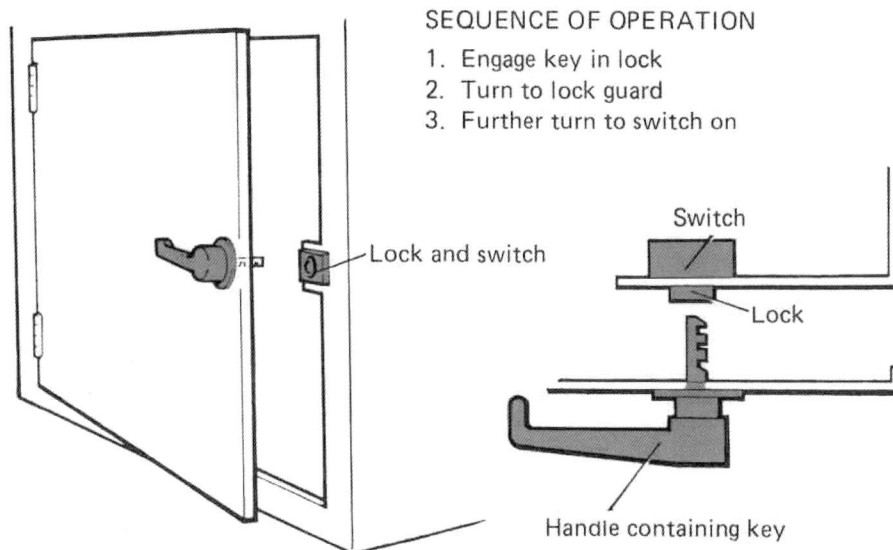

Figure C6-14: Captive key switch.   *Source: BS 5304: 1988.*

In this method of control interlocking, a combined switch and lock is attached to the machine and a key is secured to the guard. In order to engage the key in the lock, the guard has to be fully closed. This type of interlock is suitable for a hinged guard, or for a guard which can be removed bodily from the machine. Alignment of the key and switch can be aided by providing a location pin or pins which engage in bushes prior to the key entering the switch.

Time delay captive switch - The time delay commences when the machine is switched off. When the time delay is completed, the electromechanical bolt is released by energising the solenoid and the guard can be opened for access.

Trapped key system

In a trapped-key system the guard lock and switch, which also incorporates a lock, are separate as opposed to being combined into a single unit as in the captive-key switch. The essential feature of the system is that the removable key is trapped either in the guard lock, or in the switch lock. The lock on the guard has been closed and locked. This allows transfer of the key from the guard to the switch lock. Closing the switch traps the key, so that it cannot be removed while the switch is in the 'on' position. If there is more than one source of power, and therefore more than one control to be isolated, than a key exchange box should be used, to which all control isolation keys should be transferred and locked in before the access key, which is of a different configuration, can be released for transfer to the guard lock. Where there is more than one guard, the exchange box will accommodate an equivalent number of access keys.

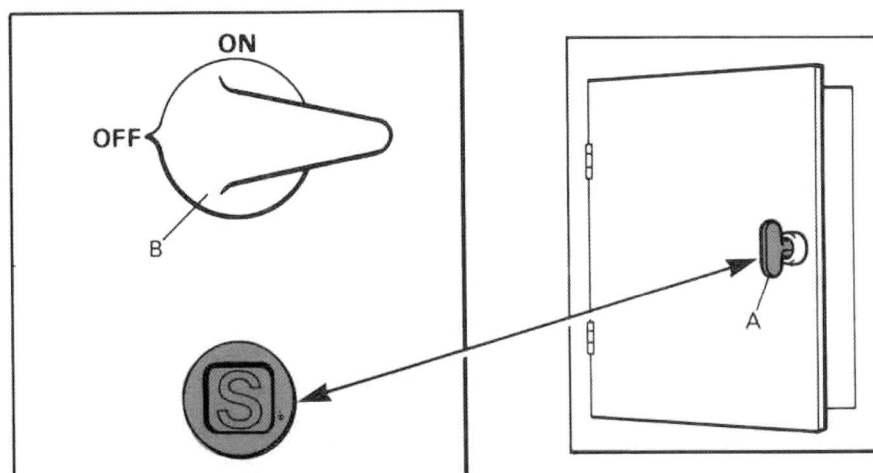

Figure C6-15: Practical application of the trapped-key control system.   *Source: BS 5304: 1988.*

Where, for the purpose of the process or of safety, a number of operations has to be carried out in a definite sequence, then the transferable key is locked in and exchanged for a different one at each stage. The exchange box can be integral with the lock.

It should be recognised that there is a danger with any interlocking system employing separate keys that the keys may be used without authorisation. The operation of such systems should therefore be restricted to responsible persons.

AUTOMATIC GUARDS

An automatic guard is a guard which is moved into position automatically by the machine, thereby removing any part of a person from the danger area. In some applications this type of guard is known as 'sweep away guard' e.g. on a guillotine.

An automatic guard operates by physically removing from the danger area any part of a person exposed to danger. The movable part of the guard should be positively actuated by the movement of the dangerous part of the machinery. The mechanism should be so designed that it will withstand long use with minimum maintenance.

It can be used only where there is adequate time for such removal to take place without introducing any further danger.

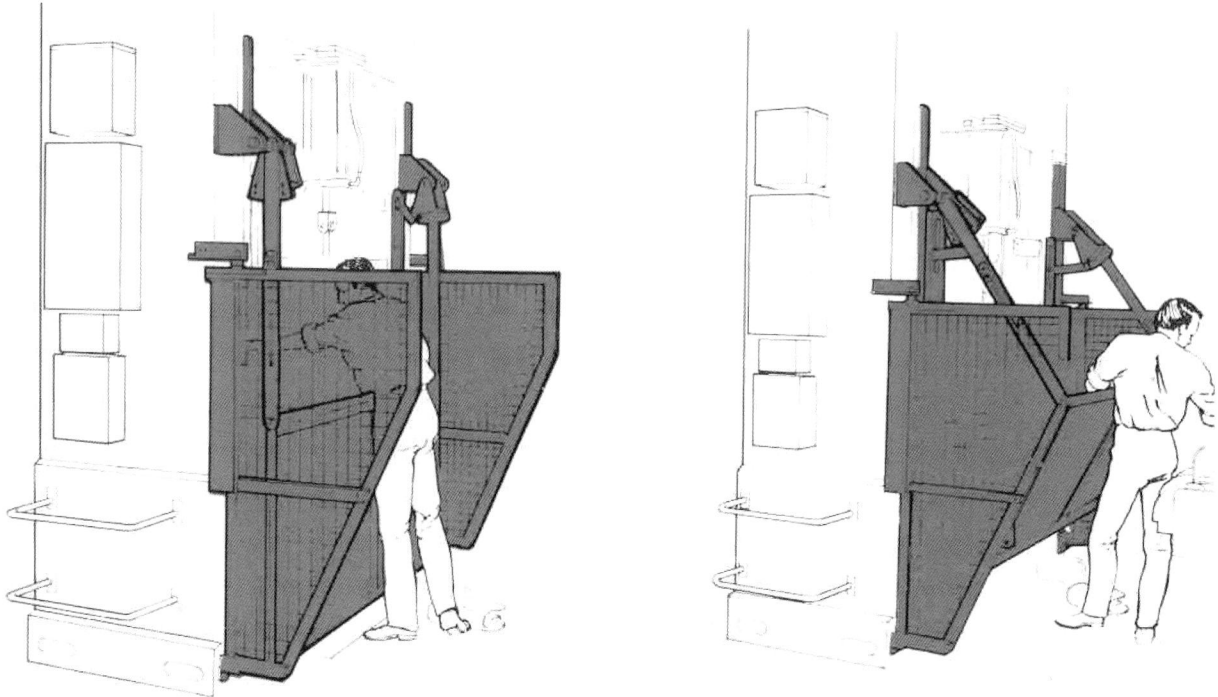

Figure C6-16: Automatic guard for a power press.

Source: BS 5304: 1988.

TRIP DEVICES

A trip device is a device which causes working machinery to stop or assume an otherwise safe condition, to prevent injury when a person approaches a danger point or area beyond a safe limit. The device will also be required to keep the machine in this condition while the person remains within the danger area unless other means of fulfilling this function are provided.

A trip device should be designed to ensure that an approach to a dangerous part beyond a safe limit causes the device to operate and the dangerous part(s) to stop before injury can be inflicted. The sensitive trip bar fitted in radial drilling machines does not exactly fit this description, but when operated on minimal deflection and properly adjusted, it prevents serious injury. The effective performance of a trip device depends on the stopping characteristics of the machinery, which should be controlled within fine limits. A brake may be necessary.

A trip device should be designed so that after it has been operated it may be re-set automatically or manually; re-starting should then be by means of the normal start button. An electrical or electronic trip device should be so designed that its effective operation will not be impaired by any function of the machinery or by extraneous influences.

There are two main types of trip device:

■ Mechanically actuated (e.g. trip wires, telescopic probes).
■ Non-mechanically actuated (e.g. photo-electric and ultra sonic devices).

Mechanical actuated devices

The essential element of a mechanical trip device is a barrier or part of the barrier, e.g. trip edge, which is moved by part of the body as it approaches a danger area. This movement operates the device which can be electrical, mechanical, hydraulic or pneumatic.

Trips can also be fitted to drills. It is important to understand that a trip is intended to prevent or minimise injury and that it does not prevent entanglement with the rotating spindle or tool. Operators should, therefore, be trained to take all necessary precautions to avoid the risk of entanglement and to use trip devices correctly.

A trip device consists of three principal components:

■ The actuating switch - usually operated from an adjustable trip probe or horizontal trip wire. Trip wires should actuate the switch in both the pulled and slack wire conditions;
■ A control unit which provides the electrical interface between the trip switch and motor. It should incorporate a reset button to ensure that after the device has been operated it must be reset before restarting the machine at the normal start control; and
■ A brake which may be either mechanical or electo-dynamic (e.g. DC injection).

TRIP DEVICE
For drilling
machines

Figure C6-17: Trip device for drilling machines (including hand drawn example).   *Source: BS 5304: 1988.*

Pressure sensitive mat system

A pressure sensitive mat contains sensors which operate when a person or object applies pressure to the mat. By their nature pressure sensitive mats are exposed to potential damage which can result in failure.

The dimensions of the mat should take account of a person's speed of approach, length of stride, and the overall response time of the safety system. Care should be taken to ensure that access cannot be gained without actuating the mat. Pressure sensitive mats should be sensitive over the whole sensing area. Where a number of mats are used together, this should include the function between adjoining mats.

A pressure sensitive mat system may be appropriate in circumstances where the use of a fixed guard or an interlocking guard is impracticable, and is particularly suitable for use as an emergency stopping device, as a means of protecting a person who may be inside machinery or in conjunction with other forms of safeguard.

The size and positioning if pressure sensitive mats should be calculated using the formula from the standard prEN 99: "The positioning of protective equipment in respect of approach speeds of parts of the human body". The standard relating to the mats themselves is contained in EN 1760-1 "Safety of machinery - Pressure sensitive devices; mats and floors". This requires that the top mat surface should be of a material capable of standing up to duty wear and be slip resistant. Where heavy loads, such as fork lift trucks, are likely then this should be made clear when specifying the mat to the manufacturer.

The standard also contains the following key points:

■   The size, force and positioning of test pieces for testing the mat sensitivity. Where an effective sensing area is built up from more than one sensor it shall have no dead zone.
■   A single sensor shall still perform its function after one million actuations by a mass of 75 kg.
■   When the actuating force is applied the output signal switching device shall change from an on state to an off state for at least as long as the acting force is applied.
■   After the actuating force has been removed the output of the output signal switching devices shall only change to on state after the application of a reset signal (applies to devices with reset).
■   For a pressure sensitive mat without reset, the output from the output signal switching device(s) shall change to an on state at power on and after the actuating force has been removed.

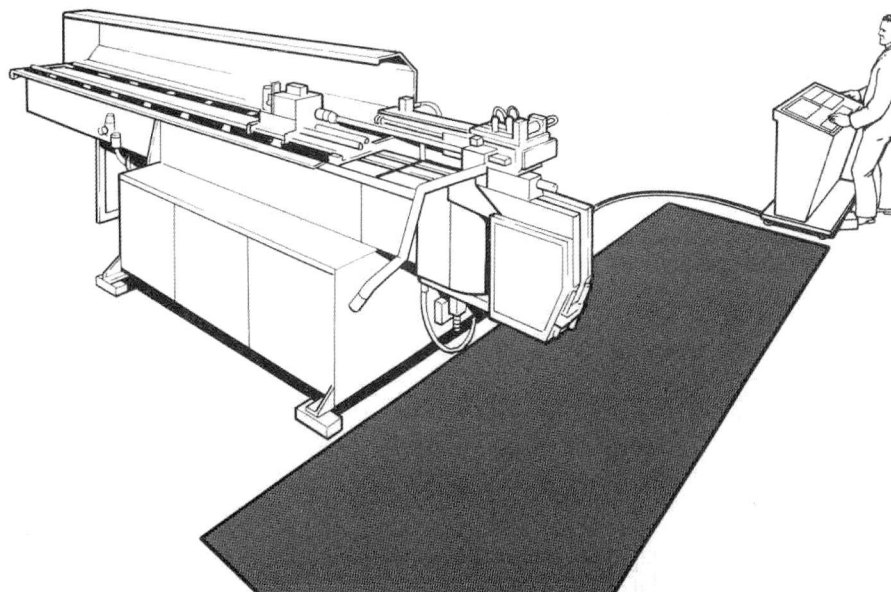

Figure C6-18: Pressure sensitive mat safeguarding the clamping and bending jaws of an automatic horizontal tube bender.   *Source: BS 5304: 1988.*

Non-mechanically actuated devices

Photoelectric safety systems

Photoelectric safety systems operate on the principal of the detection of an obstruction in the path taken by a beam or beams of light. The intangible barrier operated by this system may consist of a single beam, a number of beams of light, a curtain of light or any combination of these as necessary to provide the required safeguard. The curtain of light may be created by a scanning beam or beams, or a number of fixed beams.

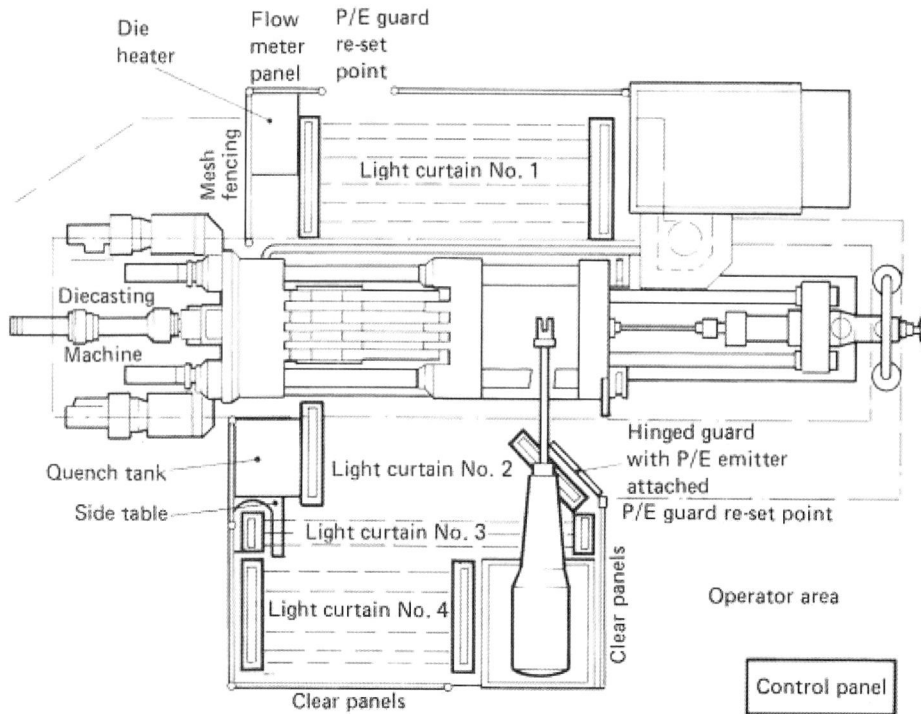

Figure C6-19: Photoelectric safety system used as a presence sensing device inside distance guards fitted around a robot served pressure die casting machine.
Source: Ambiguous.

The light may be visible or invisible, e.g. infra-red, and may be continuous or modulated, e.g. a scanning system.

Photoelectric safety system used as a presence sensing device inside distance guards fitted around a robot served pressure die casting machine.

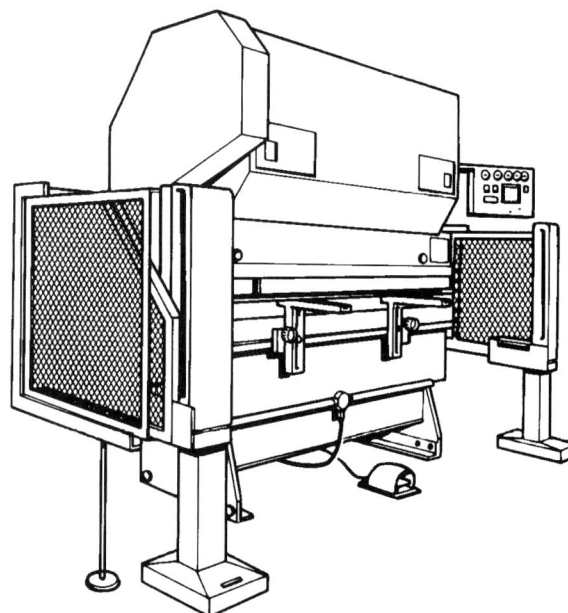

Figure C6-20: Photoelectric safety system used as a presence sensing device inside distance guards fitted around a robot served pressure die casting machine.
Source: HSG 129 Health and Safety in Engineering Workshops.

There are some factors that make photo-electric safety systems unsuitable either as trip devices or for presence detection. Factors that preclude their use as trip devices include:

- Inconsistent or inadequate machine response time/stopping performance due, for example, to:
  - The reaction characteristics of the machinery control circuitry, whether electrical, hydraulic or pneumatic;
  - Poor brake design; or
  - Variable speed, load or inertia.
- The inability of the machine to stop part-way through a cycle due to:
  - Nature of the process, e.g. a multi-station process where stopping between stations would create a production problem;
  - The method of drive, e.g. positive key clutches or similar mechanisms for engaging the drive so arranged that once started, the machinery can only be stopped when the cycle is complete; or
  - Stored energy, e.g. in the form of stored pressure in pneumatic reservoirs or hydraulic accumulators.
- Tendency for the machinery to eject materials or component parts.

Factors that preclude the use of photo-electric safety systems as trip or presence sensing devices include:

- Risk of injury from thermal or other radiation; or
- Unacceptable noise levels; or
- An environment likely to affect adversely the efficiency of the photo-electric safety system, e.g. through extraneous radiation, vibration, dust, excess water, or extremes of temperature.

However photo-electric safety systems may be acceptable if additional steps are taken to control the risks associated with the above hazards (e.g. local fixed guards to contain ejection).

The positioning of light curtains is dealt with in the standard prEN 99 "The positioning of protective equipment in respect of approach speeds of parts of the human body" and in HSE Guidance Note PM 41 "The application of photo-electric safety systems to machinery".

ADJUSTABLE / SELF-ADJUSTING GUARDS

Adjustable

A fixed guard which incorporates an adjustable element (which remains fixed for the duration of a particular operation) e.g. on a pillar drill or circular saw.

An adjustable guard provides an opening to the machinery through which material can be fed, the whole guard or part of it being capable of adjustment in order that the opening can be varied in height and width to suit the dimension of the work in hand. It is essential in such cases that the adjustment is carefully carried out by a suitably trained person.

Regular maintenance of the fixing arrangements is necessary to ensure that the adjustable element of the guard remains firmly in place when once positioned. The guard should be designed that the adjustable parts cannot easily become detached and mislaid.

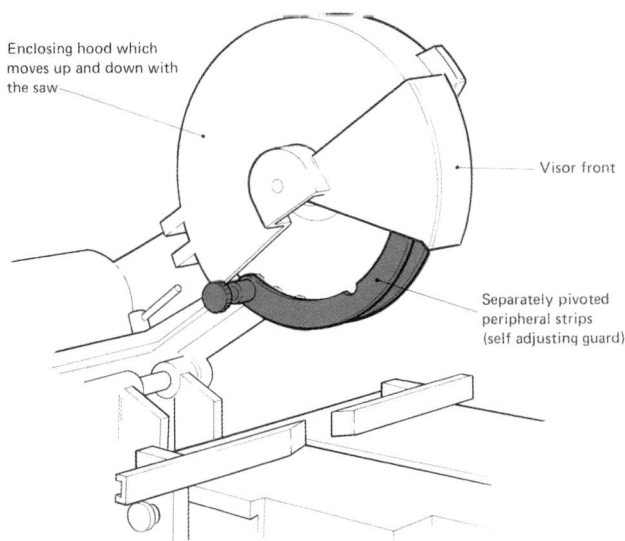

The guard is telescopic to provide ready adjustment to the surface of the workpiece and is attached to a vertical hinge to permit access to the spindle for drill changing.

Figure C6-21: Adjustable guard for a radial or pedestal drilling machine. *Source: BS 5304: 1988.*

Self adjusting

A guard which prevents accidental access by the operator, but allows entry of the material to the machine in such a way that the material actually forms part of the guarding arrangement itself e.g. hand held circular saw.

This type of protection is designed to prevent access to the dangerous part(s) until actuated by the movement of the workpiece, i.e. it is opened by the passage of the workpiece at the beginning of the operation and returns to the safe position on completion of the operation.

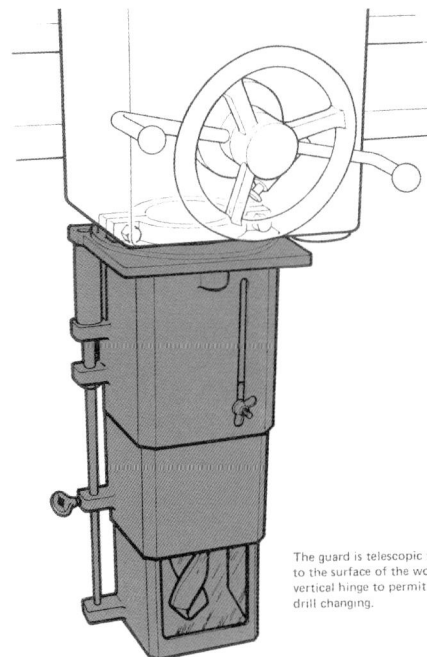

Enclosing hood which moves up and down with the saw

Visor front

Separately pivoted peripheral strips (self adjusting guard)

Figure C6-22: Self-adjusting guard arrangement for snipper cross-cutting sawing machine. *Source: BS 5304: 1988.*

Two-hand controls

A device which requires both hands to operate. Note that '2HC' devices protect only the operator and then, only provided the assistance of a colleague is not solicited to activate one control.

Where guarding is impracticable two-hand control offers a means of protecting the hands of the machine operator. It may also be used as a hold-to-run control.

A two-hand control device is a device which requires both hands to operate the machinery controls thus affording a measure of protection from danger to the machinery operator only. It should be designed in accordance with the following:

a. The hand controls should be so placed, separated and protected as to prevent spanning with one hand only, being operated with one hand and another part of the body, or being readily bridged.

b. It should not be possible to set the dangerous parts in motion unless the controls are operated within approximately 0.5s of each other. Having set the dangerous parts in motion, it should not be possible to do so again until both controls have been returned to their off position. This effectively discourages two people operating the machine together by co-ordinating their actions and also prevent the operator from locking one control in the start position which would allow him to operate the machinery by means of the other control leaving one hand free.

c. Movement of the dangerous parts should be arrested immediately or, where appropriate, arrested and reversed if one or both controls are released while there is yet danger from the movement of these parts.

Figure C6-23: Two-hand control device.   *Source: BS 5304: 1988.*

d. The hand controls should be situated at such a distance from the danger point that, on releasing the controls, it is not possible for the operator to reach the danger point before the motion of the dangerous parts has been arrested or, where appropriate, arrested and reversed.

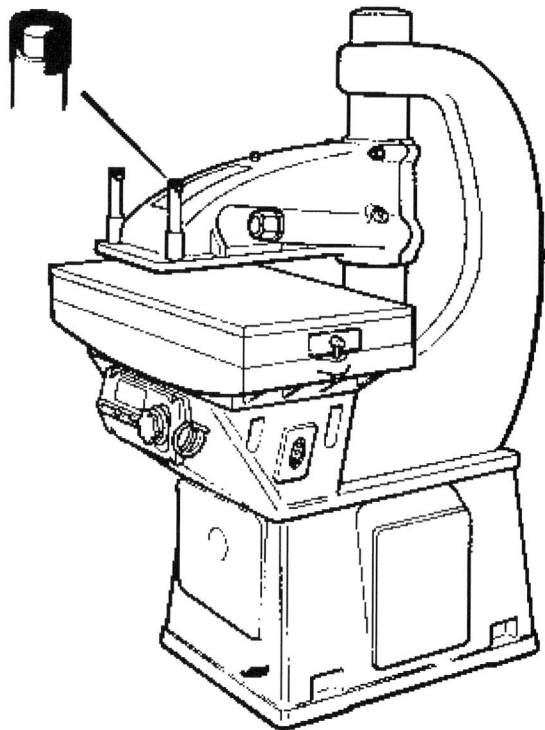

Mechanical restraints

A device which applies mechanical restraint to the dangerous part which prevents it from moving:

■ When the controls fail; or
■ When the machine is inadvertently activated.

Mechanical restraints are used to physically prevent a dangerous part of machinery from either moving into an undesired area or to stop the part moving at all during procedures such as cleaning or in transit (e.g. wedges, scotch, strut, spindle). Reliance is placed on the strength of the restraint to prevent hazardous movement such as a lift ram falling due to failure of the normal retaining system.

For example, in the plastics industry, many serious accidents have occurred during blade changing and the clearing of blockages, often due to unpowered movement of the blades in granulators. Chocks or in-built mechanical restraints should be used to stop the rotor moving during such procedures.

Jigs

Jigs and Push-Sticks are protection appliances which are used to hold or manipulate the workpiece in a way which allows people to keep their body away from the danger zone. They normally need to be used in addition to guards. Even when the best possible guarding is used, the operation of certain types of machines (e.g. woodworking machines such as a circular saw) often involves considerable risk, and wherever possible appliances such as jigs and holders, push sticks etc., should be provided and used.

Push sticks

Push sticks are used to feed timber through bench mounted circular saws. The stick is a short 12 to 24cm. length of wood used to move the last part of the timber to be cut past the blade, the stick keeps the blade; distant from the hands and the fingers. Push sticks and jigs are defined as appliances within the scope of hierarchy of PUWER for machine guarding protective devices.

Machine controls and emergency controls

Regulation 14 controls starting or making a significant change in operating conditions.

(1) Every employer shall ensure that, where appropriate, work equipment is provided with one or more controls for the purposes of -

   (a) Starting the work equipment (including re-starting after a stoppage for any reason); or

   (b) Controlling any change in the speed, pressure or other operating conditions of the work equipment where such conditions after the change result in risk to health and safety which is greater than or of a different nature from such risks before the change.

(2) Subject to paragraph (3), every employer shall ensure that where a control is required by paragraph (1), it shall not be possible to perform any operation mentioned in sub-paragraph (a) or (b) of that paragraph except by a deliberate action on such control.

(3) Paragraph (1) shall not apply to re-starting or changing operating conditions as a result of the normal operating cycle of an automatic device.

Any change in the operating conditions should only be possible by the use of a control, except if the change does not increase risk to health or safety. Examples of operating conditions include speed, pressure, temperature and power.

The controls provided should be designed and positioned so as to prevent, so far as possible, inadvertent or accidental operation. Buttons and levers should be of appropriate design, for example, including a shrouding or locking facility. It should not be possible for the control to operate itself, such as due to the effects of gravity, vibration, or failure of a spring mechanism.

Regulation 15 stop controls

(1) Every employer shall ensure that, where appropriate, work equipment is provided with one or more readily accessible controls the operation of which will bring the work equipment to a safe condition in a safe manner.

(2) Any control required by paragraph (1) shall bring the work equipment to a complete stop where necessary for reasons of health and safety.

(3) Any control required by paragraph (1) shall, if necessary for reasons of health and safety, switch off all sources of energy after stopping the functioning of the work equipment.

(4) Any control required by paragraph (1) shall operate in priority to any control which starts or changes the operating conditions of the work equipment.

The primary requirement of this Regulation is that the action of the control should bring the equipment to a safe condition in a safe manner. This acknowledges that it is not always desirable to bring all items of work equipment immediately to a complete or instantaneous stop. For example, to prevent the unsafe build-up of heat or pressure, or to allow a controlled run-down of large rotating parts. Similarly, stopping the mixing mechanism of a reactor during certain chemical reactions could lead to a dangerous exothermic reaction.

The Regulation is qualified by 'where necessary for reasons of health and safety'. Therefore accessible dangerous parts must be rendered stationary. However, parts of equipment which do not present a risk, such as suitably guarded cooling fans, do not need to be positively stopped and may be allowed to idle.

Regulation 16 emergency stop controls

The function of an emergency stop device is to provide a means to bring a machine to a rapid halt. It is provided in such circumstances where it would be of benefit and should be readily available to the operator and/or others. It should be easy to operate and clearly discernible from other controls.

(1) Every employer shall ensure that, where appropriate, work equipment is provided with one or more readily accessible emergency stop controls unless it is not necessary by reason of the nature of the hazards and the time taken for the work equipment to come to a complete stop as a result of the action of any control provided by virtue of regulation 15(1).

(2) Any control required by paragraph (1) shall operate in priority to any control required by regulation 15(1).

Emergency stops are intended to effect a rapid response to potentially dangerous situations and they should not be used as functional stops during normal operation.

Emergency stop controls should be easily reached and actuated. Common types are mushroom-headed buttons, bars, levers, kick-plates, or pressure-sensitive cables.

Regulation 17 controls

(1) Every employer shall ensure that all controls for work equipment shall be clearly visible and identifiable, including by appropriate marking where necessary.

(2) Except where necessary, the employer shall ensure that no control for work equipment is in a position where any person operating the control is exposed to a risk to his health or safety.

(3) Every employer shall ensure where appropriate -

(a) That, so far as is reasonably practicable, the operator of any control is able to ensure from the position of that control that no person is in a place where he would be exposed to any risk to his health or safety as a result of the operation of that control, but where or to the extent that it is not reasonably practicable;

(b) That, so far as is reasonably practicable, systems of work are effective to ensure that, when work equipment is about to start, no person is in a place where he would be exposed to a risk to his health or safety as a result of the work equipment starting, but where neither of these is reasonably practicable;

(c) That an audible, visible or other suitable warning is given by virtue of regulation 24 whenever work equipment is about to start.

(4) Every employer shall take appropriate measures to ensure that any person who is in a place where he would be exposed to a risk to his health or safety as a result of the starting or stopping of work equipment has sufficient time and suitable means to avoid that risk.

It should be possible to identify easily what each control does and on which equipment it takes effect. Both the controls and their markings should be clearly visible. As well as having legible wording or symbols, factors such as the colour, shape and position of controls are important.

Warnings given in accordance with regulation 17(3)(c), should be given sufficiently in advance of the equipment actually starting to give those at risk time to get clear. As well as time, suitable means of avoiding the risk should be provided. This may take the form of a device by means of which the person at risk can prevent start-up or warn the operator of his/her presence. Otherwise there must be adequate provision to enable people at risk to withdraw, e.g. sufficient space or exits.

Circumstances will affect the type of warning chosen.

PUWER - Regulation 18 control systems

(1) Every employer shall-

(a) Ensure, so far as is reasonably practicable, that all control systems of work equipment are safe; and

(b) Are chosen making due allowance for the failures, faults and constraints to be expected in the planned circumstances of use.

(2) Without prejudice to the generality of paragraph(1), a control system shall not be safe unless-

(a) Its operation does not create any increased risk to health or safety;

(b) It ensures, so far as is reasonably practicable, that any fault in or damage to any part of the control system or the loss of supply of any source of energy used by the work equipment cannot result in additional or increased risk to health or safety;

(c) It does not impede the operation of any control required by regulation 15 or 16.

Failure of any part of the control system or its power supply should lead to a 'fail-safe' condition (more correctly and realistically called 'minimised failure to danger'), and not impede the operation of the 'stop' or 'emergency stop' controls. The measures which should be taken in the design and application of a control system to mitigate against the effects of its failure will need to be balanced against the consequences of any failure. The greater the risk, the more resistant the control system should be to the effects of failure.

Stability

PUWER - Regulation 20 stability

Every employer shall ensure that work equipment or any part of work equipment is stabilised by clamping or otherwise where necessary for purposes of health or safety.

Most machines used in a fixed position should be bolted or otherwise fastened down so that they do not move or rock during use. It has long been recognised that woodworking and other machines (except those specifically designed for portable use) should be bolted to the floor or similarly secured to prevent unexpected movement.

Lighting

PUWER - Regulation 21 lighting

Every employer shall ensure that suitable and sufficient lighting, which takes account of the operations to be carried out, is provided at any place where a person uses work equipment.

Local lighting may be needed to give sufficient view of a dangerous process or to reduce visual fatigue.

Safe systems of work

It is essential to have a balanced strategy of integration of technical, procedural and behavioural controls in order to achieve safety with machinery. This means not having an over reliance on any one control but ensuring that they are integrated and complement each other. The principle of taking a risk based approach is essential. This will mean using more of the control options the higher the risk.

PERMITS

A permit-to-work system is a formal written system used to control certain types of work that are potentially hazardous. A permit-to-work is a document which specifies the work to be done and the precautions to be taken. Permits-to-work form an essential part of safe systems of work for many maintenance activities. They allow work to start only after safe procedures have been defined and they provide a clear record that all foreseeable hazards have been considered. A permit-to-work should be used whenever the method by which a job is to be done is likely to be critical to the safety of those involved, other nearby workers, the public or the plant itself. The type of work may involve:

■ Hot work of any type, or the use of tools or equipment which may create sparks, in an area where there is the possibility of fire or explosion.

■ Entry into a confined space.

■ The disconnection or opening of pipelines or vessels which have contained flammable, toxic or harmful substances.

■ Work on machinery or electrical equipment.

■ Working at height.

■ Working in excavations.

■ Pressure vessels.

Format

A permit-to-work is a document which:

■ Specifies the work to be done and the precautions to be taken.

■ Predetermines a safe procedure.

■ Is a clear record that foreseeable hazards have been considered in advance.

It defines the appropriate precautions and the sequence in which they are to be carried out.

Before maintenance work is begun, consideration should be given as to whether a permit-to-work is required.

A permit should be only as complicated as the work requires. One permit could not cover all the previously mentioned situations without being needlessly complicated for some. A permit is required when the safeguards available in normal working are no longer available and identifies those conditions required to make the operation safe.

Major features of permit systems

Identifying need

Failure to identify that a permit-to-work was needed is a frequent cause of incidents. Often it is not a failure to appreciate the risk but failure to document the procedures which lead to an incident.

Identifying hazards

A common fault with permit systems is failure adequately to consider all the possible hazards, creating a false sense of security on the part of the employees. Risks from adjacent plant are often ignored as are the introduction or creation of further hazards after a permit had been completed.

Implementation

Issuing a permit-to-work does not of itself make the job safe. It merely provides the opportunity for management to check what is necessary for the operation, to ensure that it has been done and to inform those who are to do the work how to proceed. Completing a permit without ensuring that its conditions are satisfied can be more dangerous than having no permit at all.

A number of instances have been noted where work was being carried out under a permit system but the checks had not been made to ensure compliance.

Key points of a permit-to-work

- Define the job to be done.
- Specifies the risks.
- Determine the hazards.
- Establish the controls.
- Identify responsibilities.
- Check isolation procedures are adequate.
- Define who should issue (authoriser) the permit.
- Hand over the permit to the operator (acceptor).
- Establish a time limit.
- Hand over formally if the work involves a shift change.
- Regularly monitor work standards throughout the permit duration.

ISOLATION

Regulation 19 of PUWER deals with isolation from sources of energy. The main aim of this regulation is to allow equipment to be made safe under particular circumstances, such as when maintenance is to be carried out, when an unsafe condition develops (failure of a component, overheating, or pressure build-up), or where a temporarily adverse environment would render the equipment unsafe, for example, electrical equipment in wet conditions or in a flammable or explosive atmosphere.

Isolation means establishing a break in the energy supply in a secure manner, i.e. by ensuring that inadvertent reconnection is not possible. You should identify the possibilities and risks of reconnection as part of your risk assessment, which should then establish how secure isolation can be achieved. For some equipment, this can be done by simply removing the plug from the electrical supply socket. For other equipment, an isolating switch or valve may have to be locked in the off or closed position to avoid unsafe reconnection. The closed position is not always the safe position: for example, drain or vent outlets may need to be secured in the open position.

If work on isolated equipment is being done by more than one person, it may be necessary to provide a locking device with multiple locks and keys. Each will have their own lock or key, and all locks have to be taken off before the isolating device can be removed. Keys should not be passed to anyone other than the nominated personnel and should not be interchanged between nominated people.

For safety reasons in some circumstances, sources of energy may need to be maintained when the equipment is stopped, for example when the power supply is helping to keep the equipment or parts of it safe. In such cases, isolation could lead to consequent danger, so it will be necessary to take appropriate measures to eliminate any risk before attempting to isolate the equipment.

It is appropriate to provide means of isolation where the work equipment is dependent upon external energy sources such as electricity, pressure (hydraulic or pneumatic) or heat. Where possible, means of dissipating stored energy should be provided. Other sources of energy such as its potential energy, chemical or radiological energy, cannot be isolated from the equipment. Nevertheless, there should be a means of preventing such energy from adversely affecting workers, by shielding, barriers or restraint.

Isolation of electrical equipment is dealt with by regulation 12 of the Electricity at Work Regulations 1989. Guidance to those Regulations expands on the means of isolating electrical equipment. Note that those Regulations are only concerned with electrical danger (electric shock or burn, arcing and fire or explosion caused by electricity), and do not deal with other risks (such as mechanical) that may arise from failure to isolate electrical equipment.

Thermal energy may be supplied by circulation of pre-heated fluid such as water or steam. In such cases, isolating valves should be fitted to the supply pipework.

Similar provision should be made for energy supplies in the form of liquids or gases under pressure. A planned preventive maintenance programme should therefore be instigated which assures effective means of isolation. It may be necessary to isolate pipework by physically disconnecting it or fitting spades in the line to provide the necessary level of protection. Redundancy in the form of more than one isolation valve fitted in series may also be used, but care should be exercised to check the efficacy of each valve function periodically. The performance of such valves may deteriorate over time, and their effectiveness often cannot be judged visually.

The energy source of some equipment is held in the substances contained within it; examples are the use of gases or liquids as fuel, electrical accumulators (batteries) and radionuclides. In such cases, isolation may mean removing the energy-containing material, although this may not always be necessary. Also, it is clearly not appropriate to isolate the terminals of a battery from the chemical cells within it, since that could not be done without destroying the whole unit.

Some equipment makes use of natural sources of energy such as light or flowing water. In such cases, suitable means of isolation include screening from light, and the means of diverting water flow, respectively. Another natural energy source, wind power, is less easily diverted, so sail mechanisms should be designed and constructed so as to permit minimal energy transfer when necessary. Effective restraint should be provided to prevent unplanned movement when taken out of use for repair or maintenance.

Regulation 19(3) of PUWER also requires precautions to ensure that people are not put at risk following reconnection of the energy source. So, reconnection of the energy source should not put people at risk by itself initiating movement or other hazard. Measures are also required to ensure that guards and other protection devices are functioning correctly before operation begins.

WORKING AT UNGUARDED MACHINERY

Greater reliance on information, instruction, training and supervision may be required in respect of the personnel working at unguarded machinery or involved with setting, cleaning or maintenance. The inexperience, lack of awareness of risks and immaturity of young persons should also be taken into account. While it is recognised that young people may need to carry out these operations, in the factory, as part of their course of training, such use is permitted provided it is carried out under the adequate supervision of a person who has the necessary knowledge and experience

Approach to unguarded machinery should be reduced to a minimum. Lubrication should be by remote or mechanical means. Jigs, push sticks or holders should be used where more sophisticated arrangements are not possible. Where other access is absolutely necessary, it must be strictly controlled by a safe system of work. Where it is necessary for swarf etc. to be cleared then a tool such as a swarf rake should be provided.

SETTING

The process by which the cutting tools etc. are replaced or adjusted to suit the work to be done. Setting will usually require clear access to the tools of the machine to enable adjustment or replacement. For example the dies of a power press may need to be changed and set into position to enable a new component to be produced. This type of work will usually cause the person doing the setting to open or remove the guard. The setter may be tempted to run the machine without the guard in place to test their setting arrangements. This would be a dangerous practice which must not be allowed. It is important that the guards be replaced before operational checks are made.

CLEANING

The process by which the cutting tools etc. are cleaned of waste materials such as swarf, and are periodically removed. When machines are in use and producing waste materials they may build up on the cutting tools, operators may be tempted to clean the cutting tool to remove the build up and improve the process. The machine must either be stationery to enable cleaning or the cleaning be done by the use of an appliance that keeps the operator in a safe position and free from the cutting or entanglement risk that may be associated with the cutting tools.

MAINTENANCE

Any maintenance work, including setting and cleaning, should only be done when the machine is isolated from all sources of power such as electrical, steam, compressed air and flywheels. If the potential for stored energy exists, this should be released and if necessary moving parts, for example, fans, drive shafts, mixers , etc should be physically secured to prevent movement.

6.2 - Role and application of European standards relating to machinery

TYPE A, B1, B2 AND C STANDARDS

The Supply of Machinery (Safety) Regulations 1992, were introduced in accordance with Directive 89/392/EEC, the Machinery Directive, which creates a common safety and hygiene standard for all machinery supplied within the European Union through the use of the CE Marking and the symbol $C\,\varepsilon$. *(See Element C5 – for more information on CE Marking).* The Machinery Directive differs from the Provision and Use of Work Equipment Regulations (PUWER) in that under the Machinery Directive a number of "Essential Health and Safety Requirements" (EHSRs) are established supported by a complex range and number of European Normative (EN) standards, whilst PUWER specifies only the minimum standards to be applied.

The Work Equipment Directive 89/655/EEC also refers to compliance with other directives in respect of safety and clearly identifies the user as being subject to the Work Equipment Regulations whilst the supplier/designer is subject to the full range of detailed requirements of the Machinery Directive. The only exception to this rule is the user undertakes any significant modifications to the original duty, or if the supplier undertakes a complete overhaul of the equipment. In both cases the equipment will be required to comply with the Machinery Directive and the appropriate documentation issued.

In addition the supplier/designer is also required to comply with the "new approach" mechanism which was established under a directive in 1985. This establishes a "duty for life" and the requirement to review design standards as the "state of the art" develops through the harmonised standards. This approach has been applied to a number of different European Union directives and allows the standards applicable to the conformity assessment to be modified as technology and experience develops, without the need to modify specific Directives and therefore national legislation.

The transposed harmonised standards applicable for determining compliance with the essential health and safety requirements are produced by a number of technical committees and when approved are referenced with an EN number and published in the Official Journal of the European Communities. All EN standards are translated into three languages, French, German and English, an extremely difficult task as exact translations are not always available. A box in the packaging standards became a pre-formed rigid container because of no German language equivalent.

The role of the standard in respect of the Essential Health and Safety requirements (EHSR) is clarified by considering the EHSR as being expressed in mainly general terms whilst the European Harmonised Standard should provide the detail so that the designers have clear guidance on how to achieve conformity with the directive.

However it is important to recognise that a standard is never mandatory in that the manufacturer may adopt other solutions provided that the requirements of the Regulations are met.

The manufacturer in this situation must ensure that the correct information is held in the technical file and that the standard applied is demonstrated as not introducing a lower level of protection.

The standards are divided into 4 separate categories: A, B1, B2 and C, each of which has a different intent or application in respect of the regulations process:

Type A

These are the general safety concepts and design criteria which can be applied to all machinery and are intended to provide the necessary basic information to the designer and manufacturer.

Examples: EN 292, parts 1 and 2, basic concepts, principles for design.

EN 414, rules for drafting and presentation of standards.

EN 1050, principles for Risk Assessment.

Type B

Standards which detail particular safety aspects in support of the general principles of the A standards. These are further sub-divided into:

- Type B1 - standards relating to particular safety aspects (e.g. noise, safety distances and surface temperatures).
- Type B2 - standards on safety related devices (e.g. guards, pressure sensitive devices, two handed control devices).

Examples (Type B1):   EN 294, Safety distances to prevent danger zones being reached by the upper limbs.

EN 349, Minimum gaps to avoid crushing parts of the human body.

Examples (Type B2):   Standards which provide details in respect of technical solutions involving safety devices.

EN 574, Two-hand Controllers.

EN 418, Emergency Stop Equipment.

Type C

Standards which provide details of the safety requirements or particular machines or groups of machines. This group will become the largest number of standards but will not be able to fully function until the scope and detail of the A and B standards has been completed.

Examples: EN 454, Planetary Mixers, safety and hygiene requirements.

EN 1674, Dough and Pastry Bakes, safety and hygiene requirements.

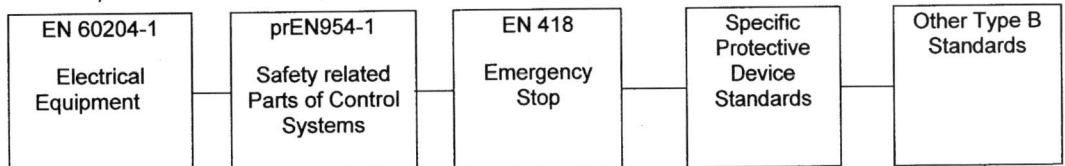

Figure C6-24: Machinery standards.

Source: ACT.

Number	Title	Type
BS EN 292-1: 1991	Safety of machinery - Basic concepts, general principles for design Part 1: Basic terminology, methodology	A
BS EN 292-2: 1991	Safety of machinery - Basic concepts, general principles for design	A
BS EN 292-2/A1:1995	Safety of machinery - Basic concepts and general principles for design. Part 2: Technical principles and specifications	A
BS EN 294:1992	Safety of machinery - Safety distances to prevent danger zones being reached by the upper limbs	B1
BS EN 349: 1993	Safety of machinery - Minimum gaps to avoid crushing of parts of the human body	B1
BS EN 28662-1: 1993	Hand-held portable power tools - Measurement of vibrations at the handle - Part 1: General (ISO 8662-1: 1988)	B1
BS EN 418: 1992	Safety of machinery - Emergency stop equipment, functional aspects - Principles of design	B2
BS EN 608: 1995	Agricultural and forestry machinery - Portable chainsaws - Safety	C
BS EN ISO 11111: 1995	Safety requirements for textile machinery. (ISO 11111: 1995)	C

Figure C6-25: Machinery standards.

Source: ACT.

The CEN technical committees standards

CEN/TC 10	Passenger, goods and service lifts.
CEN/TC 65	Portable grinding machines - Mechanical safety.
CEN/TC 98	Lifting platforms.
CEN/TC 114	Safety of machinery.
CEN/TC 122	Ergonomics.
CEN/TC 123	Lasers and laser related equipment.
CEN/TC 142	Woodworking machines - Safety.
CEN/TC 143	Machine tools - Safety.
CEN/TC 144	Tractors and machinery for agriculture and forestry.
CEN/TC 145	Rubber and plastics machines - Safety.
CEN/TC 146	Packaging machines - Safety.
CEN/TC 147	Cranes - Safety.

BS EN ISO 12100 (SUPERSEDING BS EN 292)

One of the key machinery safety standards, namely BS EN 292 Parts 1 and 2, has been superseded and replaced by BS EN ISO 12100, dated November 2003.

Safety of machinery - basic concepts, general principle for design

- Part 1, basic terminology, methodology.
- Part 2, technical principles and specifications.

Whilst the titles and content of the new standards are very similar to those of the previous standards, there are, however, some notable differences:

Parts 1 and 2 now refer only to designers, rather than 'designers, manufacturers and other interested bodies', which implies a greater responsibility for designers of machinery.

The emphasis has changed towards a more risk-based approach; for example:

Section 5 of Part 1 has been renamed 'Strategy for risk reduction' rather than 'Strategy for selecting safety measures.'

Section 3 of Part 1 contains around 60 terms and definitions, which is a substantial increase over the old standard despite the fact that some terms and definitions have been deleted.

Unlike BS EN 292-1, the new standards cross reference to other standards; this is extremely useful and helps to remove previous ambiguity.

Section 4 (Hazards to be taken into account when designing machinery) whilst similar to its counterpart in the old standard, now incorporates the additional hazards that were previously contained in Section 6. For machine designers, Section 4 represents a fairly comprehensive checklist of hazards, even extending as far as slips/trips/falls and hazards associated with the environment in which the machine is used.

An important principle contained in section 5 is that protective measures are a combination of measures taken by the designer and the user. However, it is preferable by far to use measures taken by the designer and the designer is expected to have an input into the safety measures taken by the user. Designers must also take into account the safety of the machinery during all phases of its lifecycle. Section 5.3 refers to risk assessment and states 'the designer shall estimate the risk for each hazard, as far as possible on the basis of quantifiable factors, and finally decide if risk reduction is required as a result of the risk evaluation.' Having identified and evaluated the risks, the designer must eliminate or reduce them by protective measures.

The standard refers to the 'three-step method':

Step 1   Inherently safe design measures.

Step 2   Safeguarding and complementary protective measures.

Step 3   Information for use (eg warning signs on the machine, instructions in the handbook).

For each of these three steps there is a cross-reference to Part 2 of the standard, where more information can be found.

Whilst BS EN ISO 12100 Part 2 is similar to BS EN 292 Part 2, there is much more information provided relating to inherently safe design measures and the benefits that these offer.

Part 2 includes many examples of ways in which the requirements of the standard could be met in practice. To assist in selecting the correct type of standards a useful flowchart is included.

Two areas in the new standard where there is more detail than the old standard relate to 'inherently safe design measures for control systems' and 'minimising the probability of safety function failures.' These are both contained in the new Section 4, which is similar to the previous standard, Section 3.

Section 5 (Safeguarding and complementary protective measures) is also similar to the previous Section 4, though there is more detail for topics such as sensitive protective equipment.

Sub-sections, for example 5.5.2 refers to the emergency stop function have been incorporated within Section 5 whereas they were previously contained in Section 6, which has no equivalent in the new standard. In a similar way, Section 6 of the new standard (Information for use) is very similar to the previous Section 5.

BS ENO ISO 14121 (SUPERSEDING BS EN 1050)

BS EN ISO 14121 safety of machinery - principles of risk assessment

This International Standard establishes general principles for the approach to machinery risk assessment to identify the issues which need to be addressed at the design. Factors which are considered include use and foreseeable use of the equipment through all phases of the life of the machine; this will include any accident or incident data available at time of consideration.

The Standard gives guidance on the information required to allow risk assessment to be carried out. Procedures are described for the identification of hazards and the estimation and evaluation of risk. The purpose of the Standard is to provide advice for decisions to be made on the safety of machinery and the type of documentation required to verify the risk assessment carried out. The Standard is not intended to provide a detailed account of methods for analysing hazards and estimating risk, as these techniques are varied and established elsewhere. A summary of some of the analysis techniques available is provided for information only.

6.3 - Programmable electronic systems

TYPES OF COMPUTER CONTROLLED EQUIPMENT

Definition

A PES is a computer-based system, which controls, protects or monitors the operation of plant, machinery or various types of equipment. It can range in size from a single microprocessor chip to a mainframe computer system, but the same underlying principles govern its safe incorporation into any installation and all PESs have the same basic structure. The PES may form part of an oil refinery, a chemical processing plant, a robot or a CNC (computer numerically controlled) machine.

The layout of a typical PES is shown schematically below:

Schematic diagram of the structure of a programmable electronic system (PES)

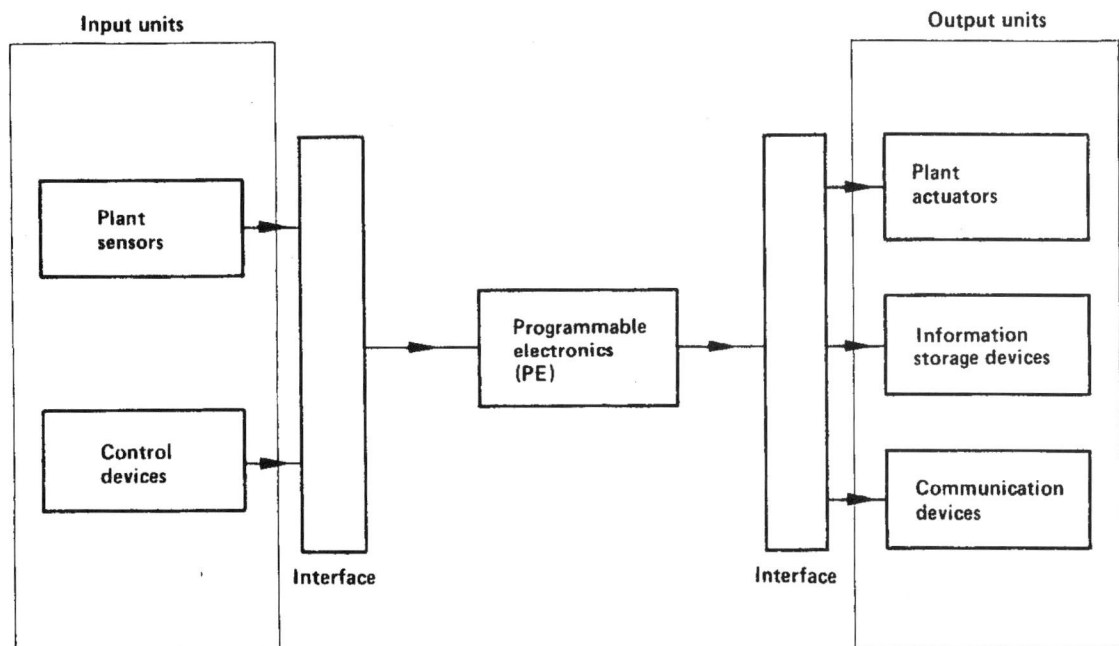

Figure C6-26: Schematic diagram of the structure of a programmable electronic system (PES).

Source: Programmable Electronic Systems (An Introductory Guide); HSE Publication - PES01.

The programmable electronics are the brain of the system. They communicate with the rest of the installation by various input and output units. The diagram above shows the input units: plant sensors and control devices. The plant sensors send messages to the programmable electronics about the state of the plant operating conditions, such as the position of a component or the temperature of a chemical reaction. The control devices allow the operator to relay instructions to the programmable electronics, for example, to tell the machine to stop one job and start on another. The programmable electronics analyse the incoming data and send the information to the output units. As the diagram shows, these are the plant actuators, information storage devices and communication devices. Information to the plant actuators could, for example cause it to move a component to the right position or to stop heating a chemical mixture because it is at a high enough temperature. Information sent to the storage devices can be retrieved and used later on. The communication devices are the monitor screens and printers, which relay the messages to the operators so they know what is going on inside the plant or machinery. The interfaces that link the programmable electronics to the input and output units organise the streams of electronic signals that are being carried along the communications channels or data highways.

PES is a computerised system that is made up of hardware and software. The hardware is the physical components of the system: monitors, wires, chips, etc., and the software is the sets of instructions that tell the computer what to do. Some software is already in the computer when it is bought, while other software can be added later. Software is sets of instructions called programs, which can be written in any one of a variety of sophisticated programming languages, and a number of other programs (compilers) reduce it to a series of binary digits (bits) that form part of the control of the machine. The basic form the program is reduced, so is the electronic signals that the PES understands.

Specific programs are used to instruct a machine to carry out a task. Further programs can be added to give new instructions that can alter or add to the task. Machines can be programmed to carry out a wide range of tasks including welding, painting, assembly fitting, and cutting intricate shapes out of metal or wood.

When safety is being evaluated, it is important to realise that programmable electronic equipment is fundamentally different from other equipment. The effects of a failure are not easy to predict, nor is it easy to find out where the fault lies. Programs can contain bugs, that is, instructions in the program that produce an effect that is not what the programmer intended and they might not show themselves until a certain sequence of events occurs. The effect of a bug is unpredictable.

There are two basic types of failure: random hardware failure and systematic failure. The hardware of a PES is comprised of many mechanical and electronic parts which will wear out or break down at different intervals. This will depend on how well the parts have been manufactured or put together in the system and how often they have been used. This means it is impossible to predict when a system will break down because of the failure of one of its parts.

Hardware failures are random events. Over time, data can be collected on how often equipment breaks down, which will help to estimate how long a component is likely to last. Because of the rapid development of computer hardware, the usefulness of the data that is collected is limited.

An effective way to help combat this is the use of redundancy. This is where a back-up component or system is used in the belief that both components or systems are unlikely to fail at the same time.

Systematic failures occur because of mistakes made at some stage in the specification, design, construction or operation of a system. Every time a particular set of conditions occurs, the system will fail. It is impossible to test for every set of conditions so the fault may remain hidden until the circumstances arise and the system breaks down. This can cause dangerous situations for people as well as operational problems.

Systematic failures can be due to specification errors, equipment errors and software errors. Specification errors can occur when the tasks to be performed by the installation were originally planned. There may be mistakes or omissions made at this early stage. Equipment errors can occur at any time in the design, manufacture, installation or operation of the equipment. Software errors can occur in the original program or later when the program is intentionally modified.

It is impossible to predict how or when a systematic failure will lead to a breakdown, so a redundancy method will probably be of no use. The working system and the backup system could both fail under the same working conditions, as they could be faulty in the same way. This is called common cause failure (CCF).

Types of failure

	Random Hardware failures	Systematic failures
Will always occur under the same conditions.	No	Yes
Effectively prevented by redundancy.	Yes	No

Figure C6-27: Types of failure. *Source: Programmable Electronic Systems (An Introductory Guide); HSE Publication - PES01.*

Examples of computer controlled equipment

Robots

A robot is defined in HSE guidance as "a manipulating machine which is automatically controlled, is reprogrammable and is capable of serving a number of different purposes". Some robots are capable of locomotion, but this is not a defining feature.

There are three categories of robot: fixed sequence, variable sequence and playback robots. Fixed sequence robots are programmed to perform successive steps of an operation in a pre-determined sequence, condition and position. Because this sequence is programmed in, it is not easy to change.

Variable sequence robots are similar to the fixed sequence except the information can more easily be changed. They have a more complex original design and are designed to fulfil a variety of movements. They have different sets of instructions/programs in order to carry out more complex tasks.

A playback robot has a memory and must be taught the sequence, positions and operations by a human operator. This information can be recalled and operations are carried out from memory.

Playback robots operate from one of two systems. They can be either point-to-point or continuous path. The point-to-point system is where the operator has a control unit to operate the robot. There are sets of instructions that are stored in the memory. The robot is moved into the start position, which is then stored in the memory. The operation is carried out in sequence with each step being stored in the memory until the final stop position is reached. The robot will repeat the taught program continuously as required. Examples of this type are the spot welding robots on a car assembly line.

With the continuous path system, all movements that are initiated by the human operator are recorded and stored in the memory. This method produces a continuous, smooth movement and requires a great deal of skill from the teacher as it also records and repeats faults. Examples of this type are paint spraying robots.

Robots are used in industrial applications where the work may be dangerous or repetitive, and in atmospheres that may be harmful to humans or atmospheres that do not support life. For example, they can be used to pick and place heavy loads, move materials around or on an assembly line.

Robots can also introduce hazards into the workplace when people have need to come into contact with them during teaching/programming, setting, tool changing/adjustment, inspection and maintenance.

A robot is a machine and presents the same hazards as other machines with regard to moving parts, ejected parts, etc.. During the phases in its sequence the robot is at its most dangerous. Not only is there a need to approach the robot, it may be that it needs to be kept "live" while work is carried out, for example, when fault finding or teaching.

The robot must be programmed to carry out its tasks and if the installation has been well thought out at the design stage, most of the teaching will be carried out outside the work enclosure. However, there will be times when the teacher will need to approach the robot. All the precautions that are discussed later in this unit should be applied, including a safe system of work to ensure the safety of the teacher and anyone else who may be likely to enter the work area.

CNC machines

CNCs are computer numerically controlled machines. Any type of machine can be CNC. The CNC refers to the control system. These machines typically drill or cut metal, plastic, wood or other similar materials into shapes that have been pre-selected. The co-ordinates of the shape are provided as instructions to the machine to control the machine movement. The axes, linear and rotary motions are provided with a standard code. The standard co-ordinate system is a right-handed rectangular Cartesian type. The CNC's usually operate a point-to-point system with little or no memory being used.

CNC machines are useful for repetitive jobs and for ease of cutting complex shapes. The items produced will all be the same dimensions and quality. The operators do not have to physically move elements of the machine as they would have to on machines controlled by other means.

CNC machines can be combined with robots to create a sophisticated production line.

Other processing plant

A PES could form part of various processing plants, for example, an oil refinery or a chemical processing plant. In a chemical processing plant, the PES may control the flow rate, the temperature and the pressure of the process. What is happening in the plant can be continuously read from the monitors. Constantly checking and adjusting the parameters of a chemical process is a complicated task for a human operator, but is competently handled by a PES.

HAZARDS ASSOCIATED WITH THE USE OF PES

With computer controlled systems the conventional operator has been largely eliminated and now, the personnel who do the setting, programming and maintenance face the greatest risk. These people must be adequately safeguarded or the risk reduced to an adequate level. In order to do this, hazard analysis should be carried out followed by a risk assessment. Identifying all the hazards is not an easy task, some may be obvious while others are difficult to foresee. For example, a robot system could go wrong while it is being set up and the setter might get hurt. It is more difficult to predict what could happen if some faulty data were recorded in the computer's memory. This might not show up until some time after.

Effective precautions are more likely to be incorporated into the system if possible hazards and their causes are thought through in advance. There are several methods of doing this, each with its own strengths and weaknesses, and the choice of which to employ depends on the application. For example, in a large chemical processing plant, a hazard and operability study (HAZOP) would be appropriate. The analysts could study what would happen if the various parameters (flow rate, temperature, pressure) deviated from the normal limits.

Hazard analysis describes the hazards that could arise when a component or a system within an installation fails and also can identify those particular systems whose failure could lead to a hazard. It is necessary to identify those systems on which the safety of the plant depends - safety related systems.

Hazards arise with the need to approach the robot. The hazards will be those associated with the use of any machinery: trapping, entanglement, impact, crushing, cutting, etc., but the reasons they occur are far more complex. With processing plant, the hazards are wider than those from a robot or a CNC machine. Failure of the controls and safeguards in a processing plant could result in explosions, fire, release of toxic gases, etc.. For example, if there is a fault with the plant sensors and they do not detect a deviant rise in pressure, they will not pass a message through the programmable electronics to the plant actuators to close down the source of the over-pressurisation. However, failure in any part of PES could have the same catastrophic result. To carry out an analysis it is necessary to:

- Define events and identify the hazards.
- Evaluate the need for access and the risk to personnel.
- Study possible failure modes and their influence on risk.
- Identify safety strategies which eliminate or minimise the risks.
- Decide on acceptable levels of safety integrity for the controls and safety interlocks.
- Assess the achieved levels of safety integrity for each part of the system and ensure that these levels are acceptable.

Risk assessment is the prediction of the likelihood of people being injured by the hazards identified, balanced with the potential severity of the injury. This enables a judgement to be made about which safeguards have adequate integrity and reliability for the job in hand.

REASONS FOR ABERRANT BEHAVIOUR

Aberrant behaviour can be defined as any unintentional or uncovenanted movement caused by a malfunction of the control system or any actuator. This can be caused by electrical interference. PESs may be affected by electrical interference just as many other types of electrical equipment. What results in the annoying flicker on a television screen can be disastrous in a computerised system. This interference can be kept to a minimum by carefully considering the system design, installation practices and by the use of an appropriate electrical interference immunity test programme.

Aberrant behaviour can also be caused by a programming fault. An error may have been made in the original program and not show until a certain sequence of events occurred. An error could be introduced when the program is being modified, which again may not show itself until a later date. The error may also be due to a transient fault. The complexity of the system makes error tracing very difficult, and even more so when attempting to foresee where errors could occur.

SAFEGUARDS THROUGH RELIABILITY

Safety integrity is the characteristic of a safety related system concerning its ability to perform the required functions in the desired manner under all the relevant conditions and on every occasion it is required to do so.

Programming faults

In determining safety integrity, all causes of failures which lead to an unsafe state should be included; for example, hardware failures and software induced failures, which could stem from design errors and failures due to electrical interference. Some of these types of failures, in particular random hardware failures, may be quantified using such measures as the failure rate in the dangerous mode of failure or the probability of a protection system failing to operate on demand. However, the safety integrity of a system also depends on many elements which cannot be quantified but can only be considered qualitatively, such as the software.

Electrical interference

Electrical interference may result from a number of sources, static build up on the equipment or materials being processed, electrical spikes on the computer supply voltage, interference from other equipment such as mobile phones or arc welding equipment. The software should be shielded from such interference to prevent spurious trips or other malfunctions

Stored energy

Stored energy should be identified at the design stage for each operational sequence of the equipment.

Aberrant behaviour can also occur due to stored energy. The robot may be powered by pneumatics or hydraulics and, after a stop signal has been received, still hold enough energy for an uncovenanted stroke to occur. This stroke may be completely unexpected both in the fact that it happened and in the way that it happened.

The robot could be halted where a part of it is in an up position and that part has enough stored energy to come down when it is not expected. The part could also fall down due to gravity. The operator may have a false sense of security because the power to the machine is cut off and very often locked off.

INTEGRITY OF CONTROL SYSTEMS

Reliability is the aspect of the safety integrity relating to random hardware failures in a dangerous mode of failure of the safety related systems. The term relates to failures in a dangerous mode. That is, those failures of a safety related system that would impair its safety integrity. The two reliability parameters that are relevant in this context are the overall failure rate and the probability of failure of demand. The former is used when it is necessary to maintain continuous control in order to maintain safety and the latter is used in the context of protection systems. The term can be used in a narrow meaning, relating only to hardware failures in a dangerous mode of failure, or as in common usage to include failure in both a safe and dangerous mode.

Random hardware failures result from a variety of normal degradation mechanisms in the hardware.

Many degradation mechanisms occur at different rates in different components and since manufacturing tolerances cause components to fail due to these mechanisms, after different times in operation, failures of total equipment comprising many components occur at unpredictable (random) times.

Systematic failures due to errors in design, construction or use of a system cause it to fail under particular combinations of inputs or under some environmental condition. Three types of systematic failure are considered:

- Systematic failures due to errors or omissions in the system requirements specification.
- Systematic failures due to errors in the design, manufacture, installation or operation of the hardware.
- Systematic failures due to errors or omissions in the software.

An 'error' is the mistake made by the programmer (designer, coder, manufacturer, etc.) which gives rise to a `fault' in the `software' or `hardware' which eventually causes a `failure' of the equipment due to time, environment, stress, etc.

No one can predict when a random failure will occur, but the risk of the installation breaking down because of systematic errors can be reduced by careful consideration and examination of the quality of the software and hardware components at every stage of their design, manufacture and use. Potentially dangerous errors can creep in at any time. Two basic considerations should be borne in mind when deciding if the overall quality of the system is high enough for it to be safe: quality of manufacture and quality of implementation.

Safety-related equipment can be divided into two major types: control systems and protection systems. Some control systems include protection features. However, if there is a failure in the control system, it could lead to a failure in its own protection features. For this reason it is strongly recommended that control and protection systems be linked to the operating equipment separately.

CONTROL AND PROTECTION SYSTEMS

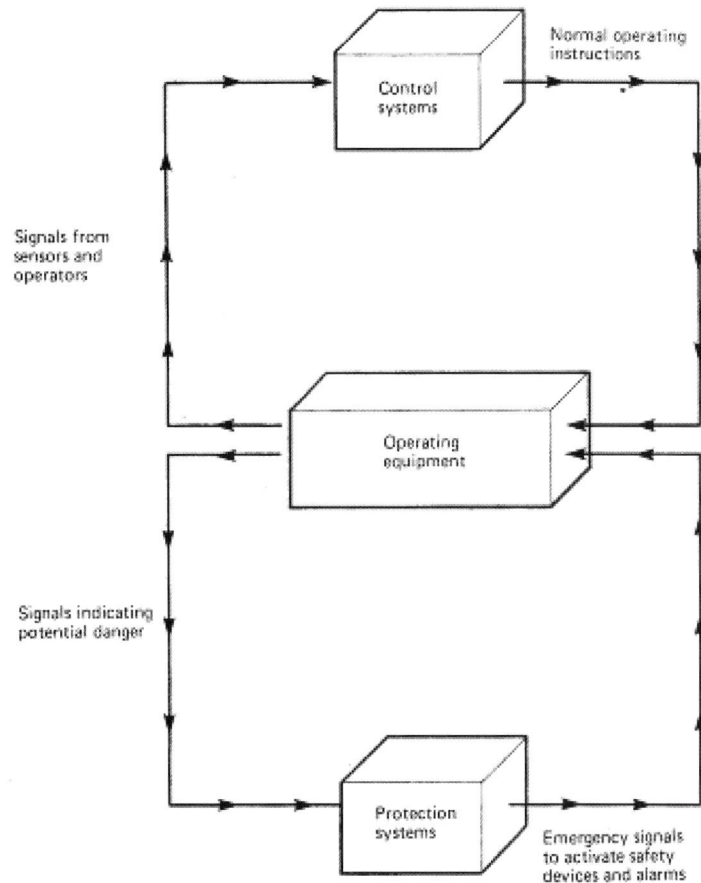

Figure C6-28: Control and protection systems.   *Source: Programmable Electronic Systems (An Introductory Guide); HSE Publication - PES01.*

The control systems govern the operation of plant, machinery and other equipment. They respond to input signals from human operators and/or other equipment, and generate output signals to the processing and manufacturing equipment. Not all the control systems are safety related.

Protection systems respond to conditions in the installation that are dangerous or could become dangerous. The protection system takes preventive action, for example, by sounding an alarm, switching the machine off or turning on water sprinklers.

SAFETY IN PROGRAMMING, OPERATION AND MAINTENANCE

Programming

The operating system's program or software provided by the robot or installation manufacturer or supplier should not be accessible to unauthorised people. The programmes should be written so that it is possible to identify which function is in operation and what stage has been reached. Programme proving procedures should be developed, for example, using computer graphics, single step facilities, slow speed and full speed dry runs. Records and documentation of changes to the program should be maintained. Copies of master programs should be carefully stored and only updated, when updates have been proved (work as designed and intended) by repeated testing under controlled, but representative work conditions.

Programming involves the teaching of position and such teaching is often done from a pendant control. This is best done from outside the enclosure if the design allows good visibility. This is to protect the programmer from any sudden, unforeseen movements of the robot. However, it may be necessary to observe part of the cycle from within the enclosure. If teaching is done within the enclosure then several measures should be taken:

- There should be a positive means of switching from automatic to teach mode. Controls for activation of power for the automatic mode must be under the control of the programmer.
- Automatic transfer of control from the console to the teach pendant and from automatic to teach mode when the pendant is activated. It should only be possible to control the robot from the teach pendant once it has been activated. Emergency stops should remain active; all other controls should be disabled.
- Switching is by key from automatic mode to teach mode - the programmer retains the key at all times whilst within the enclosure.
- Speed should automatically be restricted and where possible low torque selected. The speed must not exceed 0.25 metres per second.
- Typically speeds are limited to a maximum of between 10% or 25% of full speed although teaching is often done at speeds far slower.
- There should be provided: hold-to-run teach controls for initiating robot movement, a hard-wired emergency stop and a hard-wired deadman's handle.

After teaching or reprogramming, verification of the program is usually necessary. The reinstatement of normal control after verification should only be possible if all the safeguards are reinstated.

Operation

During normal production the system will often be capable of unattended operation and close approach should be unnecessary. If the hazard analysis has identified risks arising from the use of the robot, the safety measures should prevent operators, including material loaders, cleaners and labourers, and passers-by from gaining access to the installation.

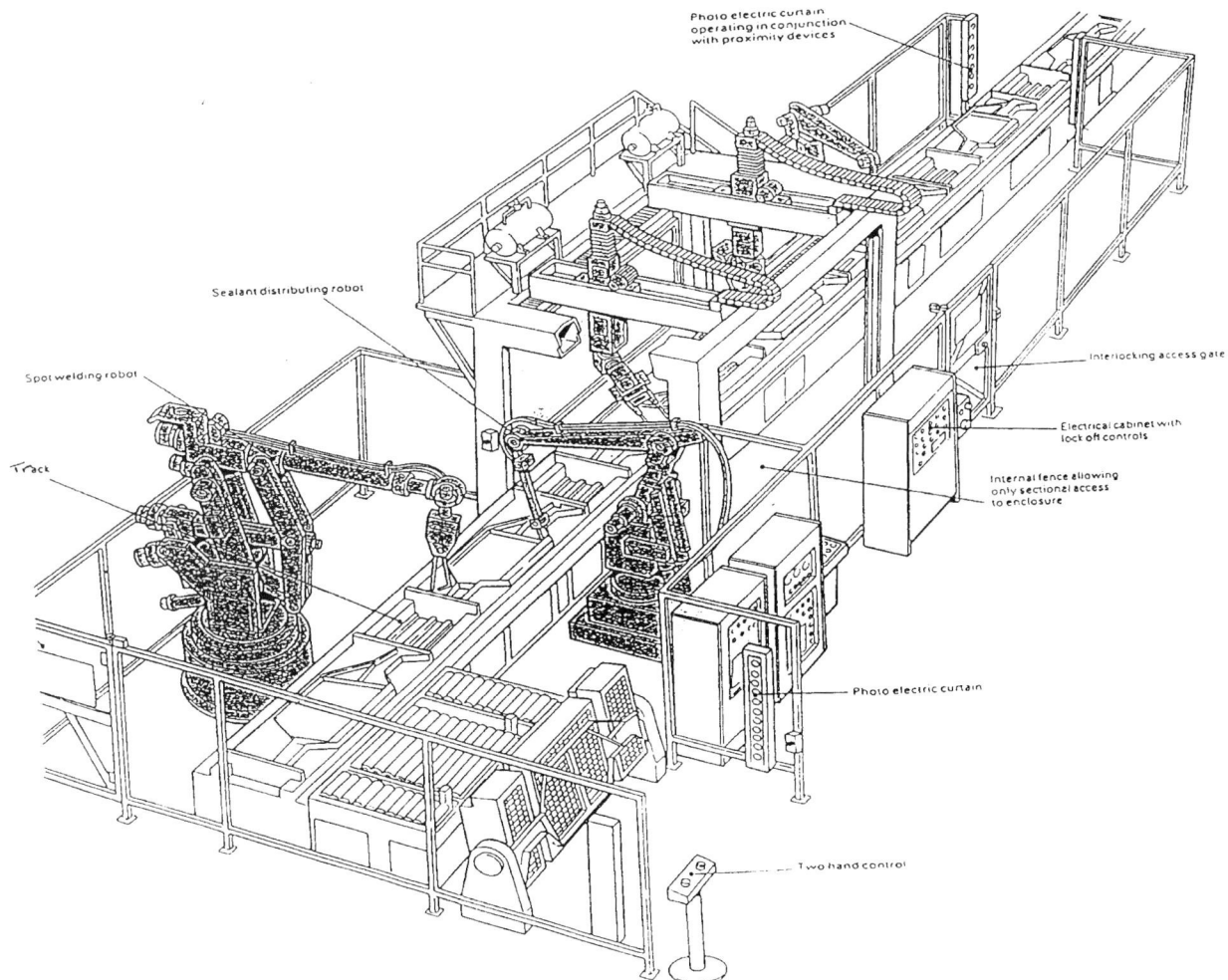

Figure C6-29: Spot welding robot.   Source: Programmable Electronic Systems (An Introductory Guide); HSE Publication - PES01.

If the operator needs to approach the robot and associated tooling during normal operation with the robot in automatic mode, it is preferable that the access arrangements require a safe controlled shutdown through the robot controller. All power to the robot axes should be cut off when the guards are opened or when the operator enters the enclosure.

If an operator has to enter a single robot cell, while other robot cells continue to operate, safeguarding arrangements should include means to prevent the operator gaining access to or being injured by other robots. Fixed barriers or electro-sensitive sensing devices may be required.

The risk posed by associated machines and equipment including feed, transfer and delivery machinery should be assessed and where appropriate safeguards applied. Safe working procedures should be developed for setting associated machines, making sure that the robot is isolated from its power source. The interlocking arrangements should not be relied on for isolation. Where the robot is working with several machines and one requires servicing or setting, special safety precautions will be necessary. Sub-routine program alterations may be needed as well as temporary or permanent safeguards, for example, barriers. Safe systems of work should be put into place to ensure that this is all carried out.

Maintenance

While robots are working automatically, there is usually no reason to approach them. However, with maintenance work, close approach will almost certainly be necessary. Because of the complex nature of robot systems, there must be carefully thought out routines to safeguard the personnel involved. Maintenance workers should have all the relevant information and be skilled and trained to an appropriate level. They should work whenever possible with the power supplies off and work in a logical sequence. The aberrant behaviour of robots makes maintenance work particularly dangerous.

Before maintenance operations are undertaken, unnecessary power supplies to the robot should be switched off to minimise the possibility of uncovenanted powered movement, residual power should be dumped and the robot should be placed in its lowest physical resting position. It may be necessary to place chocks between parts of the machinery to provide a physical restraint against stored energy movement or gravity falls. Most maintenance work can be carried out with the power off.

In addition to any interlocking arrangements, it is necessary to provide means of properly isolating and locking out the actuating power supplies: electrical, hydraulic or pneumatic. For large, complex installations, it may be necessary to use a team approach when two people are present during maintenance, each with access to an emergency stop and having personal lock out controls. If several robots are working and maintenance work is required on one part, it may not be practicable to shut everything down, nor might it be practicable to provide a physical barrier between the maintenance worker and the working robots. In this case presence-sensing devices might be an effective alternative.

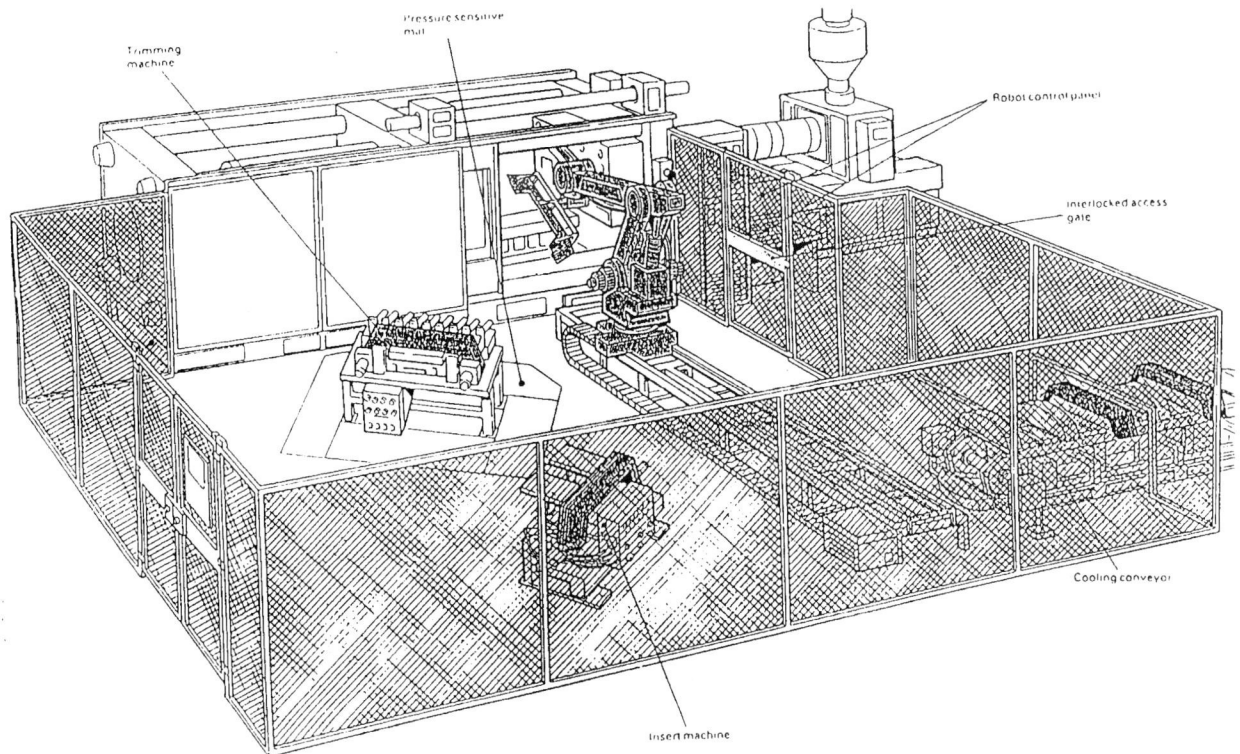

Figure C6-30: Robot retrieval machine for hot metal application. *Source: Programmable Electronic Systems (An Introductory Guide); HSE Publication - PES01.*

If reliance is placed on keeping interlocked access gates open as part of the safety procedure to prevent power being restored, they should be prevented from closing by using a trapped key exchange system or by other physical means.

Robots very often carry other tools on their manipulating arm(s), which present a risk of inadvertent operation. Suitable precautions should be taken against this happening and the maintenance staff should be fully aware of this.

Following any major maintenance work which disturbs safety devices or guards, an independent check of the safety devices and guards should be made before production is resumed.

Maintenance operations cover four main activities: routine servicing and inspection, planned preventive maintenance, fault finding (trouble shooting) and major repair.

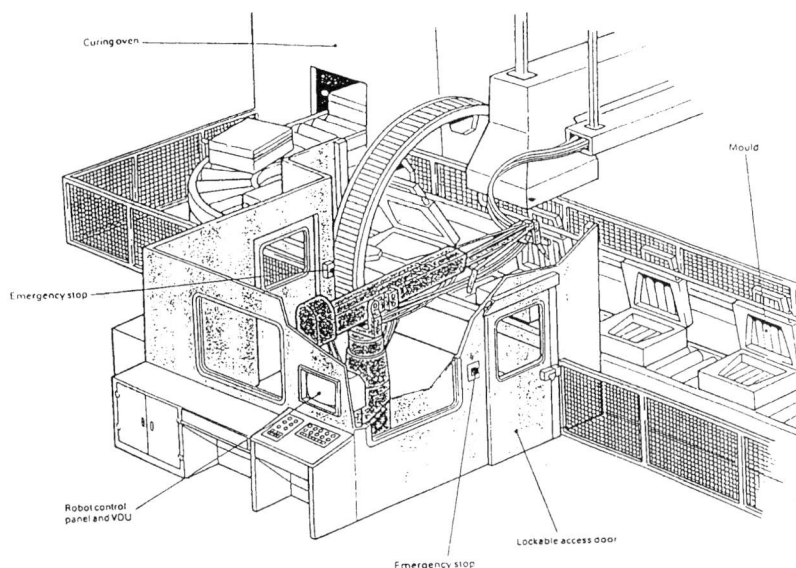

Figure C6-31: Plastic injection robot. *Source: Programmable Electronic Systems (An Introductory Guide); HSE Publication - PES01.*

The safety of routine servicing and planned preventive maintenance can be greatly improved if provision is made at the design, development and installation stages. For example, designers should arrange for maintenance to be carried out with the power off and with the minimum disruption to in-built safety features.

Diagnostic facilities such as error codes on VDU screens or indicator lamps on a diagnostic board will enable maintenance staff to identify fault areas. The monitoring system may be able to automatically override the operational programme and place the robot on servo hold until action is taken. Control panels, keyboards and terminals should be sited outside the enclosure and in such a position that the operator has a good overall view of the work process. Controls should be identified and labelled and ergonomically laid out to minimise errors. Emergency stops should be provided at each workstation. The controller should be designed so that the parts can be replaced easily. It is important to know where to stand in relation to the robot to obtain the correct control orientation. Aids to orientation including floor markings can assist this.

Figure C6-32: Spot welding robot with safety markings showing.

Source: Programmable Electronic Systems (An Introductory Guide); HSE Publication - PES01.

Safety during trouble shooting and emergencies is more difficult to achieve. A dangerous situation can arise when the trouble-shooter has to enter the robot working area because of an unplanned stoppage. Once the stoppage is cleared, the robot may continue with the cycle with the person still there. Safety devices must be used to prevent starting up with the trouble-shooter still in the enclosure. Entry to the enclosure to observe the robot or associated machinery working will require a permit to work system. Similar conditions to those that apply when teaching is taking place will be necessary, for example manual operation of the robot or machinery, or slow movements.

Appropriate tools and personal protective equipment should be provided to ensure safe maintenance work as should adequate and appropriate training. If routines are to be changed then further training will be required.

CONSIDERATIONS IN SAFEGUARDING THE WORKING ENVELOPE

Layout

Careful planning of the layout can avoid many of the hazards associated with PESs. The aim is to minimise the need to approach dangerous areas. This can be achieved by having good viewing arrangements from outside the enclosure and by providing the means to feed and remove components so no-one needs to enter the enclosure. There should be enough space around the robot so personnel can stand safely, if they need to enter when the robot is under power. It should be noted that this area might not be safe in the event of aberrant behaviour. The layout should also allow for access to an injured person who may need assistance or need to be removed. Access should be prevented by perimeter fencing. Where access is necessary it should only be possible through interlocked access gates or their equivalent that stops all dangerous movement of the robot before the person enters the enclosure.

Interlocked perimeter fencing

Perimeter fencing is positioned so that it is not possible to reach any dangerous parts of machinery. It is usually 2m high, made from rigid panels and securely fastened to the floor or a suitable structure. It should only be possible to remove fixed fencing with a tool. The fencing should be strong enough for the purpose and often a steel structure infilled with steel mesh is satisfactory. With some processes there is a danger from hot splashes, for example molten metal, or from welding flashes or ejected materials. Where these hazards could occur, the infilling should be made from sheet steel or plastic panels.

If regular access is required, the fencing may be provided with sliding or hinged interlocking access gates. There are various interlocking devices that can be used. Guard operated position switches can be used, for example positive and negative mode cam operated limit switches, cross monitored and operating in the control circuit of the robot.

The trapped key exchange method can be used. These isolate positively the power supply or the control to all or parts of the robot installation. This method uses a lock on the gate(s) of the perimeter fencing and another lock on either a valve (or isolator) controlling the robot actuators or on the robot controller. The key cannot be removed from the actuator (or control) lock to open the gate lock until a safe condition is established. For the actuator lock this may require the complete removal of the source of power (including stored energy). On the robot controller, it may be a change of control state from run to hold or slow speed.

A solenoid lock may be used. This is an electro-mechanical device activated by an electrical signal. When the signal is received the locking bolt is withdrawn allowing the access gate to be opened. This device may be used in conjunction with a time delay, which allows time for the machinery to come to rest.

Electro-sensitive safety systems

These systems provide a good standard of safety when used with conventional fencing. They may operate as trip devices by detecting the approach of persons or objects to dangerous parts of machinery, or as presence-sensing devices which will not allow dangerous parts to be set in motion as long as the person or object is detected.

Photo-electric (PE) safety systems operate on the principle of the detection of an obstruction in the path taken by a beam or beams of light. The intangible barrier operated by this system may consist of a single beam or a number of beams of light, a curtain of light, or any combination of these as necessary to provide the required safeguard. The curtain of light may be created by a scanning beam or beams, or a number of fixed beams. The light may be visible or invisible, for example infrared, and may be continuous or modulated, for example a scanning system.

Photo-electric systems have three basic uses in safeguarding: used as a trip device where the curtain is arranged vertically, as a presence-sensing device where the curtain is arranged in horizontal format and in combination where two or more PE devices are used.

PE devices are useful where a clear view of the robot is necessary and they allow zoning of human access.

PE devices are unsuitable for certain applications, for example, in certain environments where there is excessive noise, dust, heat or radiation. They are not suitable for protection against ejected parts or tools handled by the robot, nor are they suitable where a tangible barrier is required, for example adjacent to a walkway.

Pressure sensitive mats are devices that are placed on the floor around the machine. When pressure is applied to the mat the machine will stop. If a person approaches the machine, he will have to walk across the mat thereby cutting off the power to the machine. They have to take into account the speed of approach, the length of a person's stride and the response time of the system. They are useful as an emergency stop and in conjunction with other safeguards, but are not suitable for use when a high integrity of guarding is required. They are exposed to potential damage which can result in their failure.

Trip devices

These can be used to stop the robot if it comes into contact with people or associated machinery. They come in the form of sensitive edges, strip buffers or trip wires and should protect all the parts that create the hazard. When tripped, the control system should require manual resetting before the machine can be set In motion. There are difficulties with applying these devices to the robot arm and so are not normally used for the protection of people.

Positive stops and brakes

Positive stops can be used to keep the robot within its work area by limiting its movement to the part of the envelope required for the job. The robot's movements are kept within defined limits, which can prevent dangerous traps. Care must be taken in design or by shrouding so additional traps are not created.

Brakes are used when there is a danger of a fall under gravity. A brake could be applied to a robot arm as when the actuator power is removed the arm could fall. The brake should be automatically applied when motion stops and should be of the hold-off variety. They should be capable of supporting the weight of the arm plus the weight of the heaviest tool or workpiece that is likely to be used.

Emergency stop controls should be red actuators with yellow background surfaces so the actuator is clearly contrasted. In robot installations the emergency stop controls should be of the mushroom head, manually reset type. A number of emergency stops should be provided: at the control panel, on the teach control pendant, at every work station and at any other position considered necessary. The emergency stops should all be hardwired to the robot axes power switching control circuit and should stop all motion and release stored energy where practicable.

Entry procedures

Safe systems of work (SSW) are used to help ensure safety when entry is required into the enclosure. A SSW is the carefully considered analysis of the hazards taking into account all the modes of operation, the needs for approach and the types of activity, which will lead to a method of working which will ensure the safety of those engaged in the activity. It may also be necessary to introduce a permit to work system for entry, especially when the robot is to remain "live".

This page is intentionally blank

ELEMENT C6 - MACHINERY SAFETY

This page is intentionally blank

Mechanical handling

Overall aims

On completion of this Element, the student will have knowledge and understanding of:

- safety in the movement of vehicles.
- safety in the movement of people.

Content

Specific intended learning outcomes

The intended learning outcomes are that the student will be able to:

1.   identify the main hazards where lift trucks, cranes, hoists, lifts and conveyor systems are in use and suggest ways of reducing the risks where appropriate

2.   outline the specific hazards and safeguards associated with automated warehouses

Relevant statutory provisions

Workplace (Health, Safety and Welfare) Regulations (WHSWR) 1992

Provision and Use of Work Equipment Regulations (PUWER) 1998

Lifting Operations and Lifting Equipment Regulations (LOLER) 1998

7.1 - Stability of vehicles

LATERAL AND LONGITUDINAL INSTABILITY AND LOSS OF CONTROL OF VEHICLES

FLT Stability

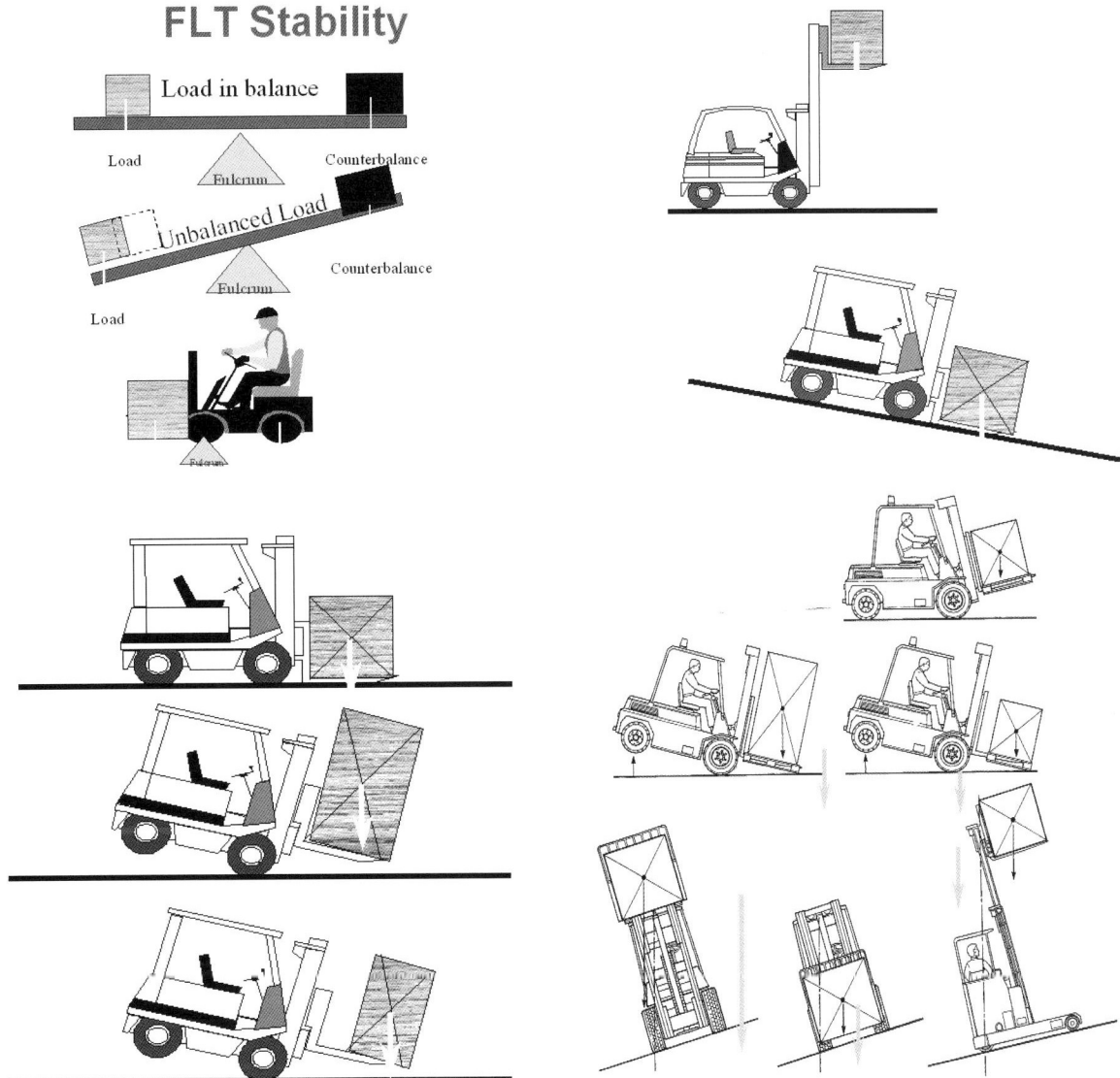

Figure C7-1: Fork lift truck stability.

Source: Ambiguous.

Factors affecting fork lift truck instability
- Overloading or uneven loading of the bucket.
- Cornering at excessive speed.
- Hitting obstructions.
- Driving too close to the edges of embankments or excavations.
- Mechanical defects.
- Inappropriate tyre pressures.
- Driving across slopes.

Factors affecting dumper truck instability
- Driving too fast.
- Sudden braking.
- Driving on slopes.
- Driving over debris.
- Under-inflated tyres.
- Driving over holes in floor, such as drains.
- Driving with load elevated.
- Overloading - exceeding maximum capacity.

Figure C7-2: Vehicle overturned. *Source: Lincsafe.*

7.2 - Safe use of lift trucks

APPLICATIONS OF DIFFERENT TYPES OF LIFT TRUCK

Counterbalance

The mass of this truck acts as a counterweight so that the truck can lift and move a load without tipping; (loads placed on the forks are counterbalanced by the weight of the vehicle over the rear wheels).

The **rated capacity** of a fork lift truck (FLT) is the maximum weight in pounds/kilos at a maximum load centre stated in inches/metres. The load centre is measured from the heel of the forks, e.g. 907 kg at 0.45 m load centre. Any deviation from the rated capacity will cause instability, as will travelling with the load raised.

Figure C7-3: Counterbalance fork lift truck.

> *Source: HSE Guidance Note PM28; Working Platforms on Fork Lift Trucks.*

Reach

With forks "out" it behaves in similar manner to the counterbalance truck. With the fork "in" and the load retracted within the wheelbase the truck is less likely to tip. (This minimises the overall working length and allows the isle width to be reduced). However, if the load is raised and the mast tilted back, there is a significant risk of tipping, particularly if the load is carried high and the wheelbase is short and on a slope.

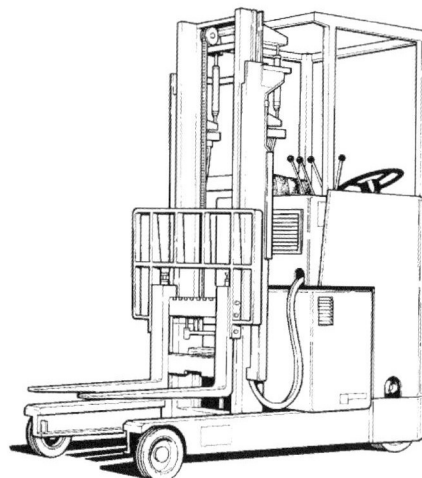

Figure C7-4: Reach fork lift truck.

> *Source: HSE Guidance Note PM28; Working Platforms on Fork Lift Trucks.*

Rough terrain

Figure C7-5: Rough-terrain forklift trucks.

Source: ACT.

Rough terrain fork lift trucks operate similarly to traditional fork lift truck equipment found within industry, the main difference being the surface on which they operate is typically unmade and not hard standing. The design employed on construction sites is usually of a heavier duty design.

Typical design differences include:

- Diesel fuelled engines to provide the greater power required.
- Increased load / lifting capacity.
- Enclosed operator cab for protection against the elements.
- Higher chassis position for uneven terrain.
- Large diameter wheels with deep tread, pneumatic traction tyres for muddy, rough terrain.
- Increased security for external siting of the vehicle.

The same stringent rules and procedures should be in place for rough terrain FLT's as there are for industrial types. Operators must be competent and licensed, loads must not exceed the safe working load and should be palletised when loading, unloading or moving.

Telescopic materials handlers

These units are often referred to as multi-tool carriers. They can be used as front-end loaders and, if fitted with a jib, for crane duties. As shown it is set up as an industrial truck:

Figure C7-6: Telescopic handler.   *Source: Ambiguous.*

Figure C7-7: Side loading trucks.   *Source: Ambiguous.*

Side loading trucks

A lift truck with a load carriage, which moves laterally to pick up or deposit a load, or to enable the centre of gravity of the load to be within the wheelbase of the truck during travelling. During travelling, the load is usually resting on the truck structure:

Pedestrian controlled trucks

May be pedestrian operated or ride on. They may be equipped with a battery powered lift facility or the lift may be powered by using hydraulic hand pump.

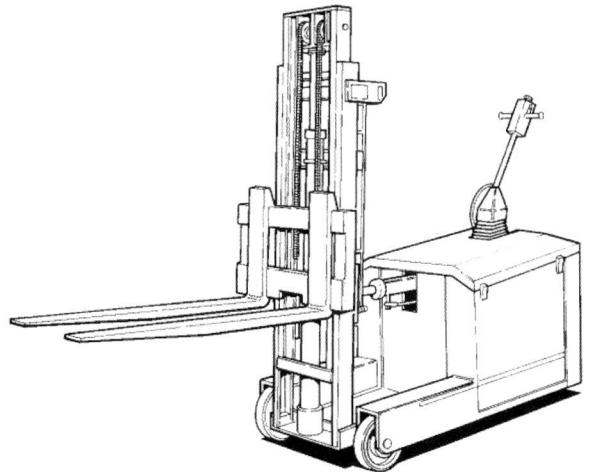

Figure C7-8: Pedestrian controlled trucks.

Source: HSE Guidance Note PM28; Working Platforms on Fork Lift Trucks.

HAZARDS ASSOCIATED WITH USE OF LIFT TRUCKS

Although the fork lift truck (FLT) is a useful machine for moving materials in many industries, it features prominently in industrial accidents. Every year about 20 deaths and 5000 injuries can be attributed to FLTs and these can be analysed as follows:

Injuries to driver	40%
Injuries to assistant	20%
Injuries to pedestrians	40%

Fractures account for some 80% of Injuries, some 60% of which include injury to ankles and feet.

Typically 45% of the accidents can be wholly or partly attributed to operator error this underlines the need for formal operator training. There are, however, many other causes of accident including inadequate premises, gangways, poor truck maintenance, inadequate lighting etc. As a lifting machine, the FLT may be overloaded or incorrectly loaded causing it to overbalance in a forward direction. It may also overbalance if it is driven on steep slopes, on uneven surfaces (unless it is a rough terrain truck), if driven too fast or overbalance laterally if traversing slopes. Also, it is essential to remember that hydrogen gas is generated during battery recharging as this is highly explosive between concentrations of 4 to 75%.

Fork lift truck hazards

Overturning

- Driving too fast.
- Sudden braking.
- Driving on slopes.
- Driving with load elevated.

Loss of load

- Insecure load.
- Poor floor surface.
- Passengers should not be carried.

Overloading

- Exceeding the maximum rated capacity.

Collision

- With buildings.
- With pedestrians.
- With other vehicles.

Failure

- Load bearing part (e.g. chain or hydraulic system).

PRECAUTIONS IN THE USE OF LIFT TRUCKS

The following basic precautions should be followed:

- No smoking or sparks anywhere in the vicinity, with warning notices to this effect.
- Adequate high level ventilation (hydrogen is lighter than air) with explosion proof motors where forced ventilation is required.
- Clear instructions and training of personnel in the handling of battery acid, spillage procedure and first aid.
- Lifting gear for handling FLT batteries.
- CO^2, powder or halon fire extinguisher.

Only trained and authorised persons to carry out battery charging.

Safe operation

- Make someone in your company responsible for transport.
- Drivers properly trained and ensure unauthorised people are not allowed to drive.
- Make sure visiting drivers are aware of your rules.
- Check vehicles daily and have faults rectified promptly.
- Keep keys secure when vehicles are not in use.
- Ensure safe vehicle movements - particularly when reversing or near blind corners.
- Keep roadways/gangways properly maintained and adequately lit.
- Separate vehicles and pedestrians where practicable.

Pre-operational checks

It is essential that the operator carries out pre-operational checks to ensure that the truck is safe for work. These should be carried out when the truck has been left standing for any length of time and especially at the beginning of each shift.

Forks	-	check for alignment and security.
Tyres	-	check for security, adequate tread, no excessive cuts, and correct pressure if pneumatic.
Hydraulic oil tank	-	check level of fluid.
Unions, pipes, jacks	-	check there are no leaks.
Seat	-	check adjustment to personal requirements.
Lift and tilt controls	-	check effectiveness.
Brakes	-	foot - Check effectiveness on level in forward and reverse.
	-	handbrake - check effectiveness on slope.
Warning device	-	check effectiveness.

If any item on the above non-exclusive list is found to be defective the fault must be reported immediately to the supervisor and the truck taken out of commission until it has been rectified and certified safe. It is recommended that each truck has an individual log where these tests as well as other checks and remedial measures are recorded. No operator or other person should make any repair or adjustment unless specifically trained and authorised to do so. A system of regular maintenance by competent persons must be in existence and records kept in the log mentioned above.

Parking areas

Sufficient and suitable parking areas should be provided away from the main work area and located where the risk of unauthorised use of the FLT will be reduced. Positive management action must be taken to control the use of FLTs by untrained/unauthorised persons. Trucks should be parked as follows:

- Clear of doorways, vehicles, fire fighting equipment and heat treatment plant.
- Brakes on.
- Controls in neutral with forks fully lowered.
- Power off, key removed and returned to supervisor.
- Wheels checked, if on incline.

Operational rules - basic fork lift truck

The following list should be used as a guide to good practice only.

- Speeds must be consistent with factory conditions, special care on greasy or wet roads.
- Operators should always face direction of travel.
- Forks should be between 10cms and 15cms from ground and parallel to ground unless travelling with a load, when the forks should be tilted back.
- The load must be seated as close to the heel of the forks as possible.
- When travelling up or down a slope the forks must always point up the slope.

- Trucks must not be driven over obstacles or holes in the road. These defects must be reported immediately to the supervisor.
- Care should be taken not to drive trucks across a slope.
- Travel slowly with due care when approaching a road junction, door opening or where pedestrians could be present. Sound horn.
- No passengers.
- All parts of driver's body must be kept within the limits of the truck and no part of the body placed between the uprights of the mast.
- The truck must be stationary with the handbrake applied when the forks are raised or lowered, whether with a load or not. (See reference for detailed instructions.)
- Trucks must not be used to pull or push loads.

Safe layout of areas where trucks are used

Management needs to consider the safe movement of FLTs and loads as part of their overall safety policy. Consideration should be given to the following:

- Separate routes, designated crossing places and suitable barriers at recognised danger spots. As far as is practicable pedestrians should be kept clear of FLT operating areas and/or notice displayed warning pedestrians that they are entering a FLT area.
- Roads, gangways and aisles should have sufficient width and overhead clearance for the largest FLT. Attention should be paid to areas where they might meet other traffic i.e. loading bays. If ramps (sleeping policemen) are used, a by-pass for the FLTs should be provided. A one-way traffic system should be considered to reduce the risk of collision.
- Clear direction signs and marking of doors and buildings can help to avoid unnecessary movement.
- Sharp bends and overhead obstructions should be avoided where possible. Hazards that cannot be removed should be clearly marked with black and yellow diagonal stripes i.e. loading bays edges, stacks, pits etc. If reasonably practicable barriers should be installed.
- The floor surface should be in good condition, free of litter and obstructions.
- Any gradient in a FLT operating area should be kept as gentle as possible. In no case should the gradient exceed the maximum gradient given in the manufacturer's specification.

Protection of pedestrians

There is a need to alert people to the hazards when working in or near a FLT operating area. Consideration should be given to the provision of protective clothing, boots, helmets and "high visibility" clothing for stores personnel etc. working in FLT operating areas.

A vigorous management policy covering operator training, truck maintenance and sound systems of work, supported by good supervision will reduce personal injury and damage to equipment and materials. This in turn will lead to better truck utilisation and increased materials handling efficiency.

USE OF LIFT TRUCKS TO MOVE PEOPLE

Conditions and equipment necessary

The use of powered lift trucks can be extended by a variety of attachments, which include:

Working Platforms - these can be used as temporary places of work or to transfer people or materials from one level to another.

Amongst other measures, the platform should be securely attached to the lift truck, the maximum allowable load should be clearly marked, and raising and lowering the platform should be controlled by the person on the platform who should be aware of the 'dead men's handle' type. When a lift truck is used in conjunction with a working platform, the safety of the unit as a whole (lift truck and platform) must be considered.

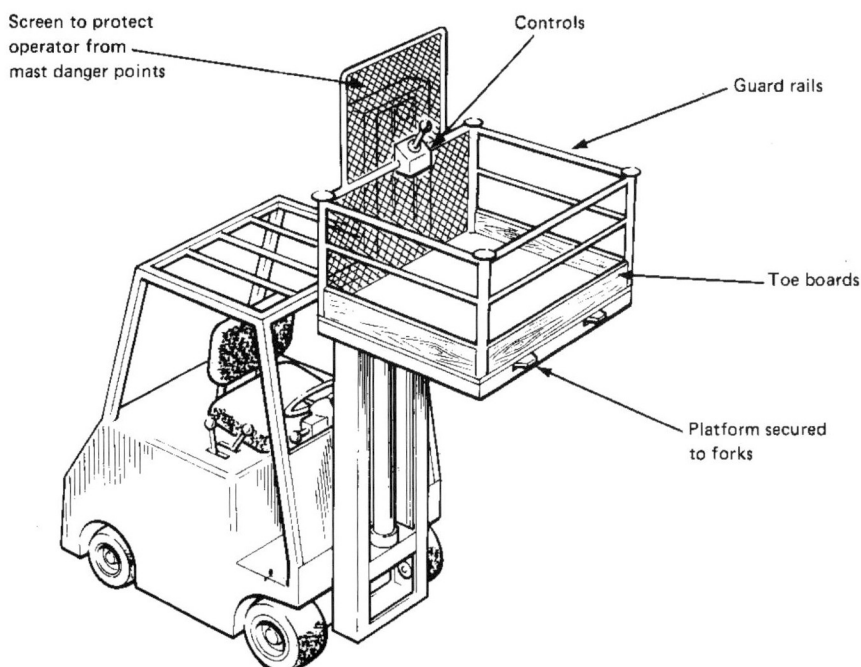

Figure C7-9: Use of working platform.   *Source: HSE Guidance Note PM28; Working Platforms on Fork Lift Trucks.*

Other attachments used on lift trucks

If a fork lift truck is to be dedicated to drum handling, or a lack of space requires that the drum is handled close to the lift truck, a carriage-mounted attachment may be an advantage.

This bucket forklift truck attachment handles any type of loose or granular material.

An example from a range of underslung attachments designed for handling typical construction materials, for use under a crane or with a forklift truck or telescopic handler.

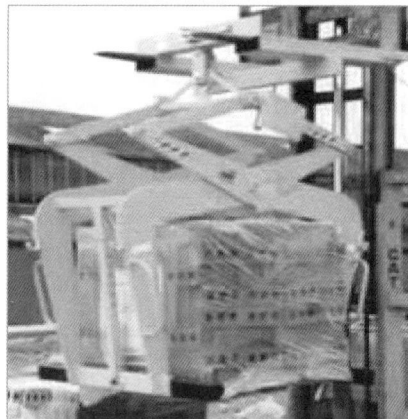

The forklift truck jib attachment for dedicated handling of un-palletised loads or product. This style of jib attachment combines the advantages of long reach with the added capability of handling to the maximum of the forklift truck's capacity closer to the mast.

Figure C7-10: Other attachments used on forklift trucks.

Source: www.forklift-attachments.co.uk.

TRAINING OF LIFT TRUCK OPERATORS

No persons should be permitted to drive fork lift trucks (FLTs) unless they have been selected, trained and authorised to do so, or are undergoing properly organised formal training.

Selection

The safe usage of FLTs calls for a reasonable degree of both physical and mental fitness and of intelligence. The selection procedure should be devised to identify people who have shown themselves reliable and mature during their early years at work. To avoid wasteful training for workers who lack co-ordination and ability to learn, selection tests should be used. Potential operators should be medically examined prior to employment/training and every five years in middle age; also after sickness or accident in order to assess the individual's physical ability to cope with this type of work.

Points to be considered are:

- *General* - normal agility, having full movement of trunk, neck and limbs.
- *Vision* - good eyesight is important as operators are required to have good judgement of space and distance. Normally distance vision should not be less than 6/12 with both eyes or corrected by spectacles or contact lenses as appropriate. Operators should have good colour vision.
- *Hearing* - the ability to hear instruction and warning signals with each ear is important.

Training operators

It is essential that immediate supervisors receive training in the safe operation of FLTs and that senior management appreciates the risks resulting from the interaction of FLTs and the workplace.

For the operator, safety must constitute an integral part of the skill training programme and not be treated as a separate subject. The operator should be trained to a level consistent with efficient operation and care for the safety of himself and other persons. On completion of training he should be issued with a company authority to drive and a record of all basic training, refresher training and tests maintained in the individual's personal documents file.

The training should consist of three stages, the last being the one in which the operator is introduced to his future work environment.

Stage one - should contain the basic skills and knowledge required to operate the FLT safely, to understand the basic mechanics and balance of the machine, and to carry out routine daily checks.

Stage two - under strict training conditions closed to other personnel. This stage should include:

a.   Knowledge of the operating principles, controls, use of any special attachments and the manufacturer's data and instructions for safe and efficient operation.

b.   Training and practice in the use of the FLT in conditions likely to be encountered i.e. gangways, slopes, cold stores, confined spaces and bad weather conditions.

c.   Training and practice in the work to be undertaken i.e. loading and unloading vehicles, stacking and de-stacking, familiarisation with the loads/materials they will be handling, including weight assessment.

Stage three - after successfully completing the first two stages, the operator should be given further instruction in the place of work. Under strict supervision he/she should be made familiar with the type of FLT he/she will be operating, site layout, company safety rules, features of the work and emergency procedures.

On completion of training the operator should be examined and tested to ensure that he/she has achieved the required standard. It is recommended that at set intervals or when there is indication of the operator not working to required standard, or following an accident, formal check tests be introduced.

If high standards are to be maintained, periodic refresher training and testing should be considered.

It should not be assumed that employees who join as trained operators have received adequate training to operate safely in their new company. The management must ensure that they have the basic skills and receive training in company methods and procedures for the type of work they are to undertake. They should be examined and tested before the issue of a driving authority.

7.3 - Safe use of cranes and lifting equipment

APPLICATIONS OF DIFFERENT TYPES OF CRANE

Mobile cranes

For combined road and off-road applications. Mobile cranes are the ultimate in mobility: they can travel up to 80 km/h and are extremely versatile due to their compact dimensions.

Figure C7-11: Mobile crane.   *Source: www.liebherr.com.*

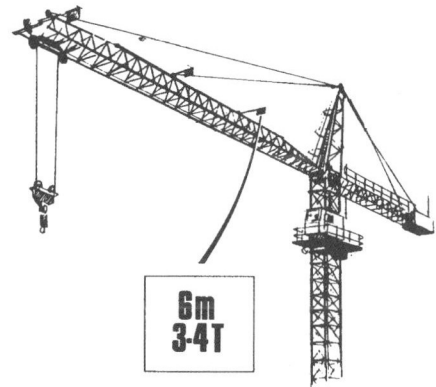

Figure C7-12: Tower crane.

Source: Construction Industry Publications Ltd for the Building Employers Confederation.

Tower cranes

These are suitable for the handling of relatively light loads to extremes of height and reach and are particularly suitable when there is limited space for a crane.

Overhead cranes

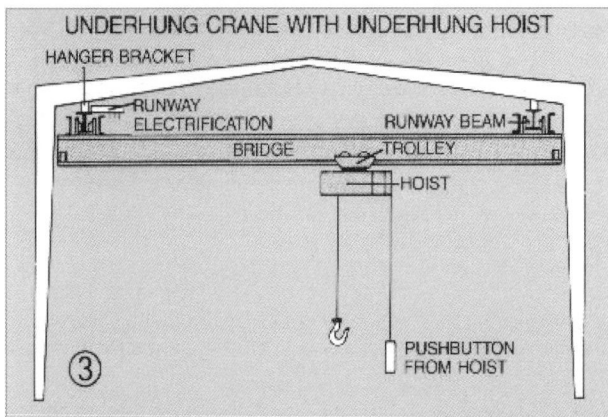

Figure C7-13: Overhead cranes.

Source: www.gaffey.com.

HAZARDS ASSOCIATED WITH CRANES AND LIFTING OPERATIONS

The principal hazards associated with any lifting operation are:

- **Overturning** which can be caused by weak support, operating outside the capabilities of the machine and by striking obstructions.
- **Overloading** by exceeding the operating capacity or operating radii, or by failure of safety devices.
- **Collision** with other cranes, overhead cables or structures.
- **Failure of load bearing part** - placing over cellars and drains, outriggers not extended, made-up or not solid ground, or of structural components of the crane itself.
- **Loss of load** from failure of lifting tackle or slinging procedure.

No matter what the type of crane, the main issues are the same:

- The ground the crane stands on - is it capable of bearing the load? Is it level? Are there any underground caverns or cellars?
- The load bearing capacity of the crane - is it sufficient for the task?
- Positioning the crane - is there enough room for the lift? Are there any overhead power lines, nearby buildings or other cranes? Will there be personnel or members of the public nearby? Is the tower crane near an airport or in a flight path?
- Adverse weather conditions.
- Structural integrity of the crane - are there signs of corrosion?
- Erecting and dismantling the crane - will other cranes be used?

In the uphill position, the greatest danger occurs when the load is set down. This can cause the crane to tip back over. In the downhill position, the load moves out of the radius which may cause the crane to tip forwards.

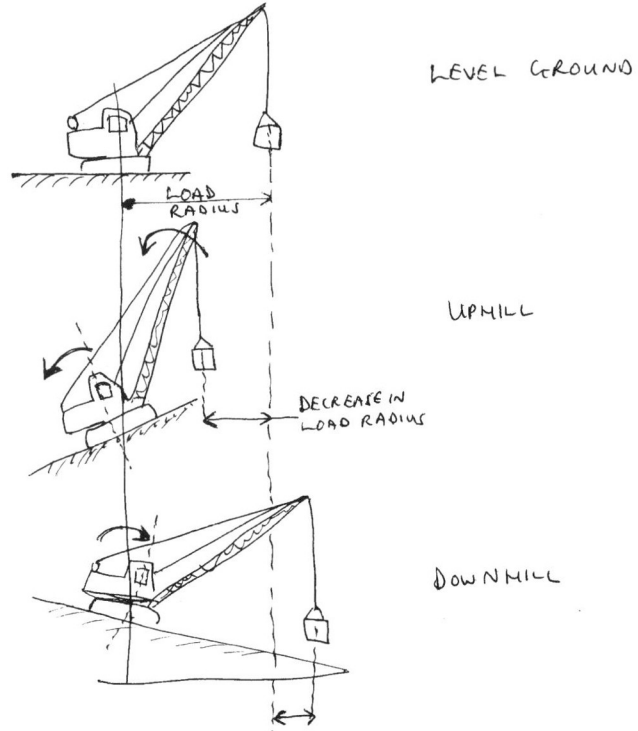

Figure C7-14: Stability of cranes (Hand-drawn). *Source: ACT.*

PRECAUTIONS IN THE USE OF CRANES

Selection

The type of crane selected will depend on a number of factors including the weight of the load to be lifted, the radius of operation, the height of the lift, the time available, and the frequency of the lifting activities. Hazards from particular types of crane, including impact with pedestrians or other vehicles relating to mobile jib cranes may suggest that alternatives such as a tower crane would be more suitable.

Cranes are often very heavy, the weight of the crane can cause the ground underneath the crane to sink or collapse, this may establish a working weight limit for any crane proposed for selection. Other factors like height and size may have to be considered as there may be limitations in site roads that are placed between structures or where overhead restrictions exist. Careful consideration of these factors must be made when selecting the correct crane to avoid the harm and consequences when the selected crane is put into use. Selecting a crane to carry out a lifting activity should be done at the planning stage, where the most suitable crane can be identified that is able to meet all of the lifting requirements and any limitations that may prevail.

Siting

Detailed consideration must be given to the location of any heavy piece of plant, and in particular crane equipment, due to the fact that additional weight is distributed to the ground through the loading of the crane when performing a lift. Surveys must be carried out to determine the nature of the ground, whether soft or firm, and what underground hazards are present such as buried services or hollow voids.

The surrounding environment must also be taken into consideration and factors may include highways, railways, electricity cables, areas of public interest. The area around where a crane is sited should be securely fenced, including the extremes of the lift radius, with an additional factor of safety to allow for emergency arrangements such as emergency vehicle access or safety in the event of a collapse or fall.

Lifting equipment must be sited in such a way as to reduce the risk, so far as is reasonably practicable, of it striking a person, structure, other equipment , natural features such as trees or power lines.

Stability of cranes

Cranes must be secured so that they do not tip over when in use. This anchoring can be achieved by securing with guy ropes, bolting the structure to a foundation, using ballast as counterweights or using outriggers to bring the centre of gravity down to the base area.

Cranes should be sited on firm ground with the wheels or outrigger feet having their weight distributed over a large surface. Care should be taken that the crane is not positioned over cellars or underground cavities, or positioned near excavations. Soft ground can be covered in timber, digger mats or hard core to prevent the outriggers sinking when under load.

Sloping ground should be avoided as this can shift the load radius out or in, away from the safe working position.

The following photograph shows the concrete plinths necessary to support this tower crane, which was about 80 meters tall.

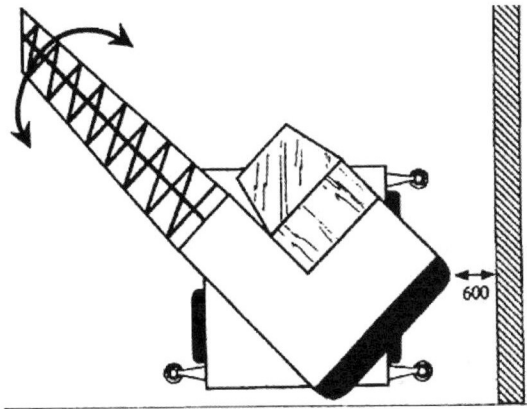

Figure C7-15: Danger zone - crane & fixed item. *Source: ACT.*

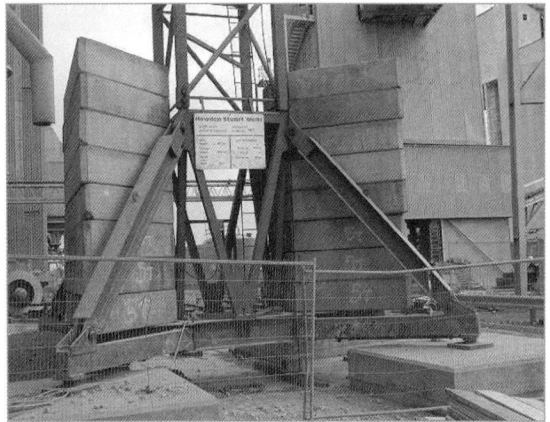

Figure C7-16: Tower crane supports. *Source: ACT.*

Figure C7-17: Mobile crane with stabilisers. *Source: ACT.*

Figure C7-18: Siting and stability. *Source: ACT.*

INTEGRITY OF LIFTING EQUIPMENT

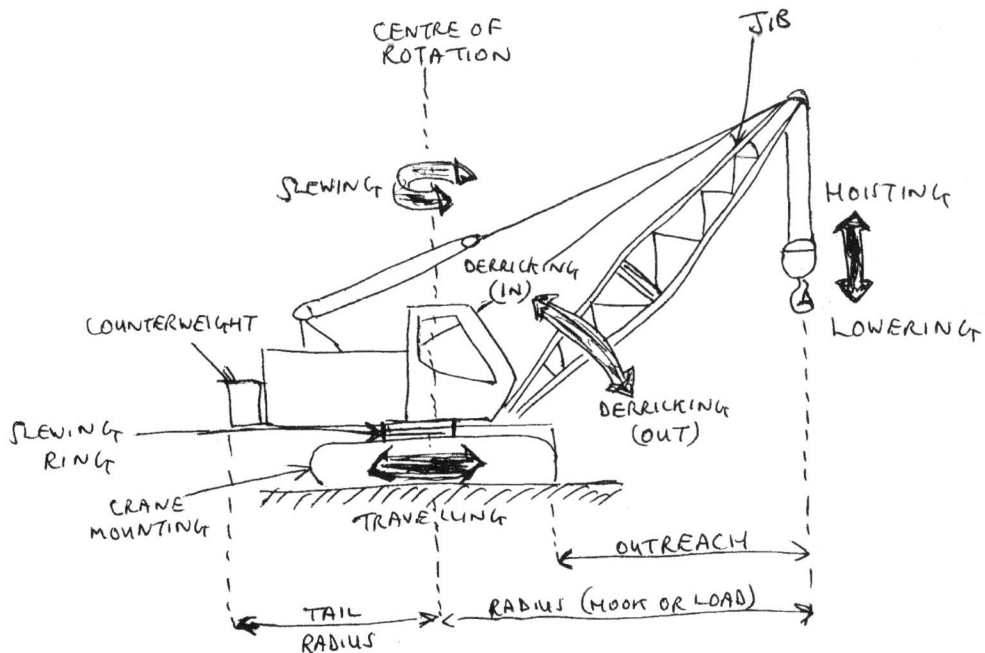

Figure C7-19: Basic terminology for jib crane. (hand-drawn). *Source: ACT.*

The main safety measures that should be incorporated to maintain the integrity of lifting equipment:

■ Pre-use check by operator.
■ Lifting equipment must be of adequate strength and stability for the load. Stresses induced at mounting or fixing points must be taken into account. Similarly every part of a load, anything attached to it and used in lifting must be of adequate strength.
■ The safe working load (SWL) must be clearly marked on lifting machinery, equipment and accessories in order to ensure safe use. Where the SWL depends on the configuration of the machinery, it must be clearly marked for each configuration used and

kept with the machinery. Equipment which is not designed for lifting persons, but which might be used as such, must have appropriate markings to the effect that it is not to be used for passengers.

- Load indicators - two types - a requirement with jib cranes, but beneficial if fitted to all cranes.
  - ✓ Load/radius indicator - shows the radius the crane is working at and the safe load for that radius. Must be visible to the driver.
  - ✓ Automatic safe load indicator - providing visible warning when SWL is approached and audible warning when SWL is exceeded.
- Controls - should be clearly identified and of the "hold to run" type.
- Over travel switches - limit switches to prevent the hook or sheave block being wound up to the cable drum.
- Access - safe access should be provided for the operator and for use during inspection and maintenance/emergency.
- Operating position - should provide clear visibility of hook and load, with the controls easily reached.
- Lifting tackle - chains, slings, wire ropes, eyebolts and shackles should be tested / examined.

COMPETENCE OF PERSONNEL

The Health and Safety at Work etc Act (HASAWA) 1974 places a duty on employers to their employees for the provision of information, instruction, training and supervision as is necessary to ensure, so far as is reasonably practicable, the health and safety at work of his employees. In addition to this general duty, a further duty exists under The Provision and Use of Work Equipment Regulations (PUWER) 1998. Employers must ensure that any person who uses a piece of work equipment has received adequate training for purposes of health and safety, including training in the methods which may be adopted when using work equipment, any risks which such use may entail and precautions to be taken.

Drivers / operators of cranes and other lifting appliances, including others involved in lifting operations (e.g. signallers), must be adequately trained, experienced and aged 18 years or over. The only exception is when under the direct supervision of a competent person for training requirements.

Under regulation 8 of the Lifting Operations and Lifting Equipment Regulation (LOLER) employers have a duty to ensure that every lifting operation involving lifting equipment for the purposes of lifting or lowering of a load is organised safely. This will include ensuring the following:

a)   Lifting operations to be properly planned by a competent person.

b)   Provision of appropriate supervision.

c)   Work is to be carried out in a safe manner.

There are various appointments with specified responsibilities in order to ensure the safety of lifting operations on site, these are as follows.

- Competent person   -   Appointed to plan the operation.
- Load handler   -   Attaches and detaches the load.
- Authorised person   -   Ensures the load safely attached.
- Operator   -   Appointed to operate the equipment.
- Responsible person   -   Appointed to communicate the position of the load (banksman).
- Assistants   -   Appointed to relay communications.

Operational rules

If the operator cannot observe the full path of the load an appointed person (and assistants as appropriate) should be used to communicate the position of the load and directions to avoid striking anything or anyone.

Where practicable, loads should not be carried or suspended over areas occupied by people. Where this is necessary appropriate systems of work should be used to ensure it is done safely.

Lifting operations should not be carried on where adverse weather conditions occur, such as fog, lightning, wind or where heavy rainfall is making ground conditions unstable. It is important that measures be used to prevent lifting equipment overturning and that there is sufficient room for it to operate without contacting other objects. Lifting equipment should not be used to drag loads and should not be overloaded. Special arrangements need to be in place when lifting equipment not normally used for people is used for that purpose, e.g. de-rating the working load limit, ensuring communication is in place between the people and operator, and ensuring the operation controls are manned at all times.

A number of safety rules are suggested as a basis of a Code of Practice for the safe operation of mobile cranes, many of which will be applicable for the operation of all types of crane (naturally circumstances differ in various workplaces and work situations and additional rules should be added to cover individual cases and conditions).

For example, before taking over a crane the operator must always check around the crane, and check the tyre pressure, the engine for fuel, lubrication oil, water and the compressed air system. Test all controls, clutches, brakes and safe load indicator; see that all ropes run smoothly, and check limit switches when fitted.

The operator should carry out the following:

- To travel unladen, lower jib onto its rest (if fitted) or to the lowest operating position and point in the direction of travel, but beware of steep hills.
- Learn the signalling system and observe the signals of the appointed banksman.
- Do not permit unauthorised persons to travel on the crane.
- Do not use the crane to replace normal means of transport, or as a towing tractor.
- Before lifting, check that the crane is on firm and level ground, and that spring locks and out-riggers (where fitted) are properly in position.
- Keep a constant watch on the load radius indicator. The driver may refuse to lift any suspected overload. Overloads are forbidden.
- All movements must be made with caution. Violent handling produces great overloads on the crane structure and machinery.
- Make allowances for adverse weather conditions.
- Do not attempt to drag loads or cause loads to swing. Always position the crane so that the pull on the hoist rope is vertical.

- Satisfy yourself that the load is properly slung. A load considered unsafe should not be lifted.
- Satisfy yourself that all persons are in a safe position before any movement is carried out.
- Make certain before hoisting that the hook is not attached to any anchored load or fixed object.
- Do not drag slings when travelling.
- If the crane is slewing, the jib, hook or load must be in a position to clear any obstruction, but the load must not be lifted unnecessarily high.
- Be on a constant lookout for overhead obstructions, particularly *electric cables*.
- Never tamper with, or disconnect safe load indicators.
- Should the hoist or jib ropes become slack or out of their grooves, stop the crane and report the condition.
- Report all defects to the supervisor and never attempt to use a crane with a suspected serious defect until rectified or certified by a competent person that it is not dangerous.
- When leaving a crane unattended, see that the power is off, the engine stopped, the load unhooked, and the hook taken up to a safe position.
- Where using special devices; e.g. magnets, grabs, etc. they must be used only for the purpose intended and in accordance with the instruction given.
- Keep the crane clean and tidy.
- When parking a crane after use, remember to apply all brakes, slew locks, and secure rail clamps when fitted. Some cranes, however, particularly tower cranes, must be left to weather vane and the manufacturer's instructions must be clearly adhered to. Park the crane where the weather vaning job will not strike any object. Lock the cabin before leaving the crane.
- When it is necessary to make a report this must be done promptly through supervision.
- Drive smoothly - drive safely. Remember, cranes are safe only when they are used as recommended by the makers. This applies in particular to speciality cranes.

Figure C7-20: Lifting operation.   Source: ACT.

Figure C7-21: Lifting points on load.   Source: ACT.

7.4 - Safe use of lifting equipment

TYPES OF LIFTING EQUIPMENT

Lifting equipment and any accessories used for lifting are pieces of work equipment under the Provision and Use of Work Equipment Regulations (PUWER) 1998. Regulation 4 states that:

'every employer shall ensure that work equipment is used only for operations for which, and under conditions for which, it is suitable in order to avoid any reasonably foreseeable risk to the health and safety of any person'.

Lifting equipment (accessories) includes slings, hooks, chains eyes and cradles. In order for lifting equipment to be suitable it must be of the correct type for the task, have a safe working load limit in excess of the load being lifted, and have the correct type and combination of lifting accessories attached.

Slings

Slings are available in single, two, three or four-leg or endless form. In practice it will be found that chain, wire rope and fibre rope slings are available in any of these configurations but that flat woven webbing is limited to single-leg and endless. Whilst round slings are only supplied in endless form. The maximum load that a sling may lift will be governed by the slinging arrangements and may vary from the marked safe working load (SWL).

Slings are normally one of the following three types:

- Steel Wire Rope (SWR)   ■ Chain   ■ Fibre Rope (natural or artificial)

Steel wire rope

A strong general-purpose sling available in a wide range of SWL, with very little stretch when subjected to a maximum permitted SWL. They can be supplied as single or multi-leg assemblies employing a wide range of terminal tackle.

Figure C7-22: Single-leg sling.

Source: Ambiguous.

They are constructed in a series of individual wires wound into strands, with a number of strands (usually six) laid in a left or right hand lay over a central strand or core. The main core helps to hold the rope together and prevent it from collapsing when bent. The core can be either fibre or steel depending on the strength and uses of the rope.

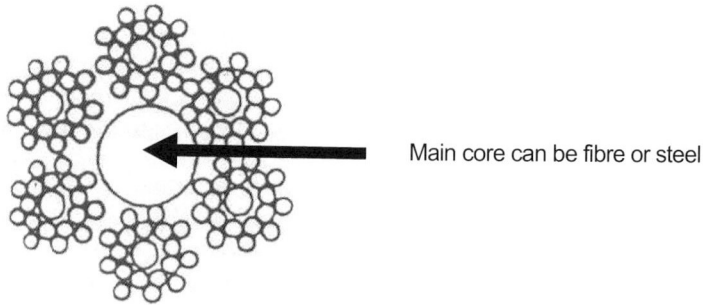

Main core can be fibre or steel

Figure C7-23: Typical wire rope construction 6 x 19 (6 strands with 19 wires in each strand). *Source: Ambiguous.*

Chain slings

Chain slings can be used as an alternative to steel wire rope (SWR). Each has its own advantages and limitations and the latter must be fully appreciated by the slinger if accidents are to be avoided. Chain slings are able to withstand rougher handling are less liable to tangle, twist or knot and they are more flexible when not under load tension than SWR. They are capable of gripping a load firmly and are not damaged as easily as SWR or fibre slings by sharp corners or edges of a load through adequate packing should still be used where necessary).

Chains are available in single, multi-leg or endless configurations and may be fitted with various types of terminal accessories such as hooks, pipe grabs, drum and case clamps etc. They are resistant to abrasion and corrosion and will give warning of excessive loading by the elongation and narrowing of links until eventually they bind together.

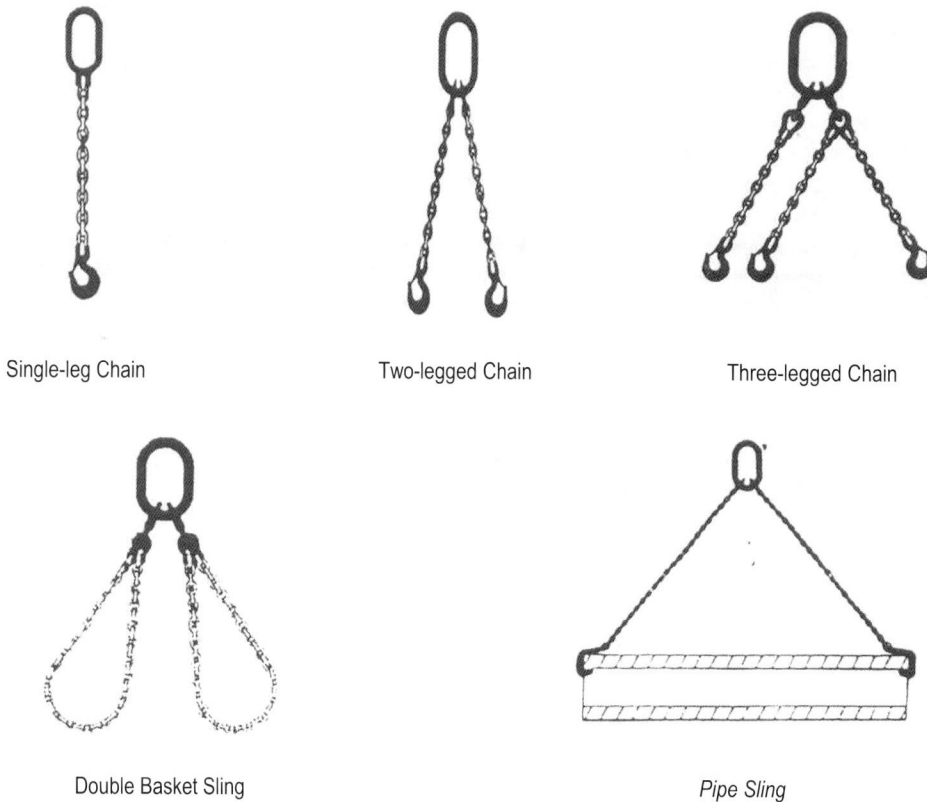

Single-leg Chain

Two-legged Chain

Three-legged Chain

Double Basket Sling

Pipe Sling

Figure C7-24: Chain slings. *Source: Ambiguous.*

Fibre rope slings

Fibre rope slings are usually constructed from one of the following materials:

Natural Fibre:

Manila, sisal, hemp

Man-made Fibre:

Terylene polyester, nylon, polypropylene

During recent years with the development of man-made fibre there has been a considerable increase in the use of this type of material for the manufacture of slings, due to its increased strength and durability. It is also less liable to damage from rot, mildew and effects from the elements. Also certain fibres are resistant to various chemical solutions. However, fibre rope slings are more suspect to damage from abrasion and cuts from steel wire rope or chain slings. This fact should always be taken into account by the slinger when selecting or inspecting these types of slings. All fibre rope slings are liable to wear and mechanical damage, and may also be weakened to some degree by various elements such as dampness, chemicals, heat and light.

Man-made fibres are resistant to the following chemicals:

Terylene polyester	High resistance to Acid solutions but is attacked by Alkali solutions
Nylon	High resistance to Alkali solutions but is attacked by Acid solutions
Polypropylene	Resistant to both Acids and Alkalis

Where artificial fibre slings are used in any chemical solution, they should be thoroughly washed and dried naturally before returning to storage. Under no circumstances should natural fibre ropes be used in chemical solutions. All fibre ropes should be stored in a cool, dry, well-ventilated storage area away from bright sunlight. Particular care should be taken to protect slings from damage caused by sharp edges on the load, by using packing or sleeves. Knots and bends tied in fibre slings will considerably reduce the Safe Working Load and should be avoided where possible. On no account should fibre rope slings of different materials be used when lifting loads due to the different stretching properties of different fibres.

Figure C7-25: Fibre rope sling.   *Source: Lincsafe.*

Figure C7-26: Fibre rope sling.   *Source: ACT.*

Eyebolts

Eyebolts are normally used for fitting to various items of equipment for the purpose of lifting anchor points when slinging. There are three common types of eyebolts:

Dynamo	To be used for straight lifts only (vertical)
Collar	For both angles (multi-leg) and straight lifts
Collar and Ring	For angle (multi-leg) lifts

Note: On no account should Dynamo Eyebolts be used for angled lifts.

Care should be taken to ensure that the load does not rotate when lifting with a Dynamo Eyebolt since the eyebolt may unscrew.

Dynamo Eyebolt   Collar Eyebolt   Collar Eyebolt with Ring

Figure C7-27: Eyebolts.   *Source: Ambiguous.*

Case or drum sling

They are only suitable for loads of less than 1 tonne. Included angle of lift should always be kept as close as possible to 60 degrees. Drum rims should always be in a sound condition when using this type of sling.

Lifting spreader beam

Plate clamp

Case or drum sling

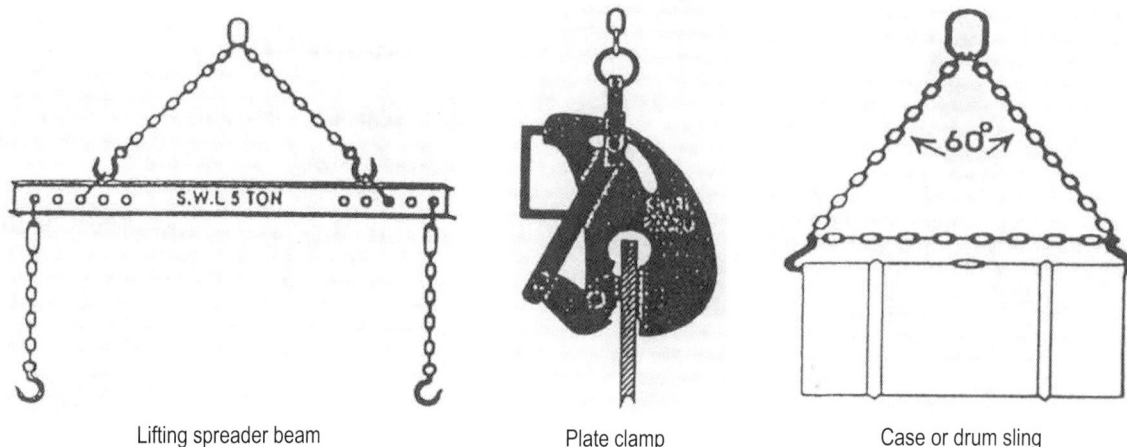

Figure C7-28: Case or drum sling.

Source: Ambiguous.

Shackles

Shackles are used as terminal tackle for securing the sling to the load or eyebolt, or to attach a number of slings to the hook of a lifting appliance. Their use is also recommended where it may be necessary to join two slings together so as increasing the sling length. All shackles should be marked with their Safe Working Load and Identification Mark.

Lifting hooks

There are several types of lifting hooks, which may be fitted to the lifting appliance or used as terminal tackle, particular on chain slings.

The type of hook will normally depend upon the type of lifting or slinging application. The slinger needs to be aware of all safe practices associated with the use of each type of hook. All hooks used for lifting must be fitted with a safety catch, or should be moused, or so shaped to prevent the sling eye or load coming off the hook.

Lifting spreader beam

Designed for the purpose of handling long loads. Can also be used in conjunction with two dynamo eyebolts since a vertical lift would be applied to the eyebolts. Must be a tested piece of lifting equipment marked with a Safe Working Load.

Plate clamp

Used for lifting sheets of metal. These must be free from oil and grease so as to prevent the load slipping. Relies on clamping force of clamp mechanism - not suitable for heavy loads. Must be a tested piece of lifting equipment marked with a safe working load.

Figure C7-29: Hook with safety latch. *Source: Corel Clipart.*

Lifting equipment is designed with the aim of assisting in lifting items without the need for manual force. Because these accessories are in a constantly changing environment and are in and out of use they need to be protected from damage, a failure of any one item could have fatal effects. For example, lifting eyes needed to be correctly fitted, slings have to be used with the correct technique and all equipment must be stored properly. Accessories must be attached correctly and safely to the load by a competent person, and then the lifting equipment takes over the task of providing the necessary required power to perform the lift.

MAINTENANCE, INSPECTION AND STATUTORY EXAMINATION OF CRANES AND LIFTING EQUIPMENT

Used lifting equipment must be thoroughly examined prior to being put into service for the first time by a new user. This does not apply to new lifting equipment (unless its safety depends on installation conditions) or equipment that conforms to EC requirements and has been certified as being examined within the previous 12 months. Suppliers of used lifting equipment are obliged to certify that a thorough examination has been carried out.

Where the safety of lifting equipment depends on the installation conditions it must be thoroughly examined prior to first use, after assembly and on change of location in order to ensure that it has been installed correctly and is safe to operate.

Lifting equipment which is exposed to conditions causing deterioration which is liable to result in dangerous situations is to be thoroughly examined:

a.   At least every 6 months for lifting equipment, for lifting persons or lifting accessories.

b.   At least every 12 months for other lifting equipment.

c.   In either case, in accordance with an examination scheme.

d.   On each occurrence of exceptional circumstances liable to jeopardise the safety of the lifting equipment.

Where appropriate, to ensure health and safety, inspections must be carried out at suitable intervals between thorough examinations. Examinations and inspections must ensure that the good condition of equipment is maintained and that any deterioration can be detected and remedied in good time.

A regular system of maintenance and inspection should be carried out. This ranges from a daily visual inspection by the driver to servicing and inspections carried out in accordance with the manufacturer's instructions. The manufacturer's instructions should be followed for any repair.

7.5 - Hoists and lifts

MAIN HAZARDS ASSOCIATED WITH THE USE OF LIFTS AND HOISTS

Gin wheel

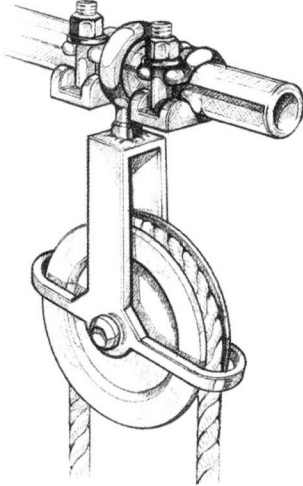

Gin wheels provide a very convenient way of raising loads. Though simple pieces of equipment, care is required when assembling and using them. Always make sure it has:

- Been securely fixed to an anchorage.
- A proper hook is being used with a safety catch to secure the load.
- A safe working platform exists from which the hook can be loaded or unloaded.

Figure C7-30: Gin wheel.

Source: HSE Guidance Note PM28; Working Platforms on Fork Lift Trucks.

Hoist/lift for passenger and goods (including construction site platform)

Hazards

In general, the hazards associated with lifts and hoists are the same as with any other lifting equipment.

- The lift / hoist may overturn or collapse.
- The lift / hoist can strike persons who may be near or under the platform or cage during normal operations.
- The supporting ropes may fail and the platform/cage may fall to the ground.
- The load or part of the load may fall.
- The lift / hoist may fail in a high position.
- Persons being lifted may become stranded if the lift or hoist fails.

Safe use and maintenance

The hoist should be protected by a substantial enclosure to prevent anyone from being struck by any moving part of the hoist or material falling down the hoist way. Gates must be provided at all access landings, including at ground level. The gates must be kept shut, except when the platform is at the landing. The controls should be arranged so that the hoist can be operated from one position only. All hoist operators must be trained and competent. The hoist's safe working load must be clearly marked. If the hoist is for materials only there should be a prominent warning notice on the platform or cage to stop people riding on it. The hoist should be inspected weekly, and thoroughly examined every 12 months (six months where it is used to lift people) by a competent person and the results of inspection recorded.

Lifts and hoists for movement of goods require:

■   Statutory safety devices.
■   Holdback gears (for rope failure).
■   Overrun tip systems.
■   Guards on hoist machinery.
■   Landing gates (securely closed down during operation).

In addition, passenger hoists require more sophisticated controls:

■   Operating controls inside the cage.
■   Electromagnetic interlocks on the cage doors.
■   The enclosing shaft must be of fire-proof construction, if within a building.

Safe use of lifts and hoists depends on:

■   Adequate design.
■   Competent operation.
■   Sound construction.
■   Regular inspection.
■   Correct selection.
■   Adequate maintenance.
■   Correct installation.

The legislation governing the construction, use and thorough examination of lifts and hoists, is the Lifting Operations and Lifting Equipment Regulations (LOLER) 1998.

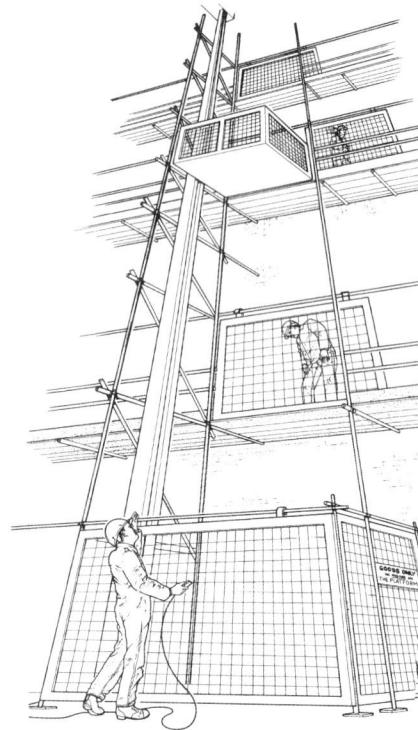

Figure C7-31: Construction lift / hoist.   *Source: HSG150, HSE books.*

Scissor

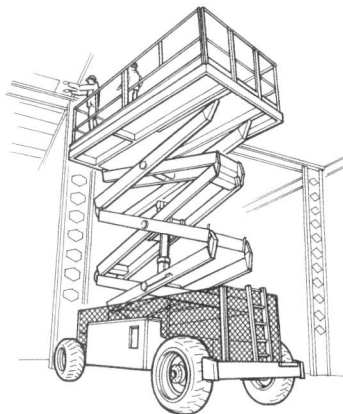

Figure C7-32: Scissor lift.   *Source: HSG150, HSE books.*

Figure C7-33: Scissor lift.   *Source: ACT.*

Hazards

■   Include crush injuries as the platform is raised to or past a fixed part of a structure.
■   People, equipment or materials falling from the platform

■   The platform overturning, particularly if used on uneven ground.
■   The sheer effect of the scissor mechanism as it closes.

Do not

■   Operate close to overhead cables or dangerous machinery.
■   Allow a knuckle, or elbow, of the arm to protrude into a traffic route when working near vehicles.
■   Overload or overreach from the platform.

■   Move the equipment with the platform in the raised position unless the equipment is especially designed to allow this to be done safely
(check the manufacturer's instructions).

Vehicle Inspection

Figure C7-34: Vehicle lift.   *Source: www.asedeals.com/scissor lifts.*

Figure C7-35: Vehicle lift.   *Source: ACT.*

Vehicle lifts come in a variety of configurations and can cause accidents if they are used unsafely or poorly maintained. There is a risk of vehicles falling/rolling off incorrectly positioned jacks or stands, particularly where they are not chocked, are one of the main causes of fatal accidents. There is an additional risk of crush injury, particularly to the feet, when the lift is lowered to the ground.

MOBILE ELEVATING WORK PLATFORM (MEWP)

Figure C7-36: MEWP.   *Source: HSG150, HSE books.*

Figure C7-37: MEWP.   *Source: ACT.*

Mobile Elevating Work Platforms (MEWPs) can provide excellent safe access to high level work. When using a MEWP make sure:

■   Whoever is operating it is fully trained and competent.
■   The work platform is fitted with guard rails and toe boards.
■   It is used on suitable firm and level ground. The ground may have to be prepared in advance.
■   Tyres are properly inflated.
■   The work area is cordoned off to prevent access below the work platform.
■   That it is well lit if being used on a public highway in poor lighting.
■   Outriggers are extended and chocked as necessary before raising the platform.
■   All involved know what to do if the machine fails with the platform in the raised position.

7.6 - Safe use of conveyors

TYPES OF CONVEYOR

Belt

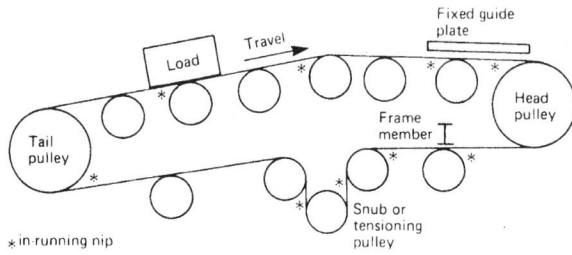

Materials are transported on a moving belt. Trapping points are created between the belt and the rotating drum. The head and tails pulleys create the main risks. Guards can be fitted enclosing the sides or at each in-running nip.

Figure C7-38: Diagrammatic layout of belt conveyor showing in-running nips.

Source: J Ridley; Safety at Work; Fourth Edition.

Roller

a. Power Driven Rollers: guards are required on power drives and in-running nips.

b. Powered and Free Running Rollers: guards are required between each pair of powered and free running rollers.

c. Free Running Rollers: no nips occur on these, but injuries can occur when people try to walk across them. This problem can be solved by providing walkways.

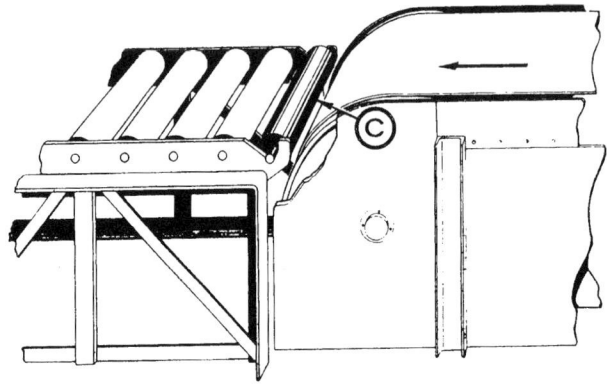

Figure C7-39: Preventing free running roller trap.

Source: J Ridley; Safety at Work; Fourth Edition - Courtesy HSE.

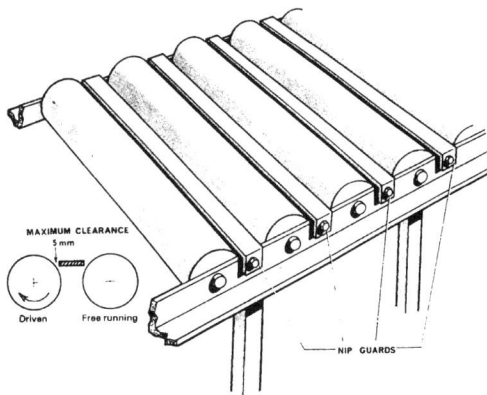

Figure C7:40: Guards between alternative drive-rollers.

Source: J Ridley; Safety at Work; Fourth Edition.

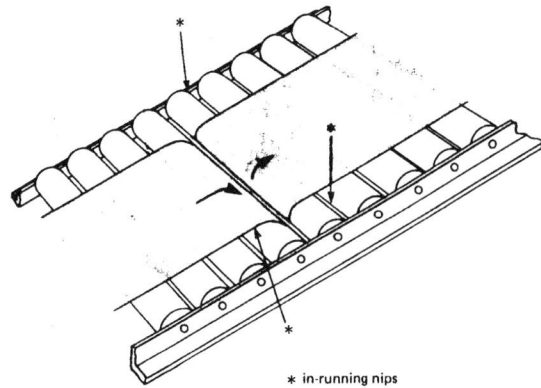

Figure C7-41: Nip points on roller conveyor with belts.

Source: J Ridley; Safety at Work; Fourth Edition.

Plate

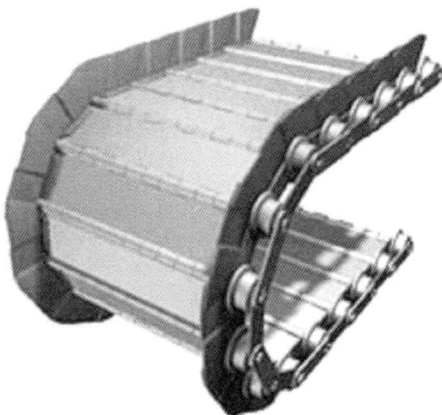

There are different versions for different applications e.g. transporting steel scrap, difficult applications e.g. domestic waste, and for carrying heavy weights.

Figure C7-42: Plate conveyor.

Source: www.mayfran.de/en/00011_00064_stahlplattenbaender.htm.

Screw

Materials are pushed forward by a rotating screw. Screw conveyors can cause terrible injuries and should be guarded or covered at all times. A locking-off system is required for maintenance and repairs.

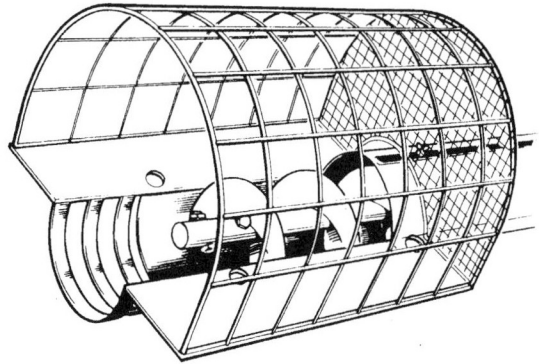

Figure C7-43: Screw conveyor guarding.

Source: J Ridley; Safety at Work; Fourth Edition - Courtesy HSE.

Monorail

The overhead monorail is a closed-loop chain conveyor system, where jobs ride on fixed centres and travel at a set speed. Jobs may be suspended from the overhead monorail chain using hangers, attachments, chains, baskets or hooks. Monorails are ideal for applications such as sub-component build lines, feeder conveyors or part delivery/storage systems. One drawback to a monorail conveyor is that it must run continuously - stopping one job requires the whole conveyor to be halted. They tend to be slow moving and are set at a height, with components hanging from them. Workers may be tempted to pass between the items being moved, with the resultant risk of being struck by items or hitting heir head on the rail as they pass under it. Careful demarcation of danger area and siting away from walk routes is essential.

Figure C7-44: Monorail conveyor system.

Source: www.aeiconveyors.com.

MAIN HAZARDS AND METHODS OF CONTROLLING RISKS FROM CONVEYORS

Hazards

- Trapping   -   Clothing or limbs being drawn in to in-running nips caused by moving parts.
- Contact   -   With moving parts.
- Entanglement   -   With rollers.
- Striking   -   Falling objects, especially from overhead conveyors.

Controls

- Fixed guards on drums.
- Enclosure of conveyed items by side guards.
- Trip wires, if necessary, along the full length of the conveyor.
- Emergency stop buttons.
- Safe access at regular intervals.
- Regular maintenance by competent people.

7.7 - Safe use of automated warehousing systems

Automated warehousing systems (AWS) avoid risk of injury to the person by excluding them from the area, thus avoiding contact with risks associated with the handling, movement and storage of materials. Automatic vehicles move goods to be stacked in cells where the bar code is read and the stock information is held on a database. As required, the truck retrieves items and returns to the loading/off loading bay. As such systems are computer controlled - the system is as good as the computer program. Problems occur when people enter the system, for repair, maintenance or performing a difficult manoeuvre that the truck cannot carry out. Hazards include:

- Manual handling at loading/off loading bay.
- Malfunctioning vehicles.
- Unknown effects of computer program bugs.
- Malfunctioning obstruction sensors.
- Damage to storage racks causing collapse or falling objects.

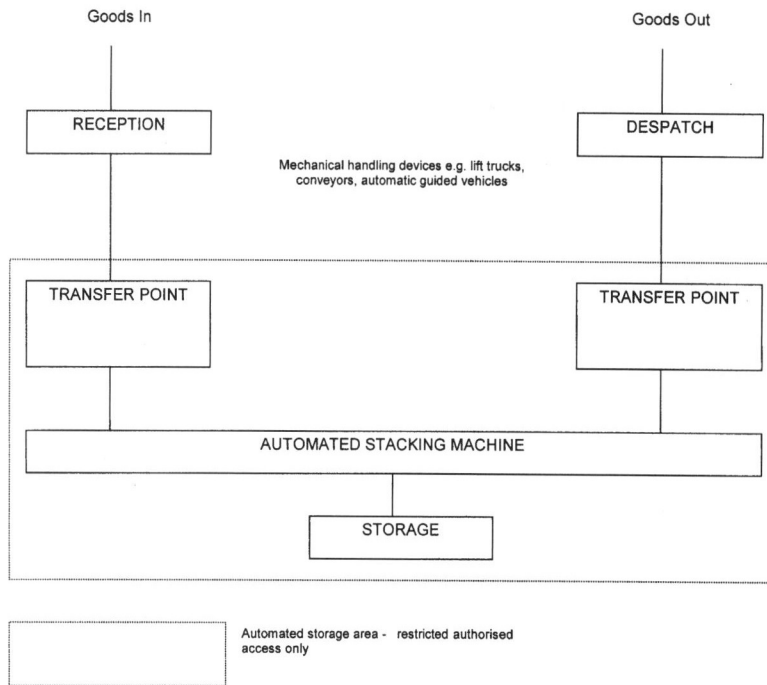

Figure C7-45: Schematic layout of an automated warehouse.

Source: Ambiguous.

Safeguarding automated warehousing systems focuses on the following main strategies:

- Risk assessment.
- Maintenance of safety devices: trip devices and obstruction sensors.
- Perimeter fencing to exclude personnel.
- Safe Systems of Work: locking off system and Permit to Work for maintenance and cleaning work.

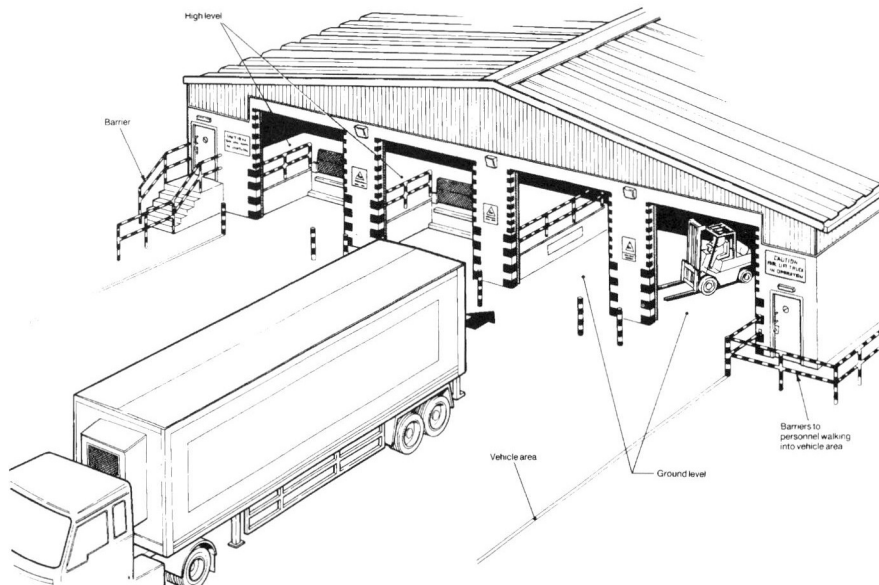

Figure C7-46: Automated warehouse.

Source: HSG76 - Health and Safety in Retail and Wholesale Warehouses.

Electrical Safety

Overall aims

On completion of this Element, the student will have knowledge and understanding of:

■ the nature of electricity.

■ the dangers of electricity and principles of first aid treatment for electrical injuries.

■ safety considerations for portable electric tools and equipment.

■ legislation relevant to the above.

Content

Specific intended learning outcomes

The intended learning outcomes are that the student will be able to:

1. identify the common hazards and evaluate the consequential risks which are likely to arise from the use of electricity

2. advise managers on the safe use and maintenance of electrical equipment

Relevant statutory provisions

Electricity at Work Regulations (EWR) 1989

Dangerous Substances and Explosive Atmospheres Regulations (DSEAR) 2002

8.1 - Basic principles of electricity

POTENTIAL DIFFERENCE

The flow of electrons through a conductor is known as current. Just as water flows through a pipe, because of the pressure behind it, the electric current flows due to differences in electrical "pressure" or potential difference as it is often known.

To further explain, current flows in a circuit as a result of a difference in potential between two points in the circuit. The potential difference between two points in a conductor is the work per unit charge done by the charge in moving from a point of higher potential to a point of lower potential.

The unit of potential difference is called the volt, **V**. One volt of potential difference exists between two points if one joule of work is done by each coulomb of charge in moving between them. Potential difference is measured by an instrument called a voltmeter.

Voltmeters are connected in parallel to the component across which one wishes to measure the potential difference. They have a resistance which is several orders of magnitude higher than the resistance of the component. The current which flows through a voltmeter is negligible.

CURRENT

Current is the flow of charge. The unit of current is the ampere, **A**.

Current is measured using an instrument called an ammeter. Ammeters are connected in series with the part of the circuit through which one wishes to measure the current, **I**, and they have negligible resistance.

RESISTANCE

For any conductor, the ratio of the potential difference across the conductor and the current flowing through it is constant. This constant is called the resistance of the conductor, **R**:

$$\text{Resistance(R)} = \frac{V}{I}$$

The unit of resistance is the Ohm, Ω.

Resistance is a property of a particular conductor and depends on:

- The material of which the conductor is made.
- The length, l, of the conductor ($R \propto l$). (Resistance is directly proportional to length).
- The cross-sectional area of the conductor. (Resistance is inversely proportional to cross-sectional area).
- The temperature of the conductor. (Resistance increases non-linearly with temperature).

IMPEDANCE

As an alternating current passes round a circuit under the action of an applied voltage it is impeded in its flow. This may be due to the presence in the circuit of resistance, inductance or capacitance, the combined effect of which is called impedance and is measured in ohms.

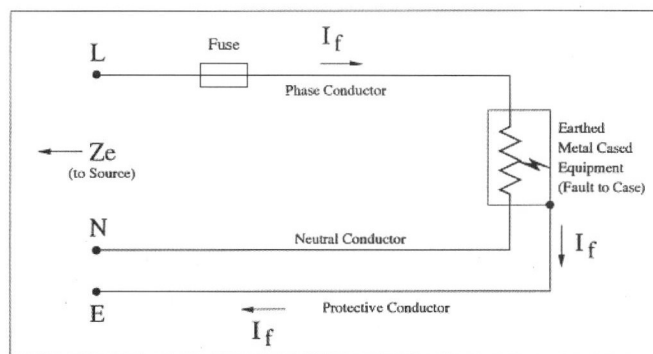

TOTAL EFLI (Z) = EXTERNAL EFLI (Ze) + CIRCUIT EFLI (Zc)

Zc = Impedance of phase conductor plus impedance of protective
      conductor (fault assumed to have negligible impedance)

Figure C8-1: Impedance.   *Source: G Self, Associate Tutor, ACT.*

OHM'S LAW

"For any particular conductor at a constant temperature, the current that flows through it is directly proportional to the potential difference applied across it."

$$I = \frac{1}{R}V \qquad \text{or IR = V or} \qquad I = \frac{V}{R}$$

There is a simple relationship between electrical pressure (volts), current and resistance represented by Ohm's Law: voltage (**V**) = current (**I**) multiplied by the circuit resistance (**R**).

$$V = I \times R \text{ or } I = \frac{V}{R}$$

Hence, given any two values, the third can be calculated. Also, if one value changes the other two values will change accordingly.

This basic electrical equation can be used to calculate the current that flows in a circuit of a given resistance or power connected to a particular voltage supply. This will need to be done to determine, for example, the fuse or cable rating needed for a particular circuit. Similarly, the current that will flow through a person who touches a live conductor can be calculated.

BASIC ELECTRICAL CIRCUITRY

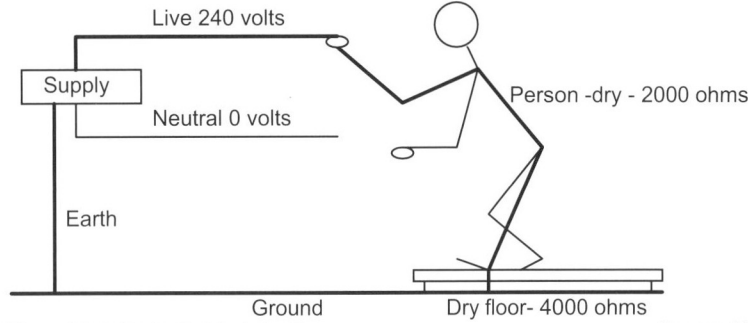

By Ohm's law:

$$Current = \frac{Voltage}{Resistance}$$

Figure C8-2: Basic electrical circuitry.   *Source: ACT.*

Resistance in a circuit is dependent on many factors. Most metals, particularly precious metals allow current to pass very easily. These have a low resistance and are used as conductors. Other materials such as plastics, rubber and textiles have a high resistance and are used as insulators.

If the person is on, say a dry concrete floor, resistance in the body will only be about 2000 ohms and the resistance in the floor about 4000 ohms therefore:

$$I = \frac{V}{R} = \frac{240 \text{ Volts}}{\approx 2000 + 4000 \text{ Ohms}} = 0.04 \text{ Amps}$$

The current flowing through the operator will be about 40 milliamps that could result in a fatal shock. *(See the diagram above).*

EARTHING PRINCIPLES

The conductive mass of the Earth, whose electric potential at any point is conventionally taken as zero helps as a protective measure.

A conductor called an earth wire is connected to the system. It is connected at one end to a plate buried into the ground and the other end connected to the metal casing of the equipment. If for any reason a conducting wire touches the casing so that the equipment casing becomes '*Live*' the current will flow to the point of lowest potential.

By fitting the earth wire the path to this point is made easier as the wire has very little resistance and therefore an easier path.

Unearthed electrical system

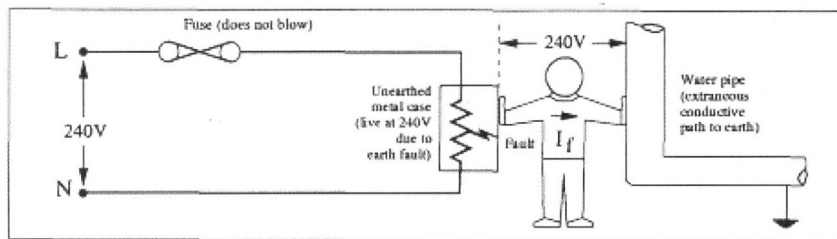

Earthed electrical system

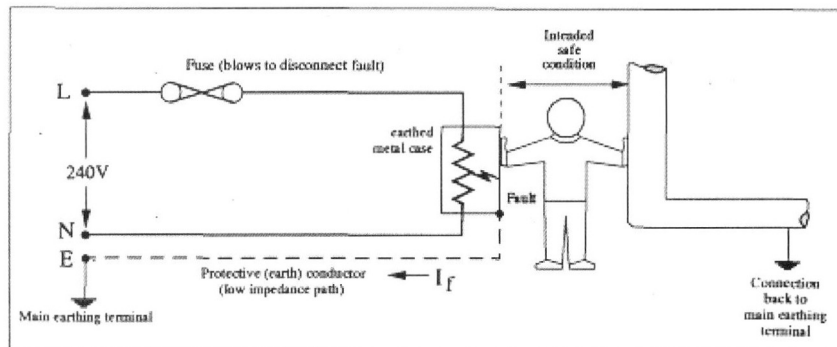

Figures C8-3 & C8-4: Unearthed and earthed electrical systems.   *Source: G Self, Associate Tutor, ACT.*

SIGNIFICANCE OF DIRECT AND ALTERNATING CURRENTS

In some systems the current flows continually in the same direction. This is known as direct current (d.c.). However the current may also constantly reverse its direction of flow. This is known as alternating current (a.c.). Most public electricity supplies are alternating current. The UK system reverses its direction 50 times per second. It has a frequency of 50 cycles per second or 50 Hertz (50 Hz). Direct current. is little used in standard distribution systems but is sometimes used in industry for specialist applications. Although there are slight differences in the effects under fault and shock conditions between alternating current and direct current, it is a safe rule to apply the same rules of safety for the treatment of electric shock.

8.2 - Dangers of electricity

ELECTRIC SHOCK

Effects on the body

Electric shock is where the injury results from the flow of electricity through the body's nerves, muscles and organs and causes abnormal function to occur. Muscular spasm may lead to significant secondary effects such as falls, falling objects and bumps. Other factors include the following:

- Pain.
- Muscular contraction.
- Respiratory failure.

- Heart fibrillation.
- Cardiac arrest.
- Internal burns.

Factors influencing severity of effects on the body

The severity of electric shock or the amount of current which flows for a given voltage will depend on the frequency of the supply voltage, on the level of the voltage which is applied and on the state of the point of contact with the body, particularly the moisture condition.

The effect of electricity on the body results from a combination of the current level and the time duration of the passage of that current. The voltage level is relevant only in that it causes the passage of the current.

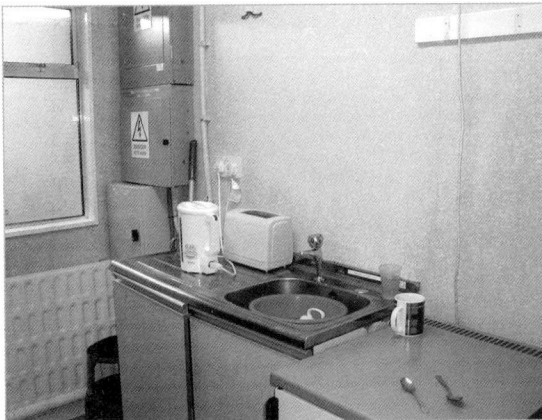

Figure C8-5: Electrical equipment near water. *Source: ACT.*

Figure C8-6: Contact with high voltage buried cable. *Source: ACT.*

Effects of current flowing in the human body

Current (mA)	Length of time	Likely effects
0-1	Not critical	Threshold of feeling. Undetected by person
2-15	Not critical	Threshold of cramp. Independent loosening of the hands no longer possible
16-30	Minutes	Cramp like pulling together of the arms, breathing difficult. Limit of tolerance
31-50	Seconds to minutes	Strong cramplike effects, loss of consciousness due to restricted breathing. Longer time may lead to fibrillation
51-500	Less than one heart period (750 ms)	No fibrillation. Strong shock effects.
	Greater than one heart period	Fibrillation. Loss of consciousness. Burn marks.
Over 501	Less than one heart period	Fibrillation. Loss of consciousness. Burn marks.

Figure C8-7: Effects of current flowing in the human body. *Source: ACT.*

The most important message to be put over to employees is that although many will have experienced shock from 230 volts, this has not been fatal because they were, for example, standing on or wearing some insulating material. It is relatively easy in the factory or office situation to receive a fatal shock from 230 volts or even lower voltage supplies because of the presence of many more low resistance paths to earth.

Direct shock - contact with a charged or energised conductor that is intended to be so charged or energised. In these circumstances the installation is operating in its normal or proper condition.

Indirect Shock - contact with a conductor that is normally at a safe potential but has become dangerously live through a fault condition. Reference is made to exposed conductive parts: these are the conducting casing etc. of the apparatus, normally safe to touch but which, under fault conditions, could become dangerously live.

Other factors include the following:

- Voltage.
- Frequency.
- Duration.

- Impedance / resistance.
- Current path.

ELECTRICAL BURNS

Electrical burns result from the heating effect of the current which burns the body tissue.

Direct

Where electric current passes through body tissues there will be a heating effect along the route. Whilst there are likely to be burn marks on the skin at the point of contact there may also be a deep seated burning within the body which is painful and slow to heal. As the outer layer of skin is burnt, the resistance decreases and so the current will increase.

Indirect

If while working on live equipment the system is short-circuited by, for example, an un-insulated spanner touching live and neutral this will result in a large and sudden current flow through the spanner. This current will cause the spanner to melt and may throw molten metal out from the points of contract.

FIRST AID TREATMENT PRINCIPLES FOR ELECTRICAL INJURIES

In case of electrical shock:

Do

- Switch off or remove the plug. Check that there is no remaining connection to the supply and, if possible, prove that the system is discharged and dead.
- Assess the situation and any remaining danger to yourself or the casualty.
- Call for qualified support which may mean the 999 emergency services.
- If safe, check the casualty's response (What is the degree of consciousness?)

Check

A - Airway   -   Is it open?

B - Breathing   -   Is the casualty breathing normally?

C - Circulation   -   Does the casualty have a normal pulse?

Action

If the airway is obstructed by teeth, food etc., remove; if the tongue obstructs tilt head back to clear, and then provide cardio-pulmonary resuscitation (**CPR**).

If trained, place in the recovery position and/or apply resuscitation as required. Cool any burns with cold water.

Keep the casualty under observation for secondary effects until you hand him/her over to a medically qualified person.

Do not

- Do not go near the casualty until the electricity supply is proven to be off. This is especially important with overhead high voltage lines: keep yourself and others at least 18 metres away until the electricity supply company personnel advise otherwise.
- Do not delay - after 3 minutes without blood circulation irreversible damage can be done to the casualty.

Figure C8-8: First aid sign.   Source: ACT.

- Do not wait for an accident to happen - train in emergency procedures and first aid now, plan procedures for an emergency (calling for help, making 999 calls, meeting ambulances etc. and leading them to the casualty) as seconds saved may save a life. Hold emergency drills.

FIRES

Electrical fires are caused by overheating or arcing apparatus in contact with a fuel.

Common causes

Much electrical equipment generates heat or produces sparks and this equipment should not be placed where this could lead to the uncontrolled ignition of any substance.

The principal causes of electrical fires are:

- Wiring with defects such as insulation failure due to age or poor maintenance.
- Overheating of cables or other electrical equipment through overloading with currents above their design capacity.
- Incorrect fuse rating.
- Poor connections due to lack of maintenance or unskilled personnel.

Electrical equipment may itself explode or arc violently and it may also act as a source of ignition of flammable vapours, gases, liquids or dust through electric sparks, arcs or high surface temperatures of equipment. Other sources are heat created by poorly maintained or defective motors, heaters and lighting. Anyone in the immediate area could receive burns from the molten metal. Other electrical sources of fire include the following:

- Overloading of conductors - overheating.
- Ignition of flammable vapour.
- Ignition of combustible material.
- Breakdown of insulation.

Figure C8-9: Used coiled up-risk of overheating. *Source: ACT.*

Figure C8-10: Max current capacity exceeded. *Source: ACT.*

ELECTRIC ARCS

Molten metal splash and radiation

An electric arc is a high temperature electrical discharge between two electrodes in close proximity. The energy released is in the form of heat and light. This extremely high temperature can result in the conductor melting. If this phenomenon is controlled it has great benefits for industry e.g. electric arc welding. However, uncontrolled it can lead to molten metal being discharged or the light (UV radiation) produced can cause burns and a condition called 'arc eye'.

8.3 - Portable electrical equipment

CONDITIONS AND PRACTICES LIKELY TO LEAD TO ACCIDENTS

Unsuitable equipment
- Unsuitable apparatus for the duty or the conditions.
- Misuse.
- Failure to follow operating instructions.
- Wrong connection of system - supply phase, neutral or earth reversed.
- Wrong voltage or rating of equipment.

Figure C8-11: Hazard - fuse wired out. *Source: ACT.*

Figure C8-12: Hazard - defective apparatus. *Source: ACT.*

Inadequate maintenance
- Inadequate maintenance of the installation and the equipment.
- Wrong or broken connection to portable apparatus.
- Inadequate earthing.
- Poor maintenance and testing.
- No defect reporting system.

Use of defective apparatus
- Faulty cables, notably extension leads.
- Plugs and sockets.
- Damaged plug or socket.
- Protection devices, such as fuses or circuit breaker, incorrect rating, damaged or missing.
- Overloaded leading to damage or over-heating.
- Short circuit leading to damage, overheating or movement.
- Isolation procedures or systems of work wrong.
- Bad circuit connections.

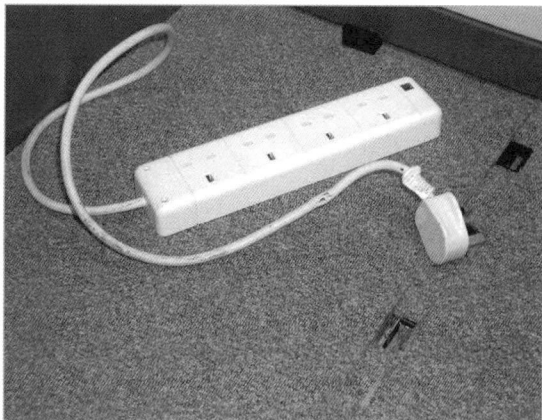

Figure C8-13: Hazard - damaged cable.   *Source: ACT.*

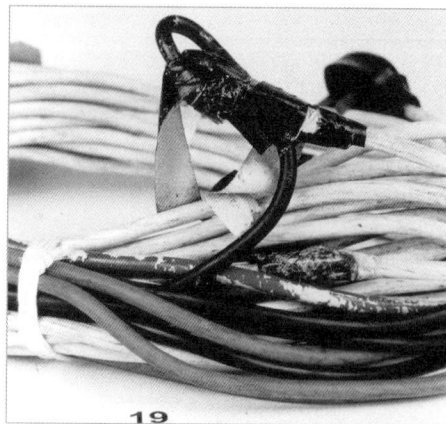

Figure C8-14: Hazard - taped joints.   *Source: ACT.*

General

- Lack of competence.
- Poor access, lighting and emergency procedures.
- No work planning including permit-to-work.

PORTABLE APPLIANCE INSPECTION AND TESTING

This should be carried out in accordance with a defined schedule of planned maintenance. Factors affecting the time scales between tests include:

- Number of work hours used.
- Environmental conditions.
- Reported defects or problems during use.
- Voltage dependant upon environment equipment used.

There are 3 types of test:

- User check - carried out by the user prior to use.
- Formal visual check - carried out by a competent person.
- Combined inspection and testing - carried out by a competent person.

Source: HSG107 - Maintaining Portable and Transportable Electrical Equipment.

8.4 - Static electricity

Static electricity is different to mains power electricity. It can be generated naturally and is familiar in everyday life as the crackling sound when we remove a woollen sweater, the tiny blue sparks seen in the dark, the clinging together of clothing, paper or sheets of material, or the sharp shock - usually just a nuisance - when we rub and separate from a dissimilar surface such as when getting out of a car and then touching the body work.

Except that the resulting jump may cause distraction and occasionally a fall, such shocks in themselves are not usually personally dangerous. The resulting jump or fall may cause injury.

CIRCUMSTANCES GIVING RISE TO THE GENERATION OF STATIC ELECTRICITY

What is static?

Static electricity consists of an excess or deficiency of electrons on the surface of materials. Its presence is normally only recognised by the occurrence of the discharging spark unless appropriate instruments are used. If two charged materials remain close together, the charges oppose each other and to external appearances the combination is neutral.

When the two surfaces are rubbed or moved apart, the two opposite charges separate and the two materials become separately and oppositely charged. The materials can remain in that state if the surroundings are sufficient to withstand the often thousands of volts between them.

There are two types of discharge:

- **Spark discharge** occurs where a charged conductor is discharged usually to earth through another conductor, for example, from an insulated charged container to an earthed vessel, or from a charged insulated vessel through a person and thence to earth. When an energetic discharge of this type occurs, the virtually instantaneous action produces a spark which is easily enough to ignite gas, vapour, dust or vapour/dust mixtures.
- **Brush discharge** occurs where a non-conducting body becomes charged and part discharges to earth. Because only the energy from around the proximity of the discharge is dispersed immediately, this type of discharge is slower, less energetic and less visible. It will ignite gas, vapour and vapour/dust mixtures but is not usually of sufficient energy to ignite dust.

Control

Spark discharge can be controlled through the bonding and earthing of all conducting surfaces and the good management of all exposed flammable materials.

Brush discharges cannot be earthed out and can only be prevented by the avoidance of non-conductors or the exclusion of oxygen.

Proper clothing will minimise production of static on people.

Knowledge of and strict compliance with safe procedures of work is essential.

Reducing static build up

- Earthing of all exposed non-current carrying metalwork.
- Maintaining an atmosphere with a high relative humidity.
- Ionising the air by controlled voltage discharge.
- Wearing special conducting footwear and clothing that does not allow static build up.
- Placing earthed metal combs or similar devices near to the source of the static.
- For some flammable liquids, a special chemical additive can be obtained to allow static to conduct through the liquid and dissipate.
- The flooding of the free space above liquids and powders with an inert gas to reduce the possibility of ignition.

Occurrence of static

Static electricity has been frequently experienced in the following situations:

- The flow of liquids and powders through pipes, filters, tanks and other non-miscible liquids.
- The pouring of powders from insulating plastic bags.
- Spraying.
- The settling of solids through liquids or bubbles rising through liquids.
- The mixing and stirring of liquids and powders.
- The sieving or grinding of powders and dusts.
- The unwinding of rolled insulating foils.
- Human movement with insulated shoes over nylon or plastic carpets or floors; similarly between layers of clothing.
- The movement of dust or liquids through air.
- The pouring of liquids, granules or powders from insulated containers.

DANGERS

Danger occurs in particular when a static spark occurs in a flammable or explosive atmosphere. Given the right mix of flammable material and oxygen, the static spark can start fire or explosion.

PRECAUTIONS

The risk of static spark can be controlled by removing one side of the fire triangle - flammable material, oxygen or ignition source.

The flammable material (whether a liquid or fine dusty solid) might be replaced by a less risky material; although this is usually impossible in the industrial process. Control by enclosure in a closed vessel or pipeline is better than carriage in open vessels and pouring from a bucket. The oxygen source can be removed by blanketing with an inert gas such as nitrogen in vessels, hoppers and transfer lines. The ignition source can be removed by removing static as well as those other sources such as smoking, naked lights, non-flameproof electrical power equipment, mechanical sparks from tools or footwear, and heat from radiators or hot processes and tools.

8.5 - Planning design and installation of electrical systems

DUTY HOLDERS

The Electricity at Work Regulations (EWR) 1989 place duties upon the following:

- Employers and self employed persons.
- Managers of quarries.
- Employees.

Employers and self employed persons

The duty imposed is to comply with the Regulations as far as they are within his/her control.

Managers of quarries

The duty here again is to comply with the Regulation as far as matters are within the Manager's control. They are defined further by saying that it is only so far as the regulations apply to the Quarry or part of the Quarry of which he/she is the Manager.

Employees

The duty imposed is a duplication of Section 7(b) of the Health and Safety at Work etc. Act (HASAWA) 1974 - Duty to Co-operate with the Employer to fulfil the employee's duties. The Regulations also place a duty for the employee to comply with the Regulations as far as they are within their control at all levels. These duties are designed to make everyone in an organisation take ownership for safety at levels and for each person to comply with all aspects of the Regulations.

CONSTRUCTION

Construction - this has a wide interpretation. It covers the physical condition and arrangement of the components of a system during its life. It includes the following stages:

- Design.
- Planning.
- Manufacture.
- Installation.
- Testing.
- Inspecting.
- Maintaining.
- Decommissioning.

Figure C8-15: Construction site generator.   *Source: ACT.*

Figure C8-16: Construction site power supply.   *Source: ACT.*

Figure C8-17: 110v generator.   *Source: ACT.*

Figure C8-18: 110v extension lead.   *Source: ACT.*

The Guidance to the EWR 1989 specifies that when assessing the suitability of electrical systems the following should be considered:

■ The manufacturer's assigned or other certified rating of the equipment.
■ The likely load and fault conditions.
■ The need for suitable electrical protective devices.
■ The fault level at the point of supply and the ability of the equipment and the protective devices to handle likely fault conditions.
■ Any contribution to the fault level from the connected loads such as from motors.
■ The environmental conditions which will have a bearing on the mechanical strength and protection required of the equipment.
■ The user's requirements of the installation.
■ The manner in which commissioning, testing and subsequent maintenance or other work may need to be carried out.

Strength and capability of electrical equipment

"No electrical equipment shall be put into use where its strength and capability may be exceeded in such a way as may give rise to danger".

Figure C8-19 Electrical equipment danger.   *Source: Regulation 5 - The Electricity at Work Regulations 1989.*

This duty requires an assessment to be made prior to connecting equipment to a system. This involves looking at the design specification and the operating limitations of the piece of equipment and considering the system it is to be used in conjunction with. In particular, attention should be paid not only to the normal operating limits of the system and equipment but also the potential consequences during fault conditions.

The 'strength and capability' refers to the ability to withstand the thermal, electro-magnetic, electro-chemical or other effects of an electrical current that the equipment will be exposed to when connected to a system.

Insulation, protection and placing of conductors

Insulation and protection

All solids contain free electrons. Substances which contain many are good conductors of electricity. Those solids that do not have many free electrons are bad conductors and are called insulators. Examples of insulators are rubber, plastic, glass. The EWR 1989 specify in Regulation 7:

"All conductors in a system which may give rise to danger shall be suitably covered with insulating material and as necessary protected to prevent, so far as is reasonably practicable, danger".

Figure C8-20 Prevention of danger.   *Source: Regulation 7 - The Electricity at Work Regulations 1989.*

Insulation specifications can be found (up to 1000 V ac) in the IEE 16th Edition regulations.

The level of insulation required will depend upon the conditions of use, environmental factors and also the voltage present. This could either be between the conductor and any other conductor near by or between the conductor and earth.

Regulation 7 also places a duty to assess whether or not, once insulation has been applied to a conductor, any mechanical protection is also required to prevent danger. An example of this is an armoured cable sheath.

Placing of conductors

Obviously due to the danger presented by a conductor the process of planning where they should be positioned is an important part of the design and planning stages of a system. Wherever possible conductors should be placed out of reach. The consideration that people move about should be given and not just normal operating procedures but also emergency or non-routine operations. An example of this would be putting supplies to a factory overhead, but failing to consider the operations of a window cleaner moving a ladder.

Reducing the risk of shock

Those designing, installing, maintaining or using electrical systems have the following means available to prevent persons or animals from contacting dangerous parts of electrical systems:

Protection from direct contact

Note - Direct contact is contact with a charged or energised conductor which is intended to be so charged or energised.

- Insulation, barriers, enclosures, obstacles, out-of-reach.
- Residual / differential current relay - Rccb/Rcd/Elcb.
- Separated extra low voltage, SELV.

Protection from indirect contact

Note - Indirect Shock is contact with a conducting part which is normally at a safe potential but has become dangerously live through a fault condition.

- Class I, earthed equipment.
- Earthed equipotential bonding and automatic disconnection of the supply, EEBAD.
- Class II, double insulated equipment.
- Non conducting location.
- Earth free local equipotential bonding.
- Electrical separation.

Protection from external influences

- Adverse conditions.
- Index of Protection - (IP codes) - finger and tool proof, dust proof, rain proof, watertight etc.
- Flora and fauna, vibration, impact, seismic, wind etc.
- Flameproof, intrinsically safe etc.

Reduced voltage and SELV

Pneumatic tools and reduced voltage tools, i.e. 110 volt centre-tapped, are readily available and should be considered. Where there is a high risk of electric shock, as with hand lamps, soldering irons, and portable tools in adverse conditions, the use of Separated Extra Low Voltage (maximum 50 volts a.c. /125 volts d.c. ripple free) is recommended.

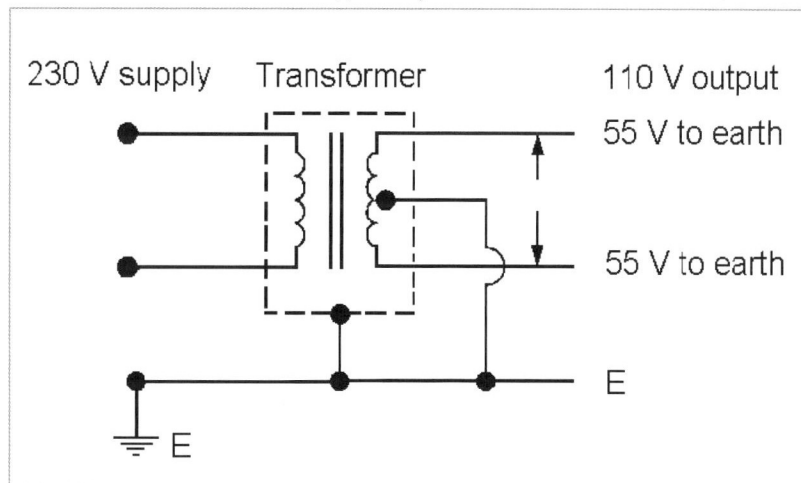

Figure C8-21: UK standard reduced voltage system.   *Source: G Self, Associate Tutor, ACT.*

Excess current protection

Excess current is also called over current. There are 2 types of over current. These are overload and fault current.

Overload

This occurs in a normally healthy electrical system when equipment has been mechanically overloaded beyond its safe operating load or an excessive number of electrical appliances have been added to the system creating excessive demands.

Two things normally happen. Due to the extra current demanded the temperature of the conductors rapidly rises and, if left undetected, this will lead to a breakdown in insulation resistance and eventually a fire.

Protection devices rely on the detection of the excess current and disconnection within designed boundaries. The current level for disconnection will always be greater than the normal operating current.

Fuses

These work on the thermal effect produced by the current and are designed to melt at predetermined temperatures which are proportional to a level of current flow. There are 2 types of fuse commonly used - cartridge fuses and HBC fuses (High Breaking Capacity).

Cartridge fuse

The body of the fuse can be either ceramic or glass with metal end caps to which the fuse element is connected. The fuse sometimes is filled with silica sand.

Advantage	Disadvantage
■ Small physical size.	■ More expensive to replace over time.
■ No mechanical moving parts.	■ Can be replaced with the wrong rated fuse.
■ Accurate current rating.	■ Not suitable for high fault current.
■ Little deterioration over time.	■ Can be shorted out.

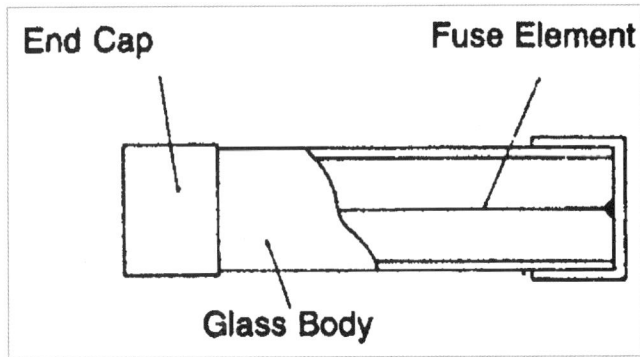

Figure C8-22: Cartridge fuse.   *Source: Ambiguous.*

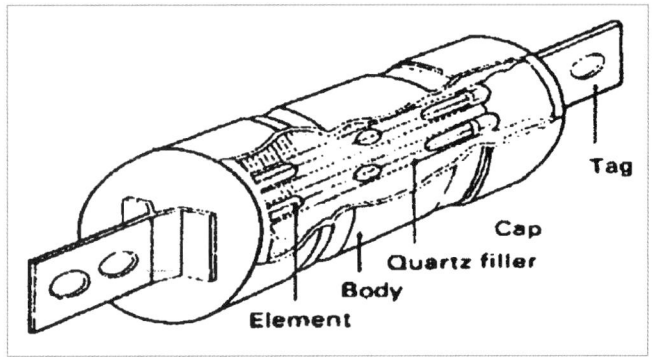

Figure C8-23: HBC fuse.   *Source: Ambiguous.*

HBC fuse

The barrel of the fuse is made from high grade ceramic to withstand the mechanical forces of heavy current interruption. The plated end caps give good levels of electrical contact. The element is machined from silver and gives precise characteristics. Some HBC Fuses are fitted with indicator bands which show when they have blown.

Advantage	Disadvantage
■ Discriminates between overload currents of short time duration and high fault currents.	■ Very expensive.
■ Simple to observe when blown.	■
■ Consistent in operation.	■
■ Reliable.	■

Circuit Breakers

These work on either thermal or magnetic field principle and have a wide range of applications and designs.

Advantage	Disadvantage
■ Tripping characteristic set during manufactured; cannot be altered.	■ Have mechanically moving parts.
■ Will trip for a sustained overload but not for transient overloads.	■ Expensive.
■ Faulty circuit is easy identified.	■ Need for regular testing to ensure satisfactory operation.
■ Supply quickly restored.	■ Characteristics affected by ambient temperature.
■ Tamper proof.	
■ Multiple units available.	

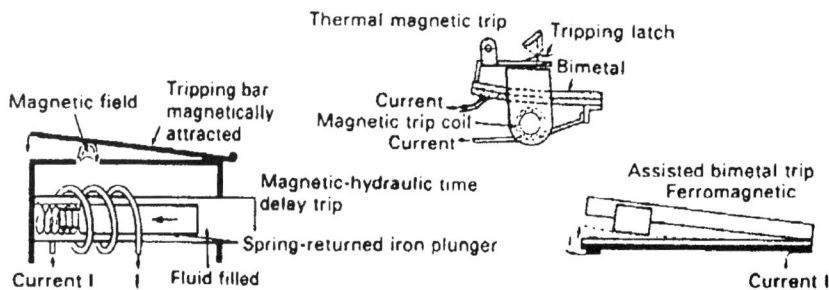

Figure C8-24: Circuit breaker.   *Source: Ambiguous.*

Fault Current

This occurs when an excess of current flows between conductors or from one or more conductors to earth due to a fault condition. The consequences may generate sufficient heat to cause fire and in this case the overload protection will normally take effect.

Under certain conditions only a small fault current will be generated but this may be sufficient to apply a live potential to the exposed casing or metalwork.

Cutting off supply and isolation

Regulation 12 of the EWR 1989 places a duty to ensure that to prevent danger, where necessary, there must be a suitable means for switching off the electrical supply to a piece of equipment.

Regulation 12 also deals with the term 'isolation'.

Isolation means 'the disconnection and separation of the electrical equipment from every source of energy in such a way that this disconnection and separation is secure'.

Figure C8-25 Isolation.

Source: Regulation 12 - The Electricity at Work Regulations 1989.

Isolation is different to switching off and this must be remembered, although there are circumstances when both will occur by the same action.

Switches

A switch is a mechanism which is able to mechanically disconnect the electrical supply from a part of an installation or an appliance. There are 2 types of switch:

Functional Switch - this is the device that the operator of a piece of equipment uses to turn the machine on or off e.g. light switch.

Emergency Switch - this is used on some equipment where a hazardous condition may occur e.g. an emergency stop on a lathe.

Note: A piece of equipment can be switched off but still be *Live*.

Figure C8-26: Power supply isolation.   *Source: ACT.*

Working space, access and lighting

Regulation 15 of the EWR 1989 states:

"For the purposes of enabling injury to be prevented, adequate working space, adequate means of access, and adequate lighting shall be provided at all electrical equipment on which or near which work is being done in circumstances which may give rise to danger".

Figure C8-27 Circumstances which may give rise to danger.

Source: Regulation 15 - The Electricity at Work Regulations 1989.

This duty does not only apply when live conductors are exposed but also when any work is conducted that may give rise to danger.

The Regulations do not specifically mention dimensions, but earlier legislation in the form of the Electricity (Factories Act) Special Regulations 1908 and 1944, which were revoked by the 1989 Regulations, did and these dimensions are still used as a guideline for voltages up to 3 kV.

The dimensions are detailed in Appendix 3 of the Guidance for the Electricity at Work Regulations 1989.

CONTROL MEASURES

Selection and suitability of equipment

The British Standard BS 7671, the Institution of Electrical Engineers (IEE) 16th edition requirements, Chapter 13 - 'Fundamental requirements for safety' - specifies the needs. Good workmanship and proper materials shall be used. Construction, installation, inspection, testing and maintenance shall be such as to prevent danger. Equipment shall be suitable for the power demanded and the conditions in which it is installed. Additions and alterations to installations shall comply with regulations. Equipment, which requires operation or attention, shall be accessible.

Concerning the supplier of equipment, the Low Voltage (Safety) Regulations 1989 refer to equipment using between 50 and 100 volts a.c. and requires it to be safe.

Construction, including flexible cables and cords, must be to EEC accepted good engineering practice standards. The Regulations are deemed satisfied if the equipment bears a recognised standard mark, certificate or other acceptable authorisation. Supply of unsafe equipment or components is prohibited.

Protective systems

Fuses

This is a device designed to automatically cut off the power supply to a circuit within a given time when the current flow in that circuit exceeds a given value. A fuse may be a re-wirable tinned copper wire in a suitable carrier or a wire or wires in an enclosed cartridge.

In effect it is a weak link in the circuit that melts when heat is created by too high a current passing through the thin wire in the fuse case. When this happens the circuit is broken and no more current flows. They tend to have rating in the order of Amperes rather than milliamperes which means it has *limited usefulness in protecting people from electric shock*. This may also act slowly if the current is just above the fuse rating. Using the wrong fuse causes many electrical problems.

The following formula should be used to calculate the correct rating for a fuse:

$$\text{Current (Amperes)} = \frac{\text{Power (Watts)}}{\text{Voltage (Volts)}}$$

For example, the correct fuse current rating for a 2-kilowatt kettle on a 240-volt supply would be:

$$\text{Fuse Current Rating (Amperes)} = \frac{2000}{240} = 8.33 \text{ A}$$

Fuses are available for appliances as 2, 5, 7, 10 and 13 Ampere ratings.

The nearest fuse just above this current level is 10 A.

Typical examples of power ratings are:

- Computer processor   350 Watts.
- Electric kettle   1850-2200 Watts.
- Dishwasher   1380 Watts.
- Refrigerator   90 Watts.

In summary a fuse is:

- A weak link in the circuit that melts slowly when heat is created by a fault condition. However, usually too slowly to protect people.
- Easy to replace with wrong rating.
- Needs tools to replace.
- Easy to override.

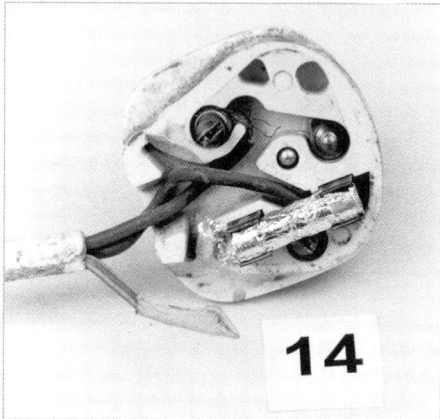

Figure C8-28: Plug-foil fuse, no earth. *Source: ACT.*

Figure C8-29: Earthing.   *Source: ACT.*

Reduced voltage systems

One of the best ways to reduce the risk from electricity is to reduce the voltage. This is achieved by the use of a transformer (step down) which will reduce the voltage. A common reduction is to 110 V. Normally, transformers that are used to reduce voltage are described as "centre tap to earth". In practice this means that any voltage involved in an electrical shock will be 55 V.

Using the earlier example of Ohms Law in practice, if the voltage is 240 V then:

$$I = \frac{V}{R} = \frac{240 \text{ Volts}}{\approx 2000 + 4000 \text{ Ohms}} = 0.04 \text{ Amperes or 40 mA}$$

However, if a centre tap to earth transformer is used, then,

$$I = \frac{V}{R} = \frac{55 \text{ Volts}}{\approx 2000 + 4000 \text{ Ohms}} = 0.009 \text{ Amperes or 9 mA}$$

The examples above clearly show how reducing the voltage ***reduces the effects of electric shock*** on the body.

An alternative to reduction in voltage is by means of a transformer to provide battery powered equipment that will commonly run on 12 V - 24 V. The common method is to use a rechargeable battery to power the equipment, which eliminates the need for a cable to feed power to the equipment and gives a greater flexibility of use for the user, e.g. drills.

Figure C8-30: 110V centre tapped earth transformer. *Source: ACT.*

Figure C8-31: Battery powered drill - 12V.   *Source: ACT.*

Figure C8-32: 110V powered drill.   *Source: ACT.*

Figure C8-33: 110V powered drill.   *Source: ACT.*

Isolation

Regulation 12 of the EWR 1989 places a duty to ensure that to prevent danger, where necessary, there must be a suitable means for switching off the electrical supply to a piece of equipment. Regulation 12 also deals with the term 'isolation'. This is defined as:

"The disconnection and separation of the electrical equipment from every source of energy in such a way that this disconnection and separation is secure".

Figure C8-34 Isolation.   *Source: Regulation 12 - The Electricity at Work Regulations 1989.*

Isolation Device

This is a device that will disconnect all supplies of electrical energy to an installation or piece of equipment. The internal design of the isolator must be such that contact separation from the electrical supply conductors is ensured. Security in the isolated position is necessary and this can be in the form of a lock off method or supervision by the user. The location of the isolator should be easily accessible and the time and effort required to use the isolator should be reasonable taking into account the circumstances in which the isolator may be used.

Residual current devices (RCDs)

RCDs are sometimes referred to as 'earth leakage circuit trips' and are an electro-mechanical switching device used to automatically isolate the supply when there is a difference between the current flowing into a device and the current flowing from the device. Such a difference might result from a fault causing current leakage, i.e. the current in the neutral (return) conductor is less than that in the phase conductor. Current leakage has possible fire risks or the risk of electric shock when a person touches a system as it provides a path to earth for the current. A typical circuit diagram for a RCD is shown below.

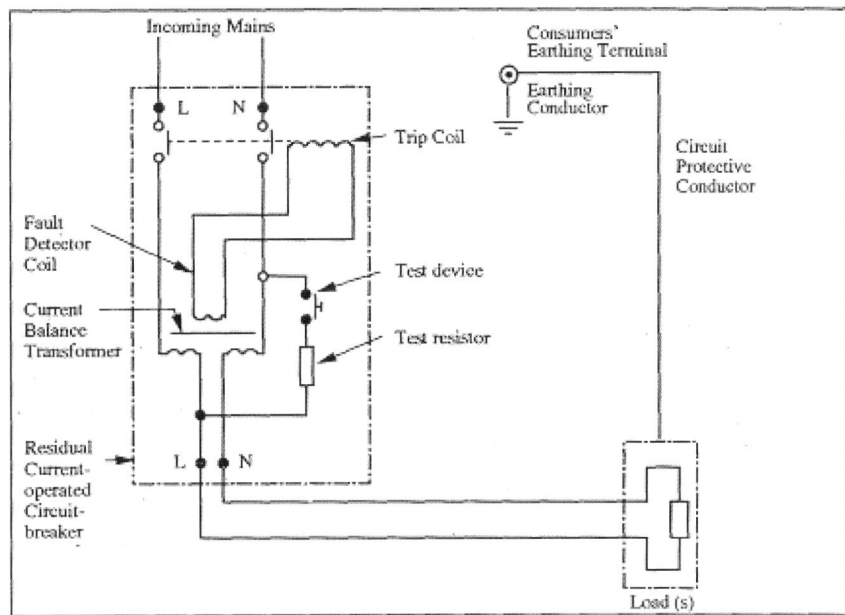

Figure C8-35: A typical circuit diagram for a RCD.   *Source: G Self, Associate Tutor, ACT.*

RCDs can be designed to operate at low currents and fast response times (a typical operating current being 30 mA, with tripping occurring within about 15-40 ms depending upon the magnitude of the current flow); and whilst an RCD will not prevent electric shock, because of its quick acting nature, any current flow through the body will hopefully be of sufficiently short duration to **reduce the effect of electric shock and prevent that shock from being fatal**.

A residual current device is:

- Rapid and sensitive.
- Difficult to defeat.
- Easy and safe to test and reset.

Figure C8-36: Residual current device.   *Source: ACT.*

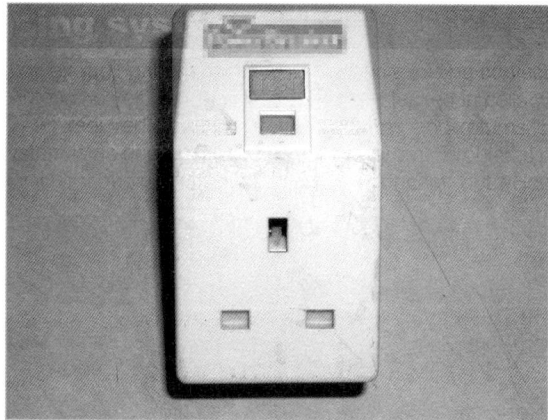

Figure C8-37: Plug-in residual current device.   *Source: ACT.*

Double insulation

This is a common protection device and consists of a second layer of insulated material being used for the casing of the equipment. Since the casing material is an insulator and does not conduct electricity, equipment having this type of protection does not normally have an earth wire. Each layer of insulation must be sufficient in its own right to give adequate protection against shock.

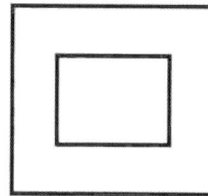

Figure C8-38: Double insulation symbol.   *Source: HSG107.*

Double insulated equipment has two layers of insulating material between the live parts of the equipment and the user. If a fault occurs with the live parts and a conductor touches the insulating material surrounding it no current can pass to the user, therefore **no shock occurs**.

Earth free zones

This is a protective measure that is used in areas where research and live testing is used. It is only to be used in an area with competent persons and effective supervision and where it has been designed and specified by suitably qualified engineers. If the area is insulated from earth, then even if live metal is touched there is no path for the electricity to flow to earth.

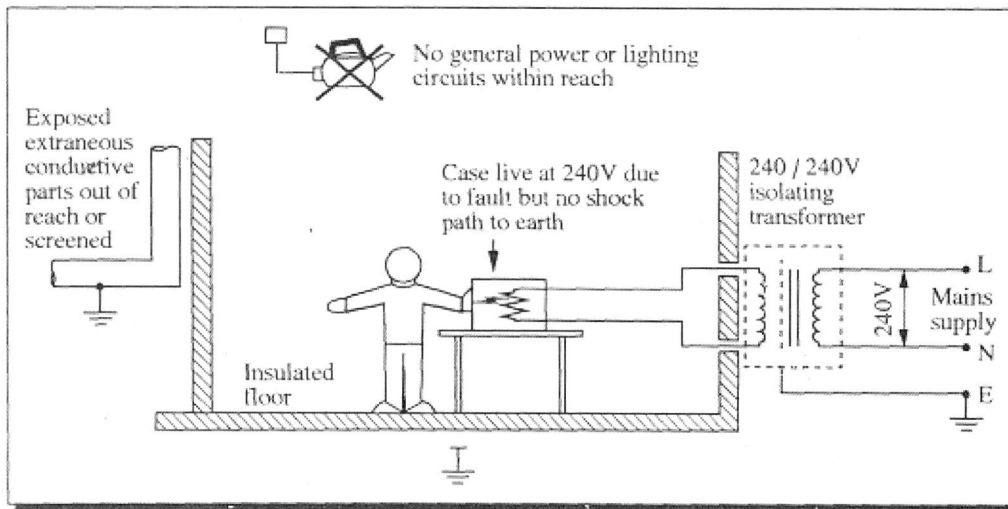

Figure C8-39: General arrangement for an earth free work environment.   *Source: G Self, Associate Tutor, ACT.*

Inspection and maintenance strategy

User checks

The user of electrical equipment should be encouraged, after basic training, to look critically at apparatus and the source of power. If any defects are found, the apparatus should be marked and not be used again before examination by a competent person. Obviously, there must be a procedure by which the user brings faults to the attention of a supervisor and/or a competent person who might rectify the fault. Checks by the user are the first line of defence but should never be the only line taken. Such inspections should be aimed at identifying the following:

- ✓ Damaged cable sheaths.
- ✓ Damaged plugs. Cracked casing or bent pins.
- ✓ Taped or other inadequate cable joints.
- ✓ Outer cable insulation not secured into plugs or equipment.
- ✓ Faulty or ineffective switches.

- ✓ Burn marks or discolouration.
- ✓ Damaged casing.
- ✓ Loose parts or screws.
- ✓ Wet or contaminated equipment.
- ✓ Loose or damaged sockets or switches.

Formal visual inspections

The maintenance system should always include formal visual inspection of all portable electrical equipment. User checks and a programme of formal visual inspections are found to pick up some 95% of faults. The frequency depends on the type of equipment and where it is used. The inspection can be done by a sensible member of staff, who has been shown what to look for and has basic electrical knowledge and common sense. They should know enough to avoid danger to themselves or others.

Visual inspections are likely to need to look for the same types of defects as user checks but should also include the following:

Opening plugs of portable equipment to check for:
- ✓ Use of correctly rated fuse.
- ✓ Effective cord grip.
- ✓ Secure and correct cable terminations.

Inspection of fixed installations for:
- ✓ Damaged or loose conduit, trunking or cabling.
- ✓ Missing broken or inadequately secured covers.
- ✓ Loose or faulty joints.
- ✓ Loose earth connections.
- ✓ Moisture, corrosion or contamination.
- ✓ Burn marks or discolouration.
- ✓ Open or inadequately secured panel doors.
- ✓ Ease of access to switches and isolators.
- ✓ Presence of temporary wiring.

Combined inspection and tests

Periodic Testing. Faults such as loss of earth or broken wires inside an installation or cable cannot be found by visual inspection, so some apparatus needs to have a combined inspection and test. This is particularly important for all earthed equipment and leads and plugs connected to hand held or hand operated equipment.

Testing procedures. The installation should be tested regularly in accordance with IEE Requirements. The word 'regularly' is not specified in terms of time intervals other than in certain special cases and a management judgment must again be made to specify an appropriate timetable.

Getting a maintenance programme started

In order to identify what systems will need maintenance, they should be listed. This same listing can be used as a checklist recording that the appropriate checks have been done. It may also include details of the type of the equipment, the checks and tests to be carried out. There is a growing trend, especially in offices, for employees to bring to work their own electrically powered equipment including calculators, radios, kettles and coffee makers. The number of electrical accidents has grown accordingly and fires from calculator chargers left on overnight are growing in number. All such equipment should be recorded and inspected by a competent person before use and at regular intervals, as if it were company property.

Records of maintenance and test

Although there is no requirement under the EWR Regulations to keep maintenance logs for portable and transportable electrical equipment, the 'Memorandum of Guidance on the EWR 1989, HSR25, HSE Books', does refer to the benefits of recording maintenance, including test results. A suitable log is useful as a management tool for monitoring and reviewing the effectiveness of the maintenance scheme and also to demonstrate that a scheme exists. It can also be used as an inventory of equipment and a check on the use of unauthorised equipment (e.g. domestic kettles or electric heaters brought to work by employees).

Source: HSG107 - Maintaining Portable and Transportable Electrical Equipment.

Frequency of inspection and testing

Question:"I have been told that I have to have my desk lamp tested every six months. Is this correct?"

Answer: "No. The law requires it to be maintained. It does not require any elaborate or rigorous system of frequent electrical testing".

Deciding on the frequency of inspection and testing is a matter of judgement by the duty-holder, and should be based on an assessment of risk. This can be undertaken as part of the assessment of risks under The Management of Health and Safety Regulations 1999 (MHSWR).

For further information, HSG107 - Maintaining Portable and Transportable Electrical Equipment, sets out a table showing the suggested frequency of formal visual inspections and electrical tests for portable and transportable electrical equipment. This table gives suggested starting intervals when implementing a maintenance programme. It is up to the duty-holder, with appropriate advice where necessary, to assess the conditions affecting equipment, which may lead to potential damage and/or deterioration and should determine the maintenance regime.

Source: HSG107 - Maintaining Portable and Transportable Electrical Equipment.

The legal duty for inspection and maintenance

The particular requirements relating to the use and maintenance of electrical equipment are contained in EWR 1989. These Regulations apply to all work activities involving electrical equipment. They place duties on employers, the self-employed and employees (the duty-holders), that are intended to control risks arising from the use of electricity. The Regulations are goal-setting, describing safety objectives to be achieved, without prescribing the measures to be taken. This allows the duty-holder to select precautions appropriate to the risk rather than having precautions imposed that may not be relevant to a particular work activity.

The EWR, Regulation 4(2) requires that:

Figure C8-40 Electrical systems maintained. *Source: The Electricity at Work Regulations 1989, Regulation 4(2).*

This requirement covers all items of electrical equipment including fixed, portable and transportable equipment. (Danger is defined as the risk of injury from electric shock, electric burn, fire of electrical origin, electric arcing or explosion initiated or caused by electricity).

Particular actions that can be taken in order to maintain portable and transportable equipment, and thereby prevent danger, are described in HSG107 Maintaining Portable and Transportable Electrical Equipment. *(See also - HSG107 - later in this Element)* For further guidance on the subject of maintenance, several British Standards (although dealing mainly with specialist areas) might also be consulted. Many manufacturers of equipment will also provide recommendations on maintenance and it would be foolish to ignore them.

In addition to the EWR, the *general duties covering the use and maintenance of work equipment* are contained in:

- *Section 2, HASAWA 1974:* " ... the provision and maintenance of plant ... so far as is reasonably practicable ... safe and without risks to health".

- *MHSWR 1999*, which require an employer to make: " ... a suitable and sufficient assessment of the risks to health and safety of employees ... for the purposes of identifying the measures he needs to take to comply with the requirements ... imposed upon him ... under other relevant law". Such a risk assessment should include risks arising from the use of electrical equipment.

- *PUWER 1998*, which require the employer (person in control) to select suitable work equipment (Regulation 5) and to: " ... ensure that work equipment is maintained in an efficient state, in efficient working order and in good repair".

Source: HSG107 - Maintaining Portable and Transportable Electrical Equipment.

What is maintenance?

Guidance from the HSE and in the IEE Code of Practice for In-Service Inspection and Testing of Electrical Equipment indicates that maintenance is a general term that in practice can include visual inspection, repair, testing and replacement. Maintenance will determine whether equipment is fully serviceable or needing repair. It further suggests that cost effective maintenance can be achieved by a combination of:

- Checks by the user.
- Visual inspections by a person appointed to do this.
- Combined inspection and tests by a competent person or by a contractor.

What needs maintenance?

The system. The Memorandum of Guidance on the EWR defines a system. In simple terms it will include any equipment which is, or may be, connected to a common source of electrical energy and includes the source and the equipment. Thus the distribution system in the plant and the apparatus connected to it are covered. The IEE requirements apply similarly to the permanent installation in the building. It must be recognised that there is little benefit in having perfect portable apparatus if it is plugged into a defective socket which may be without proper insulation, with a switch that does not work properly, with the polarity reversed or with a high resistance earth connection.

Deciding the frequency

Be aware of the manufacturer's recommendations. Any manufacturer's recommendations concerning use or limitations in use, periodic service, lubrication etc. must be noted and acted upon. User checks on more potentially dangerous types of equipment should be made whenever the equipment is used but the frequency of other types of maintenance is a matter for judgement based on the assessment of risk. Factors to be considered when assessing the risk include:

✓ Type of equipment.	✓ Age.	✓ Duration of use.
✓ Is it hand held?	✓ Working environment.	✓ Foreseeable use.
✓ Manufacturer's recommendations.	✓ Likelihood of mechanical damage.	✓ Who uses it.
✓ Its initial integrity and soundness	✓ Frequency of use.	✓ Modifications or repairs.
		✓ Past experience.

Competent persons

As defined in EWR 1989, Part II, General, Regulation 16, 'Persons to be Competent to Prevent Danger and Injury':

> "No person shall be engaged in any work activity where technical knowledge or experience is necessary to prevent danger or, where appropriate, injury, unless he possesses such knowledge or experience, or is under such degree of supervision as may be appropriate having regard to the nature of the work."

Figure: C8-41 Competent person.   *Source: Regulation 16 - The Electricity at Work Regulations 1989.*

Maintaining portable and transportable electrical equipment (HSG107)

Portable and transportable electrical equipment should only be used for its intended purpose, and in the environment it was designed and constructed for. Maintenance will not allow safe use of equipment in circumstances it is not intended for, e.g. using a table lamp as a hand lamp, or equipment that is not waterproof in a wet environment.

Maintenance can include visual inspection, testing, repair and replacement. Maintenance will determine whether equipment is fully serviceable or remedial action is necessary. Routine inspection and appropriate testing, where necessary, are normally part of any overall strategy for ensuring that work equipment is maintained in a safe condition.

Figure C8-42: PAT labels.   *Source: ACT.*

As outlined in an earlier section of this Element on 'Portable Appliance Inspection and Testing' there are 3 types of test:

- User check - carried out by the user prior to use.
- Formal visual check - carried out by a competent person.
- Combined inspection and testing - carried out by a competent person.

Management should follow up these procedures by monitoring the effectiveness of the system and taking action where faults are found, particularly when faults are frequent.

Source: HSG107 - Maintaining Portable and Transportable Electrical Equipment.

THE SIGNIFICANCE OF INSTITUTION OF ELECTRICAL ENGINEERS (IEE)

Who are they?

Founded in 1871, the IEE is the largest professional engineering society in Europe and has a worldwide membership of 120,000. These men and women, who have joined together to promote the advancement of electrical, electronic and manufacturing science and engineering, range from students to the most distinguished and highly qualified members of the profession. The IEE is a Registered Charity No. 211014.

What the IEE do

- Represents the profession of electrical, electronic, manufacturing and systems engineering and related sciences.
- Acts as the voice of the profession in matters of public concern and assists government to make the public aware of technological issues.
- Sets standards of qualifications for professional electrical, electronics, software, systems and manufacturing engineers.
- Accredits degree courses in subjects relevant to electrical, electronic, manufacturing and information engineering at universities and colleges around the world.
- Accredits professional development schemes for engineering graduates.
- Awards scholarships, grants and prizes.
- Issues regulations for the safe installation of electrical and electronic equipment and takes a leading part in the formulation of national and international standards.
- Provides an extensive range of lectures, meetings, conferences, seminars, residential vacation schools and publications.
- Sets standards for the professional conduct of its members.
- Assists government to make the public aware of technological issues.
- Offers guidance on best practice in professional development.
- Operates a career advisory service to give advice and assistance to members on various aspects of career development.
- Operates a learning resources service to provide details of potential professional development activities provided by both the IEE and other organisations.
- Operates a computer-assisted information service, 'Inspec', which has the world's largest computerised database in the English language in physics, electro-technology, computer science and control engineering.
- Provides business and technical information on electrical, electronic, IT and manufacturing subjects.

Source: www.iee.org.

REQUIREMENTS FOR ELECTRICAL INSTALLATIONS (BS7671)

The IEE prepares regulations for the safety of electrical installations for buildings. The IEE Wiring Regulations (BS7671) have become the standard for the UK and many other countries.

BS 7671:2001, 'Requirements for Electrical Installations in buildings'

From 31 March 2004 the current version of the Wiring Regulations is the 2004 revision of BS7671:2001 (incorporating Amds 1:2002 and 2:2004). This version takes account of the changes to cable core colours for fixed wiring, The Electricity Safety, Quality and Continuity Regulations 2002 (ESQCR), and updates to certain other areas. Contractors are recommended to acquire the new, amended Regulations to be able to show that they are up to date. The principal changes are:

New sections

Section 443 - Protection against overvoltages of atmospheric origin or due to switching.

Section 482 - Precautions where particular risks or dangers of fire exist.

Major revisions

Part 1 - Scope, object and fundamental principles has been updated to align with HD 384.1.

Part 4 - Changes to Chapter 43 on Protection against overcurrent. Changes to Chapter 46 on Isolation and switching.

Part 6 - Section 604, Construction site installations.

Section 607, Earthing requirements for the installation of equipment having high protective conductor currents. Section 611, Highway power supplies and street furniture. Section 601, Locations containing a bath or shower has been consolidated into the UK standard.

Regulations and tables on type 1, 2, and 3 MCBs have been replaced and extended with information on circuit breakers to BS EN 60898 and on RCBOs to BS EN 61009, including new disconnection / time graphs in Appendix 3.

Although the forms in Appendix 6 have remained unchanged (except for a few editorial changes), the Regulations implementing inspection and testing in Chapters 73 and 74 have significant changes. These include the introduction of continuous monitoring and maintenance of electrical installations. Schedules of inspections and schedules of test results have been added to Appendix 6 (similar to those in IEE Guidance Note 3, Inspection and Testing). The standards called up by BS 7671 have been updated. Amendment No 1 and Amendment No 2 to BS 7671:2001 have been issued.

8.6 - Adverse or hazardous environments

RESISTANCE TO HAZARDOUS ENVIRONMENTS

In order to protect equipment from damage by foreign bodies or liquid, and also to prevent persons from coming into contact with live or moving parts, such equipment is housed inside enclosures. The degree of protection offered by such an enclosure is the subject of: BS EN 60529 - commonly called the IP Index or Index of Protection. *The table for this is shown above*. It can be seen from the table that it specifies categories by a numbering system. The first digit represents the level of mechanical protection and the second digit the level of liquid protection.

First Numeral		Second Numeral	
(a) Protection of persons against contact with live or moving parts inside enclosure. (b) Protection of equipment against ingress of solid bodies.		Protection of equipment against ingress of water.	
No. / Symbol	**Degree of Protection**	**No. / Symbol**	**Degree of Protection**
0	(a) No protection. (b) No protection.	0	No protection.
1	(a) Protection against accidental or inadvertent contact by a large surface of the body, e.g. hand, but not against deliberate causes. (b) Protection against ingress of large solid objects less than 50mm in diameter.	1	Protection against drops of water. Drops of water falling on enclosure shall have no harmful effect.
2	(a) Protection against contact by standard finger. (b) Protection against ingress of medium sized bodies less than 12mm diameter and less than 80mm in length.	2	Drip Proof: Protection against drops of liquid. Drops of falling liquid shall have no harmful effect when the enclosure is tilted at any angle up to 15° from the vertical.
3	(a) Protection against contact by tools, wires or suchlike more than 2.5mm thick. (b) Protection against ingress of small solid bodies.	3	Rain Proof: Water falling as rain at any angle up to 60° from the vertical shall have no harmful effect.
4	(a) As 3 above but against contact by tools, wires or the like, more than 1.00mm thick. (b) Protection against ingress of small foreign bodies.	4	Splash Proof: Water splashed from any direction shall have no harmful effect.
5	(a) Complete protection against contact. (b) DUSTPROOF - Protection against harmful deposits of dust; dust may enter but not in amount sufficient to interfere with satisfactory operation.	5	Jet Proof: Water projected from a nozzle from any direction (under stated conditions) shall have no harmful effect.
6	(a) Complete protection against contact. (b) DUST TIGHT - Protection against ingress of dust.	6	Watertight Equipment: Protection against conditions on ships, decks, etc. Water from heavy seas or power jets shall not enter the enclosures under prescribed conditions.
IP CODE NOTES: The degree of protection is stated in form IPXX. Protection against contact or ingress of water respectively is specified by replacing first or second X digit number tabled, e.g. IP2X defines an enclosure giving protection against finger contact but without any specific protection against ingress of water or liquid.		7	Protection Against Immersion in Water: It shall not be possible for water to enter the enclosure under stated conditions of pressure and time.
		8	Protection Against Indefinite Immersion in Water Under Specified Pressure: It shall not be possible for water to enter the enclosure.

Figure C8-43: International protection ratings.   *Source: ACT.*

Note: use this table for general guidance only - refer to BS EN 60529 for full information on degrees of protection offered by enclosures.

Example - an enclosure with an IP value of IP56. This means that the 5 = Dust proof and the 6 = Watertight so the enclosure is protected from water and dust. The most commonly quoted IP codes are IP2X and IP4X. The X does not mean that no protection is given but that the level of protection is not specified. The IEE 16th Edition specifies the types of equipment, cables and enclosures etc. that may be required for certain environmental conditions.

Example - an enclosure housing equipment in an AD8 environment (under water) would have an IP code of IPX8.

SELECTION OF ELECTRICAL EQUIPMENT FOR USE IN FLAMMABLE ATMOSPHERES

Where flammable or explosive substances are present or likely to be present, special precaution must be taken, especially with electrical installations.

Management must first consider the practicability of elimination of or substitution for the flammable substance itself. Examples are with certain cleaning materials or paints and their solvents. In the latter, for example, a balance must be made between the costs of the delays in waiting for a less hazardous paint to harden and the costs of preventing the ignition of the solvents from a faster setting paint by use of flameproof or intrinsically safe equipment.

Where electrically powered tools might be used, consider their substitution by the use of hand or pneumatic tools. Although this will lessen the ignition risk from sparking or heat production as the source of ignition, there will still be risks to be considered from the potential of a spark or heat from cutting tools etc. Even studded or plated shoes will have to be eliminated in high risk areas.

The use of electrical equipment in areas with flammable atmospheres is a very specialist topic which must be entrusted to competent persons but the notes below are of guidance in the initial assessment of the problems and potential solutions that might be considered.

CLASSIFICATION OF HAZARDOUS AREAS - ZONING

It is the practice to classify areas according to the likelihood of the presence of and the concentration (mixture) of the flammable or explosive substance within the explosive limits where combustion can take place. Combustion is not supported below the lower explosive limit (LEL) as the fuel: air mix is too lean. Above the higher explosive limit the mix is too rich. The standard EN 60079-10:1996 (was British Standard 5345) covers area classification based on a risk assessment approach which is based on two variables - probability and duration:

- **Zone 0** - is an area in which a flammable atmosphere is known to be continuously present or present for long periods at a concentration within the upper and lower flammability or explosive limits, such as within a reactor, mixing vessel or storage tank.
- **Zone 1** - is an area in which a flammable atmosphere is likely to occur, at least during normal processing, handling or storage operations.
- **Zone 2** - is an area in which a flammable atmosphere is unlikely to occur except under abnormal conditions and then only for a period of short duration.

PRESSURISATION AND PURGING

Pressurised gasses and inert gasses are used to create a positive pressure in the equipment in comparison to the atmospheric pressure outside the equipment. By doing this it does not allow the flammable atmosphere to ingress. These types of systems are safe to use for all zones. Purging is where an atmosphere is purged with an inert gas to prevent the atmosphere becoming flammable.

INTRINSICALLY SAFE EQUIPMENT (EX I)

Firstly, the possibility of designing out the use of equipment in the work area which is likely to produce sparks or heat should be considered. Only if this is impracticable should resort be made to the use of flameproof or intrinsically safe equipment.

Intrinsically safe equipment is equipment which by design cannot produce a spark with sufficient energy to ignite the flammable substance present. The equipment is usually limited to instrumentation and low energy equipment. The limitation of energy also means that components do not become too hot. Powered respirators, test equipment and process instrumentation are commonly met examples, distinguished by their deep blue colour.

FLAMEPROOF EQUIPMENT (EX D)

This apparatus is designed and constructed to withstand an internal explosion thus preventing ignition source entering the Zone and by having such volume that any inward leakage of flammable substance is unlikely to result in a mixture above the lower flammability limit. Flameproof equipment is easily recognised by its heavy, substantial and costly construction. The suitability of the apparatus for use in a particular Zone is denoted by type and approval markings on the apparatus in accordance with BASEEFA

The flameproof quality of an area and its equipment are only as good as the cabling feeding the apparatus, its mechanical protection and the integrity of any plugs and sockets. Designers and installers must ensure that cables, glands and barriers where cables pass through walls etc., are to comparable standards.

TYPE 'N' EQUIPMENT

This equipment is designed for use in zone 2 conditions and is so constructed that, properly used, it will not ignite flammable atmospheres under normal conditions.

TYPE 'E' EQUIPMENT

This includes equipment such as transformers and squirrel cage motors. They do not produce sparks or hot surfaces and are suitable for zone 1 and 2 conditions.

Hot surface ignition and auto ignition temperature. Many substances will ignite if they come into contact with a hot surface; this phenomenon is known as auto ignition. Physical properties tables, available from suppliers, list auto ignition temperatures for many substances. It should be noted that hot surface temperature in the black heat range, up to 450 to 500 degrees centigrade will ignite many substances.

The basic concepts are detailed in BS 5345. It provides information on the selection, installation and maintenance of apparatus for use in potentially explosive atmospheres. The **apparatus group** is classified in accordance with how easily the burning gas will burn through a narrow gap and the minimum spark ignition energy. The **temperature class** is based on how hot the equipment gets in fault or worst case normal conditions.

The groups are outlined below:

Apparatus Group	Representative gas	Remarks
I	Methane.	Mining equipment only.
IIA	Propane.	Most flammable gases/vapours are Group IIA.
IIB	Ethylene.	Medium sensitive group.
IIC	Hydrogen.	Most sensitive group; consists of hydrogen, acetylene & carbondisulphide; very small sparks ignite and will burn through very small gaps.

Figure C8-44: Apparatus for use in potentially explosive atmospheres.   *Source: ACT.*

Temperature Classification	Temperature Limit
T1	below 450C.
T2	below 300C.
T3	below 200C.
T4	below 135C.
T5	below 100C.
T6	below 85C.

Figure C8-45: Temperature classification limits.   *Source: ACT.*

The temperature classification limit must be below the auto-ignition temperature of any flammable gas.

8.7 - Safe use, maintenance and repair of electrical systems

SAFE SYSTEMS OF WORK AND CRITERIA OF ACCEPTABILITY FOR LIVE WORKING

Regulation 14 Electricity at Work Regulations 1989 - work on or near live conductors

No person shall be engaged in any work activity on or so near any live conductor (other than one suitably covered with insulating material so as to prevent danger) that danger may arise unless:

a.   It is unreasonable in all the circumstances for it to be dead; and

b.   It is reasonable in all the circumstances for him to be at work on or near it while it is live; and

c.   Suitable precautions (including where necessary the provision of suitable protective equipment) are taken to prevent injury.

Figure: C8-46 Work on or near live conductors.   *Source: Regulation 14 - The Electricity at Work Regulations 1989.*

This duty means that if danger could be present, wherever possible the work should be carried out with the electrical system dead. However it also appreciates that there are times when there is work that must be done with the conductors live, e.g. taking voltage readings.

The guidance to the regulations recommends that equipment should be designed with the intent of manufacturing it so that work with the conductors live will not be necessary.

Factors that should be considered in deciding whether to work with the conductors live include:

■   When it is not practicable to carry out work with the conductors dead.
■   The creation of other hazards, by making the conductors dead such as to other users of the system, or for continuously operating process plants etc.
■   The need to comply with other statutory requirements.
■   The level of risk involved in working work with the conductors live and the effectiveness of the precautions available set against economic need to perform that work.

SAFE SYSTEMS OF WORK

Safe systems of work should be employed when carrying out work with the conductors live. The safe system of work should take into account all eventualities, and should be documented to ensure adequate management of the task involved.

Suitable precautions that are required to be taken include:

■   Only allowing authorised competent personnel to work on or near live conductors.
■   Provision of adequate information on the task to be performed.
■   The selection and use of suitable test equipment and tools to be used.
■   Competent supervision of the work either direct or indirect.
■   Maintenance of effective controls in any area where there is danger from live conductors.
■   Segregation of the workers carrying out the work with the conductors live and any other persons, vehicles or plant.
■   Ensuring adequate lighting and access is given.
■   Suitably qualified first aid trained personnel available during the work.

SAFE SYSTEMS OF WORK ON INSTALLATIONS MADE DEAD

Regulation 13 Electricity at Work Regulations 1989 - precautions for work on equipment made dead

Adequate precautions shall be taken to prevent electrical equipment, which has been made dead in order to prevent danger while work is carried out on or near that equipment, from becoming electrically charged during that work if danger may thereby arise.

Figure: C8-47 Work on electrical equipment made dead.   *Source: Regulation 13 - The Electricity at Work Regulations 1989.*

Regulation 13 EWR 1989 deals with working with the conductors dead. The main principle is that once the system is dead, then it must be proven to be dead at the point of work, and steps must be taken to prevent the system in question becoming live or charged until it is safe to do so.

'Lock Off' - once the isolator has been isolated there is a system called 'lock off' that can be employed to prevent it being made live again. This involves the personnel padlocking the isolator in the 'off' position. The padlock has a unique key which the worker keeps on him at all times. This prevents any unauthorised person inadvertently turning the electrical supplies back on.

The worker will also post warning signs to show other personnel that the electrical system is being worked on and that the isolations have been carried out and danger could be present if they are turned back on.

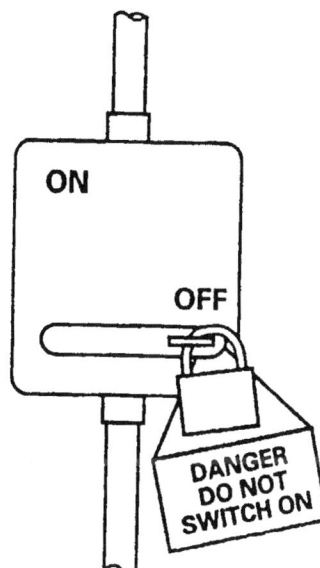

Figure C8-48: Lock off.   *Source: ACT.*

PERMITS TO WORK

These are an essential form of documentation and form part of the safe system of work employed to manage the risk of working with the conductors dead. The permit is really a form of declaration, by an authorised person in charge of the work, for the purpose of making known to other persons exactly what work is being carried out, where and when, and what safety precautions have been taken. It is the duty of the authorised person issuing the permit to work to ensure that the safety precautions have been taken, that they are adequate to prevent danger, and that the recipient is fully conversant with the task and the precautions to be taken.

'COMPETENT' PERSON

"No person shall be engaged in any work activity where technical knowledge or experience is necessary to prevent danger or, where appropriate, injury, unless he possesses such knowledge or experience, or is under such degree of supervision as may be appropriate having regard to the nature of the work."

Figure C8-49: Competent person.   *Source: Regulation 16 - The Electricity at Work Regulations 1989.*

The guidance to the Regulations informs us that the object of this regulation is to:

"Ensure that persons are not placed at risk due to a lack of skills on the part of themselves or others in dealing with electrical equipment."

In order to meet the requirements of this regulation a competent person may need:

- Adequate knowledge of electricity.
- Adequate experience of electrical work.
- Adequate understanding of the system to be worked on and practical experience of that class of system.
- Understanding of the hazards which may arise during the work and the precautions which need to be taken.
- Ability to recognise at all times whether it is safe for work to continue.

Figure: C8-50 Requirements for a competent person.   *Source: Memorandum of Guidance on The Electricity at Work Regulations 1989. HSR25.*

Advice and queries regarding qualifications and training can be directed to the IEE - Institution of Electrical Engineers, London.

8.8 - Safe working in the vicinity of high voltage systems

COMMON HIGH VOLTAGE SYSTEMS AND PREVENTION OF DANGER

High voltage systems refer to those which exceed 1000 volts. Although the EWR 1989 do not distinguish between various voltage limits, the degree of competence that a person would need to prevent danger and injury, as required by Regulation 16, would be considerably more than that needed for work at lower voltages.

The majority of industrial facilities will have a supply from the Electricity Authority coming into their facility and will have a transformer that reduces the voltage down to a useable voltage.

The normal method by which electricity is supplied to a facility is that the electricity is taken by the suppliers from the National Grid. This occurs at 400 kV to 275 kV. The supply voltage is then distributed at 132 kV and transformed down.

This reduction pattern is normally 132 kV down to 33 kV, 33 kV to 11 kV and then it will either be supplied to the facility directly at this voltage, where a substation will be positioned on site to reduce it to 415 V a.c., or it will be supplied at 415 V a.c. This is a three phase supply and a 230 V a.c. tap will be taken to supply those pieces of equipment that run at this voltage level.

Figure: C8-51 Electric supply line.   *Source: Regulation 16 of The Electricity Safety, Quality and Continuity Regulations 2002 (ESQCR).*

Exposure to high voltages normally occurs in three forms:

1. Overhead lines.
2. Underground lines.
3. Substations.

COMPETENT AND AUTHORISED PERSONS ROLE RELATED TO SYSTEM MODIFICATIONS

It must be ensured that any personnel working on high voltage systems must be competent. In assessing competence, the person's knowledge, training and experience in the particular class of work and type of system involved should be considered. The more complex the system, the higher the competence level required.

In the case of high voltage systems, most electricity supply companies organise special high voltage consumer's courses which provide legal, technical and practical guidance on distribution systems.

Safe systems of work

The risk of death or injury is significant in many high voltage, and particularly high energy systems. Safe systems of work should be employed when carrying out working with or near high voltage systems. The system should take into account all eventualities. The following general guidelines are suggested:

- Turn off the power before touching any part of a high voltage system, or even getting close to it. Secure isolation by use of a key switch or lockout device.
- High voltage capacitors may hold a charge long after power is turned off. Always discharge capacitors and keep them shorted in storage or when working on them. Even after being shorted, a capacitor can regain significant voltage when open circuited. Ideally, the system should be designed so that the capacitor shorting is failsafe.
- Make sure the metal cases of transformers, motors, control panels and other items are properly grounded (earthed).
- Keep a safe distance from energised or potentially energised components. Don't move conductive objects too close to energised components.
- Use adequate fusing of the power and/or circuit breakers to limit the maximum current.
- Spend some time laying out your circuits. Hot glue, electrical tape and exposed wiring are quick and easy, but could be lethal.

Permit to work procedures

A permit to work type system should be used to ensure adequate management of the task involved. This should form part of the safe system of work employed to manage the risk of working on or near high voltage systems. The permit states what work is being carried out, where and when, and what safety precautions have been taken. It is the duty of the authorised person issuing the permit to work to ensure that the safety precautions have been taken, that they are adequate to prevent danger, and that the recipient is fully conversant with the task and the precautions to be taken.

SAFE WORKING NEAR OVERHEAD POWER LINES

Every year people are seriously hurt by coming into contact with overhead power lines. A high proportion - about one third - prove to be fatal. These fatalities occur at voltages ranging from 400 kV to 230 V. Any lines found on a site should always be treated as live until they are proved to be otherwise.

Overhead power lines usually consist of bare (uninsulated) conductors. These are often referred to as cables. They are supported overhead in a number of ways, the most common being wooden posts or metal towers. A common problem with the type supported by wooden posts is that they are mistaken for telephone cables. As a general rule vehicles should not be brought closer than:

- 15m of overhead lines supported by steel towers.
- 9m of overhead lines supported by wooden poles.

One of the main risks is that of arcing or, as it is sometimes called, a flashover. This occurs when an object, or person, approaches the conductor, the electricity bridges the air gap between and current flows through the object or person. The risk of flashover increases significantly as the voltage applied to the conductor increases.

Regulation 19 of ESQCR places a duty for electricity suppliers to prevent access to overhead lines and to provide warning signs that are suitably positioned to 'give due warning of danger in all circumstances'.

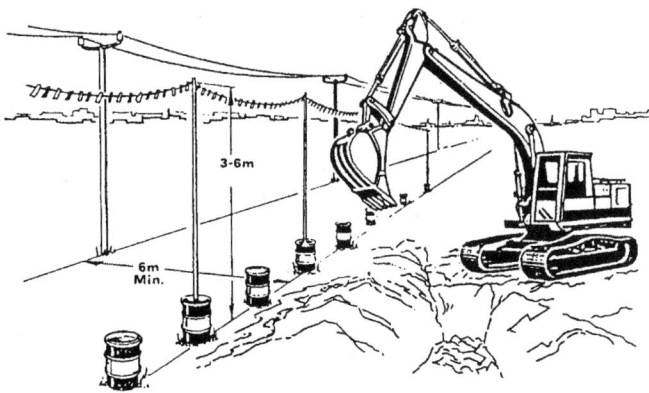

Figure C8-52: Working near power lines.   *Source: HSG144.*

Figure C8-53: Overhead power lines.   *Source: Lincsafe.*

Using the principles of prevention stated in the Management of Health and Safety at Work Regulations 1999, the following approach should be taken when working near overhead power lines:

Avoid where possible:

■   If this cannot be achieved then divert the lines clear of the work area.
■   If this cannot be done then have the lines made dead.
■   If this cannot be achieved then take suitable precautions to prevent danger.

Suitable precautions depend upon the nature of the work. There are three main categories:

1.   Work carried out near to lines.
2.   Work where items or vehicles will pass beneath the lines.
3.   Work carried out beneath the lines.

Work carried out near to lines

If work is carried out near the lines then barriers are to be used along with warning signs. The recommended minimum distance for the position of the barriers is 6m (horizontally) from the nearest line. It should always be remembered that some vehicles have a jib that extends long distances, therefore the measurement should be taken with the reach of the jib (maximum outreach) measured (horizontally) from the position of the ground barriers. For very high voltages these distances may be increased further.

Where cranes or vehicles with jibs are working, it may be necessary to place bunting to show drivers of these vehicles the position of the lines. The bunting should be placed at a height of 3 - 6m. Where it is used at a height of 6m the distance (horizontally) from the lines should be increased to a distance of 9m (horizontally) from the nearest line. The erection of bunting should be pre-planned so as to avoid coming into contact with the lines, and only competent personnel should carry out the work.

Ground barriers should be sturdy enough so that they are not moved easily and should be colour coded with red and white stripes. Types of barrier commonly used include:

■   40 gallon oil drums - filled with rubble or concrete.
■   Railway sleepers.
■   Earth bank raised to 1m height and marked by posts to prevent vehicle entry.
■   A tension wire fence with flags attached. This type of protection needs to be earthed in consultation with the electricity supplier.

Equipment and materials should never be allowed to be stored between the overhead power lines and the ground barriers.

Work where items or vehicles will pass beneath the lines

Work areas where plant will pass beneath the lines are required to have similar protection devices. The number of passing points should always be kept to a minimum. Each passing place should have a set of goal posts erected at both ends to serve as gateways between the barriers. Appropriate warning signs should be placed around these goal posts and the approaches to them, including the clearance height and notice to drivers to lower jibs.

The goal posts should be constructed of an insulating material and should be marked with red and white stripes to define them and make them visible. If work is to be carried out at night then suitable lighting levels should be achieved by site lighting to ensure good visibility.

Work carried out beneath the lines

The working height and overhead power line height should be defined and where possible ensuring materials used cannot come into contact with the line. Any mobile plant used that has a telescopic facility or raised parts should be physically limited so that it cannot strike the line.

UNDERGROUND CABLES - HAZARDS AND PRECAUTIONS

Underground lines

Part IV (regulations 12 to 15) of ESQCR specifies that any conductor that is placed below ground and is not earthed must be insulated from earth and so positioned that no damage can occur inadvertently from an excavation, tool or similar.

It is stated that, 'a conductor placed below ground used in a suppliers high voltage system but not connected with earth shall be laid in such manner as to ensure, so far as is reasonably practicable, that any person excavating the ground will receive a warning of its presence'

Suppliers of electricity must keep accurate drawings and plans of the position of where their cables are. This information is to be given to developers and construction personnel as necessary in order for them to ascertain the proximity of buried cables in relation to any excavating they may carry out.

When planning excavation work a survey needs to be carried out, not just for ground conditions and contamination levels, but also for the position of buried services. Technological advances over the last few years has made this job a lot easier than previously and various forms are available including ground radar and portable cable measuring devices.

Once identified, the locations of cables need to be marked out to warn workers of the hazard buried below ground. Colour identification can be used to distinguish between the wide range of buried services. Barriers can be used either side of where a buried cable lies to prevent digging or exploratory work being carried out.

Any services, regardless of identification or condition, should be treated as a live cable until proven otherwise. Hand methods of digging, spades and shovels rather than picks or forks, should be used to explore for the position of cables and within 0.5m of a known buried service.

SUBSTATIONS

Substations are premises where the transformation of electrical energy occurs. Some industrial complexes may have a substation on site, but employees may not have access to it; whereas other sites will have access as the ownership of the substation is theirs.

The electrical apparatus inside a substation usually includes the input and output cables, the transformer and housing, instrumentation and switchgear. This type of equipment can present high risk if operated incorrectly. With this in mind, the substation should have suitable security measures to ensure only authorised personnel are allowed to gain entry to the premises and safe systems of work employed to control the access and the work carried out within.

Live conductors should be screened or insulated to prevent danger and an adequate working area should be employed when designing the substation with regard to the nature of the work to be carried out there.

Part III (Regulation 11) of ESQCR deals with substations and places a duty on suppliers to prevent the ingress of water or gasses into any 'suppliers' works' including substations.

Substations are required to have a fence no less than 2.4m high to prevent access. Safety signs and a sign identifying the supplier, a telephone number and a contact address are to be prominently displayed. Additionally, all reasonable steps are to be taken to prevent fire.

Safety in construction and demolition

Overall aims

On completion of this Element, the student will have knowledge and understanding of:

- safe working practices associated with construction and demolition work, specifically working above, at and below ground level.
- safe use of equipment and materials.

Content

Specific intended learning outcomes

The intended learning outcome is that the student will be able to:

1.   identify common hazards and precautionary measures associated with construction and demolition work carried out on site

Relevant statutory provisions

Construction (Head Protection) Regulations (CHPR) 1989

Construction (Design and Management) Regulations (CDM) 1994

Construction (Health, Safety and Welfare) Regulations (CHSWR) 1996

Working at Height Regulations (WHR) 2004

Lifting Operations and Lifting Equipment Regulations (LOLER) 1998

Provision and Use of Work Equipment Regulations (PUWER) 1998

Control of Substances Hazardous to Health Regulations (COSHH) 2002

9.1 - General

TYPES AND CAUSES OF ACCIDENTS AND ILL-HEALTH IN CONSTRUCTION AND DEMOLITION WORK

In the year April 2001 to March 2002, 79 workers died and thousands were injured on construction sites. 68 were killed and 4,000 suffered serious injury by falling from height, which remains the most common cause of fatality. In response, the construction industry has set itself a target of reducing fatalities and major injuries by 40% next year and 66% by 2010. These statistics are made all the more tragic by the fact that every accident is preventable. The HSE reported that working at height still displayed the worst forms of bad practice and stated: 'It was not acceptable to work at height without first identifying the risks and putting into place measures to eliminate or control them'. It seems that lessons are not being learned.

In the same period, the HSE published a report entitled 'Causal Factors in Construction Accidents', assessing the causes of 100 accidents. Ten key themes to emerge from the report were:

1. Inadequate risk management was considered to be present in almost all of the accidents, and frequently risk assessments were either non-existent or superficial and unlikely to have prevented the accident.

2. Planners and designers give insufficient consideration to health & safety in designing a project despite their legal obligations to do so. Up to half of the accidents could have been avoided through a design change.

3. Price competition between contractors gives an advantage to companies that are less diligent with health and safety. Equally, whilst bonus payments act as a strong incentive to be productive, they also encourage contractors to ignore safety.

4. Essential documentation such as the Health & Safety Plan, Method Statements and Risk Assessments are being treated as a paper exercise only.

5. Lengthy sub-contractor chains mean that the workers carrying out the work are distanced from those with responsibility for management of the project. In fact in 70% of accidents assessed inadequate supervision was a factor.

6. The frequent revision of work schedules leads to difficulties with project management and undesirable time pressures. The long hours culture in the industry results in fatigue.

7. Training is seen as a solution to all problems, but the content of that training (if any) is often superficial.

8. The skill shortage in the industry has led to increasing reliance on inexperienced workers.

9. Forcing workers to use personal protective equipment in inappropriate circumstances actually contributes to accidents.

10. Many accidents occurred away from the work face, while workers were moving around the site. Accident investigations by employers and contractors are frequently superficial and of little value as a learning experience.

Source: www.andersonstrathern.co.uk.

DUTIES

Clients

- Prompt (as soon as practicable) appointment of competent Planning Supervisor and Principal Contractor.
- Ensure adequate provision of resources and time to achieve a safe working environment.
- Preparation of the pre-tender health and safety plan.
- Make reasonable site enquiries.
- Make relevant health and safety information available.
- Keep health and safety file available for inspection.

The Client may appoint an agent to undertake his duties under CDM provided that he is reasonably satisfied that the agent is competent and that the HSE are notified in writing of the appointment.

Designers

- Ensure that structures are designed to avoid risks to health and safety while they are being built and maintained.
- Ensure where it is not possible to avoid risks that they are minimised.
- Provide adequate information about materials used in the design that could affect the health and safety of persons carrying out construction work.

Planning supervisors

- Ensure that a pre-tender health and safety plan is prepared.
- Ensure that designers include among the design considerations adequate regard to health and safety.
- Ensure co-operation between different designers.
- Be in a position to give advice to clients and contractors.
- Ensure that a health and safety file is prepared.
- Ensure that a health and safety file is delivered to the client.

Principal contractors

- Take account of health and safety issues when preparing tenders.
- Develop the construction phase health and safety plan.
- Ensure co-operation between all contractors to ensure they comply with health and safety legislation.
- Take reasonable steps to ensure only authorised persons are allowed on site.
- Provide information to the Planning Supervisor for inclusion in the health and safety file.
- Enable employed persons to discuss health and safety issues.
- Arrange for co-ordinating the views of employed persons where this is important for health and safety.

Contractors

- Must co-operate with the Principal Contractor.
- Provide relevant information to the Principal Contractor on the health and safety risks created by their works and how they will be controlled.
- Comply with directions given by the Principal Contractor and any rules in the Health and Safety Plan.
- Provide the Principal Contractor with any Reporting of Injuries, Diseases and Dangerous Occurrences Regulations (RIDDOR) 1995 reports.

PLANNING AND CO-ORDINATION

Gathering as much health and safety information about the project and proposed site before work begins is important. Information available at tendering should be used so that allowance is made for time and resources to deal with problems. Particular attention should be paid to the presence of asbestos, overhead power lines, unusual ground conditions, public rights of way and any other activities going on near the site.

When Construction (Design and Management) Regulations (CDM) 1994 applies, much of this information will be found in the health and safety plan.

The method the CDM Regulations take are to:

1. Plan health and safety into construction at the design stage by improving management and co-ordination of health and safety issues.

2. Create two instruments for managing and co-ordinating health and safety:

    a. The Health and Safety Plan.

    - Pre tender stage.
    - Construction Phase.

    b. The Structure Health and Safety File.

3. Allocate adequate time and resources so that duties imposed by these and other health and safety legislation can be met.

4. Involve all participants in the achievement of safe working environments to minimise risks during construction work.

Where CDM does not apply, information gathering is still important. Health and safety issues should be considered when estimating costs and preparing the programme. If equipment is hired, the supplier has a duty to provide information.

Source: HSG150.

NOTIFICATION AND APPLICATION OF CDM

The regulations apply to projects where 5 or more people at any one time are carrying out construction work and where demolition or dismantling of a structure is taking place regardless of time or numbers. They also apply where a project is notifiable. Construction projects with a construction phase longer than 30 days or involving more than 500 person days of construction work are notifiable to the Health and Safety Executive (HSE). Notification must be in writing and can be made using the form F10 (rev).

HEALTH AND SAFETY PLAN

The Pre-tender Health and Safety Plan

The pre-tender stage health and safety plan is essentially a collection of information about the significant health and safety risks of the construction project which the principal contractor will have to manage during the construction phase. The information in the pre-tender stage health and safety plan will mainly come from:

- ***The client*** - who has to provide information relevant to health and safety to the planning supervisor. This could include existing drawings, surveys of the site or premises, information on the location of services, etc.
- ***Designers*** - who have to provide information about the risks which cannot be avoided and will have to be controlled by the principal contractor and other contractors. Typically this information may be provided on drawings, in written specifications or in outline method statements.

The pre-tender stage health and safety plan serves three main purposes:

- During its development the plan can provide a focus at which the health and safety considerations of design are brought together under the control of the planning supervisor.
- Secondly, the plan plays a vital role in the tender documentation. It enables prospective principal contractors to be fully aware of the project's health, safety and welfare requirements. This will allow prospective principal contractors to have a level playing field as far as health and safety is concerned on which to provide tender submissions.
- Thirdly, the plan provides a template against which different tender submissions can be measured. This helps the planning supervisor to advise the client on the provision of resources for health and safety and to assess the competence of prospective principal contractors.

The planning supervisor is responsible for ensuring that the pre-tender stage health and safety plan is prepared. This does not mean that the planning supervisor must produce the plan directly, but the planning supervisor must ensure that it is prepared.

Content of the pre-tender health and safety plan

The contents of the pre-tender stage health and safety plan will depend on the nature of the project itself. However, the following areas should be considered:

- Description of the project.
- Project description and programme details.
- Details of client, designers, planning supervisor and other consultants.
- Extent and location of existing records and plans.
- Client's considerations and management requirements.
- Structure and organization.

- Safety goals for the project and arrangements for monitoring and review.
- Permits and authorization requirements.
- Emergency procedures.
- Site rules and other restrictions on contractors, suppliers and others e.g. access arrangements to those parts of the site which continue to be used by the client.
- Activities on or adjacent to the site during the works.
- Arrangements for liaison between parties.
- Security arrangements.
- Environmental restrictions and existing on-site risks.
- Hazards

a. Safety hazards, including:

  - Boundaries and access, including temporary access.
  - Adjacent land uses.
  - Existing storage of hazardous materials.
  - Location of existing services - water, electricity, gas, etc.
  - Ground conditions.
  - Existing structures - stability, or fragile materials.

b. Health hazards, including:

  - Asbestos, including results of any surveys.

  - Existing storage of hazardous materials.

  - Contaminated land, including results of surveys.

  - Existing structures hazardous materials.

  - Health risks arising from client's activities.

  - Significant design and construction hazards

  - Design assumptions and control measures.

  - Arrangements for co-ordination of on-going design work and handling design changes.

  - Information on significant risks identified during design (health and safety risks).

  - Materials requiring particular precautions.

Format of the pre-tender stage health and safety plan

If the pre-tender stage health and safety plan is to be effective in helping to select a principal contractor, the planning supervisor and any other professional advisers who put together the tender documentation will need to determine what is the most suitable format for the plan. Clearly the way the pre-tender stage health and safety plan is included in the tender documentation and is structured is essential if responses on health and safety are to be made by prospective principal contractors. The pre-tender stage health and safety plan does not have to be a separate document. If the project is a large and complex one, a separate document which ensures that the key information is highlighted, makes sense. However, on small projects, some of the information outlined will already be in existing tender documentation. In this case, the key information can be highlighted in a covering letter or by use of an index pointing to which information should be considered. *Source http://www.hse.gov.uk/pubns/cis42.pdf.*

The Construction Phase Health and Safety Plan

The plan is developed by the principal contractor and is the foundation on which the health and safety management of the construction work is based. The contents of the construction phase health and safety plan will depend on the nature of the project itself. However, the health and safety plan can usefully open with:

- A description of the project.
- A general statement of health and safety principles and objectives for the project.
- Information about restrictions which may affect the work (e.g., neighbouring buildings, utility services, vehicular and pedestrian traffic flows and restrictions from the work activities of the client).
- The *management* structure and responsibilities of the various members of the project team, whether based at site or elsewhere.
- The health and safety *standards* to which the project will be carried out. These may be set in terms of statutory requirements or high standards that the client may require in particular circumstances.
- Means for *informing* contractors about risks to their health and safety arising from the environment in which the project is to be carried out and the construction work itself.
- All contractors, the self employed and designers to be appointed by the principal contractor are properly *selected* (i.e. they are competent and will make adequate provision for health and safety).
- Means for *communicating* and passing information between the project team (including the client and any client's representatives) the designers, the planning supervisor, the principal contractor, other contractors, workers on site and others whose health and safety may be affected.
- Arrangements for the identification and effective management of *activities with risks to health and safety*, by carrying out risk assessments, incorporating those prepared by other contractors, and also safety method statements which result. These activities may be specific to a particular trade or to site-wide issues.
- *Emergency* arrangements for dealing with and minimising the effects of injuries, fire and other dangerous occurrences.
- Arrangements for passing information to the principal contractor about accidents, ill health and dangerous occurrences that require to be notified to the health and safety executive (HSE) under the Reporting of Injuries Disease and Dangerous Occurrences Regulations (*RIDDOR*)
- Arrangements for the provision and maintenance of *welfare* facilities.

- Arrangements to ensure the principal contractor checking that people on site have been provided with health and safety *information and safety training*.
- Arrangements that have been made for *consulting* and co-ordinating the views of workers or their representatives.
- Arrangements for making *site rules* and for bringing them to the attention of those affected.
- Arrangements for passing on information to the planning supervisor for the preparation of the *health and safety file.*
- Arrangements should be set out for the *monitoring* systems to achieve compliance with legal requirements; and the health and safety rules developed by the principal contractor.

HEALTH AND SAFETY FILE

Preparing the health and safety file

The planning supervisor is responsible for ensuring the health and safety file is prepared. Putting together the health and safety file is a task which should ideally be a continual process throughout the project and not left until the construction work is completed. Early on in the construction project the planning supervisor may find it useful to discuss the health and safety file with the client. This will help determine what information the client requires and how the client wishes the information to be stored and recorded. When the client's requirements are known, procedures may need to be drawn up by the planning supervisor so that all those who will be contributing to the health and safety file (e.g. designers and contractors) are aware of:

- What information is to be collected.
- How the information is to be collected, presented and stored.

The planning supervisor may find it useful to detail in the pre-tender stage health and safety plan requirements on how and when the information for the health and safety file is to be prepared and passed on. The principal contractor may also find it useful to include similar procedures in the health and safety plan for the construction phase.

Throughout the project those who carry out design work (including contractors) will need to ensure so far as is reasonably practicable that information about any feature of the structure which will involve significant risks to health and safety during the structure's lifetime are passed to either the planning supervisor or to the principal contractor.

Providing this information on drawings will allow for amendments if any variations arise during construction. It will also allow health and safety information to be stored on one document, therefore reducing the paperwork. The principal contractor may need to obtain details of services, plant and equipment which are part of the structure from specialist suppliers and installers, e.g. mechanical and electrical contractors and pass this information on. Contractors have a specific duty in the CDM Regulations to pass information for the health and safety file to the principal contractor, who in turn has to pass it to the planning supervisor. This information could include 'as built' and 'as installed' drawings as well as operation and maintenance manuals.

At the end of the project the planning supervisor has to hand over the health and safety file to the client. In some cases it might not be possible for a fully developed file to be handed over on completion of the project. This may happen because the construction work was finished rapidly to meet a tight deadline and completion of the health and safety file was impossible. Clearly a common sense approach is needed so that the health and safety file is handed over as soon as practical after a completion certificate or similar document has been issued.

Contents of the health and safety file

The contents of the health and safety file will vary depending on the type of structure and the future health and safety risks that will have to be managed. Typical information which may be put in the health and safety file includes:

- 'Record' or 'as built' drawings and plans used and produced throughout the construction process.
- The design criteria; General details of the construction methods and materials used.
- Details of the equipment and maintenance facilities within the structure.
- Maintenance procedures and requirements for the structure.
- Manuals produced by specialist contractors and suppliers which outline operating and maintenance procedures and schedules for plant and equipment installed as part of the structure.
- Details of the location and nature of utilities and services, including emergency and fire-fighting systems.

Future use of the health and safety file

When the project is finished and the health and safety file has been handed over by the planning supervisor, the client should keep it available for those who need to use it. Usually this will include maintenance contractors, the planning supervisor and contractors preparing or carrying out future construction work.

Ideally, the health and safety file should be kept available for inspection on the premises to which it relates. It may be useful to store the health and safety file so that it is in two parts. One part will be more relevant for day to day use, e.g. operational and maintenance manuals. The other part will be for longer term use, e.g. drawings which will only be required when major alteration work is carried out. The health and safety file could be stored electronically or on microfiche. In whatever form it is stored, it should be easily accessible. For ease of reference it may be useful for the planning supervisor to produce a document which summarises the key elements of the health and safety file and acts as a quick guide to where the relevant information is stored. On a project which involves work on part of a structure for which there is no health and safety file, a file only has to be created in relation to the construction work carried out and not for the whole of the structure. Eventually, as further work is carried out on that structure, the health and safety file will be added to and amended. If the client sells all or part of the structure, the health and safety file, or the relevant parts of the health and safety file, should be passed to the new owner.   *Source: http://www.hse.gov.uk/pubns/cis44.pdf.*

RELEVANCE OF SITE LAYOUT

The following key considerations should be taken into account when determining the site layout:

- The provision of safe entry and exit points including adequate turning room and good visibility for operators.
- The provision and maintenance of good running surfaces including dealing with muddy areas.
- Segregation of pedestrians from vehicles. Separate site entry and exit points, barriered walkways and good visibility at crossing points can be used to achieve this.
- Consideration of a one way traffic system.

- Fitting revering alarms to vehicles.
- Use of signallers/banksmen in high risk situations.
- High visibility clothing.
- Control of plant and drivers to ensure that only authorised people who have been inducted on site rules are operating plant and machinery.
- The protection of vulnerable structures such as excavations and scaffolds.

ACCESS AND EGRESS

Access to a construction site must be planned to minimise any hazards identified during the initial assessment. When a suitable location for site access has been identified, this must be controlled at a point or points that are designated as authorised access point/s and the remainder of the construction site boundary must be secure against unauthorised access. Site safety information should be displayed at access points to inform all attendees of contact names, rules and emergency procedures. Barrier systems are normal on complex undertakings, accompanied by procedures for admittance and exit of people and plant. Special rules for site safety induction and issue of any site security identification are often used to maintain control.

Access to a construction site should be through a controlled point and requires adequate planning to take into account the surrounding area. Restrictions and hazards relating to safe access to a construction site may include the conditions of the highway from which access is being gained (size, speed, use). The traffic that will operate on the site needs to be considered (size, type, frequency, volume).

Figure C9-1: Site access. *Source: ACT.*

Figure C9-2: Means of access. *Source: ACT.*

PROTECTION OF THE PUBLIC

The boundaries of the demolition site need to be fenced off to exclude persons not involved with the work. These could be children, who are attracted to such sites, which, like construction sites are adventure playgrounds, persons sleeping rough and those who wish to salvage materials, as well as people who are just passing by. The very nature of a demolition site suggests both attraction and danger. Some form of fencing or boarding about 2.5m high would be ideal, with warning notices set up around it. Protective screens and fans should be set up around scaffolds to prevent debris falling on to passers-by.

Dust can be a nuisance and a risk to health of the public as well as of the workers. It may contain fungal and bacterial matter, which is pathogenic to humans. Dust can be damped down with water to keep it to a minimum. The closure of roads and pathways is a good precaution to keep people and vehicles away from the site, but this is not always possible.

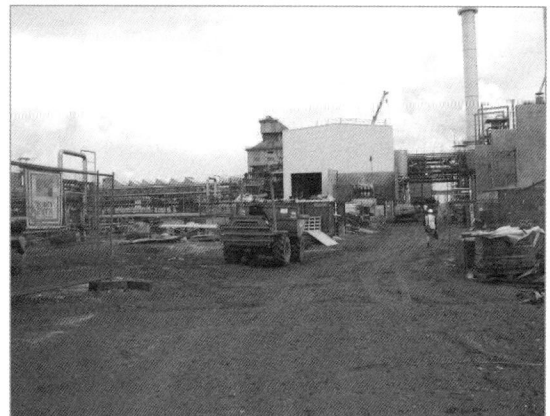

Figure C9-3: Site controls - access and roadways. *Source: ACT.*

Plant and appliances should be secured and never left with the keys in the ignition. Serious accidents have been caused by children trying to drive or operate site vehicles. Demolition sites are extremely dangerous places for experienced workers so it is essential that members of the public are kept away.

USE OF METHOD STATEMENTS AND PERMITS TO WORK

Health and safety method statements are an effective management tool for high risk work such as demolition. The method statement draws together the information concerning the hazards associated with the job and the controls that will be necessary. It takes into account the results of the assessments that have been carried out: general risk, Control of Substances Hazardous to Health Regulations (COSHH) 2002, manual handling, etc. This information will help in the planning of the job and highlight the resources that are needed for it. The method statement will also provide information for other contractors working on the site about any effects the work will have on them. With demolition, the statement will need to be revised regularly as the circumstances and conditions constantly change.

The method statement is also a useful and effective way of giving employees information about how a particular task should be carried out and what precautions are necessary. The inclusion of simple diagrams is useful as they can make it clear how a task should be carried out. It is necessary to monitor the method statements to check that what they say is being put into action.

Permits to work are used for particularly hazardous tasks such as hot work, work in confined spaces, using explosives, etc. They are a formal way of setting out what must be done to help minimise the risks involved. The competent person must sign to say everything necessary has been done according to the permit and allowing the work to go ahead. Boundaries may have to be set up to exclude personnel and warning notices posted. When the work is completed the permit must be signed off to say as much and that everything is safe to continue with the routine work.

9.2 - Working at heights

DANGERS ASSOCIATED WITH WORKING AT HEIGHTS

Fragile roofs, roof-lights and voids

Almost 20% of those killed in accidents on construction sites were doing roof work. Some fall off the edge of flat or sloping roofs but many are killed by falling through fragile materials. Asbestos cement, fibreglass and plastic deteriorate with age and become more fragile. Similarly, steel sheets may rust or may not be supported properly. This presents a serious risk to workers who work on these materials without means to prevent falls.

Before work is done on and to a roof, ensure that:

- There is safe access and egress.
- Crawling boards or roof ladders are used to spread the weight of people and materials.
- Roof openings / lights are clearly identified and protected by barriers.
- People do not attempt to walk on the purlins or the roof ridge.

Deteriorating materials

Asbestos cement, fibreglass and plastic deteriorate with age and become more fragile. Similarly, steel sheets may rust or may not be supported properly. This presents a serious risk to workers who work on these materials without means to prevent falls.

Weather

Adverse weather can have a significant effect on the safety of those working at a height. Rain, snow and ice increase the risk of slips and falling from a roof. When handling large objects, such as roof panels, then high wind can be a serious problem and may cause the person to be blown off the roof.

Extremely cold temperatures can increase the likelihood of brittle failure of materials and therefore increase the likelihood of failure of roof supports, scaffold components and plastic roof lights.

Figure C9-4: Working above ground level.   *Source: ACT.*

PROVISION OF SAFE ACCESS

Falls from height account for almost 25% of deaths at work each year. Most accidents involving falls could have been prevented if the right equipment had been provided and properly used.

Ladders are a frequent cause of accidents. They should not be used as a working platform - only for access. There are many systems available, ranging from tower and general scaffold, mobile and suspended access equipment (cherry pickers), mobile elevating work platforms (MEWPs), boatswain's chairs, rope and harness systems and ladders. If regular access is needed, modifications should be made to the plant structure to provide a safe working area. The choice of system will depend on the individual circumstances.

In order, these are the priorities when choosing the system to be used:

- Only when it is not practical to provide a work platform with guardrails, should other means of access (for example, boatswain's chairs or rope access) be used.
- Only where no other method is practicable, or when work platforms cannot comply with all the requirements for safe work (e.g. a guardrail has to be removed to land materials) should a way of arresting falls (for example, a harness and lines) be relied upon.
- A harness or nets may also be needed to protect people when putting guardrails or other protection in place.
- Ladders are a means of access, not a working platform; they should only be used as workplaces for a short time, and then only when it is safe to do so. It is generally safer to use a tower scaffold or mobile elevating work platform, even for short-term work.

Remember to allow adequate clearance when equipment is used, particularly near overhead power lines; and around nearby structures when mobile equipment is being used.

SAFE PLACE OF WORK WHEN WORKING AT HEIGHTS

Do not work at height unless it is absolutely unavoidable. If work must be performed at height, then provide a secure platform which will:

- Be securely footed on stable ground.
- Support the weight of the personnel and equipment to be used.
- Provide a stable access and will not overturn.
- Be secured to an existing structure, where necessary and wherever possible.
- Take account of the gradient of the ground, especially where mobile platforms are used.
- Provide guard rails to the platform.
- Provide barriers on open edges, holes and openings in the platform floor, the edges of roofs and working areas.

SAFE USE OF ACCESS EQUIPMENT

Ladders

Ladders are primarily a means of vertical access to a workplace. However, they are often used to carry out work and this frequently results in accidents. Many accidents involving ladders happen during work lasting 30 minutes or less. Ladders are often used for short jobs when it would be safer to use other equipment, e.g. mobile scaffold towers or MEWPs. Generally, ladders should be considered as access equipment and use of a ladder as a work platform should be discouraged. There are situations when working from a ladder would be inappropriate, for example:

- When two hands are needed or the work area is large.
- Where the equipment or materials used are large or awkward.
- Excessive height.

- Work of long duration.
- Where the ladder cannot be secured or made stable.
- Where the ladder cannot be protected from vehicles etc.
- Adverse weather conditions.

Figure C9-5: Ladder as access and workplace. *Source: ACT.*

Figure C9-6: Improper use.   *Source: ACT.*

Before using a ladder to work from, consider whether it is the right equipment for the job. Ladders are only suitable as a workplace for light work of short duration, and for a large majority of activities a scaffold, mobile tower or MEWP is likely to be more suitable and safer.

- Pre-use inspection. Make sure the ladder is in good condition. Check the rungs and stiles for warping, cracking or splintering, the condition of the feet, and for any other defects. Do not use defective or painted ladders.
- Position the ladder properly for safe access and out of the way of vehicles.
- Ladders must stand on a firm, level base, be positioned approximately at an angle of 75^0 (1 unit horizontally to 4 units vertically) and extend about 1 metre above the landing place. Do not rest ladders against fragile surfaces.
- Ladders must be properly tied near the top, even if only in use for a short time. If not tied, ladders must be secured near the bottom, footed or weighted. Footing is not considered effective on ladders longer than five metres. While being tied, a ladder must be footed.
- Keep both hands free to grip the ladder when climbing or descending, with only one person on the ladder at any time. Beware of wet, greasy or icy rungs and make sure soles of footwear are clean.

Figure C9-7: Poor storage.   *Source: Lincsafe.*

Figure C9-8: Stepladder.   *Source: ACT.*

Stepladders require careful use. They are subject to the same general health and safety rules as ladders.

However, in addition, they will not withstand any degree of side loading and overturn very easily. Over-reaching is to be avoided at all costs. The top step of a stepladder should not be used as a working platform unless it has been specifically designed for that purpose. Ladder stays must be 'locked out' properly before use.

Trestles

Trestles are pre-fabricated steel, aluminium or wood supports, of approximately 500 mm - 1 metre width, that may be of fixed height or may be height adjustable by means of sliding struts with varying fixing points (pin method) or various cross bars to suit the height required. They are used to span scaffold boards from one to the other in order to make a work platform. *These can only be used where work cannot be carried out from the ground but where a scaffold would be impracticable.* A good example would be a plasterer who is installing and plastering a new ceiling. Typical working heights when using a trestle system ranges from 300 mm to 1 metre but can be up to above 4 metres. Edge protection should be fitted wherever practical. As with any work carried out above ground level, a risk assessment (as required by the Management of Health and Safety at Work Regulations (MHSWR)1999) should be carried out and consideration given to the application of the Construction (Health and Safety) Regulations (CHSW) 1996 and/or the Workplace (Health, Safety and Welfare) Regulations (WHSWR) 1992.

Scaffolds

Independent

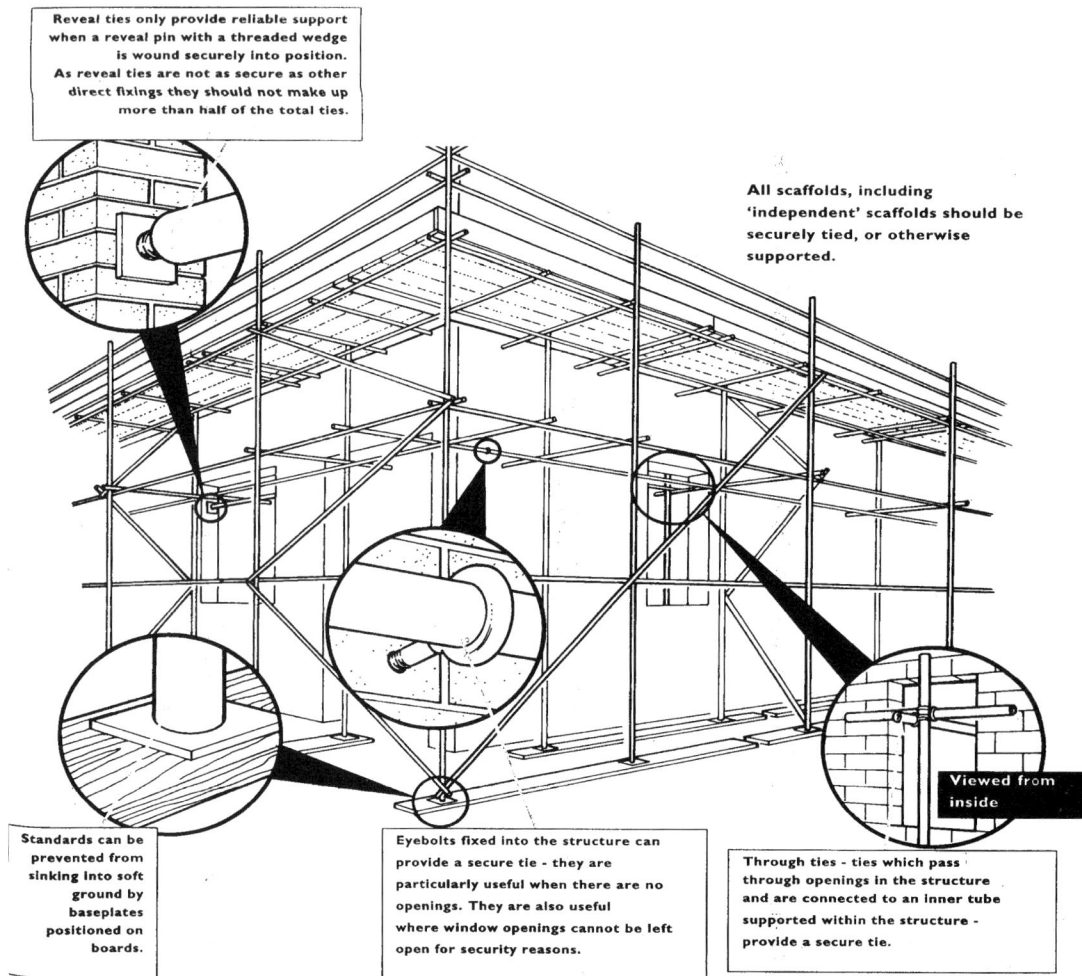

Reveal ties only provide reliable support when a reveal pin with a threaded wedge is wound securely into position. As reveal ties are not as secure as other direct fixings they should not make up more than half of the total ties.

All scaffolds, including 'independent' scaffolds should be securely tied, or otherwise supported.

Standards can be prevented from sinking into soft ground by baseplates positioned on boards.

Eyebolts fixed into the structure can provide a secure tie - they are particularly useful when there are no openings. They are also useful where window openings cannot be left open for security reasons.

Through ties - ties which pass through openings in the structure and are connected to an inner tube supported within the structure - provide a secure tie.

Viewed from inside

Figure C9-9: Scaffolds.   *Source: HSG150.*

The independent tied scaffold is classified into three main types:

- **Light duty** - only one platform is used at any one time. The distributed load and height are restricted to 73kg/m^2 and 61m respectively. This scaffold is used for stone cleaning or painting.
- **General purpose** - up to four platforms can be used. The distributed load to be carried by the scaffold depends on how far apart the standards are, i.e. the wider apart the less the load which can be supported. At 2.1m apart the maximum load should be 180kg/m^2 and at 2.5m apart is reduced to 145kg/m^2, with the maximum recommended height being 46m. This scaffold is for general work with loaded materials.
- **Heavy duty** - there are two heavy duty working platforms, maximum distributed load 290kg/m^2, and two other platforms for light duty and access, with a maximum distributed load of 180 kg/m^2. The maximum recommended height is 46m. This is used for heavy masonry work or when large building blocks are used.

As the independent tied scaffold depends on the integrity of the ground to carry its full weight including the load, it is vital that the weight is spread with the use of base plates and sole plates. They prevent the narrow ended standards being forced into the ground by the weight placed on them.

The independent tied scaffold has a double row of standards. The inner row should be set far enough out from the building to allow working clearance and to lay one width of scaffold board along its length. The outer standards should be set at a distance suitable for the number of boards used on the working platform. Platform widths can vary from three to seven boards:

- 3 boards - for footing, i.e. for persons to work without materials deposited or as a gangway.
- 4 boards - for footing and storing materials.
- 5 boards - for general work.
- 6 boards - for masons and their materials.
- 7 boards - for masons using trestles.
- All boards must be secured so they don't lift in high winds.

The working platform must be fitted with toeboards and guardrails. The toeboards are to help prevent materials falling off and injuring someone. They also help to prevent persons rolling off the platform or their feet slipping off the edge. Guardrails must be fitted around the working platform, inside the standards, at a height of between 0.9m and 1.14m.

The standards are set in the vertical position, or leaning very slightly towards the building, with the ledgers at right angles, running horizontally across the face of the scaffold. The transoms run horizontally from the front to the wall of the building. They are used for supports for the working platforms and to keep the rows of standards evenly spaced. Bracing is used to give stiffness to the structure and may be diagonal/transverse or longitudinal. The stabilising link to the structure is the ties. There are three methods that can be used: through ties, reveal ties and permanent ties.

A ***through tie*** is a tube bearing on the inside face of the wall that is used for tying in. At least 50% of the fixings should be through ties as these are the safest.

Reveal ties are where a tube is wedged between two opposite surfaces and a reveal pin is used to make jacking adjustments. Because reveal ties are not considered safe, special bolts may be used. They can have their shanks expanded into the face of the building and the scaffold can be secured to them.

Permanent ties are also used. These are set into the building during construction to allow future scaffolds to be set up.

Tower scaffolds

A mobile scaffold can become unstable very easily so certain factors are considered essential when it is in use:

- It must be set up for use on level ground;
- Access must be by the ladder fitted to the inside of the scaffold and not by climbing up the outside structure;
- The wheels must be turned outwards, which increases the base area, and locked into position;
- When the scaffold is to be moved, it must only be done by pushing or pulling at the base.
- The scaffold should never be moved when either workers or materials are on the platform.

The tall, relatively narrow structure of a mobile scaffold makes it inherently unstable unless the rules and guidelines are followed. Used correctly, they allow safe access to large areas.

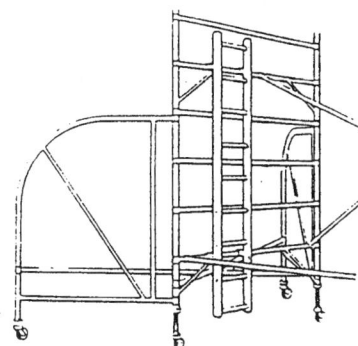

Clip-In Vertical Ladder for 'Span-Type' Tower.

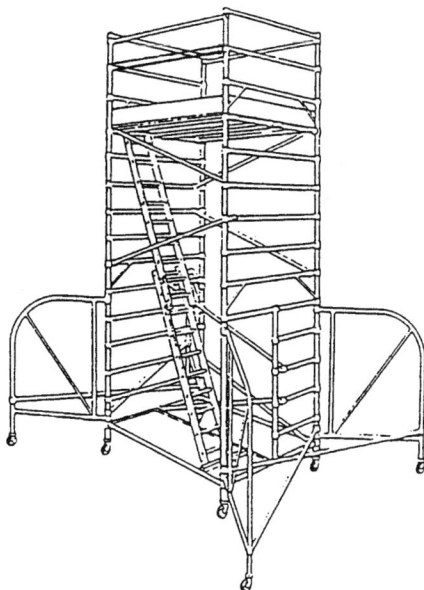

A proprietary mobile access tower with outriggers.

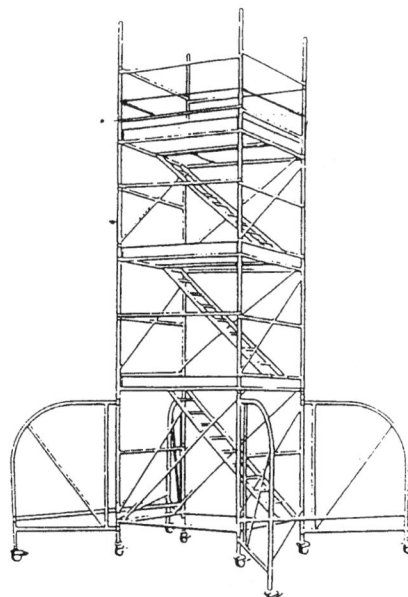

Internal Stairway.

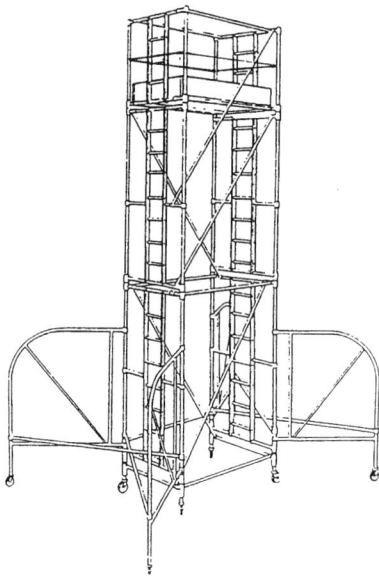

Ladder Section Integral with 'Span-Type' Frame Member.

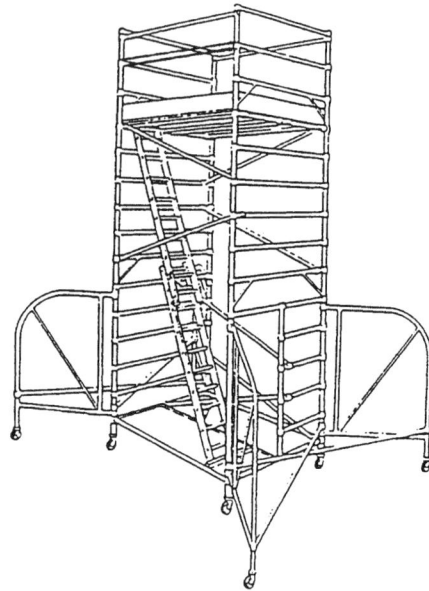

Inclined Ladder for 'Span-Type' Tower.

Figure C9-10: Tower scaffolds.

Source: Ambiguous.

PRECAUTIONS FOR SCAFFOLD HOIST TOWERS

The hoist should be protected by a substantial enclosure to prevent anyone from being struck by any moving part of the hoist or material falling down the hoist way. Gates must be provided at all access landings, including at ground level. The gates must be kept shut, except when the platform is at the landing. The controls should be arranged so that the hoist can be operated from one position only. All hoist operators must be trained and competent. The hoist's safe working load must be clearly marked. If the hoist is for materials only there should be a prominent warning notice on the platform or cage to stop people riding on it. The hoist should be inspected weekly, and thoroughly examined every 12 months (six months for hoists used for passengers) by a competent person and the results of inspection recorded. *See also – Hoists and lifts – in Element C7.*

REQUIREMENTS FOR STATUTORY INSPECTION OF SCAFFOLDS

Those in control of workplaces should ensure inspections are carried out by a competent person. All employers and people in control of construction work should make sure that places of work are safe before they allow their workers to use them for the first time or stop work if the inspection shows it is not safe to continue.

The competent person must:

- Complete the inspection report before the end of the working period.
- Provide the report or a copy to the person for whom the inspection was carried out within 24 hours.

Reports must be kept on site until the work is complete. Reports should then be kept for three months at an office of the person for whom the inspections were carried out.

A report is not needed following every inspection:

- A report is only needed for a tower scaffold if it stays in the same place for seven days or more.
- Where an inspection of a working platform or any personal suspension equipment is carried out:
  - Before being used for the first time.
  - After any substantial addition, dismantling or other alteration.

Only one report is needed for any 24-hour period.

Where an inspection of an excavation is carried out, only one written report is needed in any seven day period unless something happens to affect its strength or stability.

Your record must include the following information:

- Name and address of person on whose behalf the inspection was carried out.
- Location of the workplace inspected.
- Description of workplace or part of workplace inspected (including any plant and equipment and materials, if any).
- Date and time of inspection.
- Details of any matter identified that could lead to a risk to the health and safety of anyone.
- Details of any action taken as a result of any matter identified in the last point.
- Details of any more action considered necessary.
- The name and position of the person making the report.

General

1. The inspection report should be completed before the end of the relevant working period.
2. The person who prepares the report should, within 24 hours, provide either the report or a copy to the person on whose behalf the inspection was carried out.
3. The report should be kept on site until work is complete. It should then be retained for three months at an office of the person for whom the inspection was carried out.

Working platforms only

1. Any inspection is only required where a person is liable to fall more than two metres from a place of work.

2. Any employer or any other person who controls the activities of people using a scaffold shall ensure that it is stable and of sound construction and that the relevant safeguards are in place before their employees or people under their control first use the scaffold.

3. No report is required following the inspection of any mobile tower scaffold which remains in the same place for less than seven days.

4. A report is required where an inspection of a working platform or part thereof or any personal suspension equipment is carried out:

    i.   Before it is taken into use for the first time.
    ii. After any substantial addition, dismantling or other alteration.

Not more than one report is required for any 24 hour period.

Source: www.hse.gov.uk.

HAZARDS ASSOCIATED WITH FALLING MATERIALS

Try to avoid leaving materials on the roof when the site is closed especially at weekends and during holiday periods. If materials are left on the roof make sure that they are secured so that they cannot be blown off the roof by windy weather.

Make sure that toe boards are in place around the roof perimeter. Control other trades' access to areas underneath roofing work, unless protection such as debris netting is provided which ensures protection for anyone working underneath. In addition, methods provided should prevent materials or other objects rolling, or being kicked, off the edges of platforms. This may be done with solid barriers, brick guards, or similar at open edges. If working in a public place, nets, fans or covered walkways may be needed to give extra protection for people who may be passing below. High-visibility barrier netting is not suitable for use as a fall prevention device.

Materials such as old slates, tiles etc should not be thrown from the roof or scaffold - passers-by may be at risk of being injured. Enclosed debris chutes should be used or debris lowered in containers. Safe methods in roofwork.

ROOFWORK

Fragile roofs

On any fragile or angled roof (greater than 30^0) or on any roof which is considered hazardous because of its condition or because of the weather, suitable crawling boards must be used. They must be correctly positioned and secure. If it is obvious that the job requires a progression along the roof, extra crawling boards must be provided and no fewer than two such boards shall be taken on any job.

Flat roofs

Work on a flat roof is high risk. People can fall.

■   From the edge of a completed roof.
■   From the edge where work is being carried out.
■   Through openings or gaps.

Edge protection for flat roofs

Unless the roof parapet provides equivalent safety, temporary edge protection will be required during most work on flat roofs. Both the roof edge and any openings in it need to be protected. It will often be more appropriate to securely cover openings rather than put edge protection around them. Any protection should be:

■   In place from start to finish of the work.
■   Strong enough to withstand people and materials falling against it.

Where possible the edge protection should be supported at ground level, e.g. by scaffold standards, so that there is no obstruction on the roof. If the building is too high for this, the roof edge upstand can support the edge protection provided it is strong enough. Edge protection can also be supported by frames, counterweights or scaffolding on the roof. The protection should be in place at all times. Guarding systems are widely available that enable roof repair work to carry on without removing any guard rails.

Figure C9-11: Hazards associated with falling materials.

Source: ACT.

Where possible the edge protection should be supported at ground level, e.g. by scaffold standards, so that there is no obstruction on the roof. If the building is too high for this, the roof edge upstand can support the edge protection provided it is strong enough. Edge protection can also be supported by frames, counterweights or scaffolding on the roof. The protection should be in place at all times. Guarding systems are widely available that enable roof repair work to carry on without removing any guard rails.

Sloping roofs

On traditional pitched roofs most people fall:

- From eaves.
- By slipping down the roof and then over the eaves.
- Through the roof internally, e.g. during roof truss erection.
- From gable ends.

Edge protection for sloping roofs

Full edge protection at eaves level will normally be required for work on sloping roofs. The edge protection needs to be strong enough to withstand a person falling against it. The longer the slope and the steeper the pitch the stronger the edge protection needs to be. A properly designed and installed independent scaffold platform at eaves level will usually be enough. Less substantial scaffolding barriers (rather than platforms) may not be strong enough for work on larger or steeper roofs, especially slopes in excess of 30°. On some larger roofs, the consequences of sliding down the whole roof and hitting the eaves edge protection may be such that intermediate platforms at the work site are needed to prevent this happening. If the work requires access within 2 m of gable ends, edge protection will be needed there as well as at the eaves. Powered access platforms can provide good access as an alternative to fixed edge protection. They can be particularly useful in short-duration work *(see also - 'Short Duration Work On Sloping Roofs')* and during demolition when gaps are created in the roof.

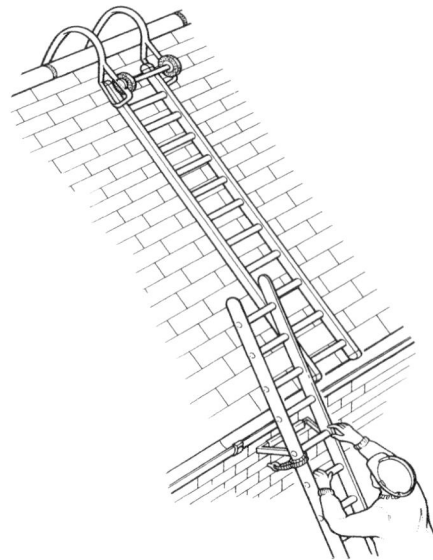

Source: www.hse.gov.uk.

Figure C9-12: Use of roof ladders.

Source: HSG150, HSE.

Short-duration work on flat roofs

Short-duration means a matter of minutes rather than hours. It includes such jobs as brief inspections or adjusting a television aerial. *Work on a flat roof is still dangerous even if it only lasts a short time. Appropriate safety measures are essential.*

It may not be reasonably practicable to provide edge protection during short-duration work. In such cases anyone working nearer than 2 m to any unguarded edge should be using a safety harness. Where safety harnesses are used they need to be:

- Appropriate for the user and in good condition - full harnesses are essential, safety belts are not sufficient.
- Securely attached to an anchorage point of sufficient strength.
- Fitted with as short a lanyard as possible that enables wearers to do their work.
- Actually used - tight management discipline is needed to ensure this.

Source: www.hse.gov.uk.

Demarcating safe areas

Full edge protection may not be necessary if limited work on a larger roof involves nobody going any closer than 2 m to an open edge. In such cases demarcated areas can be set up, outside of which nobody goes during the work or access to it. Demarcated areas should be:

- Limited to areas from which nobody can fall.
- Indicated by an obvious physical barrier (full edge protection is not necessary but a painted line or bunting is not sufficient).
- Subject to tight supervision to make sure that nobody strays outside them (demarcation areas are unacceptable if this standard is not achieved).

MEANS OF ACCESS FOR MAINTENANCE WORK

Cradles

Before use
- Equipment is installed, modified and dismantled only by competent specialists.
- There is a current report of thorough examination for the equipment.
- A handover certificate is provided by the installer. The certificate should cover how to deal with emergencies, operate, check and maintain the equipment, and state its safe working load.
- Areas of the site where people may be struck by the cradle or falling materials have been fenced off or similar. Debris fans or covered walkways may also be required.
- Systems are in place to prevent people within the building being struck by the cradle as it rises or descends and prevent the cradle coming into contact with open windows or similar obstructions which could cause it to tip.
- Supports are protected from damage (for example, by being struck by passing vehicles or by interference from vandals).
- The equipment should not be used in adverse weather. High winds will create instability. Establish a maximum safe wind speed for operation. Storms and snow falls can also damage platforms, so they should be inspected before use after severe weather.
- Only trained personnel are to operate.

At the end of each day
- All power has been switched off and, where appropriate, power cables have been secured and made dead.
- The equipment is secured where it will not be accessible to vandals or trespassers.
- Notices are attached to the equipment warning that it is out of service and must not be used.
- Check the shift report for warnings of malfunction.

Boatswains' chairs

Boatswain's chairs and seats can be used for light, short-term work. They should only be used where it is not practicable to provide a working platform.

Before use

- Installation and use of boatswain's chair to be supervised by trained, experienced and competent person.
- Chair and associated equipment carefully examined for defects.
- Confirm test / examination certificates are valid. Establish safe working load.
- Check that user is both trained and competent in the use of the chair.
- Warning notice displayed and notification of intention to carry out work given.
- Prohibit access to the area below the chair in case materials fall.

In use

- Free of material or articles which could interfere with user's hand-hold.
- The fall rope must be properly tied off in use and always under or around a cleat to act as a brake.

After use

- Chairs and rope should be left in a safe condition:
  - Top rope secured.
  - Chair and rope secured to prevent swing.
  - Raised when out of use or for overnight storage.
- Inspected for defects.
- Ropes (and chair, if timber) dried before storage.

Rope access

Often known as abseiling, this technique is usually used for inspection work rather than construction work. Like a boatswain's chair, it should only be used when a working platform cannot be provided. If rope access is necessary, then check that:

- A competent person has installed the equipment.
- The user is fully trained.
- There is more than one point securing the equipment.
- Tools and equipment are securely attached or the area below cordoned off.

The main rope and safety rope are attached to separate points.

Positioning systems

Terms such as 'safety belts' and 'lanyards', have been replaced with references to 'personal fall arrest', 'personal fall restraint' or 'positioning systems' or 'personal fall protection systems'.

MOBILE ELEVATING WORK PLATFORMS

Types and applications, hazards and precautions in use

Figure C9-13: Mobile elevated work platform "Cherry Picker". *Source: ACT.*

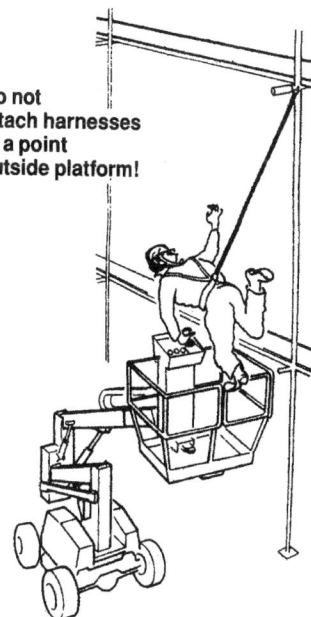

Do not attach harnesses to a point outside platform!

Figure C9-14: Use of harness with a MEWP. *Source: ACT.*

Mobile Elevating Work Platforms (MEWPs) can provide excellent safe access to high level work. When using a MEWP make sure:

- Whoever is operating it is fully trained and competent.
- The work platform is fitted with guard rails and toe boards.
- It is used on suitable firm and level ground. The ground may have to be prepared in advance.
- Its tyres are properly inflated.

- The work area is cordoned off to prevent access below the work platform.
- If being used on a public highway in poor lighting that it is well lit.
- Any outriggers are extended and chocked as necessary before raising the platform.
- Everyone knows what to do if the machine fails with the platform in the raised position.

DO NOT

- Operate MEWPs close to overhead cables or other dangerous machinery.
- Allow a knuckle, or elbow, of the arm to protrude into a traffic route when working near vehicles.
- Move the equipment with the platform in the raised position unless the equipment is especially designed to allow this to be done safely (check the manufacturer's instructions).

Figure C9-15: "Scissor lift".

Source: HSG130 - Health and Safety for Small Construction Sites.

Figure C9-16: Scissor lift.   *Source: ACT.*

Some MEWPs can be used on rough terrain. This usually means that they are safe to use on uneven or undulating ground. Always check their limitations in the manufacturer's handbook before taking them onto unprepared or sloping ground. Wearing a harness with a lanyard attached to the platform provides extra protection against falls especially when the platform is being raised or lowered.

SAFETY NETS

Safety nets are used in a variety of applications where other forms of protection are reasonably impracticable - such as steel erecting and roof work where site personnel are at risk of falling through fragile roofs onto solid surfaces or structures (steel work) below.

Safety nets will arrest the fall of an individual preventing an impact that may cause injury or death. Safety nets must be installed beneath the work area, as a minimum, and consideration should be given to an extension of the protection to allow for people working outside the planned area. Safety nets are only to be installed under supervision by competent installers and are to be inspected weekly and checked daily. It should be remembered that nets are also used to collect debris that may fall. This may be rigged to take a lesser weight than that for protection of people. It is important to identify which type of net is in use in a workplace as reliance on the wrong type may have fatal consequences.

Figure C9-17: Safety nets.   *Source: ACT.*

BELTS AND HARNESSES

There may be circumstances in which it is not practicable for guard rails etc to be provided, for example, where guard rails are taken down for short periods to land materials. In this situation if people approach an open edge from which they would be liable to fall two metres or more, a suitably attached harness and temporary horizontal lifeline could allow safe working. When using harnesses and temporary horizontal lifelines, remember:

- The harness and lanyards are made of man-made fibres and as such are prone to degradation by sunlight, chemicals etc. It is important to carry out tactile pre-use checks daily, in good light, before taking harnesses and lanyards into use. If there is the slightest doubt about a harness or the lanyard, do not use it. Faults can be noticed by discolouration, little tears, nicks and grittiness to touch.
- A harness will not prevent a fall - it can only minimise the injury if there is a fall. The person who falls may be injured by the impact load to the body when the line goes tight or when they strike against parts of the structure during the fall. An energy absorber fitted to the energy-absorbing lanyard can reduce the risk of injury from impact loads.
- Where possible the energy-absorbing lanyard should be attached above the wearer to reduce the fall distance. Extra free movement can be provided by running temporary horizontal lifelines or inertia reels. Any attachment point must be capable of withstanding the impact load in the event of a fall. Consider how to recover anyone who does fall.

- Anyone who needs to attach themselves should be able to do so from a safe position. They need to be able to attach themselves before they move into a position where they are relying on the protection provided by the harness.
- To ensure that there is an adequate fall height to allow the system to operate and arrest the fall.
- A twin lanyard may be necessary in some cases where the wearer needs to move about. A twin lanyard allows the wearer to clip on one lanyard in a different position before unclipping the other lanyard.
- Installation of equipment to which harnesses will be fixed, e.g. a suitable anchor, must be inspected regularly.
- Everyone who uses a harness must be instructed in how to check, wear and adjust it before use and how to connect themselves to the structure or safety line as appropriate.
- They should be thoroughly examined at intervals of no more than every six months.

AIR BAGS

Airbags are shock absorption devices that can be employed to protect against the effects of falls from a height. They are made of a toughened nylon or similar man-made material and are usually inflated using a powered fan device. They are designed so that should a person fall onto one, a volume of air is forced out of the bag creating a cushioning effect that does not bounce or deflect the person in another direction. This equipment must be matched to correspond to the fall height and as such must only be put into use by a competent person.

9.3 - Excavations

HAZARDS FROM EXCAVATION WORK AND EXCAVATIONS

Work in excavations and trenches, basements, underground tanks, sewers, manholes etc., can involve high risks and each year construction workers are killed with some buried alive or asphyxiated.

Contaminated ground

Digging may uncover buried materials that have the potential to be hazardous to health. The history of the site should be examined to try to identify if substances have been buried on the site during its previous use. Sites that once were used as steel works may contain arsenic and cyanide dating back many years; farmyards may have been used as graves for animals and to dispose of pesticides and organo-phosphates. There is always the presence of vermin to consider - this can increase the risk of diseases such as leptospirosis.

Toxic and asphyxiating atmospheres

Excavations can under different circumstances be subject to toxic, asphyxiating or explosive atmospheres. Chalk or limestone deposits when in contact with acidic groundwater can release carbon dioxide, and gases such as methane or hydrogen sulphide can seep into excavations from contaminated ground or damaged services in built-up areas. These atmospheres can accumulate at the bottom of an excavation and result in asphyxiation, poisoning, explosion or potential fatalities.

Figure C9-18: Buried services.   *Source: ACT.*

Figure C9-19: Excavation hazards.   *Source: ACT.*

Collapse

Often, the soil and earth that make up the sides of the excavation cannot be relied upon to support their own weight, leading to the possibility of collapse. The collapse may be sudden and unexpected providing many tonnes of earth to crush or constrict the movement of those working in the trench. Risk increases if:

- The soil structure is loose or made unstable by water logging.
- Heavy plant or materials are too close to the edge of the excavation.
- Machinery or vehicles cause vibration.
- There is inadequate support for the sides.
- Excavation below the level of the shoring provided.
- The depth, insufficient shoring and cross-bracing.

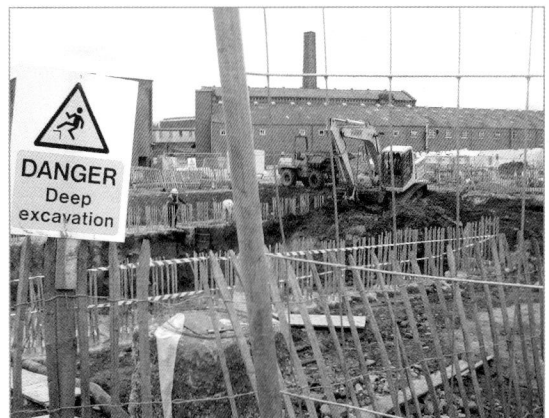

Figure C9-20: Excavation hazards.   *Source: ACT.*

Access

The absence of planned proper access into, out of, around and across excavations presents the combined hazards of slips, trips and falls. Workers may be tempted to improvise and use cut away sections of earth to get in and out, however these do not tend to last long (particularly after rain has fallen) and quickly decline in condition till they become a slide. Ladders, when provided may present a hazard due to becoming slippery or workers may fall from them after getting tired if they are too long and have insufficient resting places. An improvised crossing point, without proper edge protection represents a high risk of falling to the user. Ladders are the usual means of access and egress to excavations. They must be properly secured, in good condition and inspected regularly. The ladder should extend about one metre or three rungs above ground level to give a good handhold. To allow for emergency egress, the CHSW Regulations 1996 Approved Code of Practice (ACOP) recommends a minimum requirement of one ladder every 15 metres.

Falls

When people are working below ground in excavations, the problems are very similar to those faced when people are working at a height – falls and falling objects. Particular problems arise when:

- Materials, including spoil, are stored too close to the edge of the excavation.
- The excavation is close to another building and the foundations may be undermined.
- The edge of the excavation is not clear, especially if the excavation is in a public area.
- Absence of barriers or lighting.
- Poor positioning or the absence of access ladders allowing people to fall.
- Absence of organized crossing points.
- Badly constructed ramps for vehicle access which can cause the vehicle to topple.
- No stop blocks for back filling.
- Routing of vehicles too close to the excavation.

Where people or materials can fall a distance of more than two metres, edge protection must be provided. It is also sensible to cover shallow trenches when they are left unattended. Guardrails must meet the same standards as those provided for working platforms. Concrete or wooden blocks (usually old railway sleepers) are placed some distance from the edge to prevent vehicles from getting too close, particularly when the excavation is being 'back filled', where they provide a stop block.

Signs that comply with The Health and Safety (Signs and Signals) Regulations (SSSR) 1996 should be displayed to warn people of the excavation and any special measures to be taken. If working on a public highway, the police or the local authority must be consulted over the positioning of traffic lights. Appropriate lighting should be provided; it must provide sufficient illumination for those at work but should not create glare or other distractions for passers by, especially motorists. Battery operated headlamps (to avoid trailing cables) may be considered for individual use. If excavations are present in dark conditions they must be suitably lit to prevent vehicles or people colliding or falling into them.

Use of transport

Transport passing close to or over an excavation represents a hazard in a number of ways. In the first instance it creates an additional loading on the sides of the trench and may cause it to collapse. In addition, its close proximity to the edge of the excavation, perhaps for back filling (filling in the trench after use), could lead to the vehicle falling into the trench. Two further hazards exist in that transport may collide with equipment in use around the trench or its barriers, particularly when it is badly identified. Transport represents a source of carbon monoxide which, if traffic is heavy or vehicles wait near the trench, may present an asphyxiant hazard to workers in the trench. To prevent objects falling into excavations, the following precautions should be taken:

- Spoil and building materials must not be stacked near to the edge.
- The weight of stacks should not be enough to cause the sides to collapse.
- Designated operating areas for vehicles and machinery must be routed away from the excavation.
- Where vehicles have to approach, stop blocks must be provided to prevent overrunning.

Flooding

Unless a major watercourse is breached, leading to a massive ingress of water, drowning is not likely to be an issue. However, heavy rainfall, breaking into drains and digging below the natural water table can all lead to flooding. In deep excavations, where access is not readily available, the combined effect of water and mud could lead to difficulty in escape and risk of drowning. In addition, this can lead to the sides of the trench becoming soft and the integrity of the supports can be undermined.

Ingress of water may occur through rainfall, flood (river, sea) or when an excavation continues below the natural groundwater level. Consideration must be given to the likelihood of water entering the excavation and the measures to be implemented in order to control water levels within the excavation entering the excavation and water levels between it. Usually water is abstracted from excavations and pumped to sumps for settlement from where it can be pumped out for disposal. When an excavation is liable to water ingress the stability of walls can be undermined; this will influence the choice of shoring, for example, close boarded (Fig. c9-24) shoring rather than open (Fig. c9 -25) sheeting.

It is permissible to distribute pumped groundwater from within an excavation over grassy areas where any silt deposits can be absorbed and not have a detrimental effect on the environment. However, when works are within close proximity to a watercourse, within 10 metres, then advice should be sought on the disposal of groundwater and a 'Consent for Works Affecting Watercourses' should be obtained from the Environment Agency.

METHODS OF SUPPORTING EXCAVATIONS

"Where it is necessary to prevent danger to anybody from falls or dislodgement of materials from the side or roof of an excavation, that excavation shall as early as practicable in the course of work be sufficiently supported so as to prevent, so far as is reasonably practicable, the fall or dislodgement of materials. Suitable and sufficient equipment for supporting an excavation shall be provided to ensure the foregoing.".

Figure C9-21: Methods of supporting excavations.   *Source: Construction (Health Safety and Welfare) Regulations Regulation 12 of the CHSW.*

Precautions must be taken to prevent collapse. The methods of supporting (shoring) the sides of excavations vary widely in design depending on:

- The nature of the subsoil - for example wet may require close shoring with sheets.
- Projected life of the excavation - a trench box may give ready made access where it is only needed for short duration.
- Work to be undertaken, including equipment used - for example, the use of a trench box for shoring where pipe joints are made.
- The possibility of flooding from ground water and heavy rain - close shoring would be required.
- The depth of the excavation - a shallow excavation may use battering instead of shoring, particularly where shoring may impede access.
- The number of people using the excavation at any one time - a lot of space may be required so cantilever sheet piling may be preferred.

In order to ensure satisfactory support for excavations:

- Prevent trench collapse by battering the sides to a safe angle or supporting them with sheeting or proprietary support systems.
- Use experienced people for the erection and dismantling of timbering and other supports.
- Adequate material must be used to prevent danger from falls or falling objects.

Figure C9-22: Battering. *Source: ACT.*

Figure C9-23: Trench box - for shoring. *Source: ACT.*

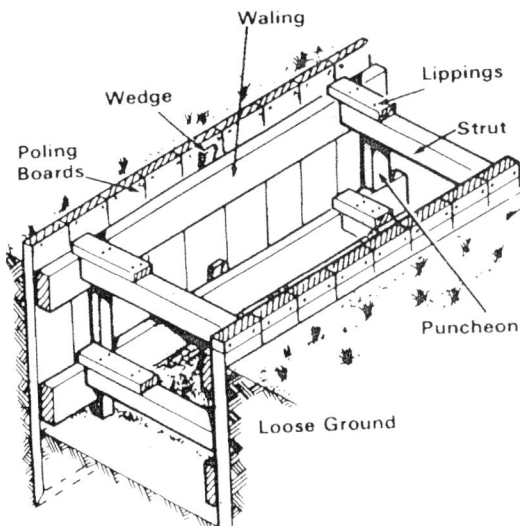
Figure C9-24: Close boarded excavation. *Source: BS6031.*

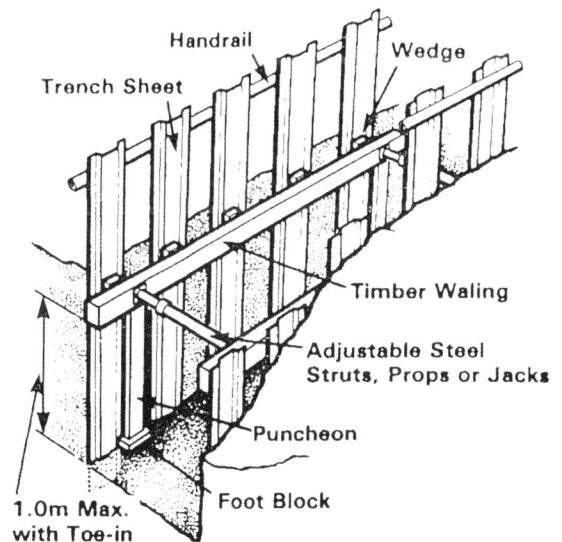
Figure C9-25: Open sheeting. *Source: BS6031.*

Figure C9-26: Close sheeting. *Source: ACT.*

Figure C9-27: Open sheeting. *Source: ACT.*

Example of a permit to dig

PERMIT TO DIG

Contract: ....   Contract No: ....

Principal Contractor: ....   Sub Contractor: ....

Permit No: ....   Date: ....

1.   Location: ....

2.   Size, detail and depth of excavation: ....

    ....

3.   Are Service Plans on site ?   YES / NO

    Comments: ....

4.   Has cable locating equipment been used to identify services ?   YES / NO

    Comments: ....

5.   Are all known services marked out ? (site inspection by relevant statutory bodies)   YES / NO

    Comments: ....

6.   Are trial holes required ?   YES / NO

    Comments: ....

7.   Have precautions been taken to prevent contact if overhead lines are in the vicinity of the operation or near approach to the operation?   YES / NO

8.   Additional precautions, i.e. Shoring/Fencing/Access/Storage/Fumes/Record of setting out points to re-establish services routes

    Comments: ....

9.   Sketch details or attach copy of plans

10.   Date and time of excavation: ....

    Signed: ....   Accepted by: ....
    For and on behalf of issuing party   (Work shall not commence unless all persons involved are aware of the safe systems of work)

        A new permit will be required for any further excavations. This permit is for guidance only.
        Persons carrying out work must take reasonable precautions when working around services.

Figure C9-28: Permit to dig.   *Source: Reproduced by kind permission of Lincsafe.*

BURIED SERVICES

Although electricity cables provide the most obvious risk, gas pipes, water mains, drains and sewers can all release dangerous substances. Gas is particularly dangerous if there is a potential ignition source close by. Fibre-optic cables may not produce a health and safety risk but are very expensive to repair.

Buried services (electricity, gas, water, etc) are not obvious upon site survey and so the likelihood of striking a service when excavating, drilling or piling is increased. The results of striking an underground service are varied, and the potential to cause injury or fatality is high. As with overhead power lines, any underground service should be treated as live until confirmed dead by an authority. Incidents can include shock, electrocution, explosion and burns from power cables, explosion, burns or unconsciousness from gas or power cables, impact injury from dislodged stones or flooding from ruptured water mains.

Types and consequences of damage

The consequences of even a minor collapse can be very serious. A minor fall of earth can happen at high speed and bring with it anything (plant and machinery) that may be at the edge. Even if the arms and head of a person are not trapped in the soil, the material pressing on the person can lead to severe crush injuries to the lower body and asphyxiation due to restriction of movement of the chest.

Excavations that are carried out within close proximity to existing buildings or structures may result in their foundations becoming undermined and create the potential for significant settling damage to occur or worse still, collapse. Consideration should be given to the effects that excavation work might have on foundations of neighbouring buildings or structures, and control measures implemented to ensure that foundations are not disturbed or undermined. Building foundations that are at a distance of less than twice the excavation depth from the face of the excavation are more likely to be affected by ground movement; underpinning or shoring of such structures may be required to prevent structural damage.

Methods of checking for buried services and Precautions to be observed

Excavation operations should not begin until all available service location drawings have been identified and thoroughly examined. Record plans and location drawings should not be considered as totally accurate but serve only as an indication of the likelihood of the presence of services, their location and depth. It is possible for the position of an electricity supply cable to alter if previous works have been carried out in the location due to the flexibility of the cable and movement of surrounding features since original installation of the cable. In addition, plans often show a proposed position for the services that does not translate to the ground, such that services are placed in position only approximately where the plan says.

It is important that 'service location devices' such as a cable avoidance tool (CAT) are used by competent, trained operatives to assist in the identification and marking of the actual location and position of buried services. When identified it is essential that physical markings be placed on the ground to show where these services are located.

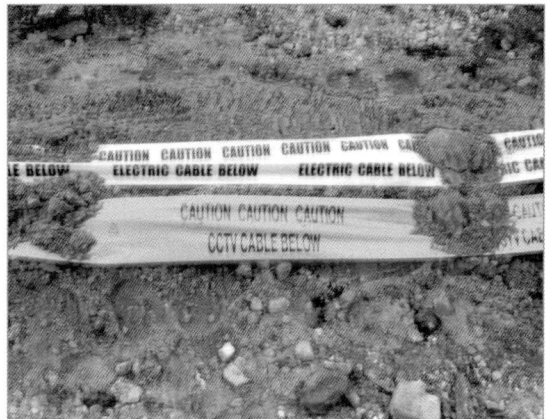

Figure C9-29: Marking of services. *Source: ACT.*

Safe digging methods

Safe digging methods should be implemented within 0.5 metres of a buried service. This involves the use of insulated hand tools such as a spade or shovel with curved edges (to be used with light force and not sudden blows). Mechanical, probing or piercing tools and equipment such as excavator's, forks, picks or drills should not be used when in the vicinity of buried services, as these may cause damage to any service if they strike it. Careful hand digging using a spade or shovel should be used instead.

STATUTORY INSPECTIONS AND EXAMINATIONS OF EXCAVATIONS

The schedule to the CHSW Regulations 1996 specifies the frequency and circumstances for inspection of an excavation.

A competent person must inspect excavations:

- At the start of each shift before work begins.
- After any event likely to have affected the strength or stability of the excavation.
- After any accidental fall of rock, earth or other material.

The written report should be made after most inspections. Stop work if the inspection shows the excavation to be unsafe.

The notes that follow the inspection report outline which places of work require inspection under the Construction (Health, Safety and Welfare) Regulations. They also specify the timing and frequency of those inspections.

The competent person must:

- Complete the inspection report before the end of the working period.
- Provide the report or a copy to the person for whom the inspection was carried out within 24 hours.
- A copy of the Reports must be kept on site until the work is complete. Reports should then be kept for three months at an office of the person for whom the inspections were carried out.

Where the person carrying out the inspection is not satisfied that it is safe to work in the excavation they must inform the person who they are doing the inspection for and work must not continue until the matters identified by the inspection have been remedied.

The inspection record must include the following information:

- Name and address of person on whose behalf the inspection was carried out.
- Location of the workplace inspected.
- Description of workplace or part of workplace inspected (including any plant and equipment and materials).
- Date and time of inspection.
- Details of any matter identified that could lead to a risk to the health and safety of anyone.
- Details of any action taken as a result of any matter identified in the last point.
- Details of any more action considered necessary.
- The name and position of the person making the report.

9.4 - Demolition work

MAIN TECHNIQUES IN DEMOLITION OF BUILDINGS

Balling machines

Considerable skill is necessary in the use of a demolition ball. The ball is a large steel, pear-shaped device, which is suspended from the jib of an appliance.

The demolition ball can be used in three main ways:

- Raised to a height and allowed to fall vertically onto the structure.
- Swung forward into the structure in line with the jib of the appliance.
- Swung sideways by slewing the jib of the appliance.

Cranes should only be used for the vertical drop method. Crane jibs are not designed to withstand the stresses created by sidewards drag or forward swinging. Excavators which can be converted into a 'crane' for drag line operations are more suited to the task.

Piecemeal

Piecemeal demolition is done by hand using hand held tools and is sometimes a preliminary to other methods. It can be completed or begun by machines. For example, when demolishing a tall chimney with occupied buildings in close proximity, the job may commence with the painstaking task of dismantling by hand - brick by brick. When the structure has been reduced to about 10 metres, then conventional heavy equipment can be used.

Controlled collapse and pre-weakening

Deliberate controlled collapse involves the pre-weakening of the structure or building. This involves removing key structural members so the remaining structure collapses under its own weight.

There are several problems associated with this method of demolition:

- The structure may collapse to a greater extent than was anticipated.
- The planned collapse may only be a partial collapse and could leave the structure hazardous and insecure.
- The resultant debris may be projected over a wider area than anticipated.
- The pile of debris that is left after the collapse of the structure may be in a dangerous condition, presenting a serious risk to those who remove it.

One method of removing the key structural members is overturning by wire rope pulling. Wires are attached to the main supports, which are pulled away using a heavy tracked vehicle or a winch to provide the motive power. The area must be cleared of workers for this operation and there must be enough clearance for the vehicle to move the distance required to pull out the structural supports.

Problems associated with this method arise when the wire becomes overstressed. If it breaks, then whiplash can occur which can have the force to slice through the human body. The forces applied may be enough to overturn the winch or the tracked vehicle. Another problem can occur when the action of pulling has begun and there is inadequate power to complete it.

Use of explosives - The use of explosives requires the expertise of an experienced explosives engineer. Also, the HSE should be consulted to ensure compliance with The Control of Explosives Regulations 1991. There are a number of factors to be considered for safe demolition with the use of explosives, which include:

- The local and structural conditions must be considered when fixing the size of the charges. The structure to be blasted can be divided into a number of sections and suitable charges applied to each section.
- Shot holes should be drilled electrically. Drilling pneumatically could cause vibration, which could result in premature collapse.
- Charges should not be placed near cast iron as it easily shatters into shrapnel.
- The area around the structure being demolished and the firing point should be barricaded and unauthorised persons not allowed to enter.
- The demolition engineer must be satisfied that no dangerous situation or condition has been left or created. The danger zone must be barricaded until rendered safe.

TYPICAL HAZARDS

Demolition is probably the most hazardous operation undertaken in the construction industry. The principal hazards are:

- Falls of men, falls of materials, flying materials, dust and debris, resulting in a wide range of injuries and conditions, some of which are of a fatal nature.
- Collapse of a building or structure, either deliberately or unplanned.
- Overloading of floors or the structure with debris, resulting in floor and/or building collapse.
- Explosions in tanks or other confined spaces.
- The presence of live electric cable or gas mains.
- The presence of dusty, corrosive and poisonous materials and/or atmospheres.
- Projecting nails in timber etc., broken glass and cast iron fragments which can penetrate the hands, feet and parts of the body.

Falling materials

Protective screens and where appropriate fans should be set up around scaffolds set around buildings undergoing demolition, to prevent debris falling on to passers-by. In addition, brick guards, debris nets and sheeting will help to contain falling materials and prevent them falling outside the framework of a scaffold erected as part of the demolition process.   There must be a clearly demarcated area where workers can tell that the specific area of the structure is being worked on and that the work in that area has a risk from falling materials. This includes buildings being demolished by hand, where a safe access route to the work place must be maintained. Warning of planned demolition stages by use of audible and visual warnings will assist in removing people from the hazards area at this time. Head protection is an essential last line of defence for workers in this environment.

Figure C9-30: Protection of public.   *Source: ACT.*

Figure C9-31: Disposal of waste.   *Source: ACT.*

Figure C9-32: Protection from falling materials.   *Source: ACT.*

Figure C9-33: Falling materials.   *Source: ACT.*

Premature collapse of buildings

The technical advances in mechanical plant have considerably reduced the risk to demolition workers of working at a height. Modern machines can be fitted with scissor jaws that can break down a wall in small pieces. Another benefit of scissor jaws is that there is less likelihood of major structural damage or premature collapse. The likelihood of premature collapse remains a consideration when using the ball and chain method or carrying out partial demolition. In some cases the façade of a building may be left intact for renovation and the rest of the structure removed. In these circumstances great care must be taken to avoid freestanding walls and to provide adequate support to the structure.

Materials of construction

- The presence of asbestos should be determined because its removal will require specialist treatment. The workers must have appropriate clothing and respirators.
- Special hazards during demolition will need to be identified, for example, reinforced concrete, pre-stressed members, arches, structural steelwork, etc.
- It is important to know the previous use of the buildings. They may still contain toxic or flammable materials or even radioactive materials or sources.

PRECAUTIONS

Safe working methods

The following precautions are necessary during the demolition process:

- Demolition should be carried out in the reverse order of erection of the building.
- No freestanding wall should be left on its own unless judged to be secure by the competent person.
- Scaffold working platforms should be used.
- Entrances, passages, stairs and ladder runs should be kept clear of all material.
- Disturbed staircases, particularly stone staircases, should not be used.
- Timber with protruding nails should have the nails removed.
- Glass in partitions, doors, roofs and windows should be removed separately.
- Adequate and suitable lighting should be provided.

Planning, structural surveys and surveys for hazardous substances

Before any work begins and usually before the contract is signed, a survey is carried out to ensure that the demolition can go ahead safely and that property surrounding the site is protected from the demolition work as it progresses.

Items which are dealt with in the survey include the following:

- Details and location of all the public services must be known and shown on a large-scale plan. Most of these will be buried services: gas pipes, electrical cables, water pipes, sewerage, etc., and could present serious risk if damaged. It is necessary to state which of these will need to be cut off and which will need further protection. It should be made absolutely clear who is responsible for each to be sure that nothing gets overlooked.
- The structural design should be examined to identify the supporting members and structures.
- Basements, cellars, wells or storage tanks need to be identified. Workers may fall through into these underground areas, while tanks pose a special risk if they have held or still hold toxic or flammable materials.
- The suitability of the ground for scaffolds, cranes, excavators and other plant needs to be established.
- Access to the site should be established to enable the large plant and appliances to be taken or driven there safely. It may also be necessary to get permission to close roads or pathways for the duration of the work.
- The recommended means of disposal of rubbish should be considered, according to The Control of Pollution Act 1974 and The Control of Pollution (Special Wastes) Regulations 1980.
- Special requirements will necessarily arise out of the survey. Drains may need to be sealed to prevent toxic and flammable gases escaping to the site and to prevent infestation of rats. The special precautions, for example, respiratory protection or for entry into confined spaces, should be written into the contract. Other requirements, such as the removal of glass from all windows should also be written into the contract.

Provision of working places and means of access / egress

Working places are ever changing on demolition sites and it is important to constantly monitor the situation. Work on the structure being demolished needs careful planning to ensure that unplanned collapse does not occur. Scaffolds are used as working platforms and rely on the structure being demolished for their stability. Constant inspection is needed to ensure the scaffold does not collapse with the building.

Lighting is important for safe working and to make sure there are no hidden tripping hazards or dark areas where holes in flooring, for example, cannot be seen.

It is difficult to maintain safe access and egress because of the nature of demolition work. Because conditions are ever changing the safety systems should be constantly reviewed and updated. Housekeeping must be maintained to a very high standard by keeping walkways free of rubble. Where scaffolds are used, platforms and gangways must be kept clear of debris and any tripping hazards. Scaffolds must be constantly checked to ensure they have sufficient ties into the building.

Where there is a chance of falling debris, there must be some way of protecting the workers and the public. Protective fans can be set up, but they must be kept clear of any debris that does fall on them, as they are not designed to carry heavy weights.

Care must be taken with ladders as the structure is demolished and the ladders are repeatedly fixed and removed, there is always the temptation to use them on occasion without securing. In certain conditions the demolition worker is required to work in precarious positions, safety harnesses should be worn and they should be attached to a secure part of the structure in these circumstances.

Where floorboards have been removed, it is important to leave some in place, a 'skeleton floor', to allow work to carry on in relative safety.

Use of method statements and permits to work

Health and safety method statements are an effective management tool for high risk work such as demolition. The method statement draws together the information concerning the hazards associated with the job and the controls that will be necessary. It takes into account the results of the assessments that have been carried out: general risk, COSHH 2002, manual handling, etc. This information will help in the planning of the job and highlight the resources that are needed for it. The method statement will also provide information for other contractors working on the site about any effects the work will have on them. With demolition, the statement will need to be revised regularly as the circumstances and conditions constantly change.

The method statement is also a useful and effective way of giving employees information about how a particular task should be carried out and what precautions are necessary. The inclusion of simple diagrams is useful as they can make it clear how a task should be carried out. It is necessary to monitor the method statements to check that what they say is being put into action.

Permits to work are used for particularly hazardous tasks such as hot work, work in confined spaces, using explosives, etc. They are a formal way of setting out what must be done to help minimise the risks involved. The competent person must sign to say everything necessary has been done according to the permit and allowing the work to go ahead. Boundaries may have to be set up to exclude personnel and warning notices posted. When the work is completed the permit must be signed off to say as much and that everything is safe to continue with the routine work.

Security of site boundaries and protection of the public

The boundaries of the demolition site need to be fenced off to exclude persons not involved with the work. These could be children, who are attracted to such sites, which, like construction sites are adventure playgrounds, persons sleeping rough and those who wish to salvage materials, as well as people who are just passing by. The very nature of a demolition site suggests both attraction and danger. Some form of fencing or boarding about 2.5m high would be ideal, with warning notices set up around it. Protective screens and fans should be set up around scaffolds to prevent debris falling on to passers-by.

Plant and appliances should be secured and never left with the keys in the ignition. Serious accidents have been caused by children trying to drive or operate site vehicles. Demolition sites are extremely dangerous places for experienced workers so it is essential that members of the public are kept away.

Protection from noise

Demolition must take into account the public and neighbour interface. Simple controls for reducing the impact of noise on others include limiting the work hours / days to those more socially acceptable. The choice of equipment and where it might be sited, may be used to limit the effects of noise, for example by locating noisy plant away from boundaries shared with those affected.

Control and protection from dust

Dust can be both a nuisance and a risk to health to those exposed; this may not only affect the site personnel but neighbours and members of the public. Dust may contain fungal and bacterial matter (e.g. demolition of empty buildings infested with vermin, pigeons etc.) which may be pathogenic to humans. Dust can be damped down with water to keep it to a minimum. The closure of roads and pathways is a good precaution to keep people and vehicles away from the site, but this is not always possible. Prevailing winds will need to be considered in order to decide the approach and order of the demolition; it may be possible for the un-demolished parts of the structure to reduce dust liberated from the site during the initial demolition phase.

Protection of the environment

Where lorries are being used to transport the demolition waste material to a disposal site, then provision should be made for wheel washes and the cleaning of the highway by a road sweeper. Waste substances, such as oils, must not be allowed to leak away into the soil and must be disposed of in a controlled manner. During demolition sewers may become exposed and be at risk of contamination from substances, and care should be taken to identify and protect them from entry of such materials. In the same way it may be necessary to establish interceptor pits to control water run off into water courses.

9.5 - Mobile equipment

TYPES OF MOBILE EQUIPMENT USED ON CONSTRUCTION SITES

See also - Mechanical Handling - Element C7

- Rough-terrain fork lift trucks.
- Telehandlers.

Dumper trucks

General piece of plant consisting of a heavy-duty chassis, body and tipping bucket on large diameter wheels and deep tread, traction tyres, used for transporting materials around a construction site or street works. The equipment is generally used as a large mechanised wheelbarrow.

Hazards include the generic hazards associated with mobile equipment. Specific hazards associated with dumper trucks are impact with pedestrians or vehicles, trap and crush beneath the tipping bucket as it discharges its contents, falling items or objects from the bucket, high pressure hydraulic lines and tipping over on unstable ground or into excavations. Other hazards include noise, chemicals and fumes produced by the running of the machinery which may find their way into places like excavations. Control measures should include trained, authorised, operatives; maintenance and inspection; segregation of pedestrians to a safe distance by the provision of suitable barriers and signs advising of the dangers of operating plant; stop blocks for tipping into excavations; seat restraints and rollover protection for the operator.

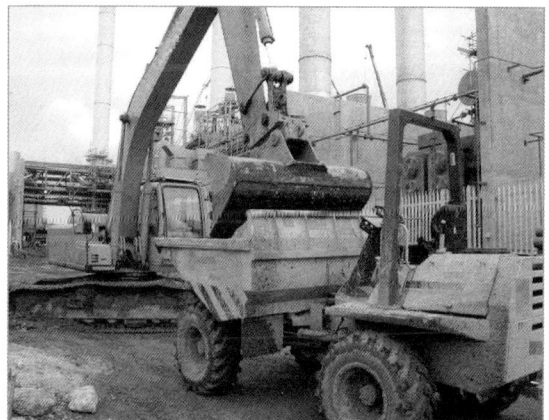

Figure C9-34: Dumper truck. *Source: ACT.*

Excavators

Consisting of a heavy duty chassis, fixed or rotating body and digging gear (jib arms & bucket) on either large diameter wheels and deep tread, pneumatic traction tyres or caterpillar track system.

REQUIREMENTS FOR SAFE USE

There are many types of truck available for a range of activities. There are many situations when specialist trucks such as reach trucks, overhead telescopic or rough terrain trucks are required. Many accidents happen due to the incorrect selection and/or use of forklift trucks.

When choosing the right truck for the job the following factors should be taken into account:

- Power source - the choice of battery or diesel will depend on whether the truck is to be used indoors or outdoors.
- Tyres - solid or pneumatic depending on the terrain.
- Size and capacity - dependent on the size and nature of loads to be moved.
- Height of the mast.
- Audible and/or visual warning systems fitted according to the proximity of pedestrians.

Figure C9-35: Excavator. *Source: ACT.*

■ Protection provided for the operator dependent on rough terrain which might increase the likelihood of overturning or the possibility of falling objects say from insecure racking.

■ Training given to operators must be related specifically to the type of truck.

Specific hazards associated with excavators are impact with pedestrians or vehicles by swinging jibs and booms, trap and crush beneath the excavator bucket as it digs into the ground or discharges its contents, falling items or objects from the bucket, high pressure hydraulic lines and tipping over on unstable ground or into excavations. Other hazards include noise, chemicals and fumes produced by the running of the equipment. Excavation equipment is generally adapted and used for a variety of different purposes that it may not specifically be designed for, including towing /shunting, lifting, loading / unloading / transport of articles and equipment. The fact that these are improvised activities increases the risk of injury. Control measures should include trained and authorised operatives; not overloading the bucket; maintenance and inspection; segregation of pedestrians to a safe distance by the provision of suitable barriers and signs advising of the dangers of operating plant; good visibility with the assistance of mirrors where necessary; high visibility clothing for those working nearby; and seat restraints for the operator who should be enclosed in a protective cage that can also act as a guard against contact with moving machinery and the effects of overturning.

Environmental pollution and waste management

Overall aims

On completion of this Element, the student will have knowledge and understanding of:

■ typical sources of environmental pollution resulting from process operations, possible hazards, control strategies and methods.

■ categories of waste and practical waste management.

■ waste treatment and disposal techniques.

■ relevant statutory provisions.

■ need for emergency response.

Content

Specific intended learning outcomes

The intended learning outcomes are that the student will be able to:

1.   identify potential sources and impacts of environmental pollution from processes

2.   identify the main categories of waste arising and give advice to management on the best practicable management and disposal options

3.   identify the need for monitoring and emergency response

Relevant statutory provisions

Environmental Protection Act (EPA) 1990

Environment Act (ENVA) 1995

Special Waste Regulations (SWR) 1996

Control of Major Accident Hazard Regulations (COMAH) 1999

10.1 - Environmental pollution

A definition of pollution:

"The introduction into the environment of substance or energy liable to cause hazards to human health, harm to living resources and to ecological systems, damage to structures or amenity or interference with the legitimate use of the environment".

Environmental pollution is a major issue today with the industrialised countries of the world concerned about the long term effects on Earth's resources and on plant, animal and human life. Major concerns on health are often blamed on pollution and there are many pressure groups that focus on environmental issues, particularly pollution.

The problem of pollution is not new; it has been with us since Roman times where the land around old lead mines is still contaminated with the heavy metal today. Since the industrial revolution industry has relied on the capacity of the environment to dilute and disperse pollutants by discharging them to the ground, water and air. This has left a legacy of polluted areas, land pollution being the most persistent, but the discharges to air and water are more global in their effect.

INTENDED RELEASES

An example of an ***intended release*** is the emission of sulphur dioxide (SO_2) and nitrogen oxides (NO^x) into the atmosphere by coal-fired power stations. This example also illustrates the global, as well as local, impact that such emissions have which, in this case, results in acid rain falling in Scandinavia which emits very little sulphur dioxide itself. A further impact by the same power station is caused by the carbon dioxide emissions that lead to global warming.

The local effects of the emission of particulates and sulphur dioxide is illustrated by the London Smogs of the 1950s, and more recently by the increase in road traffic - many cities in Britain now have pollutants above recommended limits, especially in warm, still conditions.

ABNORMAL CONDITIONS GIVING RISE TO OCCASIONAL RELEASES

Plant failure and accidents can lead to ***abnormal releases*** following higher than expected temperatures and pressures. This has led to a loss of process control with uncontrolled venting to the environment. Lack of control can lead to losses e.g. overfilling. Abnormal conditions may also occur at plant start-up or shut-down.

MAJOR RELEASES FOLLOWING PLANT FAILURE

There have been many high profile ***major releases*** of both flammable and toxic substances following plant failure. These include:

Location	Event	Factors
Flixborough **Nypro (UK)** **Limited Plant** **1974**	Unconfined vapour cloud explosion killed 28 people and injured 36 others on site. 53 casualties off site recorded. Plant totally destroyed; extensive property damage over a wide area (1,821 houses and 167 shops/factories).	▪ Reactor discovered leaking cyclohexane. ▪ Bridging pipe used to bypass reactor. ▪ The assembly was subjected to temperature and pressure more severe than had been encountered since the bypass was fitted but still within what should have been normal margins. ▪ The bridging pipe ruptured which released large quantities of cyclohexane which mixed with air to form an unconfined vapour cloud which then exploded. ▪ There was nitrate stress corrosion on the reactor and many of the stainless steel components had suffered from embrittlement and creep cavitation fractures.
Seveso **1976**	About 2 kg of TCDD (dioxin) was released over a 20 minute period in Milan and brought down by rain in Seveso (24 km from release). It contaminated about 4 km^2 of soil.	TCDD = 2,3,7,8 - tetrachloro-dibenzo-*p*-dioxin. Dioxin is extremely toxic and associated with still births, deformities, cancer, blindness and chloracne. External spillages are extremely persistent (not easily rendered harmless by exposure to the environment) Dioxin is insoluble in water. ▪ Reactor had gone out of control. ▪ Overheating caused safety valve to open. ▪ High temperature caused an abnormally high quantity of the undesired by-product TCDD to be produced. ▪ Safety valve did not vent to an enclosed system safely.
		Note: Previous accidents involving TCDD releases in much smaller quantities (10 times less) proved decontamination to be unsuccessful. The plant had to be dismantled and buried in concrete to contain the contaminant.
Bhopal **1984**	Rapid vaporisation and release of methyl isocyanate (MIC). Killing 2500 people and seriously injuring thousands of others.	MIC was stored in high-pressure stainless steel tanks designed to be at 0-15° C via a refrigeration system. ▪ Refrigerant system and flare line out of commission. ▪ Pressure and temperature increased with rapid vaporisation of MIC. ▪ Temperature and pressure indicators not working. ▪ Vent scrubbers switched off. ▪ Emergency spare tank not used for emergency transfer.

Figure C10-1: Major release following plant failure.

Source: ACT.

These accidents in Europe, Seveso in particular, have led to legislation being formed which attempts to limit the risk from these sites. *See also - Element C11 - Relevant Statutory Provisions - the Control of Major Accident Hazards Regulations (COMAH) 1999.*

BEHAVIOUR AND DISPERSION OF GASES

The dispersion and behaviour of toxic and flammable gases arising from a leak or spillage will depend on a number of factors:

- The quantity of the gas/vapour and the rate of release.
- The physical characteristics of the gas or vapour (density and temperature).
- The physical atmospheric conditions (air temperature, humidity, wind speed - direction and turbulence).
- The topographical features of the surroundings (hills, buildings etc.).

Perhaps the most important factors involved are the type of escape and the prevailing weather conditions. This will determine where the flammable gas cloud is likely to at an explosive concentration and or likely to be at a hazardous toxic level.

If the gas/vapour is escaping from a fractured vessel or pipe then the resultant plume is likely to be well mixed with air when compared to a large lagoon type spillage.

The weather conditions will also determine the rate of dispersion into the atmosphere. Stormy conditions will help to ensure a rapid dilution of the gas/vapour cloud whereas calm light winds will tend to promote concentration. This is graphically illustrated by the unconfined vapour cloud explosion that occurred in the Nypro Plant at Flixborough in 1974. Here temperature inversion conditions held the flammable cyclohexane at an explosive concentration above the plant with devastating effect.

The following factors will affect the behaviour of the gas cloud/vapour plume:

- Wind speeds and directions tend to change with height (wind speeds usually increase).
- Wind direction varies with the time of day (particularly near coastal areas).
- Temperatures decrease with height (~ 1° C per 100 metres), however, inversion conditions can occur which inhibit vertical dispersion. Temperature inversion conditions can be caused by weather fronts and sea breezes. For the first few hundred metres of the atmosphere, temperature change with height is often decreasing by day and increasing by night due to the rapid heating and cooling of the land mass.

RELEASE AND DISPERSION OF TOXIC SUBSTANCES TO GROUND, WATER AND AIR

The general principle of assessing releases of toxic substances is to consider the **Source, Pathway and Target** of a pollutant. This method will enable a focus on the actual effects of a release.

Releases to ground

The surface of the planet is made up of materials including rocks, gravels, sands, clays and soils, which are present in many combinations. Superimposed on these are the various ecosystems which combine to produce a complex system which is therefore not easy to characterise.

Glacial action has formed the landscape as the ice age retreated. Rivers, floods, earthquakes, volcanoes, winds, and all forms of life shape the surface of the planet. Each country has unique forms and habitats which provide for the great diversity of life on the planet.

Human life results in waste being generated and depending on how these are deposited pollution of the land can occur. As we have mainly populated the land masses, it is these that have traces of pollution dating back to ancient times.

Some typical pollutants and their effects include the following:

Contaminant	Hazard Pathway	Harmful Effects
Heavy metals.	Ingestion.	May cause respiratory cancers, emphysema and other lung disorders, kidney dysfunction and birth defects (teratogenicity).
Zinc, copper, nickel.	Phytotoxicity.	Can stunt plant growth, cause discoloration, shallow root system and die back.
Sulphate and sulphides.	Contact with buildings.	Can corrode and accelerate the weathering of services and structural components.

Figure C10-2: Typical pollutants.   *Source: ACT.*

Global issues

Each year about 11 million ha of arable lands are lost through erosion, desertification, toxification and cropland conversion to non agricultural uses. If this trend continues we shall have lost 275 million ha or 18% of our arable lands in the final quarter of the century. By 2025 the same amount could disappear again.

Deforestation also causes a number of environmental effects. Once trees have been burnt to clear the ground soil loss becomes very rapid when rains occur. This is because the tree roots bind the soils together and the tree canopies reduced the velocity of rain droplets. The rains now fall on exposed soils with greater energy. The soil that is removed is washed away very quickly causing silting-up of rivers and the creation of new islands.

Local issues

The United Kingdom faces a considerable and unfortunate legacy from its industrial history. The Industrial Revolution scarred the face of the landscape and left many pockets of pollution which are only now being tackled.

New legislation covering contaminated land coupled with developments in the inner cities and dock-lands means that that old industrial pollution is being tackled. British Gas owns a high number of old gas works sites which are contaminated. This land is often sited in prime areas and in order to realise its value it is investing in remediation techniques so that this land can be safely sold on. Many supermarkets are sited on old gas works sites.

Industry generates waste streams and these are classed as controlled wastes and must therefore be properly handled. This will almost certainly involve disposal into landfill sites. In the past controls on landfill sites were comparatively lax and many old landfills once forgotten are now beginning to be identified as councils are charged with listing all contaminated sites in their areas to compile a Contaminated Land Register.

Releases to water

Water composes the oceans of the world, rivers, lakes, streams and lochs. Water is also stored in the ground and is referred to as groundwater. An aquifer is a layer of permeable rock, sand or gravel that absorbs water and allows it free passage through the interstices of the rock.

Water pollutants

One way of thinking about pollution is too much of something in the wrong place and therefore there are many potential water pollutants. This fact is recognised within the European Community by the listing of Black and Grey List materials, sometimes called List I and List II substances.

Black List or List I substances are considered to be so toxic, persistent or bio accumulative in the environment that priority should be given to eliminating pollution by them. This includes substances such as organohalogens, organophosphorus, cyanide, cadmium and mercury and their compounds. Sheep-dip and solvents are included in this list.

The Grey List or List II covers those substances considered less harmful when discharged to water. Included here are metals such as zinc, nickel, chromium, lead, arsenic and copper. Also included are various biocides and substances such as phosphorus and its compounds and ammonia which are present in sewage effluent.

Diffuse and point sources

A diffuse source of pollution is one which is spread over a wide area, an example of which is the use of fertilisers over wide areas. Nitrate pollution from fertilisers represents a significant pollutant to rivers, coastal waters and seas.

A discharge from an industrial sewer represents an example of a point source.

Pollution from diffuse sources is more significant than from point sources and is much more difficult to control. In any case, any pollutant which enters the groundwater system will eventually enter watercourses, and be carried into streams, rivers, and the sea.

Global issues

Global issues concerning water and what we do with it are vast. These range from serious over-fishing of the oceans to the drying up of England's rivers during summer months.

For many years after the discontinued use of the insecticide DDT significant traces were discovered in the fat of Antarctic penguins, thousands of kilometres from source. Disasters involving super tankers occur as with the Exxon Valdez and Braer sometimes resulting in massive oil pollution. There is increasing use and pollution of groundwater as well as a reduction in water resources.

Local issues

In the United Kingdom much attention is given to both maintaining water quality and where possible improving it. Standards are set for the supply of drinking water and the water supply companies must achieve these standards.

The improvement of rivers and their water quality is a target for the Environment Agency. This is achieved by the setting of water quality objectives and many of the rivers in England and Wales are now much improved.

The Groundwater Regulations 1998 came into force on 1 January 1999 to ban or limit the amount of pollutants which reach the groundwater. This will be achieved by a system of control on substances utilising Lists I and II and authorising their use and disposal.

In terms of climatic change there may well be increased difficulties in maintaining water supplies. It is not yet clear what patterns are emerging and how the water companies will need to re-structure their supply systems.

The diagram below illustrates the routes water takes and assists the investigation of water pollution incidents.

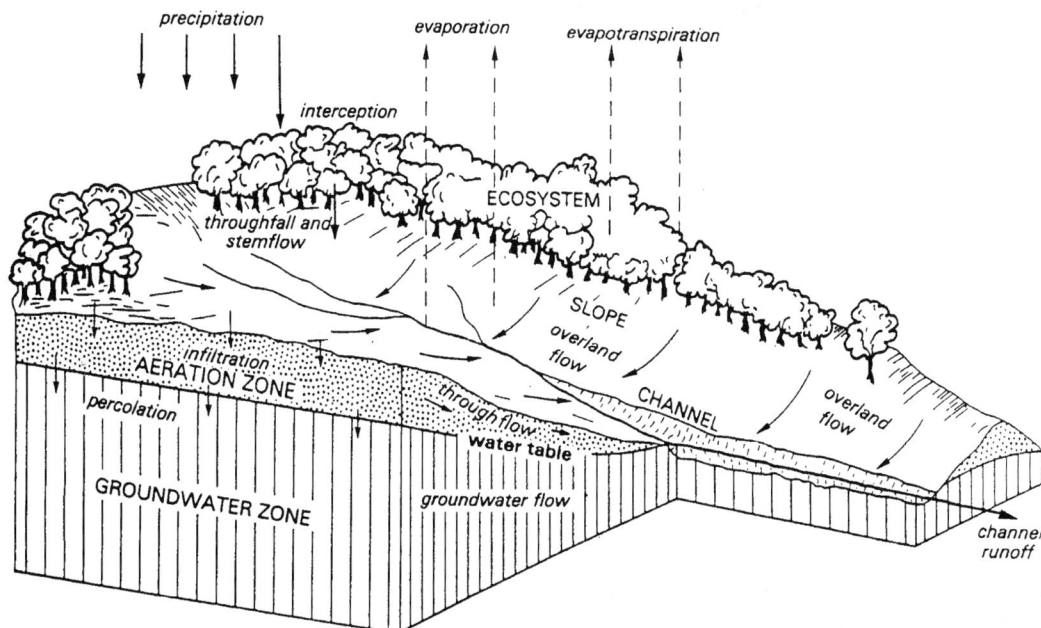

Figure C10-3: Block diagram of the catchment basin system.

Source: Environmental Systems; I D White; 1984.

Releases to air

The atmospheric system

Five gases - nitrogen, oxygen, argon, carbon dioxide and water vapour, make up 99.9% of the total volume of the atmosphere. The balance is made up of suspended particles such as water droplets, dust and soot, and the minor gases. Into this system a range of pollutants are released.

Atmospheric pollutants

Sulphur dioxide: The major source of sulphur dioxide is the combustion of fossil fuels containing sulphur. These are predominantly coal and fuel oil, since natural gas, petrol and diesel fuels have relatively low sulphur content.

Sulphur dioxide, and other pollutants emitted at high level may be transported over very large distances by the atmosphere. During such transport processes, oxidation of sulphur and nitrogen oxides to sulphuric and nitric acids occurs, hence causing "acid rain" at great distances downwind. This problem is most acute in Scandinavia which itself emits very little sulphur dioxide. Several environmental problems are associated with acid rain including the killing of fish in acidified lake waters and the leaching of nutrients from soils. Sulphur dioxide damages the human respiratory function especially when exposure is in conjunction with particulates as in the London Smogs of the 1950's. It also damages plants at modestly elevated concentrations.

Suspended Particulate Matter: The main source of primary man made particulate pollutants is combustion of fossil fuels, especially coal. Power stations use large tonnages of coal. There has been a massive decrease in urban concentrations of smoke. The main source of black smoke in urban air in the UK is diesel engined road vehicles.

Oxides of nitrogen: The most abundant nitrogen oxide in the atmosphere is nitrous oxide, N^2O and this is formed by natural microbiological processes in the soil. It is not normally considered as a pollutant, although it does have an effect upon stratospheric ozone concentrations and there is concern that use of nitrogenous fertilisers may be increasing atmospheric levels of nitrous oxide. The main concerns are nitric oxide NO and nitrogen dioxide NO^2, which together are called NO^X. The major source of NO^X is in high temperature combustion processes.

Carbon monoxide: This main source of this pollutant is petrol-engined road vehicles. Car exhaust gases contain several per cent carbon monoxide, under normal running conditions, and greater amounts when cold and choked.

Hydrocarbons: The major sources of hydrocarbons in air are the evaporation of solvents and fuels, and the partial combustion of fuels.

Carbon dioxide: Increasingly CO^2 is viewed as an air pollutant because of its importance as a "greenhouse gas". Its source lies in animal and plant respiration, and anoxic decomposition processes. It may be both absorbed or released by the oceans. Fossil fuel combustion receives a lot of attention but it is a minor source. However a small imbalance in the CO^2 cycle is leading to a steady increase in atmospheric concentration.

Ozone: Ozone is a naturally occurring gas in the atmosphere and is important in the upper reaches because it forms a protective layer (the ozone layer) to filter out potentially harmful rays from the sun.

"Holes" in the ozone layer have been discovered at both North and South poles and severe thinning over large parts of North America and Europe - people living in these areas suffer from a greater risk of skin cancer due to increased ultra violet exposure. In addition plant and aquatic life can be affected with corresponding problems for the whole food chain. The ozone depletion is primarily caused by a range of chemicals containing chlorine or bromine. Chlorofluorocarbons (CFCs) are in this group and when they react with radiation from the sun release chlorine which reacts with and destroys ozone. However, the chlorine is not destroyed and can go on to repeat the process up to 100,000 times. Other ozone depleting gases include:

- Halons.
- Carbon tetrachloride.
- 1,1,1 - trichloroethane.

Hydrochlorofluorocarbons (HCFCs) which are less harmful than CFCs have been introduced as temporary measure. Hydroflourocarbons (HFCs) are similar to HCFCs but without the chlorine they do not deplete ozone, but they do enhance the greenhouse effect.

Global issues

Air quality around the globe is a crucial issue and the top three items on the agenda are ozone depletion, global warming and acid rain. It is not known how effective measures to reduce CFC releases will be. Increased Ultra Violet penetration of the planet will affect both humans and flora and fauna. Genetic mutations are appearing and genes are known to be affected by radiation.

Global warming and changing patterns of climate will affect the whole planet and in turn all humans. Climate change is now taken to be a fact and water shortages in the United Kingdom are already appearing. Acid rain is already proven and has already caused acidification of a very large proportion of Scandinavian lakes. More than half of the 12 million tonnes of acid deposited on eastern Canada originate from the United States of America.

Local issues

In terms of local issues there is the air quality of the place where you live. Acid rain corrodes buildings; low level ozone irritates respiratory tracts. Many councils give air quality forecasts and these often advise asthma sufferers to stay indoors. Many more people now suffer from respiratory diseases.

Arrangements to manage air quality in the United Kingdom are now in place. The Government has published a National Air Quality Strategy which sets air quality standards and objectives for eight pollutants which have the most damaging effects on health, including:

- Benzene.
- Carbon monoxide.
- Sulphur dioxide.
- VOC's (Volatile Organic Compounds).

Local authorities have been given the duty of implementing the Strategy. Major pollutants have been identified and assigned control limits in Part IV of the Environment Act 1995.

Dispersion of air pollutants

Emissions to air from a polluting source may occur as follows:

- **Continuous:** for example the plume from a smoke stack.
- **Discrete:** regular short discharges from a pressure release valve.
- **Fugitive:** leaks from pipework, evaporation from uncovered containers.

When assessing a discharge to air, factors to consider include:

- Mass, volume, temperature etc of the discharge.
- Height of the discharge point above ground level.
- Prevailing wind direction.

- Local topography.
- Local population centres or other targets.

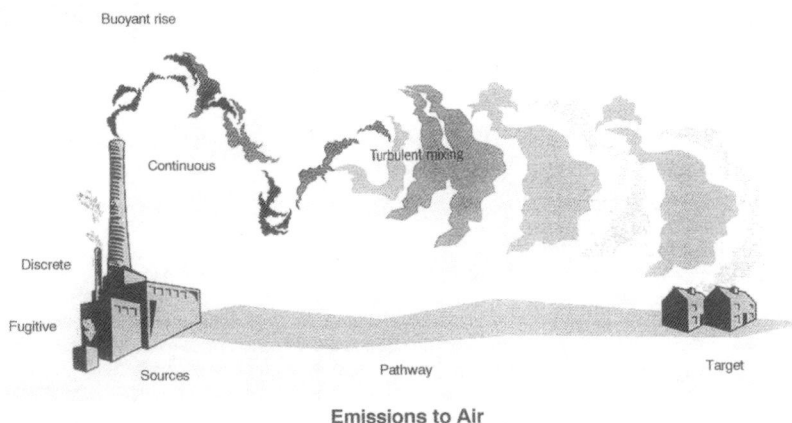

Figure C10-4: Dispersions of air pollutants.   *Source: Rapid Results College.*

ENVIRONMENTAL IMPACTS

In order to assess the environmental significance of a process or substance, the term **Environmental Impact** is used in management standards such as **BS EN ISO 14001:2004**, and legislation such as **the Environmental Impact Assessment Regulations (EIA) 1999**.

ISO 14001 definitions

- **Environmental aspect -** elements of activity that can interact with the environment.
- **Environmental impact -** any change to the environment either good or bad resulting from an organisation's activities.
- **Significant impact -** a change to the environment which could cause major concern in legislative, economic or moral terms.

An environmental risk assessment will therefore need to identify the significance of any impact before appropriate control measures are put into place. The table below could be used in order to assess the impact of a landfill site on the environment. The analysis assists in defining the source, pathway and target

Landfill site environmental impact matrix						
Activity	Environmental Impact					
	Air		Water		Land	Flora & Fauna
	Local	Global	Surface	Ground		
Solids						
General waste						
Historical contaminants						
Liquids						
Chemical storage						
Trade effluent						
Leachate						
Gas / Vapours						
Landfill gas						
Odours						
Noise						
Plant noise						
Road tankers / lorries						
Pests						
Litters						
Dusts						
Transport						
Vehicle movements						
Vehicle emissions						
Emergency conditions						
Breach consent limit						
Firewater						
Spillages - liquid / solid						

Figure C10-5: Risk assessment: a simple matrix.   *Source: Ambiguous.*

Examples of environmental impacts

Source	Pathway	Target & Impact
Mercury from spent batteries in dumped waste	Enters groundwater, stream, reservoir	Human population, flora and fauna. Cumulative poison
Sulphur Dioxide from combustion of fossil fuels	Atmosphere, acid rain falls on forests etc.	Flora and fauna, attacks buildings, pollutes lakes etc.
VOC's from chemical processes	Atmosphere	Atmosphere. Ozone depletion and greenhouse effect

Figure C10-6: Examples of environmental impacts.   Source: ACT.

POLLUTION CONTROL STRATEGIES

Prevent, minimise, render harmless

This section considers the hierarchy of pollution control. There is an enormous variety of pollutants that may be released into the environment from industrial processes. This section will describe just a few representative methods for preventing the escape of some typical air pollutants. The strategy for controlling sulphur oxides emissions, for example, can include:

1. **Prevent** - replacing fuels containing sulphur e.g. replace coal and oil with gas or expand the use of nuclear power.

2. **Minimise** - replace existing fuels by e.g. imported low-sulphur coals.

3. **Render harmless** - by removing the sulphur dioxide from the flue gases after they leave the boiler or furnace (flue gas desulphurisation). The sulphur dioxide is converted to calcium sulphite and then to calcium sulphate (gypsum) which can be used as a building material.

Methods in manufacturing, waste treatment, disposal

Methods in manufacturing

There are five key steps involved in the principles of preventing or minimising pollution during the manufacturing process:

1. **Reformulate the product** - develop a non-polluting or less-polluting product or process, by using different raw materials or feedstock.

2. **Modify the process** - change the process to control by-product formation or to incorporate non-polluting raw materials.

3. **Change the equipment** - make the equipment more efficient or allow it to use by-products from another process.

4. **Recover resources** - recycle by-products from own use or use by others.

Only after minimising wastes released to any domain of the environment do we proceed to other levels in the pollution management hierarchy.

Examples of waste minimisation which alone or in combination with other techniques can minimise air pollution include:

■ Replacing chemical processes with mechanical ones - produce more manageable emissions.
■ Replacing organic solvent-based inks, paints and coatings with water-based ones - reduces emissions of volatile organic compounds.
■ Replacing halogenated compounds with non-halogenated - reduces the impact on ozone layer.
■ Replacing mercury, cadmium and lead with other less toxic substances - reduces emissions as particulate matter or as vaporised metal.
■ Improving technology to minimise the production of pollutants from the process stream, or to return useful products to the process.
■ Installing improved process monitoring equipment to make it possible to improve and continuously maintain optimum process conditions - this improves all round efficiency and so reduces emissions.

5. **Life Cycle Assessment** - One of the key applications of the life cycle assessment (LCA) technique is to manufacturing. It may be used at a strategic level to enable key decisions to be made about product development strategy in the light of developments in the market place or with legal requirements. It may also be used at an operational level to control specific parts of the production process on a day to day basis.

It can be used as a tool to enable auditing of the production process to be carried out against specific performance requirements. LCA may also be used to evaluate the environmental performance of supply chains and enable managers to make decisions between alternative suppliers.

Methods in waste treatment and disposal

The basic principles of waste management emphasise the priority of reducing the total waste stream. This is sometimes called the *waste hierarchy*:

■ Reduce.
■ Re-use.
■ Recycle.
■ Waste to Energy.
■ Landfilling or Landraising *(see also - later in this Element)*.

Waste minimisation should be a prime objective of a company's environmental strategy and clearly set objectives should be available which are specific to each waste identified, e.g. it may be an objective to reduce the volume of contaminated plating rinse water by 30% over a 12 month period. As well as reducing the quantity of waste, it is equally important to reduce its toxicity. A concerted waste reduction programme can often be a useful component in an overall package of measures designed to reduce the environmental impact of a particular process.

This does not imply that waste should necessarily be reduced to an absolute minimum in every case, since this would not always be environmentally beneficial or economically viable. For example, if it requires a considerable input of energy to reduce the waste produced by a process to a low level, then it may be less damaging to the environment to produce a greater amount of waste, i.e. to use Best Practicable Environmental Option (BPEO).

It should be remembered that as well as saving costs in disposal of waste materials, waste minimisation programmes can also result in significant reduction in raw materials and energy usage providing additional economic incentive. Adequate resources should be made available to facilitate a suitable programme to be enacted to achieve this objective.

The main areas where waste reduction and thus lessened environmental impact can be achieved include:

Raw material changes	■ Less toxic alternatives replace solvent based materials. ■ Change specifications. ■ Re-design finished product.
Technology changes	■ Mechanical for chemical. ■ Non-solvent paints and inks. ■ Microprocessing.
Good housekeeping	■ Spill control. ■ Planned maintenance. ■ Sensors and meters.
Product innovation	■ New uses for reject/waste streams. ■ Convert wastes to saleable products. ■ Design products to aid recycling.
Process changes	■ Closed loops. ■ Production scheduling.
Inventory management	■ Reduce quantities and range of raw materials used.

Waste produced by one process may be reusable as raw materials in the same process or as feed stock to another process with little or no treatment. In the UK some 100, 000 tonnes of solvent are recovered from wastes containing solvents, since they can be down graded in specification for use as degreasing agents. Examples of materials which are recovered/recycled/re-used are given below:

■ Plating solutions with high metal content, particularly the precious metals.
■ Solvents.
■ Process waters through system for heating.
■ Plastics.
■ Scrap metal, etc.

For many products the potential for re-use is well-exploited, e.g. for packaging materials, milk bottles, etc. Where it is not possible to recycle combustible materials, burning of the waste can provide a supply of energy. Generally this takes the form of producing steam. The energy value of the waste is recovered in the form of electricity or combined heat and power.

The waste hierarchy provides three distinct levels of options for reducing the environmental impact of waste. Cleaner technology aims to find ways of production that do not create waste. Process modification seeks to achieve a reduction in waste production by modifying the production process. End of pipe technologies are the last resort and seek to deal with the waste once it has been produced. Within each level of the waste hierarchy several options exist for dealing with the waste. Exactly which option is selected for use will depend upon a variety of factors relating to the waste.

Cleaner Technology	■ Replace or eliminate. ■ Reduce consumption.
Process Modification	■ Reduce consumption. ■ Re-use in process or on site. ■ Recycle off site. ■ Treat to minimise environmental impact.
Abatement or end of pipe	■ Treat to minimise environmental impact. ■ Dispose.

Traditionally waste has most often been dealt with by disposal to landfill. More recently techniques such as incineration have been introduced for the more difficult wastes that require chemical destruction. In other cases disposal at sea has been used for low level nuclear waste that has attracted much media attention from the activities of organisations like Greenpeace. Disposal at sea has also been used for sewage sludge as well as incineration using incinerator ships like the *Vulcanus* - touring from port to port collecting and treating difficult waste.

Before the development of these techniques waste management was far less well controlled with material being disposed of on land using techniques which by today's standards would be considered to be primitive. Other historical practices such as industrial bonfires are now only rarely used as a means of waste disposal. Today there is a wide range of waste management techniques that are designed to reduce the volume of material of waste that is disposed of and to recover as much as is possible with any economic value.

Legal pressures

To increase the pressure on organisations to reduce waste, the Government takes steps to make waste more expensive to dispose of. Examples are:

■ The recovery and recycling of packaging is covered by the *Producer Responsibility Obligations (Packaging Waste) Regulations 1997* which impose a levy on anyone involved in packaging operations.
■ The cost of sending waste to landfill is made progressively more expensive by increasing the Landfill Tax.

IMPORTANT DEFINITIONS

Integrated Pollution Prevention and Control (IPPC)

Integrated Pollution Prevention Control (IPPC) is an upgrade of Integrated Pollution Control (IPC) and is a system following the *European Community Directive (96/61)* which introduces a more integrated approach to controlling pollution from industrial sources in England and Wales.

"The main aim of IPPC is to achieve:

A high level of protection of the environment taken as a whole by, in particular, preventing or, where that is not practicable, reducing emissions into the air, water and land."

The Act that makes provisions for "implementing Council Directive 96/61/EC and for otherwise preventing and controlling pollution; to make provision about certain expired or expiring disposal or waste management licences; and for connected purposes" is the *Pollution Prevention and Control Act 1999.*

This Act enabled regulations to be made in pursuance of that Directive - the *Pollution Prevention and Control (England and Wales) Regulations 2000* and the *Pollution Prevention and Control (Scotland) Regulations 2000.*

This new regime is replacing IPC and Local Air Pollution Control (LAPC), the current systems for preventing and controlling emissions under Part 1 of the *Environment Protection Act (EPA) 1990.*

The LAPC regime will be replaced by Local Air Pollution Prevention and Control (LAPPC) which is similar to IPPC in procedures, but will still only regulate emissions to air.

Applying for an IPPC permit

Operators of installations under IPPC have to apply for a permit from the Regulator (the Environment Agency). These applications have to undergo public consultation. The Regulator considers all the representations and may grant the permit subject to conditions or reject the application. If dissatisfied with the decision, an appeal can be made to the Secretary of State.

If a permit is granted, the Regulator must ensure certain general principles are adhered to:

- All appropriate preventative measures are taken against pollution, in particular through application of Best Available Technique.
- No significant pollution is caused.
- Waste production is avoided and where waste is produced, it is recovered. Where that is not possible it is disposed of in a way producing the least impact on the environment, if any impact is produced at all.
- Energy is used efficiently.
- Measures are taken to avoid accidents and limit their consequences.
- Necessary measures are taken on the closure of an installation to avoid any pollution risk and return the site to a satisfactory condition.

The operators must monitor emissions and supply the Regulator with data. The Regulator has to undertake independent monitoring and inspections of the installation to check compliance with the set emission limits. If the Regulator believes the operator is breaching the conditions of the permit, enforcement options are possible: enforcement, suspension or a revocation notice can be served. Appeals can be made to the Secretary of State.

For existing installations, IPC permits will continue until IPPC permits are phased in on a sectoral basis by October 2007.

A long term charging scheme for the new IPPC regime has been developed in consultation with interested parties.

Best Practicable Environmental Option (BPEO)

In 1988 the Royal Commission on Environmental Pollution produced the following definition of BPEO:

"The outcome of a systematic consultative and decision-making procedure, which emphasises the protection and conservation of the environment across land, air and water. The BPEO procedure establishes, for a given set of objectives, the option that provides the most benefits or the least damage to the environment, as a whole, at acceptable cost, in the long term as well as in the short term".

Figure C10-7: Definition of BPEO. *Source: Royal Commission on Environmental Pollution.*

The EPA 1990 enshrined the concept of BPEO as the cornerstone of integrated pollution control (IPC). For processes that are likely to release substances to more than one medium, the Act sets the objective that 'best available technology not entailing excessive cost' (BATNEEC) should be used 'for minimising the pollution that may be caused to the environment taken as a whole, having regard to BPEO'.

BPEO involves analysis of alternatives. The preferred option is that which minimises harm to the environment as a whole, taking account of what is affordable and practicable.

Best Available Techniques (BAT)

Defined as "the most effective and advanced stage in the development of activities and their methods of operation which indicates the practicable suitability of particular techniques for providing the basis for emission limit values designed to prevent, and where that is not practicable, generally to reduce the emissions and the impact on the environment as a whole".

This implies that BAT not only covers the technology used but also the way in which the installation is operated, to ensure a high level of environmental protection as a whole. BAT takes into account the balance between costs and environmental benefits; the greater the environmental damage that can be prevented, the greater the cost for the techniques. It seems to be halfway between practicable and reasonably practicable as understood in health and safety law.

ROLE OF THE ENVIRONMENTAL AGENCY / SCOTTISH ENVIRONMENTAL PROTECTION AGENCY

The Environment Agency (EA) & the Scottish Environment Protection Agency (SEPA) took over the responsibilities of HMIP, the NRA and the Waste Regulatory Authorities on April 1 1996. The powers to do so were provided by the Environment Act 1995. They are the principal enforcing agencies in England, Wales and Scotland.

Environment Act 1995

The Act extended environmental legislation and, as stated above, the responsibilities of the Environment Agency to cover:

- Flood defences.
- National Parks and recreational sites.
- Coastal waters.
- Contaminated land and Abandoned Mines.

- Guidance on sustainable development.
- National Air Quality Strategy.
- National Waste Strategy and Producer Responsibility.

It also instituted the Scottish Environmental Protection Agency (SEPA)

The Environment Agency (EA)

The EA is a Non-Departmental Public Body concerned with protecting and improving the land, air and water environment of England and Wales. It has a board and the board members are appointed by the Secretaries of State for the Environment and Wales and the Minister of Agriculture Fisheries and Food. The Scottish Environment Protection Agency has a similar role and function in Scotland.

The Environment Agency has eight regional offices arranged on the basis of water catchment areas for water management and political boundaries for pollution control and prevention and waste regulation functions. In Wales the boundary follows the Principality.

Aims and objectives of the Environment Agency (England and Wales)

The Environment Act 1995 sets out the aims and objectives of the Environment Agency in England and Wales. The principal aim of the Agency in discharging its functions to protect and enhance the environment is to make a contribution towards "attaining the objective of achieving sustainable development." The Act requires Ministers of State to give to the Agency statutory guidance on its objectives. The Agency must have due regard to these and these presently include:

- To adopt, across all its functions an integrated approach to environmental protection and enhancement which considers impacts of substances on all environmental media and on natural resources.
- To work with all relevant sectors of society, including regulated organisations, to develop approaches which deliver environmental requirements and goals without imposing excessive costs on regulated organisations or society as a whole.
- To adopt clear and effective procedures for serving its customers, including the development of single points of contact through which regulated organisations can deal with the agency.
- To operate to high professional standards, based on sound science, information and analysis of the environment and the processes which affect it.
- To organise its activities in ways which reflect good environmental and management practice and provide value for money to taxpayers and for those who pay its charges.
- To provide clear and readily available advice and information on its work.
- To develop a close and responsive relationship with the public, local authorities, representatives of local communities and regulated organisations.

Sustainable development

In making a contribution towards the objective of attaining sustainable development the Agency should:

- Take a holistic approach to the protection and enhancement of the environment.
- Ensure that the longer term implications and effects of actions, particularly those which appear irreversible, or reversible at high cost over a long period of time, are fully taken into account.
- Maintain biodiversity.
- Where possible, discharge its regulatory functions in partnership with business in ways which maximise the scope for cost-effective investment in improved technologies and techniques and encourage business to adopt high environmental objectives and standards.
- Develop close and responsive relationships with all sectors of the community, maximising their contributions to the achievement of sustainable development.
- Become a recognised centre of knowledge and expertise and provide readily accessible advice and information on its work and best environmental practice.

The environment agency pollution control responsibilities

The Environment Agency has a number of areas of pollution control responsibility, which can be summarised as follows:

- Authorisations, licenses and consents for emissions, discharges and disposals to air water and land; monitoring compliance and enforcement, including prosecutions under IPC and water legislation.
- Waste management licensing, including registration of carriers, regulating the import and export of waste and control over the movement of waste. The regulation of special waste and radioactive waste accumulation and disposal. Assessing waste disposal needs and priorities and the production of technical guidance on waste management.
- Regulation of contaminated land designated as special sites; to report on the state of contaminated land and as necessary produce site specific guidance to local authorities.
- Monitoring environmental conditions and publishing relevant statistics; advice to government in setting environmental quality and other standards and proposals for pollution prevention measures.
- Advice and guidance to industry and others on best environmental practice.

Scottish Environment Protection Agency

The aims of SEPA are similar to those of the EA. In their 'Outcome Objectives', the Agency outlines its brief as follows:

> *"To aim at sustainable development by ensuring the following factors are addressed.*
> - *Minimised, recovered and well-managed waste.*
> - *Good water environments.*
> - *Good air quality.*
> - *Good land quality.*
> - *A respected environment: protected, informed and engaged communities.*
> - *Economic wellbeing."*

Figure C10-8: SEPA brief.   *Source: Outcome Objectives, Scottish Environment Protection Agency.*

10.2 - Classification of waste

DEFINITIONS OF WASTE TYPES AND FORMS

Waste occurs in all three classical states of matter:

- **Solid** - household waste, tins, bottles etc.
- **Liquid** - chemical effluent etc.
- **Gas** - from burning of fossil fuels etc.

But there are definitions which are more detailed and helpful when categorising waste streams.

Hazardous and Non-Hazardous waste

Hazardous waste has physical or chemical properties that make it dangerous. For example, it may be flammable, corrosive, toxic or harmful to the environment. Examples include: flammable paints, asbestos, waste oils.

Non-hazardous waste does not have dangerous properties e.g. paper, wood, and which degrades without producing harmful decomposition products.

Difficult waste

This is not a legal definition, but is used where the waste will be difficult to process. For example, water containing a very small amount of oil as a contaminant. Purifying the water is a lengthy and expensive process.

Flammable waste

The EC Directive on flammable waste defines flammable waste: liquid substances and preparations with a flash point $\geq 21°C$ and $\leq 55°C$. This is the standard used in UK Waste legislation.

Clinical waste

This is defined under the **Controlled Waste Regulations 1992 (as amended).** In summary clinical waste is waste consisting of human or animal tissue or blood, body fluids, excretions, swabs and dressings, needles and syringes and other items or substances that may prove hazardous to or cause infection in any person coming into contact with it.

Clinical waste should be segregated from other waste by using special yellow bins, bags and sharps containers. In general, clinical waste should be incinerated to eliminate the possibility of infection. Nappies and used wound plasters in household waste are not considered as clinical waste, because they are generated from the nominally 'healthy' general population.

Biodegradable waste

Under the **Landfill (England and Wales) Regulations 2002**, this is defined as 'waste from households or other similar waste which is capable of undergoing anaerobic (oxygen absent) or aerobic (oxygen present) decomposition.

Radioactive waste

A Radioactive substance is any natural or artificial substance which emits ionising radiation spontaneously. Radioactive waste cannot be moved or disposed of without authorisation from the EA.

METHODS OF CATEGORISING WASTE

Controlled waste

This category covers the main waste streams from:

- **Household** - includes households, campsites, prisons, churches, schools.
- **Industrial** - includes factories, laboratories, workshops, bus depots, some hospital waste.
- **Commercial** - includes offices, showrooms, hotels, sports centres.

Non-controlled waste

This category includes waste materials that are taken from the ground and returned unprocessed, such as quarry waste and topsoil.

10.3 - Practical waste management

MINIMISATION

An estimated 225 million tonnes of waste is produced by industry and commerce every year, most of which is sent to landfill sites. However the country is rapidly running out of landfill sites and the costs associated with landfill are becoming prohibitive.

An organisation has a duty of care for waste "from cradle to grave" which means in effect you have to know exactly what you are dealing with. Waste can be a major contributor to an organisation's costs, as waste in all its guises extends beyond the most obvious one of waste product for disposal. We know of no way of eliminating waste production entirely, but there is considerable scope for making our waste production and management practices more sustainable. It should always be a first priority to eliminate the production of wastes; if this is not possible, efforts should be made to reduce the volume produced, or to re-use/recycle the waste. What is waste to one particular process may be a raw material to a different site operation, e.g. hot water may be available for heating purposes. On most sites, there will still be a necessity to dispose of waste materials, even if rigorous waste management control has been exercised.

We have previously mentioned the 'Waste Hierarchy' which could be expressed thus:

- Reduction/minimisation.
- Re-use/recycling.
- Treatment.
- Disposal.

Another approach is referred to as the 5Rs of Waste Management

- Reduce the amount of waste produced.
- Re-use products and energy.
- Recover energy from incineration.
- Recycle - many items can be recycled.
- Responsible disposal - manage the rest, utilising the duty of care.

Regulation will continue to play a crucial part in the implementation of sound waste management practices, providing a regulatory framework within which organisations will have to operate. Market forces will also become a clearer 'driver' of waste management practice, as disposal costs become higher, indirectly, as a result of the landfill tax.

Such changes will encourage businesses to produce less waste and manage that which they do produce in the most cost effective manner, which will include recovery, recycling, etc.

Remember: "Segregate waste and you get potential resources, mix them and you get rubbish".

The first stage of any waste management programme must be the undertaking of a site wastes audit to establish:

- Sources and location of process losses/wastes.
- Quantities and quality of waste produced.
- Efficiency of waste producing process.
- Opportunity for recycle/re-use.

STORAGE AND HANDLING

All waste holders must act to keep waste safe against:

- Corrosion or wear of waste containers.
- Accidental spilling or leaking.
- Accident or weather breaking contained waste open and allowing it to escape.
- Waste blowing away or falling while stored or transported.
- Scavenging of waste by vandals, thieves, children, trespassers or animals.

All the requirements outlined in Element C4 and Elements B3 & B4 within Unit B: Hazardous agents in the workplace, also apply.

LABELLING

Waste handed over to another person should be in some sort of containers, which might include a skip. The only reasonable exception would be loose material loaded into a vehicle and then covered sufficiently to prevent escape before being moved. Waste containers should suit the material put in them. Waste should be labelled in accordance with the *CHIP Regulations 2002*. It is *good practice* to label drums or similar closed containers with a note of the contents when stored or handed over; this could be a copy of the waste description.

CARRIAGE

A waste holder may transfer waste to someone who transports it - a waste carrier. Subject to certain exemptions, anyone carrying waste in the course of their business, or in any other way for profit, must be registered with a waste regulation authority. Each authority's register of carriers is open to public inspection. Holders may therefore for the purpose of the duty of care use these registers as a reference list of carriers who are authorised to transport waste. However, inclusion on an authority's register is not a recommendation or guarantee of a carrier's suitability to accept any particular type of waste. The holder should remain alert to any sign that the waste may not be legally dealt with by a carrier.

Anyone intending to transfer waste to a carrier will need to check that the carrier is registered or is exempt from registration. A registered carrier's authority for transporting waste is either his certificate of registration or a copy of his certificate of registration if the waste regulation authority provided it. The certificate or copy certificate will show the date on which the carrier's registration expires. All copy certificates must be numbered and marked to show that they are copies and have been provided by the waste regulation authority. Photocopies are not valid and do not provide evidence of the carrier's registration.

In all cases other than those involving repeated transfers of waste, the holder should ask to see, and should check the details of, the carrier's certificate or copy certificate of registration. In addition, before using any carrier for the first time, the holder should check with the waste regulation authority with which the carrier is registered that his registration is still valid, even if his certificate appears to be current. The waste regulation authority with whom a carrier is registered is the authority where the carrier has his principal place of business; the authority's name and other details are shown on the certificate. The holder should provide the authority with the carrier's name and registration number as shown on the certificate.

In practice, the only exempt carriers who might take waste from a holder are:

- Charities and voluntary organisations.
- Waste collection authorities (local authorities) collecting any wastes themselves (though an authority's contractors are not exempt).
- British Rail when carrying waste by rail.
- Ship operators where waste is to be disposed of under licence at sea.

Carriage of hazardous waste is covered by legislation related to the carriage of dangerous substances by road etc. *(See also - Element C4).*

DUTY OF CARE

The common law 'duty of care' is based on the neighbour principle that it is the duty of every citizen to take reasonable care to avoid acts or omissions which you can reasonably foresee would be likely to injure persons who are closely and directly affected by your acts or omissions. Under the EPA 1990 the duty is to take all reasonable measures in the particular circumstances. This duty applies to those who import, produce, carry, treat, keep or dispose of controlled waste or, as brokers, have control of such waste. *See section - Duty of Care (Environmental Protection Act 1990) - towards the end of this Element.*

10.4 - Waste disposal

PHYSICAL AND CHEMICAL TREATMENT

The aim of physical and chemical treatment of wastes is to minimise the environmental impact. Physical treatment techniques include settling, sedimentation, filtration, flotation, evaporation and distillation (e.g. the separation of oil and water using settlement lagoons or the recovery of solvents by distillation).

Chemical conversion includes processes such as *flue gas desulphurisation* - the conversion of sulphur dioxide into gypsum can render the waste inert with little or no environmental impact. Other techniques include:

- Making soluble wastes insoluble.
- Destroying toxicity (e.g. oxidation of cyanides).
- Neutralisation of acids and alkalis.

The majority of waste techniques of this type relate to waterborne contamination and particularly the Water Industry. It should be noted that treated wastes will still require final disposal of solid residues (e.g. water treatment residues).

LANDFILL SITES

Landfill sites play a crucial role in waste management alongside other methods such as incineration, waste minimisation and recycling techniques. A landfill site is a complex engineering, technical and commercial project which requires thorough planning and high standards of management to ensure that it is successful throughout its lifetime, which may be up to 50 years or more. A land raising site involves the filling of a natural geographical depression such as a valley. Land raising sites can have all the problems, which are discussed below, as can occur with a land fill site.

Any waste management company wishing to set up a landfill site must consider site selection, design and operation. Various specialist disciplines will be needed to design and operate a landfill site such as geotechnical engineers, civil engineers, construction engineers, hydrogeologists and operations managers. In order to operate a landfill site evidence of capability must be provided in the form of a Certificate of Competence.

Landfill sites are licensed under the *Pollution, Prevention and Control Regulations (PPC) 2000*.

The environmental impacts of landfill operations

The purpose of this section is to give an overview of the environmental impacts of landfilling operations, which can be considered under the three headings of air, water and land. The precise impact of any one landfill site will depend on a number of factors. These include the design of the landfill, the method of operation and the type of waste that the site receives.

In addition it is also crucial to consider the precise characteristics of the receiving environment. Receiving environments vary enormously and range from landfills in the highlands of Scotland to landfills in the soft chalk lands of Kent.

Air	Landfill gas (methane and carbon dioxide), odour, noise, visual impact, dust. Nuisances and health hazards such as seagulls and pest infestation.
Water	Surface water, ground water, leachate discharge to sewer or to surface water.
Ground	Physical contamination of surrounding soils and rock formations.

LANDRAISING

Landraising involves depositing waste on existing ground to raise the level - in contrast to landfilling, which fills up quarries etc to restore the original ground level. It may be used to raise land in order to reduce flooding risks, or to restore contaminated land from former mineral extraction sites.

Landraising suffers from the same sort of environmental problems as landfilling, but may be considered an attractive alternative because, for example:

- Leachates and gases are easier to control.
- Land can be recovered for use.
- Engineering the site is less complex than for a landfill project.

INCINERATION

Incineration falls under two main categories; the burning of:

- Municipal solid wastes (MSW).
- Hazardous wastes.

The principle of incineration of MSW is to reduce the volume of waste by burning it under controlled conditions in order to reduce volume/mass for final disposal. The heat produced can also be used as an energy source (as a fuel MSW wastes are about 30-40% that of industrial bituminous coal).

Incineration is the only really secure environmental option for most pathogens, inflammable liquids and carcinogens such as PCBs or dioxins. Thus this option represents a suitable treatment/disposal option for a waste stream if combustion or application of high temperature destroys or transforms it. Thus its potential as an environmental hazard is reduced. About 2% of controlled waste destined for disposal in the UK is incinerated. There are two main types of incinerator - thermal and catalytic.

Thermal incinerators may be used to control a wide variety of continuous emission streams containing organic compounds. The technique is typically applied to dilute mixtures of organic compounds in air, with the greatest concentration in air usually being limited by safety considerations to 25% of the *Lower Explosive Limit*. Waste gases may have sufficient energy content to sustain a flame directly, or may require a supplementary fuel. The cost of supplying this fuel is a disincentive to maintain high temperatures (say 800°C) necessary for the destruction of organic compounds (too low a temperature may lead to dioxin production) and possible odours, and lowering the temperature may result in pollution problems, such as odours from partial combustion products. It may be possible to recover some heat from the effluent from the incinerator for preheating the incoming gases.

Catalytic incinerators are similar in design to thermal incinerators, except for the addition of a catalyst to enhance the rate of combustion. As a result of the catalyst, such incinerators may be operated at lower temperatures, so offering significant fuel savings, which may be further enhanced by incorporating heat recovery. The catalytic technique is not as widely applicable as thermal incineration because the catalysts are sensitive to pollutant characteristics and the risk of poisoning.

There are some disadvantages in the use of incinerators:

- High capital cost, maintenance and monitoring costs.
- Not suitable for many difficult waste streams (aqueous, heavy metals etc.).

10.5 - Monitoring

Monitoring is not the same as a control. Monitoring indicates what has happened with emissions, and may be used to indicate whether control measures are effective.

Monitoring techniques include non-instrumental methods such as routine visual checks, site tours, review of complaints from neighbours or reports made by employees. Instrumental monitoring may be *by continuous sampling* or *grab sampling*, otherwise known as spot sampling techniques.

CONTINUOUS AND GRAB SAMPLING AND MEASUREMENT AGAINST SET STANDARDS

Monitoring techniques

Where the consequence of failure of a control would lead to serious environmental damage, continuous sampling is preferable. Emissions to air from an incinerator or to water from a landfill site may require continuous sampling to ensure no unacceptable pollution takes place. Where the consequence of failure is less severe, or the control is simple and robust, grab sampling may be adequate. The minimum monitoring requirements for compliance may be imposed on an organisation by the enforcing authority by means of a licence or consent, and may be need to comply with a British Standard or a Technical Guidance Note.

Sampling techniques

The strategy in collecting samples will include:

Location of sampling point. For example, atmospheric sampling should be where the prevailing winds normally carry emissions from a stack.

Sampling frequency and duration

- *Continuous sampling* could be with a permanently installed sensor, feeding information to a control room.
- *Grab sampling* could be accomplished by a technician on a site tour, taking measurements at key points with an instrument that gives instantaneous readings, or collects samples for later analysis in a laboratory.
- *Frequency of sampling* depends on the risks identified should control of emissions be lost. The usual advantages of producing Time Weighted Averages for monitoring results should be considered.

Type of sampling equipment. There is a wide range of techniques and equipment available, and the choice will depend on the statutory requirements and the cost-benefit of using particular types of equipment. Some examples are:

- *Flame Ionisation Detectors (FID).* Useful for detecting flammable gases.
- *Indicator tubes (stain tubes).* Gas drawn through the tube produces a colour change in crystals, the extent of change being in proportion to the concentration of gas in the atmosphere. Good for grab sampling.
- *Conductivity/pH Heads.* Measures the conductivity and acidity of water effluent. Can be used to give a continuous or spot reading.

Reference standards for monitoring results

Any equipment and methods must be standardised against reference sources to ensure that they read correctly. The EA has introduced a scheme known as MCERTS to assist organisations in meeting satisfactory standards. More information can be found on the EA's site at www.environment-agency.gov.uk.

KEEPING REGULATORY AND LOCAL AUTHORITIES INFORMED OF ENVIRONMENTAL PERFORMANCE

The authorities require evidence of environmental performance from organisations who are working under licences, consents and authorisations.

The *Environmental Protection (Applications, Appeals and Registers) Regulations 1991* as amended, and the *Pollution Prevention and Control Regulations 2000* require information from an organisation to be placed on a public register, including:

- Application documents.
- A copy of an advertisement made in the local press concerning the application for authorisation.
- Any appeals to the application.
- Any convictions.
- Monitoring data.
- Reports from the enforcing agency about the processes.
- Changes to the process or ceasing processes.
- Where relevant, particulars about landfill closure.

European Directives on the openness of information led to the *Environmental Information Regulations 1992*, which require the Government to make available to anyone who asks, information such as registers and reports of environmental interest, unless there are issues related to security, defence and commercial confidentiality in making the information available. A reasonable charge can be made for this service.

10.6 - Legal regimes applicable

CONCEPT OF 'DUTY OF CARE' (ENVIRONMENTAL PROTECTION ACT 1990)

Under Section 34 Part II the EPA 1990, all parties involved in waste handling have a duty to take all reasonable care under all foreseeable circumstances when importing, producing, carrying, treating, keeping or disposing of or, as brokers, have control of such waste.

Those subject to the duty of care must take all reasonable steps to achieve the following goals; to prevent:

- The deposit of controlled waste without a waste management licence or in breach of the licence.
- The treatment, keeping, or disposal of controlled waste except as licensed in or on any land or by means of mobile plant.
- The treatment, keeping, or disposal of controlled waste in a manner likely to cause pollution of the environment or harm to health.
- To prevent the escape of the waste under their control or that of any other person.
- On the transfer of the waste to secure that the transfer is only to authorised persons or to a authorised person for authorised transit (six categories of persons authorised to receive controlled waste are set out under section 34(3) of the EPA).
- On transfer of the waste to secure that there is transferred a written description of the waste as will enable each person to avoid contravention of the EPA and the duty to prevent the escape of waste.

Additionally, documents relating to the waste must be produced and retained.

The *Environmental Protection (Duty of Care) Regulations 1991,* with its Code of Practice, set up a system of transfer notes and record-keeping under Section 34 of the EPA. On transfer of the waste, both the producer and the receiver of the waste must complete and sign a transfer note. Each individual transfer of waste does not necessarily have to have a separate transfer note. A single note may cover multiple consignments of the same type of waste transferred at the same time or over a defined period of time, e.g. regular weekly collections.

Transfer of waste between holders needs a new transfer note at each stage of handover.

CATEGORY OF PERSONS ON WHOM DUTY IS PLACED

The producer of waste has a duty of care until its final disposal, though in practice this only extends to the point at which it loses its identity and is mixed with other waste. The duty does not apply to private householders.

Persons authorised to carry and treat waste include:

- The holder of a Waste Management Licence (under the EPA) or a waste disposal licence under the *Control of Pollution Act (COPA) 1974.*
- Any person registered as a Carrier of Controlled Waste.
- Waste Collection Authorities (Waste Disposal Authorities in Scotland).

Full information may be found in "Waste Management - Duty of Care - A Code of Practice" available from The Stationery Office.

TYPES OF WASTE AND THEIR DISPOSAL

Definition of waste

The Duty of Care Code (TSO) requires waste to be defined from the point of view of the person discarding it. Anything which is discarded must be treated as waste. This definition has led to difficult and contentious judgments in the European Court of Justice (Tombesi 1997, Wallonie 1998). In summary, one man's waste may be another man's valuable raw material, but should still be treated as waste, with the attendant legal obligations!

The following guidelines may be used to make decisions on the status of 'waste' materials:

a. Any substance which constitutes a scrap material or an effluent or other unwanted surplus substance arising from the application of any process.

b. Any substance or article which requires to be disposed of as being broken, worn out, contaminated or otherwise spoiled (excluding explosives).

It also provides a definition of *'controlled waste'* as being household, industrial and commercial waste or any such waste. *'Special waste'* is defined as that waste which is dangerous or difficult to handle, transport or treat, whilst *'hazardous waste'* relates to special waste often transported across national boundaries and derives from the Hazardous Waste Directive.

The Waste Collection Authorities were given responsibility for **collecting waste**, whilst the Waste Regulatory Authorities (WRA) were given responsibility for **licensing, inspection and regulation of waste disposal sites.**

CONTROLLED WASTE

The concept of controlled waste was incorporated into the Environmental Protection Act (EPA) 1990, which makes it an offence to "treat, keep or dispose of controlled waste without a waste management license", or, "in a manner likely to cause pollution of the environment or harm to human health".

Controlled waste is defined in the **Controlled Waste Regulations 1992** as "household, industrial and commercial" waste. N.B. Controlled waste is also known as "Directive Waste" under the **Waste Management Licensing Regulations 1994**; it is under these Regulations where the EPA's sections are implemented.

Most wastes from industry and commerce are controlled wastes, including materials that are destined for recycling. The main exemptions are wastes from agricultural premises, mines and quarries, and radioactive wastes which are regulated under other statutory regimes. Some agriculture and mines and quarry wastes may be treated as controlled waste in the near future.

Controlled waste must not be moved until a 'duty of care' note has been prepared, giving a description of the waste, the quantity being moved, the origin and destination of the waste, and information about the Waste Carriers Licence.

SPECIAL WASTE

Special waste is a controlled waste, but with certain specified hazardous properties, and therefore has its own **Special Waste Regulations 1996 (as amended)**; these regulations define special waste. Producers, carriers and disposers of waste have duties of notification and the provision of information about the waste.

Waste is deemed to be 'special' if it falls within one of some 250 categories listed under the Directive and reproduced in Schedule 2, Part I of the Regulations and has one or more of the 14 hazardous properties listed in Part II. However, because the EC list does not include all the substances previously treated as special waste under the 1980 regulations, waste which is not on the EC list will be special if it possesses one or more of six hazardous properties, subject to specific quantitative thresholds. Medicinal waste products remain as special waste.

Among the hazard categories that determine whether waste is 'Special' are materials which are:

- Explosive.
- Flammable.
- Oxidising.
- Corrosive.
- Irritant.
- Environmentally damaging.

(Note the reflection of the **CHIP Regulations** in this list).

It is forbidden to mix special waste with other waste except in certain special cases.

Special waste cannot be moved from its origin without notifying the EA using approved consignment notes.

Pre-notification (72 hours notice) is required before the waste is removed from the premises at which it is being held. The consignment note comprises five copies.

The five copies are of different colours:

- White - pre-notification copy.
- Yellow - deposit copy.
- Pink - consignor's copy.
- Orange - carrier's copy.
- Green - consignee's copy.

Each copy has the following parts to be completed:-

- Part A - consignment details - consignor completes.
- Part B - description of waste - consignor completes.
- Part C - carrier's certificate - "I collected............".
- Part D - consignor's certificate - "I certify information given in B and C is correct...........".
- Part E - consignee's certificate - "I received this waste on..........".

There is an automatic entitlement to the use of the repeat consignment procedure for a fixed period of 12 months. Only the first consignment has to be pre-notified.

Also, the standard consignment note system has been amended for carriers' rounds. This allows that all the special waste removed from a number of premises by a carrier's round, or a succession of rounds within a 12 month period, can be covered by a simplified consignment note system.

Fees are payable to the EA for consignments. Registers of consignment notes have to be kept by all parties.

See also - Element C11 - Relevant Statutory Provisions - The Hazardous Waste (England) Regulations 2005 and the introduction of the Waste Acceptance Criteria - due to come into force in July 2005.

10.7 - Emergency procedures

NEED FOR EMERGENCY RESPONSE MEASURES IN THE EVENT OF AN UNCONTROLLED RELEASE

An organisation has a duty to prepare for emergencies which may cause harm, exposure to legal sanctions, and threaten its financial security.

Uncontrolled releases of pollutants may be caused by:

a. Internal factors such as:

- Failure of control measures.
- Failure of containment measures.

- Fire.
- Runaway chemical reactions.

b. External factors such as:

- Adverse weather.
- Natural Disasters - earthquakes etc.
- Floods.

- Sabotage.
- Road Accidents.
-

Risk assessments should identify significant weaknesses and controls and procedures should be put in place to deal with any foreseeable events.

The **EPA** and **Pollution Prevention and Control Regulations 2000** both include the obligation to prepare for emergencies which may have the potential for environmental damage. The **Civil Contingencies Act 2004** goes further and provides a definition of Major Accidents To The Environment (MATTEs), which may be summarised as follows:

An event or situation which threatens serious damage to the environment of a place in the United Kingdom if it threatens contamination of land, water or air, or disrupts or destroys plant or animal life.

CONTROL OF MAJOR ACCIDENT HAZARDS REGULATIONS 1999 (COMAH)

The main aim of the COMAH Regulations is to prevent and mitigate the effects of major accidents involving dangerous substances, such as liquefied petroleum gas (LPG), chlorine, explosives and toxic chemicals such as arsenic pentoxide which can cause serious damage/harm to people and/or the environment. One of the effects of the COMAH Regulations is to treat risks to the environment as seriously as those to people.

The COMAH Regulations are enforced by a **competent authority (CA)** consisting of the HSE and respective Environment Agencies (Scotland & England and Wales).

The regulations place duties on the CA to inspect activities subject to COMAH and prohibit the operation of an establishment if there is evidence that measures taken for prevention and mitigation of major accidents are seriously deficient. It also has to examine safety reports and inform operators about the conclusions of its examinations within a reasonable time period. The CA charges for the work based on the recovery of the full costs of the time spent in carrying out COMAH-related activities for a particular establishment.

The Regulations apply mainly to the chemical industry, but also to some storage activities, explosives and nuclear sites and other industries, where threshold quantities of dangerous substances identified in the regulations are kept or used.

COMAH applies to sites which meet the criteria detailed in Regulation 3 and Schedule 1. These detail which substances and the quantities involved that the Regulations apply to. There are two thresholds (tiers) for application. Operators of sites that hold large quantities of dangerous substances ('top tier' sites) are subject to more onerous requirements than those of 'lower tier' sites.

Examples:

Substance	Lower Tier Sites	Top Tier Sites
	tonnes	*tonnes*
Liquefied extremely flammable gases (including LPG) and natural gas (whether liquefied or not)	50	200
Automotive petrol or other petroleum spirits	5,000	50,000
Arsenic pentoxide, arsenic (V) and/or salts	1	2
Chlorine	10	25

Figure C10-9: Examples of dangerous substances.   *Source: ACT.*

LOWER-TIER SITES

Key duties for operators of lower-tier sites are:

- Notify basic details to the CA.
- Take all measures necessary to prevent major accidents and limit their consequences to people and the environment.
- Prepare a major accident prevention policy.

Notify basic details to the CA

Operators who come into scope of the regulations after 1 April 1999 must submit a notification before operation begins (operation begins when the quantity of dangerous substance exceeds one of the thresholds and includes commissioning). Operators must notify certain basic details, which are given in Schedule 3 to the Regulations, to the CA. The main points include:

- Name and address of operator.
- Address of establishment.
- Name or position of person in charge.

- Details of dangerous substances on site.
- Site activities.
- Environmental details.

Operators of existing establishments who had previously submitted COMAH safety reports do not need to notify as that report contains all the necessary information.

Take all measures necessary to prevent major accidents and limit their consequences to people and the environment

This is the general duty on all operators which underpins the regulations. It is a high standard which applies to all establishments within scope. By requiring measures both for prevention and mitigation there is a recognition that all risks cannot be completely eliminated. This in turn implies that proportionality must remain a key element in the enforcement policy of the HSE and the Agencies. Thus, the phrase *'all measures necessary'* will be interpreted to include this principle and a judgement will be made about the measures in place. Where hazards are high then high standards will be required to ensure risks are acceptably low, in line with the HSE's and Agencies' policy that enforcement should be proportionate.

Prevention should be based on the principle of reducing risk to a level as low as is reasonably practicable (ALARP) for human risks and using the best available technology not entailing excessive cost (BATNEEC) for environmental risks. The ideal should always be, wherever possible, to avoid a hazard altogether.

Prepare a major accident prevention policy

Regulation 5 requires lower-tier operators to prepare a document setting out their policy for preventing major accidents (a major accident prevention policy or MAPP). Operators who come into scope of the regulations after 1 April 1999 must prepare their MAPP before operation begins. Operators of existing establishments should prepare one as soon as possible after 1st April 1999.

The MAPP will usually be a short and simple document setting down what is to be achieved but it should also include a summary and further references to the safety management system that will be used to put the policy into action. The detail will be contained in other documentation relating to the establishment e.g. plant operating procedures, training records, job descriptions, audit reports, to which the MAPP can refer.

The MAPP also has to address issues relating to the safety management system. The details are given in Schedule 2 of the regulations but the key areas are:

- Organisation and personnel.
- Identification and evaluation of major hazards.
- Operational control.
- Planning for emergencies.
- Monitoring, audit and review.

TOP-TIER OPERATORS

Top-tier operators have to comply with the above except that they do not have to prepare a separate major accident prevention policy document - their safety reports *(see below)* have to include the information that lower-tier operators provide in their MAPPs. They also have the following additional duties:

- The preparation of a safety report.
- The updating of the safety report.
- Prepare and test an on-site emergency plan.
- The supply of information to the local authorities.
- The provision of information to the public.

Prepare a safety report

A safety report is a document prepared by the site operator and provides information to demonstrate to the CA that all measures necessary for the prevention and mitigation of major accidents have been taken. The purposes and contents of a safety report are set out in Schedule 4 to the regulations.

The safety report must include:

- A policy on how to prevent and mitigate major accidents.
- A management system for implementing that policy.
- An effective method for identifying any major accidents that might occur.
- Measures (such as safe plant and safe operating procedures) to prevent and mitigate major accidents.
- Information on the safety precautions built into the plant and equipment when it was designed and constructed.
- Details of measures (such as fire-fighting, relief systems and filters) to limit the consequences of any major accident that might occur.
- Information about the emergency plan for the site, which is also used by the local authority in drawing up an off-site emergency plan.

Safety reports will be available to the public via the competent authority registers, subject to safeguards for national security, commercial and personal confidentiality.

Update the safety report every five years or after significant changes or new knowledge about safety matters

The safety report needs to be kept up to date. If there are any modifications to the plant or the way it is operated or if new facts or information become available, the safety report must be reviewed and, if necessary, revised at the time. It must be reviewed after five years even if there have not been any changes.

Prepare and test an on-site emergency plan

Top-tier operators must prepare an emergency plan to deal with the on-site consequences of a major accident.

Supply information to local authorities for off-site emergency planning purposes

Local authorities play a key role by preparing, reviewing, revising and testing off-site emergency plans for dealing with the off-site consequences of major accidents at top-tier sites. In order to fulfil this role they need information from operators. Details can be found in Schedule 5 to the regulations. Operators will need to hold discussions with their local authorities to determine their exact needs.

The information for the local authority must be supplied no later than the date the on-site emergency plan for the site has to be completed.

Provide certain information to the public about their activities

People who could be affected by an accident at a COMAH establishment must be given information without having to request it. The details are given in Schedule 6 of the regulations but include details of the dangerous substances, the possible major accidents and their consequences and what to do in the event of an accident.

As previously mentioned, safety reports will be available to the public via public registers.

The information for people who could be affected by a major accident at the establishment must be supplied 'within a reasonable period of time after the off-site emergency plan has been prepared for the establishment'. Six months would be the normal time.

Safety reports will be put on the public register shortly after receipt by the CA, unless there is a request for certain information to be withheld (for national security, commercial and personal confidentiality reasons), as provided for in the regulations.

Relevant Statutory Provisions

Content

Building Regulations 2000, Approved Document B (consolidated with 2000 and 2002 amendments)

Law considered in context / more depth in Element C3.

Outline of key points

Approved Document B is a Fire Safety document that provides practical guidance on meeting the requirements of Schedule 1 to and Regulation 7 of the Building Regulations 2000 for England and Wales. The areas covered are as follows:

- B1 Means of warning and escape.
- B2 Internal fire spread (linings).
- B3 Internal fire spread (structure).
- B4 External fire spread.
- B5 Access and facilities for the Fire Service.

The current Approved Document B provides a consolidation of the guidance previously issued in the original 2000 edition (and the subsequent amendments of it which were issued in 2000 and 2002) and is one of several Approved Documents issued by the Secretary of State that are intended to provide guidance for some of the more common building situations. However, there may well be alternative ways of achieving compliance with the requirements. Thus there is no obligation to adopt any particular solution contained in an Approved Document if you prefer to meet the relevant requirement in some other way.

B1 MEANS OF WARNING AND ESCAPE

Guidance.

Section 1:   Fire alarm and fire detection systems.

Section 2:   Dwelling houses.

Section 3:   Flats and maisonettes.

Section 4:   Design for horizontal escape – buildings other than dwellings.

Section 5:   Design for vertical escape – buildings other than dwellings.

Section 6:   General provisions common to buildings other than dwelling houses.

B2 INTERNAL FIRE SPREAD (LININGS)

Guidance.

Section 7:   Wall and ceiling linings.

B3 INTERNAL FIRE SPREAD (STRUCTURE)

Guidance.

Section 8:   Loadbearing elements of structure.

Section 9:   Compartmentation.

Section 10:   Concealed spaces (cavities).

Section 11:   Protection of openings and fire stopping.

Section 12:   Special provisions for car parks and shopping complexes.

B4 EXTERNAL FIRE SPREAD

Guidance.

Section 14:   Space separation.

Section 15:   Roof coverings.

B5 ACCESS AND FACILITIES FOR THE FIRE SERVICE

Guidance.

Section 16:   Fire Mains.

Section 17:   Vehicle access.

Section 18:   Access to buildings for firefighting personnel.

Section 19:   Venting of heat and smoke from basements.

APPENDICES

Appendix A: Performance of materials and structures.

Appendix B: Fire doors.

Appendix C: Methods of measurement.

Appendix D: Purpose groups.

Appendix E: Definitions.

Appendix F: Fire behaviour of insulating core panels used for internal structures.

Appendix G: Standards referred to/other publications referred to.

Main changes in the 2000 edition

The main changes are:

GENERAL INTRODUCTION

a. Hospitals: HTM 81 can be used instead of the Approved Document.

B1

b. *Fire alarms:*

    i. the Requirement has been expanded to include fire alarm and fire detection systems;

    ii. the guidance forms a new Section 1 and has been extended to loft conversions and buildings other than dwellings.

c. *Alternative approaches:* this guidance has been moved from Section 3 to the "Introduction" and expanded.

d. *Door width:* the definition has been modified to align with that given in Approved Document M and corresponding reductions made to Table 5 "Widths of escape routes and exits".

e. *Means of escape:*

    i. Dwellings – storeys not more than 4.5m above ground level need to be provided with emergency egress windows;

    ii. Single escape routes and exits – the limit of 50 persons has been increased to 60;

    iii. Alternative escape routes – the 45° rule has been changed;

    iv. Minimum number of escape routes – Table 4 has been simplified;

    v. Mixed use buildings – the guidance has been modified;

    vi. Door fastenings – more guidance is given;

    vii. Escape lighting – changes have been made in Table 9 regarding toilet accommodation;

    viii. Storeys divided into different uses – guidance has been added to deal with storeys which are also used for the consumption of food and/or drink by customers;

    ix. Shop store rooms – guidance is given on when these need to be enclosed in fire-resisting construction.

B2

f. *Special applications:* guidance is given on the use of air supported structures, structures covered with flexible membranes and PTFE based materials.

B3

g. *Places of special fire hazard:* these need to be enclosed in fire-resisting construction.

h. *Compartments:* maximum compartment dimensions have been extended to single storey Schools and to the Shop/Commercial purpose group.

B4

i. *Rooflights:* separate Tables are given for Class 3 and TP(a)/(b) plastics rooflights and the provisions relating to Class 3 rooflights on industrial buildings has been modified.

B5

j. *Vehicle access:*

    i. specific guidance is now included for single family houses and for blocks of flats and maisonettes;

    ii. the 9m height in Table 20 has been increased to 11m.

k. *Personnel access:*

    i. modifications have been made to the heights at which firefighting shafts are needed, with corresponding reductions to the 20m height in B1 (access lobbies & corridors), B3 (Table 12), B4 Diagram 40) and Appendix A (Tables A2 & A3);

    ii. guidance is given regarding firefighting shafts in blocks of flats and maisonettes.

Appendix A

l. *Uninsulated glazed elements:* table A4 has been modified and extended.

m. *Notional designations of roof coverings:* bitumen felt pitched roof coverings have been deleted from table A5.

Appendix B

n. *Compartment walls:* limits are now specified on the use of uninsulated doors.

Appendix E

o. *Fire separating element:* this new definition has been added to support Sections 9 to 11 in B3.

Appendix F

p. This new Appendix gives guidance on *insulating core panels*.

Carriage of Dangerous Goods and Use of Transportable Pressure Equipment Regulations 2004

Law considered in context / more depth in Elements C4 and C5.

Arrangement of Regulations

PART 1 - INTRODUCTORY PROVISIONS

1) Citation and commencement.

2) Interpretation.

3) Application.

4) Application to international carriage.

5) Application to tanks, pressure receptacles, battery-vehicles, battery-wagons, MEGCs, UN-certified MEGCs and transportable pressure equipment.

6) Application to armed forces.

7) Exemptions.

8) Competent authority.

PART 2 - REQUIREMENTS OF ADR AND RID

9) Training.

10) Safety obligations.

11) Class 7 goods for carriage by rail.

12) Safety advisers.

13) Reports on accidents or incidents.

14) Emergency plans for marshalling yards.

15) Classification of goods.

16) Prohibition from carriage.

17) Dangerous goods list and special provisions.

18) Use of packagings.

19) Use of tanks, battery-vehicles, battery-wagons, MEGCs and UN-certified MEGCs.

20) Consignment.

21) Construction and testing of packagings and packages.

22) Construction and testing of tanks, MEGCs and UN-certified MEGCs.

23) Carriage, loading, unloading and handling.

24) Vehicle crews, equipment, operation and documentation.

25) Construction and approval of vehicles.

PART 3 - COMPETENT AUTHORITY FUNCTIONS

26) Interpretation of Part 3 and Schedule 3.

27) Grant of approvals by the GB competent authority.

28) Grant of unilateral and multilateral approvals by the GB competent authority in relation to class 7 goods for carriage by rail.

29) Appointment of persons by the GB competent authority.

30) Recognition of approvals, tests, methods, standards and procedures etc. by the GB competent authority.

31) Imposing of requirements by the GB competent authority.

32) Issuing of safety adviser vocational training certificates by the GB competent authority.

33) Issuing of driver training certificates by the GB competent authority.

34) Notification under sub-section 1.8.2.2 of ADR or of RID.

35) Miscellaneous functions of the GB competent authority.

36) Exemption certificates, temporary and ad hoc exemptions.

PART 4 - TRANSPORTABLE PRESSURE EQUIPMENT

37) Interpretation of Part 4.

38) Placing on the market and use at work of transportable pressure equipment.

39) Transportable pressure equipment placed on the market and used at work exclusively in Great Britain.

40) Reassessment of conformity.

41) Periodic inspection and repeated use.

42) Notified bodies.

43) Approved bodies.

44) Appointment of notified bodies and approved bodies by the competent authority.

45) Conformity marking.

PART 5 - ADDITIONAL REQUIREMENTS TO ADR AND RID

46) Attendant for carriage of class 1 goods by road.

47) Duration of carriage and delivery of class 1 goods by road.

48) Miscellaneous security requirements for carriage of class 1 goods by road.

49) Miscellaneous security requirements for carriage of class 1 goods by rail.

50) Security requirement for carriage of class 1 goods by road or rail and class 7 goods by rail.

51) Carriage of class 1 goods in vehicles used to carry passengers for hire or reward.

52) Carriage of class 1 goods by road in motor vehicles.

53) Marshalling and formation of trains.

54) Keeping of information by carriers.

55) Placards, marks and plate markings for carriage within Great Britain.

PART 6 - MISCELLANEOUS

56) Fees for applications relating to pressure receptacles and tanks.

57) Transitional defence.

58) Defence and enforcement.

59) Amendments to the Health and Safety (Fees) Regulations 2004.

60) Amendments to Chemicals (Hazard Information and Packaging for Supply) Regulations 2002.

61) Amendments to the Classification and Labelling of Explosives Regulations 1983.

62) Consequential amendments.

63) Revocations and savings.

SCHEDULES

Schedule 1   Old tanks.

Schedule 2   Old pressure receptacles.

Schedule 3   Competent authority functions.

Schedule 4   Conformity assessment procedure.

Schedule 5   Modules to be followed for conformity assessment.

Schedule 6   Conformity reassessment procedures.

Schedule 7   Periodic inspection procedures.

Schedule 8   Conformity marking.

Schedule 9   Placards, marks and plate markings for carriage within Great Britain.

Schedule 10   Amendments to the Health and Safety (Fees) Regulations 2004.

Schedule 11   Amendments to the Chemicals (Hazard Information and Packaging for Supply) Regulations 2002.

Schedule 12   Amendments to the Classification and Labelling of Explosives Regulations 1983.

Schedule 13   Consequential amendments.

Schedule 14   Revocations.

Outline of key points

These Regulations deal with the carriage of dangerous goods by road, rail and inland waterway. The Competent Authority (CA) is the Secretary of State, the Secretary of State for Defence and HSE.

Any person involved in the carriage of dangerous goods shall ensure that he and his employees, especially the drivers, receive appropriate training. He must comply with, as they relate to matters within his control, the safety measures stated. He must appoint a safety advisor and provide copies of accidents and annual reports to the CA. Emergency plans must be prepared for marshalling yards when goods are carried by rail.

Goods carried by road or rail must be classified. A carrier must not accept goods for carriage that are prohibited from being carried. Packaging must be in accordance with the provisions and must be marked and labelled and the packaging tested and approved. Drivers must have a certificate issued by the CA. Vehicles that carry dangerous goods must be approved.

The CA may grant approvals, and may appoint persons to carry out the requirements, known as Appointed Persons. The CA notifies the relevant CA in other member states and receives notification from them.

Chemicals (Hazard Information and Packaging for Supply) Regulations (CHIP 3) 2002

Law considered in context / more depth in Element C4.

Arrangement of Regulations

1) Citation and commencement.

2) Interpretation.

3) Application of these Regulations.

4) Meaning of the approved supply list.

5) Classification of substances and preparations dangerous for supply.

6) Safety data sheets for substances and preparations dangerous for supply.

7) Advertisements for substances dangerous for supply.

8) Packaging of substances and preparations dangerous for supply.

9) Labelling of substances and preparations dangerous for supply.

10) Particular labelling requirements for certain preparations.

11) Methods of marking or labelling packages.

12) Child resistant fastenings and tactile warning devices.

13) Retention of classification data for substances and preparations dangerous for supply.

14) Notification of the constituents of certain preparations dangerous for supply to the poisons advisory centre.

15) Exemption certificates.

16) Enforcement, civil liability and defence.

17) Transitional provisions.

18) Extension outside Great Britain.

19) Revocations and modifications.

Schedule 1	Classification of substances and preparations dangerous for supply.
Schedule 2	Indications of danger and symbols for substances and preparations dangerous for supply.
Schedule 3	Classification provisions for preparations dangerous for supply.
Schedule 4	Classification provisions for preparations intended to be used as pesticides.
Schedule 5	Headings under which particulars are to be provided in safety data sheets.
Schedule 6	Particulars to be shown on labels for substances and preparations dangerous for supply and certain other preparations.
Schedule 7	British and International Standards relating to child resistant fastenings and tactile warning devices.
Schedule 8	Modifications to certain enactments relating to the flashpoint of flammable liquids.

The Chemicals (Hazard Information and Packaging for Supply) Regulations (CHIP 3) 2002 apply to those who supply dangerous chemicals. They are based on European Directives, which apply to all EU and European Economic Area (EEA) Countries. The Directives are constantly reviewed and changed when necessary. When changes do occur to the Directives, CHIP is changed as well (about once a year). CHIP may be changed by amending Regulations or if there are major changes, the principal Regulations are revised.

The Regulations are designed to protect people's health and the environment by:

■ Identification of the hazardous properties of materials (classification).

■ Provision of health and safety information to users (safety data sheet and label).

■ Packaging of materials safely.

CHIP introduces a new scheme to classify products based upon a calculation method.

Outline of key points

REGULATION 6 (1)

*'The supplier of a substance or preparation dangerous for supply **shall** provide the recipient of that substance or preparation with a safety data sheet containing information under the headings specified in Schedule 5 to enable the recipient of that substance or preparation to take the necessary measures relating to the protection of health and safety at work and relating to the protection of the environment and the safety data sheet shall clearly show its date of first publication or latest revision as the case may be.'*

The test of adequacy of the information provided in a safety data sheet is whether the information enables the recipient to take the necessary measures relating to the protection of health and safety at work and relating to the protection of the environment.

This does not mean that the safety data sheet will take the place of a risk assessment which would require specific detail of the circumstances in which the chemical is to be used.

GUIDANCE ON THE CONTENTS OF SAFETY DATA SHEETS

The headings shown here are those specified in Schedule 5 of C(HIP) 2. However, information given here is indicative of the issues to be addressed by the person compiling the safety data sheet and do not impose an absolute requirement for action or controls.

Identification of the substance/preparation and the company
- Name of the substance.
- Name, address and telephone number (including emergency number) of supplier.

Composition/information on ingredients
- Sufficient information to allow the recipient to identify readily the associated risks.

Hazards identification
- Important hazards to man and the environment.
- Adverse health effects and symptoms.

First-aid measures
- Whether immediate attention is required.
- Symptoms and effects including delayed effects.
- Specific information according to routes of entry.
- Whether professional advice is advisable.

Fire fighting measures
- Suitable extinguishing media.
- Extinguishing media that must not be used.
- Hazards that may arise from combustion e.g., gases, fumes etc.
- Special protective equipment for fire fighters.

Accidental release measures
- Personal precautions such as removal of ignition sources, provision of ventilation, avoid eye/skin contact etc.
- Environmental precautions such as keep away from drains, need to alert neighbours etc.
- Methods for cleaning up e.g. absorbent materials. Also, "Never use…."

Handling and storage
- Advice on technical measures such as local and general ventilation.
- Measures to prevent aerosol, dust, fire etc.
- Design requirements for specialised storage rooms.
- Incompatible materials.
- Special requirements for packaging/containers.

Exposure controls/personal protection
- Engineering measures taken in preference to personal protective equipment (PPE) 1992 (and as amended).
- Where PPE is required, type of equipment necessary e.g. type of gloves, goggles, barrier cream etc.

Physical and chemical properties
- Appearance, e.g. solid, liquid, powder, etc.
- Odour (if perceptible).
- Boiling point, flash point, explosive properties, solubility etc.

Stability and reactivity
- Conditions to avoid such as temperature, pressure, light, etc.
- Materials to avoid such as water, acids, alkalis, etc.
- Hazardous by-products given off on decomposition.

Toxicological information
- Toxicological effects if the substance comes into contact with a person.
- Carcinogenic, mutagenic, toxic for reproduction etc.
- Acute and chronic effects.

Ecological information
- Effects, behaviour and environmental fate that can reasonably be foreseen.
- Short and long term effects on the environment.

Disposal considerations
- Appropriate methods of disposal e.g. land-fill, incineration etc.

Transport information
- Special precautions in connection with transport or carriage.
- Additional information as detailed in the Carriage of Dangerous Goods by Road Regs (CPL) 1994 may also be given.

Regulatory information
- Health and safety information on the label as required by C(HIP) 2.
- Reference might also be made to Health and Safety at Work etc Act (HASAWA) 1974 and Control of Substances Hazardous to Health Regulations (COSHH) 2002.

Other Information

■   Training advice.
■   Recommended uses and restrictions.
■   Sources of key data used to compile the data sheet.

RISK PHRASES AND SAFETY PHRASES

More useful information to help ensure the safe use of dangerous substances comes in the form of risk phrases and safety phrases. These are often displayed either on the container label or in the safety data sheet. There are currently 48 risk phrases and 53 safety phrases. Some examples are given below and detailed information can be found in the ACOP to CHIP 3.

Risk Phrase		Safety Phrase	
R3	Risk of explosion by shock, friction, fire or other sources of ignition.	S2	Keep out of reach of children.
R20	Harmful by inhalation.	S20	When using do not eat or drink.
R30	Can become highly flammable in use.	S25	Avoid contact with eyes.
R45	May cause cancer.	S36	Wear suitable protective clothing.
R47	May cause birth defects.	S41	In case of fire and/or explosion do not breathe fumes.

Absence of hazard symbols or risk and safety advice does not mean the item is harmless.

Confined Spaces Regulations (CSR) 1997

Law considered in context / more depth in Element C1.

Arrangement of Regulations

1)   Citation, commencement and interpretation.
2)   Disapplication of Regulations.
3)   Duties.
4)   Work in confined spaces.
5)   Emergency arrangements.
6)   Exemption certificates.
7)   Defence in proceedings.
8)   Extension outside Great Britain.
9)   Repeal and revocations.

Outline of key points

The Confined Spaces Regulations (CSR) 1997 repeal and replace earlier provisions contained in s.30 of the Factories Act 1961. (Note: Factories Act 1961 has been repealed).

A failure to appreciate the dangers associated with confined spaces has led not only to the deaths of many workers, but also to the demise of some of those who have attempted to rescue them. A confined space is not only a space which is small and difficult to enter, exit or work in; it can also be a large space, but with limited/restricted access. It can also be a space which is badly ventilated e.g. a tank or a large tunnel. The Confined Spaces Regulations (CSR) 1997, define a confined space as any place, including any chamber, tank, vat, silo, pit, pipe, sewer, flue, well, or other similar space, in which, by virtue of its enclosed nature, there is a foreseeable risk of a 'specified occurrence'.

Construction (Design and Management) Regulations (CDM) 1994

Law considered in context / more depth in Element C9.

Arrangement of Regulations

1)   Citation and commencement.
2)   Interpretation.
3)   Application of regulations.
4)   Clients and agents of clients.
5)   Requirements on developer.
6)   Appointments of planning supervisor and principal contractor.
7)   Notification of project.
8)   Competence of planning supervisor, designers and contractors.
9)   Provision for health and safety.
10)   Start of construction phase.

11)   Client to ensure information is available.

12)   Client to ensure health and safety file is available for inspection.

13)   Requirements on designer.

14)   Requirements on planning supervisor.

15)   Requirements relating to the health and safety plan.

16)   Requirements on and powers of principal contractor.

17)   Information and training.

18)   Advice from, and views of, persons at work.

19)   Requirements and prohibitions on contractors.

20)   Extension outside Great Britain.

21)   Exclusion of civil liability.

22)   Enforcement.

23)   Transitional provisions.

24)   Repeals, revocations and modifications.

Schedule 1   Particulars to be notified to the Executive.

Schedule 2   Transitional provisions.

Outline of key points

The Construction (Design & Management) Regulations (CDM) 1994 came into force on 31 March 1995, with the aim of raising standards of construction site health and safety.

METHOD

The method the CDM Regulations take are to:

1.   Plan health and safety into construction at the design stage by improving management and co-ordination of health and safety issues.

2.   Create two instruments for managing and co-ordinating health and safety:

     a.   The Health and Safety Plan

         ■   Pre tender stage and,
         ■   Construction Phase

     b.   The Structure Health and Safety File.

3.   Allocate adequate time and resources so that duties imposed by these and other health and safety legislation can be met.

4.   Involve all participants in the achievement of safe working environments to minimise risks during construction work.

APPLICATION OF CDM

The Regulations do not apply to projects where fewer than five people at any one time are expected to carry out construction work and where the local authority is the enforcing authority. Only the HSE enforce CDM, where the Local Authority is the enforcing authority, they hand over to the HSE as soon as CDM applies.

The Regulations apply to projects where five or more people at any one time are carrying out construction and where demolition or dismantling of a structure is taking place regardless of time or numbers.

Projects with a construction phase longer than 30 days or involving more than 500 person days of construction work, are also notifiable to the Health and Safety Executive (HSE). Notification must be in writing and can be made using the form F10(rev).

Where there are fewer than five people CDM will still apply if the project is notifiable, e.g. a construction phase lasting 40 days with a workplace of 4.

CIVIL LIABILITY

The right to civil action is excluded under CDM except for:

■   The Client's duty to ensure that a health and safety plan is prepared before construction starts [Regulation 10].

■   The Principal Contractor's duty to take reasonable steps to control access to site [Regulation 16(1)(c)].

RESOURCES AND COMPETENCE

The Client must be reasonably satisfied as to the competence and resources of the Planning Supervisor and Principal Contractor. In this context competency and resources relate to dealing with risks to health and safety. Similar duties are imposed on anyone appointing designers or contractors such as:

■   Designers appointing other designers to assist in design work.

■   The Principal Contractor appointing contractors.

REQUIREMENTS ON DEVELOPERS

When commercial developers sell domestic premises before the project is complete (e.g. 30 houses on an estate of 100 houses are released for occupation whilst work on the remainder continues) then the developer must comply with the following:

■   Appointment of planning supervisor and principal contractor.

■   Ensure the competence of the planning supervisor, designers and contractors.

■   Be reasonably satisfied that the planning supervisor, designers and contractors has allocated or will allocate adequate resources to enable them to comply with their functions/duties etc.

- Ensure the construction phase does not start unless a construction phase health and safety plan has been prepared.
- Ensure information is available to the planning supervisor.
- Ensure the structure health and safety file is available for inspection and if their entire interest in the property has been disposed of, the person acquiring the property is aware of the nature and purpose of the file.

KEY PARTIES

A number of key parties identified in the regulations have specific duties:

Client:

a. Prompt (as soon as practicable) appointment of competent Planning Supervisor and Principal Contractor.

b. Ensure adequate provision of resources and time to achieve a safe working environment.

c. Preparation of the pre-tender health and safety plan.

d. Make reasonable site enquiries.

e. Make relevant health and safety information available.

f. Keep health and safety file available for inspection.

The Client may appoint an agent to undertake his duties under CDM provided that he is reasonably satisfied that the agent is competent and that the HSE are notified in writing of the appointment.

Designer:

a. Ensure that structures are designed to avoid risks to health and safety while they are being built and maintained.

b. Ensure where it is not possible to avoid risks that they are minimised.

c. Provide adequate information about materials used in the design that could affect the health and safety of persons carrying out construction work.

d. To co-operate with the planning supervisor and other designers.

Planning Supervisor:

a. Ensure that a health and safety plan for the pre-tender stage is prepared.

b. Ensure that designers include among the design considerations, adequate regard to health and safety.

c. Ensure co-operation between different designers.

d. Be in a position to give advice to clients and contractors.

e. Ensure that a health and safety file is prepared.

f. Ensure that a health and safety file is delivered to the client.

Principal Contractor:

a. Take account of health and safety issues when preparing tenders.

b. Develop the construction phase health and safety plan.

c. Ensure co-operation between all contractors to ensure they comply with health and safety legislation.

d. Take reasonable steps to ensure only authorised persons are allowed on site.

e. Provide information to the Planning Supervisor for inclusion in the health and safety file.

f. Enable employed persons to discuss health and safety issues.

g. Arrange for the co-ordinating the views of employed persons where this is important for health and safety.

Contractors:

a. Must co-operate with the Principal Contractor.

b. Provide relevant information to the Principal Contractor on the health and safety risks created by their works and how they will be controlled.

c. Comply with directions given by the Principal Contractor and any rules in the Health and safety Plan.

d. Provide the Principal Contractor with any Reporting of Injuries, Disease and Dangerous Occurrences Regulations (RIDDOR) reports.

INSTRUMENTS

The Pre-tender Health and Safety Plan

The contents of the pre-tender plan will depend on the nature of the project, however, the following areas should be considered:

- Description of project.
- Client's considerations and management requirements.
- Environmental restrictions and existing on-site risks.
- Significant design and construction hazards.
- The health and safety file.

THE CONSTRUCTION PHASE HEALTH AND SAFETY PLAN

The plan is developed by the principal contractor and is the foundation on which the health and safety management of the construction work is based. The contents of the pre-tender stage health and safety plan will depend on the nature of the project itself. However, the following areas should be considered.

a.   The management structure and responsibilities of the various members of the project team, whether based at site or elsewhere.

b.   The health and safety standards to which the project will be carried out. These may be set in terms of statutory requirements or high standards that the client may require in particular circumstances.

c.   Means for informing contractors about risks to their health and safety arising from the environment in which the project is to be carried out and the construction work itself.

d.   All contractors, the self employed and designers to be appointed by the principal contractor are properly selected (i.e. they are competent and will make adequate provision for health and safety).

e.   Means for communicating and passing information between the project team (including the client and any client's representatives) the designers, the planning supervisor, the principal contractor, other contractors, workers on site and others whose health and safety may be affected.

f.   Arrangements for the identification and effective management of activities with risks to health and safety, by carrying out risk assessments, incorporating those prepared by other contractors, and also safety method statements which result. These activities may be specific to a particular trade or to site-wide issues.

g.   Emergency arrangements for dealing with and minimising the effects of injuries, fire and other dangerous occurrences.

h.   Arrangements for passing information to the principal contractor about accidents, ill health and dangerous occurrences that require to be notified to the Health and Safety Executive (HSE) under RIDDOR.

i.   Arrangements for the provision and maintenance of welfare facilities.

j.   Arrangements to ensure the principal contractor checking that people on site have been provided with health and safety information and safety training.

k.   Arrangements that have been made for consulting and co-ordinating the views of workers or their representatives.

l.   Arrangements for making site rules and for bringing them to the attention of those affected.

m.   Arrangements for passing on information to the planning supervisor for the preparation of the health and safety file.

n.   Arrangements should be set out for the monitoring systems to achieve compliance with legal requirements; and the health and safety rules developed by the principal contractor.

THE HEALTH AND SAFETY FILE

The health and safety file should include information about all the following topics, where this may be relevant to the health and safety of any future construction work. The level of detail should be proportionate to the risks likely to be involved in such work.

1.   A brief description of the work to be carried out.

2.   Residual hazards and how they have been dealt with (e.g. surveys or other information concerning asbestos, contaminated land, water bearing strata, buried services).

3.   Key structural principles incorporated in the design of the structure (e.g. bracing, sources of substantial stored energy – including pre- or post- tensioned members) and safe working loads for floors and roofs, particularly where these may preclude placing scaffolding or heavy machinery there.

4.   Any hazards associated with the materials used (e.g. hazardous substances, lead paint, special coatings which should not be burnt off).

5.   Information regarding the removal or dismantling of installed plant and equipment (e.g. lifting arrangements).

6.   The nature, location and markings of significant services, including fire-fighting services.

7.   Information and as-built drawings of the structure, its plant and equipment (e.g. the means of safe access to and from service voids, fire doors and compartmentation).

Construction (Head Protection) Regulations (CHPR) 1989

Law considered in context / more depth in Element C9.

Arrangement of Regulations

1)   Citation, commencement and interpretation.

2)   Application of these Regulations.

3)   Provision, maintenance and replacement of suitable head protection.

4)   Ensuring suitable head protection is worn.

5)   Rules and directions.

6)   Wearing of suitable head protection.

7)   Reporting the loss of, or defect in, suitable head protection.

8)   Extension outside Great Britain.

9)   Exemption certificates.

Outline of key points

ENSURING SUITABLE HEAD PROTECTION IS WORN

Reg. 4(1)   Every employer shall ensure so far as is reasonably practicable that each of his employees who is at work on operations or works to which these Regulations apply wears suitable head protection, unless there is no foreseeable risk to injury to his head other than by his falling.

4(2)   Every employer, self-employed person or employee who has control over any other person who is at work on operations or works to which these Regulations apply shall ensure so far as is reasonably practicable that each such other person wears suitable head protection, unless there is no foreseeable risk of injury to that other person's head other than by his falling.

RULES AND DIRECTIONS

Reg.5(1)   The person for the time being having control of a site where operations or works to which these Regulations apply are being carried out may, so far as is necessary to comply with regulation 4 of these Regulations, make rules regulating the wearing of suitable head protection on that site by persons at work on those operations or works.

5(2)   Rules made in accordance with paragraph (1) of this regulation shall be in writing and shall be brought to the notice of persons who may be affected by them.

5(3)   An employer may, so far as is necessary to comply with regulation 4(1) of these Regulations, give directions requiring his employees to wear suitable head protection.

5(4)   An employer, self-employed person or employee who has control over any other self-employed person may, so far as is necessary to comply with regulation 4(2) of these Regulations, give directions requiring each such other self-employed person to wear suitable head protection.

WEARING OF SUITABLE HEAD PROTECTION

Reg.6(1)   Every employee who has been provided with suitable head protection shall wear that head protection when required to do so by rules made or directions given under regulation 5 of these Regulations.

6(2)   Every self-employed person shall wear suitable head protection when required to do so by rules made or directions given under regulation 5 of these Regulations.

6(3)   Every self-employed person who is at work on operations or works to which these Regulations apply, but who is not under the control of another employer or self-employed person or of an employee, shall wear suitable head protection unless there is no foreseeable risk of injury to his head other than by his falling.

6(4)   Every employee or self-employed person who is required to wear suitable head protection by or under these Regulations shall do so properly.

REPORTING THE LOSS OF, OR DEFECT IN, SUITABLE HEAD PROTECTION

Reg. 7   Every employee who has been provided with suitable head protection by his employer shall take reasonable care of it and shall forthwith report to his employer any loss of, or obvious defect in, that head protection.

Construction (Health, Safety and Welfare) Regulations (CHSW) 1996

Law considered in context / more depth in Element C9.

See also – Work at Height Regulations (WAH) 2005 – on page 305.

Arrangement of Regulations

1)   Citation and commencement.

2)   Interpretation.

3)   Application.

4)   Persons upon whom duties are placed by these Regulations.

5)   Safe places of work.

6)   Falls.

7)   Fragile material.

8)   Falling objects.

9)   Stability of structures.

10)   Demolition or dismantling.

11)   Explosives.

12)   Excavations.

13)   Cofferdams and caissons.

14)   Prevention of drowning.

15)   Traffic routes.

16)   Doors and gates.

17)   Vehicles.

18)   Prevention of risk from fire etc.

19)   Emergency routes and exits.

20)   Emergency procedures.

21)   Fire detection and fire-fighting.

22)   Welfare facilities.

23)   Fresh air.

24)   Temperature and weather protection.

25)   Lighting.

26)   Good order.

27)   Plant and equipment.

28)   Training.

29)   Inspection.

30)   Reports.

31)   Exemption certificates.

32)   Extension outside Great Britain.

33)   Enforcement in respect of fire.

34)   Modifications.

35)   Revocations.

Schedule 1.   Requirements for guard-rails etc.

Schedule 2.   Requirements for working platforms.

Schedule 3.   Requirements for personal suspension equipment.

Schedule 4.   Requirements for means of arresting falls.

Schedule 5.   Requirements for ladders.

Schedule 6.   Welfare facilities.

Schedule 7.   Places of work requiring inspection.

Schedule 8.   Particulars to be included in a report of inspection.

Schedule 9.   Modifications.

Schedule 10.   Revocations.

Outline of key points

DUTY HOLDERS UNDER THE REGULATIONS

The main duty-holders under these Regulations are employers, the self-employed and those who control the way in which construction work is carried out. Employees too have duties to carry out their own work in a safe way. Also, anyone doing construction work has a duty to co-operate with others on matters of health and safety and report any defects to those in control.

SAFE PLACES OF WORK (REGULATION 5)

A general duty to ensure a safe place of work and safe means of access to and from that place of work

This Regulation sets out a general requirement which applies to all construction work. It applies equally to places of work in the ground, at ground level and at height. In essence it requires that 'reasonably practicable' steps should be taken to provide for safety and to ensure risks to health are minimised. This means that action to be taken should be proportionate to the risk involved.

PRECAUTIONS AGAINST FALLS (REGULATIONS 6 AND 7)

■   Prevent falls from height by physical precautions or, where this is not possible, provide equipment that will arrest falls.

■   Ensure there are physical precautions to prevent falls through fragile materials.

■   Erect scaffolding, access equipment, harnesses and nets under the supervision of a competent person.

■   Ensure there are criteria for using ladders.

Falls account for more than half of the fatal accidents in construction. The aim of the Regulations is to prevent falls from any height, but there are specific steps to be taken for work at heights of two metres or more.

1)   At or above two metres, where work cannot be done safely from the ground, the first objective is to provide physical safeguards to prevent falls. Where possible, means of access and working places should be of sound construction and capable of safely supporting both people and the materials needed for the work. Guard rails and toe boards or an equivalent standard of protection   should be provided at any edge from which people could fall.

2)   If it is either not possible to provide the above safeguards or the work is of such duration or difficulty that it would not be reasonably practicable to do so consider using properly installed personnel equipment such as rope access or boatswain's chairs.

3)   If, for the same reasons these methods of work cannot be used, it will be necessary to consider equipment which will arrest falls, i.e. safety harnesses or nets with associated equipment. Scaffolds, personnel harnesses and net equipment have to be erected or installed under the supervision of a competent person.

FALLING OBJECTS (REGULATION 8)

■   Where necessary to protect people at work and others, take steps to prevent materials from falling.

■   Where it is not reasonably practicable to prevent falling materials, take precautions to prevent people from being struck, e.g.

■   covered walkways.

- Do not throw any materials or objects down from a height if they could strike someone.
- Store materials and equipment safely.

The first objective is to prevent materials or objects from falling in circumstances where they could strike someone. Only where it is not reasonably practicable to do so, should other means, e.g. covered walkways, be used.

WORK ON STRUCTURES (REGULATIONS 9, 10 AND 11)

- Prevent accidental collapse of new or existing structures or those under construction.
- Make sure any dismantling or demolition of any structure is planned and carried out in a safe manner under the supervision of a competent person.
- Only fire explosive charges after steps have been taken to ensure that no one is exposed to risk or injury from the explosion.

Every year there are structural collapses which have the potential to cause serious accidents. The CHSW Regulations set a high standard to prevent collapses which involves taking into account the hazard during the planning stage. Demolition or dismantling are recognised as high risk activities. In any cases where this work presents a risk of danger to anyone, it should be planned and carried out under the direct supervision of a competent person.

EXCAVATIONS, COFFERDAMS AND CAISSONS (REGULATIONS 12 AND 13)

- Prevent collapse of ground both in and above excavations.
- Identify and prevent risk from underground cables and other services.
- Ensure cofferdams and caissons are properly designed, constructed and maintained.

From the outset, and as work progresses, any excavation which has the potential to collapse unless supported, should have suitable equipment immediately available to provide such support. Underground cables and services can also be a source of danger. These should be identified before work starts and positive action taken to prevent injury.

PREVENTION OR AVOIDANCE OF DROWNING (REGULATION 14)

- Take steps to prevent people from falling into water or other liquid so far as is reasonably practicable.
- Ensure that personal protective and rescue equipment is immediately available for use and maintained, in the event of a fall.
- Make sure safe transport by water is under the control of a competent person.

TRAFFIC ROUTES, VEHICLES, DOORS AND GATES (REGULATIONS 15, 16 AND 17)

- Ensure construction sites are organised so that pedestrians and vehicles can both move safely and without risks to health.
- Make sure routes are suitable and sufficient for the people or vehicles using them.
- Prevent or control the unintended movement of any vehicle.
- Make arrangements for giving a warning of any possible dangerous movement, e.g. reversing vehicles.
- Ensure safe operation of vehicles including prohibition of riding or remaining in unsafe positions.
- Make sure doors and gates which could present danger, e.g. trapping risk of powered doors, have
- suitable safeguards.

PREVENTION AND CONTROL OF EMERGENCIES (REGULATIONS 18, 19, 20 AND 21)

- Prevent risk from fire, explosion, flooding and asphyxiation.
- Provide emergency routes and exits.
- Make arrangements for dealing with emergencies, including procedures for evacuating the site.
- Where necessary, provide fire-fighting equipment, fire detectors and alarm systems.

These Regulations require the prevention of risk as far as it is reasonably practicable to achieve. However, there are times when emergencies do arise and planning is needed to ensure, for example, that emergency routes are provided and evacuation procedures are in place.

These particular Regulations (as well as those on traffic routes, welfare, cleanliness and signing of sites) apply to construction work which is carried out on construction sites. However, the rest of the Regulations apply to all construction work.

The HSE continues to be responsible for inspection of means of escape and fire-fighting for most sites. However, fire authorities have enforcement responsibility in many premises which remain in normal use during construction work. This continues the sensible arrangement which ensures that the most appropriate advice is given.

WELFARE FACILITIES (REGULATION 22)

- Provide sanitary and washing facilities and an adequate supply of drinking water.
- Provide rest facilities.
- Provide facilities to change and store clothing.

There is an important additional duty in this Regulation. Anybody in control of a site has to ensure that there are reasonable welfare facilities available at readily accessible places. This does not necessarily mean, for example, that the main contractor has to provide these facilities, but they should check that others who have duties are making this provision.

A number of the Regulations are supported by explanatory Schedules. For welfare, the Schedule is fairly detailed and explains what is a reasonable standard of welfare in line with the duration of work and site activities.

SITE-WIDE ISSUES (REGULATIONS 23, 24, 25, AND 26)

- Ensure sufficient fresh or purified air is available at every workplace, and associated plant is capable of giving visible or audible warning of failure.
- Make sure a reasonable working temperature is maintained at indoor work places during working hours.
- Provide facilities for protection against adverse weather conditions.
- Make sure suitable and sufficient emergency lighting is available.
- Make sure suitable and sufficient lighting is available, including providing secondary lighting where there would be a risk to health or safety if primary or artificial lighting failed.
- Keep construction sites in good order and in a reasonable state of cleanliness.
- Ensure the perimeter of a construction site to which people, other than those working on the site could gain access, is marked

- by suitable signs so that its extent can be easily identified.

Note that **Regulation 27** (the duty to ensure that plant and equipment is safe, of sound construction and to ensure maintenance and safe use) has been revoked and replaced by the Provision and Use of Work Equipment Regulations (PUWER) 1998. All of these duties (with the exception of those for lighting) are governed by the term 'so far as it is reasonably practicable'.

TRAINING, INSPECTION AND REPORTS (REGULATIONS 28, 29 AND 30)

- Ensure construction activities where training, technical knowledge or experience is necessary to reduce risks of injury are only carried out by people who meet these requirements or, if not, are supervised by those with appropriate training, knowledge or experience.
- Before work at height, on excavations, cofferdams or caissons begins, make sure the place of work is inspected, (and at subsequent specified periods), by a competent person, who must be satisfied that the work can be done safely.
- Following inspection, ensure written reports are made by the competent person.

Lack of training has been identified as one of the major contributory factors in accidents and ill health in construction. Many activities are made safe simply by ensuring that those doing the work have knowledge of and understand the importance of safe practices.

The frequency of inspections depends on the nature and place of work. For example, following the initial inspection, work at places over two metres in height require weekly inspections. In contrast, for work in excavations (including shafts and tunnels), inspections are necessary at the beginning of every shift. Inspections help to ensure that safety is monitored during changing site conditions.

Reports detailing inspections are generally required every time an inspection is carried out, but there are exceptions. For example, weekly reports only are needed for inspections of excavation work, and unless the tower scaffold remains erected in the same place for seven days or more, inspections of tower scaffolds do not have to be recorded.

Control of Major Accident Hazard Regulations 1999

Law considered in context / more depth in Elements C4 and C10.

Arrangement of Regulations

PART 1 - INTRODUCTION

1) Citation and commencement.
2) Interpretation.
3) Application.

PART 2 - GENERAL

4) General duty.
5) Major accident prevention policy.
6) Notifications.

PART 3 - SAFETY REPORTS

7) Safety report.
8) Review and revision of safety report.

PART 4 - EMERGENCY PLANS

9) On-site emergency plan.
10) Off-site emergency plan.
11) Review and testing of emergency plans.
12) Implementing emergency plans.
13) Charge for preparation, review and testing of off-site emergency plan.

PART 5 - PROVISION OF INFORMATION BY OPERATOR

14) Provision of information to the public.
15) Provision of information to the competent authority.
16) Provision of information to other establishments.

PART 6 - FUNCTIONS OF COMPETENT AUTHORITY

17) Functions of competent authority in relation to the safety report.
18) Prohibition of use.
19) Inspections and investigations.
20) Enforcement.
21) Provision of information by competent authority.
22) Fee payable by operator.

PART 7 - AMENDMENTS, REVOCATIONS, SAVINGS AND TRANSITIONAL PROVISIONS

23) Amendments.
24) Revocations and savings.
25) Transitional provisions.

SCHEDULES

Schedule 1   Dangerous substances to which the regulations apply.

Schedule 2   Principles to be taken into account when preparing major accident prevention policy document.

Schedule 3   Information to be included in a notification.

Schedule 4   Purpose and Contents of Safety Reports.

Schedule 5   Emergency Plans.

Schedule 6   Information to be supplied to the public.

Schedule 7   Criteria for notification of a major accident to the European Commission and information to be notified.

Schedule 8   Provision of information by competent authority.

Outline of key points

The Control of Major Accident Hazards Regulations 1999 (COMAH) came into force on 1 April 1999. These Regulations implemented the Seveso II Directive (except for the land use planning requirements), and replaced the Control of Industrial Major Accident Hazards Regulations 1984 (CIMAH).

An Amendment Directive broadening Seveso II is planned for implementation by July 2005.

COMAH applies mainly to the chemical industry, but also to some storage activities, explosives and nuclear sites, and other industries where threshold quantities of dangerous substances identified in the Regulations are kept or used.

Their main aim of COMAH is to prevent and mitigate the effects of a major accident involving dangerous substances, such as chlorine, LPG, explosives and arsenic pentoxide which can cause serious damage/harm to people and/or the environment. COMAH treats risks to environment as seriously as those to people.

The main duty is to prepare a safety report which will include:

- A policy on how to prevent and mitigate major accidents.
- A management system for implementing that policy.
- An effective method for identifying any Major Accidents that may occur.
- Measures (safe plant and procedures) to prevent and mitigate major accidents.
- Information on safety precautions built into the plant when designed and constructed.
- Details of measures(fire fighting, relief systems, filters, etc) to limit the consequences of any accident.
- Information about the emergency plan for the site, this is used by the Local Authority for their off site plan.

Control of Substances Hazardous to Health Regulations (COSHH) 2002

Law considered in context / more depth in Element C9.

Arrangement of Regulations

1)   Citation and commencement.

2)   Interpretation.

3)   Duties under these Regulations.

4)   Prohibitions on substances.

5)   Application of regulations 6 to 13.

6)   Assessment of health risks created by work involving substances hazardous to health.

7)   Control of exposure.

8)   Use of control measures etc.

9)   Maintenance of control measures.

10)   Monitoring exposure.

11)   Health surveillance.

12)   Information etc.

13)   Arrangements to deal with accidents, incidents and emergencies.

14)   Exemption certificates.

15)   Extension outside Great Britain.

16)   Defence in proceedings for contravention of these Regulations.

17)   Exemptions relating to the Ministry of Defence etc.

18)   Revocations, amendments and savings.

19)   Extension of meaning of "work".

20)   Modification of section 3(2) of the Health and Safety at Work etc Act 1974.

Schedule 1   Other substances and processes to which the definition of "carcinogen" relates.

Schedule 2   Prohibition of certain substances hazardous to health for certain purposes.

Schedule 3   Special provisions relating to biological agents.

Schedule 4	Frequency of thorough examination and test of local exhaust ventilation plant used in certain processes.
Schedule 5	Specific substances and processes for which monitoring is required.
Schedule 6	Medical surveillance.
Schedule 7	Legislation concerned with the labelling of containers and pipes.
Schedule 8	Fumigations excepted from regulation 14.
Schedule 9	Notification of certain fumigations.
Appendix 1	Control of carcinogenic substances.
Annex 1	Background note on occupational cancer.
Annex 2	Special considerations that apply to the control of exposure to vinyl chloride.
Appendix 2	Additional provisions relating to work with biological agents.
Appendix 3	Control of substances that cause occupational asthma.

NOTE the main impact to the latest version of the COSHH Regulations concern the control of substances that cause occupational asthma.

Outline of key points

REGULATIONS

Reg. 2
Interpretation

"Substance hazardous to health" includes:

1) Substances which under The Chemicals (Hazard Information and Packaging) Regulations (CHIP 3) 2002 are in categories of very toxic, toxic, harmful, corrosive or irritant.

2) A substance listed in Schedule 1 to the Regs or for which the HSC have approved a maximum exposure limit or an occupational exposure standard.

3) A biological agent.

4) Dust in a concentration in air equal to or greater than:

- 10 mg/m^3 inhalable dust as an 8hr TWA, or
- 4mg/m^3 respirable dust as an 8hr TWA.

5) Any other substance which creates a health hazard comparable with the hazards of the substances in the other categories above.

Reg. 3
Duties

Are on employer to protect:

Employees

Any other person who may be affected, except:

- Duties for health surveillance do not extend to non-employees.
- Duties to give information may extend to non-employees if they work on the premises.

Reg. 4
Prohibitions on Substances

Certain substances are prohibited from being used in some applications. These are detailed in Schedule 2 to Regs.

Reg. 5
Application of Regs. 6 - 13

Regs. 6 - 13 are made to protect a person's health from risks arising from exposure. They do not apply if:

The following Regs already apply:

- The Control of Lead at Work Regulations (CLAW) 2002.
- The Control of Asbestos at Work Regulations (CAWR) 2002.

The hazard arises from one of the following properties of the substance:

- Radioactivity, explosive, flammable, high or low temperature, high pressure.
- Exposure is for medical treatment.
- Exposure is in a mine.

Reg. 6
Assessment

Employer must not carry out work which will expose employees to substances hazardous to health unless he has made an assessment of the risks to health and the steps that need to be taken to meet the requirements of the Regs.

The assessment must be reviewed if there are changes in the work and at least once every 5 years.

A suitable and sufficient assessment should include:

- An assessment of the risks to health.
- The practicability of preventing exposure.
- Steps needed to achieve adequate control.

An assessment of the risks should involve:

- Types of substance including biological agents.

- Where the substances are present and in what form.
- Effects on the body.
- Who might be affected.
- Existing control measures.

Reg. 7 ## Control of Exposure

1) Employer shall ensure that the exposure of employees to substances hazardous to health is either prevented or, where this is not reasonably practicable, adequately controlled.

2) So far as is reasonably practicable (1) above except to a carcinogen or biological agent shall be by measures other than personal protective equipment (PPE).

3) Where not reasonably practicable to prevent exposure to a carcinogen by using an alternative substance or process, the following measure shall apply:

- Total enclosure of process.
- Use of plant, process and systems which minimise generation of, or suppress and contain, spills, leaks, dust, fumes and vapours of carcinogens.
- Limitation of quantities of a carcinogen at work.
- Keeping of numbers exposed to a minimum.
- Prohibition of eating, drinking and smoking in areas liable to contamination.
- Provision of hygiene measures including adequate washing facilities and regular cleaning of walls and surfaces.
- Designation of areas/installations liable to contamination and use of suitable and sufficient warning signs.
- Safe storage, handling and disposal of carcinogens and use of closed and clearly-labelled containers.

4) If adequate control is not achieved, then employer shall provide suitable PPE to employees in addition to taking control measures.

5) PPE provided shall comply with The Personal Protective Equipment at Work Regulations, 2002 (dealing with the supply of PPE).

6&7) For substances which have a maximum exposure limit (MEL), control of that substance shall, so far as inhalation is concerned, only be treated if the level of exposure is reduced as far as is reasonably practicable and in any case below the MEL.

Where a substance has an occupational exposure standard (OES), control of that substance shall, so far as inhalation is concerned, only be treated as adequate if the OES is not exceeded or if it is, steps are taken to remedy the situation as soon as reasonably practicable.

8) Respiratory protection must be suitable and of a type or conforming to a standard approved by the HSE.

9) In the event of failure of a control measure which may result in the escape of carcinogens, the employer shall ensure:

- Only those who are responsible for repair and maintenance work are permitted in the affected area and are provided with PPE.
- Employees and other persons who may be affected are informed of the failure forthwith.

Reg. 8 Employer shall take all reasonable steps to ensure control measures, PPE, etc. are properly used/applied.

Employee shall make full and proper use of control measures, PPE etc. and shall report defects to employer.

Reg. 9 ## Maintenance of Control Measures

Employer providing control measures to comply with Reg.7 shall ensure that it is maintained in an efficient state, in efficient working order and in good repair and in the case of PPE in a clean condition, properly stored in a well-defined place checked at suitable intervals and when discovered to be defective repaired or replaced before further use.

- Contaminated PPE should be kept apart and cleaned, decontaminated or, if necessary destroyed.
- Engineering controls - employer shall ensure thorough examination and tests.
- Local exhaust ventilation (LEV) - Once every 14 months unless process specified in Schedule 4.
- Others - At suitable intervals.
- Respiratory protective equipment - employer shall ensure thorough examination and tests at suitable intervals.
- Records of all examinations, tests and repairs kept for 5 years.

Reg. 10 ## Monitoring Exposure

Employer shall ensure exposure is monitored if

- Needed to ensure maintenance of adequate control.
- Otherwise needed to protect health of employees.
- Substance/process specified in Schedule 5.

Records kept if:

- There is an identified exposure of identifiable employee - 40 years.
- Otherwise - 5 years.

Reg. 11 ## Health Surveillance

1) Where appropriate for protection of health of employees exposed or liable to be exposed, employer shall ensure suitable health surveillance.

2) Health surveillance is appropriate if:
- Employee exposed to substance/process specified in Schedule 6.
- Exposure to substance is such that an identifiable disease or adverse health effect can result, there is a reasonable likelihood of it occurring and a valid technique exists for detecting the indications of the disease or effect.

3) Health records kept for at least 40 years.

4) If employer ceases business, HSE notified and health records offered to HSE.

5) If employee exposed to substance specified in Schedule 6, then health surveillance shall include medical. surveillance, under Employment Medical Adviser (EMA) at 12 monthly intervals - or more frequently if specified by EMA.

6) EMA can forbid employee to work in process, or specify certain conditions for him to be employed in a process.

7) EMA can specify that health surveillance is to continue after exposure has ceased. Employer must ensure.

8) Employees to have access to their own health record.

9) Employee must attend for health/medical surveillance and give information to EMA.

10) EMA entitled to inspect workplace.

11) Where EMA suspends employee from work exposing him to substances hazardous to health, employer of employee can apply to HSE in writing within 28 days for that decision to be reviewed.

Reg. 12
Information etc.

Employer shall provide suitable and sufficient information, instruction and training for him to know:
- Risks to health.
- Precautions to be taken.

This should include information on:
- Results of monitoring of exposure at workplace.
- Results of collective health surveillance.

If the substances have been assigned a maximum exposure limit, then the employee/Safety Representative must be notified forthwith if the MEL has been exceeded.

Reg. 13
Arrangements to deal with accidents, incidents and emergencies.

To protect the health of employees from accidents, incidents and emergencies, the employer shall ensure that:
- Procedures are in place for first aid and safety drills (tested regularly).
- Information on emergency arrangements is available.
- Warning, communication systems, remedial action and rescue actions are available.
- Information made available to emergency services: external and internal.
- Steps taken to mitigate effects, restore situation to normal and inform employees.
- Only essential persons allowed in area.

These duties do not apply where the risks to health is slight or measures in place Reg 7(1) are sufficient to control the risk.

The employee must report any accident or incident which has or may have resulted in the release of a biological agent which could cause severe human disease.

NOTE the main impact to the latest version of the COSHH Regulations concern the control of substances that cause occupational asthma.

APPENDIX 3 CONTROL OF SUBSTANCES THAT CAUSE OCCUPATIONAL ASTHMA

This relates certain regulations specifically to substances with the potential to cause asthma.
- Regulation 6 - assessment of risk to health created by work involving substances hazardous to health, (i.e. substances that may cause asthma).
- Regulation 7 – prevention or control of exposure to substances hazardous to health, (i.e. substances that may cause occupational asthma).
- Regulation 11 – health surveillance, (for employees who are or may be exposed to substances that may cause occupational asthma).
- Regulation 12 – information, instruction and training for persons who may be exposed to substances hazardous to health, to include: typical symptoms of asthma, substances that may cause it, the permanency of asthma and what happens with subsequent exposures, the need to report symptoms immediately and the reporting procedures.

Training should be given, including induction training before they start the job.

SCHEDULE 3 ADDITIONAL PROVISIONS RELATING TO WORK WITH BIOLOGICAL AGENTS

Regulation 7(10)

Part I Provision of general application to biological agents

1 Interpretation.

2   Classification of biological agents.

The HSC shall approve and publish a "Categorisation of Biological Agents according to hazard and categories of containment" which may be revised or re-issued.

Where no approved classification exists, the employer shall assign the agent to one of four groups according to the level of risk of infection.

Group 1 - unlikely to cause human disease.

Group 2 - can cause human disease.

Group 3 - can cause severe disease and spread to community.

Group 4 - can cause severe disease, spread to community and there is no effective treatment.

3   ## Special control measures for laboratories, animal rooms and industrial processes

Every employer engaged in research, development, teaching or diagnostic work involving Group 2, 3 or 4 biological agents; keeping or handling laboratory animals deliberately or naturally infected with those agents, or industrial processes involving those agents, shall control them with the most suitable containment.

4   ## List of employees exposed to certain biological agents

The employer shall keep a list of employees exposed to Group 3 or 4 biological agents for at least 10 years. If there is a long latency period then the list should be kept for 40 years.

5   ## Notification of the use of biological agents

Employers shall inform the HSE at least 20 days in advance of first time use or storage of Group 2, 3 or 4 biological hazards. Consequent substantial changes in procedure or process shall also be reported.

6   ## Notification of the consignment of biological agents

The HSE must be informed 30 days before certain biological agents are consigned.

Part II Containment measures for health and veterinary care facilities, laboratories and animal rooms.

Part III Containment measures for industrial processes.

Part IV Biohazard sign. The biohazard sign required by regulation 7(6)(a) shall be in the form shown below –

Figure C11-1: Biohazard sign.

Source: Stocksigns.

Part V Biological agents whose use is to be notified in accordance with paragraph 5(2) of Part I of this Schedule

- Any Group 3 or 4 agent, or
- Certain named Group 2 agents.

Dangerous Substances (Notification and Marking of Sites) Regulations 1990

Law considered in context / more depth in Element C4.

Arrangement of Regulations

1)   Citation and commencement.

2)   Interpretation.

3)   Exceptions.

4)   Notification.

5)   Access Marking.

6)   Location marking.

7)   Signs to be kept clean, etc.

8)   Enforcing authority.

9)   Exemption certificates.

10)   Transitional provisions.

11)   Repeals.

Schedule 1	Exceptions.
Schedule 2	Matters to be notified.
	Part I - Particulars to be notified under regulation 4(1).
	Part II - Changes to be notified under regulation 4(2).
Schedule 3	Table of classifications and hazard warnings.
Schedule 4	Repeals and enabling powers.

Outline of key points

These Regulations are for persons who control sites where hazardous substances that are dangerous for conveyance are stored. If there is a total quantity of 25 tonnes or more of a hazardous substance, the person in control must notify in writing the fire authority and the enforcing authority; for regulations 5 – 7 this will be HSE.

Safety notices must be displayed with specific direction and location to warn fire fighters who may come on site in an emergency. The safety notices must bear the hazard-warning symbol and be of the standard colour and shape. The signs must be kept clean and free from obstruction.

Dangerous Substances and Explosive Atmospheres Regulations (DSEAR) 2002

Law considered in context / more depth in Unit 15.

Arrangement of Regulations

1) Citation and commencement.
2) Interpretation.
3) Application.
4) Duties under these Regulations.
5) Risk assessment.
6) Elimination or reduction of risks from dangerous substances.
7) Places where explosive atmospheres may occur.
8) Arrangements to deal with accidents, incidents and emergencies.
9) Information, instruction and training.
10) Identification of hazardous contents of containers and pipes.
11) Duty of co-ordination.
12) Extension outside Great Britain.
13) Exemption certificates.
14) Exemptions for Ministry of Defence etc.
15) Amendments.
16) Repeals and revocations.
17) Transitional provisions.

Schedule 1.	General safety measures.
Schedule 2.	Classification of places where explosive atmospheres may occur.
Schedule 3.	Criteria for the selection of equipment and protective systems.
Schedule 4.	Warning sign for places where explosive atmospheres may occur.
Schedule 5.	Legislation concerned with the marking of containers and pipes.
Schedule 6.	Amendments.
Schedule 7.	Repeal and revocation.

Outline of key points

These new regulations aim to protect against risks from fire, explosion and similar events arising from dangerous substances that are present in the workplace.

DANGEROUS SUBSTANCES

These are any substances or preparations that due to their properties or the way in which they are being used could cause harm to people from fires and explosions. They may include petrol, liquefied petroleum gases, paints, varnishes, solvents and dusts.

APPLICATION

DSEAR applies in most workplaces where a dangerous substance is present. There are a few exceptions where only certain parts of the regulations apply, for example:

- Ships.
- Medical treatment areas.

- Explosives/chemically unstable substances.
- Mines.
- Quarries.
- Boreholes.
- Offshore installations.
- Means of transport.

MAIN REQUIREMENTS

You must::

- Conduct a risk assessment of work activities involving dangerous substances.
- Provide measures to eliminate or reduce risks.
- Provide equipment and procedures to deal with accidents and emergencies.
- Provide information and training for employees.
- Classify places into zones and mark zones where necessary (to be phased in) -

Workplace in use by July 2003	-	Meet requirements by July 2006
Workplace modified before July 2006	-	Meet requirements at time of modifications
New workplace after 30 June 2003	-	Meet requirements from start.

The risk assessment should include:

- The hazardous properties of substance.
- The way they are used or stored.
- Possibility of hazardous explosive atmosphere occurring.
- Potential ignition sources.
- Details of zoned areas (July 2003).
- Co-ordination between employers (July 2003).

SAFETY MEASURES

Where possible eliminate safety risks from dangerous substances or, if not reasonably practicable to do this, control risks and reduce the harmful effects of any fire, explosion or similar event.

Substitution - Replace with totally safe or safer substance (best solution).

Control measures - If risk cannot be eliminated apply the following control measures in the following order:

- Reduce quantity.
- Avoid or minimise releases.
- Control releases at source.
- Prevent formation of explosive atmosphere.
- Collect, contain and remove any release to a safe place e.g. ventilation.
- Avoid ignition sources.
- Avoid adverse conditions e.g. exceeding temperature limits.
- Keep incompatible substances apart.

Mitigation measures - Apply measures to mitigate the effects of any situation.

- Prevent fire and explosions from spreading to other plant, equipment or other parts of the workplace.
- Reduce number of employees exposed.
- Provide process plant that can contain or suppress an explosion, or vent it to a safe place.

ZONED AREAS

In workplaces where explosive atmospheres may occur, areas should be classified into zones based on the likelihood of an explosive atmosphere occurring. Any equipment in these areas should ideally meet the requirements of the Equipment and Protective Systems Intended for Use in Potentially Explosive Atmospheres Regulations (ATEX) 1996. However equipment in use before July 2003 can continue to be used providing that the risk assessment says that it is safe to do so. Areas may need to be marked with an 'Ex' warning sign at their entry points. Employees may need to be provided with appropriate clothing e.g. anti static overalls. Before use for the first time, a person competent in the field of explosion protection must confirm hazardous areas as being safe.

ACCIDENTS, INCIDENTS AND EMERGENCIES

DSEAR builds on existing requirements for emergency procedures, which are contained in other regulations. These may need to be supplemented if you assess that a fire, explosion or significant spillage could occur, due to the quantities of dangerous substances present in the workplace. You may need to arrange for:

- Suitable warning systems.
- Escape facilities.
- Emergency procedures.
- Equipment and clothing for essential personnel who may need to deal with the situation.
- Practice drills.
- Make information, instruction and training available to employees and if necessary liaise with the emergency services.

Electricity at Work Regulations (EWR) 1989

Law considered in context / more depth in Unit 14.

Arrangement of Regulations

PART I - INTRODUCTION

1) Citation and commencement.
2) Interpretation.
3) Persons on whom duties are imposed by these Regulations.

PART II - GENERAL

4) Systems, work activities and protective equipment.
5) Strength and capability of electrical equipment.
6) Adverse or hazardous environments.
7) Insulation, protection and placing of conductors.
8) Earthing or other suitable precautions.
9) Integrity of referenced conductors.
10) Connections.
11) Means for protecting from excess of current.
12) Means for cutting off the supply and for isolation.
13) Precautions for work on equipment made dead.
14) Work on or near live conductors.
15) Working space, access and lighting.
16) Persons to be competent to prevent danger and injury.

PART III - REGULATIONS APPLYING TO MINES ONLY

17) Provisions applying to mines only.
18) Introduction of electrical equipment.
19) Restriction of equipment in certain zones below ground.
20) Cutting off electricity or making safe where firedamp is found either below ground or at the surface.
21) Approval of certain equipment for use in safety-lamp mines.
22) Means of cutting off electricity to circuits below ground.
23) Oil-filled equipment.
24) Records and information.
25) Electric shock notices.
26) Introduction of battery-powered locomotives and vehicles into safety-lamp mines.
27) Storage, charging and transfer of electrical storage batteries.
28) Disapplication of section 157 of the Mines and Quarries Act 1954.

PART IV - MISCELLANEOUS AND GENERAL

29) Defence.
30) Exemption certificates.
31) Extension outside Great Britain.
32) Disapplication of duties.
33) Revocations and modifications.

Schedule 1.   Provisions applying to mines only and having effect in particular in relation to the use below ground in coal mines of film lighting circuits.

Schedule 2.   Revocations and modifications.

Outline of key points

SYSTEMS, WORK ACTIVITIES AND PROTECTIVE EQUIPMENT (REGULATION 4)

The system and the equipment comprising it must be designed and installed to take account of all reasonably foreseeable conditions of use.

- The system must be maintained so as to prevent danger.
- All work activities must be carried out in such a manner as to not give rise to danger.
- Equipment provided to protect people working on live equipment must be suitable and maintained.

STRENGTH AND CAPABILITY OF ELECTRICAL EQUIPMENT (REGULATION 5)

Strength and capability refers to the equipment's ability to withstand the effects of its load current and any transient overloads or pulses of current.

ADVERSE OR HAZARDOUS ENVIRONMENTS (REGULATION 6)

This regulation requires that electrical equipment is suitable for the environment and conditions that might be reasonably foreseen. In particular, attention should be paid to:

- *Mechanical damage* caused by for example; vehicles, people, vibration, etc.
- Weather, natural hazards, temperature or pressure. Ice, snow, lightning, bird droppings, etc.
- *Wet, dirty, dusty or corrosive conditions.* Conductors, moving parts, insulators and other materials may be affected by the corrosive nature of water, chemicals and solvents. The presence of explosive dusts must be given special consideration.
- *Flammable or explosive substances.* Electrical equipment may be a source of ignition for liquids, gases, vapours etc.

INSULATION, PROTECTION AND PLACING OF CONDUCTORS (REGULATION 7)

The purpose of this regulation is to prevent danger from direct contact. Therefore, if none exists, no action is needed. Conductors though will normally need to be insulated and also have some other protection to prevent mechanical damage.

EARTHING OR OTHER SUITABLE PRECAUTIONS (REGULATION 8)

The purpose of this regulation is to prevent danger from indirect contact. Conductors such as metal casings may become live through fault conditions. The likelihood of danger arising from these circumstances must be prevented by using the techniques described earlier in this section i.e. earthing, double insulation, reduced voltages etc.

INTEGRITY OF REFERENCED CONDUCTORS (REGULATION 9)

In many circumstances the reference point is earthed because the majority of power distribution installations are referenced by a deliberate connection to earth at the generators or distribution transformers. The purpose of this regulation is to ensure that electrical continuity is never broken.

CONNECTIONS (REGULATION 10)

As well as having suitable insulation and conductance, connections must have adequate mechanical protection and strength. Plugs and sockets must conform to recognised standards as must connections between cables. Special attention should be paid to the quality of connections on portable appliances.

MEANS FOR PROTECTING FROM EXCESS CURRENT (REGULATION 11)

Faults or overloads can occur in electrical systems and protection must be provided against their effects. The type of protection depends on several factors but usually rests between fuses and circuit breakers.

MEANS FOR CUTTING OFF THE SUPPLY AND FOR ISOLATION (REGULATION 12)

Means must be provided to switch off electrical supplies together with a means of isolation so as to prevent inadvertent reconnection.

PRECAUTIONS FOR WORK ON EQUIPMENT MADE DEAD (REGULATION 13)

Working dead should be the norm. This regulation requires that precautions be taken to ensure that the system remains dead and to protect those at work on the system. Any or all of the following steps should be considered:

- Identify the circuit. Never assume that the labelling is correct.
- Disconnection and isolation. These are the most common methods: isolation switches, fuse removal and plug removal.
- Notices and barriers.
- Proving dead. The test device itself must also be tested before and after testing.
- Earthing.
- Permits to work.

WORK ON OR NEAR LIVE CONDUCTORS (REGULATION 14)

Live work must only be done if it is unreasonable for it to be done dead. If live work must be carried out then any or all of the following precautions should be taken:

- Competent staff (see reg. 16).
- Adequate information.
- Suitable tools. Insulated tools, protective clothing.
- Barriers or screens.
- Instruments and test probes. To identify what is live and what is dead.
- Accompaniment.
- Designated test areas.

WORKING SPACE, ACCESS AND LIGHTING (REGULATION 15)

Space. Where there are dangerous live exposed conductors, space should be adequate to:

- Allow persons to pull back from the hazard.
- Allow persons to pass each other.

Lighting. The first preference is for natural lighting then for permanent artificial lighting.

PERSONS TO BE COMPETENT TO PREVENT DANGER AND INJURY (REGULATION 16)

The object of this regulation is to 'ensure that persons are not placed at risk due to a lack of skills on the part of themselves or others in dealing with electrical equipment'.

In order to meet the requirements of this regulation a competent person would need:

- An understanding of the concepts of electricity and the risks involved in work associated with it.
- Knowledge of electrical work and some suitable qualification in electrical principles.
- Experience of the type of system to be worked on with an understanding of the hazards and risks involved.
- Knowledge of the systems of work to be employed and the ability to recognise hazards and risks.
- Physical attributes to be able to recognise elements of the system e.g. colour blindness and wiring.

Advice and queries regarding qualifications and training can be directed to the IEE - Institute of Electrical Engineers, London.

DEFENCE (REGULATION 29)

In any Regulation where the absolute duty applies, a defence in any criminal proceedings shall exist where a person can show that: *"He took all reasonable steps and exercised due diligence to avoid the commission of the offence."*

Is there a prepared procedure (steps), is the procedure being followed (diligence) and do you have the records or witness to prove it retrospectively?

Environment Act 1995

Law considered in context / more depth in Element C10.

Outline of key points and arrangement of regulations

THE ENVIRONMENT AGENCY AND THE SCOTTISH ENVIRONMENT PROTECTION AGENCY

The 1995 Environment Act provided the powers for the formation of the Environment Agency in England and Wales and the Scottish Environment Protection Agency. Both agencies are charged with making a contribution towards achieving the objective of sustainable development. This is likely to become a major issue.

Contaminated land and abandoned mines

Section 57 of the Environment Act 1995 applies to contaminated land and the Act inserts a new Part II A into the Environment Protection Act 1990, after section 78. The new sections are numbered 78A to 78Y, which is a total of 25 new sections.

It provides new powers in the identification of contaminated land which local authorities are required to do. Where contaminated land is identified a notice will be served on the person liable to clean it up. If the person does not comply with the notice then they will be liable to prosecution.

National parks

The Act provides the powers for the establishment of National Parks Authorities and covers their general purposes and powers. Several additions are made to the National Parks and Access to the Countryside Act 1949. Each National Park is required to produce a National Park Management Plan.

Air quality

The Act requires the Secretary of State to prepare and publish a statement with respect to the assessment or management of the quality of air, to be known as the National Air Strategy. Local authorities are required to review the quality of air within their areas. Where it appears that air quality standards are not being achieved then an air quality management area will be designated and a plan produced to improve air quality.

THE ENVIRONMENT ACT HAS FIVE MAIN PARTS TO IT, AS FOLLOWS:

Part 1 The Environment Agency and the Scottish Environment Protection Agency.

Part 2 Contaminated Land and Abandoned Mines.

Part 3 National Parks.

Part 4 Air Quality.

Part 5 Miscellaneous, General and Supplemental Provisions.

PART I - THE ENVIRONMENT AGENCY AND THE SCOTTISH ENVIRONMENT PROTECTION AGENCY

Unit I - The Environment Agency

Sections

1 Establishment of the Agency.

2-10 Transfer of functions, property etc. to the Agency.

11-13 Advisory committees.

14-19 Flood defence committees.

Unit II - The Scottish Environment Protection Agency

Sections

SCHEDULES

Schedule 1   The Environment Agency.

Schedule 2   Transfers of property etc.: supplemental provisions.

	Part I	Introductory.
	Part II	Transfer schemes.
	Part III	General provisions with respect to transfers by or under Section 3 or 22.

Schedule 3   Environmental protection advisory committees.

Schedule 4   Boundaries of regional flood defence areas.

Schedule 5   Membership and proceedings of regional and local flood defence committees.

	Part I	Membership of flood defence committees.
	Part II	Proceedings of flood defence committees.

Schedule 6   The Scottish Environment Protection Agency.

Schedule 7   National Park authorities.

Schedule 8   Supplemental and incidental powers of National Park authorities.

Schedule 9   Miscellaneous statutory functions of National Park authorities.

Schedule 10   Minor and consequential amendments relating to National Parks.

Schedule 11   Air quality: supplemental provisions.

Schedule 12   Schedule 2A to the Environmental Protection Act 1990.

Schedule 13   Review of old mineral planning permissions.

Schedule 14   Periodic review of mineral planning permissions.

Schedule 15   Minor and consequential amendments relating to fisheries.

Schedule 16   Pollution of rivers and coastal waters in Scotland: amendment to the Control of Pollution Act 1974.

Schedule 17   Statutory nuisances: Scotland.

Schedule 18   Supplemental provisions with respect to powers of entry.

Schedule 19   Offences relating to false or misleading statements or false entries.

Schedule 20   Delegation of appellate functions of the Secretary of State.

Schedule 21   Application of certain enactments to the Crown.

	Part I	Enactments relating to England and Wales.
	Part II	Enactments relating to Scotland.

Schedule 22   Minor and consequential amendments.

Schedule 23   Transitional and transitory provisions and savings.

	Part I	General transitional provisions and savings.
	Part II	Transitory provisions in respect of flood defence.

Schedule 24   Repeals and revocations.

Environmental Protection Act (EPA) 1990

Law considered in context / more depth in Element C10.

Introduction to the EPA 1990

Concern about the UK's fragmented approach to environmental protection led to the formation of a Royal Commission on the Environment in 1970. The Commission recommended the introduction of legislation which would feature an integrated pollution control (IPC) approach. As a result of this, and European Union initiatives the Environmental Protection Act (EPA) was introduced in 1990.

The main features of EPA 1990, affecting *industry* are:

- The introduction of Integrated Pollution Control (IPC) and Air Pollution Control by Local Authorities (LAAPC).
- The classification of Part A - Environment Agency and Part B - LAAPC processes, depending on the type of material being processed and size of facility.
- The provision to make regulations defining prescribed substances.

- The introduction of the concept of **B**est **A**vailable **T**echniques **N**ot **E**ntailing **E**xcessive **C**ost (BATNEEC), EPA s.7.
- The introduction of the concept of **B**est **P**racticable **E**nvironmental **O**ption (BPEO). In IPC Applications operators must show that their chosen abatement technique represents the BPEO.

The powers of the Environment Agency (EA) are affected by:

- Part B processes in regard to air pollution control, being dealt with by local authorities.
- The relationship between the Environment Agency and HSE (Health and Safety Executive) - there are potential problems over the CoSHH (Control of Substances Hazardous to Health) Regulations 1999 and extracting workplace pollutants and venting to atmosphere directly.

Outline of key points and arrangement of regulations

"An Act to make provision for the improved control of pollution arising from certain industrial and other processes;

to re-enact the provisions of the Control of Pollution Act 1974 relating to waste on land with modifications as respects the functions of the regulatory and other authorities concerned in the collection and disposal of waste and to make further provision in relation to such waste;

to restate the law defining statutory nuisances and improve the summary procedures for dealing with them, to provide for the termination of the existing controls over offensive trades or businesses and to provide for the extension of the Clean Air Acts to prescribed gases;

to amend the law relating to litter and make further provision imposing or conferring powers to impose duties to keep public places clear of litter and clean;

to make provision conferring powers in relation to trolley abandoned on land in the open air; to amend the Radioactive Substances Act 1960;

to make provision for the control of genetically modified organisms; to make provision for the abolition of the Nature Conservancy Council and for the creation of councils to replace it and discharge the functions of that Council and, as respects Wales, of the Countryside Commission; to make further provision for the control of the importation, exportation, use, supply or storage of prescribed substances and articles and the importation, exportation, use, supply or storage of prescribed substances and articles and the importation or exportation of prescribed descriptions of waste; to confer powers to obtain information about potentially hazardous substances; to amend the law relating to the control of hazardous substances on, over or under land;

to amend section 107(6) of the Water Act 1989 and sections 31 (7)(a), 31 A(2) (c)(i) and 32(7)(a) of the Control of Pollution Act 1974;

to amend the provisions of the Food and Environmental Protection Act 1985 as regards the dumping of waste at sea;

to make further provision as respects the prevention of oil pollution from ships; to make provision for and in connection with the identification and control of dogs;

to confer powers to control the burning of crop residues;

to make provision in relation to financial or other assistance for purposes connected with the environment;

to make provision in relation to financial or other assistance for purposes connected with the environment;

to make provision as respects superannuation of employees of the groundwork Foundation and for remunerating the chairman of the Inland Waterways Amenity Advisory Council; and

for purposes connected with those purposes." [1st November 1990].

THE EPA 1990 HAS 9 MAIN PARTS PLUS 16 SCHEDULES, THE MAIN PARTS ARE AS FOLLOWS:

Part I Integrated Pollution Control and Air Pollution Control by Local Authorities.

Part II Waste on Land.

Part III Statutory Nuisances and Clean Air.

Part IV Litter etc. (provisions relating to litter and abandoned trolleys).

Part V Amendment of the Radioactive Substances Act 1960.

Part VI Genetically Modified Organisms.

Part VII Nature Conservation in Great Britain and Countryside Matters in Wales

Part VIII Miscellaneous (Other controls on substances, articles or waste, Pollution at sea, Control of dogs, Straw and stubble burning and Environmental expenditure)

Part IX General

Schedules

Schedule 1 Authorisations for Processes: Supplementary Provisions.

Part I Grant of Authorisations.

Part II Variation of Authorisations.

Schedule 2 Waste Disposal Authorities and Companies.

Part I Transition to Companies.

Part II Provisions regulating Waste Disposal Authorities and Companies.

Schedule 3 Statutory Nuisances: Supplementary Provisions.

Schedule 4 Abandoned Shopping and Luggage Trolleys.

Schedule 5 Further Amendments of the Radioactive Substances Act 1960.

Fire Certificates (Special Premises) Regulations (FCSPR) 1976

Law considered in context / more depth in Elements C3 and C4.

Outline of key points

It was recognised, when the Fire Precautions Act (FPA) 1971 was compiled, that there are special industrial and commercial installations and processes which present particularly significant hazards, not only to people at work, but also to members of the public. In these types of premises, expertise in the administration and enforcement of safety provisions derives from the technical knowledge of the materials and processes in question and their potential hazards, including the risk of fire and explosion. It was decided, therefore, that the additional fire regulations to be made due to the certification under the FPA, should be administered by the same enforcing authority who should control other safety issues within the site. It is for this reason that these regulations are enforced by the Health and Safety Executive (HSE).

It is estimated that between 1,000 and 2,000 premises come under these regulations.

The system laid down in the regulation for the application for, issue of, contents, conditions and amendment to fire certificates is similar to that prescribed under the FPA. However, the variations are highlighted under the requirements for the types of premises that need fire certificates under the Special Premises Regulations.

The main types of premises requiring fire certificates under the Special Premises Regulations are those which:

1. Have more than 50 tonnes of a flammable liquid which is at a pressure greater than atmospheric pressure, and above it boiling point.

2. Manufacture expanded cellular plastics and have quantities of 50 tonnes or more per week.

3. Store 100 tonnes or more of L. P. G.s unless it is for use as a fuel or for heat treatment methods.

4. Store 100 tonnes or more of liquefied natural gas unless it is solely for use as a fuel at the premises themselves.

5. Store 100 tonnes or more of liquefied flammable gas predominantly of methyl acetylene unless it is solely to be used as a fuel at the premises.

6. Store 135 tonnes or more of oxygen or liquid oxygen.

7. Store 50 tonnes or more of chlorine, unless it is solely stored for the purpose of water purification.

8. Storage of 250 tonnes or more of ammonia at premises which manufacture artificial fertilisers.

9.   The following quantities or more of materials are in process, manufacture, use or storage:

Phosgene	5 tonnes
Ethylene Oxide	20 tonnes
Carbon Disulphide	50 tonnes
Acrylonitrile	50 tonnes
Hydrogen Cyanide	50 tonnes
Ethylene	100 tonnes
Propylene	100 tonnes
Any highly flammable liquid	4,000 tonnes

10.   Explosive factories or magazines licensed under the Explosives Act 1875.

11.   Any building on the surface of any mine under the Mines and Quarries Act 1954.

12.   Certain sites which involve nuclear installations.

13.   Certain sites involving radioactive substances.

Fire Precautions (Workplace) Regulations (FPWR) 1997

Law considered in context / more depth in Element C3.

See also – Management of Health and Safety at Work and Fire Precautions (Workplace) (Amendment) Regulations 2003 – on page 293.

Arrangement of Regulations

PART I - PRELIMINARY

1)   Citation, commencement and extent.

2)   Interpretation.

PART II - FIRE PRECAUTIONS IN THE WORKPLACE

3)   Application of Part II.

4)   Fire-fighting and fire detection.

5)   Emergency routes and exits.

6)   Maintenance.

PART III - AMENDMENT OF THE MANAGEMENT OF HEALTH AND SAFETY AT WORK REGULATIONS 1992

7)   Amendment of the 1992 Management Regulations: general provisions.

8)   Amendment of the 1992 Management Regulations.

PART IV - ENFORCEMENT AND OFFENCES

9)   Disapplication of the 1974 Act.

10)   Enforcement.

11)   Serious cases: offence.

12)   Serious cases: prohibition notices.

13)   Serious cases: enforcement notices.

14)   Enforcement notices: rights of appeal.

15)   Enforcement notices: offence.

16)   Enforcement orders.

PART V - FURTHER, CONSEQUENTIAL AND MISCELLANEOUS PROVISIONS

17)   Application of the 1971 Act.

18)   Application to the Crown.

19)   Application to visiting forces, etc.

20)   Application to premises occupied by the UK Atomic Energy Authority.

21)   Employee consultation.

22)   Disapplication of section 9A of the 1971 Act.

Outline of key points

INTRODUCTION

The Fire Precautions (Workplace) Regulations (FPWR) 1997 came into force on the 1st December 1997, and have been amended on 1st December 1999. Note: FPWR also amended again as a result of the Management of Health and Safety at Work and the Fire Precautions (Workplace) (Amendment) Regulations 2003.

APPLICATION

There are few additional responsibilities for the majority of employers. However the Regulations do differ slightly from traditional fire legislation. The main difference is that the regulations apply to all workplaces (with a few exceptions), regardless of the number of employees that work there, unlike the Fire Precautions Act (FPA) 1971.

OBLIGATIONS

The regulations require employers to provide minimum fire safety standards in workplaces.

Where an employer does not have control over parts of the workplace, there is a responsibility on the occupier, owner or landlord to ensure compliance with the regulations.

MAIN REQUIREMENTS

The main requirements of the regulations are as follows:

- Employers to assess the fire risks in the workplace (either as part of existing risk assessment requirements or as a separate area. This is a requirement of the Management of Health and Safety at Work Regulations (MHSWR) 1999.
- Employers must check that a fire can be detected in reasonable time and that people can be warned.
- Employers are to ensure that people who may be in the building can evacuate safely.
- Provide reasonable fire fighting equipment.
- Employers are to check that people in the workplace know what to do if there is a fire.
- Fire safety equipment in the workplace is to be maintained and monitored, to ensure it is in a safe working condition.
- Employer has to nominate employees to implement fire-fighting measures as necessary, and to ensure there are sufficient numbers, equipment, and training.
- Arrange necessary contacts with emergency services, particularly with regard to rescue work and fire fighting.

Fire Precautions Act (FPA) 1971 (as amended by the Fire Safety and Safety of Places of Sport Act 1987)

Law considered in context / more depth in Element C3.

Outline of key points

The FPA requires that a fire certificate be issued for certain premises based on the concept of "designated use". These include:

FACTORY, OFFICES AND SHOPS

Where:

- There are more than 20 persons at work in total.
- There are more than 10 persons (in total) on anything other than the ground floor.
- Adjoining premises, which are not fire separated, accumulate to more than these numbers.
- There are explosives or flammable liquids stored or used.

HOTELS AND BOARDING HOUSES

Where sleeping accommodation is provided for staff or guests:

- For more than six people.
- At basement level.
- Above the first floor level.

Fire Certificates may also be required for premises defined as special premises under the Fire Certification (Special Premises) Regulations 1976.

CONTENTS OF A FIRE CERTIFICATE

Include the specification of:

- Use of premises.
- Means of escape.
- Means of securing safe escape. i.e. provision of suitable extinguishers, alarms, fire doors etc.
- Special requirements for explosives, flammables etc.
- Maintenance of fire escape routes.
- Training of employees in fire safety, use of extinguishers etc.
- Maximum number of people in the building at any one time.

Health and Safety (First-Aid) Regulations (FAR) 1981

Law considered in context / more depth in Element C1.

See also – Health and Safety (Miscellaneous Amendments) Regulations (MAR) 2002 – below.

Arrangement of Regulations

1) Citation and commencement.

2) Interpretation.

3) Duty of employer to make provision for first-aid.

4) Duty of employer to inform his employees of the arrangements.

5) Duty of self-employed person to provide first-aid equipment.

6) Power to grant exemptions.

7) Cases where these Regulations do not apply.

8) Application to mines.

9) Application offshore.

10) Repeals, revocations and modification.

Schedule 1 Repeals.

Schedule 1 Revocations.

Outline of key points

2) Regulation 2 defines first aid as: '…treatment for the purpose of preserving life and minimising the consequences of injury or illness until medical (doctor or nurse) help can be obtained. Also, it provides treatment of minor injuries which would otherwise receive no treatment, or which do not need the help of a medical practitioner or nurse.'

3) Requires that every employer must provide equipment and facilities which are adequate and appropriate in the circumstances for administering first-aid to his employees.

4) An employer must inform his employees about the first-aid arrangements, including the location of equipment, facilities and identification of trained personnel.

5) Self-employed people must ensure that adequate and suitable provision is made for administering first-aid while at work.

Health and Safety (Miscellaneous Amendments) Regulations 2002

Law considered in context / more depth in Elements C1, C5, C6, C7 and C9.

See also – First Aid 1981 (page 282), PPER 1992 (page 295), WHSWR 1992 (page 307), PUWER 1998 (page 300) and LOLER 1998 (page 288).

These Regulations make minor amendments to UK law to come into line with the requirements of the original Directives and came into force on 17th September 2002. In relation to this publication, the Regulations that are effected by the amendments are:

- Health and Safety (First-Aid) Regulations 1981
- Personal Protective Equipment at Work Regulations 1992.
- Workplace (Health, Safety and Welfare) Regulations 1992.
- Provision and Use of Work Equipment Regulations 1998.
- Lifting Operations and Lifting Equipment Regulations 1998

Arrangement of Regulations

1) Citation and commencement.

2) Amendment of the Health and Safety (First-Aid) Regulations 1981.

3) Amendment of the Health and Safety (Display Screen Equipment) Regulations 1992.

4) Amendment of the Manual Handling Operations Regulations 1992.

5) Amendment of the Personal Protective Equipment at Work Regulations 1992.

6) Amendment of the Workplace (Health, Safety and Welfare) Regulations 1992.

7) Amendment of the Provision and Use of Work Equipment Regulations 1998.

8) Amendment of the Lifting Operations and Lifting Equipment Regulations 1998.

9) Amendment of the Quarries Regulations 1999.

Outline of key points (relevant to this publication only)

REGULATION 3 - AMENDMENT OF THE HEALTH AND SAFETY (FIRST AID) REGULATIONS 1981

The Health and Safety (First Aid) Regulations 1981 shall be amended by adding the following paragraph -

(5)   "Any first-aid room provided pursuant to this regulation shall be easily accessible to stretchers and to any other equipment needed to convey patients to and from the room and be sign-posted, and such sign to comply with regulation 4 of the Health and Safety (Safety Signs and Signals) Regulations 1996 as if it were provided in accordance with that regulation.".

REGULATION 5 - AMENDMENT OF THE PERSONAL PROTECTIVE EQUIPMENT AT WORK REGULATIONS 1992

The Personal Protective Equipment at Work Regulations 1992 shall be amended -

(a)   by substituting for sub-paragraphs (a) and (b) of paragraph (3) of regulation 4 the following sub-paragraphs -

"(a) it is appropriate for the risk or risks involved, the conditions at the place where exposure to the risk may occur, and the period for which it is worn;
(b) it takes account of ergonomic requirements and the state of health of the person or persons who may wear it, and of the characteristics of the workstation of each such person;";

(b)   by adding to regulation 4 the following paragraph -

"(4) Where it is necessary to ensure that personal protective equipment is hygienic and otherwise free of risk to health, every employer and every self-employed person shall ensure that personal protective equipment provided under this regulation is provided to a person for use only by him.";

(c)   in paragraph (2) of regulation 6, by adding the following sub-paragraph -

"(d) an assessment as to whether the personal protective equipment is compatible with other personal protective equipment which is in use and which an employee would be required to wear simultaneously.";

(d)   in paragraph (1) of regulation 9 by adding after sub-paragraph (c) the words "and shall ensure that such information is kept available to employees"; and

(e)   in paragraph (3) of regulation 9 by adding the following paragraph -

"(3) Without prejudice to the generality of paragraph (1) the employer shall, where appropriate, and at suitable intervals, organise demonstrations in the wearing of personal protective equipment.".

REGULATION 6 - AMENDMENT OF THE WORKPLACE (HEALTH, SAFETY AND WELFARE) REGULATIONS 1992

The Workplace (Health, Safety and Welfare) Regulations 1992 shall be amended -

(a)   in regulation 2(1), by inserting, before the definition of "new workplace", the following definition -

"disabled person" has the meaning given by section 1 of the Disability Discrimination Act 1995;

(b)   in the definition of "workplace" in regulation 2(1), by deleting the words "but shall not" to the end of the definition;

(c)   by inserting after regulation 4 the following regulation -

" **Stability and solidity**
4A. Where a workplace is in a building, the building shall have a stability and solidity appropriate to the nature of the use of the workplace.";

(d)   in regulation 5(3) -

(i) by deleting the word "and" after sub-paragraph (a);
(ii) by adding the word "and" after sub-paragraph (b); and
(iii) by adding the following sub-paragraph -

" (c) equipment and devices intended to prevent or reduce hazards";

(e)   by deleting regulation 6(3);
(f)   in regulation 7, by inserting the following paragraph -

" (1A) Without prejudice to the generality of paragraph (1) -

(a) a workplace shall be adequately thermally insulated where it is necessary, having regard to the type of work carried out and the physical activity of the persons carrying out the work; and
(b) excessive effects of sunlight on temperature shall be avoided.";

(g)   in paragraph (2) of regulation 24, by adding the words "and the facilities are easily accessible, of sufficient capacity and provided with seating";

(h)   in regulation 25, by substituting for paragraph (3) the following paragraph -

" (3) Rest rooms and rest areas shall -

(a) include suitable arrangements to protect non-smokers from discomfort caused by tobacco smoke; and
(b) be equipped with -

(i) an adequate number of tables and adequate seating with backs for the number of persons at work likely to use them at any one time; and
(ii) seating which is adequate for the number of disabled persons at work and suitable for them.";

(i)   by inserting after regulation 25 the following regulation -

" **Disabled persons**
25A. Where necessary, those parts of the workplace (including in particular doors, passageways, stairs, showers, washbasins, lavatories and workstations) used or occupied directly by disabled persons at work shall be organised to take account of such persons.".

AMENDMENT OF THE PROVISION AND USE OF WORK EQUIPMENT REGULATIONS 1998

The Provision and Use of Work Equipment Regulations 1998[7] shall be amended -

(a)   by substituting for paragraphs (1) and (2) of regulation 10 the following paragraphs -

10.   (1)   "Every employer shall ensure that an item of work equipment conforms at all times with any essential requirements, other than requirements which, at the time of its being first supplied or put into service in any place in which these Regulations apply, did not apply to work equipment of its type.

        (2)   In this regulation "essential requirements", in relation to an item of work equipment, means requirements relating to the design and construction of work equipment of its type in any of the instruments listed in Schedule 1 (being instruments which give effect to Community directives concerning the safety of products)";

(b)   by substituting for paragraph (2) of regulation 11 the following paragraph -

11. (2)   "The measures required by paragraph (1) shall consist of -

        (a)   the provision of fixed guards enclosing every dangerous part or rotating stock-bar where and to the extent that it is practicable to do so, but where or to the extent that it is not, then

        (b)   the provision of other guards or protection devices where and to the extent that it is practicable to do so, but where or to the extent that it is not, then

        (c)   the provision of jigs, holders, push-sticks or similar protection appliances used in conjunction with the machinery where and to the extent that it is practicable to do so, and the provision of such information, instruction, training and supervision as is necessary.";

(c)   by substituting for paragraph (1) of regulation 18 the following paragraph -

18.   (1)   "Every employer shall ensure, so far as is reasonably practicable, that all control systems of work equipment -

        (a)   are safe; and

        (b)   are chosen making due allowance for the failures, faults and constraints to be expected in the planned circumstances of use.";

        (d)   in paragraph (2) of regulation 35, by substituting for the words "33(1)(a)(ii) or (2)(b)" the words "33".

AMENDMENT OF THE LIFTING OPERATIONS AND LIFTING EQUIPMENT REGULATIONS 1998

The Lifting Operations and Lifting Equipment Regulations 1998 shall be amended:

(a)   in the definition of "accessory for lifting" in regulation 2(1), by substituting for the word "work" the word "lifting";

(b)   in regulation 3(4), by substituting for the words "(5)(b)" the words "(3)(b)".

SUMMARY OF AMENDMENTS

- Minor changes to the Health and Safety (First Aid) Regulations 1981 regarding accessibility and sign posting to the first aid room.
- Regarding amendments to the Personal Protective Equipment At Work Regulations 1992 - PPE must be appropriate for the risk or risks, the conditions in the workplace where exposure to the risk may occur and the period it is to be worn. It must also take into account ergonomic requirement, the state of health of the person wearing it and the workstation characteristics.
- Minor changes to the definitions in the Workplace (Health, Safety and Welfare) Regulations and to the wording about thermal insulation of buildings and avoidance of excessive effects of sunlight. Also requires rest rooms to include suitable arrangements to protect non-smokers from smoke discomfort, to have adequate tables and seating with backs and an adequate amount of suitable seating for the disabled.
- Regarding amendments to the Provision and Use of Work Equipment Regulations 1998 - all items of work equipment must conform at all times with any essential requirements; 'essential requirements' being requirements relating to the design and construction of work equipment as listed in Schedule 1. Also, the required measures for machinery guarding or protection devices or the provision of jigs and push-sticks or similar protection devices; plus the provision of information, instruction, training and supervision as is necessary. Also, the requirements regarding control systems of work equipment.
- Minor changes to the definitions in the Lifting Operations and Lifting Equipment Regulations 1998.

Health and Safety (Safety Signs and Signals) Regulations (SSSR) 1996

Law considered in context / more depth in Elements C1, C3 and C4.

Arrangement of Regulations

1)   Citation and commencement.

2)   Interpretation.

3)   Application.

4)   Provision and maintenance of safety signs.

5)   Information, instruction and training.

6)   Transitional provisions.

7)   Enforcement.

8)   Revocations and amendments.

Outline of key points

The Regulations require employers to provide specific safety signs whenever there is a risk which has not been avoided or controlled by other means, e.g. by engineering controls and safe systems of work. Where a safety sign would not help to reduce that risk, or where the sign is not significant, there is no need to provide a sign.

They require, where necessary, the use of road traffic signs within workplaces to regulate road traffic.

They also require employers to:

- Maintain the safety signs which are provided by them.
- Explain unfamiliar signs to their employees and tell them what they need to do when they see a safety sign.

Regs cover 4 main areas of signs:

1)   *PROHIBITION* - circular signs, prime colours red and white. e.g. no pedestrian access.

2)   *WARNING* - triangular signs, prime colours black on yellow.   e.g. overhead electrics.

3)   *MANDATORY* - circular signs, prime colours blue and white e.g. safety helmets must be worn.

4)   *SAFE CONDITION* - oblong/square signs, prime colours green and white e.g. fire exit, first aid etc.

Supplementary signs provide additional information.

Supplementary signs with yellow/black or red/white diagonal stripes can be used to highlight a hazard, but must not substitute for signs as defined above.

Fire fighting, rescue equipment and emergency exit signs have to comply with a separate British Standard.

Health and Safety at Work etc. Act (HASAWA) 1974

Law considered in context / more depth in Element C1 (HASAWA Section 2(2)(d) and(e).

Arrangement of Act

PRELIMINARY

1)   Preliminary.

GENERAL DUTIES

2)   General duties of employers to the employees.

3)   General duties of employers and self-employed to persons other than their employees.

4)   General duties of persons concerned with premises to persons other than their employees.

5)   [repealed].

6)   General duties of manufacturers etc. as regards articles and substances for use at work.

7)   General duties of employees at work.

8)   Duty not to interfere with or misuse things provided pursuant to certain provisions.

9)   Duty not to charge employees for things done or provided pursuant to certain specific requirements.

THE HEALTH AND SAFETY COMMISSION AND THE HEALTH AND SAFETY EXECUTIVE

10)   Establishment of the Commission and the Executive.

11)   General functions of the Commission and the Executive.

12)   Control of the Commission by the Secretary of State.

13)   Other powers of the Commission.

14)   Power of the Commission to direct investigations and Inquiries.

HEALTH AND SAFETY REGULATIONS AND APPROVED CODES OF PRACTICE

15)   Health and safety regulations.

16)   Approval of codes of practice by the Commission.

17)   Use of approved codes of practice in criminal proceedings.

ENFORCEMENT

18)   Authorities responsible for enforcement of the relevant statutory provisions.

19)   Appointment of inspectors.

20)   Powers of inspectors.

21)   Improvement notices.

22)   Prohibition notices.

23)   Provisions supplementary toss. 21 and 22.

24)   Appeal against improvement or prohibition notice.

25)   Power to deal with cause of imminent danger.

26)   Power of enforcing authorities to indemnify their inspectors.

OBTAINING AND DISCLOSURE OF INFORMATION

27)   Obtaining of information by the Commission, the Executive, enforcing authorities etc.

28)   Restrictions on disclosure of information.

SPECIAL PROVISIONS RELATING TO AGRICULTURE

29-32)   [repealed].

PROVISIONS AS TO OFFENCES

33)   Offences.

34)   Extension of time for bringing summary proceedings.

35)   Venue.

36)   Offences due to fault of other person.

37)   Offences by bodies corporate.

38)   Restriction on institution of proceedings in England and Wales.

39)   Prosecutions by inspectors.

40)   Onus of proving limits of what is practicable etc.

41)   Evidence.

42)   Power of court to order cause of offence to be remedied or, in certain cases, forfeiture.

FINANCIAL PROVISION

43)   Financial provisions.

MISCELLANEOUS AND SUPPLEMENTARY

44)   Appeals in connection with licensing provisions in the relevant statutory provisions.

45)   Default powers.

46)   Service of notices.

47)   Civil liability.

48)   Application to Crown.

49)   Adaptation of enactments to metric units or appropriate metric units.

50)   Regulations under the relevant statutory provisions.

51)   Exclusion of application to domestic employment.

52)   Meaning of work and at work.

53)   General interpretation of Part I.

54)   Application of Part I to Isles of Scilly.

Outline of key points

AIMS

1)   To protect people.

2)   To protect the public from risks which may arise from work activities.

THE MAIN PROVISIONS - SECTION 1

a)   Securing the health, safety and welfare of people at work.

b)   Protecting others against risks arising from workplace activities.

c)   Controlling the obtaining, keeping, and use of explosive and highly flammable substances.

d)   Controlling emissions into the atmosphere of noxious or offensive substances.

Duties imposed on:

a)   The employer.

b)   The self employed.

c)   Employees.

d)   Contractors and subcontractors.

e)   Designers, manufacturers, suppliers, importers and installers.

f)   Specialists - architects, surveyors, engineers, personnel managers, health and safety specialists, and many more.

EMPLOYER'S DUTIES - [TO EMPLOYEES]

Section 2(1)

To ensure, so far as *reasonably practicable*, the health, safety and welfare at work of employees.

Section 2(2)

Ensuring health, safety and welfare at work through:

a)   Safe plant and systems of work e.g. provision of guards on machines.

b)   Safe use, handling, storage and transport of goods and materials e.g. good manual handling of boxes.

c)   Provision of information, instruction, training and supervision e.g. provision of induction training.

d)   Safe place of work including means of access and egress e.g. aisles kept clear.

e)   Safe and healthy working environment e.g. good lighting.

Further duties are placed on the employer by:

Section 2(3)

Prepare and keep up to date a written safety policy supported by information on the organisation and arrangements for carrying out the policy. The safety policy has to be brought to the notice of employees. If there are fewer than five employees, this section does not apply.

Section 2(4)

Recognised Trade Unions have the right to appoint safety representatives to represent the employees in consultations with the employer about health and safety matters.

Section 2(6)

Employers must consult with any safety representatives appointed by recognised Trade Unions.

Section 2(7)

To establish a safety committee if requested by two or more safety representatives.

EMPLOYER'S DUTIES - [TO PERSONS NOT HIS EMPLOYEES]

Section 3

a)   Not to expose them to risk to their heath and safety e.g. contractor work barriered off.

b)   To give information about risks which may affect them e.g. location induction for contractors.

Figure C11-2: Risks from road side work.   *Source: ACT.*

Figure C11-3: Risks from street light repair or tree felling. *Source: ACT.*

SELF EMPLOYED DUTIES

Section 3

a)   Not to expose themselves to risks to their health and safety e.g. wear personal protection.

b)   Not to expose other persons to risks to their health and safety e.g. keep shared work area tidy.

Some of the practical steps that an organisation might take in order to ensure the safety of visitors to its premises are:

- Identify visitors by signing in, badges etc.
- Provide information regarding the risks present and the site rules and procedures to be followed, particularly in emergencies.
- Provide escorts to supervise visitors throughout the site.
- Restrict access to certain areas.

PEOPLE IN CONTROL OF PREMISES

Section 4

This section places duties on anyone who has control to any extent of non-domestic premises used by people who are not their employees. The duty extends to the provision of safe premises, plant and substances, e.g. maintenance of a boiler in rented out property.

MANUFACTURERS, DESIGNERS, SUPPLIERS, IMPORTERS, INSTALLERS

Section 6

This section places specific duties on those who can ensure that articles and substances are as safe and without risks as is reasonably practicable. The section covers:

- Safe design, installation and testing of equipment (including fairground equipment).
- Safe substances tested for risks.
- Provision of information on safe use and conditions essential to health and safety.
- Research to minimise risks.

EMPLOYEES' DUTIES

Section 7

a)   To take reasonable care for themselves and others that may be affected by their acts / omissions e.g. wear eye protection, not obstruct a fire exit.

b)   To co-operate with the employer or other to enable them to carry out their duty and/or statutory requirements e.g. report hazards or defects in controls, attend training, provide medical samples.

Additional duties created by the Management of Health and Safety at Work

Regulations employees' duties:

- Every employee shall use any equipment, material or substance provided to them in accordance with any training and instruction.
- Every employee shall inform (via supervisory staff) their employer of any (a) risk situation or (b) shortcoming in the employer's protection arrangements.

OTHER DUTIES

Section 8

No person to interfere with or misuse anything provided to secure health and safety - e.g. wedge fire door open, remove first aid equipment without authority, breach lock off systems.

Section 9

Employees cannot be charged for anything done or provided to comply with a specific legal obligation e.g. personal protective equipment, health surveillance or welfare facilities.

OFFENCES COMMITTED BY OTHER PERSONS

Section 36

- Where the commission by any person of the breach of legislation is due to the act or default of some other person, that other
- person shall be guilty of the offence and may be charged with and convicted of the offence whether or not proceedings are
- taken against the first mentioned person.
- Case law indicates that 'other person' refers to persons lower down the corporate tree than mentioned in section 37, e.g.
- middle managers, safety advisors, training officers; and may extend to people working on contract e.g. architects, consultants
- or a planning supervisor.

OFFENCES COMMITTED BY THE BODY CORPORATE

Section 37

- Where there has been a breach of legislation on the part of a body corporate (limited company or local authority) and the offence can be proved to have been committed with the consent or connivance of or to be attributable to any neglect on the part of any director, manager, secretary or similar officer of the body corporate, he, as well as the body corporate, can be found guilty and punished accordingly.

ONUS OF PROOF

Section 40

In any proceedings for an offence under any of the relevant statutory involving a failure to comply with a duty or requirement:

- to do something so far as is practicable or
- to do something so far as is reasonably practicable.

it shall be for the accused to prove that the requirements were met rather than for the prosecution to prove that the requirements were not met.

Lifting Operations and Lifting Equipment Regulations (LOLER) 1998

Law considered in context / more depth in Elements C5, C7 and C9.

See also – Health and Safety (Miscellaneous Amendments) Regulations (MAR) 2002 – on page 282.

Arrangements of Regulations

1)   Citation and commencement.

2)   Interpretation.

3)   Application.

4)   Strength and stability.

5)   Lifting equipment for lifting persons.

6)   Positioning and installation.

7)   Marking of lifting equipment.

8)   Organisation of lifting operations.

9)   Thorough examination and inspection.

10)   Reports and defects.

11)   Keeping of information.

12)   Exemption for the armed forces.

13)   Amendment of the Shipbuilding and Ship-repairing Regulations 1960.

14)   Amendment of the Docks Regulation 1988.

15)   Repeal of provisions of the Factories Act 1961.

16)   Repeal of section 85 of the Mines and Quarries Act 1954.

17)   Revocation of instruments.

Schedule 1.   Information to be contained in a report of a thorough examination.

Schedule 2.   Revocation of instruments.

Outline of key points

The Lifting Operations and Lifting Equipment Regulations (LOLER) 1998 impose health and safety requirements with respect to lifting equipment (as defined in regulation 2(1)). They are not industry specific and apply to almost all lifting operations.

The Regulations place duties on employers, the self-employed, and certain persons having control of lifting equipment (of persons at work who use or supervise or manage its use, or of the way it is used, to the extent of their control (regulation 3(3) to (5)).

The Regulations make provision with respect to:

- The strength and stability of lifting equipment (regulation 4).
- The safety of lifting equipment for lifting persons (regulation 5).
- The way lifting equipment is positioned and installed (regulation 6).
- The marking of machinery and accessories for lifting, and lifting equipment which is designed for lifting persons or which might so be used in error (regulation 7).
- The organisation of lifting operations (regulation 8).
- The thorough examination (defined in (regulation 2(1)) and inspection of lifting equipment in specified circumstances, (regulation 9(1) to (3)).
- The evidence of examination to accompany it outside the undertaking (regulation 9(4)).
- The exception for winding apparatus at mines from regulation 9 (regulation 9(5)).
- Transitional arrangements relating to regulation 9 (regulation 9(6) and (7)).
- The making of reports of thorough examinations and records of inspections (regulation 10 and Schedule 1).
- The keeping of information in the reports and records (regulation 11).

Management of Health and Safety at Work Regulations (MHSWR) 1999

Law considered in context / more depth in Elements C1 and C3.

See also – Management of Health and Safety at Work and Fire Precautions (Workplace) (Amendment) Regulations 2003 – on page 293.

Arrangement of Regulations

1)   Citation, commencement and interpretation.

2)   Disapplication of these Regulations.

3)   Risk assessment.

4)   Principles of prevention to be applied.

5)   Health and safety arrangements.

6)   Health surveillance.

7)   Health and safety assistance.

8)   Procedures for serious and imminent danger and for danger areas.

9)   Contacts with external services.

10)   Information for employees.

11)   Co-operation and co-ordination.

12)   Persons working in host employers' or self-employed persons' undertakings.

13)   Capabilities and training.

14)   Employees' duties.

15)   Temporary workers.

16)   Risk assessment in respect of new or expectant mothers.

17)	Certificate from a registered medical practitioner in respect of new or expectant mothers.

18)	Notification by new or expectant mothers.

19)	Protection of young persons.

20)	Exemption certificates.

21)	Provisions as to liability.

22)	Exclusion of civil liability.

23)	Extension outside Great Britain.

24)	Amendment of the Health and Safety (First-Aid) Regulations 1981.

25)	Amendment of the Offshore Installations and Pipeline Works (First-Aid) Regulations 1989.

26)	Amendment of the Mines Miscellaneous Health and Safety Provisions Regulations 1995.

27)	Amendment of the Construction (Health, Safety and Welfare) Regulations 1996.

28)	Regulations to have effect as health and safety regulations.

29)	Revocations and consequential amendments.

30)	Transitional provision.

Schedule 1.	General principles of prevention.

Schedule 2.	Consequential amendments.

Outline of key points

The Management of Health and Safety at Work Regulations (MHSWR) 1999 (and as amended 2003) set out some broad general duties which apply to almost all kinds of work. They are aimed mainly at improving health and safety management. You may already be familiar with broad health and safety law of this kind - as it is the form taken by the Health and Safety at Work Act (HASAWA) 1974. The Regulations work in a similar way, and in fact they can be seen as a way of fleshing out what is already in the HASAWA. The Management of Health and Safety at Work Regulations and the Fire Precautions (Workplace) (Amendment) Regulations 2003 amend the MHSWR 1999; which previously replaced the MHSWR 1992, the MHSW (Amendment) Regulations 1994, the Health and Safety (Young Persons) Regulations 1997 and Part III of the FPWR 1997. The Principal Regulations are discussed below.

RISK ASSESSMENT (REGULATION 3)

The regulations require employers (and the self-employed) to assess the risk to the health and safety of their employees and to anyone else who may be affected by their work activity. This is necessary to ensure that the preventive and protective steps can be identified to control hazards in the workplace.

A *hazard* is defined as something with the potential to cause harm and may include machinery, substances or a work practice.

A *risk* is defined as the likelihood that a particular hazard will cause harm. Consideration must be given to the population, i.e. the number of persons who might be exposed to harm and the consequence of such exposure.

Where an employer is employing or about to employ young persons (under 18 years of age) he must carry out a risk assessment which takes particular account of:

■	The inexperience, lack of awareness of risks and immaturity of young persons.

■	The layout of the workplace and workstations.

■	Exposure to physical, biological and chemical agents.

■	Work equipment and the way in which it is handled.

■	The extent of health and safety training to be provided.

■	Risks from agents, processes and work listed in the Annex to Council Directive 94/33/EC on the protection of young people at work.

Where 5 or more employees are employed, the significant findings of risk assessments must be recorded in writing (the same threshold that is used in respect of having a written safety policy). This record must include details of any employees being identified as being especially at risk.

PRINCIPLES OF PREVENTION TO BE APPLIED (REGULATION 4)

Regulation 4 requires an employer to implement preventive and protective measures on the basis of general principles of prevention specified in Schedule 1 to the Regulations. These are:

1)	Avoiding risks.

2)	Evaluating the risks which cannot be avoided.

3)	Combating the risks at source.

4)	adapting the work to the individual, especially as regards the design of workplaces, the choice of work equipment and the choice of working and production methods, with a view, in particular, to alleviating monotonous work and work at a predetermined work-rate and to reducing their effect on health.

5)	Adapting to technical progress.

6)	Replacing the dangerous by the non-dangerous or the less dangerous.

7)	Developing a coherent overall prevention policy which covers technology, organisation of work, working conditions, social relationships and the influence of factors relating to the working environment.

8)	Giving collective protective measures priority over individual protective measures.

9)	Giving appropriate instructions to employees.

HEALTH AND SAFETY ARRANGEMENTS (REGULATION 5)

Appropriate arrangements must be made for the effective planning, organisation, control, monitoring and review of preventative and protective measures (in other words, for the management of health and safety). Again, employers with five or more employees must have their arrangements in writing.

HEALTH SURVEILLANCE (REGULATION 6)

In addition to the requirements of specific regulations such as Control of Substances Hazardous to Health (COSHH) and Asbestos regulations, consideration must be given to carry out health surveillance of employees where there is a disease or adverse health condition identified in risk assessments.

HEALTH AND SAFETY ASSISTANCE (REGULATION 7)

The employer must appoint one or more competent persons to assist him in complying with the legal obligations imposed on the undertaking (including Part II of the Fire Precautions (Workplace) Regulations (FPWR) 1997 - Note: FPWR amended 2003). The number of persons appointed should reflect the number of employees and the type of hazards in the workplace.

If more than one competent person is appointed, then arrangements must be made for ensuring adequate co-operation between them. The Competent person(s) must be given the necessary time and resources to fulfil their functions. This will depend on the size the undertaking, the risks to which employees are exposed and the distribution of those risks throughout the undertaking.

The employer must ensure that competent person(s) who are not employees are informed of the factors known (or suspected) to affect the health and safety of anyone affected by business activities.

Competent people are defined as those who have sufficient training and experience or knowledge and other qualities to enable them to perform their functions.

Persons may be selected from among existing employees or from outside. Where there is a suitable person in the employer's employment, that person shall be appointed as the 'competent person' in preference to a non-employee.

PROCEDURES FOR SERIOUS AND IMMINENT DANGER AND FOR DANGER AREAS (REGULATION 8)

Employers are required to set up emergency procedures and appoint **competent persons** to ensure compliance with identified arrangements, to devise control strategies as appropriate and to limit access to areas of risk to ensure that only those persons with adequate health and safety knowledge and instruction are admitted.

The factors to be considered when preparing a procedure to deal with workplace emergencies such as fire, explosion, bomb scare, chemical leakage or other dangerous occurrence should include:

- The identification and training requirements of persons with specific responsibilities.
- The layout of the premises in relation to escape routes etc.
- The number of persons affected.
- Assessment of special needs (disabled persons, children etc.).
- Warning systems.
- Emergency lighting.
- Location of shut-off valves, isolation switches, hydrants etc.
- Equipment required to deal with the emergency.
- Location of assembly points.
- Communication with emergency services.
- Training and/or information to be given to employees, visitors, local residents and anyone else who might be affected

CONTACTS WITH EXTERNAL SERVICES (REGULATION 9)

Employers must ensure that, where necessary, contacts are made with external services. This particularly applies with regard to first-aid, emergency medical care and rescue work.

INFORMATION FOR EMPLOYEES (REGULATION 10)

Employees must be provided with relevant information about hazards to their health and safety arising from risks identified by the assessments. Clear instruction must be provided concerning any preventative or protective control measures including those relating to serious and imminent danger and fire assessments. Details of any competent persons nominated to discharge specific duties in accordance with the regulations must also be communicated as should risks arising from contact with other employer's activities (see Regulation 11).

Before employing a child (a person who is not over compulsory school age) the employer must provide those with parental responsibility for the child with information on the risks that have been identified and preventative and protective measures to be taken.

CO-OPERATION AND CO-ORDINATION (REGULATION 11)

Employers who work together in a common workplace have a duty to co-operate to discharge their duties under relevant statutory provisions. They must also take all reasonable steps to inform their respective employees of risks to their health or safety which may arise out of their work. Specific arrangements must be made to ensure compliance with fire legislation (i.e. the Fire Precautions (Workplace) Regulations (FPWR) 1997 - Note: FPWR amended 2003).

PERSONS WORKING IN HOST EMPLOYERS' OR SELF EMPLOYED PERSONS' UNDERTAKINGS (REGULATION 12)

This regulation extends the requirements of regulation 11 to include employees working as sole occupiers of a workplace under the control of another employer. Such employees would include those working under a service of contract and employees in temporary employment businesses under the control of the first employer.

CAPABILITIES AND TRAINING (REGULATION 13)

Employers need to take into account the capabilities of their employees before entrusting tasks. This is necessary to ensure that they have adequate health and safety training and are capable enough at their jobs to avoid risk. To this end consideration must be given to recruitment including job orientation when transferring between jobs and work departments. Training must also be provided when other factors such as the introduction of new technology and new systems of work or work equipment arise.

Training must

- Be repeated periodically where appropriate.
- Be adapted to take account of any new or changed risks to the health and safety of the employees concerned.
- Take place during working hours.

EMPLOYEES' DUTIES (REGULATION 14)

Employees are required to follow health and safety instructions by using machinery, substances, transport etc. in accordance with the instructions and training that they have received.

They must also inform their employer (and other employers) of any dangers or shortcoming in the health and safety arrangements, even if there is no risk of imminent danger.

TEMPORARY WORKERS (REGULATION 15)

Consideration is given to the special needs of temporary workers. In particular to the provision of particular health and safety information such as qualifications required to perform the task safely or any special arrangements such as the need to provide health screening.

RISKS ASSESSMENT IN RESPECT OF NEW OR EXPECTANT MOTHERS (REGULATION 16)

Where the work is of a kind which would involve risk to a new or expectant mother or her baby, then the assessment required by regulation 3 should take this into account.

If the risk cannot be avoided, then the employer should take reasonable steps to:

- Adjust the hours worked, or
- Offer alternative work, or
- Give paid leave for as long as is necessary.

CERTIFICATE FROM A REGISTERED MEDICAL PRACTITIONER IN RESPECT OF NEW OR EXPECTANT MOTHERS (REGULATION 17)

Where the woman is a night shift worker and has a medical certificate identifying night shift work as a risk then the employer must put her on day shift or give paid leave for as long as is necessary.

NOTIFICATION BY NEW OR EXPECTANT MOTHERS (REGULATION 18)

The employer need take no action until he is notified in writing by the woman that she is pregnant, has given birth in the last six months, or is breastfeeding.

PROTECTION OF YOUNG PERSONS (REGULATION 19)

Employers of young persons shall ensure that they are not exposed to risk as a consequence of their lack of experience, lack of awareness or lack of maturity.

No employer shall employ young people for work which:

- Is beyond his physical or psychological capacity.
- Involves exposure to agents which chronically affect human health.
- Involves harmful exposure to radiation.
- Involves a risk to health from extremes of temperature, noise or vibration.
- Involves risks which could not be reasonably foreseen by young persons.

This regulation does not prevent the employment of a young person who is no longer a child for work:

- Where it is necessary for his training.
- Where the young person will be supervised by a competent person.
- Where any risk will be reduced to the lowest level that is reasonably practicable.

(Note: Two HSE publications give guidance on the changes. HSG122 - New and expectant mothers at work: a guide for employers and HSG165 - Young people at work: a guide for employers.)

EXEMPTION CERTIFICATES (REGULATION 20)

The Secretary of State for Defence may, in the interests of national security, by a certificate in writing exempt the armed forces, any visiting force or any headquarters from certain obligations imposed by the Regulations.

PROVISIONS AS TO LIABILITY (REGULATION 21)

Employers cannot submit a defence in criminal proceedings that contravention was caused by the act or default either of an employee or the competent person appointed under Regulation 7.

EXCLUSION OF CIVIL LIABILITY (REGULATION 22)

Breach of a duty imposed by these Regulations shall not confer a right of action in any civil proceedings for those other than employees.

REVOCATIONS AND AMENDMENTS (REGULATIONS 24-29)

The Regulations:

- Revoke regulation 6 of the Health and Safety (First-Aid) Regulations (FAR) 1981 which confers power on the Health and Safety
- Executive to grant exemptions from those Regulations.
- Amend the Offshore Installations and Pipeline Works (First-Aid) Regulations 1989.
- Amend the Mines Miscellaneous Health and Safety Provisions Regulations 1995.
- Amend the Construction (Health, Safety and Welfare) Regulations 1996.

The Regulations provide that, with some exceptions, the Fire Precautions (Workplace) Regulations (FPWR) 1997 are to be considered as health and safety regulations within the meaning of the Health and Safety at Work etc Act (HASAWA) 1974. The Regulations also make amendments to the statutory instruments as specified in Schedule 2.

TRANSITIONAL PROVISION (REGULATION 30)

The Regulations contain a transitional provision (regulation 30). The substitution of provisions in the 1999 Regulations for provisions of the Management of Health and Safety at Work Regulations (MHSWR) 1992 shall not affect the continuity of the law; and accordingly anything done under or for the purposes of such provision of the 1992 Regulations shall have effect as if done under or for the purposes of any corresponding provision of these Regulations.

Management of Health and Safety at Work and Fire Precautions (Workplace) (Amendment) Regulations 2003

Law considered in context / more depth in Elements C1 and C3.

See also – Management of Health and Safety at Work Regulations (MHSWR) 1999 – on page 289.

See also – Fire Precautions (Workplace) Regulations (FPWR) 1997 – on page 280.

Arrangement of Regulations

1)   Citation and commencement

2-6)   Amendments to the Management of Health and Safety at Work Regulations 1999

7-13)   Amendments to the Fire Precautions (Workplace) Regulations 1997

Outline of key points

AMENDMENTS TO MANAGEMENT OF HEALTH AND SAFETY AT WORK REGULATIONS 1999

2.   The Management of Health and Safety at Work Regulations 1999[5] shall be amended in accordance with regulations 3 to 6 of these Regulations and any reference in those provisions to any specified provision shall, unless the context requires otherwise, be taken to be a reference to the provision so specified of the Management of Health and Safety at Work Regulations 1999.

3.   For regulation 2 there shall be substituted the following regulation -

" Disapplication of these Regulations 2. -

(1) These Regulations shall not apply to or in relation to the master or crew of a ship, or to the employer of such persons, in respect of the normal ship-board activities of a ship's crew which are carried out solely by the crew under the direction of the master.

(2) Regulations 3(4), (5), 10(2) and 19 shall not apply to occasional work or short-term work involving work regarded as not being harmful, damaging or dangerous to young people in a family undertaking.

(3) In this regulation -

"normal ship-board activities" include -

(a) the construction, reconstruction or conversion of a ship outside, but not inside, Great Britain; and

(b) the repair of a ship save repair when carried out in dry dock; "ship" includes every description of vessel used in navigation, other than a ship belonging to Her Majesty which forms part of Her Majesty's Navy.".

4.   In regulation 3(3) the words "and where" to the end shall follow and not appear in subparagraph (b).

5.   Regulation 19(4) shall be omitted.

6.   For regulation 22 there shall be substituted the following regulation - " Restriction of civil liability for breach of statutory duty 22. Breach of a duty imposed on an employer by these Regulations shall not confer a right of action in any civil proceedings insofar as that duty applies for the protection of persons not in his employment."

AMENDMENTS TO FIRE PRECAUTIONS (WORKPLACE) REGULATIONS 1997

7.   The Fire Precautions (Workplace) Regulations 1997[6] shall be amended in accordance with regulations 8 to 13 of these Regulations and any reference in those provisions to any specified provision shall, unless the context requires otherwise, be taken to be a reference to the provision so specified of the Fire Precautions (Workplace) Regulations 1997.

8.   In regulation 9(1) there shall be omitted the words "provisions of health and safety regulations or".

9.   In regulation 9(2)(a)(ii), for the words "premises to which" there shall be substituted the words "premises of a description specified in Part I of Schedule 1 to" and the word "apply" shall be omitted.

10.   For paragraph (ii) of regulation 9(2)(b) there shall be substituted the following paragraph -

" (ii) have effect in relation to a workplace in Great Britain other than -

(a) an excepted workplace, or

(b) any workplace referred to in paragraphs (i) and (ii) of paragraph (2)(a), other than a building on the surface at a mine,".

11.   After regulation 9(2) there shall be inserted the following paragraph -

" (2A) Notwithstanding that the provisions of Part II of these Regulations are not provisions forming part of the relevant statutory provisions, the provisions of Part II shall, in so far as they apply to any workplace referred to in paragraphs (i) and (ii) of paragraph (2)(a) other than a building on the surface at a mine, be deemed to be health and safety regulations for the purposes of sections 16 to 24, 26, 28, 33 to 40, 42, 46 and 47 of the 1974 Act.".

12.   At the end of regulation 9 there shall be inserted the following regulation -

" Civil liability for breach of statutory duty 9A. - (1) Subject to paragraph (2), and notwithstanding section 86 of the Fires Prevention (Metropolis) Act 1774[7], breach of a duty imposed on an employer by the workplace fire precautions legislation shall, so far as it causes damage, confer a right of action in civil proceedings.

(2) Breach of a duty imposed on an employer by the workplace fire precautions legislation shall not confer a right of action in civil proceedings insofar as that duty applies for the protection of persons not in his employment".

13.   In regulation 17 -

(a) in paragraph (2), the words "27A (civil and other liability)" shall be omitted;

(b) at the end of paragraph (5) there shall be inserted the following paragraph -

" (6) Insofar as Part II of these Regulations contains any provision which is made under the 1971 Act, section 27A(a) of the 1971 Act shall not apply in respect of any contravention of such provision.".

Notification of Installations Handling Hazardous Substances Regulations 1982 (as amended)

Law considered in context / more depth in Element C4.

Arrangement of Regulations

1)   Citation and commencement.

2)   Interpretation.

3)   Notification of installations handling hazardous substances.

4)   Updating of the notification following changes in the notifiable activity.

5)   Re-notification where the quantity of a substance is increased to 3 times that already notified.

6)   Exemption certificates.

7)   Enforcing authority.

8)   Transitional provision.

Schedule 1   Part I   Named substances.

                Part II   Classes of substances not specifically named in Part I.

Schedule 2   Part I   Particulars to be included in the notification of a site.

                Part II   Particulars to be included in a notification relating to a pipeline.

Outline of key points

These regulations specify dangerous substances; the quantities of which trigger *obligations to notify the HSE of their use 3 months before such use commences*. The list of notifiable hazardous substances is divided into specifically named substances and classes of substances not specifically named; the related notifiable quantities of such substances are also listed in Schedule 1.

Examples from Schedule 1 are shown on the next page ...

SCHEDULE 1 - LIST OF HAZARDOUS SUBSTANCES - EXAMPLES

Named substances		Classes of substances not specifically named	
Substance	Notifiable quantity (tonnes)	Substance	Notifiable quantity (tonnes)
Phosgene	2	1. Gas or any mixture which is flammable in air and is held in the installation as a gas.	15
Sulphur dioxide	20		
Ammonium nitrate and mixtures of ammonium nitrate where the nitrogen content derived from the ammonium nitrate exceeds 15.75%* of the mixture by weight other than - (a) mixtures to which the Explosives Act 1975 applies; or (b) ammonium nitrate based products manufactured chemically for use as fertiliser which comply with the Council Directive 80/876/EEC. * (Formerly 28% before these regulations were amended).	150		

Figure C11-4 Schedule 1 examples.   *Source: Notification of Installations Handling Hazardous Substances Regulations 1982 (as amended).*

Note: the **Notification of Installations Handling Hazardous Substances (Amendment) Regulations 2002 (into force 30th December 2002)**, amended the original regulations with regard to **ammonium nitrate**. For example, quantities of ammonium nitrate trigger an obligation to notify the HSE of its use at least **4 weeks** before such use commences; also, the **notifiable quantity** was amended from 500 to **150 tonnes**.

Personal Protective Equipment at Work Regs (PPER) 1992

Law considered in context / more depth in Units 6, 8 -10, 12, 16 & 17.

See also – Health and Safety (Miscellaneous Amendments) Regulations (MAR) 2002 – on page 282.

Arrangement of Regulations

1) Citation and commencement.

2) Interpretation.

3) Disapplication of these Regulations.

4) Provision of personal protective equipment.

5) Compatibility of personal protective equipment.

6) Assessment of personal protective equipment.

7) Maintenance and replacement of personal protective equipment.

8) Accommodation for personal protective equipment.

9) Information, instruction and training.

10) Use of personal protective equipment.

11) Reporting loss or defect.

12) Exemption certificates.

13) Extension outside Great Britain.

14) Modifications, repeal and revocations directive.

Schedule 1   Relevant Community.

Schedule 2   Modifications.

Part I	Factories Act 1961. (Repealed).
Part II	The Coal and Other Mines (Fire and Rescue) Order 1956.
Part III	The Shipbuilding and Ship-Repairing Regulations 1960.
Part IV	The Coal Mines (Respirable Dust) Regulations 1975.
Part V	The Control of Lead at Work Regulations 2002.
Part VI	The Ionising Radiations Regulations 1999.
Part VII	The Control of Asbestos at Work Regulations 2002.
Part VIII	The Control of Substances Hazardous to Health Regulations 2004.
Part IX	The Noise at Work Regulations 1989.
Part X	The Construction (Head Protection) Regulations 1989.

Schedule 3   Revocations.

Outline of key points

2)   Personal protective equipment (PPE) means all equipment (including clothing provided for protection against adverse weather) which is intended to be worn or held by a person at work and which protects him against risks to his health or safety.

3)   These Regulations do not apply to:

- Ordinary working clothes/uniforms.
- Offensive weapons.
- Portable detectors which signal risk.
- Equipment used whilst playing competitive sports.
- Equipment provided for travelling on a road.

     The Regulations do not apply to situations already controlled by other Regulations i.e.

- Control of Lead at Work Regulations 2002.
- Ionising Radiation Regulations 1999.
- Control of Asbestos at Work Regulations 2002.
- Control of Substances Hazardous to Health Regulations 2004.
- Noise at Work Regulations 1989.
- Construction (Head Protection) Regulations 1989.

4)   Suitable PPE must be provided when risks cannot be adequately controlled by other means. Reg. 4 shall ensure suitable PPE:

- Appropriate for the risk and conditions.
- Ergonomic requirements.
- State of health of users.
- Correctly fitting and adjustable.
- Complies with EEC directives.

5)   Equipment must be compatible with any other PPE which has to be worn.

6)   Before issuing PPE, the employer must carry out a risk assessment to ensure that the equipment is suitable.

- Assess risks not avoided by other means.
- Define characteristics of PPE and of the risk of the equipment itself.
- Compare characteristics of PPE to defined requirement.
- Repeat assessment when no longer valid, or significant change has taken place.

7)   PPE must be maintained.

- In an efficient state.
- In efficient working order.
- In good repair.

8)   Accommodation must be provided for equipment when it is not being used.

9)   Information, instruction and training must be given on:

- The risks PPE will eliminate or limit.
- Why the PPE is to be used.
- How the PPE is to be used.
- How to maintain the PPE.

     Information and instruction must be comprehensible to the wearer/user.

10)   Employers shall take reasonable steps to ensure PPE is worn.

- Every employee shall use PPE that has been provided.
- Every employee shall take reasonable steps to return PPE to storage.

11)   Employees must report any loss or defect.

The Guidance on the Regulations points out:

"Whatever PPE is chosen, it should be remembered that, although some types of equipment do provide very high levels of protection, none provides 100%"

PPE includes the following when worn for health and safety reasons at work:

- Aprons.
- Adverse weather gear.
- High visibility clothing.
- Gloves.
- Safety footwear.
- Safety helmets.

- Eye protection.
- Life-jackets.
- Respirators.
- Safety harness.
- Underwater breathing gear.

Pressure Equipment Regulations 1999

Law considered in context / more depth in Element C5.

Arrangement of Regulations

PART I - PRELIMINARY

1) Citation and commencement

2) Interpretation

PART II - APPLICATION

3) Pressure equipment and assemblies

4) Excluded pressure equipment and assemblies

5) Pressure equipment and assemblies placed on the market before 29th November 1999

6) Exclusion until 30th May 2002 of pressure equipment and assemblies complying with provisions in force on 28th November 1999

PART III - GENERAL REQUIREMENTS

7) General duty relating to the placing on the market or putting into service of pressure equipment

8) General duty relating to the placing on the market or putting into service of assemblies

9) Requirement for pressure equipment or assemblies to comply with sound engineering practice

10) General duty relating to the supply of pressure equipment or assemblies

11) Exceptions to placing on the market or supply in respect of certain pressure equipment and assemblies

12) Classification of pressure equipment

13) Conformity assessment procedures for pressure equipment

14) Conformity assessment procedure for assemblies

15) Exclusion for pressure equipment and assemblies for use for experimentation

16) CE marking

17) European approval for materials

18) Notified bodies

19) Recognised third-party organisations

20) Notified bodies and recognised third-party organisations appointed by the Secretary of State

21) Fees

22) User inspectorates

23) Conditions for pressure equipment and assemblies being taken to conform with the provisions of these Regulations

PART IV - ENFORCEMENT

24) Application of Schedule 8

25) Offences

26) Penalties

27) Defence of due diligence

28) Liability of persons other than the principal offender

29) Consequential amendments

SCHEDULES

Schedule 1   Excluded pressure equipment and assemblies

Schedule 2   Essential safety requirements (Annex I to the Pressure Equipment Directive)

Schedule 3   Conformity assessment tables (Annex II to the Pressure Equipment Directive)

Schedule 4   Conformity assessment procedures (Annex III to the Pressure Equipment Directive)

Schedule 5   CE marking (Annex VI to the Pressure Equipment Directive)

Schedule 6   EC declaration of conformity (Annex VII to the Pressure Equipment Directive)

Schedule 7   European approval for materials

Schedule 8   Enforcement

Outline of key points

These regulations set out the general requirements relating to the placing on the market or putting into service of pressure equipment and assemblies by a **responsible person** (a person who manufactures the pressure equipment or assemblies for his own use or imports pressure equipment or assemblies from a third party, where it is in the course of business). Pressure equipment or assemblies must satisfy the relevant essential requirements and be safe with the appropriate conformity assessment procedure carried out (unless the equipment is to be used for experimentation). A declaration of conformity must be drawn up and a CE mark affixed.

Where pressure equipment or assemblies fall below the limits prescribed in the Pressure Equipment Regulations, it must be designed and manufactured in accordance with sound engineering practice, be accompanied by adequate instructions for use, bear markings to permit identification of the manufacturer or his authorised representative established within the EU, and be safe.

Pressure Equipment (Amendment) Regulations 2002

The *Pressure Equipment (Amendment) Regulations 2002 (into force 30th May 2002)*, amended the original regulations as follows -

After regulation 2(3) there shall be inserted the following paragraph -

(4)   "For the purposes of these Regulations, an item of pressure equipment or an assembly which is made available for the first time in the Community whether for reward or free of charge shall not be regarded as having been placed on the market where: -

(a)   it has been manufactured within the Community or imported from a country or territory outside the Community; and

(b)   prior to its being made so available it has been used otherwise than in the course of business at all times since its manufacture or import."

For regulation 26(1) there shall be substituted the following -

26(1) "   A person guilty of an offence under regulation 25(a) shall be liable -

(a)   on summary conviction, to a fine not exceeding the statutory maximum or to imprisonment not exceeding three months or to both;

(b)   on conviction on indictment, to a fine or to imprisonment for a term not exceeding two years or to both.".

In Schedule 8, sub-paragraph 2(d), for the reference to sub-paragraph "(b)" there shall be substituted a reference to sub-paragraph "(c)".

Pressure Systems Safety Regulations 2000

Law considered in context / more depth in Element C5.

Arrangement of Regulations

PART I - INTRODUCTION
1)   Citation and commencement.
2)   Interpretation.
3)   Application and duties.

PART II - GENERAL
4)   Design and construction.
5)   Provision of information and marking.
6)   Installation.
7)   Safe operating limits.
8)   Written scheme of examination.
9)   Examination in accordance with the written scheme.
10)   Action in case of imminent danger.
11)   Operation.
12)   Maintenance.
13)   Modification and repair.
14)   Keeping of records, etc.
15)   Precautions to prevent pressurisation of certain vessels.

PART III - MISCELLANEOUS
16)   Defence.
17)   Power to grant exemptions.
18)   Repeals and revocations.
19)   Transitional provision.

SCHEDULES
Schedule 1   Exceptions to the Regulations.
Schedule 2   Modification of duties in cases where pressure systems are supplied by way of lease, hire or other arrangements.
Schedule 3   Marking of pressure vessels.

Outline of key points

PRESSURE SYSTEMS SAFETY REGULATIONS 2000

The Pressure Systems Safety Regulations 2000 (PSSR) are primarily concerned with matters affecting the mechanical integrity of pressure-containing parts. As in the HSW Act, the duties imposed by the Regulations are shared between a number of persons, e.g. designers, manufacturers, suppliers, importers, installers, users, maintainers and repairers.

It should be noted therefore that the overall intention of the PSSR is to prevent the risk of serious injury from stored energy as a result of the failure of a pressure system or part of it. Apart from scalding risks from steam, the Regulations are concerned with the contents of the system only in so far as some contents and operating procedures are liable to accelerate wear in the system and thereby cause a more rapid deterioration in its condition, so leading to increased risk of failure.

The Regulations are concerned with steam, gases under pressure or fluids which are artificially kept under pressure and become gases on release to the atmosphere. The Regulations do not apply to purely hydraulic systems, systems containing traces of dissolved gas or to liquids in storage tanks which exert a static pressure. The Regulations thus apply to steam systems and systems in which gases exert a pressure in excess of half a bar above atmospheric pressure (0.5 bar).

1 bar = 14.5038 psi (pounds per square inch).

A Summary of the Pressure Systems Safety Regulations 2000

These Regulations re-enact with the Pressure Systems and Transportable Gas Containers Regulations 1989 as amended. As with the 1989 Regulations, safety requirements are imposed with respect to pressure systems which are used or intended to be used at work. They also impose safety requirements to prevent certain vessels from becoming pressurised. Thus the aim is to prevent people being injured by unintended releases of gas or fluid from pressure systems or equipment.

The 2000 Regulations modify and extend provision for sending, keeping and passing on in electronic form reports of examinations. It also provides that references to anything in writing or written includes it being in a form in which it is capable of being reproduced as a written copy. The regulations no longer requires a report to be signed; and requires information to be kept and passed on, whether or not it has been supplied as a document. This is in keeping with the trend towards allowing the use of computer software systems to store and transmit statutory documents. *A pressure system is defined in the Regulations as:*

- a system comprising one or more pressure vessels of rigid construction, any associated pipework and protective devices.
- the pipework with its protective devices to which a transportable gas container is, or intended to be connected; or
- a pipeline and its protective devices

which contains or is liable to contain a relevant fluid. The definition does not include a transportable pressure receptacle.

The Regulations apply to pressure systems if there is a relevant fluid in the system (i.e. a compressed or liquefied gases including air) above 0.5 bar or steam, the pressure volume (PV) product of the largest rigid pressure vessel in the system is grater than 250 bar litres, you are the User or Owner and there is no exemption under Schedule 1 then Regulations 7 and 8 apply. You are required to determine the extent to which a Written Scheme applies to your system.

A competent person is required to draw up or certify written schemes of examination and to carry out examinations. The level of competence, access to specialist services and organisational requirements varies according to the category of the system.

Designers, manufacturers, importers or suppliers of any pressure system or any article which is intended to be a component part of any pressure system must ensure that the pressure system or article is:

- properly designed and properly constructed from suitable material so as to prevent danger;
- designed and constructed so that all necessary examinations for preventing danger can be carried out;
- provided with the necessary protective devices for preventing danger; and
- ensuring that any such device designed to release contents shall do so safely.

In addition, where the pressure system has any means of access to its interior, it must be designed and constructed as to ensure, so far as practicable, that access can be gained without danger.

In practical terms, safety equipment includes:

- control equipment to enable safe operation
- protective devices to limit or relieve pressure
- measuring devices to indicate conditions of operation
- access door safety devices to ensure interlocking for regularly used doors, etc.

Adequate information about the pressure system must be passed on to the user. This should include:

- safe operating limits
- scheme of examination
- design standards and constructional materials
- certificates of conformity
- design pressures and temperatures
- intended contents, flow rates, capacities, etc.

Installers to ensure installation does not cause danger. This might include controlling any welding work during installation, ensuring adequate foundations are provided, ensuring no obstruction of access, protection from vehicle impacts etc.

System users must use the information provided by the designer to ensure safe operation and proper maintenance. The extent of duty depends upon the system type.

A written scheme of examination must be available before any system is used. This should be drawn up by a competent person and should include:

- pressure vessels
- pipework and valves
- protective devices
- pumps and compressors

Examination intervals should be specified, though these may be different for different parts of the system, so that deterioration, etc. can be detected before danger arises. An initial examination should be done before use. Any repairs or modifications should be controlled. Factors to be taken into account when deciding upon the frequency of examination will include:

- previous intervals and system records
- standards of supervision and routine checks
- type and quality of fluids in the system

- the likelihood of creep, fatigue, etc. failures
- corrosion potential and effect
- presence of heat sources etc.

The type of examination should also be specified.

Examinations must be carried out in accordance with the written scheme and the system adequately assessed for fitness for continued use. Appropriate preparations for and precautions during examination should be arranged for by the user. A report with any conditions or limitations on use should be prepared on completion of the examination.

Where the competent person's examination identifies imminent danger then a report must be made to the user who should ensure the system is not used further and a report sent to the relevant enforcing authority.

Anyone operating a pressure system must be given adequate and suitable instructions for safe operation and emergency action. This instruction should form part of the operating instructions for the plant and should include information on start-up, shutdown, normal operation, functions of controls, emergency procedures, etc. Doors providing routine access should be dealt with by specific instructions covering interlocking checks, opening and closing precautions, failure signs, etc.

Routine and regular maintenance should be carried out including periodic checks and inspections of important parts or components.

Adequate records of examinations, repairs, modifications etc., should be kept at the premises where the system is used.

Precautions must be taken to prevent unintentional pressurisation of parts of any system not designed for pressure.

Provision and Use of Work Equipment Regulations (PUWER) 1998

Law considered in context / more depth in Elements C6, C7 and C9.

See also – Health and Safety (Miscellaneous Amendments) Regulations (MAR) 2002 – on page 282.

See also – Work at Height Regulations (WAH) 2005 – on page 305.

Arrangement of Regulations

PART I - INTRODUCTION

1) Citation and commencement.

2) Interpretation.

3) Application.

PART II - GENERAL

4) Suitability of work equipment.

5) Maintenance.

6) Inspection.

7) Specific risks.

8) Information and instructions.

9) Training.

10) Conformity with Community requirements.

11) Dangerous parts of machinery.

12) Protection against specified hazards.

13) High or very low temperature.

14) Controls for starting or making a significant change in operating conditions.

15) Stop controls.

16) Emergency stop controls.

17) Controls.

18) Control systems.

19) Isolation from sources of energy.

20) Stability.

21) Lighting.

22) Maintenance operations.

23) Markings.

24) Warnings.

PART III - MOBILE WORK EQUIPMENT

25) Employees carried on mobile work equipment.

26) Rolling over of mobile work equipment.

27) Overturning of fork-lift trucks.

28) Self-propelled work equipment.

29) Remote-controlled self-propelled work equipment.

30) Drive shafts.

PART IV - POWER PRESSES

31)   Power presses to which Part IV does not apply.

32)   Thorough examination of power presses, guards and protection devices.

33)   Inspection of guards and protection devices.

34)   Reports.

35)   Keeping of information.

PART V - MISCELLANEOUS

36)   Exemption for the armed forces.

37)   Transitional provision.

38)   Repeal of enactment.

39)   Revocation of instruments.

Schedule 1   Instruments which give effect to Community directives concerning the safety of products.

Schedule 2   Power presses to which regulations 32 to 35 do not apply.

Schedule 3   Information to be contained in a report of a thorough examination of a power press, guard or protection device.

Schedule 4   Revocation of instruments.

Outline of key points

These Regulations impose health and safety requirements with respect to the provision and use of work equipment, which is defined as 'any machinery, appliance, apparatus, tool or installation for use at work (whether exclusively or not)'. These regulations:

- Place general duties on employers.
- Certain persons having control of work equipment, of persons at work who use or supervise or manage its use or of the way it is used, to the extent of their control.
- List minimum requirements for work equipment to deal with selected hazards whatever the industry.

'Use' includes any activity involving work equipment and includes starting, stopping, programming, setting, transporting, repairing, modifying, maintaining, servicing and cleaning.

The general duties require you to:

- Make sure that equipment is suitable for the use that will be made of it.
- Take into account the working conditions and hazards in the workplace when selecting equipment.
- Ensure equipment is used only for operations for which, and under conditions for which, it is suitable.
- Ensure that equipment is maintained in an efficient state, in efficient working order and in good repair.
- Ensure the inspection of work equipment in specified circumstances by a competent person; keep a record of the result for specified periods; and ensure that evidence of the last inspection accompany work equipment used outside the undertaking.
- Give adequate information, instruction and training.
- Provide equipment that conforms with EU product safety directives.

SPECIFIC REQUIREMENTS COVER

- Guarding of dangerous parts of machinery.
- Protection against specified hazards i.e. falling/ejected articles and substances, rupture/disintegration of work equipment parts, equipment catching fire or overheating, unintended or premature discharge of articles and substances, explosion.
- Work equipment parts and substances at high or very low temperatures.
- Control systems and control devices.
- Isolation of equipment from sources of energy.
- Stability of equipment.
- Lighting.
- Maintenance operations.
- Warnings and markings.

MOBILE WORK EQUIPMENT MUST HAVE PROVISION AS TO:

- Its suitability for carrying persons and its safety features.
- Means to minimise the risk to safety from its rolling over.
- Means to reduce the risk to safety from the rolling over of a fork-lift truck.
- The safety of self-propelled work equipment and remote-controlled self propelled work equipment.
- The drive shafts of mobile work equipment.

This did not apply to existing mobile work equipment (in use before 5 Dec 1998) until 5 Dec 2002 for existing mobile work equipment.

PUWER ALSO APPLIES TO CERTAIN POWER PRESSES

The Regulations provide for:

- The thorough examination (defined in regulation 2(1)) of power presses and their guards and protection devices (regulation 32).
- Their inspection after setting, re-setting or adjustment of their tools, and every working period (regulation 33).
- The making (regulation 34 and Schedule 3) and keeping (regulation 35) of reports.
- The regulations implement an EC directive aimed at the protection of workers. There are other directives setting out conditions which much new equipment (especially machinery) will have to satisfy before it can be sold in EC member states.

Simple Pressure Vessels (Safety) Regulations 1991 (as amended)

Law considered in context / more depth in Element C5.

Arrangement of Regulations

1) Citation and commencement

2) Interpretation.

3) Application (now amended to 'Interpretation of the principle Regulations').

4) Safety requirements (now amended to 'Implementation of the CE Marking Directive').

5) Obligations of manufacturers, suppliers and importers.

6) Transitional and other exceptions.

7) Approved bodies.

8) Fees.

9) Safety clearance.

10) EC certificate of adequacy.

11) EC type-examination certificate.

12) EC verification certificate (now amended to 'EC verification').

13) EC certificate of conformity.

14) The EC mark (now amended to 'CE mark').

15) Retention of documentation.

16) Special provisions applying to vessels in Category A.2.

17) Functions of approved bodies in course of EC surveillance.

18) Report by United Kingdom approved body concerning contraventions.

19) Enforcement.

20) Offences.

21) Power of the court to require matter to be remedied.

22) Defence of due diligence.

23) Liability of persons other than the principal offender.

24) Consequential amendment of United Kingdom law.

Outline of key points

The ***Simple Pressure Vessels (Safety) (Amendment) Regulations 1994 (into force 1st January 1995)*** amended the Simple Pressure Vessels (Safety) Regulations 1991; and apply to the following:

■ Simple pressure vessels i.e. welded vessels made of certain types of steel or aluminium, which are intended to contain air or nitrogen under pressure and are manufactured in series.

■ Relevant assemblies, i.e. any assembly incorporating a pressure vessel.

Important definitions relating to these regulations are:

Vessel - this means a simple pressure vessel that has been welded and is intended for the storage of nitrogen or air at a gauge pressure greater than 0.5 Bar but not exceeding 30 Bar.

Series manufacture - this is where more than one vessel of the same type are produced during a given period by the same continuous process. The regulations only apply to series manufactured vessels. **The regulations do not apply to:**

■ Fire Extinguishers

■ Vessels intended for use in the propulsive systems of ships, aircraft

■ Vessels intended for nuclear use where if a failure occurs, a release of radioactivity would occur.

CATEGORISATION OF VESSELS

The regulations specifically categorise vessels into 2 classes:

Category A	A.1	3000 - 10,000	Bar litres
	A.2	200 - 30000	Bar litres
	A.3	50 - 200	Bar litres
Category B		50 Bar litres or less	

PRINCIPAL REQUIREMENTS

A vessel with a stored energy in excess of 50 Bar litres must, if supplied in the UK:

■ Ensure that materials used in its construction must meet relevant safety requirements.

■ Be certified safe for use by an appropriate body.

■ Bear the CE mark and any other relevant inscriptions.

■ Follow the CE mark by the identification number of the approved body responsible for EC verifications or EC surveillance.

■ Must bear at least the following information -

- the maximum working pressure (PS in bar);

- the maximum working temperature (Tmax in °C);

- the minimum working temperature (Tmin in °C);

- the capacity of the vessel (V in litres);

- the name or mark of the manufacturer;

- the type and serial or batch identification of the vessel; and

- the last two digits of the year in which the CE marking was affixed.

(If a data plate is used, it must be so designed that it cannot be re-used and must include a vacant space to enable other information to be provided).

■ Have a set of manufacturers work instructions and guidance
■ Be safe as defined by the regulations.

A vessel with a stored energy up to 50 Bar litres must, if supplied in the UK:

■ Be safe as defined by the regulations.
■ Bear specific inscriptions but not the CE mark.
■ Be engineered and manufactured to a recognised suitable standard within the Community Country.

Exports

The regulations do not apply to any vessel supplied outside of the European Community.

Prosecution

Failure to comply with these regulations will result in the following:

■ Fine of up to £2,000.00 and/or imprisonment of up to three months.
■ The vessels cannot be sold legally.

Approved bodies

These are designated by the Secretary for Trade and Industry and the bodies are given certain rights of power with regard to surveillance of vessels. These powers include:

Powers of entry

■ To take samples.
■ To acquire information.

■ To compile reports on surveillance operations.
■ To report to the secretary of state cases of wrongful application, and failures by manufacturers in respect of their legal duties.

Special Waste Regulations 1996 (as amended)

Law considered in context / more depth in Element C10.

Arrangement of Regulations

1) Citation, commencement, extent, application and interpretation

2) Meaning of special waste.

3) Certain radioactive waste to be special waste.

4) Coding of consignments.

5) Consignment notes: standard procedure.

6) Consignment notes: cases in which pre-notification is not required.

7) Consignment notes: procedure where pre-notification is not required.

8) Consignment notes: carrier's rounds.

9) Consignment notes: removal of ships' waste to reception facilities.

10) Consignment notes etc.: duty of consignee not accepting delivery of a consignment.

11) Consignment notes: duties of the Agencies.

12) Consignment notes: provisions as to furnishing.

13) Consignment notes: importers and exporters.

14) Fees.

15) Registers.

16) Site records.

17) Restrictions on mixing special waste.

18) Offences.

19) Responsibilities of the Agencies.

20) Transitional provisions for certificates of technical competence.

21) Amendment of regulations relating to the assessment of environmental effects.

22) Amendment of the Controlled Waste (Registration of Carriers and Seizure of Vehicles) Regulations 1991.

23) Amendment of the Environmental Protection (Duty of Care) Regulations 1991.

24) Amendment of the Controlled Waste Regulations 1992.

25)	Amendment of the Waste Management Licensing Regulations 1994.

26)	Revocations and savings.

SCHEDULES

Schedule 1	Forms of consignment note and schedule.

Schedule 2	Special waste.

Schedule 3	Amendments to the Waste Management Licensing Regulations 1994.

Outline of key points

The **Special Waste Regulations 1996 (as amended),** implement the European Hazardous Waste Directive 91/689/EEC. The purpose of these regulations is to provide an effective system of control for wastes that are difficult to handle. The regulations ensure that dangerous wastes are soundly managed from their production to their final destination for disposal or recovery.

Recent updates* to the regulations mean that the previous Environment Agency guides, Special Waste Information Sheets 1, 2 and 3, are now out of date. They have been replaced by a single document, 'A Guide to the Special Waste Regulations 1996 (as amended) version 2, November 1st 2001' (referred to below as the Guide).

The Guide aims to assist readers in the following:

■	Assessment procedure, using a flowchart, for classifying special waste using the principles described within the Special Waste Regulations 1996 (as amended),.

■	Use and completion of the consignment note that must accompany every movement of special waste.

■	Where to obtain and send consignment notes.

■	Site records and registers - how long parties involved with the transfer of special waste are required to retain copies of the consignment notes.

■	Data sources and other information - the Guide contains a bibliography of pertinent legislation and publications for special waste.

* Special Waste (Amendment) (England and Wales) Regulations 2001 and the corresponding Special Waste (Amendment) (Wales) Regulation 2001.

Source: www.environment-agency.gov.uk.

Supply of Machinery (Safety) Regulations (SMSR) 1992

Law considered in context / more depth in Element C6 (scope and application).

Outline of key points

GENERAL ADVICE

The Supply of Machinery (Safety) Regulations (SMSR) 1992 came into force on 1 January 1993 and implement the EC Machinery Directive (89/392/EEC) and its first amendment (91/368/EEC). Duties are placed upon those who supply machinery. 'Supply' is given a broad definition and those covered by the Regulations include manufacturers, importers and others in the supply chain. There is a transitional period from January 1993 to January 1995, during which time suppliers can either meet the users' national laws in force before 1993 or these Regulations. Machinery first supplied after 1 January 1995 must comply with these Regulations. These Regulations are being mirrored in other EC countries and also those not in the EC but within the European Economic Area (EEA) (EC and EFTA countries except Switzerland), so that there will eventually be uniformity in legislation, and legal barriers to trade within the EEA will be removed. The machinery covered is very wide ranging. There are some exclusions, however, such as most manually powered machines, machinery for medical use and most means of transport (see Schedule 5 of the Regulations). Machinery whose risks are mainly electrical are also excluded.

AMENDING REGULATIONS

In 1994 the Supply of Machinery (Safety) Regulations were extended so as to implement two more recent European Directives. The principal effect of this has been to apply the above requirements, as from 1 January 1995, to safety components, as defined, and widens the scope to include a greater range of lifting machines (but not classical passenger lifts and other specified exclusions). There is a further two year transitional period from January 1995, during which time compliance with the new requirements is optional with certain conditions.

MEETING THE REQUIREMENTS

The duty to meet the requirements mainly falls to the 'responsible person' who is defined as the manufacturer or the manufacturer's representative. If the manufacturer is not established in the EEA, the person who first supplies the machinery in the EEA may be the responsible person, which can be a user who manufactures or imports a machine for his/her own use.

There are basically three steps to dealing with the requirements.

Step 1 - Conformity assessment

The responsible person should ensure that machinery and safety components satisfy the essential health and safety requirements (EHSRs), and that appropriate conformity assessment procedures have been carried out. The EHSRs are laid out in the Directive and repeated in the Regulations (Schedule 3). This can be done either by reference directly to these requirements or to a relevant transposed harmonised standard where one exists. Harmonised standards are currently being prepared by the European Standards Organisations, CEN and CENELEC, before formal adoption by the European Commission. Harmonised standards will be available for a wide range of industrial machinery, including agricultural, textiles, engineering, construction, machinery. In addition, the responsible person must draw up a technical file (see below).

For certain classes if dangerous machine and safety component, a more rigorous procedure is required. Such products are listed in Annex 4 of the Directive and reproduced in Schedule 4 of the Regulations. In additional to the above requirements, the responsible person must arrange for type-examination of these produces by an approved body if there are no harmonised standards formally adopted by the EC for them, or if they are not manufactured to such standards. The Department of Trade and Industry (DTI) has appointed approved bodies in the UK for this purpose. Details are available from: DTI, Technology and Innovation Policy Division, 151 Buckingham Palace Road, London SW1W 9SS (Tel: 0171 215 5000).

Step 2 - Declaration procedure

The responsible person must issue one of two forms of declaration.

Declaration of conformity

This declaration should be issued with the finished product so that it is available to the user. It will contain various details such as the manufacturer's address, the machinery type and serial number, and Harmonised European or other Standards used in design.

Declaration of Incorporation

Where machinery is intended for incorporation into other machinery, the responsible person can draw up a declaration of incorporation. This should state that the machinery must not be put into service until the machinery into which it is to be incorporated has been given a Declaration of Conformity. A CE mark is not affixed at this intermediate stage.

Step 3 - Marking

When the first two steps have been satisfactorily completed, the responsible person or the person assembling the final product should affix the EC mark.

ENFORCEMENT

In this country the Health and Safety Executive is responsible for enforcing these Regulations in relation to machinery designed for use at work. Trading Standards Officers are responsible for enforcing these Regulations in relation to consumer goods. *After 1 January 1995 it is an offence for the responsible person to supply machinery which does not comply with these requirements. It is also an offence for any supplier to supply machinery which is not safe (and which was not first supplied before 1 January 1995).*

Detailed advice for the designer and manufacturer.

TECHNICAL FILE CONTENTS

The responsible person (defined above) is required to draw up a technical file for all machinery and safety components covered by these Regulations. The file or documents should comprise:

a)   An overall drawing of the product together with the drawings of the control circuits.

b)   Full detailed drawings, accompanied by any calculation notes, test results etc. required to check the conformity of the product   with the essential health and safety requirements.

c)   A list of the essential health and safety requirements, transposed harmonised standards, national standards and other technical specifications which were used when the product was designed.

d)   A description of methods adopted to eliminate hazards presented by the machinery or safety component.

e)   If the responsible person so desires, any technical report or certificate obtained from a component body or laboratory.

f)   If the responsible person declares conformity with a transposed harmonised standard, any technical report giving the results of tests.

g)   A copy of the instructions for the product.

For series manufacture, the responsible person must also have available documentation on the necessary administrative measures that the manufacturer will take to ensure that the product meets requirements.

TECHNICAL FILE PROCEDURE

The technical file document need not be on a permanent file, but it should be possible to assemble and make them available to an enforcement authority. The technical file documents should be retained and kept available for at least ten years following the date of manufacture of the product or of the last unit produced, in the case of a series manufacture. If the technical file documents are drawn up in the United Kingdom, they should be in English unless they are to be submitted to an Approved/Notified Body in another Member State, in which case they should be in a language acceptable to that approved Body. In all cases the instructions for the machinery should be in accordance with the language requirements of the EHSRs.

Work at Height Regulations (WAH) 2005

Law considered in context / more depth in Elements C1 and C9.

See also - PUWER 1998 (page 300), WHSWR 1992 (page 307) and CHSWR 1996 (page 262).

Arrangement of Regulations

1)   Citation and commencement.
2)   Interpretation.
3)   Application.
4)   Organisation and planning.
5)   Competence.
6)   Avoidance of risks from work at height.
7)   Selection of work equipment for work at height.

8)   Requirements for particular work equipment.
9)   Fragile surfaces.
10)   Falling objects.
11)   Danger areas.
12)   Inspection of work equipment.
13)   Inspection of places of work at height.
14)   Duties of persons at work.
15)   Exemption by the Health and Safety Executive.
16)   Exemption for the Armed Forces.
17)   Amendment to the Provision and Use of Work Equipment Regulations 1998.
18)   Repeal of section 24 of the Factories Act 1961.
19)   Revocation of instruments.

SCHEDULES

Schedule 1   Requirements for existing places of work and means of access or egress at height.

Schedule 2   Requirements for guard-rails, toe-boards, barriers and similar collective means of protection.

Schedule 3   Requirements for working platforms.

        Part 1   Requirements for all working platforms

        Part 2   Additional requirements for scaffolding

Schedule 4   Requirements for collective safeguards for arresting falls.

Schedule 5   Requirements for personal fall protection systems.

        Part 1   Requirements for all personal fall protection systems.

        Part 2   Additional requirements for work positioning systems.

        Part 3   Additional requirements for rope access and positioning techniques.

        Part 4   Additional requirements for fall arrest systems.

        Part 5   Additional requirements for work restraint systems.

Schedule 6   Requirements for ladders.

Schedule 7   Particulars to be included in a report of inspection.

Schedule 8   Revocation of instruments.

Introduction

Falls from height at work are the most common cause of fatality and the second most common cause of major injury to workers and during the period between 2001/2002 resulted in 68 fatalities and approximately 4,000 serious injuries.

Health and Safety Commission (HSC) consultation on these regulations ended in April 2004, resulting in the production of a draft regulation. An additional consultative document was also issued concerning retention of the above 'two metre rule'; consultation on this ended in December 2004. The final version of the regulations, designated the **Work at Height Regulations 2005** came into force 6th April 2005.

Under these regulations the interpretation of 'work at height' includes any place of work at ground level, above or below ground level that a person could fall a distance liable to cause personal injury and includes places for obtaining access or egress, except by staircase in a permanent workplace.

Amendments to other regulations as a result of the Work at Height Regulations 2005

These regulations make an amendment to the Provision and Use of Work Equipment Regulations 1998; they also replace certain regulations in the Workplace (Health and Safety) Regulations; and amend definitions in the Construction (Health, Safety and Welfare) Regulations -

Regulation 17 - amendment of the Provision and Use of Work Equipment Regulations 1998. There shall be added to regulation 6(5) of the Provision and Use of Work Equipment Regulations 1998 the following sub-paragraph -

(f)   "work equipment to which regulation 12 of the Work at Height Regulations 2005 applies".

Schedule 8 - revocation of instruments

    Workplace (Health and Safety) Regulations 1992 - extent of revocation: regulation 13(1) to (4).

    Construction (Health, Safety and Welfare) Regulations 1996 - extent of revocation: in regulation 2(1), the definitions of "fragile material", "personal suspension equipment" and "working platform"; regulations 6 to 8; in regulation 29(2) the word "scaffold" in both instances; regulation 30(5) and (6)(a); Schedules 1 to 5; and the entry first mentioned in columns 1 and 2 of Schedule 7.

Outline of key points

Regulation 4 states that all work at height must be properly planned, supervised and be carried out so far as is reasonably practicable safe. Planning must include the selection of suitable equipment, take account of emergencies and give consideration to weather conditions impacting on safety.

Regulation 5 states that those engaged in any activity in relation to work at height must be competent; and, if under training, be supervised by a competent person.

Regulation 6 states that work at height must only be carried out when it is not reasonably practicable to carry out the work otherwise. If work at height does take place, suitable and sufficient measures must be taken to prevent a fall of any distance, to minimise the distance and the consequences of any fall liable to cause injury. Employers must also make a risk assessment, as required by regulation 3 of the Management of Health and Safety at Work Regulations.

Regulation 7 states that when selecting equipment for use in work at height the employer shall take account of working conditions and any risk to persons in connection with the place where the equipment is to be used. The selection of work equipment must have regard in particular to the purposes specified in regulation 6.

Regulation 8 sets out requirements for particular equipment to conform to standards expressed in schedules to the regulations. It includes guard-rails, toe-boards, working platforms, nets, airbags, personal fall arrest equipment rope access and ladders.

Regulation 9 states that every employer shall ensure that suitable and sufficient steps are taken to prevent any person at work falling through any fragile surface; and that no work may pass across or near, or work on, from or near, fragile surfaces when it is reasonably practicable to carry out work without doing so. If work has to be from a fragile roof then suitable and sufficient means of support must be provided that can sustain foreseeable loads. No person at work should be allowed to pass or work near a fragile surface unless suitable and sufficient guard rails and other means of fall protection is in place. Signs must be situated at a prominent place at or near to works involving fragile surfaces, or persons are made aware of the fragile roof by other means.

Regulation 10 states that every employer shall take reasonably practicable steps to prevent injury to any person from the fall of any material or object; and where it is not reasonably practicable to do so, to take similar steps to prevent any person being struck by any falling material or object which is liable to cause personal injury. Also, that no material is thrown or tipped from height in circumstances where it is liable to cause injury to any person. Materials and objects must be stored in such a way as to prevent risk to any person arising from the collapse, overturning or unintended movement of the materials or objects.

Regulation 11 states that every employer shall ensure that where an area presents a risk of falling from height or being struck from an item falling at height that the area is equipped with devices preventing unauthorised persons from entering such areas and the area is clearly indicated.

Regulation 12 states that every employer shall ensure that, where the safety of work equipment depends on how it is installed or assembled, it is not used after installation or assembly in any position unless it has been inspected in that position. Also, that work equipment is inspected at suitable intervals and each time that exceptional circumstances which are liable to jeopardise the safety of the work equipment occur. Specific requirements exist for periodic (every 7 days) inspection of a working platform where someone could fall 2 metres or more.

Regulation 13 states that every employer shall ensure that fall protection measures of every place of work at height are visually inspected before use.

Regulation 14 states the duties of persons at work to report defects and use equipment in accordance with training / instruction.

Workplace (Health, Safety and Welfare) Regulations (WHSWR) 1992

Law considered in context / more depth in Elements C1, C6 and C7.

See also – Health and Safety (Miscellaneous Amendments) Regulations (MAR) 2002 – on page 282.

See also – Work at Height Regulations (WAH) 2005 – on page 305.

Arrangement of Regulations

1) Citation and commencement.
2) Interpretation.
3) Application of these Regulations.
4) Requirements under these Regulations.
5) Maintenance of workplace, and of equipment, devices and systems.
6) Ventilation.
7) Temperature in indoor workplaces.
8) Lighting.
9) Cleanliness and waste materials.
10) Room dimensions and space.
11) Workstations and seating.
12) Condition of floors and traffic routes.
13) Falls or falling objects.
14) Windows, and transparent or translucent doors, gates and walls.
15) Windows, skylights and ventilators.
16) Ability to clean windows etc. safely.
17) Organisation etc. of traffic routes.
18) Doors and gates.
19) Escalators and moving walkways.
20) Sanitary conveniences.
21) Washing facilities.

22) Drinking water.

23) Accommodation for clothing.

24) Facilities for changing clothing.

25) Facilities for rest and to eat meals.

26) Exemption certificates.

27) Repeals, saving and revocations.

Schedule 1   Provisions applicable to factories which are not new workplaces, extensions or conversions.

Schedule 2   Repeals and revocations.

Outline of key points

SUMMARY

The main requirements of the Workplace (Health, Safety and Welfare) Regs 1992 are:

1) *Maintenance* of the workplace and equipment.

2) *Safety* of those carrying out maintenance work and others who might be at risk (e.g. segregation of pedestrians and vehicles, prevention of falls and falling objects etc.).

3) Provision of *welfare* facilities (e.g. rest rooms, changing rooms etc.).

4) Provision of a safe *environment* (e.g. lighting, ventilation etc.).

ENVIRONMENT

Reg 1	New workplaces, extensions and modifications must comply now. Older workplaces have until 1 January 1996 to get up to standard.
Reg 4	Requires employers, persons in control of premises and occupiers of factories to comply with the regulations.
Reg 6	Ventilation - enclosed workplaces should be ventilated with a sufficient quantity of fresh or purified air (5 to 8 litres per second per occupant).
Reg 7	Temperature indoors - This needs to be reasonable and the heating device must not cause injurious fumes. Thermometers must be provided. Temperature should be a minimum of 16oC or 13oC if there is physical effort.
Reg 8	Lighting - must be suitable and sufficient. Natural light if possible. Emergency lighting should be provided if danger exists.
Reg 10	Room dimensions and space - every room where persons work shall have sufficient floor area, height and unoccupied space (min 11 cu.m per person).
Reg 11	Workstations and seating have to be suitable for the person and the work being done.

SAFETY

Reg 12	Floors and traffic routes must be of suitable construction. This includes absence of holes, slope, uneven or slippery surface. Drainage where necessary. Handrails and guards to be provided on slopes and staircases.
Reg 13	Falls or falling objects - suitable and effective measures shall be taken to prevent persons falling or being struck by falling objects. Tanks and pits must be covered or fenced.
Reg 14	Windows and transparent doors, where necessary for health and safety, must be of safety material and be marked to make it apparent.
Reg 15	Windows, skylights and ventilators must be capable of opening without putting anyone at risk.
Reg 17	Traffic routes for pedestrians and vehicles must be organised in such a way that they can move safely.
Reg 18	Doors and gates must be suitably constructed and fitted with any necessary safety devices.
Reg 19	Escalators and moving walkways shall function safely, be equipped with any necessary safety devices and be fitted with emergency stop.

HOUSEKEEPING

Reg 5	Workplace and equipment, devices and systems must be maintained in efficient working order and good repair.
Reg 9	Cleanliness and waste materials - workplaces must be kept sufficiently clean. Floors, walls and ceilings must be capable of being kept sufficiently clean. Waste materials shall not be allowed to accumulate, except in suitable receptacles.
Reg 16	Windows etc. must be designed so that they can be cleaned safely.

FACILITIES

Reg 20	Sanitary conveniences must be suitable and sufficient and in readily accessible places. They must be adequately ventilated, kept clean and there must be separate provision for men and women.
Reg 21	Washing facilities must be suitable and sufficient. Showers if required (a table gives minimum numbers of toilets and washing facilities).
Reg 22	Drinking water - an adequate supply of wholesome drinking water must be provided.
Reg 23	Accommodation for clothing must be suitable and sufficient.
Reg 24	Facilities for changing clothes must be suitable and sufficient, where a person has to use special clothing for work.
Reg 25	Facilities for rest and eating meals must be suitable and sufficient. Non smokers must be protected from discomfort caused by tobacco smoke.

Summary of relevant forthcoming legislation

Current at time of publication.

Regulatory Reform (Fire Safety) Order (RRFSO) 2004/2005

INTRODUCTION

At present we have to consider 5 principal pieces of legislation when considering fire safety in the workplace:

- Fire Precautions Act (FPA).
- Fire Precautions (Workplace) Regulations (FPWR).
- Management of Health and Safety at Work Regulations (MHSWR).
- Dangerous Substances & Explosive Atmosphere Regulations (DSEAR).
- Regulatory Reform Fire Safety Order (RRO) – due to be introduced in 2005.

In addition to the above we would also need to consider common law.

FIRE PRECAUTIONS ACT

This legislation is due to be repealed when the RRO is introduced in 2005.

FIRE PRECAUTIONS WORKPLACE REGULATIONS

This regulation outlines the fire safety measures that need to be achieved via the risk assessment of fire and management of fire safety within a workplace. These regulations will be repealed when RRO is implemented however they have been incorporated within the RRO.

MANAGEMENT OF HEALTH AND SAFETY AT WORK REGULATIONS

It is this regulation that makes the legal requirement for fire risk assessments, at present. In addition, it makes various requirements for the management of fire safety within workplaces. This regulation will continue as a stand alone health and safety regulation in the future. Again the relevant fire aspects of this regulation have been incorporated within the RRO.

DANGEROUS SUBSTANCES & EXPLOSIVE ATMOSPHERE REGULATIONS

This regulation outlines the safety and control measures that need to be taken if dangerous or flammable / explosive substances are present. This regulation will continue as a stand alone health and safety regulation in the future. Again the relevant fire aspects of this regulation have been incorporated within the RRO.

REGULATORY REFORM (FIRE SAFETY) ORDER 2004/2005

This is a new, all encompassing, fire safety order is due to be implemented in 2005. As shown above it will have aspects of other legislation within it and has been compiled in such a way as to present a 'one stop shop' for fire safety legislation.

The order is split into 5 parts:

- Part 1   General
- Part 2   Fire Safety Duties
- Part 3   Enforcement
- Part 4   Offences and appeals
- Part 5   Miscellaneous

Each part is then subdivided into the individual points or articles as they are called in the order.

Outline of key points

PART 1 - GENERAL

This part covers various issues such as the interpretation of terminology used, definition of responsible person, definition of general fire precautions, duties under the order, and its application.

PART 2 - FIRE SAFETY DUTIES

This part imposes a duty on the responsible person to carry out a fire risk assessment to identify what the necessary general fire precautions should be. It also outlines the principles of prevention that should be applied and the necessary arrangements for the management of fire safety. The following areas are also covered:

- Fire-fighting and fire detection.
- Emergency routes and exits.
- Procedures for serious and imminent danger and for danger areas.
- Additional emergency measures re dangerous substances.
- Maintenance.
- Safety assistance.
- Provision of information to employees, employers and self employed.
- Capabilities and training.
- Co-operation and co-ordination.
- General duties of employees.

PART 3 - ENFORCEMENT

This part details who the enforcing authority is, (which in the main is the Fire Authority), and it states they must enforce the order. It also details the powers of inspectors. It also details the different types of enforcement that can be taken:

- Alterations notice.
- Enforcement notice.
- Prohibition notice.

PART 4 - OFFENCES AND APPEALS

This part details the 13 offences that may occur and the subsequent punishments and appeals procedure. It also explains that the legal onus for proving that an offence was not committed is on the accused. A new disputes procedure is also outlined within this part.

PART 5 - MISCELLANEOUS

Various matters are covered within this part the principal points being:

- 'Fire-fighters switches' for luminous tube signs etc.
- Maintenance of measures provided for the protection of fire-fighters.
- Civil liability.
- Duty to consult employees.
- Special provisions for licensed premises.
- Application to crown premises.

There is then a schedule that covers the risk assessment process, plus details of the various legislation that will be repealed or amended.

Hazardous Waste (England) Regulations 2005 and the introduction of the Waste Acceptance Criteria

INTRODUCTION

These regulations will replace the existing Special Waste Regulations 1996 (as amended); the new regulations are due to come into force in July 2005. Although still in draft, the key changes to the Special Waste Regulations have been set out by the Department for Environment Food and Rural Affairs (DEFRA) in their consultation paper 'Proposals for replacement Hazardous Waste Regulations and List of Waste Regulations'.

Outline of key points

IMPORTANT CHANGES

1) The term "special waste" will be replaced by "hazardous waste".

2) The European Waste Catalogue (EWC) and the Hazardous Waste List (part of the EWC) will be formally transposed into UK legislation. All wastes will need to be characterised by their EWC code.

3) 200 additional wastes have been added to the Hazardous Waste List. Among them are everyday items such as fluorescent tubes, fridges, TVs, computer monitors and end of life vehicles. You may therefore be classed as a "new" producer of hazardous waste.

4) There are new requirements on hazardous waste producers (registration, inspections, consignment notes, record keeping).

5) Mixing of hazardous wastes with other hazardous wastes and with non-hazardous wastes will not be permitted, except under license.

You may need to apply to the Environment Agency to have your current Waste Management License or permit reviewed, in light of the new regulations.

From 16 July 2005 all treated hazardous waste accepted into hazardous or special 'cells' of a non-hazardous landfill site must comply with the full Waste Acceptance Criteria (WAC), as required by the Landfill Regulations 2002.

EXCLUSIONS

The only hazardous waste type excluded from the regulations will be 'domestic wastes', arising from households.

THE NEED TO REGISTER WITH THE ENVIRONMENT AGENCY AS A HAZARDOUS WASTE PRODUCER

If you produce hazardous waste (as defined in the Hazardous Waste List of the EWC) you will be classed as a producer of hazardous waste. Each hazardous waste production site must be registered annually with the Environment Agency.

Registration will also apply to the site where separately collected fractions of domestic waste are bulked up (CA site, transfer station, etc). These sites are classed as sites of production. Notification fees will apply.

DEFRA is proposing to exempt so-called "low risk" commercial and industrial and 'domestic wastes' producers (for example, offices, shops, residential homes, educational establishments, hospitals or nursing homes, prisons and public meeting places) from the notification (registration) requirement.

Exemptions would apply for:

(a)   Less than 200 kg of hazardous waste produced per year.

(b)   200 kg per year for Waste Electrical and Electronic Equipment (WEEE) and batteries.

THE PROPOSED RULES FOR NOTIFICATION AND RECORD KEEPING

1)   Consignment Notes will stay, but no 72 hour pre-notification to the Environment Agency will be required before hazardous waste is moved.

2)   The Environment Agency has proposed that quarterly consignee returns will replace the present system of the consignee copying each Consignment Note to the Environment Agency. Electronic transfer is to be encouraged.

3)   Sites exempt from waste management licensing will need to send quarterly returns to the Environment Agency.

4)   The consignee must send returns to waste producers notifying them of the receipt of their wastes. It will be an offence to collect hazardous waste from non-notified premises if the producer is not exempt.

HOW THE CHANGES WILL AFFECT THE COLLECTION OF WASTE

Waste producers cannot mix different categories of hazardous waste or mix hazardous waste with non-hazardous waste, except under license.

If multiple hazardous waste streams from industrial or commercial premises are deposited within a single container, all the individual EWC codes must accompany the consignment note, which must contain the relevant EWC codes.

Both individual and multiple collections of hazardous wastes can be arranged. There is likely to be one consignment note for multiple collections with space in an annex for the details of individual loads rather than completely separate consignment notes for each collection.

For waste collections using multi-lift vehicles and single compartment tankers, a transfer note will exist for each waste producer. Differences in the contents of the individual containers must be recorded in the individual written descriptions.

DUTIES RELATING TO THE WASTE ACCEPTANCE CRITERIA

From 16 July 2005 all hazardous and non hazardous wastes destined for disposal in landfill have to meet the WAC before they can be deposited. WAC contain the 'quality standards' wastes have to comply with before they are allowed to be placed in inert, non hazardous or hazardous landfills.

The waste producer is under a duty of care to ensure the characterisation of the waste to establish its key characteristics as specified in the Regulations. That is, to assess the physical and chemical properties to identify if they classify as hazardous, non hazardous or inert waste. In particular, details of the chemical composition and leaching behaviour of the waste are required. The flow chart below illustrates the procedure.

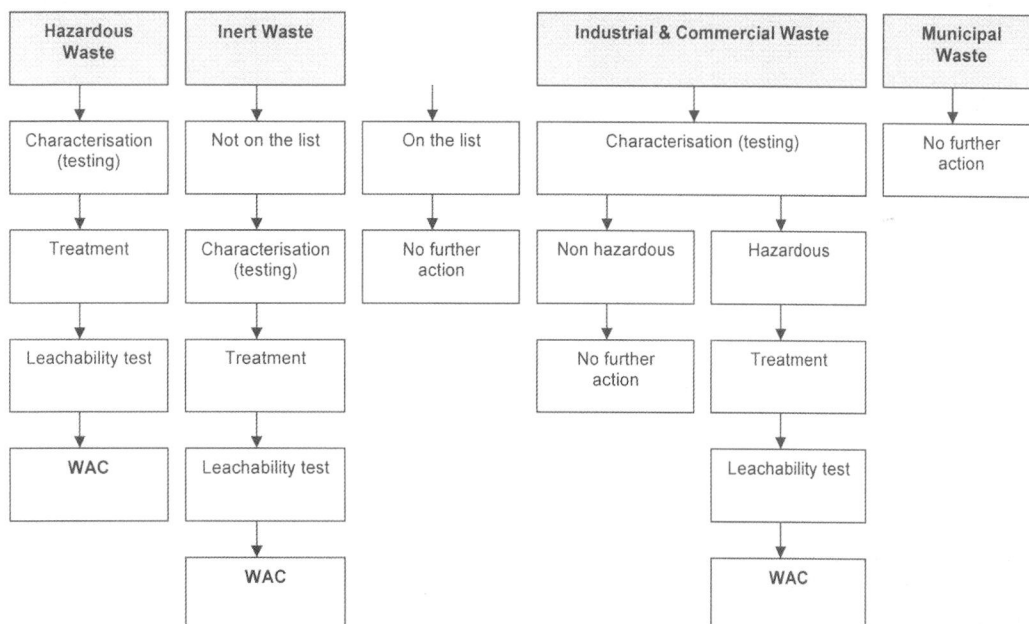

Figure C11-5: Flowchart - characterisation of waste.   *Source: SITA.*

This assessment takes the form of sample testing, whereby a representative sample of your waste arisings is sent away for scientific analysis. Once the results have been returned and assessed, you can then receive advice on how your waste may be disposed of.

THE NEW INSPECTION REGIME

If you are a hazardous waste producer, the Environment Agency intends to periodically inspect your premises and assess the following:

(a)   Does the site produce hazardous waste?

(b)   Has the site been notified (i.e. registered)?

(c)   Is mixing carried out?

(d)   Are the Consignment Note records complete?

(e)   Is the waste moved by a registered carrier …

(f)   … and taken to a permitted consignee?

(g)   If going to landfill how are the Waste Acceptance Criteria being met?

The Environment Agency also intends to issue fixed penalties (spot fines) for:

- Failing to notify premises.
- Failing to complete consignment notes.
- Failing to apply for review of existing permit.

ARE YOU PREPARED?

Do you know whether you are producing hazardous waste, or will now be producer of "newly" hazardous waste? If so:

1)   How much hazardous waste do you produce annually?

2)   Are you above or below the proposed exemption limits for registration with the Environment Agency as a hazardous waste producer?

3)   Have you established whether your current Waste Management License or permit needs to be reviewed by the Environment Agency?

4)   Do you know the EWC codes for your individual waste streams, in order to fill in your consignment notes correctly?

5)   Is your hazardous waste being collected in a container separate from non-hazardous waste? If not, you will need to consider new arrangements for segregated storage and collection.

6)   Have you made arrangements with your collection and disposal services, to prepare for the Consignment Note forms and quarterly returns?

7)   If your waste is consigned to landfill, are you familiar with the Waste Acceptance Criteria that you will have to meet after 16 July 2005 ?

8)   Have you adequately characterised your waste in order to select appropriate treatment for your waste prior to landfilling, in accordance with the Waste Acceptance Criteria

Source: www.sita.co.uk. Document code M141, Review of the Hazardous Waste (England) Regulations 2005 and the introduction of the Waste Acceptance Criteria.

Index

NOTES